REALMS OF BEING

Realms of Being

By

GEORGE SANTAYANA

One-Volume Edition

WITH A NEW INTRODUCTION BY THE AUTHOR

NEW YORK

Charles Scribner's Sons

1942

PREFACE TO REALMS OF BEING

THE world is old, and can have changed but little since man arose in it, else man himself would have perished. Why, then, should he still live without a sure and sufficient philosophy? The equivalent of such a philosophy is probably hereditary in sundry animals not much older than man. They have had time to take the measure of life, and have settled down to a routine of preferences and habits which keeps their heads, as a race, above water; and they are presumably visited at appropriate seasons by magic images, which are symbols to them for the world or for the cycles of their destiny. Among groups of men an equilibrium of this moral sort has been sometimes approached—in India, in China, under the Moslem or the Catholic regimens; and if socialist or other panaceas now exercise such a strange influence over men's hearts, it is perhaps because they are impatient of being so long the sport of divers ignorant dogmas and chance adventures, and aspire to live in a stable harmony with nature.

In fact, beneath these various complete systems which have professed but failed to be universal, there is actually a dumb human philosophy, incomplete but solid, prevalent among all civilised peoples. They all practise agriculture, commerce, and mechanical arts, with artificial instruments lately very much complicated; and they necessarily possess, with these arts, a modicum of sanity, morality, and science requisite for carrying them on, and tested by success in doing so. Is not this human competence philosophy enough? Is it not at least the nucleus of all sound philosophy? In spite of the superficial confusion reigning in the world, is not the universal wisdom of the future actually gathering about this human competence in engineering, in chemistry, in medicine, in war?

It might seem so, since the sort of knowledge involved in the arts, though it may not go very far, is The realm compulsory so far as it goes, and being of matter. sanctioned by success, it ought to be permanent and progressive. There is indeed a circle of material events called nature, to which all minds belonging to the same society are responsive in common. Not to be responsive to these facts is simply to be stupid and backward in the arts; those who explore and master their environment cannot help learning what it is. In this direction competence involves enlightenment. Among minds forming a moral society, and able to compare their several opinions, this enlightenment in the expert is coercive over the layman also, because the same facts confront them both. Did not the same facts confront them, communication would be impossible between them, or if communication was reputed to exist by magic there would be no possible conflict or progress among their opinions, because they would not refer to the same events. Even if each declared himself competent and prosperous in his own world, he would know nothing of the world of his neighbours. Their several minds would simply be variously or similarly brilliant, like jewels, signifying nothing to one another.

If any mind hopes to address another (or even itself) persuasively, as I now wish to address the reader and my own thoughts, it must assume a single system of events to which both minds are responsive, and which includes their respective bodies and actions.

Assuming such a common world, it is easy to see how animals may acquire knowledge of it and may communicate it. Material events will arouse in them intuitions conformable to their several stations, faculties, and passions; and their active nature (since they are animals, not plants) will compel them to regard many of the essences so given in intuition as signs for the environment in which they move, modifying this environment and affected by it. This assumption justifies itself at every turn in practice, and establishes in the habits of all men, in proportion to their competence, an appropriate adjustment to the *Realm of Matter*, and in their imagination a suitable picture of the same.

Nevertheless, since the station, faculties, and passions of all men are not identical, these pictures will not be similar. Different observers may be The realm addressed to different regions of nature, or of essence. sensitive to different elements in the same region; thus dwellers in distinct planets must evidently have distinct geographies, and the same battle in the clouds will be known to the deaf only as lightning and to the blind only as thunder, each responding to a different constituent of the total event, and not simultaneously. So an eclipse—itself but one aspect of a constellation of events in the heavens—may be known in various entirely different terms; by calculation before it occurs, by sense when it is occurring, by memory immediately afterwards, and by reports to posterity. All these indications are entirely inadequate to the facts they reveal in the realm of matter, and qualitatively unlike those facts; they are a set of variegated symbols by which sensitive animals can designate them. Of course, the existence and use of such languages is an added fact in nature—a fact so important and close to the egotism of the animals themselves as perhaps to obscure all else in their eyes. Their instinct, indeed, keeps their attention stretched upon the material world that actually surrounds them; but sometimes sensation and language, instead of being passed over like the ticking of the telegraph, may become objects in themselves, in all their absolute musical insignificance; and then animals become idealists. The terms in which they describe things, unlike the things they meant to describe, are purely specious, arbitrary, and ideal; whether visual, tactile, auditory, or conceptual these terms are essentially *words*. They possess intrinsically, in their own ontological plane, only logical or æsthetic being; and this contains no indication whatever of the material act of speaking, touching, or looking which causes them to appear. All possible terms in mental discourse are essences existing nowhere; visionary equally, whether the faculty that discovers them be sense or thought or the most fantastic fancy.

Such diversity in animal experience taken in itself exhibits sundry qualities or forms of being, a part of the infinite multitude of distinguishable ideal terms which (whether ever revealed to anybody or not) I call the *Realm of Essence*. Pure intuition, in its poetic ecstasy, would simply drink in such of these essences as happened to present themselves; but for a wakeful animal they are signals. They report to his spirit, in very summary and uncertain images, the material events which surround him and which concern his welfare. They may accordingly become terms in knowledge if interpreted judiciously, and if interpreted injudiciously they may become illusions.

The dumb philosophy of the human animal, by which he rears his family and practises the arts and All mental finds his way home, might take definite shape discourse is and establish a healthy routine in all his deal-more or less significant ings with matter (which includes society), poetry. and yet his imaginative experience might retain all its specious originality. The control which

the environment exercises over the structure and
conduct of animals is decidedly loose. They can
live dragging a long chain of idle tricks, diseases, and
obsolete organs; and even this loose control fails
almost entirely in the case of alternative senses or
languages, one of which may serve as well as another.
Many species survive together, many rival endowments and customs and religions. And the same control fails altogether in regard to the immaterial essences
which those senses or languages call up before the
mind's eye. Adaptation is physical, and it is only the
material operation in sensation or speech that can
possibly be implicated in the clockwork of nature. The
choice of those visionary essences which meantime
visit the mind, though regular, is free; they are the
transcript of life into discourse, the rhetorical and
emotional rendering of existence, which when deepened
and purified, becomes poetry or music. There can be
no reason why differences in these spheres, even among
men of the same race, should not be perpetual. It
would be mere sluggishness and egotism to regret it.
Such differences are not merely added like a vain
luxury to a sane recognition, in other conscious terms,
of the facts of nature. The "sane" response to nature
is by action only and by an economy which nature can
accept and weave into her own material economy; but
as to the terms of sense and discourse, they are all from
the very beginning equally arbitrary, poetical, and (if
you choose) mad; yet all equally symptomatic. They
vary initially and intangibly from mind to mind, even
in expressing the same routine of nature. The imagination which eventually runs to fine art or religion
is the same faculty which, under a more direct control
of external events, yields vulgar perception. The
promptings and the control exercised by matter are
continuous in both cases; the dream requires a material
dreamer as much as the waking sensation, and the latter

is a transcript of his bodily condition just as directly
as the dream.   Poetic, creative, original fancy is not a
secondary form of sensibility, but its first and only
form.   The same manual restlessness and knack which
makes man a manufacturer of toys makes him, when
by chance his toys prove useful, a manufacturer of
implements.   Fine art is thus older than servile labour,
and the poetic quality of experience is more fundamental than its scientific value.   Existence may revert
at any moment to play, or may run down in idleness;
but it is impossible that any work or discovery should
ever come about without the accompaniment of pure
contemplation, if there is consciousness at all; so that
the inherent freedom of the spirit can never be stamped
out, so long as spirit endures.

    Nor is it safe to imagine that inspired people,
because they dream awake in their philosophy,
The realm must come to grief in the real world.   The
of spirit.   great religious and political systems which
I mentioned above have had brilliant careers.   Their
adepts have been far from making worse soldiers than
sceptics make, or worse workmen than materialists;
nor have they committed suicide or been locked up in
the madhouse more often than exact philosophers.
Nature drives with a loose rein, and vitality of any sort,
even if expressed in fancy, can blunder through many
a predicament in which reason would despair.   And
if the mythical systems decline at last, it is not so much
by virtue of the maladjustments underlying their speculative errors—for their myths as a whole are wisely
contrived—as because imagination in its freedom
abandons these errors for others simply because the
prevalent mood of mankind has changed, and it begins
dreaming in a different key.   Spirit bloweth where it
listeth, and continually undoes its own work.   This
world of free expression, this drift of sensations, passions, and ideas, perpetually kindled and fading in the

light of consciousness, I call the *Realm of Spirit*. It is only for the sake of this free life that material competence and knowledge of fact are worth attaining. Facts for a living creature are only instruments; his play-life is his true life. On his working days, when he is attentive to matter, he is only his own servant, preparing the feast. He becomes his own master in his holidays and in his sportive passions. Among these must be counted literature and philosophy, and so much of love, religion, and patriotism as is not an effort to survive materially. In such enthusiasms there is much asseveration; but what they attest is really not the character of the external facts concerned, but only the spiritual uses to which the spirit turns them.

A philosopher cannot wish to be deceived. His philosophy is a declaration of policy in the presence of the facts; and therefore his first care must be to ascertain and heartily to acknowledge all such facts as are relevant to his action or sentiment—not less, and not necessarily more. The range of reasonable curiosity. The pursuit of truth is a form of courage, and a philosopher may well love truth for its own sake, in that he is disposed to confront destiny, whatever it may be, with zest when possible, with resignation when necessary, and not seldom with amusement. The facts to which it is prudent and noble in him to bare his bosom are the morally relevant facts, such as touch his fortunes or his heart, or such as he can alter by his efforts; nor can he really discover other facts. Intuition, or absolute apprehension without media or doubt, is proper to spirit perusing essences; it is impossible to animals confronting facts. Animals know things by exploration, reaction, and prophetic fancy; they therefore can know only such parts and depths of nature as they explore materially and respond to vitally. The brave impulse to search may, indeed, become eager and may wish to recognise no limits; and there may be spirits so utterly practical and serious that the pursuit of material facts absorbs them altogether, to the exclusion of all play of mind. Yet such hectic exactitude is an expression of fear, and automatic rather than rational. Curiosity in an animal always has limits which it is foolish to transgress, because beyond them theory insensibly lapses into verbal myths, and if still taken for true knowledge defeats the honest curiosity that inspired it. What renders knowledge true is fidelity to the object; but in the conduct and fancy of an animal this fidelity can be only rough, summary, dramatic; too much refinement renders it subjective, as does too much haste. This is true of mathematical refinements no less than of verbal pedantries. The realm of matter can never be disclosed either to hypothesis or to sensation in its presumable inmost structure and ultimate extent: the garment of appearance must always fit it loosely and drape it in alien folds, because appearance is essentially an adaptation of facts to the scale and faculty of the observer.

There are also moral limits to seriousness and utter literalness in thought. The tragic compulsion to honour the facts is imposed on man by the destiny of his body, to which that of his mind is attached. But his destiny is not the only theme possible to his thought, nor the most congenial. The best part of this destiny is that he may often forget it; and existence would not be worth preserving if it had to be spent exclusively in anxiety about existence.

It follows from all this that knowledge of facts merely because they are facts cannot be the ultimate *Relativity of* object of a philosopher, although he must *knowledge.* wish to know the whole unvarnished truth about relevant matters. A liberal mind must live on its own terms, and think in them; it is not inferior to what surrounds it; fact-worship on its part would accordingly be a fault in taste and in morals. What is the function of philosophy? To disclose the absolute truth? But is it credible that the absolute truth should descend into the thoughts of a mortal creature, equipped with a few special senses and with a biassed intellect, a man lost amidst millions of his fellows and a prey to the epidemic delusions of the race? Possession of the absolute truth is not merely by accident beyond the range of particular minds; it is incompatible with being alive, because it excludes any particular station, organ, interest, or date of survey: the absolute truth is undiscoverable just because it is not a perspective. Perspectives are essential to animal apprehension; an observer, himself a part of the world he observes, must have a particular station in it; he cannot be equally near to everything, nor internal to anything but himself; of the rest he can only take views, abstracted according to his sensibility and fore-shortened according to his interests. Those animals which I was supposing endowed with an adequate philosophy surely do not possess the absolute truth. They read nature in their private idioms. Their imagination, like the human, is doubtless incapable of coping with all things at once, or even with the whole of anything natural. Mind was not created for the sake of discovering the absolute truth. The absolute truth has its own intangible reality, and scorns to be known. The function of mind is rather to increase the wealth of the universe in the spiritual dimension, by adding appearance to substance and passion to necessity, and by creating all those private perspectives, and those emotions of wonder, adventure, curiosity, and laughter which omniscience would exclude. If omniscience were alone respectable, creation would have been a mistake. The single duty of all creatures would then be to repair that creative error, by abolishing their several senses and desires and becoming indistinguishable from one another and from nothing at all; and if all creation could attain to this sort of salvation, the absolute substance, in whose honour all else had been abandoned, would become unconscious. The time will doubtless come for each of us, if not for the universe at large, to cease from care; but our passage through life will have added a marvellous episode to the tale of things; and our distinction and glory, as well as our sorrow, will have lain in being something in particular, and in knowing what it is.

Thus if there is a sense in which all special and separable existence is illusion, there is another sense in which illusion is itself a special and separable existence; and if this be condemned for not being absolute substance and for excluding knowledge of the absolute truth, it may also be prized for these very reasons. Sensation is true enough. All experience yields some acquaintance with the realm of essence, and some perspective of the material world; and this would always be a true perspective (since things seen at that angle and with that organ really look like that) if the appearance were not stretched to cover more than it covers in reality. Of such true perspectives the simplest and most violently foreshortened may be as good as the most complicated, the most poetical or pictorial as good as the most scientific, not only æsthetically but even cognitively; because it may report the things concerned on that human scale on which we need to measure them, and in this relation may report them correctly. Nor is the error which such very partial knowledge may breed, when inflated by pre-cipitate judgements and vanity, altogether unavoidable. The variety of senses in man, the precarious rule of his instincts, and the range of his memory and fancy, give rise in him eventually to some sense of error and even of humour. He is almost able to pierce the illusions of his animal dogmatism, to surrender the claim to inspiration, and in one sense to transcend the relativity of his knowledge and the flightiness of his passions by acknowledging them with a good grace.

This relativity does not imply that there is no absolute truth. On the contrary, if there were no absolute truth, all-inclusive and eternal, the desultory views taken from time to time by individuals would themselves be absolute. They would be irrelevant to one another, and incomparable in point of truth, each being without any object but the essence which appeared in it. If views can be more or less correct, and perhaps complementary to one another, it is because they refer to the same system of nature, the complete description of which, covering the whole past and the whole future, would be the absolute truth. This absolute truth is no living view, no actual judgement, but merely that segment of the realm of essence which happens to be illustrated in existence. The question whether a given essence belongs to this segment or not—that is, whether a suggested idea is or is not true—has a tragic importance for an animal intent on discovering and describing what exists, or has existed, or is destined to exist in his world. He seldom has leisure to dwell on essences apart from their presumable truth; even their beauty and dialectical pattern seem to him rather trivial, unless they are significant of facts in the realm of matter, controlling human destiny. I therefore give a special name to this tragic segment of the realm of essence and call it the *Realm of Truth*.

The knowledge of relevant truth, while it has this fundamental moral importance, is far from being our only concern in the life of reason. It comes in only incidentally, in so far as a staunch and comprehensive knowledge of things makes a man master of things, and independent of them in a great measure. The business of a philosopher is

The realm of truth.

Human values of knowledge.

rather to be a good shepherd of his thoughts. The share of attention and weight which he gives to physical speculation or to history or to psychology will express his race and disposition, or the spirit of his times; everyone is free to decide how far material arts and sciences are worth pursuing, and with what free creations they shall be surrounded. Young and ardent minds, and races without accumulated possessions, tend to poetry and metaphysics; they neglect or falsify the truth in the heat of their imaginative passion. Old men, and old nations, incline to mix their wine with larger dilutions of reality; and they prefer history, biography, politics, and humorous fictions; because in all these, while the facts are neither conceived nor tested scientifically, the savour of earth and of experience remains dominant.

By the philosopher, however, both the homeliest brew and the most meticulous science are only relished as food for the spirit. Even if defeated in the pursuit of truth, the spirit may be victorious in self-expression and self-knowledge; and if a philosopher could be nothing else, he might still be a moralist and a poet. He will do well to endow his vision of things with all the force, colour, and scope of which his soul is capable. Then if he misses the truth of nature, as in many things is probable, he will at least have achieved a work of imagination. In such a case the universe, without being mapped as a whole in the fancy, will be enriched at one point, by the happy life enacted there, in one human focus of art and vision. The purer and more distinct the spirit which a philosopher can bring to light in his thoughts, the greater the intellectual achievement; and the greater the moral achievement also, if the policy so set forth is actually carried out in his whole life and conversation.

As for me, in stretching my canvas and taking up my palette and brush, I am not vexed that masters

should have painted before me in styles which I have
no power and no occasion to imitate; nor do I expect
future generations to be satisfied with always   Legitimate
repainting my pictures. Agreement is sweet,   variety in
being a form of friendship; it is also a   speculation.
stimulus to insight, and helpful, as contradiction is not;
and I certainly hope to find agreement in some quarters.
Yet I am not much concerned about the number of
those who may be my friends in the spirit, nor do I
care about their chronological distribution, being as
much pleased to discover one intellectual kinsman in
the past as to imagine two in the future. That in
the world at large alien natures should prevail, innumerable and perhaps infinitely various, does not
disturb me.   On the contrary, I hope fate may manifest to them such objects as they need and can love;
and although my sympathy with them cannot be so
vivid as with men of my own mind, and in some cases
may pass into antipathy, I do not conceive that they
are wrong or inferior for being different from me, or
from one another. If God and nature can put up
with them, why should I raise an objection?   But let
them take care; for if they have sinned against the
facts (as I suspect is often the case) and are kicking
against the pricks of matter, they must expect to be
brought to confusion on the day of doom, or earlier.
Not only will their career be brief and troubled, which
is the lot of all flesh, but their faith will be stultified by
events, which is a needless and eternal ignominy for the
spirit.   But if somehow, in their chosen terms, they
have balanced their accounts with nature, they are to
be heartily congratulated on their moral diversity.   It
is pleasant to think that the fertility of spirit is inexhaustible, if matter only gives it a chance, and that the
worst and most successful fanaticism cannot turn the
moral world permanently into a desert.
    The pity of it is only that contrary souls should often

fight for the same bodies, natural or political, as if
space and matter in the universe were inadequate (as
on earth indeed they are) for every essence in its own
time to see the sun. But existence is precipitate and
blind; it cannot bide its time; and the seeds of form
are often so wantonly and thickly scattered that they
strangle one another, call one another weeds and tares,
and can live only in the distracted effort to keep others
from living. Seldom does any soul live through a
single and lovely summer in its native garden, suffered
and content to bloom. Philosophers and nations cannot be happy unless separate; then they may be single-
minded at home and tolerant abroad. If they have a
spirit in them which is worth cultivating (which is not
always the case) they need to entrench it in some consecrated citadel, where it may come to perfect expression. Human beings allowed to run loose are vowed
to perdition, since they are too individual to agree and
too gregarious to stand alone. Hence the rareness of
any polity founded on wisdom, like that of which
ancient Greece affords some glimpses, and the equal
rareness of a pure and complete philosophy, such as
that of Dante or of Spinoza, conceived in some moment
of wonderful unanimity or of fortunate isolation.

My own philosophy, I venture to think, is well-
knit in the same sense, in spite of perhaps seeming
eclectic and of leaving so many doors open
both in physics and in morals. My eclec-
ticism is not helplessness before sundry influences; it is detachment and firmness in taking each
thing simply for what it is. Openness, too, is a form
of architecture. The doctrine that all moralities equally
are but expressions of animal life is a tremendous
dogma, at once blessing and purging all mortal passions;
and the conviction that there can be no knowledge save
animal faith positing external facts, and that this
natural science is but a human symbol for those facts,

The temper
of this
system.

also has an immense finality: the renunciation and the assurance in it are both radical and both invincible.

In confessing that I have merely touched the hem of nature's garment, I feel that virtue from her has passed into me, and made me whole. There is no more bewitching moment in childhood than when the boy, to whom someone is slyly propounding some absurdity, suddenly looks up and smiles. The brat has understood. A thin deception was being practised on him, in the hope that he might not be deceived, but by deriding it might prove he had attained to a man's stature and a man's wit. It was but banter prompted by love. So with this thin deception practised upon me by nature. The great Sphinx in posing her riddle and looking so threatening and mysterious is secretly hoping that I may laugh. She is not a riddle but a fact; the words she whispers are not oracles but prattle. Why take her residual silence, which is inevitable, for a challenge or a menace? She does not know how to speak more plainly. Her secret is as great a secret to herself as to me. If I perceive it, and laugh, instantly she draws in her claws. A tremor runs through her enigmatical body; and if she were not of stone she would embrace her boyish discoverer, and yield herself to him altogether. It is so simple to exist, to be what one is for no reason, to engulf all questions and answers in the rush of being that sustains them. Henceforth nature and spirit can play together like mother and child, each marvellously pleasant to the other, yet deeply unintelligible; for as she created him she knew not how, merely by smiling in her dreams, so in awaking and smiling back he somehow understands her; at least he is all the understanding she has of herself.

xxv

CONTENTS

CONTENTS

THE REALM OF TRUTH

INTRODUCTION

For this compact edition of *Realms of Being* the publishers desired a new Introduction. The work had been originally issued in four separate volumes at intervals of years, but an introduction to the whole was not lacking. An elaborate one had previously appeared under the title *Scepticism and Animal Faith*; yet although expressly written to introduce *Realms of Being*, this earlier book was essentially more sophisticated than the later volumes and less friendly to the fundamental convictions of mankind. As my purpose in discriminating these realms of being had been to reassert those fundamental convictions, there was a tactical circumlocution, and perhaps a misleading one, in beginning by a *reductio ad absurdum* of modern paradoxes. The reconstruction of common sense on that radically sceptical foundation found the reader confused, and not inclined to recognise and recover his natural reason under the name of animal faith. I am therefore not sorry to see *Realms of Being* reappear without that retrospective prologue. This is not an exercise in controversy but in meditation. It addresses itself less to the professional philosophers of the day than to the reflective moments and speculative honesty of any man in any age or country.

In this spirit I afterwards composed the briefer and more direct introduction contained in the general Preface that here immediately precedes. It indicates how these kinds of reality may come to be distin-

guished by an animal mind in the presence of nature.
Such an articulation of thought and language has
nothing compulsory about it; it can be neither complete nor exclusive, and other animal minds may come
to clearness differently. Mankind, drowning observation in myth, has gone and continues to go much farther afield than I should venture in composing religions and philosophies. I offer only a sketch of the
logical and moral economy that has imposed itself on
my free thoughts.

Recently, by friendly solicitations coming from outside, I have been led to write a somewhat biographical
and controversial *Apologia* for my way of thinking;[1]
and this might serve as a third Introduction to *Realms
of Being*, perhaps the best for that part of the public
which is more interested in an author's life and in
what people say of him than they are in his works.
Yet so labyrinthine an approach may block the way
as much as it guides, and may end in utter confusion;
because in my defence I am compelled to wander into
artificial problems and hopeless misunderstandings,
that for my ultimate purpose had better be disregarded. Each critic inevitably has his preconceptions
and his characteristic blind-spots, no worse doubtless
than mine, but not helpful to an innocent reader who
would like to understand my unadulterated doctrine.

Philosophical innocence, neutrality in regard to
modern professional philosophy, will indeed be a help
in understanding this book; because after having
cleared my own mind as much as possible of traditional sophistry, I have endeavoured to recover the
natural and inevitable beliefs of a human being living
untutored in this world, but having a reflective mind.
He need not be ignorant of the systems of mythology,
religion, or philosophy that ingenious or inspired wits

[1]In volume second of *The Library of Living Philosophers:*
Northwestern University, Evanston & Chicago. 1940.

have constructed, as he need not be ignorant of genuine science and history: but all this will merely complicate for him, in a challenging fashion, the landscape of nature; and his allegiance need not begin to be engaged to anything speculative until he has seen its place, as an arbitrary or as an inevitable conception, in the life of mankind.

Great difficulties beset any man who in a sophisticated age asks himself what are the inescapable elements in his own beliefs and conceptions. He has been using for years a complicated language in which contrary metaphors and logics are imbedded; and the problems that have been presented to him as pressing are very likely quite accidental or perverse, such as would not arise in a clear development of intelligence. The earth, as Nietzsche said, has been too long a madhouse. We need to purify the air of all the miasmas of the past, and still more of those of the present which are even more likely to choke us. A man so immersed in local and momentary affairs, and in the interests of his profession or party, as to think them fundamental either in the world or in his own heart, may be most useful to the useless projects of others, but he can never be a philosopher.

Technical philosophy itself abounds in unnecessary problems, which the truly wise will not trouble about, seeing that they are insoluble or solved best by not raising them. Nevertheless it may be enlightening to study these puzzles historically, to understand, to situate, and to disinfect them. This is what I instinctively endeavoured to do for many years in my reading and teaching respecting the whole of Greek and modern philosophy: not learnedly or anxiously, but as the subject-matter at each point might suggest to my free mind. I had no thought of constructing any rival system; yet my sincere reaction to one system after another gradually revealed to me the unformulated principles that guided my judgment; so that my system, if system it can be called, was not so much formed by me as discovered within me. A brand new system could never tempt me. I should hear the tramp of the next new system at its heels. This philosophy that I have unearthed within me is ancient philosophy, very ancient philosophy. Indeed, my endeavour in putting it into words has been to retreat to the minimum beliefs and radical presuppositions implied in facing a world at all or professing to know anything: beliefs and presuppositions that it is impossible for me to deny honestly, although I may seldom or never have conceived them clearly.

For when I speak of *minimum* beliefs and *radical* presuppositions I do not in the least refer to the *earliest* notions in my own mind or in the minds of children or savages. My investigation is not anthropological, but critical and analytic and made in the full light of human experience and history. The notions of savages and children, if allowed to grow wild, are extravagantly fanciful and confused; and much of this confusion and extravagance seems to me to subsist in traditional philosophy. It remains superstitious in principle whenever it fails to distinguish the two elements in childish apprehension: on the one hand the real contact with things, the cognitive intent, justified faith, and prompting to inquiry that are proper to *knowledge ;* on the other hand the pictures, emotions, and ideal relations that are proper to *imagination.* Superstition, and sometimes philosophy, accepts imagination as a truer avenue to knowledge than is contact with things; but this is precisely what I endeavour to avoid by distinguishing matter, or the substance of dynamic things, from essence, or the direct datum, sensuous or intelligible, of intuition. Intuition represents the free life of the mind, the poetry native to it, which I am far from despising; but this is the subjective or ideal element in thought which we must discount if we are anxious to possess true knowledge.

In saying, then, that my philosophy is ancient I do not mean that it is traditional or reactionary. On the contrary, it is as personally sceptical and independent as I am able to make it; although I think it reasonable to suppose that the beliefs that prove inevitable for me, after absolutely disinterested criticism, would prove inevitable also to most human beings. The trouble is that for them many other beliefs and superstitions prove inevitable also; and they take their first principles to be no more fundamental than their accidental prejudices. Moreover, if they are professional philosophers or inspired prophets they may even embrace some decidedly secondary and accidental notion as alone requisite or true, and in its name they will then contradict their own inevitable first principles. So, in the interests of idealism, they may verbally deny the existence of matter, or in the vortex of romanticism they may flout the reality of truth. Yet they are plainly heretics, since they retract the primary presuppositions of intelligence implied in their own arguments.

The sum of all that I find myself compelled to assume is not large; and the endless investigation of the fields that I see open before me I frankly abandon to more diligent or more competent inquirers. I am no scientific man, no mathematician, no historian; so that the details of the realms of matter, essence, and truth extend in all directions far beyond my ken, and I do not pretend to foresee what may be eventually discovered there. Even in the sphere of morals and politics, where I feel more at home, I do not wander in this book beyond the rudiments; because it is only the rudiments that an individual can discover by analysing his own passions. In primitive societies, where custom is sacred and the passions are all choral and collective (unless sneakingly criminal), it is still the individual that is gregarious and swayed by the mood of the little circle in which he moves and which forms the whole world for his conscience. Whether we remain childishly gregarious or become at moments childishly petulant and conceited, is again an individual question. There is no human nature except in particular men, and no social power except over individuals. If society evolves, it does so by obeying or imposing a change of habit in the animal psyches of its members. Such mutations are provoked by men of action or announced prophetically by men of genius, who possess unusual insight into the interplay between human nature and the material conditions of life. The task I have undertaken here is at once more modest and more intimate. I study only the revelation made inwardly to the spirit, while the psyche undergoes those material mutations or asserts itself among them. For besides governing the organism and its action, the psyche *feels* what it does and what it suffers; and this inner echo of all that happens in the body in its contacts with surrounding things, I call the life of spirit. It is evidently only as affecting the spirit and as enlightening the spirit that a rational moralist need consider the world.

In an animal psyche as complex and as delicately organised as the human, the spirit has a wider basis and comes to light in more ways and in more places than we might at first suspect. And at each point where it flowers at all, it flowers into something original. The ear yields one unprecedented character to the sum of existence in yielding sound, and the eye another unprecedented element in yielding visual light and colour. The same organic machinery, in other places and motions, yields the unprecedented elements of pleasure and pain and all the emotions. Nor is the originality of the pigments the whole originality in the spiritual picture. Memory lights up perspectives which in nature can subsist only as dead relations between dead facts; and expectation, contradiction, doubt and surprise vivify the mechanism of instinct and turn plodding existence into a series of comedies. It is only by being reported through the senses to the spirit that the world puts on this wedding garment and can be admitted to the feast of life. We should never become poets in the end had we not been essentially poets from the beginning.

There is a strange servility in conventional sentiment on this subject. People admire the mind as a most opportune and useful servant of the body, to warn it of dangers and opportunities and to guide it in constructing artificial instruments. In nature I suppose that nothing arises for the sake of anything else, but everything only when other things permit and favour it. Thus mind in particular seems to awake in animals when they become physically capable of long-range reactions upon surrounding events; and this extension of life over a web, as it were, of aerial relations, in the act of giving birth to intelligence becomes, for the observer from without, evidence that intelligence has been born. We may even, if we like, give the name of intelligence directly to this aerial organisation of material motions, ignoring for the moment the inner side of life. But this use or abuse of language will not abolish the actuality of consciousness in each animal on those occasions; much less will it determine the moral question whether we shall prize mind for its utility in serving matter or matter for its utility in serving mind. In any case, before there was mind, nothing could have been created with malice prepense, least of all mind itself; for evidently before there was consciousness there would not have been any idea of consciousness, or any insight into its possible uses, if introduced into the interstices of material events. And anything capable of being so introduced and of having such uses would seem to me not to deserve the name of mind at all, but to be, by definition, a material agent. That may be only a question of words. What I should say without hesitation is that, for mental life, the body and the world cannot be dispensed with; from physical and social health comes the very existence of mind and all its happiness; yet the only use of health and of a good social regimen is to permit the mind to flourish more freely.

What is this free life of mind ? What are the necessary and sufficient themes that may occupy it ? What troubles does it suffer from, when do they vanish, and in what then may it find a positive joy ? Such are the questions that ultimately concern me in this book. Romantic souls, who think that spirit is an unharnessed Pegasus tumbling among the clouds, will find nothing here to their purpose. The great characteristic of the human spirit, as I see it, is its helplessness and misery, most miserable and helpless when it fancies itself dominant and independent; and the great problem for it is salvation, purification, rebirth into a humble recognition of the powers on which it depends, and into a sane enjoyment of its appropriate virtues. Such salvation and rebirth must come by gift of nature, but they are not impossible. On the contrary, they tend to be re-established automatically, through the self-elimination of extreme madness, and the natural fertility of health. At any moment spirit unexpectedly flowers; a little earth and a little sunshine are sufficient for it. It overflows in the play of children, as in the wit and wisdom of mature minds; for spirit may readily overcome the world without doing it violence, by transmuting it into terms of art, of love, and of reflection.

GEORGE SANTAYANA

January, 1942.

THE REALM OF ESSENCE

Ἔστιν . . . πρῶτον διαιρετέον τάδε· τί τὸ ὂν ἀεί, γένεσιν δὲ οὐκ ἔχον . . . ἀεὶ κατὰ ταὐτὰ ὄν.—The first distinction to make is this: What is that which always is, having no origin, and being always identical with itself?—PLATO.

Buddha teaches that all beings are from eternity abiding in Nirvana.—Dasgupta's *History of Indian Philosophy.*

Per Deum intelligo ens absolute infinitum, hoc est, substantiam constantem infinitis attributis, quorum unumquodque aeternam et infinitam essentiam exprimit. . . . Quod autem absolute infinitum est, ad ejus essentiam pertinet quidquid essentiam exprimit.— By God I understand Being absolutely infinite, that is, substance consisting of infinitely numerous attributes, each of which expresses eternal and infinite essence. . . . For if a thing is absolutely infinite, whatsoever expresses any essence belongs to the essence of that thing.—SPINOZA.

Le néant . . . est infini; il est éternel; il a bien des attributs communs avec Dieu; il comprend une infinité de choses, car toutes celles qui ne sont point sont comprises dans le néant, et celles qui ne sont plus sont rentrées dans le néant.—The Non-existent . . . is infinite, it is eternal; it possesses many attributes in common with God; it includes an infinity of things since all those which never exist belong to the Non-existent, and those which exist no longer have fallen back into the Non-existent.—LEIBNIZ.

CHAPTER I

VARIOUS APPROACHES TO ESSENCE

THE modern or romantic man is an adventurer; he is less interested in what there may be to find than in the lure of the search and in his hopes, guesses, or experiences in searching. Essence is perfectly indifferent to being discovered and unaffected by the avenue through which any discoverer may approach it; and for that very reason the explorer ignores it, and asks what it can possibly be. Now the subjective attitude in philosophy is not only prevalent in these times, but always legitimate; because a mind capable of self-consciousness is always free to reduce all things to its own view of them. Before considering the realm of essence in itself, therefore, I will indicate some paths by which even the most rambling reflection may be led to it. Essence is indeed everywhere at hand; and a scrupulous scepticism, falling back on immediate appearance, is itself a chief means of discovering the pervasive presence of essences.

All approaches are adventitious.

In a volume on *Scepticism and Animal Faith*, to which the present work is a sequel, I have described in detail the approach to essence through scepticism. Knowledge such as animal life requires is something transitive, a form of belief in things absent or eventual or somehow more than the state of the animal knowing them. It needs to be informa-

Approach through scepticism: Nothing indubitable save the character of some given essence.

tion. Otherwise the animal mind would be the prisoner of its dreams, and no better informed than a stone about its environment, its past, or its destiny.

It follows that such transitive knowledge will always be open to doubt. It is a claim or presumption arising in a responsive organism; yet in spite of this biological status, it ventures upon assertions concerning facts elsewhere. This boldness exposes it to all sorts of errors; for opinion will vary with its organ and, on that irrelevant ground, will make varying assertions about its outlying objects. Nor is it to be presumed that initially the terms in which objects are conceived are their intrinsic qualities; the terms may be, in quality as in existence, generated in the organ of sense, as are words or optical perspectives. Knowledge of nature or of absent experience is accordingly no less questionable in its texture than in its scope. Its validity is only presumptive and its terms are merely symbols.

The sceptic once on this scent will soon trace essence to its lair. He will drop, as dubious and unwarranted, the belief in a past, an environment, or a destiny. He will dismiss all thought of any truth to be discovered or any mind engaged in that egregious chase; and he will honestly confine himself to noting the features of the passing apparition. At first he may still assume that he can survey the passage and transformation of his dreams; but soon, if he is truly sceptical and candid, he will confess that this alleged order of appearances and this extended experience are themselves only dreamt of, like the future or the remoter past or the material environment—those discarded idols of his dogmatic days. Nothing will remain but some appearance now; and that which appears, when all gratuitous implications of a world beyond or of a self here are discarded, will be an *essence*. Nor will his own spirit, or spirit absolute (which grammar may still seem to insert, under the form of the pronoun I, as a prior agent in this intuition of essence) be anything but another name for the absolute phantom, the unmeaning presence, into which knowledge will have collapsed.

This approach to essence through scepticism is by no means the only one possible, even for a critic of knowledge. Scepticism can impugn only such knowledge as is a form of faith, and posits a removed object; but the dialectician ignores this sort of knowledge as much as he can, and by his initial attitude plants himself in the realm of essence, and wishes to confine himself to it. What is dialectic? Precisely an analysis or construction of ideal forms which abstracts from such animal faith as might be stimulated by their presence, and traces instead the inherent patterns or logical relations of these forms as intuition reveals them. To the dialectician animal faith seems wanton and superfluous, and in his overt reasoning, if not in his secret assumptions, he neither posits any objects of natural knowledge nor seeks to describe them. Such preoccupation with dark external facts and hidden events seems to him but a grovelling instinct; and the persuasion that one's ideas describe natural objects, though inevitable perhaps in sniffing one's way through this nether world, he laughs at as a vain presumption, unworthy of the name of science. In practice, as a man amongst men, the dialectician may have mixed views. If he is an enthusiast or a naturalist in disguise, using dialectic for some ulterior purpose, he will probably embrace his conclusions not merely as implications of his premisses, but as objects of hot animal faith; and he may even think he has discovered a metaphysical world, when in truth he has merely elaborated a system of essences, altogether imaginary, and in no way more deeply rooted in reality than any system

[marginal note:] Approach through dialectic: every term intuited or defined is an essence.

of essences which a poet or a musician might compose. This eventual mystification, however, by which dialectic is represented as revealing facts, does not destroy its native competence to describe essences; in its purity it will be free from error, because free from any pretence to define ulterior existences. Now this very purity, this identity of the object envisaged with the definition given to it in thought, seems to the dialectician the perfection of science, because it is the last refuge of certitude. But certitude and dialectical cogency are far removed from animal faith, and unnecessary to it; and animal faith, when it describes in suitable symbols (of which a dialectical system may be one) the objects encountered in action, is what I call knowledge. The question of titles and preferences does not concern me here; in any case the dialectician, whether his art be called knowledge or not, has discovered the realm of essence (or some province in it) and has devoted himself to exploring it.

This acquaintance with essence I call intuition, whether it be passive, æsthetic, and mystical, or on the contrary analytical and selective, as in reasoned discourse; because at every point demonstration or inference depends for its force on intuition of the intrinsic relation between the given terms. So in planning a series of moves in chess, as in originally inventing that game, the mind *sees* the consequences implied at each stage by the rules of procedure: these rules are mere essences, but their implications are precise in any hypothetical position of the pieces. If chess were not a well-established game and if material chess-boards and chess-men had never existed, a day-dream in which particular imaginary matches were traced out, could hardly be called knowledge: but every possibility and every consequence involved at each juncture would be equally definite, and the

Distinguishable essences, such as the terms of dialectic, are the most real of beings.

science of chess—even if chess never had existed in the world—would be an exact science. Evidently an exact science is not without an object, ideal as this object may be: indeed, the ideal definition of that object, the absence of all ambiguity as to what it is, renders exact science of it possible. Such definable non-existent objects of exact science have being in an eminent degree; their nature and their eternal intrinsic relations to other comparable natures are perfectly determinate. They are what they are; and of all the meanings of the word *is*—existence, substance, equivalence, definition, etc., the most radical and proper is that in which I may say of anything that it is what it is. This asseveration does not commit me to any classification of the object or to any assertion of its existence. I merely note its idiosyncrasy, its qualitative identity, which enables me to distinguish it, study it, and hold it fast in my intent, so that I may eventually frame a definition of it, and perhaps assert or deny its existence. If any object had no such specific character, there would be no truth in saying that *it* was before me, or could ever again be the theme of memory or discourse. Essences, by being eternally what they are, enable existence to pass from one phase to another, and enable the mind to note and describe the change.

That what I see, I see, or what I am, I am, may seem a vain assertion: practical minds are not interested in anything except for the sake of something else. They are camp-followers or heralds of events, without self-possession. They are the only staunch possessions of the mind. Yet if that which is actual and possessed at the moment never had a satisfying character, no satisfaction would ever be possible; the mind could never dip twice into the same subject or know its friends from its enemies, and life would be what a romantic philosophy would make it—an idle escape from one error into another. Radical flux is indeed characteristic of existence, where it is innocent, since there can be no mistake or regret where there is no purpose: but the mind, even if describing only the series of its own illusions, attempts to describe it with truth: and it could not so much as fail in this attempt unless that series of illusions and each of its terms had a precise inexpungible character. Then the question whether in some ulterior sense those phases were illusions or not, becomes a subsidiary question. In any case, internally, they were what they were; and to a simple and recollected spirit the obvious often is enough. Its identity may have a deep charm, like that of a jewel. I may long ruminate upon it and impress it upon myself by repetitions, which to a lover never seem vain. Even in the midst of distractions, if I say to myself "No, no", or "Business is business", the repetition serves to detach and to render indubitable the essence meant; it raises that material accident to the intellectual level, where my judgement henceforth may recognise it to the exclusion of circumstances, which do not alter essences, but only cases.

Sometimes sense itself, without any dialectical analysis, distinguishes essences from facts, and recognises them in their ideal sphere. This happens for a very simple reason. The stimulus that calls animal attention to some external fact, in provoking an act of the body, also presents some image to the mind. Moreover this labour of perception may be more or less welcome, pleasant, or life-enhancing, apart from its ulterior uses; and sometimes this incidental emotion is so strong that it overpowers the interest which I may have had originally in the external facts; and, I may suspend my action or continue it automatically, while my thought is absorbed in the image and arrested there. As I was jogging to market in my village cart, beauty has burst

Approach through contemplation: Every intelligible pattern or harmony is an essence.

upon me and the reins have dropped from my hands. I am transported, in a certain measure, into a state of trance. I see with extraordinary clearness, yet what I see seems strange and wonderful, because I no longer look in order to understand, but only in order to see. I have lost my preoccupation with fact, and am contemplating an essence.

This experience, in modern times, is called æsthetic; but it has no exclusive connection with the arts or with the beautiful. It is really intellectual, and the high Platonic road. That the clearest and purest reality should be formal or ideal, and something on which no animal instinct could possibly be directed, may seem a paradox; it may be denied by cynics—often very dull people; it may be used by metaphysicians as an argument for the supernatural origin and destiny of the soul. It is important at once to discard any such inferences, not only because they are in themselves mistaken, thin, and superstitious, but particularly, at this point in my argument, because they encumber the notion of essence with a moral significance quite extraneous to it, and may distort and discredit it altogether. When a thing is beautiful, I stop to look at it; and in this way its beauty helps me to drink in the actual appearance, and to be satisfied with that ethereal draught. But if the thing were ugly or uninteresting, it would have an absolute appearance just as much, and would present an essence to intuition; only that in that case I should have no motive—no vital animal motive—for dwelling upon that essence, or noticing it at all. If the thing is beautiful, this is not because it manifests an essence, but because the essence which it manifests is one to which my nature is attuned, so that the intuition of it is a delightful exercise to my senses and to my soul. This pleasure and refreshment welling up in me, I

Essences are beautiful when congruous with human faculty.

courteously thank the object for, and call its intrinsic charm : but an intrinsic charm is a contradiction in terms, and all that the object possesses is affinity to my life, and power over it, without which it would be impossible for me to observe it or to think it beautiful.

The beautiful is itself an essence, an indefinable quality felt in many things which, however disparate they may be otherwise, receive this name by virtue of a special emotion, half wonder, half love, which is felt in their presence. The essence of the beautiful, when made an object of contemplation by itself, is rather misleading: like the good and like pure Being, it requires much dialectical and spiritual training to discern it in its purity and in its fullness. At first the impetuous philosopher, seeing the world in so many places flowering into beauty, may confuse his physics with a subjective or teleological reference to the beautiful, thereby turning this essence, which marks a spiritual consummation, into a material power: or, if he is not an enthusiast, he may dwell so much on the instinctive and pleasant bonds which attach men to what they call beautiful, that he may bury the essence of the beautiful altogether under heavy descriptions of the occasions on which perhaps it appears. I will not stop to discuss these complications: however apt to become entangled itself, the beautiful is a great liberator of other essences. The most material thing, in so far as it is felt to be beautiful, is instantly immaterialised, raised above external personal relations, concentrated and deepened in its proper being, in a word, sublimated into an essence: while on the other hand, many unnoticed Platonic ideas, relations, or unsubstantial aspects of things, when the thrill of beauty runs through them, are suddenly revealed, as in poetry the secret harmonies of feelings and of words. In this way innumerable natural themes of happiness,

Beauty detaches them for contemplation from the flux of nature.

which no one could possibly mistake for things, become members of the human family, and in turn restore the prodigal mind, perhaps long wasted on facts, to its home circle of essence.

This native affinity of the mind to essence rather than to fact is mind itself, the very nature of spirit or intellectual light.   The sort of intelligence There is which adapts one natural being to another, concomitant and may be found in the conduct of animals, contempla-or even in the structure of their bodies, does midst of not consist in thinking; it is an adaptation action of life to its conditions, a form of behaviour action is in matter, which must exist and flourish masterly. before thinking or even feeling can arise at all.   Intuition would be impossible without an underlying animal life, a psyche; for how should the sheer light of intuition actualise itself, or choose the essence on which it should fall?   A psyche, the hereditary organisation and movement of life in an animal, must first exist and sustain itself by its "intelligent" adaptations to the ambient world: but these adaptations are not conscious until, by virtue of their existence, intuition arises; and intuition arises when the inner life of the animal, or its contact with external things, is expressed in some actual appearance, in some essence given in feeling or thought.   The psyche and the material circumstances, by their special character and movement, determine the choice and succession of themes on which intuition shall be employed in some particular person; in so far as spirit is kindled there at all, it will have raised those themes to the plane of essence; the whole movement of nature and of human affairs, which imposes those themes, becomes itself only another theme for contemplation, if present to the mind at all.   This contemplation does not require a man to shut his eyes or to fix them exclusively on the stars; it does not require him to stop living or acting.   Often the most contemplative

minds are the most worldly-wise, and the most capable
of directing business. But though they may survey or
foresee action, they do not live in action, because they
see it in its wholeness and in its results; as a spectator
who sees the plot of a play understands the emotions of
the characters; but does not succumb to them; or
as a writer, very busy with his pen and conveying much
ink from inkstand to paper, may be thinking of his
subject; and the words will probably come most aptly
when, as words, they come unconsciously, and when
the truth which they express absorbs the whole mind.
The same thing happens in a game of ball, or in the
game of politics, when the player is good; the quick
adjustment of his faculties and organs, being automatic,
kindles in his mind a graphic image and a pure
emotion, to be the signs of his achievement to his inner
man.

The natural and the spiritual fruits of life are not
opposed, but they are different. Its natural fruits are
more life, persisting through readjustments
and an incessant generation of new forms,
so that youth may fill the place of age and
attain an equal, though not identical, perfection. It is in these perfections, or in approaches which partly anticipate them, that
the spiritual fruits are found. As we have seen,
they may ripen early, and may be gathered at all
seasons, when any phase of life is perfected in action;
but the spiritual fruits are internal or tangential to this
action, not consequent upon it, like the natural fruits:
they may be omnipresent in existence, but only by
everywhere transmuting existence into essence. Spirit
is life looking out of the window; the work of the
household must have been done first, and is best done
by machinery. Moral triumphs are not æsthetic,
because they have other occasions, but they are equally
intellectual when realised in the spirit; they lie in the

Moral as
well as
æsthetic
virtue is
realised in
the con-
templation
of essence.

joy of having done *this*: they are a passage into essence. Finality, though it is not felt as beauty, marks the great moments of passion satisfied or purposes achieved. Into some scene, into some phrase, into some gesture in itself trivial, the whole burden of a long experience may then be cast, and happiness may be centred and realised in some simple event or in some silent moment.

I should need but to enlarge this canvass in order to paint the whole happiness possible to man. In what should it lie? In going on, and simply not stopping? In passing to some better experience? But in what would it be better? In being fuller or longer? I think the longer and the fuller a bad life is, the worse it is. How, then, should it be made better? Only surely, by bringing all its activities, as far as possible, to intrinsic perfection and mutual harmony, so that at each step, and in every high moment of synthesis and reflection, intuition may fall on an essence beyond which it need not look, finding in it peace, liberation, and a sufficient token that fate, so far as that expression of spirit is concerned, has lost its terrors. Without such vision realised at each of its stages, life would be a mere fatality, automatism at odds with itself, a procession of failures. Spirit would have been called into being by a false promise; its only hope would be that by sleep supervening, or by distraction so extreme as to destroy the organic harmonies on which intuition depends, that mistake should be corrected and forgotten.

This possible conflict between matter and spirit is a family quarrel; it is not a shock between independent forces brought together by accident, since spirit cannot exist except in matter, and matter cannot become interested in its formations and fortunes save by creating a spirit that may observe and celebrate them. How happily spirit and matter may lead their common

In normal life, as in play, intuition is the innocent expression of action.

life together appears in play at the beginning, and in contemplation at the end. It is only in the middle when animal faculties are inwardly perfect and keen enough to be conscious, but are outwardly ill-adjusted and ignorant, that trouble arises; because the mind sees and wants one thing, and circumstances impose something different, requiring a disposition and a form of imagination in the animal to which his play-life is not adapted. Spirit—the voice of the inner nature in so far as it is already formed and definite— accordingly suffers continual defeats, by the defeat of those animal impulses which it expresses; and if these impulses become confused or exhausted, it sinks with them into vice or discouragement. It would soon perish altogether, and annul the moral problem which its existence creates, unless in some way a harmony could be re-established between the individual and the world. This may be done in society at large by some firm political and moral regimen; or it may be done religiously by the discipline of the inner man, so that a part of him is weaned from the passions and interests which distract the world and is centred upon purely intellectual or spiritual aspiration. Religion is hard for external events to defeat, since ill-fortune stimulates it as much at least as good fortune. Thus within strict limits, and in a soberer garb, the play-life of childhood is restored to the soul.

Hence that happy quarrel of philosophers—happy because both parties are right—as to whether wisdom is a meditation on life or on death. But in the midst of one we are in the other, not only in that existence is transition, but far more remarkably, in that life triumphant is life transmuted into something which is not life— into union with essence, with so much of the eternal as is then manifested in the transitory. This manifestation, with all the approaches to it, is life itself;

Life, death, and immortality all hang on the relation of existence to essence.

and death is the fading of that vision, the passing of that essence back into its native heaven, depriving us by its obscuration of a part of ourselves, so that existence in us must lapse into some different phase, or into total darkness. Life, if by this word we understand the process of mutation, is itself death; to be fed is to kill, to advance is to reject and abandon. The truly creative movement is only upward, and life, in so far as it means light and accomplishment, is only some pre-destined intuition achieved, some wished-for essence made manifest. Existence itself is a momentary victory of essence : a victory over matter, in that matter, which might have taken any other form, takes this particular one and keeps circling about it, as if fascin-ated; not that there is really any magic here, but that matter, which has to have some form or other, is willing enough to be true to the one it has, and (so indifferent is it to form) to renounce for an indefinite time its native right to inconstancy : as a hardened traveller, not caring what inn he stays at, may remain good-naturedly at the one in which he happens to be lodged. Essence is victorious also over spirit, and no less amiably victorious; since it is in essence that spirit aspires to lose itself and to find its quietus, as it was from essence that matter managed to borrow some character and some beauty. What Spinoza meant by meditation on life was, I take it, the effort to wrest the truth of nature out of empirical confusion, so that all the vicissitudes of things might appear under the form of eternity; and what Socrates and Plato meant by meditation on death was almost the same thing. Only the Greeks, by distinguishing many gods and many divine ideas, could humanise and make friends with at least some of them; and in sympathy with those beautiful immortals they could survey and dismiss earthly existence with a touch of disdain; whereas the piety of thrifty and moralising nations, when enlightened, issues only in a scrupulous natural philosophy. Being overawed by the facts, and eager for existence and prosperity, they miss the liberal life; they prefer perpetual servitude, if well fed, to emancipation, such as interest in pure essences affords; and often (though not in Spinoza) they substitute a troubled hope in some fabulous resurrection for the present union with the eternal which is natural to spirit.

Thus scepticism, dialectic, contemplation, and spiritual discipline, all lead to the discrimination of essence; and anyone who has trodden any of these paths to the end will not need to be told what essence means, or that it is a most real and interesting realm of being. But it is not the whole of being : on the contrary, were there nothing but essence, not one of these approaches to it would be open : there would be no possible movement, no events, no life, and no preference. Considered in itself, essence is certainly the deepest, the only inevitable, form of reality; but I am here speaking of approaches to it, that is, of considerations drawn from human experience that may enable us to discern that primary reality and to recognise it to be such in contrast to our own form of being. We stand, then, on another plane, the plane of scattered experience, brute fact, contingent existence; if we did not, the discernment of essence would have no novelty for us, it would reveal no night-firmament behind our day, it would not liberate us from ourselves or from the incubus of accidental things. If we were prompted, then, by our new insight to cry that our old life was all illusion, we might be turning this insight into a new folly. Enlightenment itself would be impossible if chance experiences had not preceded, perfectly real in their own way; indeed existence (something that has no foothold whatever in the realm of essence) is presupposed and contained in any assertion or denial, and

Essence, to which spirit is addressed, is not the source of spirit or of any existing fact.

in the intuition of essence itself.   The existence and distribution of enlightenment, as of any other fact, places us to begin with in another realm, the realm of matter, which must be begged separately: without it there could be no manifestation of essence, whether in nature or in discourse.

The priority of the realm of essence is therefore not temporal or dynamic.   It is an infinite field for selection; evidently it cannot select or em- phasise any part of itself.   When the selection takes place, we accordingly refer it to a different principle, which we may call chance, fact, or matter: but this principle would be a mere word, a term without indicative force, if it did not select some feature of the realm of essence to be its chosen form: in other words, if this brute accident were not some accident in particular, contrasted with the infinity of other forms which it has not chosen.   To appeal to fact, to thump existence with empirical con- viction, is accordingly but to emphasise some essence, like a virtuous bridegroom renouncing all others: the exclusion is opportune, but the bride after all is only one of a million, and the mind has simply wedded an essence.   The principle of constancy, or perhaps of inconstancy—the selective principle—is matter; yet whatever way it may turn, it must embrace one essence or another.

Matter is the selective principle even among essences.

The approaches to essence are therefore as various as those predispositions in matter which deter- mine the poses of life.   Or we may say that for the mind there is a single avenue to essence, namely, attention.   Awaken attention, intensify it, purify it into white flame, and the actual and unsubstantial object of intuition will stand before you in all its living immediacy and innocent nakedness.   But notice: this atten- tion, discovering nothing but essence, is itself an

Through animal passions and interests, matter directs attention upon essence.

animal faculty: it is called forth by material stress, or
by passion. The passions, in so far as they are impulses to action, entangle us materially in the flux of
substance, being intent on seizing, transforming, or
destroying something that exists: but at the same time,
in so far as they quicken the mind, they are favourable
to the discernment of essence; and it is only a passionate soul that can be truly contemplative. The
reward of the lover, which also chastens him, is to
discover that in thinking he loved anything of this
world he was profoundly mistaken. Everybody strives
for possession; that is the animal instinct on which
everything hangs; but possession leaves the true lover
unsatisfied: his joy is in the character of the thing
loved, in the essence it reveals, whether it be here or
there, now or then, his or another's. This essence,
which for action was only a signal letting loose a generic
animal impulse, to contemplation is the whole object
of love, and the sole gain in loving. Naturally essences
seem thin abstractions to those absorbed in action,
whose heart is set on the eventual, and to whom the
actual is never anything: the actual in experience is
never more than an echo or supplement to deeper facts,
a shimmer on the surface of the great sea labouring
beneath; yet the actual in experience is never an
abstraction from experience itself; it is the whole
fruit of that hidden labour, the entire reality for the
spirit. It is therefore not as a quality attributed to
external things that essence is best distinguished; for
the colour or the shape of an apple may be supposed
to exist in it, and when drawn out and imagined existing alone they may seem ghostly; neither the roundness nor the redness of the apple would be edible. To
a greedy child they would be miserable cheats; but
not so to the painter or the geometer. The child might
be better initiated into the nature of essence (which
is not far from the innocent mind) if he chose as an

instance the pleasure of eating the apple, or of snatching
it from another boy's hand; essences which he would
distinguish ~~~~~~~~~~~~~~~~~~~~~~~~~~~ nd which he
~~~~~~~~~~~~~~~~~~~~~~~~~~~~~~~~~ apples.   A
~~~~~~~~~~~~~~~~~~~~~~~~~~~ at these in-
~~~~~~~~~~~~~~~~~~~~~~~~~~~ les, and not
~~~~~~~~~~~~~~~~~~~~~~~~~~~ inter of still
~~~~~~~~~~~~~~~~~~~~~~~~~~~ gs are mere
~~~~~~~~~~~~~~~~~~~~~~~~~~~ e essential.
~~~~~~~~~~~~~~~~~~~~~~~~~~~ ecise char-
~~~~~~~~~~~~~~~~~~~~ at the mind can take
~~~~~~~~~~~~~~~~~~~~ of essence.   Herein
~~~~~~~~~~~~~~~~~~ al or poetical virtue
~~~~~~~~~~~~~~~~~~ dominating it is, the
~~~~~~~~~~~~~~~~~ hich may control its
~~~~~~~~~~~~~~~~~ ly it addresses itself
~~~~~~~~~~~~~~~~ t is, to the essences
~~~~~~~~~~~~~~~~ if it were pure and

CHAPTER II

THE BEING PROPER TO ESSENCES

THE principle of essence, we have seen, is identity: the being of each essence is entirely exhausted by its definition; I do not mean its definition in words, but the character which distinguishes it from any other essence. Every essence is perfectly individual. There can be no question in the realm of essence of mistaken identity, vagueness, shiftiness, or self-contradiction. These doubts arise in respect to natural existences or the meanings or purposes of living minds : but in every doubt or equivocation both alternatives are genuine essences; and in groping and making up my mind I merely hesitate between essences, not knowing on which to arrest my attention. There is no possibility of flux or ambiguity within any of the alternatives which might be chosen at each step.

Each essence is by being identical and individual.

This inalienable individuality of each essence renders it a universal; for being perfectly self-contained and real only by virtue of its intrinsic character, it contains no reference to any setting in space or time, and stands in no adventitious relations to anything. Therefore without forfeiting its absolute identity it may be repeated or reviewed any number of times. Such embodiments or views of it, like the copies of a book or the acts of reading of it, will be facts or events in nature (which is a net of external

Also universal.

18

relations); but the copies would not be copies of the
same book, nor the readings readings of it, unless (and
in so far as) the same essence reappeared in them all.
Physical obstacles to exact repetitions or reproductions
do not affect the essential universality of every essence,
even if by chance it occurs only once, or never occurs
at all; because, in virtue of its perfect identity and
individuality, it cannot fall out of the catalogue of
essences, where it fills its particular place. If I try to
delete it, I reinstate it, since in deleting *that* I have
recognised and defined it anew, bearing witness to its
possessing the whole being which it can claim as an
essence. There accordingly it stands, waiting to be
embodied or noticed, if nature or attention ever choose
to halt at that point or to traverse. it. Every essence
in its own realm is just as central, just as normal, and
just as complete as any other : it is therefore always
just as open to exemplification or to thought, without
the addition or subtraction of one iota of its being.
Time and space may claim and repeat it as often or as
seldom as they will : that is their own affair. The flux
is free to have such plasticity as it has, and to miss all
that it misses; and it is free to be as monotonous as it
likes, if it finds it easier to fall again and again into the
same form, rather than to run away into perpetual and
unreturning novelties. The realm of essence is the scale
of measurement, the continuum of variation, on which
these repetitions or these novelties may be plotted and
compared. Re-embodiments or re-surveys of an
essence (if they occur) bind the parts of the flux
together ideally, and render it amenable to description.
The essential universality of these forms makes any
fact, in so far as it exhibits them, distinct and knowable :
the universal and the individual being so far from
contrary that they are identical. I am not myself
unless I re-enact now the essence of myself, which I
may re-enact at all times and places.

Since essences are universals not needing to figure in any particular place or time, but fit to figure in any, it is not possible to investigate the realm of essence by empirical exploration. You cannot go in search of that which is nowhere. Some essences will appear or occur to you, since whatever intuition life may awaken in you must light up some essence or other; but what further essences, if any, there may be is not discoverable by simply waiting for them to turn up. Nature is indeed very rich in forms, compared with the inertia and monotony of experience in home-keeping animals, revolving in their private circle of habits and ideas; but nature too is built on a single plan—all nuclei and planets, all life and death— and as much a slave of routine as any of her creatures. The unexemplified is not exemplified there, the unthought of is not thought of : not because in itself it resists being created or described, but because nature and thought happen not to bloom in any way but that in which they have taken to blooming. In part, indeed, this restriction may be due to local prejudice and ignorance in the observer, who draws the periphery of nature with his compass. Another man, a different animal, a spirit native to another world may even now be greeting the essences which it has not entered into my heart to conceive. Evidently my limitations cannot forbid them to rejoice in their different experience; nor can the limitations of any actual experience forbid the essences it leaves out to be just those which are absent. An essence is an inert theme, something which cannot bring itself forward, but must be chosen, if chosen, by some external agent; and evidently the choice made by this agent, contingent as it is and wholly arbitrary, cannot render unavailable the other inert themes which other agents, or itself in a different moment of its flux, might choose instead. The very contingency of existence, the very blindness of life,

Essences are infinite in number.

throw the doors wide open towards the infinity of being.   Even if some philosopher or some god thought himself omniscient, surprises might be in store for him, and thoughts new to his thought; nay, even supposing that his whole experience and the entire history of his world lay synthesised before him under the form of eternity, and that he was not a victim of sheer egotism in asserting that nothing more could ever exist, still the wanton idiosyncrasy of that total fact, the enormity of that accident, could not be blustered away.   Existence is irrational for a deeper and more intrinsic reason than because one part of it may not be deducible from another : any part, and all its parts together, are irrational in merely existing, and in being otherwise than as essences are, that is, identical with themselves and endowed with that formal being which it is impossible that anything, whatever it be, should not possess.   Not that essence can resist or resent this irrational selection which existence makes of its riches: on the contrary, essence is a sort of invitation to the dance; it tempts nature with openings in every direc-tion ; and in so doing it manifests its own inexhaustible variety.   Its very being is to set no limits to the forms of being.   The multitude of essences is absolutely infinite.

This assertion has an audacious sound, and I should not venture upon it, had it not a counterpart or corollary which takes away all its venom, namely, that But non-essences do not *exist*.   If I were in pursuit of existent; substance (as I shall be in the Second Book) they form an indelible I should distrust any description of it not background purely tentative, empirical, and scrupulously transitory modest: but the bold definition which Spinoza facts. gives of what he calls substance that it is Being absolutely infinite, seems to me a perfect and self-justifying definition of the realm of essence: because in conceiving and defining such an object we prove it to possess the only being which we mean to ascribe to it. Denying it to be infinite, or denying that any supposed element in it existed, we should be designating these missing elements and that absent infinity: whereby we should be instituting them ideally, and recognising them to be essences. The realm of essence is comparable to an infinite Koran—or the Logos that was in the beginning—written in invisible but indelible ink, prophesying all that Being could ever be or contain: and the flux of existence is the magical reagent, travelling over it in a thin stream, like a reader's eye, and bringing here one snatch of it and there another to the light for a passing moment. Each reader may be satisfied with his own verse, and think it the whole of Scripture: but the mere assertion of this limit, or suspicion that other readers might find other texts, is enough to show that the non-existent cannot be limited, since the limits of the existent might always be changed. To deny the being of essence, because it may happen to be unrealised, is self-contradictory: for if it is not realised, it must have a quality, distinguishing it from realised forms. Unrealised forms may not interest a sluggish mind: an arithmetician who was happy in the thought of whole numbers, might deprecate all mention of vulgar fractions or repeating decimals, and might swear to die without them, lest his safe and honest arithmetic should be complicated with unrealities. But unrealities of that sort nevertheless envelop his realities on every side; and it is his arrest at his realities that, if you like, is unreal; there is no reason in it, and no permanence; whereas the unrealities are unchangeable, inevitable, and always standing behind the door. Even if the whole realm of essence (as Spinoza assumed) were realised somewhere at some time in the life of nature, essence would remain a different and a non-existent realm: because the realisation of each part

could be only local and temporary, and for all the rest
of time and in all the worlds that excluded it, each fact
would fade into the corresponding essence, and would
remain certain and inevitable as an essence only, and as
a fact merely presumptive.

Essence so understood much more truly *is* than any
substance or any experience or any event: for a substance, event, or experience may change its Existence
form or may exist only by changing it, so that and truth
borrow their
all sorts of things that are proper to it in one individuality
phase will be absent from it in another. It from essence
will not be a unit at all, save by external delimitation.
Perhaps some abstract constancy in quantity, energy,
or continuity may be discovered to run through it, but
this constant element will never be the actual experience, event, or substance in its living totality at any
moment. Or perhaps all the phases of such an existence may be viewed together and synthesised into one
historical picture; but this picture would again not be
the existent substance, experience, or event unrolling
itself in act. It would be only a description of that
portion of the flux seen under the form of eternity;
in other words, it would be an essence and not an
existence. Essence is just that character which any
existence wears in so far as it remains identical with
itself and so long as it does so; the very character which
it throws overboard by changing, and loses altogether
when it becomes something else. To be able to
become something else, to suffer change and yet endure,
is the privilege of existence, be it in a substance, an
event, or an experience; whereas essences can be exchanged, but not changed. Existence at every step
casts off one essence and picks up another: we call it
the same existence when we are able to trace its continuity in change, by virtue of its locus and proportions;
but often we are constrained to give up the count, and
to speak of a new event, a new thing, or a new experi-

ence. The essences or forms traversed in mutation render this mutation possible and describable: without their eternal distinctness no part of the flux could differ in any respect from any other part, and the whole would collapse into a lump without order or quality. So much more profound is the eternal being of the essences traversed in change, than that of the matter or attention or discourse which plays with those essences at touch and go.

Nothing, then, more truly *is* than character. Without this wedding garment no guest is admitted to the feast of existence: whereas the unbidden essences do not require that invitation (with which very low characters are sometimes honoured) in order to preserve their proud identity out in the cold. There those few privileged revellers will soon have to rejoin them, not a whit fatter for their brief surfeit of being. After things lose their existence, as before they attain it, although it is true of them that they have existed or will exist, they have no internal being except their essences, quite as if they had never broached Existence at all: yet the identity of each essence with itself and difference from every other essence suffices to distinguish and define them all in eternity, where they form the Realm of Essence. True and false assertions may be made about any one of them, such, for instance, as that it does not exist; or that it includes or excludes some other essence, or is included or excluded by it.

Notion of the Realm of Essence.

Here is a further character inseparable from essence: all essences are eternal. No hyperbole or rhetorical afflatus is contained in this assertion, as if some prophet pronounced some law or some city to be everlasting. That any existing thing should be everlasting, though not impossible, is incongruous with the contingency of existence. God or matter, if they are everlasting, are

Its eternity is the counterpart of its non-existence.

so by a sort of iterated contingency and perpetual reproduction; for it is in the nature of existence to be here and perhaps not there, now and perhaps not then; it must be explored to discover how far it may stretch; it must wait and see how long it shall last. The assumption that it lasts or stretches for ever can be made only impetuously, by animal enthusiasm, when the feeling of readiness and omnipotence makes some living creature defy all threats of disaster. Yet so long as we live in time, the ghost of the murdered past will always fill the present with a profound uneasiness. If the eternity of essence were conceived after that fashion, it would indeed be a rash boast; no essence has an essential lien on existence anywhere, much less everywhere and always. Its eternity has nothing to do with such mortal hazards. It is merely the self-identity proper to each of the forms which existence may put on or off, illustrate somewhere or perhaps illustrate always, or very likely never illustrate at all.

CHAPTER III

ADVENTITIOUS ASPECTS OF ESSENCE

THE realm of essence, like the empyrean, is a clear and tranquil region when you once reach it; but for the observer from the earth clouds may inter-vene, or his eye may be arrested at some nearer sphere which, just because it has some opaqueness, he may think the true blue. Instead of conceiving essences he may conceive possible beings, problematical facts, forms of things, abstractions, thoughts, sensations, or natural elements. Of course such intermediate objects, however they be defined, will exhibit some essence, since some essence cannot help appearing in any chosen thing whatsoever; but in the categories just mentioned there is some ambiguity, some reference to contingent existence, which limits their scope, and renders them altogether confusing, if taken as synonyms for essential being.

In many impure speculative terms essence is fused with existence.

The word " possible " is slippery and treacherous. It is commonly applied to anything that the speaker can readily imagine, especially when he is ignorant whether it is a fact or not. In this sense the whole future, and much of the past, is called possible when imaginable. But in another sense the whole past and future, even when unimaginable, must have been possible too. The materially possible threatens to coincide with the actual course

Essence not possible being.

26

of nature: and then the term possible begins to mean the materially impossible, provided it is imaginable. The imagination, however, is itself something existent, and extremely elastic: a little shake, or a new stimulus, will cause it to conceive many new possibilities. Can these have been impossibilities before? Perhaps we may take refuge in the notion that everything is possible except what is self-contradictory: in other words, things are not possible merely because they are actual, or merely because they are imagined, but if they are such as not to preclude being imagined. But how should anything preclude being imagined, if an imagination arose capable of imagining it? The meaning can only be that my own imagination, in some particular instance, has got into a tangle, and that in speaking of the round square or of the son of a barren woman I have lost the meaning of my terms; and what I call an impossibility is only the suspense of my thought between two possibilities. Nothing contradicts itself, not even this state of confusion in my thinking. It is a perfectly possible muddle. This process of fluctuating from one object to another has a character easily recognisable; its essence, like every essence, is individual and (since it may reappear) is universal. Contradiction is a vice into which discourse may fall when it blurs the inherent distinctness of different essences. Determination, individuality, variety infinitely precise and indelible (degrees of articulation being themselves all equally distinct) is the very being of essence. Howsoever monistic physics may choose to be, the realm of essence is the home of eternal and irreducible plurality.

The terms " possible " and " impossible " have, then, no proper application in the realm of essence; even to facts in nature they are applicable only in view of human ignorance or imagination. Their true field is that of discourse, where the intent to consider one essence binds the mind to fidelity and consistency, and excludes the substitution of another essence under the same name—excludes it, I mean, if the intent is maintained to express the essence originally chosen. Hence the extension of the " possible " and the " impossible " to natural facts, in so far as their names or relations are assumed to prejudge their character: in a given world, describable by a given essence, anything contrary to that essence is impossible. In the actual universe, its essence being completely determined by the events which compose it, all that is actual is necessary and all else is impossible. But this of course does not preclude the possibility of any different world; and so long as the complete essence of the actual universe is unknown to us, we may give its name to almost any extensions or transformations of the part which we presume to know: so that the known world will be free to become, or to have been, almost anything.

Nothing impossible, except that one essence should be another.

The contingency of existence, though intrinsic to it, and the hypothetical nature of all reasoning about it, are a trial to logicians: they would like their art to rule *a priori*. Many of them, in their eagerness to make logic dominant, betray it, by reducing it to a description of what they presume to be the natural movement of thought or of history: but there are some too devoted and clearheaded for such a subterfuge, who nevertheless wish to chain existence to their chariot. How do so? I know only of one way: to assert that the whole realm of essence is realised in existence. The existence of an infinity of worlds irrelevant to ours, and utterly undiscoverable by us, cannot be precluded by our ignorance of them: the supposition is merely idle. But another consequence involved in this hypothesis is positively repugnant to common sense; and this is, that an infinity of worlds almost identical with ours,

Natural necessity is not logical.

but differing from it in some detail, must exist too. An infinite number of solar systems, for instance, must have begun as ours began, but each of them must have deviated at one point from ours in its evolution, all the previous incidents being followed, in each case, by a different sequel. The interest in natural derivation which animates the observant and artful mind is thus outraged by the demand for logical completeness in things: and there can be little doubt to which side the sense for fact, which alone can judge of facts, will incline the naturalist.

By a somewhat different opposition to accidental facts, essence might be called "the imaginary". This designation is popular and poetically very appropriate, since the realm of essence is unsubstantial, remote from existence, and in-finitely more extensive. In broaching it we escape the limitations of fortune, as the poet does in his fictions; and yet the objects that greet us there may be more definite, memorable, and beautiful than the sordid facts, which we live among without feeling for them, perhaps, any intellectual affinity. But the danger in calling essence imaginary is that, like poetry, we should identify it with the imagined. The imagined is indeed unsubstantial, but it is selected, insecure, and de-pendent for its specious actuality on the vapours of some animal psyche. The imagined is not, as essence is, a field from which all facts must gather their tem-porary forms; it is only a replica or variant of some of these facts — namely, of human sensations — richer perhaps in spots than material reality, but on the whole far thinner and less extensive. Images drifting through idle heads are in their psychological dimension a part of the actual, since the intuition of those imaginary objects occurs at definite times and places. The im-aginary, if it is to mean essence, is the infinite fairy-land of which such dreams are glimpses. The moral

[margin note: Essences are not the imaginary.]

connotation of the word imaginary is also ambiguous. Actual images, being generated in the living psyche, may be very apposite fulfilments to her previous experience or to her instinctive needs, and therefore very beautiful; and actual dreams, even if for the most part silly and fatiguing, are sometimes pleasant and even prophetic. Nothing of the sort can be said of the imaginary as a whole, conceived as the realm of essence. Not being selected or produced by any living soul, but inert, infinite, and latent, it contains an appalling multitude of vain and ugly themes, as well as the few which are relevant to human interests and fit for human contemplation.

If free imagination presents stray essences to the mind, attentive perception presents others, to which studious people give greater importance. The flux of nature could not be a flux, nor at all perceptible, unless it was a flux through essences, that is, through forms of being differing from one another. It is as the forms things wear to the senses or to the practised intellect that essences are first noticed; in this capacity, or as definitions of current terms, they appear in the Socratic school. Geometrical figures, fixed by intent, are certainly essences; so too are any types of animal bodies or human institutions which may be arrested in thought : but so also are all the qualities of sensation despised by Platonism and all the types of change or relation neglected by that philosophy. This neglect was ominous, because if essences had been studied for their own sake they would have been found everywhere, as they are by the poet or the mathematician. To discern them only in natural or moral units, and to think of them as perfections towards which things aspire, is not merely to omit noticing them elsewhere but to regard them as natural magnets, as a background of metaphysical powers, more selective than nature itself, and

Nor the forms of things.

constituting a world of substances behind the flux of appearance. Physics and theology may appeal to such patron substances if they think fit; but in the theory of essence they have no place whatever. Essences are not substances containing a matter that can assume a different essence : they cannot be the material source of anything. Nor have they any relevance to particular places and times, so that one might be conceived to preside over one part of nature, and another over another. The essence of a bridge cannot build bridges or breed them; and when a bridge falls and the matter of it becomes a heap of stones, the essence of that bridge is not a surviving ghost haunting the spot, and seeking to restore the structure. A material bridge-builder must return to the work: and the resulting form will hardly repeat exactly the one that has disappeared; nor will that discarded essence fight against reform, or in any way complain or avenge itself, if presently bridge-builders come no more to the spot, and the placid stream flows on unspanned, reflecting no shadow of any human contrivance. So it is also, in spite of superstition, with the essences of living beings, which reproduce themselves for generations with little change of type. Their conservation is physical and an elaborate instance of rhythm and habit in matter. Here too a material seed must transmit the substance that is to run through the ancestral cycle and embody that familiar essence: let the seed fail, or circumstances modify it, and at once that prescribed form is forsaken and forgotten, relegated to the realm of essence and reduced to the same impotence, or left in the same peace, as all its sister essences that time has never brought to existence.

The most stubborn misunderstanding of essence arises, however, from thinking and calling it an abstraction. In a popular sense the epithet is natural and harmless : it means only that essence is immaterial.

So mathematics is called an abstract science and music an abstract art; they do not describe particular parts of the material world or particular historical events; they may therefore seem unreal and superfluous to the man in the street. But the mathematician or the musician will hardly call them *abstract*, since his apprehension of them is direct and his interest in them primary.

No doubt the material world, especially in his own person and life, supplies a suggestion and an organ for those intuitions; but their object is so far from being drawn out of existing things that it never exists in them in its ideal perfection, and the study of it requires a special imaginative faculty, a profound application, and a great exactitude. It is the very complexity and precise definition of this realm—its essential concreteness—that renders it difficult and vague to the gross mind: and it is called abstract not because it is drawn from existence but because it is not found there.

It is an accident to essence to be manifested; but not to be manifested is also an accident; it means simply that matter or intellect happen never to have traversed that form. A different plasticity in existence might make any essence an appearance; and evidently in a given appearance there can be nothing abstract— nothing verbal, unrealisable, or cognitively secondary. Each appearance (and therefore every essence, since it might well appear) is an obvious and complete being; and if essences when simple are indefinable, that fact only proves that they are the original elements of any description. Far from being creatures of language, they suffer from not being commonly named, since names are hurriedly clapped on things and persons, however ill perceived, which move as material units; whereas the most evident features in immediate experience receive no separate names, until perhaps some logician, poet, or madman grows conscious of their perpetual presence, and borrows some title for them from the vocabulary of physics; as I have borrowed this term "essence," once used by chemists for their drugs, in order to designate every specious object actually present to intuition. Language is responsible, not for these objects, but for the prejudice against them. An essence, if un-named, is thought to be imperfect and but half real. An unchristened child has to be called So-and-So's baby, and a stranger in the street has to be pointed at dumbly; yet it would be too egotistical even for human nature to assert that the waif or the stranger possessed no being of his own, but was essentially an abstraction from our social circle, because he could be described in our language only relatively and peripherally. It is not otherwise with the immediate, radical, nameless phantoms of feeling and intuition. They are just the appearances they are, exactly determinate and perfect at each moment, and different in some precise way from whatever else may be felt before or after or by other people; and the necessary defects, or rather the proper summary function, of language or reflection, must not be charged against those primary appearances as a defect of essence.

When a term is felt to be disparaging, as the term abstract has become for some writers, it can easily be passed on from one bad thing to another. If the parts, Instead of designating defect of form abstract- when de-ness may designate defect of quantity. In tached from a whole, an etymological sense any part of a thing, be called like the skin of an apple when peeled off, abstractions, might be called an abstraction from the whole, are abstrac-especially when the part abstracted happens tions from not to have existed separately in the beginning, of essence. as do the bricks of a house, but to have grown up together with the whole, and been first found there. Hence a well-known doctrine that only the Absolute is concrete and that every particular fact or observation is an abstraction. In this sense of the word, every essence would be an abstraction from the realm of essence, but no essence, much less the realm of essence in its entirety, would be an abstraction from existing things: on the contrary, existing things would be abstractions from their essences, which in the realm of essence possess much richer essential relations than those which in existing instances are abstracted and realised materially. The rind of the apple, peeled and curling casually on a plate, would be a miserable abstraction from all the spirals and all the patterns implied in its geometrical essence and in its pictorial aspect.

Abstraction, however, in the proper sense of the word, is possible only for a mind: things and essences, whatever may be their unions or separations, are never in their own being abstractions from anything else. A term can be abstract only relatively: how should anything be abstract in itself? None of the constituents of a thing or of an essence is an abstraction from it; each is a thing or an essence in its own right. To find abstractions we must enter the psychological sphere and consider the casual history of human ideas. A late idea, though its object may be perfectly concrete and definite, like the sphere, may be simple in comparison with some early impression—say, that of an apple—which may have first suggested it: and if the variegated essence was really distinguished first (which is not always the case) and the simple one —roundness—was only noticed afterwards as an element included in the other, then, for that person the sphere will be something abstract, not indeed in its essence, but in its mode of reaching manifestation: an act of abstraction happens first to have revealed this essence to this man. But such an approach is accidental: a true psychologist would often record that in

Abstraction is an operation in discourse, relative, adventitious, and alien to the essences concerned.

looking at some roundish thing he first noticed and intuited nothing but roundness, perfect, Platonic, and unadulterated. The clumsiest spheroid cannot convey to an innocent mind any idea save that of a simple sphere; and our first impression of a world in which everything is crooked is that everything is straight. The enormity of our childish idealism would prove immediately fatal if we needed to have a true idea of things in order to act properly in their presence. But ideas which are ridiculous as descriptions may be adequate as signals: all animals eat and breed without any notion of calorics or eugenics: hunger and love are moral overtones quite sufficient to express for them their share in the rude economy of nature. The mind is not a fifth wheel to her coach, but her observations on the journey. Conventional psychology is misled by a primitive gnostic theory to the effect that things ought normally to appear to sense in their full and exact nature. Nothing could be further from the fact, or more incongruous with animal life and sensibility. That which appears to sense is determined at each moment by the liveliness and direction of the psyche in her current reactions. Things are thereby "known" in the sense that they are named, and distinguished by their rough aspect and occasions; they are not known at all in the sense of being disclosed in their inner nature, either totally or partially. The specious essence intuited is the *name* given by the psyche to the material force encountered or exerted; it is a spontaneous symbol, not abstract even in its origin; as the word cat is not drawn out of the domestic animal, yet serves to designate it in its entirety, and is much simpler.

Repetition is impossible in the realm of essence; two essences, if not different, will be one essence; if different they will be two essences, and not repetitions of the same essence. Repetition is possible only among objects which are particular but not individual; that is, when they exist and are distinguished by their external relations, even if internally they should happen Essences not general terms. to be precisely similar, and should have but one individuality or essence. An individual may change his relations and have different moments and places of existence, so that here he may be surrounded by one environment and there by another. This possibility of iterating or repeating an essence is what, from the point of view of existence, makes essences seem abstract or general, when in reality they are the only individuals. An essence is not the thing which it defines, and may define many things numerically distinct: what is ordinarily called one thing or one person has many separable moments of existence, between any two of which it may perish: they will be moments of one thing or one person only in so far as one individual essence pervades those moments. As nothing can be abstract in itself, so nothing can be general in itself. Every essence is universal not because there are repeated manifestations of it (for there need be no manifestations at all) but because it is individuated internally by its character, not externally by its position in the flux of nature: and no essence is general for the same reason. However it may be related to particular existences, its own nature is complete and intrinsic; whereas a term can be said to be general only if it happens to be predicable of a number of scattered things, none of which, perhaps, it defines intrinsically. Yet everything that is at all must be something intrinsically: had a term no individual essence there would be no meaning in predicating it, and it could not be predicated of two things in the same sense, since it would have no sense. Before essences can be called—occasionally and in relation to natural things—either abstract or general, it is requisite that in themselves they should be concrete and individual.

The organ of intuition is an animal psyche, governed by the laws of material life, in other words, by habit: so that it is normal for intuitions to be recur- *In dis-* rent, in so far as circumstances allow. Dis- *course,* course, in which intuitions subserve intent, *intent supervenes* requires intended essences to recur identically, *on passive* and imputes identity to them even when they *contempla- tion, and* are different, if their difference is irrelevant *only the essence* to the cogency of discourse, and incom- *meant is* patible with it. It is these intended essences, *considered.* identical for intent on various occasions, but never actually intuited, that might well be called abstractions: they are like points of the compass, or limits of un- ending approaches, ideal in the sense of being never realised, although clearly indicated and definable by their relation to other terms which are actually given. The identity of an essence with itself is absolute and constitutional, but the identity of the essence given in one intuition with that given in another is an identity assumed and always unverifiable. It is impossible to arrest the two intuitions and compare their objects: to do this would be to supersede both by a third in which perhaps twin objects were presented: but it would remain an assumption that one twin repeated the datum of one intuition, and the other twin the datum of the other. Yet the impetuosity of life, which dis- course cannot help sharing, brushes aside these scruples: habit—iteration of words, gestures, and sentiments— sufficiently identifies the essence meant at one moment with that meant at another, in contempt of the varying context in which they may appear. This essence, not the context, is probably the only object distinctly noticed, or designated expressly. Thus the essence of straightness is continually intuited afresh, and is absolutely identical at each recurrence. It is irrele- vant that the material object evoking this essence may be different in each instance, and never quite straight:

that context, even if vaguely pressing on the psyche, remains unsynthesised, unnoticed, and unintended. When on looking at a palm tree, a Roman road, or the horizon, I say to myself, How straight! I have exactly the same clear feeling: and this pure essence, not its irrelevant context, is what actually fills my mind, and is the essence apprehended. All the concomitant stuff, if it were noticed in turn, would merely supply other essences of the same universality. It is impossible that anything should appear which is not universal: for it is definite and might evidently appear again. Hence the possibility of discourse: its terms are coined into fixed values, and can pass from mind to mind, retaining their original meaning.

But mind is not a subject congenial to psychologists: they would like it either to reproduce material facts or to take its place among them, or even to swallow them up and be another name for them. Since the edges of material things are known to be broken and warped in fact, it is presumed that we must actually see all lines curved or broken. But mind is intrinsically and initially mind: it is poetical and Platonic from the beginning; and it is only by a painful eventual reinspection that it can correct its first impressions and allow that material things have in fact forms too complicated for the eye to trace, and a substance too remote in its pregnant texture from the scale of sense to be easily imagined, or to be imaginable by man at all. All this subterranean obscurity, however, is in its place: a wise man will not repine at it. Where clearness belongs, clearness enough may be found: the essences actually defined by attention are plain, brilliant, and homely, like the words of the vernacular. The psyche, a plodding beast, needs but to fall into her old paces for the old visions to reappear. It is essences, not things, that are on the human scale—

Living mind, which is intellect in act, ignored by psychology.

not all essences, of course, but those which the mind evokes spontaneously : whereas things, if humanised at all, can be humanised only by a long architectural labour —a labour which their insidious lapse very soon defeats and annuls.

That essences, though universals, are individual and are given bodily in intuition, may be better understood if we consider those existing things which are supposed to be concrete in contrast to essences. Their existence, we shall find, depends on their external relations, on their inclusion in the flux of nature; and science, in proportion as it penetrates to their dynamic structure and movement, becomes more and more mathematical, that is, operates with categories and terms more and more remote from pictorial physics. It is only when some portion of this inconceivably rapid and complicated flux of matter becomes recognisable and traceable in some respect, that a somewhat concrete thing can be found to exist. In other words, the concreteness of things is borrowed from the presence in them of some essence supposed to be abstract. Only when the flux, by its concentrations and sustained rhythms, manifests for a while locally some recognisable identity of form, can we speak of a concretion in existence, that is, of a thing. Abandon that essence, and that thing has dissolved. Certainly this essence, if it is to qualify existence, must be manifested or embodied in some nexus of events, amid variable external relations; but the flux of events itself would be the most empty of unrealities if it still pretended to flow after having obliterated within itself all distinctions of quality, direction, or phase—that is, all self-identical essences. Essences are definite and thinkable: existence is indefinite and only endured. That is the Platonic experience which I cannot help repeating and confirming at every turn; only that by

Things and facts are essences sustained in the flux of nature.

"thinkable" we must not understand definable in words, but open to intuition in the terms of any sense or of any logic. The flux flows by flowing through essences; and essences are manifested as the flux of matter or of attention picks them up and drops them.

An essence, then, is no abstraction, no unrealisable generality, but any actual aspect which anything can wear, determining its nature, or revealing it to an attentive mind. The sweetness I may taste is not dependent in the order of knowledge or of being upon abstraction from anything else. In my experience it is very likely the first indication I have of any substance called sugar existing near me, to be appropriated or investigated further. When I have gathered all I can learn about sugar, the sweetness originally tasted cannot become an abstraction from this much more remote and hypothetical object. It remains a self-sufficient essence, perhaps the only one given at the moment; but its appearance has now become, for my discursive thinking and belief, a symptom of certain chemical facts in the posited material world which I believe myself to inhabit.

Objects, whether essences or facts, may be considered recurrently, on separate occasions and by separate minds: otherwise discourse and experience could have no sanity, and could accumulate knowledge on no subject. On each occasion, however, the intuition, sensation, or thought turned upon that object is a fresh event, not only numerically but almost certainly by virtue of variations in its quality, context, and mental fringe; so that the living feeling or experience of the moment is something in flux, unseizable, not recoverable, and never, even when it existed, brought under the unity of apperception. Experience is something that just because it exists (without rising to the actuality of spirit) never exists all at once as a unit but only by

Essences not active ideas, sensations, or thoughts.

virtue of its parts, its movement, and its stress. Its parts exist, as it does itself, by occurring in a system of changes and conjunctions never given in such fleeting intuitions as it may include, and probably never given in intuition at all, even in the most accurate retrospect; because these moving clouds of sensibility and intent—the waking dreams of the psyche—are not objects which human attention is fitted or required to apprehend; they are complexes of no stability or importance as units; nothing matters in them save the objects discerned by them, or discerned by us afterwards as the goals of their movement. In discerning any of these objects, whether they be essences or things, animal life becomes intuition, the synthesis of attention by which an essence appears; but this intellectual act is wholly focussed on its object and unified only there. Taken as tension or potential perception, sensibility is diffused through indefinite time and through many vital functions; it would never exist actually and become a sensation unless it became the sensation of something; the intuition of some essence, like a pain or a sound.

An essence is, then, not at all a mental state, a sensation, perception, or living thought; it is not an "idea", as this word is understood in British philosophy. It is an "idea" only in the Platonic or graphic sense of being a theme open to consideration. Mental facts are not units either in nature or in logic; they are sub-divisions made by literary psychologists in the flux of experience considered romantically, as a biography abstracted from its organs and from its natural setting. The dream of life exists: it is going on perpetually in each of us; but its parts, called feelings and thoughts, are individuated only by the essences they discern, which are not the essences of those feelings or thoughts taken existentially, as moments in a dream, but are the essences of anything and everything under heaven or over it. If I think of God, the essence before me, my passing notion of the divine nature, individuates that thought of mine, and makes it possible for discourse afterwards to attribute it to me; but my thought was not God as it conceived God; it was a wretched mixture of words, memories, and dialectical gropings in my heated brain. So far is an existing idea from being the essence which it conceives.

If a romantic psychologist ever succeeded in reconstructing a moment of mental life exactly as it existed, he would be reconstructing (in the fresh setting of his own thoughts) an event itself perfectly particular and never destined to recur. But evidently, since his reconstruction is accurate, the essence given in that past moment is given again to him now; and it must recur in so far as any historian afterwards conceives that experience truly. The repetition of events is impossible, the recovery of essences is easy. Many a dead man, for instance, has considered the dyad in the form of twins, two shillings, or the numeral 2; and twins, two shillings, and the numeral 2 are still found in the world. This dyad, though I give it a learned name, is, indeed, the burden of a primitive intuition. The cat has it when she misses one of her two kittens, and the foreigner conveys it by holding up two fingers: it is not the fingers or the absent kitten that then absorb attention, but the instantly felt difference between one and two. In the midst of various vague and unsteady fields of experience quick intuition continually recovers this important primary essence. Hugging it, the mind can fly from world to world, and can make something definite and concrete out of their chaos, in so far as the dyad finds application there.

Animals live huddled among things and necessarily watchful of them, except in those hours of stolid composure in which they seem to be contemptuously

Mental events are particular and indefinable: essences are obvious and universal.

availing themselves of the chance not to think; whenever they think, however, whether in dreams or in action,
they can think only in terms of essences: and Finally,
hence that fundamental illusion, that hypo- essences
stasis of given essences, which the philosopher are not
constituent
should regard as normal and amiable, while parts of
avoiding it in his own person as far as things.
possible. He will succeed in this self-discipline in
proportion as his interests are intellectual and set
on essences rather than on things; he will then
feel the sharp contrast between the clear hypothetical
pictures in his thoughts and the dark complexities of
nature: he will be constantly aware of being an im-
pressionist in physics, a dramatist in psychology, a
novelist in history, and a pure dialectician in mathematics. But other philosophers are not lacking to
defend the illusion which animal faith imposes on
everybody until criticism comes to distinguish the
sphere of action from the language in which imagination expresses its adventures there. When intuition
remains closely attached to urgent action—in hunting,
for instance, or in pain—the essences appearing seem
actually to inhabit the material object or the bodily
member into which perception projects them. Given
essences then seem to be constituents of substances,
even when they are descriptive of perfectly immaterial
facts, like intentions and feelings: such sentiments, as
imagined by the observer, are boldly attributed to
other people, and thought of as agencies at work within
them. This dramatic sort of hypostasis is after all the
most defensible, because if the observer and the
observed are similar creatures in similar circumstances,
they will really be having similar intuitions; so that
our wild shot will hit the bull's eye by a pre-established
harmony. The transcript of nature in discourse will,
of course, remain poetical, since a man's sentiments are
but unrhymed poems which nature improvises within

him; but one poet may truly understand and repeat another.

It is harder to conceive how the form of a hollow sphere and the colour blue can help to compose the substance of aerial space, or where exactly they shall be deputed to lodge: nor is it clear how these essences can occupy some nearer locus, such as a nerve or a brain. It will not help to call these appearances qualities of things, rather than parts, if the qualities are supposed to be intrinsic: the intrinsic qualities of a thing compose its essence, and its essence, when caught in external relations, is the thing itself. If on the contrary by calling appearances qualities rather than parts of things, it be meant that these qualities are adventitious and relative, the contention is valid; because any aspect, effect, or relation accruing to a thing justifies a new epithet being assigned to it, as on my birth a whole series of dead men, up to Adam, suddenly became my ancestors. So when a human eye is turned skyward, the sky truly acquires the quality of looking blue and round: those are its real qualities in relation to such an observer, as certain substances are truly poison for rats.

But appearances, which are essences, are the qualities of things for experience.

These ulterior questions, however, cannot arrest the impetuous dogmatic instinct which asserts things to be what they seem and to exist in the very terms in which they appear. The stones would laugh, if they got wind of this human assurance; but meantime it is not useless in developing human acquaintance with essences: because this incongruous dignity attributed to them, of being material things, has the merit of attaching practical minds to them; and later, if these wise men discover their error, they may have acquired the habit of defining essences, and may find them worth cleaving to for their own sake.

CHAPTER IV

PURE BEING

OF all essences the most lauded and the most despised, the most intently studied in some quarters and the most misunderstood in others, is pure Being. Confusions It has been identified with nothing, with about pure matter, and with God; and even among those Being. who regard it in its logical purity, it is sometimes said to be the richest and most comprehensive of essences and sometimes the poorest and most abstract.

No essence, as we have seen, is abstract essentially, since it defines itself and might appear alone to an intellect strung to that key: and in the case of pure Being we have high testimony (which there is no reason to distrust) assuring us that, in fact, it appears alone to the human intellect in its ultimate reaches; and even when not realised separately in intuition, it can be discerned both analytically and intuitively in every essence whatsoever. Pure Being supplies, as it were, the logical or æsthetic matter which all essences have in common, and which reduces them to comparable modes on one plane of reality. Pure Being is thus found in all essences somewhat as light is in all colours or life in all feeling and thought; and philosophers like Parmenides and Spinoza (not to speak here of the Indians) assure us that we always have an adequate intuition of this pure Being, usually buried under vain illusions, but when unearthed and isolated seen to be

45

very mighty in itself and easily recognisable. Nevertheless such assurances may mean little to other mortals. Language at these depths of attentiveness is perforce the language of solitaries. When repeated it may not carry with it the intuition which it was first meant to record. The very logicians who distinguish this essence, because they call it Being, may conclude that nothing else can *be*—a most perplexing inference and, in view of the many meanings of the word *is*, a most misleading one; while other logicians, because pure Being is different from all other essences, may hastily identify it with nothing, by a strange equivocation between nothing and nothing else.

Confusion in this matter comes chiefly from the equivocation between being and existence. Initially this equivocation is normal, innocent, and even expedient, like any substitution of names for things: it is only when defended theoretically that it becomes perverse. Intelligence begins with it: animals are surrounded by things that affect their condition and prompt their reactions, so that their attention is necessarily intent upon existing things; yet the intellectual transcript of their condition, in that agony of attention, is only some intuited essence, some sensuous or logical term, which being their sole description for the object before them, they take to be that object itself in its whole existing nature. So individual forms of being stand in discourse for particular things. But sometimes, rather than some specific thing, a certain equilibrium of influences absorbs attention: a noon pause comes in our labour; and more special sensations being fused and blurred, we endure dull strain and duration without diversity —a vast, strange feeling. We return, then, as it were, to the sleep preceding life, to the peace of the womb: there is vitality without urgency, pressure without light, potential movement without object or express

The sense of existence is not the intuition of pure Being.

direction. Such, we may fancy, might be the inner
sense of matter: perhaps some forms of animal or
vegetable life never yield any other experience. A
vague world is posited as existing; for in expectation
and intent, as in memory and the sense of movement,
there is a tacit assumption of things removed, threatening, eventual, as yet unknown. There is accordingly
nothing pure in this sense of existence, simple or vague
as its deliverance may seem; for this vagueness and
simplicity are uneasy. The peace of the womb is precarious; it is but a muffled and initial phase of distraction, confusion, hope, and fear. Care fills its
heart, as it does our dreams; and we might identify it
with the Universal Will of German transcendentalism,
vaguely pregnant with worlds and worlds. But slumber
is not contemplation, and the buzz of matter *Profound*
is not the beatific vision. The pleasure, if *contrast*
pleasure be found in it, is that of original sin: *between*
the father of lies is whispering in that paradise. *of existence*
The intuition of pure Being looks in the op- *and the*
posite direction. In order to reach it, attention *pure Being.*
would need to abandon all concern for transi-
tions, events, ulterior or external facts, and to concentrate all its light on the positive intrinsic nature of the
present datum; nor would that suffice, but from this
special essence it would need to pass to the inner
essence of all those alien half-known things, all those
absent times, and eventual passions, which animal faith
may posit, or fancy may conceive; since pure Being
resides in them all equally, no less than in the here
and now. The force of insight would thus have to
vanquish all will and transcend all animal limitations,
cancelling every fear, preference, or private perspective
which a station now and here would involve. In other
words, in order to reach the intuition of pure Being,
it is requisite to rise altogether above the sense of
existence.

The reason for this lies in the very nature of existence, which is flux and, as Plato would say, non-being.
Flux eludes The more truly existence is felt, therefore,
intuition. the less possible it is to concentrate attention
on anything, and to say, Existence is this. He is
closest to existence, and most at its heart, who lives
on the wing, intent always on the not-given; and even
when the present fact is atrociously absorbing, as in
pain, the sense of existence remains empty essentially
and indescribable, by the very force and distraction
of its presence. If we are asked to describe it, we are
reduced to naming the circumstances or using some
metaphor; and if in the midst of it we pause to consider the internal character of that which we feel,
raising it thereby for the first time to distinct intuition,
the distraction, the belief, the assurance of existence
which filled us before have *ipso facto* disappeared:
some image, some word, some finely shaded sensible
essence alone is left. In other words, the proper
nature of existence is distraction itself, transition at
least virtual; so that it cannot be synthesised in intuition without being sublimated into a picture of itself,
and washed clean of its contradiction and urgency.
The relations which were external from the station of
each of the parts as it arose separately, now become
internal to the system of the whole; and the intuition
in which this whole is synthesised drops the flux of
existence in order to retain only its form and the truth
about it.

If, then, being and existence seem in common parlance almost interchangeable terms, it is only so long
The one is as their respective objects are merely named
primitive, or designated from the outside: when they
the other are conceived positively and at close quarters
ultimate. they turn out to be exact opposites. Existence
exists by virtue of oppositions in the place, time, and
exclusive characters of particulars: being has being by

virtue of its universal identity. This is true of the
being of each individual essence; and it is true pre-
eminently of pure Being. Its identity is omnipresent
and internal everywhere; it equalises those centres of
existence which in their single blindness become nests
for external relations; it makes all times simultaneous;
and by excluding change renders existence, from its
point of view, inconceivable. Moreover, in reducing
all things and all external relations to their internal
being, that is, to their essences, it transports them
into a realm of being which is necessarily infinite,
in which their presence, therefore, is no temporary
accident, as is their existence in the world: so that
the existent becomes continuous with the non-existent,
and neither more nor less real than any other eternal
essence.

This contrast between being and existence is indicated by calling being pure. "Pure" is an epithet
proper to all essences. Objects become pure
when intuition permeates them and rests in   Every
them without the intervention of any ulterior   essence is
intent or cross-lights, as we speak of pure   pure, by its
mathematics or pure pleasure. Purity of this   freedom
sort is no thinness of form, but the perfection ventitious
of it. It admits any amount of detail, if it is all overt
and clear, on the plane of actuality, and not latent. In
this acceptation of the word "pure", pure Being is no
purer than any other essence, but all are pure in so far
as they are considered in their proper character, freed
from the irrelevancies that may encumber them when
they figure for a moment in some material world or in
some labouring mind.

It would therefore be useless and redundant
habitually to speak of "pure Being" if nothing were
meant save that Being is an essence. What is indicated is that pure Being is related to other essences
very much as any essence is related to its existing

manifestations; for whereas any special essence, such as colour or sound, sky-blue or B flat, is exclusive and

Pure Being is so, by its freedom from internal diversity. definable by contrast, pure Being is present in them all, somewhat as space is in all geometrical figures, at once permeating and transcending each of them; for this essence, if not fertile casually as facts are fertile, is in its own way infinitely pregnant. The nature of pure Being anywhere implies the whole realm of essence, since being could not possess its full extension if any sort of being were forbidden to be.

That pure Being, in the sphere of essence, should have this simple, intense, and pervasive sort of reality,

Easy but fatal confusion of pure Being with substance. provokes afresh in the minds of dialecticians that tendency to identify essence with existence which is native to the animal mind. For in the natural world too there seems to be an omnipresent, simple, intensely real something which dwells in particular things, is transmitted from one to another, and compels them to arise in their infinite variety and endless succession. This omnipresent something is called substance. Might not then pure Being, which lies in all essences and therefore also in all existing things, be the substance of these things, and the universal internal cause of their existence? This is a suggestion which has worked powerfully in the thoughts of those metaphysicians, like the Eleatics, whose physics has been dominated by dialectic. Nor is the suggestion altogether false. That something exists, that there is a world, is very true; also that whatever else this world may be, it is substantial—that is, exists in itself independently of all report or opinion. The hypostasis of being into substance is therefore no error, but a first awakening of curiosity and belief, which in so far as it posits the existence of something errs only by its extreme inadequacy. It honestly sets about using the category of substance, but without

any notion of what, in detail, this substance is. This
inadequacy itself is inevitable: how should animals in
the womb, or just out of it, conceive truly that constitution of the world which is not disentangled even to-day
by science or philosophy? Positive error only appears
when this natural inadequacy of our ideas is denied,
and when mere being is deputed to reveal the whole
substance and complete reality of things. The belief
in substance, which should have been the beginning of
art and science, then suddenly makes an end of them;
for if there were truly nothing in nature or in experience
except mere being, all events and appearances would
be sheer illusions, since in reality they would be all
identical.

I shall return to this subject in considering the
properties requisite in any substance fit to subtend
appearances and the life of nature; such
a substance must be unequally distributed
and in motion; its proper name is matter.
Here I will only notice in passing how the notion of
pure Being is likely to be contaminated in the effort
to identify it with substance. Pure Being—as is indicated by calling it infinite and eternal, if we ponder
these epithets—is utterly absolved from all sub-
servience to contingent facts and to the momentary
casual forms of human experience; it is the most
immaterial, untameable, inexhaustible of essences. Yet
Parmenides—no tyro in dialectic—denied that it was
infinite, because it had to give body to an existing
spherical cosmos; and indeed, apart from ancient
astronomy, existence always involves a certain concentration and contrast with what is not, and thereby
excludes infinity. Again, we find Spinoza asserting
that the entire nature of being—which he actually calls
substance—must be manifested in existence, and that
all these manifestations must be parallel to the forms
of the material world, of which indeed those other

*Examples of
Parmenides
and Spinoza.*

manifestations can be only complementary aspects, by chance unknown to us. Here is the cosmic frog prodigiously swollen in rivalry with the ontological ox; but the ox, lest that ambition should seem too absurd, is accommodated to the frog nature, and pure Being is thought of as a sort of matter or force resident in natural things and lending them their existence, while at the same time enriching them with an infinite number of attributes which they hide from view.

On the one hand, then, if pure Being is substance, existence must be illusion; and on the other hand pure Being must be, not the infinite essence which it is, but a hard kernel for existence. Hence the sea-saw in the views of those metaphysicians who hypostatise pure Being; sometimes their substance annuls all particulars, and sometimes it supports them. Pure Being excludes particular determinations within its own bosom, but it does not annul them in the world, because it is not on the plane of existence at all: it is by no means a matter within particulars which lends them existence. Substance, on the other hand, is such a matter; and by its movements and redistribution it gives rise in turn to every fact and relation in the natural world. Were pure Being an existing substance, nothing else could exist or arise, not even the occasional intuition of pure Being. All that exists exists by being other than pure Being, under circumstances which themselves are particular and contingent; and if substance were not contingent, unequally distributed, and in motion, it would evidently not be the ground of any event or of any actual appearance.

Thus the hypostasis of pure Being, after being fatal to the reality of all facts, is fatal to respect for pure Being itself; because, considered as a substance, it would be useless, unknowable, and nowhere to be

Substance is thereby deprived of its natural function, nature is abolished, and pure Being is obscured.

found. Pure Being, although a supreme degree of detachment and concentration be requisite to conceive it adequately, is, like any other essence, perfectly open to intuition; its sublimity is not obscurity; and it is excluded from "knowledge" only in the sense in which any immediate object, being an object of intuition, need not and should not be posited as a removed existence, by the transitive and precarious sort of knowledge by which facts may be known. But pure Being hypostatised into substance is a metaphysical spectre: matter congealed, arrested, emptied, and deprived of its cosmic fertility.

Pure Being, conceived as a substance or an existence, might indeed almost justify the well-known gibe that pure Being and pure nothing are identical. This sophism is complementary to those misunderstandings; the same misplaced preoccupation with physics has ended in impatience of logic and of honest intent. Of pure Being, which is not a romantic object, *Pure Being identified with nothing: psychological character of the latter idea.* the moderns have little experience: the idea of nothing is easier and far more familiar to them. We all know the feeling of contrast and disappointment which comes over the senses when they are robbed of their habitual entertainment, as, for instance, the sensation of darkness when the lights suddenly go out. The psyche, continuing to live her incessant life, feels cheated of her food and bereft of her employment. This is perhaps the origin of that horror of non-existence which afflicts so many mortals; a horror which would be evidently objectless and impossible if really nothing existed, and the poor wights were not there to shiver in the cold. But the psyche, feeling or imagining the sudden disappearance of her supports, finds her own existence empty and abortive: she does not know where to turn or what to expect, and this anguish is her acquaintance with nothingness.

For experience, then, "nothing" means a void caused by the absence of some expected thing. The

fact that such a thing fails to exist is logically dependent on the reality of its form of being, its designated and recognisable essence; and the sense that there is nothing there, is dependent for its existence on a psyche missing some particular thing, and feeling a specific emptiness. Negation, no less than doubt, assertion, or faith, requires the prior individuality of ideal terms; and to predicate non-existence is in that measure to recognise essence. Being and the non-existent here actually coincide; not because both are nothing, but because both are being. If all existence could be abolished, all essence would resume its equable reign: and the absence of rude emphasis or blind exclusion would leave the infinite variety of being subsisting in peace: although this fullness, even if an animal imagination could conceive it, might seem nothing to it, singly preoccupied as it must be with the flux of facts.

The fact of non-existence, then, is a natural alternative to that of existence, in many cases familiar, and in others feared or desired. Like every fact, it is contingent, coming and going at will, and leaving the eternal manifold of being exactly as it was. "The non-existent" is accordingly not a bad name for the realm of essence, seen from the point of view of existence. But this point of view is adventitious; no essence is non-existent intrinsically, since for all it contains or suggests it may very well exist; that is, some existence somewhere may for a time embody or manifest it; and even if this contingent occurrence were by chance perpetual—if, for instance, the essence of Euclidean space were frozen into an omnipresent everlasting fact in nature—this persistent accident would not touch the status of mathematical space in its own realm, a status which is simply irrelevant to existence and not contrary to it.

When the word "nothing" denotes non-existence it is fundamentally exclamatory: it expresses a feeling or an encounter rather than an idea. But the same word may be applied descriptively within the realm of essence, to express non-being or privation of essence; "nothing", then, means "nothing of that sort". *Privation or not-being presupposes essence and defines it.* This mixture of privation distinguishes every essence, since in being itself it is necessarily no other. This is true even of the most comprehensive essences. A statue which includes the head excludes the special individuality of the same head reproduced in a bust: the different limits individuate not only the two material blocks but the two compositions. So the realm of essence, which is the full-length portrait of being, while it contains everything, drops in everything that isolation which makes it, when taken singly, seem the whole of being: it shatters the illusion of so many philosophers that they have found "the only possible" this or "the only possible" that.

Indeed, the essential mixture of privation in all being is more uncompromisingly evident among essences than among existences, because existence, in admitting change, seems to have found a way of circumventing definition. The expedient is not successful, save in so defining an existence *Change and existence cannot elude essential limitation.* that it may include successive phases, as a man's life does: but both the incidents and the life still depend for their being on their essential exclusions. The bachelor becoming a Benedict does not succeed in combining contraries; his singleness is gone; any backward glances or truancies which he may indulge in only spoil and deepen his married state, in which he then feels henpecked or adulterous. Wisdom lies in voluntary finitude and a timely change of heart:

until maturity, multiplying the inclusions, up to the limit of natural faculty and moral harmony; afterwards, gladly relinquishing zone after zone of vegetation, and letting the snow-peak of integrity rise to what height it may. Becoming, therefore, does not unite being and privation more closely than being unites them in itself, even without change or existence. The full character of each essence is inevitably absent from every other essence; but this relative privation or absence of what is alien is the consequence of possessing a positive character. Had each term no private, indefinable, positive essence of its own, it could not justify those exclusions by which we define it, nor could it fill its appointed place and spread out its eternal intrinsic relations in the realm of essence.

Pure Being, like any other essence, is individual and distinguished by exclusions, for it excludes those *Privation is* limitations which render all other essences *a relative* specific; somewhat' as light, which fills up *non-entity,* *but absolute* and dynamically constitutes all colours, never-*non-entity* theless excludes each particular tint. This is *is an im-* far from being a reason for calling pure Being *possible* a non-entity: the exclusion of all exclusions *term.* renders it infinite, not vacant. Vacancy and nothingness are terms applicable to existence, to which external relations are indispensable, and which at any moment may lapse, so that the place thereof knows it no more; they are meaningless in respect to essences each of which, including pure Being, is grounded in itself, and like a jewel or a star, shines all the brighter in isolation. Non-entity figures, indeed, in the realm of essence, because it is eternally impossible that anything there should be anything else; there are therefore always many things which anything is not. This non-entity is purely relative; an absolute non-entity would be self-contradictory, a false suggestion of discourse like the round square or the son of the barren woman. You cannot make a void of the realm of essence, as you so easily might of existence, by waving a magic wand. Its indestructibility is not an accident, a stubborn matter of fact, like that of matter or of God. If you flatter yourself to abolish the realm of essence, you actually refer to it and reinstate it; if you deny it, you affirm it. The only negation of it which, in one sense, might be staunch, would be utter oblivion; but oblivion is subjective. It destroys nothing save the feeling or thought by which something was formerly recognised.

All essences, therefore, partake of non-being, and pure Being does so in an eminent degree, since it excludes the special forms of being proper to *Pure Being* all the others. Bread partakes of non-being *is infinitely* by not being meat; but food, or pure suc- *positive.* culence, partakes of it doubly, by not being either bread or meat specifically; yet it is the positive being in both, in so far as they can sustain life. This pure essence of food is something positive, present in both but limited to neither. Pure Being, like all essences, rejects alien attributes by virtue of its positive character. When an infinite amount of entity has been denied of it, an infinite amount remains, compelling those denials. For the relative non-entity of all essences comes to them in so far as they exclude one another's characters, whereas the positive character of each is its share of being; and pure Being, far from falling outside, is the absolute being in each. It is also the totality of all, when they are regarded not in their distinction (in which they form the realm of essence) but in their continuity and in their common latency within the essence of pure Being itself; because we may say (though such language is figurative and inadequate) that pure Being contains all essences within itself virtually or eminently, since, though it cannot be any of them, it requires each of them to be what it is. The essence of food (for we are not talking of accidental facts) requires and includes all substances that could be turned into flesh and blood. The very non-exclusiveness or intensive infinity of pure Being opens the way for all essences equally, and, since each is something, cannot suffer any of them not to be. It denies each because it remembers all.

In some sense, evidently, pure Being is the supreme being: may it, then, be identified with God? I think *It is not an existence or a power; therefore not the God of theism or of pantheism.* that a religion is possible which should have pure Being for its object, and that it might even become a popular cult; Brahmanism, as the initiated explain it, seems actually to be such a religion. In theory it is entirely directed to identification with Brahma, that is, to eluding all finitude and existence; and the Mohammedans have a somewhat similar discipline, in so far as they abstain from all petitions, and cultivate absolute conformity to the will of Allah. But human religion inevitably has another side. Prudence and piety require a wise man to study the ways of nature, to cleave to good and to eschew evil. Among Greeks and Romans, Jews and Christians, the object of worship is fundamentally a fostering power; God is a dominant force in nature, creating, thundering, issuing commandments sanctioned by rewards and punishments, and in his inner being conceived to be a spirit, thinking, willing, loving, offended, and propitiated. A piety of this sort tends towards natural religion; its superstitions, if it remains superstitious, are superstitions about fortune; forces and events are its sole objects of reverence, and pure Being is nothing to it. The very earnestness of the fact-seeker compels him to reduce all myths as far as possible to literal science. Salvation he will identify with prosperity, eternity with survival, God with nature, or with some flattering purpose seeming to preside over human destinies. Divine com-

mandments, or the will of God, will become in his lips
merely an archaic phrase for the discoverable conditions of human well-being; divine omniscience will
become the truth of things, and divine love their
friendliness and beauty.

This makes a perfect religion for the irreligious; it
means death to the spirit; but the spirit is not so easily
killed. Action, like physical life, is free to _Yet in_
perfect itself, if it can, in its own plane, ad- _natural_
justing itself absolutely to its conditions and _piety
spirituality_
carrying out all its impulses in harmony; this _intervenes._
executive success, far from abolishing consciousness, will
clarify it and make it musical. As the flux of matter,
however self-contained and self-forgetful, cannot avoid
casting an eternal shadow of its every phase upon the
page of truth, so physical life cannot, by becoming
very economical, avoid kindling all the more brightly
the light of spirit: natural existence has these spiritual
extensions, whether it will or no. And in respect to
the realization of pure Being, ultimate and supremely
difficult as it is to achieve ascetically, instinctively it
lies curiously near to the simple heart. Wherever there
is peace—not the peace of death, but that which comes
of liberation from constraint or distraction—there is
a beginning of spirituality. Consciousness is nothing
but intuition thwarted or achieved. Even distraction, until it disrupts consciousness, is tossed between
intuitions; it can therefore turn into contemplation
at any favourable moment, by the mere suspension
of animal will, anxiety, and care. Certainly the dark
peace of the womb is far removed from the peace of
the mountain-top, all clear articulation and self-con-
suming vision; yet animal consciousness, when perfect,
is not unspiritual. It may rest on nothing more recondite than a warm heart or a sound digestion, or
the overwhelming magic of some absolute lure: yet
in its contemplative simplicity, in its disregard of all

ambushed alternatives and material threats, it brings a foretaste of superhuman sympathies, which discipline might one day render disillusioned and habitual. When the object is pure, the spirit intent upon it is pure also.

Hence that strange solace which so many millions find in their religious devotions; under some disguise of fable or image, pure Being is their sanctuary from the world and their liberation from themselves. Natural religion itself, when reflected upon, drives them in this direction. Force and fact are reverenced by the humanist because in them he finds the sources of his happiness; but as he watches and studies them his reverence changes its hue; it becomes disinterested, sacrificial, liberating. Contemplation, even of destiny, neutralises the will. The exuberance of nature, the disproportion between her wantonness and the clean interests of man, must give the humanist pause; he will find the world cruel, and he may react on its cruelty by asking himself what thoughtless pledge he has given to it, that he should be subject to these vain torments. His piety will still forbid him to rebel against fate; rebellion would be a fresh form of vanity. There is no reason why man, or the transitory world in which he finds himself living, should have any prerogative amongst the realms of being. Traditional religion, for all its motherly coddling of human conceit, is not without a door towards the infinite. Theology must somehow reconcile the special mercies and graces coming to men from God, with the immutability and eternity attributed to him. Nor is this an idle theoretical question; for of what ultimate use would the graces and mercies be, if they did not lead men to share that immutability and eternity? In order to keep well and live long hygiene is better than religion. If the fear of power—that is, of matter—was the beginning of wisdom for the natural man, the possession

Contempla-tion of pure Being is the last phase of spiritual progress.

of power cannot be the end of wisdom for the spirit; and the spirit will not permanently worship in God a life inferior to that which it enjoys in itself. Power is a relation between existences; but where did existence and power come from, and how long will they last? There can be no safety in existence even for the gods. Safety in a living world means only forgetfulness of danger, because perhaps, on the scale and in the habitat of that particular being, danger may not be imminent. True safety, spiritual peace, profound reconciliation with fate, lie in another dimension: they spring from a new and superhuman direction of the affections. Piecemeal, amid the accidents of existence, ultimate good is attained whenever the senses and the heart are suddenly flooded by the intuition of those essences to which they were secretly addressed: synthetically, for perfect recollection, it is realised by the contemplative intellect absorbed in pure Being.

This absorption, the union or ecstasy of which mystics speak, has always been the goal of religious discipline in India, and wherever else the spiritual life has been seriously cultivated. This union is sacrificial, like that of the insect in its bridal flight. In it the spirit loses its self-consciousness, the sense of its own or any other separable existence: and it loses this existence actually, because it cannot attain that ecstasy without dropping all connection with its body—that is, without dying. The body may subsist afterwards automatically, or perhaps generate new sensations and dreams; but these will not belong to the liberated spirit, which will have fled for good, fled out of existence altogether. It would seem, then, to unspiritual apprehension, that the end of spiritual life is an end indeed: it is annihilation. This is the plain truth of the matter, when spirit is regarded from the outside, psychologically and

The perfect realisation of it is incompatible with continued existence.

historically. Intuitions are placed and dated in the natural world by their occasions and their organs : an actual intuition of pure Being—something absolutely infinite—is evidently irrelevant to any place or time, and disproportionate to any natural organ. We may safely say, therefore, that it cannot exist. Yet if we transfer our point of view to that of the spirit itself, and energise with it and by it, we shall see that intellectually and morally the spirit is fulfilled by the being of its object, not by its own existence. The soul, says Aristotle, is everything that it knows: but then, we may add with equal truth, the soul is no longer itself, nor a soul at all. There lies the selfless nature of intellect, that existence is indifferent and imperceptible to it, either in other things or in itself: so that in losing its existence—if it has died victorious—it has lost what was no part of its prize, and in attaining its prize it has saved itself entire. Certainly a song that ends full in the quieting of all its impulses and the synthesis of all its notes comes to an end just as truly as if it had broken down in the middle; both the soul saved and the soul lost cease living in time; yet what a strange blindness there would be in giving to both the same evil name, and making no difference between dying defeated and being perfected in death! If in the act of union with pure Being the spirit drops the separate existence which it had before, it drops only what it wished to drop; its separation consisted in not having yet attained perfect intuition, which must be without a natural centre or personal perspectives. On attaining that intuition the spirit abolishes itself by passing into that which it wished to find. Whether saved or lost, liberated or dissolved, the soul ceases to exist equally; but this fact does not touch the interests of the spirit seeking liberation, whose office, even from the beginning, was worship, not thrift or self-assertion.

It is only when we have thoroughly renounced self-

assertion and thrift that we can begin to understand
the spiritual view, which otherwise might seem to
contradict what the psychologist knows about spirit.
But there is no real contradiction: there is only a
transference of exclusive attention from one plane of
reality to another. Wherever spirit exists, it exists at
some particular place and time, by the operation of
its natural organs; but wherever it thinks, it regards
only some essence, eternal and non-existent, a more or
less ample manifestation of pure Being. It is perfectly
possible for any one who will consider the realms of
being together, to honour each in its place and to disregard the scorn which those who have eyes for one
only must needs pour upon the others.

If, then, contemplation of pure Being ever becomes
the last secret of a religious life, it does so only when
religion is transformed into a purely intellectual and sacrificial discipline. Positively
religious or moral feelings then drop into
their very small, very human places. Where
otherwise would be the transforming force,
the sublimity and sure finality, of this insight?
No fond eulogistic words such as "high",
"deep", "living", "spiritual", "true", patter any
longer about it; they have lost their afflatus and their
contraries have lost their sting. It is not because the
sage finds more in pure Being than pure Being itself
that he aspires to union with it, but exactly because he
does not find more. The fervent estimation in which
he held it before he possessed it would render possession
of it impossible if it continued afterwards. Like every
other object, pure Being appears under the form of the
good only to those who are moving towards it, or are
carried away from it against their will. Both creation
and contemplation are vital processes which lend a
relative value to their chosen ends; and when in a
religious life the end happens to be union with

It implies no precepts or scale of values, and does not command the worship which it may receive.

pure Being, this union becomes as precious and as legitimate as any other natural end could be to any spirit, but in no way more legitimate or more precious. Pure Being itself is neither ruffled nor flattered by these opposite currents in the flux of existence. Its authority—if we figuratively assign authority to it—cannot be invoked by either party, but both parties, like everything actual or conceivable, have its connivance and silent toleration. The artist and the moralist may shudder at pure and infinite Being, and may diversify and limit it in their own spheres to their heart's content; but understanding also has licence to be; it, too, is free to choose a good and perhaps to realise it; and it may weave again all those diversities and contrasts into the seamless but many-coloured garment which wraps Brahma in his slumber. There no praise or dispraise can intrude; all this flutter of spirits escapes from it unheeded and returns to it uncalled.

Here, before leaving this subject, I beg the reader to allow me a personal confession, lest he should misunderstand the temper in which I approach these speculations. Every pursuit has a certain warmth about it and sees its object in a golden light which, from that point of view, is a part of the thing discerned; and he who so sees it can hardly avoid using disparaging terms in regard to those who miss that revelation or are indifferent to it. So any artist in regard to his art, or any patriot in regard to his country. For the same reason the intellectual or spiritual life, especially when cultivated in unison with some long-established religious tradition, sets up its precise standards and prizes them absolutely: whatsoever satisfies other ambitious seems to it either a stepping-stone in its own path or else sheer vanity and illusion. Nevertheless it would be senseless to demand insight

The estimation in which pure Being is held is optional and relative to some finite nature.

of a stone; in the spiritual life there is nothing obligatory. Those who have spirit in them will live in the
spirit, or will suffer horribly in the flesh; but this very
insight into pure Being and into the realm of essence
shows that both are absolutely infinite, the one implicitly, the other explicitly; they therefore release the
mind from any exclusive allegiance to this or that good.
It is only by the most groundless and unstable of
accidents that any such good has been set up, or any
such world as that to which this good is relevant; and
only to the merest blindness does *this* world or *this*
good seem absolute or exclusive. Now it would be
stupid in a blind man, because he was blind, to deny
the greatness of a painter who was admittedly supreme
in his art, or the sanctity of a saint, or the insight of
some thoroughly trained, purged, and disinterested
intellect; yet that blind man would by no means be
bound in his own person to begin for that reason to
paint, to pray, or to go into the Indian wilderness and
contemplate pure Being. Humility in these respects
is not incompatible with freedom. Let those excel
who can in their rare vocations and leave me in peace
to cultivate my own garden. Much as I may admire
and in a measure emulate spiritual minds, I am aware
of following them *non passibus aequis*; and I think their
ambition, though in some sense the most sublime open
to man, is a very special one, beyond the powers and
contrary to the virtues possible to most men. As for
me, I frankly cleave to the Greeks and not to the
Indians, and I aspire to be a rational animal rather than
a pure spirit. Preferences are matters of morals, and
morals are a part of politics. It is for the statesman
or the humanist to compare the functions of various
classes in the state and the importance or timeliness of
various arts. He must honour the poets as poets and
the saints as saints, but on occasion he is not forbidden
to banish them.

CHAPTER V

COMPLEX ESSENCES

By one of the uses or abuses of the word *is*, one thing is often said to be another. This absurdity (as a pure logician might think it) flows out of the natural relation of essences with things and serves clumsily to express it. A thing naturally has many appearances—lights, sounds, temperatures, perspectives; and it may conventionally have many names. Each of these essences, as it crosses the field of intuition, is verbally identified with that thing; but good sense, unless a sophistical attempt at accuracy trips up its honest intentions, will easily perceive that none of these names or appearances *is* the existing thing; nor are they the existing thing when added together, but still only a collection, indefinitely variable and extensible, of its names and appearances. The thing is a strand in the flux of matter which, apart from all appearances and names, passes at its own rate through a continuous series of states, until that strand merges into others and the substance of it goes to form other things. So a man, or other natural being, has a material continuity, from birth to death, apart from the sensations which he may desultorily cause in others, or in himself, and apart from the names which he may receive.

Loose logic, incident to such naming and recognition of things, runs over into human thinking even

about essences, because these first attract attention as
signs for things, or as sensuous names; and it takes
time and speculative faculty to discern their intrinsic
nature.   If five potatoes go to the pound, those five
potatoes are said to *be* one pound of potatoes ; and it is
quite true that "five" and "one" are in this case alternate descriptions, in different conventional terms, for
the same parcel of matter.   Yet conceived apart from
that material signification, "one" is evidently not "five",
nor is number weight ; and when essences are envisaged directly, in abstraction (as people say) from all
that is irrelevant to them, nobody would be tempted
to identify one essence with another, or any essence
with any changeable thing.   Why confuse obvious
objects by trying to interpret or transform them at all,
as if their entire and individual nature were not given
in each instance from the beginning?   If the obvious
defies description, it does not require it.   Only it
happens that language, and the other laborious instruments of life, being addressed to the medley of things,
distract us from the obvious and render it ambiguous.
We form the habit of asking what a thing is, a habit
absurd if extended to essences.   Essences do not need
description, since they are descriptions already.

Nevertheless the attempt to describe certain essences
instead of simply inspecting them has some justification and meets with some success.   There
are memorable ideas which we may wish to   Essences
revive; incidental means of reviving them   not given
may be at hand, since intuition has a   in intuition
physical basis determining the essence that   may be
shall appear.   So written music is a means   reported
of reviving melodies; the phonograph is   circum-
stantially.   another;
and even verbal descriptions and similes may not
be useless in suggesting musical essences and distinguishing them clearly in their own category.
Intuition is thought, and anything that clarifies

thought enriches intuition. Less artificially, by the innate phonography of the psyche, much that is not given at the moment may be adumbrated and felt to lie in a certain direction within predeterminate limits of character. The intuitions with which the psyche is pregnant would actually arise if the living process that would generate them could be carried a little further: so our convictions are big with eloquence and our passions with predestined objects, which even if never realised are a sure unconscious criterion for accepting or rejecting anything that may be proffered in their name. The most interesting essences, like the thoughts of ancient philosophers, may be at some remove ; how should they be known in their absence except by description? The imaginative inquirer is reduced to retailing the circumstances or to specifying sundry qualities in which the intended object presumably differs from those within his ken, until he catches or thinks he catches a glimpse of the essence sought.

An ulterior essence may thus be approached as a thing is approached, by laying siege to it and attempt-ing to conquer it bit by bit ; and the same uncertainty always hangs about the most confident success in such an endeavour; because although the mind possesses at the end the essence it possesses, it cannot know that this essence is the one intended, pos-sessed elsewhere by an intuition numerically different and historically remote. The entire historical study of ideas, of which romantic idealism is so fond, is irrelevant to ideas. Interesting as may be an im-provised reconstruction of things past, and fascinating the learned illusion of living again the life of the dead, it distracts the mind from mastering whatever the past may have mastered; it inhibits pure intelligence, and substitutes for it the pleasures of sympathetic fiction.

Knowledge of removed essences is proble-matical like knowledge of facts.

Those ultimate visions are missed on which pure thought would rest, and which lend its only interest to rambling experience ; and even experience itself is surveyed in a false perspective, created by the special frame which the present provides for it, a present always casual and new; so that ancient history needs to be rewritten from the beginning by each generation of romanticists. Indeed, the object of interest in such reconstructions is not a moral revelation, not the rediscovery of an essence formerly discerned or prized, but only the fact that people once entertained some such idea ; and naturally the dates and the names of dead men become more important, and are easier to determine, than the truths or beauties which they may have known. Essences here, as in physics, serve only to supply names for divisions in the flux of matter; for after all this flux could not be distinguished into phases at all unless some essences were discerned in it. It is for this reason that minds fundamentally without loyalties, and incapable or fearful of knowing themselves, pursue subjects like the history of art or of culture. The illusion that they are interested in things beautiful or noble accompanies their purely material investigations, and they trace the genesis of every school of life without understanding the life of any, like eunuchs studying the physiology of love.

The first precaution, therefore, which the description of a removed essence imposes is to discount the method of approach, the position and habit of the observer. He must beware of repeating here the error common and excusable in the perception of things, that of hypostatising symbols and hastily identifying views with the objects viewed. He must not project, for instance, on a complex essence like Euclidean space, the emotional simplicity of a blue sky or a dark room, nor upon a simple essence like pure Being the miscellany of those

A complex essence may be indicated simply, and *vice versa*.

natural facts or human ideas by which pure Being may be manifested to him. The most complex approach will not complicate that which itself is simple, the setting will not carve the jewel; nor will the blank wonder of an eye seeing only simple bulks remove complexity from the intrinsically complex.

In what sense can any essence be intrinsically complex, seeing that every essence has its eternal and Three kinds indivisible unity? This question will answer of unity: itself if we ask another, namely, What is qualitative, quantitative, unity? because if there is a unity incompatible and formal. with complexity, there is another essential to it. Pure unity is qualitative, like that of a scent or a note, or like that of pure Being. Such unity is indivisible and defies analysis. But a pure quality may pervade a continuum: the scent may be diffused, the note prolonged, and pure Being may be contemplated. The unity of this continuum is quantitative and merely specious or imputed; it subsists because by chance the component parts of it are not discriminated. A continuum offers an opportunity for variation and the interweaving of qualities — something impossible without a common medium or field; quantity will then become order, it will display a form or system. The imputed or specious unity of the continuum will not be in the least jeopardised by this internal complexity; on the contrary, the complexity presupposes the unity, otherwise the elements would not figure in the same context or fall into those relations which knead them together into a particular compound. These elements would then remain separate simples, like colours in tubes; before they can form any picture a canvas or an eye must compose them into a complex essence, itself, like every essence, perfectly single and individual. Thus a third sort of unity, that of order, system, or form, is presupposed in any actual complexity of being; and the doubt whether an indivisible and eternal essence can be complex dissolves in the fuller insight into what essence means. This complexity is not material; it is not the factual coexistence of elements themselves self-centred and self- existent. It is the essential complexity of a form, in which the relations of the parts are internal relations in the whole; so that both the total unity and the contrasting parts are pure essences. Every landscape seen, as actually seen (not as confusedly supposed to exist semi-materially like a natural stage-setting) is an eternal and indivisible unit; the least derogation from its complete essence substitutes a different essence for it. *That* spread of light, *that* precise emphasis of line, *that* mixture of suggestions, are no material facts collected into an existing object; they form the very individuality of the composition momentarily intuited, which any one who would ever behold the same landscape ("the same", spiritually speaking) must evoke anew in its perfect identity.

> A particular complexity is of the essence of most essences.

In most essences complexity is obvious: a line is drawn-out-ness, progression leaving a trail; a direction is a goal of progression chosen among others avoided. Every articulated image offers some spatial or temporal pattern which is essential to that essence. There is no limit to this complexity in unity: the system of any world is one essence; the whole realm of essence is one essence. There is therefore one essence which is absolutely infinite in complexity; but doubtless many others are infinitely complex in particular respects or categories, as number is; they would seem no less hostile and exorbitant to human imagination.

> Complexity may be infinite.

The reader must forgive me if I repeat a warning; a certain lofty and idealistic sound in the word essence should not tempt his tender mind to regard essence as somehow more human than matter.

> Inhumanity of essence.

Let him be disabused ; the friendliness of essence is not intrinsic to that eternal sort of being, but hangs on two circumstances : one, that being non-existent, all essence is *innocent* and incapable of injuring or threatening him materially; the other, that when actually given in intuition, every essence is *luminous* and not estranged from him by any doubt or veil. Matter is neither luminous nor innocent; it is therefore no object for contemplation; but nevertheless there lie all his hopes; hence he sprang, on that he feeds, and there he must leave his mark if he would render existence more friendly to the spirit. It is by the shifts of matter, in the world or in the brain, that essences are revealed; very few can appear to human intuition at all, and still fewer to a sane human mind; happy the man who, in bringing to light those which to him can be enlightening and congenial, leaves all the others to loom for ever in the distance, like ancient gods respected but not worshipped: monstrous, tedious, occult, and inhumanly complicated.

In essences actually given the complexity possible is limited by the intellectual scope of the thinker; and Poverty of human intuition. this is not great. Man, harassed as he is by pricks of fortune and irrelevant calls, has to rely on the organisation of his thoughts to make up for their poverty ; if he does not misread his signals he seems intelligent, though his spirit may be a blank or stream of ticking trivialities, like the sound of the telegraph. The greatest men hardly have one great moment; their minds seem great only when the historian reviews their various actions or accomplishments, and pieces together a mythical source for them which he calls a great mind. There was never an actual greatness, a living thought mastering and directing the whole; and the historian himself is as incapable as his hero of gathering up that desultory competence into an actual intuition of the whole achievement.

Eloquence, or the spell of some rite, serves at best to hint at such an unrealised greatness; and man must commit to monuments, to books, to institutions, the suggestion of those visions which he never had. So seeds carry over from generation to generation a labouring something which we call life; it has an inward determinate potentiality, there is something which it would be; but when and where, in what joyful bridal or victorious cry, is that potentiality realised? The best seems still more than half hope and a strange uncertainty; and when we look at our clearest thought, at our most comprehensive intuition, we find in it almost nothing: we are always at cross-roads in a narrow valley, the whole world but a vague object of faith, only this poor halting-place actually ours.

So much is nature the mother of spirit, a child at the breast; it must be fed at every turn by things, resigning to their ministry that authority which it can- not exercise over itself. These things, when great originally or made great by material labour, first suggest to the spirit what ought to be its stature, if it aspires to comprehend them. It is they that keep it plodding in the path of progress, and compel its lantern-light to creep wonderingly over their vast breadth. Thinking is like telling one's beads; the poor repeated mutterings of the mind compose, beyond themselves, a single litany, a path leading humbly step by step, past every mystery, up the mountain of knowledge. It makes no difference to posterity how violent or prolonged may have been those effervescing thoughts which left this sediment of habits and institutions; what still matters is the seed-like power in this sediment, when stirred afresh, to generate in other spirits intuitions purer, juster, more classical than those into which nature might have budded untaught. The syntheses of art are far greater

Spirit is great only vicariously by virtue of its objects.

and more comprehensive than those of life. If many poets had collaborated to produce the works of Homer or of Shakespeare, these works would still be what they are: in any case, each poet is many poets in act, as many as he has moments of poetic inspiration; and the psychic continuity of his animal person, crammed full of idiocies and vain prose, is far less rigidly pertinent to his message than is the material collection of his works. Material works, customs, and ceremonies are the stay of the mind; in them it grows sober, madcap that it is in its dreams; without them its fine thoughts would go out like sparks, accruing to nothing and transmissible to nobody. Even such familiar unities as we all profess to survey clearly—a landscape, a political event, a system of philosophy—are commonly unrealised mythical objects: we observe some casual feature and implicitly assume a system of other features which we might observe *seriatim*, had we the time and the patience; and the prophetic heat with which we hail this reality is out of all proportion to our actual understanding. We are satisfied if we can go on believing that the hidden truth would justify our sentiments, could we survey it synthetically; and what we call our knowledge is really only a string of miserable phrases and small points, supported by the rash conviction that behind them lies a great truth, a familiar friendly reality from which we are never far and about which we are never wrong.

There has been much play of dialectic (for instance, in the *Parmenides* of Plato) about the One and the Many, The One or without ostensible result. Unity and plural-the Many, if ity are essences; they find an obvious and, hypostatised, up to a certain point, a sure application in make an impossible things: to which circumstance they doubtless physics. owe the clearness and confidence with which we conceive them. But they cannot be expected to be the intrinsic essences of anything existent; the existent will be many and one in a thousand ways without being one or many absolutely. Pure unity cannot exist, because existence by definition involves external relations, which will render many variable assertions true of that unit; and it would be by virtue of these relations, not of its inner unity, that such a unit would exist. If the One exists, then, as Plato says, it is Many. But if the Many exist, they are also One, since they could not exist without mutual relations which would bind them into one system. There are other reasons or relations which justify the same dialectical paradoxes: for instance, in so far as the Many are many, they are *each* one, as well as being One in their totality. There is no natural end to this shuffling of aspects; in the realm of existence, as Heraclitus and Hegel have urged, unity is manifold. Things are without other individuality than that which they acquire by proxy when some essence is embodied in them; and as substance is indefinitely plastic and forms are infinitely various, this world is much more emphatically a medley than a unit; and yet it is one in some respects, as in its dynamic continuity and in its speculative totality or system. An extreme violence is done to nature when such simple ethereal essences as unity and multiplicity are hypostatised. The result is a metaphysics which excludes the possibility of any physics—that is, of the only element in metaphysics which describes matters of fact; and the more intense the realisation of these essences is in intuition, the farther the contemplative mind flies from nature, and from any understanding of existence or any belief in it.

When, however, an essence with some precise articulation actually appears in thought, the alleged conflict between unity and plurality is perfectly solved, or rather is proved never to have existed. Suppose that in an architectural mood I stop really to consider and

In given essences, they are correlatives.

survey a façade; could it, in an æsthetic sense, be a
façade if it was not one composition? Could it be
a composition if it had no parts? Could it be this
individual composition if not composed of precisely
these elements in precisely these relations? Of course
I am not speaking of the stones and mortar and
their chemical constituents; from them, as from the
instruments of an orchestra, are wafted to me certain
material influences which kindle my intuition and, at
this juncture, evoke this vision. I am speaking of this
revelation of a moment, of something homeless in the
world though visiting me there under the gracious
influence of this place and hour; I am speaking of an
essence. I am satisfied if in respect to any and every
essence all cavil ceases, and it is heartily acknowledged
to be just as much one and just as complicated as
it happens to be, the complexity being complex
because synthesised in a single medium, and the unity
specific because composed of just these elements,
merged or contrasting in just this manner.

This perfect and eternal individuality of every complex essence is a point worth meditating upon; it helps
to make evident the infinity and, so to speak, the
democracy intrinsic to the realm of essence, and the
admirable absence from it of such things as scale, transition, genesis, or contiguity between its members. I
say, between its members, because of course *within* one
essence or another these relations, like all other forms of
being, are bound to be contained. Duration, specious
time, change, repetition, etc., are all essences perfectly
open to inspection, if not to description; the idiosyncrasy of each is absolute; and when they appear, the
peculiar relation between their parts (which is their
very essence) appears within them. But this very
idiosyncrasy renders it impossible that one should
become the other, or be composed otherwise than as,
in act, it already is; in such suppositions we are shifting

our attention from the complex essence to be inspected and substituting some view of our previous experience or of the material conditions which we presume have brought that essence to our notice. These historical vistas may be true ; but they could not be so if the synthesis which composes the vista did not faithfully render, here and now, the method by which events have unrolled themselves then and there. The question of the truth or descriptive propriety of an essence is therefore a second question, entirely subsequent to the question, or fact, of what this essence is. That change occurs continually in nature is true; but only because in the essence of change we have given together, in a single image, the successive phases of an event which, when change is enacted, are necessarily alternative. This power of projecting given essences and assigning them to things as their characters or as their relations, enables discourse to thread the labyrinth of nature dialectically. Far from removing from the complex essences so projected and used their perfect individuality, it presupposes this individuality, to which it assimilates the untraceable flux of material events. Whatever, then, may be the history of nature, or the genesis of intuition in us, all the forms which nature may assume are ontologically equally primary, and all the essences that may appear in intuition are equally fresh and original.

CHAPTER VI

IMPLICATION

SINCE any essence is an eternal form of being, each is grounded in itself without reference to any other. All essences Thus the realm of essence is an infinite are indi- plenum or continuum, in which every essence vidual and self- is surrounded by others differing infini- sufficient. tesimally from it in character. This realm is an absolute democracy by virtue of the indefeasible right of every member to its self-made place in it; and whereas in earthly democracies it suffices to be born in order to acquire every civic right, in this celestial republic even those who have not taken that risk and trouble possess full citizenship. Nor is any one threatened here by the pressure of the hard-hearted majority, or by any rude government. Here is perfect anarchy in perfect peace. The population is infinite, no legislation is possible, and everybody is safe.

In one sense, indeed, the being of any essence implies that of every other; for if any one essence is assured of its being because it is a distinguishable something, obviously every other distinguishable something is assured of its being on the same ground; so that an infinite multitude of essences is implied, if you will, in the being of any essence. Certainly no essence can create any other or remove it or pre-empt its place, that ontological place being all that an essence is. To play the dog in the manger is proper to things; essences

are always in their respective kennels.   The principle of
identity (when the accident of existence is disregarded)
renders the number of individuals spontaneously
infinite; but this principle is no force exercised somehow extraneously on individuals, or which they could
pass on to one another.   Nor will so liberal an implication ever help thought to pass from a given essence to
any other essence in particular.   The intuition of the
essence to be thought of next, even in the most obvious
inference or deduction, must be generated by the
movement of living discourse, and by the circumstances
of some animal life.   Essences are unsubstantial: the
psyche, or matter elsewhere, is the substance at work.
The essence last thought of was an essence only; it
can trail no consequences and involve no sequel.   To
attribute consequences to essences is superstition.

Such developments, then, as take place in nature or
in discourse are all generated materially.   As they
were first initiated contingently, because some   Their
parcel of matter happened to exist at some   emergence
place and time, so the phases they traverse   contingent.
afterwards are generated, if not by chance, by some
impulse which happens to be native to that structure
or to the material circumstances that feed and transform
it.   At every stage such a development picks up one
essence and drops another; each essence, like Michael-
angelo's statues lying unhewn in the block, is intrinsically no better fitted for existence than any other, and
cries for it no more loudly.   The choice, as in the case
of the statue, must be made by the genial fertility of
things already existing—the artist, his habits, his surroundings.   The artist is alive; his surroundings are
full of fashions and movements; all these existing
motions have directions; they leap and mingle and
disappear like rills down a mountain-side.   The forms
they create, they create spontaneously.   The aspect
they assume may be unprecedented; and even if

familiar, it is but a haunting essence, without power to reproduce itself or to exclude any particular sequel.

Hence the earnestness and honesty with which the defenders of free-will assert at once two incompatible A side-light things: indetermination and power. They on free-will. are expressing the life of matter, which is indeed not determined exactly to reproduce its previous forms, but tumbles forward to fresh collocations; and the power in it is truly internal—not a compelling magic exercised by any fixed form, energising either out of the past or out of the future, but indeed a potentiality or propensity within the substance concerned, a part of that blind impulse and need to shift which is native to existence; and as this universal dance was groundless in the beginning, so it remains groundless at every stage and in every factor, whether the figures of it be novel or habitual. This groundless pervasive power, with its tireless inner monotony and its occasional outward novelties, is matter thumping in the hearts of the free-willists much more loudly than in those of their opponents. Believers in necessity have caught sight of some essence—a law or habit or rule of some kind—which they make haste to clap upon nature, as if nature had no further depth, and they had touched bottom with their proverbs; as knowing people are always incredulous of things not within their experience or their books. At some depth, and in terms not at all on the human scale, nature may very well be mechanical—I shall return to this question in its place; but each factor in that mechanism would remain perfectly spontaneous; for it is not the essence illustrated here that can produce the essence illustrated there. One configuration cannot even suggest another, save to an idle mind playing with the rhymes of appearance; but substance throughout continues groundlessly to shift its groundless arrangement. One inert essence after another is thereby embodied in things—essences inwardly irrelevant, and associated even in thought only when thought has been tamed and canalised by custom. The method of this transformation may contain repetitions, and to that extent it will be mechanical; but it will never become anything but a perpetual genesis of the unwarrantable out of the contingent, mediated by a material continuity impartial towards those complications. So the common man feels that he is the source of his actions and words, though they spring up in him unbidden; and he weaves a sophisticated moral personage, all excuses, fictions, and verbal motives, to cover the unknown currents of his material life. Philosophers are not wanting to do the same for mankind at large, or even for the universe.

Any essence is a model of explicitness; it is all surface without substance. When it appears, it appears entire. How, then, should any essence have implications? Implication is something in which obscurity and fate seem to be lurking; if so, it must be something imposed on essences by human discourse, leaning, not on logic, but on the accidents of existence. And yet in dialectic we are supposed to be elucidating the meaning of pure ideas without any reference to their truth, as if the realm of essence were a second cosmos, or rather a first cosmos, the eternal intellect or Logos of God, pre-existing by a fatality deeper than any creation, and imposing itself on every possible world. *No pure essence can have implications.*

By insisting on the infinity of essence I have, in one sense, already discarded any metaphysical rationalism which should attribute this sort of prior existence and authority to any system of logic or grammar. Essences are prior to existence, but being infinitely various they cannot determine existence to take one form rather than another. Moreover, if there be a divine Logos composed of particular essences or ideas forming *The realm of essence is no particular Logos, logic, or grammar.*

a closed system, it is evident that other systems, differently compacted or anarchical, would appear in the background, since the Logos would explicitly exclude them from its own panorama: the pre-eminence of this Logos would therefore not be essential, but due to a quasi-existence, to a fact or an accident. This is perhaps the reason why Plotinus and the Christian theologians have posited the One or the Father to be the source of the Divine Intellect; as this Intellect is presumed to be specific, and not the infinite realm of essence, it expresses, by that limitation, a factual principle, a primary accident, existence, or power. Much in the same way the transcendental logic of the Germans, supposed to control existence, has to be referred mythically to a Will or a Deed itself an absolute accident. In contrast to such a Logos, the realm of essence forms rather a chaos than a cosmos. Any special system has alternatives, and must tremble for its frontiers; whereas the realm of essence, in its perfect catholicity, is placid and safe and the same whatever may happen in earth or heaven.

No essence, accordingly, can imply any other in the sense of excluding from the realm of essence the opposite of the essence implied, or any different complement. From itself an essence may exclude anything; in fact, it excludes everything not itself; but when a thing or a thought is said to preclude another, this happens only by virtue of adventitious laws of nature. A man cannot be in two places at once, not because the two places are not equally habitable or perhaps present to his spirit, but because they are assumed to lie apart farther than the span of his body. In what passes for logical exclusion or implication such a reference to existence is sometimes covert, but often it is quite direct and undisguised. All hangs on the

Implication and impossibility hang on an accepted order in nature.

usual connotations of language, on presumptions about the course of nature, and on the *argumentum ad hominum* addressed to the mental habits of mankind.

Implication in the first instance is indeed a physical relation, like that of surface to volume; such a bottle implies such a quantity of wine. Implication is the tacit commitment by which all the material detail and destiny of an object becomes relevant to intent when we point to that object or name it. So when a witness is called up in court all his past, which may presently be unearthed in cross-examination, is implied and is set vibrating, as it were, by that summons; and this even if most of those details are then absent from his thoughts or perhaps unknown to him; he may be astonished to find, by the implications of the evidence, that like Oedipus he is a parricide. At bottom the same concretions in existence govern the deductions of logic. If in looking at an object I notice that it has three corners, this specious essence, three - corneredness, which is called up in intuition, becomes itself as it were a summons to all the other essences which might be found in the same object upon further scrutiny. I note next, perhaps, that there are also three sides, of a length not irrelevant to the breadth of the opposite angles; and all my supervening geometry will be developed, not by deductions from the original specious triangle, but by continued inspection and comparison of the forms of things. I may afterwards arrange my observations dialectically, re-defining my terms so as to include in them the material implications discovered in nature, as Spinoza arranged his psychology; the whole system will tend to become a single essence, in which all the parts are contained by definition; but my guide to the choice and discrimination of that particular system will be, and will remain, observation of nature. The truth of each term, and that of their

Implication may denote: (1) physical inclusion.

arrangement, will be still empirical.   This is necessarily
the case in regard to the *truth* of dialectic, at any level
and in any degree of internal elaboration; because
truth is subsequent to existence, being truth about it.
Euclid or Plotinus or Hegel might be dialectical jewels
without a flaw, and yet the whole truth of their systems
would lie in the existence of a world which happened
to exhibit the very special form of those systems with
a miraculous fidelity.

Truth, however, is one thing and implication
another.   May not one part somehow involve another
(2) Descrip-   in a purely ideal system?   Yes; because,
tive equiva-   apart from material truth, an essence fixed
lence.   in discourse at one moment may become
an object of inquiry and intent at another moment.
When these moments are continuous, or deputed to
be continuous, the specious essence first given may
remain sensibly the same, and yet may be re-surveyed
and described in a new order, enriched by fresh
analogies, measurements, or internal discriminations;
and since all this subsequent analysis is but more
inspection of the original essence, the new essences
coming to light in the analysis (for they *are* new) are
said to be implied in the essence analysed.   This is not
strictly the case; the intuition of three-corneredness
is innocent of the Pythagorean proposition and might
be prolonged for all time without revealing it.
But when geometry, the measurement of fields or of
building-plots, has reached such a proposition, the
mind does not lose its old object in the new, but superposes this upon that, and feels their identity for intent;
the second is but an elaboration of the first, describes
without falsifying it, and transforms it only by seeing
it better.   In other words, a substitution occurs which
is felt to be materially valid, especially when it may be
reversed, and the two essences may alternate without
inconvenience in the description of the same facts;

as sense and calculation continually relieve each other
in the practical arts. This reversible equivalence in
terms is something steadying to the mind; it is attentive science; altogether different from the stray
fertility of some fact or of some fancy, materially
dissipated in unreturning ways.   In natural evolution
the original is destroyed, or if reproduced, as by a seed,
it is reproduced in a new instance, in a new setting,
with a destiny and a face never identical; but in dialectic the original theme subsists entire; it remains the
perpetual point of reference and criterion in implication;
its children surround it only to honour it.   The most
mathematical triangle still has three corners; and all
the descriptions and analyses by which an essence may
be elaborated dialectically leave it as limpid as the sky
after navigators have crossed it with their parallels and
meridians, or painters have mixed their viscous pigments to match its lights.

Implication, then, cannot enter into the realm of
essence or become truly native to an idea unless it is
turned into explicitness;   that is, unless it (3) Logical
means the actual inclusion of a part in a whole. inclusion
The triangle, in so far as its three lines are of these
                                               parts in this
included in the intuition which defines it, whole.
involves the lines so enumerated and synthesised; and
each of these lines, as found in that concretion and as
parts of that essence, implies the rest, as every stroke
in a picture, if taken as part of that picture, implies the
remainder.   In other words, pure logical implication
is but analysis reversed, and subsists only so long as the
whole subsists and supplies the lines of tension and the
specific termini of those implications.   But the moment
the given concretion is dispersed, the elements which
were parts of it stand alone, and no one of them implies
that whole any longer, or implies any of the other parts.
Neither the three angles separately, nor one or the other
of the sides, implies any triangle; each element is now

a complete essence, open to separate intuition, and not manifesting any need or proclivity to be united with any other essences into a whole centred elsewhere. Nor does it ask to be elaborated inwardly into any one of those patterns which might be introduced into it without destroying its outline and its present definition. Any such elaboration, if by chance it grows manifest, sets a new total essence before intuition, and abolishes the former object in its specious simplicity; for the outline preserved in the more complex essence, being but an outline there, is not the same actual object as the similar outline given pure and apart, though discourse may substitute the one for the other at its own convenience. Thus logical implication is unilateral; every essence involves its parts, considered as the elements which integrate it; but these elements, considered as separate essences and individual units (which all essences are) do not in turn imply any whole into which they may enter elsewhere; for they may enter into all sorts of concretions, and their only essential being is their own and what is intrinsic to their individuality.

Logical implication interests the contemplative mind because it enriches intuition; but the only implications that concern discourse are transitive and therefore borrowed from the flux of nature. Wherever there is growth towards maturity or through some biological cycle, an eye familiar with that round may see in the earlier phases a promise of the later. The grub, for the naturalist, prophesies the butterfly, although presumably the essence of the butterfly is totally absent from the aspect of the grub and from its mind. There is only, I suppose, a mechanism which eventually brings about that complete transformation; but without needing to trace this substantial continuity, the naturalist may observe

Nature gives play to logic in so far as continuity, repetitions, or fulfilments are to be found in her.

the gross phases and outer habits of nature, as if forms
bred one another directly; and this regularity in
phenomena may become for him a sort of implication,
as the flight of birds became an omen to the attentive
augurs. In an empirical system causation is reduced
to superstition, skipping from fact to observed fact
without attempting to penetrate any of them or to
examine the medium which connects them substantially.
It attributes to a juxtaposition of appearances a
mysterious power to reproduce itself. Unfortunately
in immediate experience there are, strictly speaking, no
repetitions. The word *and* occurs often; but never,
for actual feeling, in exactly the same context, or with
exactly the same emphasis and colour. Empirical
philosophy, if sincere, ought to become mystical and
to deny that the flux of events has any articulation or
method in it. The fertility of being would then be
devoid of all implication; no involution would justify
evolution or give it direction.

Even a pictorial physics, however, may discover in
the flux of things something besides continuity: there
is inheritance. A son may not only appear as if by
chance in his father's family, but he may have his
father's nose. So in any moral heritage there is a
survival of early features in the midst of accretion
and change. The Old Testament is not merely bound
among us in the same volume with the New, but the
New quotes the Old, and the Old is said to prophesy
the New. In asking any question we demand a
relevant answer: the missing feature must not only
come into a given field but must somehow fit into it
essentially. A satisfying answer, while certainly not
implied in the question, responds to the essence of that
question in a way predetermined within logical limits;
it is pertinent. Pertinence is a loose or partial implication, as inheritance is a loose and partial repetition;
when these are added to continuity we have perhaps as

much logical coherence before us as can be demanded
of phenomena.

I have said that logical implication is explicit
inclusion of a part in a whole; but what is inclusion?

The
essential
elements of
an essence
are insepar-
able from it. When one essence is said to include another,
an identification has taken place *in discourse*
between an element in the inclusive essence
and the whole of the included one; but no
essence can *be* another, so that in this identification (which is the first principle and condition of
reasoning) there is something non-logical, not to say
absurd.[1]   We may say, and must say, if we discourse on
the subject at all, that pure Being includes unity and
that unity includes pure Being; yet if pure Being were a
part of unity, unity would not be one; and if unity were
a part of pure Being, pure Being would not be pure.
It is language and thought that create this confusion
by giving the same names, "being" or "unity", to
essences not in themselves identical; because the
being included in unity is not the individual essence of
pure Being: the nature of essence is pluralistic and
excludes pantheism. So the unity included in pure
Being is not the individual essence of unity, but an
inseparable pervasive and unique something found in
pure Being by human intuition and identified abusively,
but inevitably, with the essence of unity when inspected
apart.   Identification is approximate only, and therefore inclusion is fictitious. Not that identification
need be erroneous, as if, for instance, the unity in pure
Being were not truly unity but plurality.   Unity is the
right name for it; the essence of unity as contemplated
separately is the right one to assimilate to pure Being,
since in discourse assimilations are inevitable; but the
point is that the most proper identification is still the
act of calling one essences which are individually two:
a trick of discourse and language.

[1] Compare *Scepticism and Animal Faith*, pp. 111-115.

Thus pure Being is truly included in light, as in all essences, and may be discerned by intense attention in the given essence of light; but light is *Abstraction, analysis, and predication substitute fresh complete essences for the elements present in the essence considered.* nevertheless not compounded of pure Being, present also to mere wakefulness in the dark, and a second factor, light without being. The second factor, whatever else it was, would include pure Being as much as the supposed compound includes it. Predication is therefore not a discovery of composition. As a thing is not a compound of its appearances, so an essence is not a compound of the terms into which it may be analysed. Analysis yields something specific-ally different from the object that justifies the analysis: an essence never *is* any description of it. Essences have no origin, and in that sense no constituents; their elements are only their *essential* features, which define them and are defined by them. A straight line may be intuited alone, say by an organic motor impulse felt in a dream: you traverse it, you have an im-mediate acquaintance with its absolute nature. You may think that you find it again by inspecting the edges of a triangle; but here the object, "straight line", has become the object of a different sense, sight, and appears in a context, the visible triangle, absent before, and strictly excluded by the original intuition expressing only a motor impulse within the organism. The identification of the straight line there with the straight lines here is therefore intentional only, not actual. It expresses an affinity between the two intuitions, their partial equivalence in discourse; and perhaps the separate occurrence of the first may have contributed, through the preparation and enrich-ment of the psyche, to the present complexity of the second.

Such conventional dialectic, in which intuition is submerged in the rush of animal discourse, is facilitated by words and other rude symbols. Human intelligence is strangely materialistic, not in respect of matter, where materialism would be in place, but in logic; it begs of signs, which it assumes to remain materially identical, to assure it of the identity of the essences signified. Whenever we use the same word we suppose ourselves to have the same idea; and in any long or accurate argument direct intuition must give place to guidance by a conventional notation: discourse becomes a sort of calculating machine, by which material counters are shuffled materially and intuition is only required, if at all, to read off the result attained mechanically. Demonstration at best is something verbal and technical; logic is a kind of rhetoric. It marshals intuitions in ways which are irrelevant to them: in time, in the order of complexity, by analysis, or by synthesis; so it considers terms only from the outside, as if in the end everything did not hang on what they are intrinsically. Colour, for instance, being revealed by the same sense that simultaneously reveals extension, is felt to be inseparable from it, or even from the material object believed to exist in three dimensions. Yet colour in itself is a most pungent and positive essence, which can come and go while extension remains the same; and it is only an accident of human sensibility that no organ yields something which might be called colour without extension, as the ear yields high notes comparable to violet and low notes comparable to deep red. If this analogy were felt a little more strongly, every one might indulge in the licence of symbolistic poets who tell us that treble *is* azure and bass *is* crimson: they are only letting the cat out of the bag and betraying the secret that all identifications are matters of discursive impulse, intentional and poetical. Nothing *is* anything else; all essences, however complex, are individuals, and they are individuals, however

Logic is a path traced by habitual discourse in a field of relevant essences.

simple. Their parts are parts only of that whole, as the right half of a picture is to the right and is a half only when the whole is given with it; otherwise it makes a whole picture by itself, and its centre is in the middle of it, not at the left-hand edge. But the simplicity of intuition makes the knowing mind impatient: it must get on, even if it gets into trouble. It loves generalities; but generality is a property only of animal attitudes, or of names in respect to the range of their application. Many persons may be called John; many essences may be called triangles, including the various definitions of the triangle itself; for this is not a generality but an individual essence which is, or might be, discovered separately. It is not likely that the same essence should ever appear twice in human experience: of course, any essence *may* reappear, since it is a universal; but the complexity and fluidity of life make exact repetitions unlikely in actual intuition. The essences about which discourse hovers and to which it repeatedly refers are objects of intent, just as things are; they are common goals for miscellaneous vital approaches; and if an intuition of them were ever attained, intent and animal faith would still be requisite in order to identify the object present at the end with the object intended at the beginning.

No essence is general: generality is a function of terms in external relations, i.e. in a dynamic physical context.

The realm of essence, then, while it is infinite, continuous, and compact, nevertheless leaves each of its elements entirely alone and self-centred; it is the home of indelible multiplicity and eternal individuality. No essence, not even pure Being, has any moral prerogative or any cosmic influence by virtue of its essential being: those functions belong to contingent existences, by virtue of their dynamic relations with one another, which traverse and

The absence of all material implications leaves every essence equally innocent, inviolate, and profound.

underlie the varying forms which they wear. Poetry and music lie as deep in the realm of essence as any logic; the thread of humour runs through it as essentially as that of fate. Pure sense has no object but essence; every contravention of human logic or natural law, as by chance established, is as firmly rooted in that laughing firmament as are Euclid and the Ten Commandments. A mock solemnity has too long made humanity pose as absolute; its virtues would be safer and more amiable if they recognised their relativity, and the spirit would be freer to recognise its superhuman affinities—because there is no reason why spirit should be merely human in its interests. Even nature likes to slip the gossamer bonds of human propriety and expectation, which entangle the fancy only of special individuals or nations; for matter resembles a lady often divorced, though never without a husband. The realm of essence is the playground of an even greater freedom, in a far more real singleness and integrity of being: because it justifies and exemplifies constancy no less than variety. Variability is hardly freedom, since it undermines the soul which aspired to be free. The desire to break away from an established system of life is after all a sign of weakness: the man has failed to become willingly and perfectly what he was attempting to become blindly. The truly radical liberty which the realm of essence opens before us is liberty to be something positive: as positive, precise, elaborate, and organic as it is in us to make it. Essence is an eternal invitation to take form. And the virtue of this invitation is not exhausted by being once accepted. All the possibilities remain always open ideally; and when the earth of a particular world quakes under it, and it fears to be lost for ever, its own essence, among the essences of all the other worlds, stands by in an ironical eternity, waiting for it to dissolve, and perhaps to be born again.

NOTE

In this discussion I have endeavoured to keep my eye on the living subject-matter, and to make my language as plastic as possible in the description of it. But there are learned men whose notion of clearness is always to use words as they have been used before; they may find my view confused, and may ask indignantly whether I am a realist, a conceptualist, or a nominalist. Let me observe in the first place that even among the Scholastics these positions were held exclusively only by partisans and heretics; the orthodox doctrine included and required the three views in their respective places. Universals lay in the mind of God before the creation, and guided it. They therefore were *ante rem*. But according to classical natural history and morals, all created beings were inwardly addressed to determinate types, so that perfection and depravity were possible, and souls could be saved or lost. Universals lay therefore *in re*, and were the souls of things. Finally, human observation might gradually discover and define these universals, by giving a common name to their various instances as they appeared, for example, in disease or in beauty. Universals, for human experience, were therefore *post rem*.

Remove, now, the Platonic Ideas in their moral exclusiveness, and substitute an infinite realm of essence. All universals will still be prior to existence; all possible natural types, classes, or ideals will be found among them, as well as repeated in the pattern of nature; and every concept of thought, as well as every image in sense, will be found there also, and will be a universal. Universals are individual, not general: terms can be general only in use, never intrinsically; but the individual is an essence, not an existing particular. The latter is not a possible object of intuition and has no place in logic: it is some fragment of the flux of nature, posited in action, and by virtue of that status for ever external to thought. My position, then, is simply the orthodox Scholastic one in respect to pure logic, but freed from Platonic cosmology and from any tendency to psychologism.

CHAPTER VII

THE BASIS OF DIALECTIC

IF essences have no external relations, and therefore
no implications, what can be the source of dialectic?

The force
and direc-
tion of
inference
cannot be
native to
essence.

When a man is inconsistent, we seem to distinguish that which should follow logically in
his thought or action from that which ensues
actually. Whence this distinction? And
whence that systematic extension of concepts,
so vast in scope and so specific, which the
mathematician pursues, and which leads him sometimes
to revolutionary discoveries? Whence that pregnancy
in ideas, political or theological, which often renders
them ominous, secretly absurd, and as it were hypocritical, having at heart implications which on the
surface they disown?

The very notion of pregnancy gives, I think, a hint
of the answer. Pregnancy belongs to matter, not to
essence. The difference between what follows logically and what follows actually cannot be due to the
conflict of two different orders of existence, one logical
and the other natural. An existing logical order would
be something metaphysical, a monster half essence and
half force. The difference must be due rather to two
levels of natural organisation, one cosmic and inanimate, the other animate and proper to the innate
involution of the psyche in man, which opens to his
imagination and reason paths other than those actually

traced by outer nature even in his own action or explicit discourse.

In the realm of essence, if ever we shake ourselves loose from our animal distractions and presumptions, everything that appears at all, appears patently; but in reasoning there is initially a hidden affinity or tendency in the terms, which does not become patent until the conclusion is reached. Then indeed the implication of those terms in this conclusion becomes clear, because they now simply define a new essence to which they are intrinsic. This new essence I know by intuition: no dialectic is involved in seeing or defining it to be thus. When the number *two* is given in intuition, the number *one*, repeated, is involved in it: this repetition of *one* is the very essence in view. But when the number *one* is given first, it is an accident whether I begin to count, and whether I go on living until I reach the notion of *two*. Therefore it is possible for me to define or deduce the number *one* by analysis when I have the number *two*, but not possible to define *two* when I have only *one*. On the other hand, it is quite possible, by living, to climb to the notion of *two* from that of *one*, but impossible to climb to *one* from *two*, because *one* is then already in my possession and under my foot.

I may observe in passing (confirming what I have said above about pure Being) that dialecticians who find in *one* the root of all numbers, or in the One the fountain of the universe, seem to be at heart less lovers of essence than of substance; they are not intent on form, but are searching for ultimate elements in the depths of time or of evolution, for something materially radical and indestructible in this existing world. High numbers do not satisfy them, and seem to them secondary, as they seem unreal or even humorous to idle human fancy: yet in the realm of essence all numbers are equally primitive and equally in the foreground. The parity and

The pre-eminence of the number one not essential.

eternity of all essences has hardly dawned on the minds of philosophers—at least not in the West.

Dialectic evidently involves transition; it is progressive; but any actual transition transcends the realm of essence (where every term traversed must always retain its intrinsic character) and proves that an existential and moving factor is at work, namely, attention and whatever may be the basis or organ of attention and of its movement. In a word, a psyche is involved, which herself involves (as we shall see) an existing material world. But dialectic contains more than transition, since this transition is often assumed to be a reversion; in reasoning, intent continually harks back to the object of a previous intuition and compares it with that of the present one. This feat is materially impossible; but it suffices if we perform it presumptively, by assuming that our successive objects are identical and that we should find them to be so if it were possible for us to observe them simultaneously. To transition, then, reasoning professes to add repetition and the assurance of repetition; so that besides a series of intuitions we must admit a power in thought which is not intuition but intent, since its object is something not given, but posited at a distance and identified in character only, not in position, with the given term. Intent is a sort of projection through faith, positing a relation of which only one term is given, the terminus or point of origin here, together with a gesture, word, or sense of direction indicating what and where the other term ought to be. This assumption—logically entirely in the air—is necessary to establish any instance of cogency, contradiction, or fallacy in reasoning; for the obvious disparity of two terms given simultaneously (whence comes all the emotional and essential assurance that the square is not round) does not prove any contradiction in discourse, until we assume that these very

Transition, repetition, and comparison are external to essences.

essences were present to some mind professing to identify them; and this assumption is very likely to be false, and is always hazardous. It is the great source of futility in argument. The first postulates of dialectic, therefore, the constant meaning of terms and the principle of contradiction, are rooted in animal faith. The light of intuition cannot avail to establish that use of them which alone renders them potent in discourse, or applicable to any subject of ulterior interest. The obvious is obvious, but terminates in itself; that which we say *must* be so, need not be so unless our habits of inference are independently justified by the course of nature.

Now that part of nature which is the organ of mind, the psyche, is a relatively closed system of movements, and hereditary; the living seed, as it matures, puts forth predeterminate organs and imposes specific actions and feelings on the young creature: he must eat, fall in love, build a nest, resent interference or injury. But this pre-determination is not exact, only generic; the seed develops as it can, under fire of the environment; the psyche in each individual grows into a somewhat different system of organs and habits, and these vary with time, not merely according to the predetermined sequence of phases in the race, but according to the fortunes of the individual. This partial predetermina-tion of life—which in man is especially imperfect, and dependent on the chances of education and experience— is the source of the generic; the general, absent from the realm of essence, is omnipresent in impulse and action. Every living creature aims at and needs some-thing generic, not anything in particular: *some* food, *some* shelter, *some* mate, *some* offspring, *some* country, *some* religion. The impetuous soul, half-baked and addressed only to the generic, pounces on what it happens to find; it receives it into the stomach, or

Biological nature of the generic or general.

into the mind, and digests it if it can; but there remains almost always a distinct disparity between hereditary capacities and demands, in their potent vagueness, and the satisfaction provided for them. *Not this, not all this, not merely this*, says the psyche at every turn; and her sustenance leaves her half-disgusted and half-hungry. Experience at the same time clarifies the instincts which it disappoints; and it is in terms of actual perceptions, expurgated or transformed, that secret ideals can first come to expression.

Dialectic is fledged in this nest, and obeys the same conjoined forces of innate impulse and casual experi-

The generic prejudices of the psyche are hardened and made specific by habit.

ence. Each thought, in its existence, is due equally to the predisposition of the psyche and to the course of nature outside; but the *presumptions* inherent in the thought, or accompanying and flowing out of it, are determined by the psyche alone, by the momentum and direction of her life at that moment. Hence the whole moral conflict and tragedy between reason and fact, desire and event, the ideal and the actual, nature according to philosophers and nature according to nature. In pure reasoning this conflict takes the form of opposing relevance, consistency, and implication to wandering thoughts or chance perceptions; but the force of logic, as we have amply seen, does not reside in the essences actually inspected, which have no transitive relations, but expresses the habit and range of the psyche in the thinking animal. A mind not buffeted by change, in a world in which rain and shine were not alternate, would never think of any complements to a present object; it might even passionately deny their essential reality, and might call China impossible, life in the water unthinkable, and any morality but the familiar one self-destructive. In minds, as in insects, the vehemence of littleness is remarkable. Man although born plastic and immature, soon borrows fixed prejudices from casual experience; he is teachable, and achieves littleness, or has it thrust upon him by custom and dogma. Acquaintance with facts—and with how many facts is any man acquainted? —narrows his generic native demands into specific requirements; he must now have only *this* food, *this* shelter, *this* mate, *these* children, *this* country, *this* religion. In the same way the mind, when indoctrinated, will suffer only *this* physics, and only *this* logic. Nevertheless, any given world or any given flow of imagination is an accident; its very character would be inexpressible were it not surrounded in the realm of essence with an infinitude of variations any one of which, had it been realised instead, would have been equally accidental. Even the true sage, who passes through the school of experience and learning only to recover his spiritual freedom, cannot range impartially over the realm of essence; the paths he traces in that labyrinth are imposed on him by accident, because a psyche is at work within him obeying special instincts and biassed by a special experience. Even in him the transitions of dialectic and the course of contemplation are not determined by the structure of the realm of essence, since the realm of essence, by definition, is the home of all possible structures.

Dialectic, then, while ostensibly following ideal implications absolved from any allegiance to facts or to actual instances of reasoning, secretly expresses a material life, and this in two stages. The psyche is predetermined at birth to certain generic conceptions and transitions; and these are rendered precise and irrevocable by habits formed under the pressure of circumstances.

Everything in dialectic hangs upon strength of soul; it is an effort to carry over intuition from one moment to another, to be true to oneself, and to wander into no vision not congruous with one's first insight, and complementary to it, so that at the end the mind may believe that it has gathered in and preserved all Moral its riches, and unearthed the secret of all its function of objects. This is something which no living dialectic. mind does or can do; and in so far as the ambition to do it is successful, the success is balanced by a great illusion, almost inevitable to the complete logician; the unity which his discourse has achieved he imposes on the realm of essence and on the existing world as if it drew their circumference and repeated their intrinsic order. This illusion does not destroy the dialectical coherence of the system which occasions it; but the philosopher probably aspires to describe the truth; and in that he fails, in proportion to the vehemence with which he posits his system, with its dialectical structure, in lieu of essence in its infinity and nature in her unknown depths. Dialectic is the conscience of discourse and has the same function as morality elsewhere, namely, to endow the soul with integrity and to perfect it into a monument to its own radical impulse. But as virtue is a wider thing than morality, because it includes natural gifts and genial sympathies, or even heroic sacrifices, so wisdom is a wider thing than logic. To coherence in thought it adds docility to facts, and humility even of intellect, so that the integrity of its system becomes a human virtue, like the perfect use of a single language, without being an insult to the nature of things or a learned madness.

Being *a priori*, that is, being the assertion in the face of things of a pre-formation in the soul, dialectic *A priori* is fundamentally romantic; but its roman- *logic* ticism may become austere and ascetic, in *expresses* so far as it desists from professing to drag *physio-* *logical pre-* the world with it in its speculative flight. *formations.* How far the *a priori* rules in a mind is a bio- logical accident; we may imagine some insect or some angel, created full-fledged, in whom it should rule exclusively; and we might perhaps find fanatics in whom it rules exclusively in speculative matters, once they have been thoroughly indoctrinated. For we must not suppose that anything is *a priori* in origin; every instinct and organ has its history, just as every custom has; but once the organ formed, it imposes *a priori* certain responses on the body and certain ideas on the mind. The *a priori* is such only in function. So when an intuition has become dominant, and has established its settled affinities in a well-organised mind, the further march of mundane experience becomes useless to the logician, or even distracting. As young poets on a slender experience sometimes reach the greatest heights and the greatest depths, finding nothing to intercept the impetuous flight of their spirits, so the dialectician who most resolutely hedges-in his thought in one lane of logic, may go farthest in that direction, and most unerringly. He unveils some integral pattern, perhaps never copied by things, in the realm of essence; the integrity of his pure intent and undivided attention have enabled him to unveil it. He has laid on himself the difficult task of being consistent, of being loyal, not to the realm of essence, which cannot be betrayed, but to his own commitments; he is determined to find and clarify the meaning of his spoken thoughts. Dangers lie to right and left of his path: he may slip into a change in his premises or into forgetfulness of his goal. Fulfilment is moral, even in logic. The mind bears burdens no less than the body, from which indeed the mind borrows them; and the pregnancy and implication of ideas are signs of that vital bias.

Intuitions are themselves incidental to animal life; in revealing the purest essence, like a colour or a number, they remain rooted in the soil, and render every image symbolic of the conditions under which it arises.   Thus colour brings with it extension, form, position, and an aerial emotional redolence drawn from the vital influence of light and room upon the psyche; number suggests a certain particularity in its units, as if it were a mere aggregate, yet this particularity is proper only to the moments or parts of existence and is absent from the constituents of number in its purity; for in a number the logical units numbered are merely fractions of that number, not particulars in themselves.   Yet these physical roots of intuition are far from jeopardising the essential purity of the flower to which they lend these human affinities. Horticulture simply becomes more varied and expression richer.   Intuition lyrically marks the chief crises in material life, when some organ composes and accelerates its movement, turning it into a musical note.   Dialectic is merely a change of scope in this organic synthesis by which a new essence is substituted for the one first given, that is, for the theme and terms of the analysis or deduction; a change by which the original essence, in disappearing, is identified with a part of the new one, or with a whole of which the new one is a part.   The transitions are discursive, their necessity is merely psychical; but they lead to intuitions in which essences appear having intrinsically a logical complexity corresponding more or less perfectly to the stages of discourse which preceded; this correspondence, so far as it goes, makes the validity of dialectic, a validity which cannot be intrinsic to the essence reached in the conclusion, since it is the validity of a process, of a series of substitutions and identifications.

Essences are related to dialectic somewhat as things are related to experience.   A stock or stone, dead in itself, may exercise a living influence on the imagination.   If I strike it, or if it falls upon me, or if I take

Intuitions have a natural context with which the essences revealed are associated in discourse.

shelter beside it, I encounter a reality unfathomable in its complexity and pre-established in its station; but in my romantic experience it has become an enemy or a friend. So the terms of discourse, taken in themselves, are passive and complete, implying no development; but I have arrived at them by the quick exercise of my senses or by a concretion of elements in my thought; there is a history and a momentum in my apprehension of them, and it is by no means indifferent to me, as it is to them, how they shall be superseded or transformed. Most sequels open in the realm of essence (and these sequels are infinite), or even most sequels likely in a dream, would prove irrelevant to the interest dominating waking discourse, which is not these pure appearances but some problem in the material or moral world.

The progression of discourse is a natural flux, controlled physically.

Discourse is not contemplation; dialectic is more laboriously intertwined with the accidents of existence than is intuition. It is selective, responsible, perilous; like everything in flux it moves forward by a kind of treachery to its parent world, and subtly pretends to fulfil that which it is destroying. The continuity is physical, not logical. The navigators who in the age of discovery followed in one another's traces or sought to outdo one another's exploits, had a common background and a common field; otherwise their new worlds, however marvellous, would have added nothing to the old world, and would not have discovered one another; America, China, and India would have retained their ancient self-sufficiency; while Castile and Aragon, England and Holland, would have grown no richer and no wiser. So with every problem, however ethereal. A problem is a natural predicament, a living perplexity, limiting the relevance of the solution sought and creating its value. Discourse would not be cumulative, it would set and solve no problems, if it did not share and express the adventures of a psyche in a material world; for the controlling force in reasoning is not reason, but instinct and circumstance, opening up some path for the mind, and pledging it to some limited issue.

Dialectic, like investigation, is a path to an end; it is instrumental. When successful and finished, it yields to intuition, for which the facts and relations discovered become an ordered system, a single complex essence. Then the predicament and the problem lose their malignity; they survive only in the interest or beauty which, in dying, they bequeath to the new object spread before the mind. Contemplation becomes disinterested, but remains pleasant; for it is not the contemplation of *any* essences at random, but of those precisely to which a vital affinity drew the current of my blood, the hidden essences to which my nature was directed, partly from birth, partly by ingrained habit and arts learned by experience. It is the consecutive sanity and moral integrity of a mind that hold it down to dialectical consistency. There are goals in animal thought, as in animal action and passion, of which thought, in its material basis, is indeed an integral part. These goals are set by the nature of the organs at work, a nature in its turn more or less adapted to its external opportunities; so that the goals of a healthy intellect—for instance, geographical knowledge—like those of hunger or love, are not unattainable, except by misadventure. When a geometer analyses the triangle or a lawyer points out the implications of an alleged fact, he is appealing to a fund of principles domesticated in the minds of his hearers, principles which he may call axioms or simply common sense. His dialectic will be cogent if it leads in the end to an intuition in which all the details gathered during the argument may find their places: that is, although the successive intuitions

The end of discourse, intuition, is itself a function of animal life.

and the essences they revealed will have disappeared, the stimulus and momentum which created them will proceed synthetically to a fresh intuition, as it were their joint heir, combining them without loss or friction. This total intuition will perfect the operation of its organ, raising rational life at that point to its natural entelechy. The many by-paths of fancy or logic either not traced or explicitly excluded will be called false or irrelevant; and so they will be in this final system to which they are logically repugnant; but they cannot be false or irrelevant in themselves, nor in such other systems as they might help to build up. These other systems are rejected, not by logic but by the structure of the psyche and of her environment. Thus Euclid clarifies the intuition of space which the Egyptian builders, and earlier perhaps their arboreal ancestors, had gathered in the prosperous course of their sports; Euclid brings to light the real implications of such building and such swinging. His science guides those early arts to their ultimate self-knowledge. That those first terms of animal observation and this ultimate geometry are alike well chosen is a truth of physics and morals; their application is perfect in the fields from which they were drawn; they give the true rationale of human building and swinging. But the realm of essence cannot suffer violence, and the constructions favoured by man or by nature do not prevent the same elements from entering, if occasion arises, into other designs.

The purely logical cogency of a system lies accordingly in the internal relations of that system when completed. The included elements have no Absolute intrinsic obligation to belong to such a evidence system; but if they fall within the intuition is intuitive and internal of a living mind, which if well knit can have to essence. only one such ulterior system for its natural goal, they should be, and probably will be, addressed by that mind to that system. Were the elements left detached, or combined into other wholes, the dialectic proper to that mind would be lost in the sands of a vain experience, and its congenial system would never take shape. If, for instance, any other man had undertaken to compose this book, it is certain that at every cross-road in the argument he would have taken a turn somewhat different from mine, without necessarily doing more violence to the elements combined. Our systems might have been equally coherent, if in each case the elements became parts of a single essence, clearly intuited; but each system would have been a monument to a different spirit and a different life.

The value of two such logical systems for the description of nature would be a second and distinct

Validity in a system can be only symbolic and moral. question. The more cogent system might easily be the more extravagant or childish one, if the elements combined were few or fantastic, or the harmony sought merely poetical. On each animal species, on each man and nation, nature imposes a special way of thinking, and they would be foolish to quarrel with their endowment; they will not attain truth, or anything else, by eluding it. Their thought will issue in a coherent system if their original intuitions were sharp, the synthesis of them broad, and the interpretation honest. Then all random trains of thought inconsistent with that system will be instinctively discarded; and through many a council and controversy, as in the formation of Christian dogma, heresies will be excluded as they suggest themselves, and the scattered original revelations will be interpreted in such a sense that the spirit which originally received them may honour them together. Every science and language and religion is big with unsuspected harmonies; it is for the genuine poet or philosopher to feel and to express them. Only an orthodoxy can possibly be right, as against the bevy of its heresies, which represent wayward exclusions, or a fundamental disloyalty. But no orthodoxy is right as against another orthodoxy, if this expresses an equal sensitiveness to the facts within its purview and an equal intellectual power. All values are moral, and consistency is but a form of honour and courage. It marks singleness of purpose, and the pressure of the total reality upon an earnest mind, capable of recollection. The spirit of system, though it so often renders the mind fanatical and obdurately blind to some facts, is essentially an effort to give all facts their due, not to forget things once discovered and understood, and not to leave illusions and vices comfortably unchallenged. Certainly the total reality will elude any human system; but that is no reason why human nature, which is itself a system, should not exist and assert itself; and it cannot exist congenially without intellectual clearness or without translating its natural economy into a system of ideas. In the realm of essence no such system can have any pre-eminence over any other; each is the pattern of only one possible world; but it may be the full revelation which the existing world brings to one particular creature, and it may render valid, for his description of things, those dialectic bonds which are internal to it.

CHAPTER VIII

ESSENCES AS TERMS

NAMES are normally given to things rather than to essences, and are then proper names; that is, they are indications like a gesture, designating a natural object without describing it. Although words like " table " and " John " may be names common to many natural objects, each of these objects is an existence containing much more than the fact that it is a table or is called John; therefore in giving the name " table " or " John " to that object when encountered, I do not mean to distinguish an essence, either intuited or intended, but to indicate a thing distinguished by its position relatively to me in the natural world, and by its general potentialities and connections there. I do not profess, in so naming this object, to exhaust its nature, but merely to point to an existence in a certain quarter, with a casual, relative, and summary characterisation of it. I should indeed not call this object " table ", unless it were a piece of furniture of a certain height with a flat top; and I should not call the other object " John " unless it were a male inhabiting an English-speaking country; but these conditions for applying those names are far from being the objects; the objects named are particular, natural, fluid, and indefinable.

It is possible, however, to apply names to essences also, as, for instance, to the triangle or to beauty; and then these names are inaptly called general. I say inaptly, because they do not designate classes of things, but in designating an essence they leave open the question whether any or many things exist describable by that term. Names then designate not particulars but universals.

The application of names (or other signs) to essences has an important consequence: it permits reasoning. Things have no dialectical relations, their very existence and fluidity being a defiance to dialectic. The unity of a thing is not perfect and definable, as if a thing were an essence hypostatised. It is a partial, dynamic, historical unity, in that a thing remains traceable for a time in the flux of the world; until according to the conventional use of language that particular thing is said to perish. Everything would be continually perishing, and nothing would endure for two moments, if a thing were the essence which for one moment it exemplifies; and everything might be everlasting were a thing the substance which is transmitted, within the conventional boundaries of that thing, from each of its moments to the next. A thing is a part of nature, a mode of substance, a parcel of matter that plays a certain part and wears a certain mask in the comedy of change, and only so long as it does so; when the same matter puts on a new mask and begins to speak in another voice, it has become another thing. Socrates is a part of the flux of nature, between limits fixed by the birth and death of one animal. Neither his aspect nor his thoughts at any one moment are Socrates; and the essence which his life embodies when taken as a whole is also not Socrates, but is only the truth of his life, seen under the form of eternity. His opinions may have dialectical relations, but he and his actual faith in them cannot have them. Existence itself is a surd, external to the essence which it may illustrate and

(margin note: Things, being in flux, elude dialectic.)

irrelevant to it; for it drags that essence into some here and now, or some then and there; and the things so created, far from being identical with their essence at any moment, exist by eluding it, encrusting it in changing relations, and continually adopting a different essence; so that nothing accurate can be said of a thing supposed to bridge two moments of time. Yet to bridge two moments, in some sense, is indispensable to existence.

The essence of a process, if we turn to that, is also not that process in act. The actual process is an existence inwardly unstable, and all I have just said of momentary being applies to any stretch of existence; the span of any event is just as truly a moment as the minimum duration which human wit can conceive. Sense, history, science, and poetry are all in the same case: they arrest essences, exclamatory visions, and apply them as names to the flux of nature, which they can neither fathom nor arrest.

Dialectic, then, though itself a movement in thought, can weave together only eternal essences; and the pattern it thus designs is an eternal essence in its turn. In reasoning, attention passes and re-passes between these fixed terms, and if by chance any of the terms were exchanged for another, the reasoning would be fallacious, becoming to that extent an irresponsible dream. Now there is a psychological difficulty in reverting in intuition to exactly the same essence. In a mind so volatile as the human, it is not to be expected that the entire complex essence present at one moment should ever be present again. The organ of thought being in flux, the terms of thought can hardly be repeated. The purposes of communication and reasoning would therefore not have been served by attempting to name and recall the entire actual burden of any moment. Only in dramatic and lyric poetry do we approach any

Fancy, in "breeding flowers will never breed the same".

such effort at complete personal expression. Even here, of course, success in reviving or communicating a moment of actual life is never more than approximate. Readers of poetry feel that the poet has been well inspired, and that they have rekindled his very soul, if *any* full, new, and vivid moment of intuition is begotten by his words in their own bosoms; and the more the inspiration is the reader's, and not the poet's, the greater the poet is thought to be. The irony of fate in this may wound a man's vanity, who hopes to be immortal in his own person, and to impose his opinions or his loves on mankind for ever; but humility and elevation of mind (which go together) will not take offence. The poets have had their own visions, the truth and beauty of which are hidden in God; and their works have been so closely knit into the instruments and traditions of human expression as to be fertile there in many a new pleasure and fresh thought. Reasonable minds will not ask for more. Whether the exact intuitions which they have reached can ever come to any other mortal, is a question not even to be broached; for the function of poetry is not to convey information, not even to transmit the attitude of one mind to another, but rather to arouse in each a clearer and more poignant view of its own experience, longings, and destiny. To this end the elastic connotation of words, with the intrinsic dignity of phrases (as in the English Bible), is a positive advantage in poetry. It enables the same symbol to quicken images in various minds, according to their several capacities, stirring them to a true sincerity. Hence the musical, inspired, and untranslatable nature of poetry, which lies more in the assault, relief, and cadence of the utterance, carrying with it a certain sensuous thrill and moral perspective, than in the definable meaning of the poet's words.

In prose, on the contrary, words are primarily signs for some fact which they serve to record or announce.

The sounds themselves, and the other essences, emotional or pictorial, which in intuition convey such information, are passed over. They are mere In specifying facts, intent is controlled by action. instruments — the claw with which intent clutches the potent fact. Nor is the intrinsic essence of this fact that which, in prose, words profess to describe. It would be a vain speculation, akin to poetry, to consider what a stone, or a sheep, or an enemy may be in themselves: such a question would invite not to action but to self-forgetfulness and sympathy — a dissolving sympathy with dramatised things which is idle or even dangerous. I might soon find myself refusing to eat mutton, or going over to the enemy, or disproving the existence of stones. The tight mainspring of action and thought keeps me ticking without such scruples, or if they intervene, condemns them to futility. Prose, like perception, designates things only externally, things which, since they act and are acted upon, are substances. I have found that substances posited by animal faith are identified, not by specifying their essence, but by indicating their place and function in that field of receding events called nature, of which any act is the centre. The existence of nature is involved in the execution of any act, since this act is a link in a flux of events extending beyond it. At the same time belief in nature is involved in the intent and eagerness which in consciousness express action, or readiness for action.

Thus the profit of bestowing names on things and of speaking in prose, like the profit of being sensible at all to external objects, does not lie in revealing the essence of these objects, but in expediting action amongst them. The whole network of appearance and language may accordingly remain a miracle of æsthetic and grammatical design spun in its own colours and suspended in the air without inconvenience or anomaly, if the connections meantime established between action and action are still quick and nicely adjusted. The whole rumble of the discoursing mind is music on the march, and no sane man expects it to join in battle or to describe the enemy fairly.

As music, however, may occasionally become an object of thought in itself, and may be elaborately described by the musician, so many an *In specify-* essence which in the apprehension of things *ing essences,* was only a symbol or an emotion may be *intent is controlled* arrested in reflection, and receive a name. *by language.* The name, with its valence, so to speak, or its atmosphere of suggestion, now becomes the datum in actual intuition; and the essence which formerly occupied that place and was a symbol for some material fact, now recedes into an object of intent and a theme for consecutive description.

Speech and writing are a complication in nature; as they exist substantially they are subtle secondary figures and rhythms impressed on matter, which serve mankind to record or forecast those larger rhythms and figures, called real things and true events, in which human existence is itself implicated. Thus language, like sensation, becomes significant by virtue of the animal faith which vivifies it; and this significance is its moral being. The same framework of spontaneous belief, readiness, memory, and expectation on which understanding of nature is stretched, stretches and projects also the force of words, making them indicative of absent and eventual objects. If the object is an essence, it nevertheless is identified only by being placed in some natural perspective, borrowed by language from the material world. An absent essence can be indicated only as the essence meant by a sign, which is commonly a word, and the sense of this word can be revived and realised only by reverting in fancy to the natural environment in which it was first uttered.

Thus description in words or other signs is indispensable for making an essence an object of intent when it is no longer, or not yet, an object of intuition. The torments suffered by the souls in Dante's *Inferno*, for instance, are not intuited by the poet or the reader in their intended essence, for then he would be enduring those torments actually: yet he knows what he means by them; the words or images that suggest them are significant, and in proportion as they are well chosen, they converge upon the object, the unrealised essence of those torments, as they would be if actually felt. Such convergence, while it might render the description perfect in the language used, would not at all tend to reproduce the pains, by bringing their essences into living intuition. On the contrary, it would be the essence of poetry that would actually fill the mind with verbal harmonies and sensuous vistas continually opening and closing; if there was any touch of repulsion or actual distress, it would be by a lapse from pure discourse, as when Dante becomes political, or a childish reader takes alarm, fearing that the material world may contain the bodies and places where such torments occur, and that there is danger of deserving them. In meaning an essence we accordingly by no means tend or wish to intuit it; but just as in the case of material objects of intent, we indicate its locus in the realm to which it intrinsically belongs, here the realm of essence as there the realm of matter, without at all requiring to create, in the realm of spirit, an intuition of that object as it is in itself.

Symbols have their own essences which alone are immediate in discourse.

It appears, then, that just as the whole world of common sense, history, and physics is posited, not experienced, so the whole world of dialectic—the labyrinth of essences studied in mathematics, logic, grammar, and morals—is meant and not intuited. Of course to posit any-

Essences signified need not be intuited.

thing is itself an experience, and in meaning something
I must have some intuition of my terms and some feeling of intent; but the actual experience of knowing is
not the object known, and the essence intuited in
reasoning about essences is not those essences; for
either the essence meant is a part only of the given
field of intuition, or it is not given at all, but indicated
by converging symbols as the object of an eventual,
perhaps unattainable, intuition. Thus π is an essence
meant, which can enter unequivocally into an equation;
but it is not expressible in arithmetical figures, nor
in any sensuous experience; its nature is known by
circumstantial definition; it is a goal of thought, the
exact proportion between the circumference of a circle
and its diameter. When I think of π this exact proportion is signified but not intuited: what is actually
before my mind is the Greek letter, its sound, and a
shooting vista into a world of words, human mathematics, breaking here and there into images of specious
circles, visual or given by gesture; a psychic sea
through which intent can nevertheless easily steer
towards the fixed but unattainable object defined as π.

Even when an essence is present, like the colour of
the sky, I must retreat a little and revert to it from a
different intuition in order to identify or to mean it; and
this different intuition is commonly that of the word
" blue ", the name of that colour. It need not be this
particular word: the Spanish word *azul* in my case
would do just as well; a fact which shows how separate
the intuition is in intending from the intuition in seeing,
and how disparate. Or possibly, in taking in or apper-
ceiving the evident blue and describing it, I may use as
a point of vantage the visual memory of some material
object, say the background of Titian's " Bacchus and
Ariadne", thinking to myself, This blue is that blue!
A wafted image, referred to some natural object, and
to the occasion and place where I encountered it (for

London and youth hang for me about that picture), may thus take the place of verbal predicates to define an intended essence and keep it as an object of perpetual reference. Merely to prolong a present intuition will never turn the essence presented into a goal of intent or a term useful in discourse; such a term must be kept constant in its absence, and must be often absent if it is to be always the same.

Intended essences thus acquire, through the machinery of identification, projection, and intent, a certain remoteness and mystery; they become concepts or ideals. Not that when they swim into intuition, if they ever do so, they are not perfectly individual and concrete; this blue which now floods the sky and my own being is the most obvious of realities, and the nearest at hand. So, in its essence, is that blue which is now not here, but which I evoke sentimentally out of a remote context in the world of hearsay and of memory, and which I identify with this blue, because this blue has awakened in me a state of feeling and a train of associations, ending in a revival of the circumstances of that lost intuition and (as I fondly assume) in a recovery of that lost essence. *This* blue is still the only essence before me: that this blue was also *there* is an assertion not founded on a simultaneous inspection of the two objects, which is impossible, but on enveloping the given essence in the old atmosphere and calling it by an old name. This identification is hazarded: thought and belief (even if to be verified) are shots in the air when they are actual; but the irresponsible movement by which intent posits its object takes nothing away from the intrinsic reality of this object, be it a thing or an essence. I may, if I have the necessary indications, intend and refer to things in their absence, without compromising them or reducing them to abstractions from my present beggarly self.

They lose nothing thereby in reality.

Homer was better inspired in speaking of winged words than those philosophers who call words sounds or movements of the larynx. Material organs and material occasions are no doubt indis- pensable to the birth of language, to its evolution, and to its utility. So a flying arrow requires a bow and a target, and the material reed and feathers that are its substance. But discourse is flight, it is signification; and the more we scrutinise its actual being, the more unsubstantial, fugitive, and transitive its essence appears. Not only can it never alight or become anything but a flying intent, but even the hits it makes (not to count the misses) are achievements only con- ventionally; it dies on arrival, and can never know whether it has killed its bird. It is for the gamekeepers that follow in its wake to collect the bag; and how different is this dead booty of mundane routine and prosperity and plodding art from the gleaming flight, the intent aim, the miraculous shot of actual thinking!

The intrinsic flight of discourse.

If any one in his speculative ambition is bent on seizing the veritable essence of substance, I hardly know what comfort can await him; but if his satis- faction was rather in the patterns and harmonies of essence, which he hoped to disentangle dialectically, he need not be disappointed; because even if the terms of his demonstrative science are remote terms, always objects of intent and never of intuition, yet at this remove and in that shadowy precision they form an actual perspective, a present theme for the mind. Essences are omnipresent; and while attention remains awake, you cannot shut off one without presenting another. If the objects of intent remain remote, as the persons of a novel and their career remain imaginary, the discourse which is the seat of those in- tentions must always be actual, like the crowding words, images, and excitements loved by the authors and readers of novels. The medium is always immediate.

The life of language, of poetry, of dialectic, is a keen and an innocent life. It has, by virtue of its roots in It circles with enough fidelity about the flux of nature. the body and the control of its development by circumstances, a quite sufficient relevance to material facts, a quite respectable value as a record and forecast of human destiny. Intrinsically it has its own vital, expressive, æsthetic intensities. It is not an illusion, unless it is turned into illusion by inexperience or equivocation. Love, for instance, arising irrepressibly in each successive generation, is a genuine revelation, not rebuked at all by the knowledge that it has often existed before towards other objects; if it involves illusions, they regard only ulterior facts, less important than itself. So the literary or mathematical or grammatical medium of discourse, with all the logical and moral zeal which it involves, is genuine life, full of intent and intuition. Why rebel against spirit, and ask it to be something other than it is? The flight of the arrow, in spite of Zeno, is as true a fact as the ulterior positions between which it flies or the rest which it dreams of but excludes by flying. So the intrinsic essence of discourse is signification, a flight in which the wings are words or other signs, alone actually present, and the goal, alone valued or considered, is descried simply as the point of the compass, perhaps receding and unattainable, towards which those wings are straining. It is in the act of traversing data in such a specific direction (to which a living animal holds much more unswervingly than to the intuition of any datum) that names, which are cries, come to the lips; and as these cries are habitual and very limited in number compared with the cloud-like drift of intuitions, they serve to mark the goals of thought far more clearly and unambiguously than its actual being. So things are better defined in discourse than sensations, and intended essences better than essences given.

CHAPTER IX

SINCE pure Being is infinite and contains all essences, how can anything else be? In other words, what is there in existing things besides their essences?

That this question can be asked is a proof that it is a legitimate question and admits of an answer; for if there were nothing but essences, and if pure Being, because infinite, exhausted all possible modes of being, there would be no discourse, no ignorance, no knowledge, and conse- quently no questions. In the realm of essence all equally is open, safe, and per- spicuou one essence cannot slily entrench itself on a sort of egotistical eminence, from which to survey, attack, or deny any other essence. Since this, neverthe- less, is done in what we call life or existence, and since I am doing it at this moment in this inquiry, it is certain that pure Being is not all being, and that in existence Being is impure, having in it something more or something less than any essence. This is but another way of asserting that there is a world, that there are facts, and that there is a difference between truth and error. Such a thickening and self-contra- diction by which essences become things may irritate the dialectician and may disturb the contemplative mind; but any attempt to deny the fact would be idle; the denial itself would reintroduce the very

Any instance of an essence proves that essence is not the only realm of being.

119

categories of existence, flux, self-transcendence, and truth which it professed to dismiss. Could a man really be sublimated into his essence, he would be silent, as pure Being is silent. Let him who will by all means ascend into that blessedness, if he can; but he must leave philosophy to poor living mortals whose minds are crepuscular and in whose impure world much is past, much is distant, and all is obscure.

To pursue this subject would be to broach at once those realms of being which are not that of essence; here I must leave the question of their precise nature in suspense. But I can hardly avoid some examination of the effect which they have on the manifestation of essence to the human mind; for in making this manifestation possible, they intervene in it, mingling with it an urgency and obscurity which no essence can have of itself. Manifestation is an event, and although that which is manifested there can be only an essence, the occasion and the setting transpose it into a new plane of being, the plane of phenomena or of descriptions, and render it, as the Platonists said, other than itself. It is intrinsically and inalienably eternal, yet here are temporal instances of it; it is a universal, but it appears in particulars, lending them such positive characters as they may have; it is perfectly unambiguous, and nevertheless it is merged and confused with other essences in the flux of things and of language.

Exemplification transplants essences from their proper soil.

Realisation of essence, by an ironical fate, is accordingly a sort of alienation from essence. We call it " realisation ", when from being perfectly real in its own fashion, it becomes an illusion in some mind, or the momentary form of some treacherous matter. Or perhaps we call it "manifestation," when that which manifests it, some existing thing or phase of discourse, distracts us from it, and scarcely suffers us to observe it

for its own sake.[1]   Instances are indeed occasions for
deviation: they are cross-roads at which two worlds
meet.   One set of relations exhibits the instance as
an essence; another set exhibits it as a fact.   The idiosyncrasy of the essence there realised alone enables the
fact to be distinguished from the rest of the natural
medium in which it exists; if we were interested in true
being, in the actual and moral quality of things, it is
accordingly that essence, and its essential relations,
that would absorb all our attention.   But we are
animals swimming for dear life in the same flux in
which this instance of essence has appeared: it is the
movement of that medium, what will happen to us
next, that preoccupies us; and therefore, probably, we
neglect the intrinsic being of that occasion, and of all

[1] There are various phrases capable of expressing the relation between
an essence and the instances of it; each phrase represents some perspective
view of the same actual relation.   We may call it *participation*, in that
every instance shares with the other instances the whole nature of the
essence; but this term may lead to misunderstandings, if we infer that an
essence has parts, one of which may fall to each instance, or that an essence
is a class or collection of particulars.   If we express the matter in a religious
myth, as the story of the fallen soul, instances may be said to *remind* us of a
divine original, that essence in its purity; and then, in a cosmological myth,
this original may be conceived as a magnet attracting matter (when matter
is sensitive to that particular attraction) into a likeness of that essence; so
that any existing instance of an essence might be called an *imitation* or *copy*
of it.   Such copies, if subsisting only in the mind, would be *recollections*.
A less picturesque name for instances is *phenomena*, that is, *manifestations*
of an essence; but these terms, for a modern, suggest a subjective seat for
the instance, whereas of course many phenomena are manifestations of
essences in matter: in other words, temporal things.   A safer word for
instances in general is accordingly *exemplification*.   This covers both
embodiment of essences in matter or in events, and *revelation* of essences in
intuition.   A synonym for exemplification might be *realisation*; but it has
the disadvantage of suggesting that essences when not exemplified are not
real, and that reality means existence; whereas unexemplified essences are
perfectly real in their own sphere, and many of those exemplified, being
only imagined, do not exist in the sense of being the forms of any substance.
The term realisation is convenient to express the passage from an incipient
to a clear thought, or from an unfulfilled to a fulfilled perfection in things;
in the former case we may also say that the essence has been *defined*, and in
the latter that it has been *materialised*.   The great difference in all cases is
that instances can occur only once, while essence may recur any number of
times; that which is local in the occurrence is the instance, that which might
be identical in various occurrences is the essence.   If I write the same word
twice, the word which is the same is the essence and the words which are
two are its instances.

occasions, in our haste to trace one occasion out of another.　The net of existence in which the instances of essence are caught even seems, perhaps, to our rude philosophy to create the fish which it catches: we deny their prior reality, their intrinsic being; they are to us only the contents of our net; and we shut our eyes as we swallow them.　The matter of them may still nourish us; but our attention, to that extent, has deviated from the intuition of essence, which is its only spiritual function, into tracing the labyrinth of fact; we have chosen the endless path leading from existence to existence—as indeed any instance of essence, since it must come before us on some natural occasion, invites us to do.　As in translating a language we must abandon it, so in recognising an essence we must half materialise it; in existence, in sense, and in thought it has become impure; its essential character now figures in a substance, a medium, or a context which are alien to it.

This incarnation of essences in particulars must not be supposed either to alter the essences (which are all incorruptible) or to be an imperfect incarnation, so that a part of the divinity, so to speak, descends into the world and another part remains in heaven.　Certainly in any assignable world or portion of a world only an individual essence can be realised; but of *that* essence the realisation there will be perfect.　The infinity of pure Being renders it inevitable that whatsoever form an existence may happen to assume, that form will be some precise essence eternally self-defined; for however fast the world may change or however confused chaos may become, events can never overtake or cover the infinite advance which pure Being has had on existence from all eternity.　And whichever of those prefigured forms a thing may choose to realise, that form it must realise perfectly; as an aerolith, if it falls

Instances perfectly exemplify their actual essences.

to the earth at all, must strike some pre-existing spot on its surface.

So, too, in the history of existence, as it picks up and drops these multitudinous characters, there is also no ambiguity. Substance, in the act of taking on and shuffling these forms, merely connects them in a voluminous flux alien to their several qualities. The dance falls into figures and generates relations, which each essence taken individually did not contain or imply. *The birth of spirit complicates the exemplification of essences without confusing it.* And if further facts arise out of this movement, as spirit arises in animals, the characters and complexion of these hyperphysical existences are also just what they are; feelings and discourse take on such colour or intent as they have without dislocating in the least the order of nature which they enrich. The pearls may be inwardly more precious and opalescent than the thread on which they are strung; or they may seem superfluous and negligible to a science or action so economical as to trace the thread only; but whether prized or ignored, the pearls shine by their own light in their assigned places quite unequivocally. In a word, there is no ambiguity in the truth; it enshrines all the facts, no matter how complex, with their exact configuration. Inexactitude, approximation, imperfection, are not possible in the relations of things to their essences; each thing at each moment is just what it is; it is transformed as it is transformed, related as it is related; and the sum of these changes and of these infinite cross-lights is just what it is under the eye of eternity.

Nevertheless, from the moral point of view, imperfect realisation is not a meaningless phrase. Imagination, language, and interest are finite; the categories of human discourse, though somewhat variable, are constitutional and limited; they need to be so in order to fulfil their cognitive and imaginative function, since knowledge is an adaptation of fancy to practice, a rational eloquence, not a reduplication of things as they were before life or imagination arose among them.

Confusion arises only when discourse assigns to things essences which are not theirs. Every name and every desire accordingly suggests an essence to the psyche which may fail to be realised in the world, or may be realised there only approximately; the fact that another somewhat different essence is realised there leaves human attention cold; it asked for bread and receives a stone, and to point out that the stone was a perfect stone would seem sheer mockery. The disharmony between the psyche and the rest of nature runs even deeper; for the essence actually realised in the facts may be not merely unwelcome or uninteresting; it may be nameless altogether and inconceivable. Every name and every concept which bewildered man will impose on those facts will then fit them imperfectly; and being without intuition of their true essence, he will call them vague facts, formless, elusive, or defective. For his senses have their stock responses, like birds of one note, or of very few; so too the passions and the theories of which his imagination is capable. His discourse moves within a private museum of ideal and general natures, the few essences distinguished by language; and it is only in his finer or his idler moments (if he has them) that he looks between the meshes of that logical net, and catches unauthorised glimpses of the flux of things with all its irrelevant marvels. Essences, then, may be said to be manifested imperfectly, when they are not the essences of things, but are prescribed for them by the senses and passions of some egotistical animal whose mind is like a stomach limited in its powers of digestion and obliged to treat all foreign substances as approximations—how questionable and half-baked !—to its ideal victuals.

If, then, it is possible to assign to anything an essence which is not its essence, this possibility arises because

the essences first and normally manifested in feeling
and thought are not the essences that have been
embodied multitudinously and successively
in things since the beginning of the world, Originality in ideas is
and that now define their dynamic nature. a beauty but becomes
Yet merely this disparity between ideas and a snare
things would be no anomaly, because when they are used as
ideas are not things but ideas; and ideas, predicates
like words, may be excellent signs for for things.
events in the field of action, without in the least re-
sembling them, if only the mechanism which controls
these ideas does not precipitate any assertion, expectation, or attitude which events within or without the
psyche do not justify.   The justification required is
not that the essence given in discourse should repeat
the essence embodied in material events—a repetition
which is unlikely, superfluous, and incongruous with
the summary function of sensation, as well as of significant or poetic thought; for in naming, reporting, or
prefiguring events, discourse will necessarily add an
intellectual syntax, a moral perspective, and a mocking
humour which are not in them.   What is required is
such a vital harmony between the life of thought and
that of things as may render discourse appropriate
and adorning.   But often — and here's the rub —
maladaptation exists in their respective movement and
rates of change between a psyche and her environment,
so that the essences revealed imaginatively to that
psyche are late or early or out of key with the march
of events, not only outside, but in the residual parts
of her own life.   Then, in her assertiveness (since she
is engaged in action) she will impose on things that
which she adds, and deny that which she leaves out;
and this hypostasis of her fancies or of her ignorance
will become unfathomable error about the facts encountered by her in action and prompting her to this
fond discourse.   Thus discourse, while manifesting

perfectly at each moment certain specious essences to the spirit, and embodying perfectly the essence of spirit itself, may involve confusion regarding the objects which it intends to describe, as well as ignorance of its own basis, nature, and history.

In the study of nature philosophers are much influenced by the love of economy. They wish, on this The error of intellectual parsimony. subject, to have as few ideas as possible; they may even hope to be monists and to have only one. This ideal of simplicity is imposed on nature by the mind in its desire to be clear, comprehensive, and curt; it is an extension of the dogmatic impulse involved in action by which the most conspicuous essence given in sense is taken for the essence of the object encountered. The philosopher merely repeats this form of judgement when he assumes that the simplest theory which his wit can frame must be the essence of the universe. In the study of essence, the ruling interest being more contemplative, we may perhaps avoid this haste. Illusions are no less truly essences than truths are; and no confusion will arise from complications or diversities in essences if only we abstain from asserting them of the same substances. Now I believe that more essences, and of more kinds, are exemplified in nature than the student of nature is inclined to notice: they are not realised only in single file or on one plane of being; and they are not all predicable of the same substance nor all predicable of anything. There are many open to our inspection which are not descriptive of material things even indirectly; and on the other hand, there are presumably embodied in matter many essences, of many kinds, which it has not entered into the heart of man to conceive. Such considerations are not useless in stating, if not in solving, the problems of natural philosophy; but for the moment I must be satisfied with a word about the essences which must be exemplified, some in one way, others in another, in order that discourse may move at all, and ideas may describe, or fail to describe, their intended objects.

The character of the particular world in which we find ourselves has been richly and ignorantly reported in the poetry and science of all ages; it is not for me, in passing, to revise those reports. There is avowedly a great inorganic cosmos, astronomical, geographical, chemical; and on earth at least there are living organisms capable of adjusting themselves progressively to their environment, and of modifying that environment for their future convenience. The essence of human life thus runs over and engages parts of the outer world in its rhythms, in what we call the arts; and this seems a miraculous subjugation of matter by mind. But if we look closer, the rhythm of mind seems itself to be but an extension of that of matter. Organisms, in their reproduction, pass through the most curious seminal and embryonic phases, in which nothing human appears; essences seem to descend on things like doves out of the blue. But they have their periods, conditions, and fatal exits: they compose the forms of organic behaviour, or enacted intelligence, observable in the world. Enacted intelligence, observable sensibility, discoverable languages and works of art, though they are understood to express feeling, contain no feeling in their recognisable structure: all the essences which they can possibly embody, however subtle, prolonged, or interwoven, are essences embodied in matter; they are complexities in the one flux of events in space and time which is called nature. They are all open to scientific discovery and measure, being intrinsically dated, localised, and traceable in their genesis and effects within the material sphere.

I have mentioned feeling, supposed to be expressed in some of these observable facts; and although I

The essence of this world.

have not mentioned it, there is implied throughout a transcendental observer, a spirit to whom these essences Life, besides are evident and who takes note of their em- being a form bodiment, position, and physical inter-relation. of behaviour, The natural philosopher may well protest that kindles an inner light no feeling and no spirit is discernible in the called spirit. field of his observation; and how should they be discernible there, when that is not their place nor their mode of being? Nevertheless, he is reckoning without his host and forgetting his own existence, in so far as all that he recognises, including his own body, is from time to time focussed and actually present to him in the light of spirit; a fact patent to reflection and recorded perpetually in any honest confession or bit of autobiography, such as human discourse and conversation are chiefly composed of. Remove this pedestal and the whole conception of nature has nothing to stand on, no means of entering into the moral world, no claim upon the living philosopher. He is a discoursing spirit by nature and a discoverer of this world only by accident, in that this world forces itself at present on his attention and belief. Until, therefore, he finds a means of integrating somehow his spiritual being with the realm of matter, there can be no solidity in his doctrine; for all knowledge of the world, when he is collected and self-conscious, will seem to him mere babble; and at the same time he will marvel, and even tremble, at the incredible tenuity of his actual being. He has but to shut his eyes for all that painted world to vanish; he has but to arrest the inner rumble of words for his memory and life to become a forgotten story; he has but to fall asleep for the lever of reason to lose its fulcrum altogether, and the whole argument to lapse. We may insist that his extinction makes no difference to the realm of essence and little difference to the universe; but this very fact, since this extinction makes all the difference to him,

establishes the ineradicable diversity between his spirit
on the one hand and the universe with the realm of
essence on the other.

There is in fact another way altogether, besides
embodiment in matter, by which essences may be
exemplified: they may be imagined. Even
those which are embodied passively or for- Unembodied
essences
mally in things, if any one is ever to see or may appear
to attribute them, must also (perhaps at quite to spirit.
a different time) be imagined, felt, conceived, contemplated, or somehow directly revealed to spirit. This
presence of essences occasionally to imagination was
very accurately called by the Scholastics their *objective*
being, contrasted with the intrinsic or logical being
which they had in themselves, and with the formal
embodiment which they might have in things; but in
the utter confusion of modern philosophy, substances
being denied in one breath and imagination in the
next, " the objective " has come to mean that which
is independent of intent or attention fixed upon it;
which is precisely what *the objective* can never be. It
is indeed the intuition of essences in their own category,
when the things that may embody them are absent or
non-existent, that makes up the essence of spirit, in its
various forms of feeling, sense, thought, memory, or
knowledge. Spirit is the actuality of the unsubstantial.

It belongs to the nature of spirit to be cognitive;
for even when intuition is pure and unmixed with
intent, so that there is no claim to transitive Essence of
knowledge, no positing of facts, intuition spirit.
must reveal an object other than its own spiritual being
and activity. The intrinsic action of spirit, like that of
existence (of which spirit is a special instance), cannot be
itself an object of intuition: it can be exemplified only
by being enacted and realised by a transition in neither
term of which it could be realised separately. If
spirit were ever suspended, if it ceased to live, to drink

in and to peruse its object, it would have literally lost itself in that object; there would be no spirit, no intuition, any longer, but only some essence; and this essence for its part would no longer have any adventitious prominence in the realm of essence; no emphasis or actuality would fall upon it; and no instance of it would have occurred. It is the act of attention, synthesis, and apprehension, performed by the psyche animating some animal, that lends to any essence its *objective* actuality, or ideal presence; and in so doing, and inseparably, the same act embodies and exemplifies the essence of spirit in a particular instance.

There are accordingly two disparate essences exemplified in every instance of spirit; one is the essence of spirit, exemplified *formally* and embodied in the event or fact that at such a moment such an animal has such a feeling; the other is the essence then revealed to that animal, and realised *objectively* or imaginatively in his intuition. The character of this given essence serves to distinguish morally this phase of spirit from other possible phases. Any essence whatever, if the psyche at work has the requisite energy and scope, may appear in intuition; even the essences of existence and of spirit may be defined in reflection, as I have been endeavouring to define them here; but nothing follows as to the truth or relevance to existence of any such visionary term; if these essences are embodied in nature, it is because nature of her own will embodies them in their natural places, not because I here, and at this remove, define them in my thought. They are by no means embodied formally in the thought that conceives them, so as to be predicable of this thought: my idea of God is not God, and does not bring God into existence on its precise model; nor does my idea of matter perform a corresponding miracle. My ideas merely take their places among ideas, as being images or hypotheses of a certain quality, which any one else, if he can and will, is at liberty to conceive also; it is the occasions on which they arise, their several organs in nature, that will distinguish their instances historically, as well as bring them into existence. Thus my thoughts in this book are distinguished physically, as events in the world, by belonging to my person and buzzing in my brain at the dates and places where I rehearse them; but the same thoughts, as essences then conceived by me, are distinguished morally by their scope and subject-matter; eternal essences having eternal relations of contrast or affinity with .he other essences which employ my thoughts or those of other philosophers, and beyond that to all other essences that might be instead the theme of any discourse.

This diversity of status between an essence embodied and the same essence conceived remains complete even when in its two disparate instances the essence is identical; but this is not normally the case. The essences embodied even in the human body and total human career are not such as human imagination can easily conceive; and the essences embodied in the depths and unattainable dimensions of nature escape us altogether. On the other hand, the æsthetic and sentimental essences which fill human discourse are often, by their very nature, incapable of passive embodiment: they *cannot* be true, save in the historical sense that it may be true that some one has entertained them. So, for instance, any quality or intensity of pain; such an essence can be exemplified only spiritually, never materially; its instances must be feelings. No cataclysm of nature, however disruptive, can ever embody evil. Evil can be realised there only if, in virtue of a previous organic harmony, a spirit was there incarnate, in which the disruption could generate the intuition of a hated change.

Moral essences can be realised only in spirit.

The same originality of spirit appears in the normal perspectives of memory and history, even when, con-

So, too, all human perspectives of nature and history.

ventionally speaking, they are true enough. My knowledge of Julius Cæsar obviously differs in date from its object; but it differs from it avowedly also in essence, since I cannot pretend to know the whole truth of Julius Cæsar, nor any part of it with complete accuracy. The most scrupulous and exhaustive historian would be satisfied with recovering a few salient particulars, revivifying these in his own fancy—that of a modern— and surrounding them with comparisons, judgements, and emotions adventitious to the inner being of Julius Cæsar and of his age. History is a poetic art; the Muse, Clio, must inspire it; and the existing correlate or controlling cause of the historian's thoughts, even when they are true, is not the object described, Cæsar, but the historian's person, his documents, studies, passions, and abilities.

Mind accordingly comes to enrich the essence of the world, not to reproduce it. Condensation, expression,

Spirit is nature's comment on herself, concise and emotional.

comparison, are also enrichments; it is not so much by repeating some literal aspect of something remote that this remote thing can be called to mind, as rather by modifying the present in deference and with reference to it; for instance, by giving it a new name or a new tragic or pictorial embodiment. The living poet and his contemporary world, in evoking this new essence, grow sensitive to that remote object, and truly intend, salute, and describe it. This they may do, because description, no less than intent or homage, are relative: the attitude and contribution of the observer are integral to it. Material, even if subtle, influences, descending from that object have stimulated him to this fresh conception; and the conception will be just and true in so far as, in the language native to this

later and living world, it expresses that influence
adequately in its present ramifications; for new state-
ments about a thing may be perfectly true, if they are
made from new points of comparison. Thought is
normally relative, expressing relations that accrue with
time; it may occasionally include a rapt imaginative
reproduction of something distant, though hardly to a
great extent or to much purpose.

Reproduction, again, is not the normal relation
between essences embodied in matter and those
revealed to spirit. Where this relation seems to obtain,
as between an architect's first idea and the building that afterwards realises it, the echo or fulfilment
really belongs to the same realm—imagination—as
the original conception. That which resembles the
visionary project, and repeats it, is not the material
house—which is a mass of whirling atoms, or invisible
energy, or something no less recondite—but simply the
aspect which this house presents to the architect's own
eye, or to that of a man like him. In registering such
similarities between images he has not issued from the
realm of spirit. So the reputed likeness of images
discoverable in the retina, or in a photographic plate,
to segments of the originals in nature, is a likeness
between the essence revealed to a living spirit on one
occasion and that revealed to it on another. There
is no probable or discoverable likeness between the
material composition of an eye, of a country side,
and of a sensitized plate. A living psyche must
react upon these divers substances before the actual
vision arises in any of the three cases; that three
so dissimilar substances should be able to occasion
a similar image, only proves that relatively to the
organ of sense affected they serve the same purpose
and offer an equivalent stimulus; as a gramophone,
although materially so unlike a band of rapturous
and sweating musicians, may serve the same purpose

to the ear and may offer, up to a certain point, an equivalent stimulus.

Shall we say that the exemplifications of essence in nature and in thought, although composed of very unlike forms, yet flow in parallel streams? If by parallel we understand simply not intermingled I should answer, Yes; but if by parallel we understand running side by side all the way and corresponding throughout, I should say, No. For it is contrary to the nature of spirit to arise in dead or inorganic things; and where it arises, its vistas radiate from that point, according to the material tensions present in it, forward and back along the stream of material events, and tangentially into all sorts of supervening images and rhymes. Spirit is what is called epi-phenomenal, although this word is very ill-chosen, since neither substance nor spirit is phenomenal; but the essences embodied in matter and those revealed to intuition are indeed deployed in two different media: the spiritual perspective being at each point dependent for its existence and its character upon the balance and movement of the vital process beneath. But these spiritual perspectives are called forth only occasionally, as matter rolls on; and they open out at right angles, to any distance, into the realms of truth and of essence. There are not, then, two parallel streams, but rather one stream which, in slipping over certain rocks or dropping into certain pools, begins to babble a wanton music; not thereby losing any part of its substance or changing its course, but unawares enriching the world with a new beauty. Feeling, intuition, prophetic and synthetic intelligence, are spiritual facts utterly alien to the pedestrian flux of the materially successive. They, too, are transitory, subsisting only so long as the material foci in which they are collected remain in being; but spirit, though the occasions on which it

It is occasional, symbolic, and made in view of eternity.

arises are material, is itself an imponderable and invisible fact; and although its interests are borrowed
from the impulses and contacts of animal life, the
terms in which it expresses those interests are original
and poetic; and by translating nature into those terms
it paints, as it were, her immortal portrait.

Which of the essences conceived by the human mind,
if any, may be credited with being the absolute and
intrinsic essences of the natural world, is a Conception
question to be left to the judgement and of facts
modesty of natural philosophers; I may say literal or
something about it on another occasion, in adequate.
so far as the matter interests a moralist or can fall
within his competence. Here I will only note that while
such coincidence is possible, all essences whatsoever
being open to potential intuition, every presumption
is against it. Nature, if nature exists at all, is not a
hypostasis of essences defined in human discourse;
she is the matrix, incalculably ancient and vast, of
human nature and human ideas, ideas which by their
origin and their function express the sensibility and
reactions of the human organism, and nothing else.
To suppose that these ideas reproduce and literally
define the intrinsic essence of nature is accordingly an
illusion: excusable because inevitable in an animal
at once active and ignorant; yet such, when maintained doggedly, as to excite inextinguishable laughter
in the immortal gods.

But let us suppose that, by a singular miracle,
human experience were clairvoyant, and assigned to
all parts of nature, in so far as they were en- Alleged
countered materially, their intrinsic essences. introjection
It would follow that whenever the mind or bifurca-
conceived them, the essences of things would sequent on
be exemplified twice over: once formally in jection of
the flux of matter and again imaginatively in appearances.
that of mind. The stream of existence would " bifur-

cate ", and the two currents, strangely diverse in substance but strangely similar in form, would flow side by side mirroring one another. Or if it were found impossible, as it would be, to regard all given essences as embodied in natural things, first illusions, then secondary qualities, and finally primary qualities, would have to be " introjected" and sucked in into the mental sphere; the natural world would have become a nonentity, and the result would be idealism. All this confusion comes of originally supposing that things are graphically copied in sense, and nature in science; a belief founded on the projection of the essences given to spirit, as if the world had been created and were now deployed on the model of human ideas. But the essences given to spirit are forms of imagination and thought: they never were and never will be the essences of things; and it is only by poetic licence and conventional symbolism that we are compelled to clothe things in the garb of our sensations and rhetoric. Introjection is therefore only the counterpart of a false earlier projection, and bifurcation the inevitable consequence of a pictorial physics. Nature, let me repeat, is not a visual image hypostatised : she has embodied, from indefinite past time, whatever essences she has embodied without asking our leave or conforming beforehand (as philosophers seem to expect) to the economy and logic of our thoughts. These thoughts and images of ours, with their economy, are not irrelevant to nature, since she produces them at stated junctures; our imagination and logic, as far as they go, are her own logic and imagination, by which here, at least, she finds it possible to possess and to celebrate herself spiritually; they are therefore true enough, and a different logic or a different imagination would probably be no truer. They have the value of signs and are felt to have it; because the spirit which evokes them is incarnate, with transitive and not contemplative interests predominant in it, so that it takes all its visions, when it can, for omens of collateral powers.

By the birth of spirit nature is certainly complicated and rendered heteroclite, as animal life is later by the birth of language; but spirit can never contain any portion, not to say the whole, of the material flux that generates it. This new form of existence is immaterial, synthetic, cognitive, emotional; and any of the feelings or intuitions which compose it, when they contain a vista, contain it spiritually only, focussed and seen, not enacted piecemeal and irrevocably self - substitutive, as an actual flux must be. For the fountain of conception is internal, it is the heart; and its deliverances, being fundamentally exclamatory, pictorial, and intellectually creative, can be brought round only poetically to describe the profound dynamic structure and order of things.

Science, no less than theology, is a form of discourse.

CHAPTER X

ESSENCES ALL PRIMARY

COMPLEX essences, as we have seen, are not compounded: this is one of the most fruitful reflections which speculation about essence can suggest. It can cure us of the most stubborn prejudices in physics; it can show us the vanity of any psychologism, mental chemistry, or attempt to generate ideas out of ideas; and it can help us to place the realm of essence where it belongs at an infinite remove from the accidents of any evolving world or any intellectual or moral scale.

In the material sphere it is common for complex things, such as plants, to be formed out of others, such In material as seeds, earth, sunshine, and water, which compounds to human apprehension are more simple. the essence of the whole The arts visibly continue this process of conis not com- struction; an architect, for instance, deliberpounded of ately causes various materials to be collected the essences of the parts. and built into his edifice; and the finished building is evidently an assemblage of substances and patterns, each of which was known first in isolation, and now contributes, mechanically or æsthetically, to a result which, since the architect half-intended, half-desired, and half-directed it, seems to him an achievement. At the same time the very certainty that he has selected these elements and combined them, and that they undoubtedly conspire more or less obviously to produce the result, may cause him some disappointment and, if he is metaphysically inclined, some perplexity; for many of those elements, æsthetically considered, have disappeared or have changed their character; and even the total effect, or actual uses, of the structure, in carrying out approximately his material specifications, are unprecedented, and fall together otherwise than he expected. Indeed, the poverty of the result, artistic and moral, may be out of all proportion to the richness of detail and the careful intentions which occupied him in making the plans. The angels that watched his labour will not revisit the finished work; the essence of the whole is not compounded of the essences of the parts, but is a new essence, a summary unity, perhaps simpler, and at any rate original.

A thorough appreciation of this point would save philosophers from many a false assumption and insoluble problem. Things are never compounded of their qualities, but of their substances. If the composite thing retains vestiges of the original qualities of the parts, this is due to an imperfect fusion of the materials, such that each part remains a separate fact, still separately observable; this happens in discursive painting or description of mere aggregates, never in living intuition or in theoretic insight. Again, even when the compound is single and new, the effect of it on some organ blunt to this new order of essences may be very like the effect of one or other of the original objects; as when we complain how monotonous and equivalent things or persons are in this world, in spite of their newness. It follows that any degree of composition in a thing may go with a perfect simplicity in its total essence, be this essence formal or specious; nor can this resulting essence have been native to any of the components. It has been embodied, or has appeared (as the case may be) by a formal necessity or by a natural mutation, upon the juxtaposition of those elements. So a spark may result from the friction of two bodies, who knows how complex; a pure pain may result from an elaborate disorder; a rounded blue sky may result from a flat sea of refracting atoms caught in an earthly eye. The living transcript of facts into sensations, without ceasing to be a mystery (as all existence must be) thus ceases to seem an anomaly; for if anything new was ever to arise or to be revealed to sense, it *had* to assume an essence not the essence of its compound conditions; and it simply remains for observation to specify, when it can, what the normal transformations are for the time being in our parts of the universe.

When the material complex is an animal reaction, the specious essence evoked in sense is single and novel.

There is a stock objection to materialism that looks very foolish when seen in the light of these essential necessities. Matter, it is said, cannot explain the origin of life, of consciousness, or of morals. Matter here means the *essence* which some philosopher attributes, or is alleged to attribute, to matter; this essence has probably suggested itself to the philosopher's imagination after much consideration of the ways of nature; it is a simple, perhaps a merely mathematical term. Now no essence can be the origin of anything: not even of another essence, much less of any fact. But the forms which nature wears could not be successive, or be embodied anywhere, if matter did not assume, connect, and exchange them. Of course this real matter, coming down through the ages, and falling into all these forms, is not anybody's *idea* of matter: its intrinsic essence is unknown, and if we prefer for that reason to call it by another name, we are at liberty to do so, provided we honestly attribute to it, under that sweeter name, all the relations and functions by which the existence of matter has become certain to common sense, and has been assumed by science and

A vain objection to materialism.

the arts, since the beginning of history. The essence which any man attributes to matter expresses his own experience much better than it does the nature of matter itself; but it will be a true idea, as a sensation or a maxim may be true, if it exactly reports some circumstance or relation or specious quality which it interests us to discover in that province of nature. The point that interests us in practical science and art is the method of genesis in things, which determines the successive embodiment of essences in them, their quantity and distribution. The essences distinguish the occasions, but the movement of matter produces them in their places, and makes those essences relevant to existence at all. The incapacity of the materialist to deduce logically from the terms of his theory—such as extension, atoms, electric charges, energy, or what not—the other variegated terms in which our senses or imagination may picture the world, is therefore a matter of course; far from being a defect, this is a sign that his theory is not merely verbal but may have penetrated beneath the confused surface of events and partly traced their dynamic thread; whereas a pictorial physics that should literally reproduce everything just as it appears would be entirely unintelligent and perfectly useless.

There is a more speculative prejudice which should also vanish before the equal primacy of all essences: it is the feeling that complexity, beyond a certain point, is something difficult, unlikely, and incredible. This feeling is human, too human; it expresses our scepticism or amusement or despair before any object that stretches too much our powers of intuition. It is relative to the human scale, and has no meaning in the field of being as a whole. The measure of complexity or of unity that best suits the human mind is itself variable; but wherever it may be fixed, it

In the realm of essence the true has no priority over the false, nor the natural over the unnatural.

will mark one degree in an infinite series of proportions, each neither more nor less central or proper than any other degree. Even nature seems to be full of a vastness and a minuteness that baffle us, yet are her homeliest accidents; and disproportionate as her scale may be to our fancy, she after all contains us and this fancy of ours; and at bottom she may be composed in a fashion relatively sympathetic to our categories of thought, for instance, atomically, monotonously, or subject to calculation; so that to speak of composition, elaboration, and a precarious evolved complexity, may not be meaningless in respect to natural things. Even size, childish as the notion seems, might have a natural measure: for instance, if the more atoms a thing contained the larger it should be said to be, or if the organising forces emanating from one nucleus had a greater scope than those emanating from another, so that the smaller organism might be enveloped in the larger and be a part of it. If a thing is finite either inwards or outwards, forward or back, a scale may be fixed by which it may be internally measured. But in the realm of essence all such foothold fails for human prerogative. Here every degree of complexity is as calmly enthroned as every other: none is more primitive or natural or safe than the rest, since all are necessary and all eternal. The most agitated *Paradiso* ever painted by Tintoretto, the most insane *Walpurgisnachtstraum*, is as elementary and fundamental an essence as the number one or the straight line. The realm of essence never was formed; there are no seeds or accretions in it; and we may as legitimately imagine the simple, the monotonous, or the chaotic to be derogations from some organic form, as this organic form to be a composition out of those elements. Existence, that everlasting Penelope, may sometimes embroider and sometimes undo; but all the mornings and all the evenings are one eternity, in which the finished work and the ultimate elements are equally present.

Nor is this parity of all essences confined to those which may figure in the evolution of a single world, from its atoms to the idea of its total system, seen under the form of eternity: the parity extends to the unused essences as well. Existence, infinite as it may be in some directions and by a perpetual budding, is narrowly hedged in at every step; it is all bias and exclusions. Not so the depths of pure Being: there all is simultaneous, nothing forbidden, nothing pre-eminent. The homelessness or even terror which sometimes assaults the mind at the thought of so many stars and planets, so many animals and cross-purposes even on earth, is redoubled when we consider the truly remorseless infinity of essence. It contains with perfect placidity, and without begging leave either of God or man, everything whatsoever. The selections which nature may make out of that manifold store, whether she picks a simple thing out first or a complex thing first (and who shall say which she picks out first, if she has been picking them out alternately for ever?), establish no essential priority among them. It is as easy for Being to be great as to be little: no effort is concerned, no probability; all great things and all little things are equally integral to the infinite.

It follows that all psychologisms, all attempts to analyse given essences into original elements or to assign to them a history or a meaning, are so many materialisms in disguise. Those elements are not elements of the given essence, but are other whole essences which might have been given when the material situation was different. Such history is not the history of these ideas (which have no history) but of the natural course of events which led up to the moment which begat these ideas; a course of

Nor the existent over the non-existent.

Essences have no family tree.

events which, at various points, may have begotten other ideas introducing those now alive, and having (for the best of reasons) a family likeness to them. Finally those meanings are not proper to those essences (which are what they are and have no further meaning) but express the residual pregnancy of the mind, tempted to wander dramatically, and to trace the material agencies, past or future, which may have flowed into or may flow out of the present event, in which now, like bursting rockets, these essences shine forth. Such past and future events will bear names, and will be indicated by imaginary terms which are themselves essences; but the whole force of the felt derivation will come, not from these terms or names, but from an impulse sweeping through them, rehearsed in discourse, and covering the unspecified flux of material forces actually carrying events forward from phase to phase. If the reader will recall the method of Hegel or that of Taine, he will understand what I mean: a set of brilliant dramatic sketches or notes of moral attitudes, strung together so as to suggest a voluminous current of evolution carrying these various spiritual moments on the crest of its waves. It is a material movement sketched by romantic suggestion and wrapped in moralistic eloquence or even in prophecy.

The only veritable idealism is Platonic: it sees in essences the essences themselves, self-enclosed and insulated, ultimate and eternal. The occasions on which they are manifested may be traced according to the physics or theology in vogue: that temporal underpinning cannot change their intrinsic nature. And as the means of purifying and coming truly to possess an essence is simply to contemplate it, so the means of conceiving the essences given elsewhere, for instance in the feelings and thoughts of other men, is poetic imagination, dramatic sympathy. Shakespeare is your only psychologist: the others are

Their only genealogy is that of their occasions.

physiologists or external observers who entangle their poetic science in a net of scholastic fictions. The mechanism of life being very obscure and remote from gross observation, it is inevitable that it should be adumbrated at first in fables and metaphors. When the notion of matter is crude and pictorial, there is need of piecing it out with crude and pictorial notions of souls, psychic mechanisms, laws of association, moral dialectic, and blasts of supernatural influence. These are only other names for veritable matter and its secret work; but they point to facts which science may overlook, if it has grown up in the practice of mechanical arts. Maturity, in the rhetorical school of physics, will render these myths more and more harmless and transparent, as it will all other forms of rhetoric; while maturity in the scientific school, if it is ever attained, will reduce those pictorial models more frankly to symbols, and the field of science to the field of action. But it is not the reform of science that interests me here; I am concerned to rescue from oblivion one of those preliminary facts which the science of things external ignores, although it is the breath of its nostrils: I mean intuition, with the inevitable unity and originality of the essence which that intuition defines from moment to moment.

There is no reason to suppose that nature began by being simpler than she is; we may rather suppose that she has cycles, perhaps local cycles, of relative complication with intervals of dissolution or chaos. And the beginnings of intuition can be reasonably looked for only at the height, or near the height, of this complication; intuition presupposes reactive adjustment, psychic inertia or propulsion, and therefore an elaborate hereditary life such as only a most delicately-balanced cosmos could contain. Yet though begotten and nurtured in the lap of complexity, intuition opens

Essences given on complex occasions may be simple and must be unitary.

its childish eyes upon blank light; experience does
begin with the simple, although nature does not.   The
intuition of a simple essence is called a feeling; and the
essence given in a primitive feeling is likely to be some
truly simple, quite stupid, essence, such as sheer intensity.   This intensity, when there is some concomitant
motion excited in the animal, may seem vaguely to have
a seat and to lie in some quarter; and it may be coloured
with an incipient tint of uneasiness or of contentment.
Above all, this intensity will be felt to wax and wane;
it comes as a waxing, an interruption to repose; and
the interruption over or gulped down, repose comes
slowly back.   So at least I conceive it: nature may
have many different ways of calling forth intuition,
here stealthily, there perhaps suddenly with a flare of
trumpets, and with a consciousness of having always
existed and of being omniscient.   Suffice it that this
first revelation, whether to worm or god, is a specious
thing, having a specious unity, and a precise specious
character; the vagueness or abstractness imputed to it,
when compared with the supposed material circumstances, are its very definition and familiar aspect
taken in itself.   It may be a whiff of emotion; it may
be a perception; it may be a moral sentiment redolent
of a thousand high thoughts and profound tragedies:
in each case it will be a complete apparition, born at
that moment and dying with it.   The onlooker, if
informed of its existence, may understand its origin,
its truth or falsity, its promise for the future; these are
relations external to it, physical or historical.   They
can be disclosed only when all the postulates of physics,
which are those of action, have been made by the
discursive intellect in the service of animal faith.   In
itself the given essence signifies only that which it is;
its inner perspectives, if any, are of its essence; such
reports or imaginations of things beyond as may trouble
it are elements in its being.   It is the deliverance of a

dream: the remote exists in it only as a part of the immediate. There is no complexity and no length of evolution which the immediate may not synthesise in one picture and possess in its essence. If experience in the child begins with the simple, in the wise man it begins with the complex; and his wisdom need not trouble to banish that complexity and revert to the simple, if it can learn to envisage the complex as a pure essence, in its harmless immediacy. Whether his spirit rests on a simple or a complex essence will make no difference to the purity of his contemplation, but will turn on his mood or the accidents of his life and education—things irrelevant to spiritual insight.

When I say that in a given essence all its parts are given, is not this an enormous exaggeration? It would be, if I meant the material or natural parts of an existing object; these would not only be impossible to assemble into any human view, but would be impossible to define or distinguish individually; for the structure of things is fluid, their composition perhaps infinite inwards, and their relations outwards certainly inexhaustible. But I am speaking of the features actually composing a given essence, and these by definition are all there. They are not, and can never be, anywhere else; for they are merely the features found as they are found, and where they are found, possessing the precise degree of definition, separation, and connection which they have in that living moment. As to be a living act of spirit is the nature of intuition, so to be an individual unity is the nature of essence.

Let me give three familiar illustrations of this: one drawn from emotion, one from perception, and one from imagination.

Suppose that in a Spanish town I come upon an apparently blind old beggar sitting against a wall, thrumming his feeble guitar, and uttering an occasional hoarse wail by way of singing. It is a sight which I have passed a hundred times unnoticed; but now suddenly I am arrested and seized with a voluminous unreasoning sentiment—call it pity, for want of a better name. An analytic psychologist (I myself, perhaps, in that capacity) might regard my absurd feeling as a compound of the sordid aspect of this beggar and of some obscure bodily sensation in myself, due to lassitude or bile, to a disturbing letter received in the morning, or to the general habit of expecting too little and remembering too much; or if the psychologist was a Freudian, he might invoke some suppressed impression received at the most important period of life, before the age of two. But since that supposed impression is forgotten and those alleged causes are hypothetical, they are no part of what I feel now. What I feel is simply, as Othello says, " the pity of it ". And if I stop to decipher what this *it* contains, I may no doubt be led, beyond my first feeling, to various images and romantic perspectives. My fancy might soon be ranging over my whole universe of discourse, over antiquity, over recent wars, over so many things ending in smoke; and my discursive imagery would terminate in dreary cold facts, the prose of history, from which my emotion would have wholly faded. The pity is not for them: it is not for the old man, perhaps a fraud and a dirty miser; it is pity simply, the pity of existence, suffusing, arresting, rendering visionary the spectacle of the moment and spreading blindly outwards, like a light in the dark, towards objects which it does not avail to render distinguishable. There is, then, in this emotion, no composition. There is pregnancy, a quality having affinity with certain ulterior things rather than with others; but these things are not given; they are not needed in the emotion, which arises absolutely in its full quality and in its strong simplicity. My life might have begun and ended there. Nothing is too

Illustrations: First, the emotion of pity.

complex to be primitive; nothing is too simple to stand alone.

Suppose now that I turn through the town gates and suddenly see a broad valley spread out before me with the purple sierra in the distance beyond. This expanse, this vastness, fills my intuition; also, perhaps, some sense of the deeper breath which I draw as if my breast expanded in sympathy with the rounded heavens. Here the psychologist intervening may demur, and say that I cannot see depth, because depth is a straight line terminating in the eye, along which it is impossible for the eye to travel. Distance, he will assert, must be conveyed to me through a muscular sense and the suggestion of motion; and my perception of the landscape must be compounded of a flat picture in the retina *plus* sensations in the muscles of the eye or (as I was innocently confessing) elsewhere in the body, conveying to me the suggestion of a great opportunity to move. *Second, the perception of distance.*

It is very true that pictorial space, or the specious essence of extension, appears in intuition to animals capable of locomotion, whose attention has a forward direction—that of action—so that they are capable of feeling the difference between right and left, up and down, forward and back, here and there. All the internal and external organs of their bodies are engaged in these movements, and it is fair to suppose that they all contribute something to the picture of space which, in living, dominates their spirits. But this picture is not, in itself, laid out in three dimensions. These are first discriminated by the geometry of builders in their material blocks and stones, and are specified in their working drawings and calculations. To attempt to piece together pictorial space out of imaginary earlier intuitions of dismembered geometrical elements would be the height of artifice. The third dimension does not need to be added to the *Sensible space is a single essence.*

other two, because the other two never appear without it. Breathing, stifling, writhing, and running are not felt, or seen, to occur in flatland before they are felt and seen to occur in space. Perhaps, since the possibilities of pure intuition are infinite, some paralytic geometer might see a plane in two dimensions at no distance and in no direction from himself—the pure essence of flatness lying nowhere or lying just there, in its own flat world; and nothing militates against the possibility of conceiving a mathematical plane, if circumstances lead some rapt spirit to lose itself in that essence. But such an essence would be no part of the specious essence of extension as given to ordinary mortals: it would not even be, in any literal sense, an abstraction from the latter, but an essence of a different kind (as algebraic essences are different from geometrical, or writing from speech); and nevertheless it might serve to describe in part the same material objects. A plane actually imagined is a feature in pictorial space, not an antecedent to it; the plane is viewed from a point outside and in front of it; its length and breadth are relative to the distance at which it lies. Animals surely begin by seeing moving objects in a particular quarter beyond themselves, away from the occupied centre of their own bodies; else seeing would not be looking, as it is in the play of action.

Even if we suppose that originally the intuition of extension was not a perception but only a diffuse feeling without indicative force, this felt extension would be spread in all directions, spherical and roomy, and by no means a surface without space before and behind it. For the analysis of such essences given in intuition, which is a literary task, all physiological or metaphysical hypotheses are worse than useless; they are sophistical and blinding, and tend only to falsify the honest face of experience. The question whether I see distance is a

All genetic psychology is a disguised materialism.

question not for science but for me. If I see distance
I see it; if I infer it—as when I ask myself how far a
distant object may be—I infer it; but the contention
that when I see it I must nevertheless be inferring it, is
impertinent. From what should I infer it, when the
result of the supposed inference is the only essence
before me? Nothing is present to the spirit at any
time but what is then present to it; this cannot be in
the least altered by the fact that other things may have
been present to it, or to other spirits, at other times.
These other moments will have, no doubt, an equal
importance to themselves; and memory or theory,
surveying them in their imagined order, may see a
plot or development in them, which may seem more
interesting than any of them in isolation; but this
history or plot exists for the spirit only in that contemplative or retrospective moment in which, as at the end
of a Greek tragedy, it is summed up and proclaimed.
Such a plot is a perspective in the imagination, a poetic
or philosophic idea, itself a surface view of surfaces;
the causes of all these incidents, of their existence as
well as their sequence, lie far beneath. Ideas are not
material things, or tribes of animals, though idealists
might seem to think so; in tracing their genesis or
evolution through the world, it is the movement of the
world, of the conditions and causes of those ideas, that
we are tracing under their name. An intuition is like
a flame; if the substance that fed it can continue to feed
it, or can kindle it again, it may endure or revive, in the
midst of such other intuitions as the flux of life may
involve. Discourse thus proceeds in a connected but
spasmodic manner, expressing at each moment the
cumulative energies, habits, and impulses of the
psyche, herself a mode or cycle of physical events; but
the phases of spirit, the actual intuitions and emotions
which diversify experience, are as little capable of
adding themselves up as the kisses of yesterday are

of building nests in the air and hatching the kisses of
to-morrow.

Suppose, finally, a Chinaman at the Louvre invited
to admire the Venus of Milo. The admiration expected
of him is to be a spiritual emotion, an actual
flight or transport into a fresh region of
the beautiful. It will not do if intellectually
he is able to recognise the master-lines of the statue,
although broken or because broken; nor if he can
recall the place which our historians of art may assign
to such a theme in the development of sculpture. I
will assume that he is a man of cultivated taste, accustomed to the arts of his own country, so full of delicate
ministrations to the senses and so flattering to the
ironies, perhaps to the cruelties, of the mind. He will
relegate to their place the keys to universal history
offered by philosophers, and the technical devices that
may seem for the moment the whole of art to the snobs
of the studio; and after listening to both he may continue to feel in his heart that this leaning block of
marble is blank and heavy; that a Greek goddess is
but a stalwart washer-woman; and that such monumental designs are thick, vacant, chalky, clumsy, and
rude. He will remain cold, because he will miss here
the things which in his case can work the miracle and
entrance the mind: things minute, ornate, suave, parti-
coloured, fragrant, incidental.

The sense of beauty is not a feeling separable from
some intuition of form; on the other hand, it is a feeling,
not a verbal or intellectual judgement. It
arises by the convergence in the psyche of
many assaults and many reactions, from far
and near. Some of these influences may
come from the region which the æsthetes of
the last generation denounced as morality,
or from that which the æsthetes of to-day denounce as
literature; some may come from erotic sensibility,

Third, the sense of beauty.

The sources and their composition belong to the material life of the psyche.

from familiarity, from lucidity, from harmony with other esteemed things. The Venus of Milo will not seem beautiful, in any deep sense, to any one incapable of feeling the luminous scorn, the victorious perfection, of the Greek immortals. But all this composition, though we may give moral names to its elements, occurs underground: it is physical and merely preliminary to the beauty realised in intuition. This realised beauty is not compounded of those miscellaneous extinct impressions: it could certainly not be bred in a soil which these impressions had not raked and watered, but it is a fresh flower, with its own form, its own scent, and its own naughtiness. For this reason too it cannot be preserved mummified in any external object; it can belong to things only by being attributed to them by some living soul. Those who insist that the marble Venus must be either beautiful or ugly in itself, apart from all Greeks and Chinamen, are allowing a grammatical form of judgement to mislead them about the subtler ways in which essences may be manifested in the world. Not the marble which a man without any sense of beauty might see, is the seat of beauty; the contrary quality may be as truly attributed to it. The only Venus which is inalienably beautiful is the divine essence revealed to the lover as he gazes, perhaps never to be revealed to another man, nor revealed to himself again. In this manifest goddess (for so the gods were originally revealed) her beauty is indeed intrinsic and eternal; and it is as impossible that its particular quality should be elsewhere, as that she should be without it.

The beauty felt is unprecedented, single, and revealed only to enthusiasm.

The nature of essence appears in nothing better than in the beautiful, when this is a positive presence to the spirit and not a vague title conventionally bestowed. In a form felt to be beautiful an obvious complexity composes an obvious unity: a marked intensity and individuality are seen to belong to a reality utterly immaterial and incapable of existing otherwise than speciously. This divine beauty is evident, fugitive, impalpable, and homeless in the world of material fact; yet it is unmistakably individual and sufficient unto itself, and although perhaps soon eclipsed is never really extinguished: for it visits time, but belongs to eternity.

CHAPTER XI

COMPARISON WITH SOME KINDRED DOCTRINES

THE type of being which I call essence has long been familiar to philosophers, and it is unfamiliar to the man in the street, not because it is too remote _{Pure essence} from him but because it is too near. I might _{discerned by} almost say that my theory is a variant of _{Plato and materialised} Platonism, designed to render Platonic logic _{by him.} and morals consistent with the facts of nature. I am afraid, however, that this readjustment unhinges Platonism so completely that I have no right to call my doctrine Platonic. In the realm of essence as I conceive it, the sphere of Socratic Ideas is infinitely extended and freed from all confusion with natural forces. I am no pupil of Plato's in all that phase of his thought in which he seems to supply the lack of a cosmology by turning moral and ideal terms into supernatural powers. The supernatural is nothing but an extension of the natural into the unknown, and there is infinite room for it; but when these deeper or remoter parts of nature are described in myths evidently designed for the edification or easier government of human society, I distrust the fiction. I distrust it, I mean, as a piece of physics, or information about matters of fact; but it may be a genuine and beautiful expression of the moral experience and the moral interests which have prompted it. In this capacity even the myths and the cosmology of Plato are memorable; they become again pure essences for poetic contemplation, like the Ideas; and their moral significance helps to render them warm and interesting to a man of feeling without deceiving him about the conditions of his natural life.

In calling his Ideas ideas and his myths myths, Plato seems to acknowledge that they are, after all, nothing but essences; the power which they were represented as exercising over nature was not their chief claim to respect. Nature was a phenomenon to be superseded; the material image once shattered, the god which it represented so imperfectly would appear in his proper glory. His power was an accidental effect due to the proximity of a matter capable of reflecting his likeness, and of preserving it for a time; his intrinsic and eternal being was that of an essence. Such, I think, was the fundamental conviction of Plato, in his free moments; at least such was afterwards the experience of many a Platonising soul, in ages more religious than that of Plato.

This materialisation only incidental.

Without any pretence to be religious or mystical I find myself daily in that case. I cannot read a book or think of a friend or grieve or rejoice at any fresh event, without some essence rising sensibly before me, the sole actual harvest to me of that labour. At every moment the rattle of the machine of nature, and of my own engine, unless I lose the sense of it altogether, is at once revealed and hidden by some immediate essence, which it wears like a shining garment, or more often, perhaps, merely suggests to me as its meaning, its beauty, or its secret. How should spirit ever come upon anything else? Yet this trick of arresting the immediate is in one sense an interruption to life; it is proper only to poets, mystics, or epicureans; it was incompatible with the political, censorious

Essence appears pure in poetic immediacy and disinterestedness.

temper of a traditional Greek philosopher. Socrates and Plato on the whole were conservative. They were absolutely serious only in their patriotism, in their legislative convictions, in their zeal for a well-ordered life. The rest of their philosophy was designed to be a safeguard or an ornament for the perfect citizen. They were content that his mind should dwell in a castle of words, in a mythical world no matter how fantastic, if only his hand was strengthened thereby and his will concentrated on maintaining intact the stone walls and the iron laws of his city. The same sentiment is perennial with conservatives, and would be reasonable if any city or any morality could really be conserved; but substance is in flux, in spite of the cries of all tragic heroes. Myths, maintained artificially, cannot restore morality; but a new harmony in life, defining a new morality, will clothe itself spontaneously in some new myth. Socrates and Plato could not revive the Greek city which they loved, but they facilitated the triumph of Christianity, which would have filled them with horror. The stone walls crumbled and the air-castle remained. Essence thus came to its own again, but abusively, pretending to be more than essence; and mankind has been divided ever since between the impulse to admire the vision and the impulse to denounce the lie.

If a philosophy like Platonism, founded on the intuition of essences, so soon materialised them into existences, spirits, and powers (objects of belief not amenable to intuition), no wonder that other systems, initially interested only in alleged facts, physical, psychological, or theological, should have overlooked essences altogether. Not that the most distracted or dogmatic mind ever ceases in fact to contemplate mere essences, namely, the terms in which it frames its views, and the emotions with which it views them; but the object it is

It is normally overlooked in science and experience.

intent upon is always an ulterior object, an existing world, where the things and events it believes in shall stand or move in a framework of external relations. When it calls these existences sensations, atoms, space, time, or persons, and wonders which of these names describes them best, the test does not lie in any comparison of the essences evoked by those names and the essences of the existing objects, for since these objects are removed facts their essences cannot be present to intuition. The consequence is that even in thought the given essences lose their interest; you stop asking yourself what positive notion you have of a person or an atom, of space or of time, or of a sensation; the choice between these notions becomes like the choice of words in a sentence, not determined so much by their intrinsic character as by the relations into which they fall and the current of intent and expectation that runs through some in one direction and through others in another. In other words, what concerns the naturalistic philosopher in his choice of terms is the external relations which, in using them, he is led to attribute to the pressing events which they designate. For his purposes an atom is the unit (whatever it may be) in physical transformations; a sensation is a means (no matter what) of registering a fact; a person is a centre (be it what it will) of observation or opinion. In this way not only physics but psychology comes to disregard the actual terms in which it frames its system, and empiricism overlooks the only objects of immediate experience.

Nevertheless the bias of such an outlook exclusively towards existence is too violent not to have its nemesis. Essences neglected here will assert themselves there; they will invade and perhaps absorb the ultimate description of what is supposed to be an existing world. Those who reject essences as terms swallow them as myths. Descriptions of the universe, when clear, are so fantastic, so

But, in-
evitably
intervening,
fills both
with
illusions.

evidently mere essences evoked in human thought, that the very interest in existence which begat those descriptions presently disowns them, and everybody wonders how such studious and earnest men could be the dupes of their own fables. But in reality those fables are not more fantastic than the daily aspect of the sunset or the grammar of common speech. They are essences appearing just as immediately to the mind, only more laboured and articulate; and as symbols for the facts of nature they may be just as true. Indeed, their immediate charm sometimes overcomes philosophers at the end of their speculation, as it overcomes artists and poets at the beginning; they see that what delights them is not a fact, not even a truth, but an absolute essence. This ultimate recognition of essence is normal in mathematics; nor can it be easily avoided in metaphysics, especially when mathematics, logic, or poetry becomes dominant there, and takes the bit in its teeth.

When Descartes, for example, identified matter with extension, he substituted essence for substance: an improvement, no doubt, for mathematical purposes, but an abdication in genuine physics, which is founded on animal faith. Substance was what Descartes meant to describe; it moved, and extension, being an essence, cannot move. When he imagined geometrical figures, indistinguishable in scale, parts, or quality, and bounded by merely ideal lines, nevertheless moving in reference to one another, he was substituting a possible *pattern* of nature for living nature herself. The essence in his clear and distinct intuition seemed to him fundamental and final; and so it would be to pure spirit; he forgot that a spirit cannot be born, die, or have a local habitation in the bosom of an essence. The only substance remaining in his system—the only being self-existent in all its parts and in actual flux—was accordingly the

Descartes, by substituting essences for substances, unintentionally left pure discourse to be the only existence.

discourse in which the material world might appear
as a picture. Descartes thus became the father of
psychologism against his will; and the scientific reform
which he meant to establish liberated mathematics
and mechanics, but otherwise left confusion worse
confounded.

It was reserved for Spinoza, still under the persuasion
that he was describing substance, to conceive the
realm of essence in its omnimodal immensity.
Human vanities, whether in speculation or
in manners, were not for him. He had a just
conception of man's place in nature, and in the
presence of the infinite, love cast out both fear and
greed from his mind. His approach to essence is the
more interesting for not being guided by any Platonic
motive; as he never cultivated poetry or sentimental
theology, so he might have neglected essence altogether,
if he had taken it merely for what it is. All that his
pious heart respected was substance—that which exerts
force, works in nature, and might feed or threaten him
in his contentment. In spite of his speculative scope,
his wisdom was Levitical; he craved above all things
to be safe and sure in his corner of the Lord's house.
This safety had, as it were, two phases, or two dimensions: materially, in the lea of the tempest, the swallow
might build his temporary nest; such happiness was a
part of what universal nature provided; but ideally he
might borrow the wings of the storm, and enjoy perfect
freedom in identity with that force which in creating
and destroying all things is never exhausted or defeated.

It was the plethora of this passion, at once sacrificial
and omnivorous, that carried Spinoza into the realm
of essence, and made him gloat on its infinity.
He found a cruel pleasure in asserting that
every part of it existed, thereby putting to
shame the conceit of mankind, and in that
abasement finding a fanatical compensation for his

[marginal notes:] Spinoza discerns the
infinity of
the realm
of essence.

His pan-
theist zeal
leads him to
hypostatise
it.

own frailty. Why, indeed, should not all essence exist? If extension be the essence of matter, every possible geometrical figure, in every possible super-position and substitution, must be equally real at every point in nature; and yet at all points pure extension, motionless and undivided, must be somehow the only reality. So in the other, the psychological, world. If thinking be the substance of all thoughts, all possible thoughts should be equally present in every act of thinking, and yet nothing in any thought should be real except the act of thinking in its purity.

This tragic contradiction—tragic because so many instincts and passions meet and destroy themselves there — comes of hypostatising essence and attempting to rationalise substance. The substance of this world (as I may have occasion to argue in its place) is no mere essence, such as extension, pure Being, or pure consciousness, hypostatised in its bareness: it is an existential flux, of unknown extent and complexity, which when it falls into certain temporary systems which we call living bodies, kindles intuition there, and brings various essences to light, which become terms in belief and knowledge; but substance, although thus posited and symbolised by the animal mind, always remains obscure to it. How should the essences, mainly emotional and inwardly elicited, which events evoke in this or that sensitive organism, reveal substance in its inmost constitution and total extent? That substance, at this point, has produced those appearances is indeed one of its characteristics, and so much we may safely assert of it forthwith; but to legislate for substance in our private parliament, or to assert that the whole realm of essence must somewhere be reduced to act (as Spinoza supposed) is perfectly gratuitous. More-over, when the definition of the realm of essence—all distinct beings of all kinds—is turned into a definition

The principle of existence cannot be rational.

of substance, it contradicts another definition—pure Being—which Spinoza could not help regarding, with equal rashness, as the essence of substance in some deeper sense. Natural substance must be allowed to rejoice in whatever essence it has, and to change it as often as it will, and to bring to intuition in our scattered minds such visions as it likes; and meantime, in the realm of essence, pure Being and all beings may lie eternally together like the lion and the lamb, in the peace of non-existence. Very likely, in its chosen ways, the existing world may be infinite; but the inevitable absolute infinity of the realm of essence (a matter of definition) does not justify me in ascribing a fabulous infinity to substance.

In Leibniz (who had a wonderfully clear head) the realm of essence appears in sharp distinction from

In Leibniz it reappears both infinite and pure, but in a dubious theological context. existence, under the name of "all possible worlds"; but this notion is introduced almost playfully, in the midst of a theological myth. We are invited to assist at the deliberations of the Creator when in his primeval solitude he debated which of the worlds that he could imagine might most congenially keep him company; for it was not good, he felt, for God to be alone. Now, if we take this fable literally, the Creator already existed and was himself one of the possible worlds, and a very special one; for he possessed an intuition of the whole realm of essence, and, beneath that, a mysterious propulsive nature of his own which inclined him to create other living beings, and enabled him to distinguish a better and a worse among mere possibles. Indeed, if we remember the religious sources of this conception, which Leibniz was obliged to treat with respect, we may safely say that this gallery of possibles present to the Creator's mind is not the realm of essence at all, but an emanation of his particular existing nature; just as it is not the realm of essence in its entirety that swims before a novelist when he debates what conclusion to give to his novel; but the alternatives that suggest themselves are only a few, such as lie within his experience and conspire with his purpose and are compatible with the plot of the novel as far as it has gone.   This Creator would then be a perfectly contingent existence, a particular being finding himself already at work.   He could not have asked himself, before he existed, whether he would be the best possible God.   The fabled problem of creation must already have been solved before it could be proposed; and a mind considering which world to choose is a world existing without ever having been chosen. The notions of the possible and the best, otherwise unintelligible, become significant in reference to the accidental potencies and preferences of that existing being.   His creations, like those of any living artist, would then be naturally in his own image, and it would turn out that of all those possible worlds only the best was really possible, since a motive for creating one of the others would necessarily be wanting: the best would be simply the one which the Creator actually preferred and must have preferred unless (what is inadmissible) he did not know his own mind.   I need not enter into the moral difficulties which this rigid monotheism involves; suffice it that the realm of essence has dropped out of sight, and our philosophy is reduced to an account, credible or incredible, of some natural events and some natural existences.

But perhaps we should not press in this manner words which a philosopher could only have meant figuratively.   Leibniz makes some explicit reservations about time: the original solitude of God was ontological only, not historical, and time, being an integral part of creation, could not have preceded the creative act.   In reality, then, this creative act would be the perpetual process of nature,

<!-- marginal note -->
How this might be rationalised.

viewed under the form of eternity and represented
poetically as deliberate and voluntary. If we allowed
ourselves to continue this method of rationalisation,
perhaps the realm of essence would come into its own
again, and the mind of the Creator surveying all
possible worlds would be only a dramatic metaphor
for that immutable background which the realm of
essence supplies for all the shifts of existence. Perhaps,
too, the moral compulsion which, according to Leibniz,
God was under, to distinguish and to create the best
of possible worlds, might be interpreted as inverting
mythically a homely truth: namely, that the best and
only possible world for a creature to live in is the world
that produced him. We may grumble and we may
suffer, but we should not have been ourselves in any
other world or nation or family; the circle of our
demands and ideals is but a floating expression of the
faculties which reality has fostered in us. The actual
world, in type if not in detail, is therefore always such as
it would be if the good to which it aspires had created it.
This is the reason why at bottom most people are so
well satisfied with their country and with themselves,
and why existence is normally regarded as a benefit.

Leibniz could be a very great philosopher when he
chose, when the press of business allowed, or when
some Serene Highness commanded it; but he was a
diplomatist even in philosophy, and his chief preoccupation was to reconcile powerful opinions and to
recommend himself to the orthodox as well as to the
competent. He could play as readily with the notion
of essence as with any other notion, but his sincerity
was not of that profound sort which gives to human
conceptions their radical values, and his system was a
masterpiece of artificiality in which nobody—not even
himself—could very heartily believe.

Essence was familiar to Descartes, Spinoza, and
Leibniz, because even if not scholastic themselves they

were trained in the scholastic tradition, which was itself but Platonism made prosaic and Christian; but the same cannot be said of the British and German philosophers. Yet both psychology and the criticism of knowledge ought to bring essence to light, since essences are the only objects of indubitable and immediate experience. A profound confusion, however, intervened. The objects of experience were confused with experience itself, which was assumed to be self-conscious, a series of states of mind which know what they are and are what they know. Essence accordingly became a needless if not impossible conception; because the only essences that could then be found or thought of would be essences existing and knowing themselves to exist; in other words, they would not be essences but (what is a contradiction in terms) facts given in intuition. The insecurity and anarchy prevailing in these schools allow them to traverse the ground in a thousand directions without ever disengaging the radical possibilities and principles involved; for instance, they almost always combine their axiom that existence is self-conscious with a naturalistic view of the course of human experience, deployed in time and distributed among well-known persons and nations —a combination which would be impossible if either of the two views had been thoroughly analysed. The notion that existence is self-conscious, and conscious only of the state of mind which it is, excludes the possibility of any transitive knowledge or even belief, because it reduces every object, whether of intuition or intent, to the process of thinking it. The notion of a flux of experience or thought, reporting one of its parts to another of its parts, is accordingly excluded; and yet, without such naturalistic history and psychology, self-consciousness would lose all its interest, because it would be conscious of not being knowledge, but of

Modern idealism should admit only given essences, but is too distracted to rest in them.

being only the intuition of an essence devoid of meaning.

Of late, however, various judicious persons, trained in these schools, have begun to confess that conscious- ness is not aware of itself but of objects variously styled sense-data or concepts or neutral entities (neither mental not material), or simply " objects ", meaning essences present to sense or thought as opposed to the events in nature which they symbolise.   But it is events, in natural knowledge, that are the true objects; and the given essences are only the terms in which those events are described.   If these terms are hypostatised and set in a network of natural relations, as if they were things, the result will be a pictorial physics which may have its merits, but which is not the realm of essence; to reach the latter conception it would be necessary to remember that what is given never has any relations but those which are given with it.   It is therefore always an eternal essence and never a natural fact.   Natural facts are objects of intent only; and then the propriety of the names, images, categories, or other essences which we use in conceiving them becomes problematical.

All science has need of remembering that it is only discourse.

On the other hand, essences problematical as descriptions of facts are manifest as ideas.   The more hypotheses we try, and the more alternatives we consider, whether we attain absolute truth or a sufficient symbolic truth, or no truth at all, we are still entertained by ideas which are innocent if we do not abuse them, and perhaps beautiful and significant if they express our own playful or creative impulses.   Nor is this entertainment with essence a trivial bond with reality.   Facts, however momentous, are transient and local, and truths, however eternal, are relative to these transient and local facts; but every essence, whether it ever have or not the adventitious dignity of a truth, is in

And that the realm of essence is the infinite background of every- thing.

its own right a something—a verse or a letter in that infinite Koran sealed from all eternity in the bosom of Allah, of which the trembling angel of life may read to us a few Surahs.   That it should be these and not those is the tragic mystery of our fate, and of all existence; that others also should some day be manifested in other worlds or to other spirits, would be a further decree of fate; but that all should lie for ever in the realm of essence is a luminous necessity raised far above any accident of destiny or decree of power.   It could not be otherwise.   If you deny that realm, you acknowledge it.   If you forget it, you consent that it should silently laugh at you in your sleep.

POSTSCRIPT

CORROBORATIONS IN CURRENT OPINION

AFTER revolving these things in my mind for many years in intellectual solitude, when at last I was bringing this book to a close—not without profound disappointment that for all my labour it should be no better than it is—I have had the satisfaction of finding that quite independently, in the most various quarters, the same intuition is returning to the world. Not that in my own mind it needed confirmation: these are not eventual matters of fact on which testimony is needed or witnesses are to be counted like so many head of cattle; but after all, a book is addressed to the public, and the impulse towards expression and communication would remain abortive if no one was ready to listen or to understand. True, my doctrine was neither new nor extinct. Platonism was still remembered; round the corner, though strangely out of sight, there was always Catholic philosophy; and far away Indian philosophy loomed impressively in its unravelled labyrinth. But the notion of essence in these systems seemed to be either incomplete or impure, or both impure and incomplete: they were accidental traditional faiths borrowing from logic such helps or extensions as they could welcome; they had not that honest personal seat nor that fearless outlook which amid so many weaknesses made the strength of modern philosophy. My allegiance is rather to the earlier Greeks, who looked freely and ingenuously on the universe with the curiosity of children, but of children bred nobly and protected from false terrors by a manly civilisation. The autonomy of reason which they so beautifully and simply achieved is not to be surrendered. In part, indeed, it had been recovered by the modern mind, in its romantic Protestantism; but without the Greek clearness and inner freedom. The British and German schools in which it

168

had been my fate to be educated, were themselves obscurely rooted in religious confusions. For three hundred years they had hardly been able to distinguish the universe or the realm of essence from the vapours of animal feeling.

Of late, however, various rifts or transparencies have appeared in the low sky of subjectivism; and curiously, it is the realm of essence that seems to become visible first—the stars, as it were, before the sun. Matter, though so much nearer and dearer to the heart of mankind, is even harder to define and to situate from a psychological point of view; for the more "objective" a psychological idealist wishes to render his "realities", the more empirical and sensualistic they must become: in other words, the more subjective. If an idea develops within its bosom a theory of its own origin or environment, it remains a mere idea more elaborate than it was, but not more cognisant of anything beyond; whereas if it is satisfied to contemplate and to define its internal theme or quality, it thereby begins to dominate a field of logical relations independent of its momentary attention or existence. Thus intelligence, like the dove after the Flood, escapes from the Ark of subjectivism more easily through the window than through the door.

Three recent descriptions of the realm of essence, one English, one German, and one French, lie at this moment before me. Perhaps a brief report of them may serve to convince the reader that in all this I am not dreaming alone, but that on the contrary I am introducing him to an eternal background of reality, which all minds when they are truly awake find themselves considering together.

1. In a volume entitled *The Concept of Nature*, by A. N. Whitehead, a systematic distinction is drawn between "events" on the one hand—which is the name there given to all self-existing facts or portions of nature, and on the other hand "sense objects" and "scientific objects"—which are the names given to essences, or at least to such essences as the author is concerned with. That he should recognise essences clearly, yet should call them by names so adventitious to their intrinsic nature, is an anomaly easily explained by the circumstances. Whitehead is primarily a mathematician, naturally at home amongst essences; but he is an Englishman, and was drawn toward metaphysics at a time and in a circle in which an

intense local reaction was taking place in British philosophy in favour of realism, but of a realism that should be still empirical and moralistic. It is characteristic of British reformers to disown the distressing consequences of some traditional principle, in order to be free to cling to it with a happier mind; and as an Anglican Catholic must denounce the Pope, so an Anglican realist must eschew matter. Here the traditional principle was that of Berkeley, that the only objects of knowledge are inert ideas, or the immediate data of experience; and the distressing consequence was that in that case nothing latent or dynamic could exist in nature or could be made an object of study. This consequence, at first blush, had seemed to Berkeley a palmary argument for religion, and later it was deliberately made the corner-stone of transcendental idealism; but it was wormwood now in the mouths of the new realists, engrossed as they were in dogmatic judgement, in mathematics, and in cosmological physics. Might not this consequence be denied, while maintaining that principle, if we alleged that things are in reality compacted of ideas, of "objects" immediately given in experience but existing independently of knowledge? All would then be reality and nothing appearance, yet nothing would exist otherwise than just as it appeared. Events, or the substantial facts in nature, would be concretions of human "sense objects" and of human "scientific objects"; they would no longer be free to embody, to the confusion of sense and science, any essences whatsoever which the Creator might have wished them to possess.

How these human "objects" enter into events and compose them I will abstain from inquiring; suffice it that in themselves these "objects" are evidently essences and not existing elements. Whitehead continually calls them "eternal objects"; and that is final. Nothing can be more opposite to an event, or more remote from natural existence, than any eternal being. Yet that the *terms*—not indeed the intended *objects*—of sense and science are eternal essences could not escape so accomplished a mathematician. In his early collaboration with Bertrand Russell, at a time when the latter shared with G. E. Moore a virgin enthusiasm for ideal entities, Whitehead could daily measure the gulf which separates the realm of logic from that of fact. It was a saying of his in those days—for youth sometimes has a shrewdness denied to distracted age—that some truths could be proved but were unimportant, and others were

important but could not be proved.   Logic evidently was never
quite satisfying to this logician;   even while feeding on its
manna, he yearned for the flesh-pots of fact.   Tastes are free;
but as the whole virtue of flesh-pots is to be eaten, so the whole
virtue of events is to be enacted;   an effort to describe the
cuisine of nature exhaustively, were success in it possible,
would yield dreadful literature and no food.   If, nevertheless,
any one had a desire for such preternatural knowledge, would
he be likely to attain it by overlaying the current cook-book of
science, which after all has a relative validity, with rich metaphysics of his sheer invention?

In a later book on *Science in the Modern World*, Whitehead
has distinguished essences even more clearly from the occasions
on which they may be realised.   "Each eternal object," he
tells us, "is an individual which, in its own peculiar fashion,
is what it is."   "Each eternal object is just itself, in whatever
mode of realisation it is involved.   There can be no distortion
of the individual essence without thereby producing a different
eternal object."   "Thus actualisation is a selection among
possibilities."   Each "is systematically and by the necessity of
its nature related to every other eternal object ".   "The realm
of eternal objects is properly described as a 'realm', because
each eternal object has its status in this general systematic
complex of mutual relatedness."   "A limited set of such
objects is itself an eternal object; it is those eternal objects in
that relationship."   "Thus the complexity of an eternal object
means its analysability into a relationship of component eternal
objects."   "An eternal object, such as a definite shade of
green, which cannot be analysed into a relationship of components, will be called 'simple'."

The nature of essence could hardly be recognised more
frankly: it is eternal, compacted of internal relations, indifferently simple or complex, and at every level individual.   It
composes an infinite pure Being.   If there are impurities in
Whitehead's description they arise, not from his conception
of the field of essence itself, where his mathematical expert-
ness gives him an enviable scope and fertility, but rather
from refraction in the thicker atmosphere through which he
approaches it.

2. Entirely free from these entanglements, though perhaps
caught in others, is the view of essence contained in the *Pure*

Phenomenology of Edmund Husserl.[1]   He is an analytic psychologist of the most conscientious systematic kind, never forsaking the plane of reflective autobiography; and to boot he is a convinced transcendental idealist, always remembering the activity of thought involved in the contemplation or definition of any object; so that his theory is like those early maps of the known world in which the geographer, proud of his young art, placed in the foreground a representation of the compass, sextant, and telescope, which had served him in his construction; while in another part, to fill in some large tract of *terra incognita*, he might show us the gallant ship in which he made his voyages of discovery, or a group of the naked savages found at the antipodes.   Such marginal decoration is not without its charm; and the modern reader, accustomed to romanticism even in philosophers, may be more willing to look on essence if he is told at the same time that he is looking at it, and how the vision has been achieved.   Autobiography may be enlightening even in logic: it reminds us that our map is a map; but it is also grotesque, since it is not the map's business to describe cartography; and thought turns towards essence for the sake of essence, not for the sake of thought.   Yet there are advantages in this circumspection or contortion; it is not so easy in learned Germany as in England or America for the gay philosopher to ignore transcendental criticism and psychological fact simply because they were known to some past generation, or because they annoy him and he is interested in something else.

Husserl accordingly professes to study "phenomena", which the Platonic tradition identifies with appearances and the positivistic tradition with events; and we might doubt for a moment whether he is considering essences at all, and not rather facts or existing objects.   But no: all the emphasis falls on the word *pure*; objects, in order to enter the realm of this phenomenology, must be thoroughly *purified*.   This purification consists in reducing the object to its intrinsic and evident character, disregarding all question of its existence or nonexistence, or of its locus in nature; or, in my language, it consists in suspending animal faith, and living instead con-

---

[1] *Ideen zu einer reinen Phänomenologie und phänomenologischen Philosophie*, von Edmund Husserl ; Halle, 1922.   I translate the thankless text rather freely for the reader's convenience, supplying the original phrases in parentheses where fairness seems to demand it.

templatively, in the full intuition of some essence. This essence may be as complex and as rich in inner perspectives as imagination can make it; it may span any depth of specious time, or intuited duration; every idea which science or faith may turn into a creed, or use in the description of existence, is in its spiritual immediacy a pure essence, a term given to contemplation, distinct logically and æsthetically; otherwise science and faith would be mere chatter, verbiage accompanying certain turns in action, not inner possessions or forms of thought. Nothing is therefore removed from experience by purifying it, except its distraction; and an essence, far from being an abstraction from a thing, is the whole of that thing as it ever can be directly given, or spiritually possessed. "Instead," says Husserl, "of setting up a natural world by a transcendental act of naive assertion, and being driven by the implications of that assertion to posit other transcendent things one after another, we put all these positings aside, we refrain from becoming accomplices in that act; and we direct our discerning, scrutinising, contemplative glance upon the field of pure intuition in its absolute intrinsic being. . . . We live henceforth in these acts of supervening attention, ranging over the infinite field of absolute immediacy—the bed-rock of phenomenology."

"Geometry and phenomenology," we read in another place, "being sciences of pure essence, lay down nothing concerning real existences. Hence clear fictions will not only serve just as well for these constructions as do actual perception and experience, but often much better." "Pure or transcendental phenomenology is not a science of fact but a science of essences or forms. The phenomena of transcendental phenomenology are in their nature non-existent (*characterisiert als irreal*). All immediate data (*Erlebnisse*) transcendentally purified are non-existent, and are situated out of all local relation (*Einordnung*) to the 'real world'." "As the datum of personal experimental perception is a particular thing, so the datum of intuition is a pure essence." "Every science of fact or of experience must needs draw the fundamental terms of its theory from some formal ontology." "Immediate vision, not necessarily sensuous observation of things, but awareness yielding any original datum, no matter of what quality, is the ultimate source of validity for all rational assurance." "All that I believe to exist in the world of things has, in principle, only a presumptive

existence." And finally, in answer to the inevitable reproach—
as if it were a reproach!—of being a Platonist, the author says:
"If 'object' meant 'existing object', and 'reality' meant
'existing reality', then indeed to call Ideas objects and realities
would be to indulge in a perverse hypostasis; but when the
two are explicitly opposed, and when 'object' is defined as any
theme of discourse whatsoever, what can be the remaining
objection?" "Between immediacy and existence yawns a
veritable abyss in the quality of being (*Sinn*). Existence is
posited in perspectives, never given absolutely as it is, and
has an accidental and relative status: whereas being in the
immediate is certain and unconditioned, and by its very nature
not subject to perspective or given in an external view."

Such a firm adherence to transcendental principles serves
to bring out the fundamental and ultimate part played by
essence in knowledge, and its own immaterial and incorruptible
nature; but perhaps this phenomenology is itself only an
external view and a perspective, since the fact that experience
must play with terms or essences does not imply that all
essences must figure in experience. No doubt the field of
possible intuition, the range of pure spirit, is infinite, and none
other than the realm of essence itself; but is pure spirit itself
possible, or does actual intuition realise all essences, or even as
many as are realised in the unprobed structure of nature? A
naturalist must be allowed to doubt it; and also to look for the
genesis and meaning of immediate experience in the material
and animal world, where a malicious transcendentalism, one
that isolates mind in mind, cannot consistently look for them.

3. If a mathematical physicist can vindicate the eternity of
essences, and a psychologist their purity, a pupil of the Oriental
school may well vindicate their infinity; he will help to dis-
sipate any lingering suspicion that they might be dependent for
their being on human intuition or on embodiment in nature.
In the books of René Guénon [1] the study of essence in its own
absolute sphere is called metaphysics. The proper, and even
the etymological, sense of this word, he tells us, "is that by
which it designates whatever lies beyond physics, provided we
understand by physics, as the ancients always did, the whole
of all the sciences of nature". "Nothing can be metaphysical

---

[1] Especially *Introduction générale à l'étude des doctrines hindoues*, 1921,
and *L'Homme et son devenir selon le Vedânta*, 1925.

except that which is absolutely stable, permanent, independent of all events and in particular of all historical circumstances." Metaphysics is the consideration of the universal, of the absolutely unlimited; not of matters which "special sciences may leave out because their present development is more or less incomplete, but rather of what, by its every nature, eludes the touch of these sciences." In the domain of metaphysics no experience, no contact with fact, is possible. "Being beyond physics, we are also, for that very reason, beyond experience", that is, our thought is not intent on surrounding existences, but on the nature and relations of essences chosen and defined by that thought itself. "Hence, in questions of metaphysics, all that can change with times and places is merely the mode of exposition . . . that which is beyond nature, is also beyond change. . . . No discoveries are at all possible in metaphysics. . . . All that is discoverable may have been equally known by certain men in all ages: and such is, in fact, what we may gather from a profound examination of traditional metaphysical doctrines. . . . Metaphysics excludes hypothesis; whence it follows that metaphysical truths cannot be in the least doubtful in themselves; if there is ever occasion for discussion or controversy, it can only be on account of some defect in exposition or in comprehension." "Metaphysical truths can be conceived only by a faculty which, because its operation is on the immediate, we may call intuitive; if it be thoroughly understood that it has absolutely nothing in common with what certain contemporary philosophers call intuition, a merely sensitive and vital faculty properly inferior to ·discursive intelligence and not superior to it. . . . We speak here of intellectual intuition, which is necessarily infallible, not being actually distinct from its object. Such is the essential basis of metaphysical certitude"; whereas reasoning "is evidently fallible in consequence of its discursive and mediate character ".

This use of the term metaphysics would be unobjectionable, if it could be adhered to with constancy, and by general agreement: but metaphysics has always been, and is to-day, an attempt to establish truths about nature and existence otherwise than by observation, measurement, and experiment: nor am I sure that the Indians, and their French interpreter after them, do not attribute to their metaphysics any physical prerogatives, or to their intuition any feminine or Bergsonian privilege of being a miraculous substitute for intellect and a short cut to knowledge of fact. There is a sense, indeed, in which all existing things depend upon the non-existent realm of pure essence, since they could not be what they are, either intrinsically or in their internal relations to every other nature, did they not realise and illustrate some part of that primordial structure of being; so that any elucidation of pure essences explores a part of those essences one or another of which actual things must assume if they are to exist at all, or allow anything to be seen or said of them; but so long as the study of essences is *a priori*, imaginative and metaphysical, there is no likelihood or presumption that *those* essences will be found realised in anything existent. Before any such assumption can be made legitimate, we must turn with an absolutely docile and clear mind to the empirical aspects and relations of the facts themselves, as exploration and practical mastery unroll them before us; and then, when we have ascertained what essence, in some measure and in some respect, these existing things possess, we may freely develop the dialectical relations of that essence and deepen thereby our intellectual understanding of those things: as, for instance, has been done in mathematics to every one's satisfaction. But if arithmetic and geometry had not been originally the coinage of mechanical art, stamped upon the mind by commerce with things, they would have had no application to existence, and no authority over it—as indeed they have not over the whole field of psychic and moral being. Pure metaphysics, then, must call for aid on sense before it can claim to describe existence; it becomes impure and abusive, and such metaphysics as we are all accustomed to, when it presumes to describe nature without her consent. And can we doubt that Indian metaphysics does so at least as boldly as the metaphysics of the West? Else how comes it infallibly to distinguish five physical elements, neither more nor less, or to know that qualities of human sensation, such as sound, are intrinsic to those elements, or to assume the transmigration of souls, or to posit Ishwara and other existing deities between man and the impersonal infinite? Far be it from me to quarrel with the ideology of holy men; my wish is rather to understand and revivify as far as possible the essences which any spiritual tradition has made symbols of fate or themes for profound contemplation: my own native themes and symbols are probably not better. Only I would not let the lust of imposture, in others or in myself, distort that meditation. Delusion is the greatest enemy to peace.

How perfect such intellectual peace may ultimately become, how remote from all bias or presumption, appears in the direction of all Indian discipline upon deliverance from existence. Of course, this deliverance can be imaginative only, else peace would never be realised: but to exist as if not existing is a blessed deliverance, not only from the troubles of the flesh, but from the illusions of philosophy: it is the enlightenment which the philosopher seeks. Existence produces a false isolation and a vain reinforcement of some fragment of essence which by the logical necessity of its being forms part of an infinite and eternal realm. We therefore escape and overcome existence automatically in the act of understanding what existence is—that it is blindness to almost everything: although this blindness comes of being dazzled by a few features which matter, the principle of existence, happens to embody and to press upon the attention of the organisms which it forms.

The universe, then, is but a stain in the purity of the infinite,[1] of that non-existence by accident which is pure Being by necessity. Such bandying about of dark phrases need not irritate a tolerant mind, that knows the various realms of being in their disparate sorts of reality. Thus Guénon himself uses the word Being, not, indeed, for existence, but for only so much of essence as is illustrated there: precisely for that segment of essence which I call the realm of truth. "If ontology or the science of Being", he writes,[2] " is subordinate to metaphysics and belongs to it, it is far from identical with metaphysics as a whole: because Being does not signify the non-manifested absolutely, but only the principle of the manifested part"; that is, Being is so much of the eternal script as the reagent is destined to render visible at one time or another. "Consequently that which lies beyond Being is of much more importance metaphysically than is Being itself: in other words, it is Brahma, not Ishwara, that must be acknowledged to be the Supreme Principle."

According to this use of language, metaphysics would mean the description of the realm of essence, ontology that of truth, and physics or natural philosophy that of existence: existence

---

[1] "L'univers n'est qu'un défaut dans la pureté du Non-Être ": Paul Valéry; L'Ébauche d'un serpent, in the volume of poems entitled Charmes.
[2] L'Homme et son devenir, p. 45.

having an urgent sort of reality, but a derivative and a lame sort. "Being, while it is properly the principle of universal manifestation", the essence which is temporally embodied in the universe, "lies outside and beyond this manifestation of it—and here we may call to mind the 'unmoved mover' of Aristotle." The existing world, as well as its eternal essence, "is no doubt real, but only in a relative fashion, by virtue of its subordination to its principle, and, in so far as something of this principle is reflected in it, as an image reflected in a mirror draws all its reality from the object, without which it would have no existence. But this subordinate reality, which is only borrowed, is illusory in comparison with the supreme reality" —that is, with the eternal essence there momentarily exemplified—"even as the image in the mirror is illusory in comparison with the object: and if we attempted to cut the image off from its original, the illusion would vanish into nonentity pure and simple"—for then, besides being unsubstantial and impermanent it would not even deceptively manifest any essence. "From this we may understand that existence, or conditioned and exemplified Being, is at once real in one sense and illusory in another; a point which people in the West have never rightly understood."

In invoking the authority of the Indians and of their lucid French interpreter, I wish I might invoke it without reserve; but there is a mass of cosmological and historical extravagance, entangled with their "metaphysics," which is nothing to my purpose. Tradition is venerable, where it transmits a unanimous spiritual discipline, by which the souls of essential hermits, in every age and country, have been made sensitive to the contingency of fact and the eternity and infinity of pure Being; but superstitions too are traditional, and not for that reason respectable. Superstition prevails also in traditional philosophy in the West, not only in theology, but in biology and psychology; it is maintained there by an ancient and stubborn confusion of formal with efficient causes. The forms which things wear, since these things could not be themselves without those forms, are said to *make* the things what they are; and so the essence by which a thing is classified and named is introduced among the efficient conditions which have ushered it into existence and endowed it with that particular form: conditions which are all ultimately material. Matter is requisite for continuity in change, or for brotherly existence.

This is often implied and sometimes confessed by the most sweeping idealisms: thus Guénon himself writes,[1] "Individual modifications, such, for instance, as pleasure and pain . . . all proceed from the plastic principle, *Prakriti* or *Pradhâna*, as from their only root. It is in this substance, containing potentially all the possibilities of manifestation, that the modifications are produced in the phenomenal order, by the mere unfolding of these possibilities, or, to use Aristotelian terms, by their passage from potentiality into act. 'Every modification (parinâma), says Vijnâna-Bhikshu, from the original formation of the world (that is, of each cycle of existence) until its final dissolution comes exclusively out of *Prakriti* and its derivatives.'" Whence, indeed, should change come, except from a region of changes? Where else should existence be enacted, save in a medium where forms may arise and lapse, may be irrationally conjoined, and may quarrel for their substance and transmit it to one another? The realm of essence, or a pure spirit eternally contemplating that realm, since it is immutable and incapable of any local emphasis or arbitrary exclusion, can have no influence whatsoever on the production of anything.

Nevertheless, bewildering equivocations continue to play about the word *make*. What makes this table a table? Surely, we may innocently answer, its form and its uses. Therefore, in contempt of the wood and the carpenter, the metaphysician may proceed to assure us that the essence of tabularity or the essence of utility is the true and only creator of this table. An air of profundity may be given to this nonsense by the fact that the genesis of things in nature is mysterious, and untraceable by human fancy; while we reconcile ourselves habitually to our own being and actions, merely by naming and expecting them. As within us, so without us, the flux of matter, amid a welter of waste and chaos, is rich in transitory harmonies; and this world is truly miraculous, in the sense in which any existing world was bound to be so. The verbiage of metaphysics might therefore pass as decent drapery for our ignorance or eloquent expression of it; but the trouble is that when some good critic detects that innocent imposture, he may extend his scorn to the realm of essence in its legitimate prerogatives. These do not include any power of piecing out the imperfections of physics; the forms of things conceived to exist

[1] *L'Homme et son devenir*, p. 69.

before the things and to call them into existence would, indeed, be *chimaerae bombinantes in vacuo*. Nevertheless the forms which things assume, when they assume or suggest them, are clearer, more interesting, and more beautiful than their substance or their causes. It would be a pity if the abuse of logic hardened men's hearts against poetry, and made them enemies to their own intellectual life. The metaphysicians, in their impatience of pure essences, which are their appointed food, are to blame for this misunderstanding: they insist that their clairvoyance is historical or physical knowledge; but this pretension is not only easily disproved, but is unworthy of their contemplative vocation. This expressly carries their thoughts beyond the accidents of life, and lifts them into communion with another realm of being, more akin to the spirit, since there an infinite variety, a boundless freedom, coincides with peace, and possession with security.

THE REALM OF MATTER

Thou hast ordered all things in number
and measure and weight.
—Wisdom of Solomon.

Nil natum est in corpore ut uti
Possemus, sed quod natum est, id procreat
usum.

Nothing has arisen in the body in order
that we may use it, but when anything has
arisen it creates its use.—LUCRETIUS.

Καὶ γὰρ εἰ αὐτὴ ἡ ψυχὴ τῇ ὕλῃ ἐγέννησε
παθοῦσα, καὶ εἰ ἐκοινώνησεν αὐτῇ καὶ ἐγένετο
κακή, ἡ ὕλη αἰτία παροῦσα· οὐ γὰρ ἂν ἐγένετο
εἰς αὐτὴν μὴ τῇ παρουσίᾳ αὐτῆς τὴν γένεσιν
λαβοῦσα.—For if the (heavenly) soul, having
become subservient to matter, passed into
process, and if by communion with matter
she was corrupted, extant matter by its
presence was the cause thereof; for the
(heavenly) soul would not pass into matter,
if matter was not at hand to lend her a
changeful existence.—PLOTINUS.

PREFACE

THERE is a prejudice in some quarters against the word Matter, even where the thing and all its uses are most honoured. Matter seems an evil to the sour moralist because it is often untoward, and an occasion of imperfection or conflict in things. But if he took a wider view matter would seem a good to him, because it is the principle of existence: it is all things in their potentiality, and therefore the condition of all their excellence or possible perfection. In metaphysics, however, the objection to matter is not that matter is evil, but that it is superfluous, unknowable, or even non-existent; and I might easily have avoided certain antagonisms by giving to matter a more fashionable name and speaking instead of the realm of events or of space-time or of evolution. I might even have taken refuge in that half-poetical language to which I am not disinclined, and might have called the realm of matter simply nature. But nature, events, space-time, and even evolution (when this means simply metamorphosis) are indicative terms, containing no ontological analysis: my problem is precisely to distinguish in this vast flood of existence the planes and qualities of reality which it contains or presupposes. I wish to note the differences and the relations between

183

the animate and the inanimate, the physical and the moral, the psychological and the logical, the temporal and the eternal.   It is very true that one and the same flux of events exemplifies now one and now another of these realms of being, or variously impinges upon them; but this amphibious character of existence is far from being a reason for not distinguishing those realms. On the contrary, besides the inherent differences in them which nothing can ever obliterate, there is an added reason why the naturalist should discriminate them.   He is not merely living, like the animals, but professing to describe the world; and the sense of existence would remain a merely emotional burden, and life a blind career, unless he began by discriminating the essences which it discloses, in their heterogeneity, hierarchy, and succession.

If, then, in turning to the study of existence I had avoided the word matter, there would have been a sort of treason in that subterfuge. I do not mean treason so much to matter itself, because the intrinsic essence of matter being unknown, it may be figured almost indifferently by any image of sense or thought, as by " the gods " or " the devil ", provided that expectation and action are not misled by that symbol. I mean rather treason to spirit, to truth, to essence, to those trembling immaterial lights and that infinite immutable background which, unless sharply contrasted with the matter which they surround, may be transposed in confused apprehension to the plane of matter, and saddled with material functions. Have not both truth and spirit, not to speak of essence, been represented in our day as things physical, temporal, instrumental, and practical? Ontologically, this attitude is absurd, and a mere failure in discernment; but taken apostolically—for it is zealously espoused—it expresses a genuine and perfectly legitimate allegiance: that respect for matter only, which characterises the psyche when absorbed in action and in circumstances. Life marks a mechanical complication, maintained in a world where it did not always exist; and the psyche, in her fundamental impulse, is perfectly content that all her ardent labour should end in a vain redistribution of matter, or should never end. It would seem idle from her point of view, and rather mad, that any spirit should ever disengage itself from that process and should come to find in it some satisfying essence, so that in discerning and possessing this essence it might transcend that remorseless flux and might look away from it to an eternal world. In the reversion of philosophy (which in spite of itself is a form of spirit) to exclusive sympathy with the flux of matter, there is accordingly a too domestic virtue or exaggerated piety, like that of a fair daughter devoting her whole existence to nursing her old mother. Free spirit lets the dead bury their dead, and takes no thought for the morrow; and it redeems the labouring world by bringing joy into it.

Theoretical scruples about the reality of matter are of two sorts: they may be sceptical and empirical, based on the fact that matter is no immediate datum of intuition; or they may be scientific and logical, based on the suspicion that some particular idea of matter may be unfit or inadequate to express its true nature. These two kinds of objection are mutually contradictory; for the one condemns matter for not being a human sensation, and the other condemns matter for being only a human idea. The first objection involves a retreat to the subjective sphere; and however legitimate such a retreat may be in romantic soliloquy, it is in principle destructive of all science or even belief. The postulate of substance—the assumption that there are things and events prior to the discovery of them and independent of this discovery— underlies all natural knowledge. The refinements which may supervene on this conviction ought never to shake it, and do not do so when they are fruitful. Therefore the first sort of objection against matter— that it is a thing-in-itself antecedent to human experience—may be dismissed at once as vain and sophistical; for it rescinds that animal faith, or that common sense, which is the beginning of art and of science and their perpetual presupposition.

There remains the second difficulty: the suspicion, or the clear perception, that some special description of matter—say that of Democritus or that of Descartes —is inadequate or mistaken. But of course all human notions of matter, even if not positively fabulous, must be wholly inadequate; otherwise the natural philosopher would be claiming a plenitude of miraculous illumination such as no prophet ever thought to possess. Human ideas of matter are initially as various as human contacts with it, and as human sensations in its presence. These ideas are sensuous and pictorial from the beginning. They are then variously sifted and refined according to people's progress in the arts of comparison and calculation. In popular speech the word matter continues to suggest the popular aspects of natural things; in scientific speech, at each stage of it, the word comes to denote such aspects of those same things as have become calculable at that stage. Thus to a stone-cutter extension and impenetrability may well seem the essence of matter; the builder, intent on the strains and dangers of position, will add degrees of cohesion and weight to his definition. At this stage metaphysicians and moralists will look down on matter as something gross and dead, and will imagine that motion and organisation must be imposed on matter from without: not seeing that this external force, if it governed and moved matter, would be the soul of matter, and much nearer to its proper essence than the æsthetic aspects which its aggregates may wear to the human eye. Yet what could be more obviously material than thunder and lightning, sunshine and rain, from which the father of the gods borrowed his poetic substance? Weight and figure are not more characteristic of matter than are explosiveness, swiftness, fertility, and radiation. Planters and breeders of animals, or poets watching the passing generations of mankind, will feel that the heart and mystery of matter lie in the seeds of things, *semina rerum*, and in the customary cycles of their transformation. It is by its motion and energy, by its fidelity to measure and law, that matter has become the substance of our world, and the principle of life and of death in it. The earliest sages, no less than the latest moderns, identified matter with fire, æther, or fluids, rather than with stocks and stones; the latter are but temporary concretions, and always in the act of growing or crumbling. Even those who, partly for dialectical reasons, reduced matter to impenetrable atoms, attributed all its fertility to the play of collisions which swept perpetually through the void and drove those dead atoms into constellations and vortices and organisms. This endless propulsion and these fated complications were no less material, and far more terrible, than any monumental heap into which matter might sometimes be gathered, and which to a gaping mind might seem more substantial. If any poet ever felt the life of nature in its truth, irrepressible, many-sided, here flaming up savagely, there helplessly dying down, that poet was Lucretius, whose materialism was unqualified.

Finally, in our own times, when physics speculates chiefly on bodies so remote or minute as to be known only through variations in light, matter seems to evaporate into these visible variations, as if light had no source, or as if man had no contact with nature except through the eye. But the seat of these perceptions is not the heavens or the æther, but the human organism; and even if the human organism were composed of these or of other such perceptions, the conditions for the existence of these elements and their relation to the heavens, the æther, and one another, would constitute a material world. A psychological nature might thus be ascribed to matter, in its unapproachable internal essence; but that hypothesis, or rather myth, would materialise a late human idea, removed by the whole diameter of evolution and mundane time from the primeval matter which was its object; an object which cannot be found in the landscape of intuition, but must be posited in action, from the outside, in its dynamic and truly material capacity. Criticism, I think, would induce us to stop with this functional definition of matter, which represents our actual approach to it. We should then attach the landscape of intuition to matter only at the summit of evolution, when the psyche becomes a poet, and learns to transcribe her material passions and experiences into terms of essence.

All these partialities in the conception of matter are honest and inevitable. Each view, in stretching its special language as far as possible, may serve to disclose some side of the true order of nature. But this order is that of actual generation and existential flux, something that happens and is not conceived; so that no sensuous or graphic or mathematical transcript of it should be so pressed as to be substituted for it. Nor is it reasonable for those familiar with one side of nature to deride those who, seeing some different side, unsuspectingly identify it with the substance before them: They are wrong; but the critic would be wrong also if he did not tolerate their error, and even prize it for its measure of subjective truth.

The realm of matter, then, from the point of view of our discovery of it, is the field of action: it is essentially dynamic and not pictorial. Moreover, our action is interpolated in a world already in existence. Our existence and purposes are things of yesterday; they were evidently drawn from that very world on which they react. From the point of view of origins, therefore, the realm of matter is the matrix and the source of everything: it is nature, the sphere of genesis, the universal mother. The truth cannot dictate to us the esteem in which we shall hold it: that is not a question of fact but of preference. Yet natural philosophy may disclose the source of our preferences and their implications, so that it may lead us to reconsider them, or to express them differently. So if, with this conception of the realm of matter before us, we turn back to the moral prejudices against matter, we shall be amazed at their levity. A spiritual mind might well look over the head of nature to a First Cause, and beyond the vicissitudes of life to a supreme good: therein there would be a genuine aversion from the realm of matter, and absorption in essences which, at best, existence can illustrate or suggest for a moment to the mind, as it does beauty or the laws of number. But, though not prized for itself, the realm of matter would remain standing; otherwise those divine essences would never have been illustrated or suggested at all. If in clinging to the immaterial we denied the material, it would not be merely ashes or dust that we should be despising, but all natural existence in its abysmal past and in its indefinite fertility; and it would be, not some philosopher's sorry notion of matter that we should be denying, but the reality of our animal being, the fact that we are creatures of time, rooted in a moving universe in which our days are numbered. And rather than blaspheme in this way against our own nature and origin, we might well say with the Irish poet:[1]

> Who is that goddess to whom men should pray,
> But her from whom their hearts have turned away,
> Out of whose virgin being they were born,
> Whose mother-nature they have named with scorn,
> Calling her holy substance common clay. . . .
>
> Ah, when I think this earth on which I tread
> Hath borne these blossoms of the lovely dead,
> And makes the living heart I love to beat,
> I look with sudden awe beneath my feet—

---

[1] " A. E." (George Russell) in " The Virgin Mother ".

and here the poet adds the questionable line:

As you with erring reverence overhead.

If I look overhead, I see the cosmic spaces, the sun or the stars: all this is as much a part of nature, and a source of life, as the nether earth. Or if by " overhead " we understand the spiritual sphere, why should it not be looked upon with as much respect as that realm of matter which, for a free spirit, can be only a means and an instrument? But I think I understand what the poet means, and the justness of his sentiment. *Reverence* is something due to antiquity, to power, to the roots and the moral supports of existence; it is therefore due really to the realm of matter only, and there is a profound error and self-deception in attributing those genetic functions, or directing that piety, to ideal objects. Towards these the appropriate feeling is not reverence so much as love, enthusiasm, contemplative rapture, mystic union: feelings which it would be as silly to address to matter as to address a dutiful reverence to essences or to attribute power to them. In reality, the realm of matter contains more than half of that which from the dawn of life has been the object of human religion: it contains " the gods ", or the veritable influences represented by their names and conciliated by the worship of them. Hell and heaven, for any honest and serious religion, are parts of nature; if ever they cease to be so regarded, they are immediately replaced, as among liberal Protestants, by the goods and evils of this world. The residue of human religion is something private, generous, and not obligatory: it rises from the earth in incense and music, never to return; it forms a spiritual life, akin to poetic love, to happiness, to philosophy. In contrast with it, the tremendous sanctions and fixed duties of established religion, being instinct with prudence and great hopes, belong to the sober economy of life; and they all regard, if people's eyes were only unsealed, this despised realm of matter.

CHAPTER I

THE SCOPE OF NATURAL PHILOSOPHY

THE measure of confidence with which I have spoken
of essence forsakes me when I approach existence.
Logic, grammar, and poetry are free; no   Contrast
alien fact, no vociferation, can prevent intui-   between
tion from beholding what it actually beholds.   ideal and
natural
The public censor has indeed some rights over   science.
the persons in whom intuition arises, and may condemn
their habit of mind if he thinks that it comports idleness
or the disruption of happy national conventions; but,
in this instance, fortune having relegated me, like the
gods of Epicurus, to the interstices of the worlds, I
may escape that censure or disregard it. Who knows?
Perhaps some kindred spirit may tell me that I have
chosen the better part. In any case, I deny nothing
and prejudge nothing concerning the intuitions of
others; if I cultivate my own with a certain ardour,
it is only as any man cultivates his language and tastes,
if his mind is at all liberal; and I am confident no god
or man will be justly angry with me for browsing so
innocently in my own pasture. But when the active
impulse of curiosity and dogmatism asserts itself in its
turn, as it must in the most contemplative mind, and
I ask myself what dark objects or forces have created
or are threatening my contemplation, then indeed I
am at a loss: and as in positing such natural agencies
at all I assume that they are objects obligatory to every

193

other mind with which I can communicate, I bind myself to make my opinions conformable with their reports, and my reports agreeable to their experience. Of course the belief that I can communicate with other minds, and that the reports reaching me signify an experience of theirs over and above my own, is a part of this extraordinary compulsory assumption which I make in living; the assumption that I am surrounded by a natural world, peopled by creatures in whom intuition is as rife as in myself: and as all my concern in perception and action turns on what those external things may do, so half my interest in my own thoughts turns on what other people may be thinking.

It is not the task of natural philosophy to justify this assumption, which indeed can never be justified. Its task, after making that assumption, is to carry it out consistently and honestly, so as to arrive, if possible, at a conception of nature by which the faith involved in action may be enlightened and guided. Such a description of nature, if it were ever completed in outline, would come round full circle, and in its account of animals it would report how they came to have intuitions (among them this natural philosophy) and to use them in the description of the world which actually surrounded them. The whole field of action and of facts would then be embraced in a single view, summary and symbolic, but comprehensive.

Assumption of an existing world.

The dream of the natural philosopher would be to describe the world from its beginning (if it had a beginning), tracing all its transformations; and he would like to do this analytically, not pictorially—that is, not in the sensuous language of some local observer composing a private perspective, but in terms of the ultimate elements (if there are ultimate elements) concerned in the actual evolution of things. Out of those elements he would conceive each observer

Inevitable attempt to describe it.

and his perspective arising, and of course varying from moment to moment. Even if the natural philosopher were an idealist, and admitted only observing spirits and their perspectives, he would endeavour to trace the evolution of these intuitions, which would be his atoms, in their universal order and march, by no means contenting himself with one intuition and one perspective; for, if he did so, his idealism (like that of some philosophies of history) would not be a system of physics or of logic, but a literary entertainment, the lyrical echo of many verbal reports in a romantic imagination. This echo might be interesting in itself: but it would remain only an incident in that natural world which indeed it presupposed, but which it deliberately ignored. So that when the idealist became a man again in the world of action, and began to live (as he must) by animal faith, his philosophy would entirely forsake him; yet it is in the service of this animal faith that philosophy exists, when it is science and wisdom. Indeed, a theoretical refusal to trust natural philosophy cannot absolve the most sceptical of us from framing one, and from living by it. I *must* conceive a surrounding world, even if in reflection I say to myself at every step: Illusion, Illusion. It then becomes almost as interesting to know what sort of illusions must accompany me through life, as it would be to imagine what sort of world I really live in. Indeed, if all spurious substitutes for natural philosophy were discarded (spurious because irrelevant to the animal faith which alone posits existence) those two positions might coincide, since the picture of the natural world framed by common sense and science, while framed with the greatest care, would be admittedly only a picture; and belief in the existence of that world, though assumed without wobbling, would be admittedly but an article of inevitable faith.

Non-scientific beliefs about existence, whether inspired by religious feeling, reasoning, or fancy, are alternatives to the current natural philosophy, or extensions of it. Nobody would believe in his ideas if he had not an initial propensity to believe in things, as if his ideas described them. Dogmatic religions are assertions about the nature of the universe; what is called supernatural is only ultra-mundane, an extension of this world on its own plane, and a recognition of forces ruling over it not reckoned with in vulgar commerce. The assertions made by such religious faith, if not superstitious errors, are ultimate truths of natural philosophy, which intuition or revelation has supplied in advance of experiment: but if the assertions are true at all, experiment might one day confirm them. Thus Christian orthodoxy maintains that men will carry their memories and their bodies with them into hell or heaven. Theology is the natural philosophy of that larger world which religion posits as truly existing: it therefore has precise implications in politics and science. The absence of such implications and commitments, far from showing that religion has become spiritual, proves it a sham; it is no longer a manly hypothesis, honestly made about the world confronted in action. No doubt there is an inner fountain of religious feeling which a person accepting his theology on hearsay might wholly lack; but it was religious instinct of some kind that originally prompted those hypotheses about the hidden nature of things, and if this instinct is lacking those hypotheses will soon be discarded. On the other hand, religious feeling may not always require ultra-mundane extensions of the natural world; it may find a sufficient object and sanction in the course of earthly history and domestic life, as was the case, at bottom, with Jewish and Protestant righteousness: the politics and science dictated by religious faith will then coincide with those recommended by worldly wisdom.

Positive religions involve cosmologies.

Religious feeling may take still other forms; for instance, it may smile mystically at action and belief altogether, retreating into the invisible sanctuary of the spirit, or floating incredulously amid mere music and dreams. But mysticism, whether austere or voluptuous, since it regards the absolute, ceases to regard existence which, by definition, is relative, since it consists in having external relations. Positive and virile minds may find indulgence in such mysticism irreligious, because their earnestness is directed upon alleged facts, in this world or in another: facts essentially relevant to action and policy, and open to natural philosophy.

Much restraint, and some disillusion, may enable a man to entertain ideas without believing them to describe any matter of fact: such ideas will be avowedly mere terms of grammar, logic, or fancy, to be discarded, or at least discounted, on broaching a serious natural philosophy. Idolatrous character of metaphysics. They may still be indispensable as a medium, as some language is indispensable to science; but they will be optional and interchangeable, as the scientific part of a book of science (which is never the whole of it) is perfectly translatable from one language into another. This is not to say that the medium of intuition, even in natural philosophy, is indifferent in itself; nothing is dearer to a man or a nation than congenial modes of expression; I would rather be silent than use some people's language; I would rather die than think as some people think. But it is the quality of life that is concerned here, not the truth of ideas. To attempt to impose such modes of intuition or expression, as if they were obligatory tenets, is metaphysics: a projection of the constraints or the creations of thought into the realm of matter. The authority of intuition would be entire if it kept to the definition of essences, and of their essential relations; but when zeal intervenes, and we profess to find our favourite dialectic in things, we are betrayed into disrespect for nature, and are inflating our egotism into cosmic proportions. At best the metaphysician has given a useful hint to the naturalist: he has supplied categories which may be convenient or even indispensable for expressing the ways of nature in human discourse. The palmary instance of this is mathematics, which, long after having ceased to be empirical and become dialectical, still continues to serve for construction and even for prophecy in the material sphere: yet the symbols employed grow more abstruse and tenuous as they grow more exact, so that people are little tempted to substitute the notation for the thing denoted; and they thus escape metaphysics.

When the experience interpreted is spiritual or passionate, the categories used are, as in religion and poetry, clearly mythological: yet they are not without a real, though indirect, object in the realm of matter. This object is the psyche, with all those profound currents in her life which create the passions, and create the spirit which expresses the passions, yet which in expressing them is so entangled that it often comes to regard them as its enemies. Those psychic currents, being dynamic, are material; but they are hidden from the eye of spirit, which alone is spiritual, by layer upon layer of vague sensation, rhetoric, and imagery.

Belief, in its very soul, is belief about nature; it is animal faith. To entangle belief in anything non-natural, or avowedly tangential to action, would be to cheat at the game. Honest speculative belief is always speculative physics. But its terms are inevitably the essences present to intuition; and the very faith which, in the presence of these essences, posits existing things, drags something of the given apparition into the presumed

Nature is the nexus of all substances and forces.

substance of the thing revealed: the theophany human-
ises the god. In correcting this illusion, and in discarding one mythical or metaphysical image after
another, science must still retain some symbol for the
overpowering reality of the world. This reality is not
that symbol itself, nor a collection of such symbols: if
we cling to these we shall never quit the realm of essence.
Nor am I sure that the most learned symbols are the
least deceptive; if any human ideas must be idolized,
I should almost prefer those of the senses and of the
poets. Yet it would be ignominious for a philosopher
voluntarily to succumb to illusion at all, when the
artificiality and relativity of all human views, especially
of learned and beautiful systems, is so patent to reflection. Yet views we must have, none the worse,
surely, if they are beautiful and learned; so that the
natural philosopher is driven to a deeper question, to
which I mean to devote this book: How much, when
cleared as far as possible of idolatry, can sense or science
reveal concerning the dark engine of nature? In what
measure do they truly enlighten animal faith?

In broaching this question I am not concerned with
repeating, correcting, or forecasting the description
which men of science may give of the world. How far is
I accept gladly any picture of nature honestly science
drawn by them, as I accept gladly any picture knowledge?
drawn by my own senses. Different circumstances or
different faculties would certainly have produced different pictures. From Genesis to Thales, to Ptolemy,
to Copernicus, to Newton, and to Einstein the landscape has pleasantly varied; and it may yet open other
vistas. These variations and prospects show the
plasticity of human thought, for it is not the facts that
have much varied, nor the material station of man, nor
his senses and destiny. The incubus of existence
remains exactly the same. Is it merely imagination that
has become more laboured but no less fantastic? Or

has the path of destiny been really cleared and the forces that control destiny been better understood? Within what limits does any description of nature, picturesque or scientific, retain its relevance to animal faith and its validity as knowledge of fact, and at what point does it become pure speculation and metaphor? That is the only question which I shall endeavour to answer.

My survey of the realm of matter will accordingly be merely transcendental, and made from the point of view of a sceptic and a moralist criticising the claims of experience and science to be true knowledge.

By transcendental reflection I understand reversion, in the presence of any object or affirmation, to the immediate experience which discloses that object or prompts that affirmation. Transcendental reflection is a challenge to all dogmatism, a demand for radical evidence. It therefore tends to disallow substance and, when it is thorough, even to disallow existence. Nothing is ultimately left except the passing appearance or the appearance of something passing. How, then, if transcendental reflection disallows substance, can it lead me to distinguish the properties of substance?

The transcendental method applied to animal faith.

In *Scepticism and Animal Faith* I have considered the transcendental motives which oblige me to believe in substance. The belief must always remain an assumption, but one without which an active and intelligent creature cannot honestly act or think. Transcendentalism has two phases or movements—the sceptical one retreating to the immediate, and the assertive one by which objects of belief are defined and marshalled, of such a character and in such an order as intelligent action demands. The enterprise of life is precarious, and to the sceptic it must seem an adventure in the dark, without origins or environment or results. Yet this flying life, by its forward energy, breeds from within certain postulates of sanity, certain conceptions of the conditions which might surround it and lend it a meaning, so that its own continuance and fortunes may be conceived systematically and affirmed with confidence. Thus the faith that posits and describes a world is just as transcendental as the criticism which reduces that world to an appearance or a fiction. If so many transcendental philosophers stop at the negative pole, this arrest is not a sign of profundity in them, but of weakness. It is by boldly believing what transcendental necessity prompts any hunting animal to believe, that I separate myself from that arrested idealism, and proceed to inquire what existences, what substances, and what motions are involved in the chase.

In the chase, for those who follow it, the intensity of experience is not like the intensity (limitless if you will) of contemplating pure Being—immutable, equable, and complete. The hunter and the hunted believe in something ambushed and imminent: present images are little to them but signs for coming events. Things are getting thick, agents are coming together, or disappearing: they are killing and dying. The assurance of this sort of being is assurance of existence, and the belief in this sort of agent is belief in substance. If this belief and assurance are not illusions (which the acting animal cannot admit them to be), several properties must belong to substances and to the world they compose. These properties I may distinguish in reflection and call by philosophical names, somewhat as follows.

Action posits a field existing substantially for science to describe.

CHAPTER II

INDISPENSABLE PROPERTIES OF SUBSTANCE

1. SINCE substance is posited, and not given in intuition, as essences may be given, *substance is external to the thought which posits it.*

2. Since it is posited in action, or in readiness for action, the substance posited is external not merely to the positing thought (as a different thought would be) but is external to the physical agent which is the organ of that action, as well as of that thought. In other words, *Substance has parts and constitutes a physical space.* Conversely, the substantial agent in action and thought is external to the surrounding portions of substance with which it can interact. *All the parts of substance are external to one another.*

A world in which action is to occur must be external, spatial, and temporal, possessing variety and unity.

3. Since substance is engaged in action, and action involves change, *substance is in flux and constitutes a physical time.* Changes are perpetually occurring in the relations of its parts, if not also in their intrinsic characters.

4. Since the agents in action and reaction are distinct in position and variable in character, and since they induce changes in one another, *substance is unequally distributed.* It diversifies the field of action, or physical time and space.

5. Since there is no occasion for positing any

substance save as an agent in the field of action, all recognisable substance must lie in the same field in which the organism of the observer occupies a relative centre. Therefore, wherever it works and solicits recognition, *substance composes a relative cosmos.*

A mutual externality, or *Auseinandersein*—an alternation of centres such as moment and moment, thing and thing, place and place, person and person —is characteristic of existence. Each centre is equally actual and equally central, yet each is dependent on its neighbours for its position and on its predecessors for its genesis. The existential interval from one centre to another is bridged naturally by generation or motion— by a transition actually taking place from one moment, place, or character to another, in such a manner that the former moment, place, or character is abandoned and lost. The same interval may still be bridged cognitively by faith or intent, cognition being a substitute for a transition which cannot be executed materially, because the remote term of it is past or not next in the order of genesis or transformation. But this interval can never be bridged by synthesis in intuition. Synthesis in intuition destroys the existential status of the terms which it unites, since it excludes any alternation or derivation between them. It unites at best the essences of some natural things into an ideal picture. On the other hand the conjunction of existences in nature must always remain successive, external, and unsynthesised. Nature shows no absolute limits and no privileged partitions; whereas the richest intuition, the most divine omniscience, is imprisoned in the essence which it beholds. It cannot break through into existence unless it loses itself and submits to transition; and the foretaste or aftertaste of such transition, present in feeling, must posit something eventual, something absent from intuition, if

The first property, externality to thought belongs to all existence.

even the sense or idea of existence is to arise at all. Then the mind engaged in action may begin to live by faith in the outlying conditions of life, and by an instinctive tension towards obscure events.

It might seem that memory eludes this necessity, and actually encloses some parts of the past in the present, and brings the movement of events bodily within the circle of intuition. But this is an illusion founded on the fact that memory contains both imagery and knowledge: the imagery is all present, but that of which it gives knowledge, when memory is true, is past and gone. Even if, by a rare favour, the original aspect of the past experience should be reproduced exactly, it will not be the past event, nor even the present one, that will be given in intuition, but the dateless essence common to both.

Memory, when cognitive, a relation between separate natural facts.

The cognitive value of this apparition will hang on the ulterior fact that such an apparition, or the event which it reports, occurred before, at a point of time which was its own centre, and not a marginal feature in the present perspective. Memory, then, in so far as it is, or even claims to be, knowledge, is faith in the absent, and bridges external relations by intent only, not by synthesis in intuition.

A mutual externality is also requisite among the instances of spirit, that is, among thoughts that are to be regarded as existences and events. This at first sight might seem contrary to the apparent self-existence and self-evidence of conscious being, and to the transcendental status of spirit, which, because it is a logical counterpart to any datum, might be alleged to be an omnipresent fact, existing absolutely. But this, although it may pass for criticism, is the sophistry of reflection, which can readily take its verbal terms

Existing thoughts are separate events lodged each in its place in nature.

for existences or substances, and ignore the natural springs of feeling and of reflection itself. An instance of spirit, a pure feeling or intuition, if it had no date or place in nature, would not be an event or existence at all, but only another name, and a mythical name, for the essence conceived to be present there. The life of thought, in its conscious intensity, lies in the syntheses which it is perpetually making among its changing materials. These acts of synthesis, these glances and insights, are historical facts; they arise and are distinguishable on the level of experience from their material conditions; but they are not substances. Their substance is their organ in its movement and in its changing tensions: it is the psyche. The case is like that of a collision between two vehicles, or checkmate in a game of chess. The collision is a new fact, on the plane of human affairs, as is the checkmate which ends the game; so, too, are the chagrin or the severe pain which these events may occasion. But the pain or the chagrin could no more arise, or come into existence, without the living persons who endure them—persons moving in the realm of matter—than the checkmate could occur without the match, or the collision without the vehicles. If a feeling or thought is to be actual, and not a metaphorical name for some eternal essence, it must therefore arise out of material events, and in the midst of them: it must stand in external relations.

Thus the first indispensable condition for the being of substance is indispensable also to any form of existence, mental or historical as well as physical. Existence, like substance, is essentially diffuse and many-centred. One fact can be reached cognitively from another fact only by faith, and materially only by transition; and the cognitive or the initial fact itself can exist only by virtue of its position or action in a natural system extending beyond it.

It follows that substance is in flux, virtual, if not actual. External relations are such as are due to the Existence position, not to the inherent character, of the being contingent is terms. They are, therefore, always variable, essentially and existence, although it may endure by unstable. accident for any length of time, is inherently mortal and transitory, being adventitious to the essences which figure in it. When Hamlet says, *To be or not to be*, he is pondering the alternative between existence and non-existence, and feeling the contingency of both. The question is not whether he shall be or not be Hamlet: death might cause him to forget his essence, but could not abolish it or transform it into another essence. In the realm of essence all these essences are eternally present and no alternative arises: which is perhaps the ultimate truth conveyed by the doctrine of eternal salvation or punishment. But the accidents of death, or dreams, or oblivion continually confront this life, and existence is an optional form of being. Shall this beloved or detested essence presently lose it? And on what other essence shall it fall next? To this pressing question the realm of essence supplies no answer, and the contemplative mind is hopelessly puzzled by it. *Solvitur ambulando*: the event, the propulsive currents of substance merging and rushing into new forms, will precipitate a solution without ever considering alternatives; and it is perhaps because they never stop to think before they act, that they are able to act at all.

Something not essence, then, actualises and limits the manifestation of every essence that figures The substance in nature or appears before the mind. To which determines this dark principle of existence we give the termines events is name of substance; so that substance, by definition, is the soil, the medium, and the creative motion. force which secretly determines any option like that of Hamlet. Every such option is momentary and local; for although substance is external to essence and to thought, and its parts are external to one another, yet substance is internal to the things which it forms by occupying those contrasted places and assuming these various qualities.   It is *their* substance, the principle of their existence, the ground of all the spontaneous changes which they undergo.   It is indefinitely, perhaps infinitely, deep and inhuman; but whatever else its intrinsic essence may be, it is certainly complex, local, and temporal.   Its secret flux involves at least as many contrasts and variations as the course of nature shows on the surface.   Otherwise the ultimate core of existence would not exist, and the causes of variation would not vary.   But how shall that which puts on this specious essence here and not there, be in the same inner condition in both places?   Or how shall that which explodes now, have been equally active before?   Substance, if it is to fulfil the function in virtue of which it is recognised and posited, must accordingly be for ever changing its own inner condition.   It must be in flux.

Undoubtedly the word substance suggests permanence rather than change, because the substances best known to man (like the milk and the wet sand of the young architect) evidently pass from place to place and from form to form while retaining their continuity and quantity.   Such permanence is not contrary to flux, but a condition of flux.   The degree of permanence which substance may have in any particular process, and the name which should be given to this permanent factor, are questions for scientific discussion. They may not, and need not, receive any ultimate answer. But that *some* permanence, not the casual persistence of this or that image, is interwoven with the flux of things, follows from the reality of this flux itself.   If change were total at any point, there transformation

Permanence need not be attributed to substance otherwise than as implied in flux.

and existence would come to an end. The next, completely new, fact would not be next; it would be the centre, or the beginning, of a separate world. In other words, events, if they are to be successive or contiguous, must be pervaded by a common medium, in which they may assume relations external to their respective essences; for the internal or logical relations between these essences will never establish any succession or continuity among them, nor transport them at all into the sphere of existence. The critics of empiricism who have insisted that a series of sensations is not the sensation of a series, might well have added that the sensation of a series is no more than an isolated term on its own account, unless there is a background common to those terms and to this synthetic idea—a background in relation to which they may respectively take such places as shall render them contiguous or successive, although there is nothing within any of them to indicate such a position. This background, for human perception, is the field of vision symbolising the field of action; in this specious field the position of objects is distinguished before the objects are clearly specified or posited; but this unity of perspective, relative to the momentary station and thought of the observer, cannot embrace the existential flux itself, in which the events reported and the observer, with his thought, are incidental features. For the continuity and successiveness of this existing series, synthesis in apprehension is useless: it merely creates one more item—a living thought—to be ranged among its neighbours in the flux of existence. That which is requisite is the *natural derivation* of one phase in this flux from another, or a *natural tension* between them, determining their respective characters and positions. Such derivation and such tension, essential to action, involve a substance within or between events. There may be very much more in substance than that; but this is enough to disclose the existence of a substance, and to begin the human description of it by its functions.

Permanence, therefore, need not be set down separately among the radical properties attributed to substance: it is sufficiently expressed in the possibility of change, of continuity, of succession, and of the inclusion of actual events in a natural series, which shall not be a mere perspective in imagination.

Action and animal faith look in some specific direction; the butt of action, which is what I call substance, must be particular, local, and circumscribed. It must be capable of varying its position or its condition; for otherwise I could neither affect it by my action, nor await and observe its operation. In battle, in the chase, or in labour, attention is turned to a particular quarter, to something substantial there: it would defeat all action and art if all quarters were alike, and if I couldn't face a fact without turning my back on exactly the same fact in the rear; and the price of bread would be indifferent, if one substance being everywhere present I could find the same substance in the air. Action evidently would be objectless in an infinite vacuum or a homogeneous plenum; and even the notion or possibility of action would vanish if I, the agent, had not distinguishable parts, so that at least I might swim forward rather than backward in that dense vacuity.

Action presupposes a diversified field.

A field of action must, then, be diversified substantially, not pictorially only; that which is at work in it here must not be equally at work in it there; the opportunities which it opens to me now must not be the same which it opened and will open always. Any conception of substance which represents it as undivided and homogeneous is accordingly not a conception of nature or of existence: and if such an object is ever called substance, it must be in

The substance of things is physical: metaphysical substance is only a grammatical term.

a metaphysical sense which I do not attach to the word. One test of such evasions into the realm of essence is ability, or ambition, to give a precise definition of what substance is. *Materia prima* may be defined—Plotinus has an admirable exposition of it, like the Athanasian creed—because it is avowedly something incapable of existence, and at best one of those ideal terms which serve to translate nature into the language of thought. *Materia prima* is a grammatical essence, comparable to the transcendental ego, the " I think ", which according to Kant must accompany all experience. The discrimination of such essences distinguishes one logic from another, and leaves everything in nature, except human language, just as it was. The existing substance of things, on the contrary, is that which renders them dynamic; it is wherever dynamic things are, not where they are not; it determines their aspects and powers; and we may learn, since it exists in us also, to play with it and to let it play on us, in specific ways. But it would be frivolous to attempt to define it, as if a set of words, or of blinking ideas, could penetrate to the heart of existence and determine how, from all eternity, it must have been put together. What we may discover of it is not its essence but its place, its motion, its aspects, its effects. Were it an essence given in intuition, a visionary presence to sense or to language, it would forfeit those very functions which compel us to posit it, and which attest its formidable reality. Chief of these functions is a perpetual and determinate revolution in the heavens, and fertility and decay upon earth. In this flux there is a relative permanence and continuity; but substance is not for that reason less agitated than the familiar face of nature, or nearer to the impassibility of an eternal essence. Far otherwise. Investigation rather shows that this substance (which may be traced experimentally in many of its shifts) is in a continual silent ferment, by which gross visible objects are always being undermined and transformed: so much so that science often loses its way amid those subtle currents of the elements, and stops breathless at some too human image.

There are certain celebrated doctrines which, in their forms of expression, are excluded at once from natural philosophy by these considerations. In physics I may not say, for instance, with Parmenides that Being is and Not-Being is not, if what I am seeking to describe is the substance of nature. If for dialectical reasons, which are not directly relevant to physics, I wished to regard pure Being as the essence of matter, I should be compelled to distribute this pure Being unequally in a void: a result which would contradict my premise that Not-Being is not, since this void would not only exist but would be the only true theatre of existence, because it would be the only seat of change. The pure Being or matter distributed in it, by hypothesis, is impassible and everywhere identical. Nature and life would therefore be due to the redistribution in the bosom of Not-Being of a pure Being in itself immutable. We should thus be led to the system of Democritus: a possible and even a model system of physics, although, in its expression, too Eleatic, and borrowing from that dialectical school a false air of necessity.

Parmenides must give way to Democritus.

Similarly, at the threshold of natural philosophy, the Vedanta system must yield to the Samkhya: and this the Indians seem to have admitted by regarding the two systems as orthodox and compatible. It might be well if in the West we could take a hint from this comprehensiveness. The unity and simplicity of pure Being is not incompatible with the infinite variety of essences implied in it; and many things are true in the realm of essence which, if taken to describe existence, would be unmeaning or contrary to fact. It would suffice to

The Vedanta must give way to the Samkhya system.

distinguish the two spheres more carefully, for the legitimacy of systems, verbally most unlike, to become equal: although certainly those which were drawn from insight into essence would be more profound and unshakable than those drawn from observation of nature, since nature might as well have offered quite a different spectacle. On the other hand, it is the order and ground of this spectacle that interests the natural philosopher; and to him that more inward and more sublime intuition of essential Being is a waste of time, or a rhetorical danger.

One more illustration: the language of Spinoza about substance ought to yield, in physics, to that of Aristotle, in spite of the fact that a follower *And Spinoza must give way to Aristotle.* of Descartes could not help being more enlightened in mechanical matters than a follower of Socrates. Nevertheless it was Aristotle who gave the name of substance to compound natural things actually existing, and Spinoza who bestowed it on an ambiguous metaphysical object, now pure Being, now the universe in its infinity—in either case an ideal unity and an essence incapable of realisation all at once, if at all, in any natural locus. No discrimination of infinite Being into infinitely numerous attributes would ever generate existence, since all would remain eternal; and no enumeration of the possible modes of each attribute would turn them into particular things or into living minds, since each mode would imply all the others, and all would be equally rooted everywhere. In Aristotle, on the contrary, the name of substance is given where the office of substance is performed, and where one fact here asserts itself against another fact there; so that substance is the principle of individuation and exclusion, the condition of existence, succession, and rivalry amongst natural things. Even if these things, as conceived by Aristotle, have too much of an animate unity, and are mysteriously fixed in their genera and species, and redolent of moral suggestions, all this is but the initial dramatic rendering of their human uses, and the poetry of good prose. It does not prevent a more disinterested analysis, a microscopic and telescopic science, from disclosing in time the deeper mechanisms and analogies of nature, and its finer substance: just as the static zoology and the political psychology of Aristotle do not prevent us from peeping into the seething elementary passions beneath those classical masks. Things have not ceased to wear the sensuous and moral forms which interested the Greeks; but we may discover how those shells were generated, and what currents of universal substance have cast them up.

Finally, the practical intellect, in positing substance, imposes on it a certain relevance to the agent, who is to be in dynamic relations with it. The objects which art and sanity compel me to recognise as substantial, must affect me together, even if in very different ways. They must all impinge, directly or indirectly, on my action now; and it is by this test that I distinguish fact from fiction and true memory from fancy. Facts are dynamically connected with that which I now posit as substantial, and objects of fancy are not so connected. The field of animal faith spreads out from a living centre; observation cannot abandon its base, but from this vital station it may extend its perspectives over everything to which it can assign existence. Among these accredited things there may be other centres of observation, actual or eventual; but if the original organ and station, and these other stations and organs accredited by it, were not parts of one and the same substantial world, no means would remain of identifying the objects observed from one centre with those observed from another. I can acknowledge the existence

The field of action must have a dynamic unity.

of other moral centres in the world which I posit, but only if these centres are agencies, earthly or celestial, at work in my field of action, and dynamically connected with my own existence. All credible animation, of ascertainable character, must animate substances found in the same world with myself, and collateral with my own substance.

Perhaps this argument has some analogy to Spinoza's proof of the unity of substance. He tells us that substance is one, because if there were two or more substances they could bear no relation to one another. In other words, there can be but one universe, since anything outside, by being outside, would be related to it and collateral, and so after all would form a part of it. Yet if one universe, or one substance, can exist absolutely, and out of all relation to anything else, why should not any number of them exist, each centred in itself? The necessity of lying in external relations in order to exist, far from proving that only one system of facts is possible, proves that any closed circle of facts, in interplay with one another and with nothing else, will form a complete universe. Each part of this system will exist by virtue of its active position there, and may be discovered by any members of it who are sufficiently intelligent and adventurous; but from no part of that universe will anything beyond that universe be discoverable. Does this fact preclude the being of a different system, a separate universe, possessing the same sort of inward life and reality? I cannot think so. Transcendental necessities are relative to particular centres of experience; they have no jurisdiction beyond. Those other universes, to us, would be undiscoverable; but ours, too, would be undiscoverable to them; and yet we exist here without their leave. Might they not exist without ours?

What logic enables us to assert, therefore, is not

This system is relative and need not cover all reality.

that there is only one universe, but that each universe must be one, by virtue of a domestic economy determining the relative position and character of the events which compose it. Anything beyond this dynamic field is beyond the field of posited existence and possible knowledge. If there are other centres and active substances moving in other spheres, the relation of these disconnected spheres is not a physical relation: no journey and no transformation can bridge it: it lies in the realm of truth. Each of these worlds will exemplify its chosen essence; and the internal and unchangeable relations between these essences will be the only relations between those worlds. One will not exist before the other, nor will they be simultaneous; nor will either lie in any direction from the other, or at any distance. No force or influence will pass between them of any traceable physical or historical kind. If omniscience should see any harmony, contrast, or mutual fulfilment between their natures, that spiritual bond would be of the sort which links essences together by a logical necessity, and which a contemplative spirit may stop to disentangle and admire if it can and will.

If there are many worlds their mutual relations are not physical, but are the eternal relations of their essences in the realm of truth.

Indeed, we may go further and say even of a single universe taken as a whole that its status is that of a truth rather than of an existence. Each part of it will exist, and if animate may truly feel its internal tension and life, and may truly assert the existence of the other parts also; yet the whole system—perhaps endless in its time and space—never exists at once or in any assignable quarter. Its existence is only posited from within its limits: externally its only status is that of a truth. Its essence was not condemned to be a closet-tragedy; living actors have been found to play it and a shifting stage to exhibit for a moment those convincing scenes. This essence has therefore the eternal dignity of a truth: it is the complete description of an event. Yet this event, taken as a whole, being unapproachable from outside, dateless, and nowhere, is in a sense a supernatural event. Those scenes are undiscoverable, save to those who play them, and that tumult is an ancient secret in the bosom of truth.

Indeed, good sense might suffice to convince anyone that no arguments or definitions can prevent things from being as numerous and as separate as they may chance to be. There is an infinite diversity of essences: what shall dissuade the fatality of existence, which must be groundless, from composing such changeful systems as it likes, on planes of being utterly incommensurable and incommunicable? The most a man can say for himself, or for any other element from which exploration may start, is that whatever is to enter his field of action must belong to the same dynamic system with himself. In experience and art, as in the nebular hypothesis, this dynamic oneness of the world is primitive. It is not put together by conjoining elements found existing separately, but is the locus in which they are found; for if they were not found there, they would be essences only and not facts. In mature human perception the essences given are doubtless distinct and the objects which they suggest are clearly discriminated: here is the dog, there the sun, the past nowhere, and the night coming. But beneath all this definition of images and attitudes of expectancy, there is always a voluminous feeble sensibility in the vegetative soul. Even this sensibility posits existence; the contemplation of pure Being might supervene only after all alarms, gropings, and beliefs had been suspended—something it takes all the discipline of Indian sages to begin to do. The vegetative soul enjoys an easier and more Christian blessedness: it sees not, yet it believes. But believes in what? In

The first object of animal faith is nature as a whole.

whatever it may be that envelopes it; in what we, in our human language, call space, earth, sunlight, and motion; in the throbbing possibility of putting forth something which we call leaves, for which that patient soul has no name and no image. The unknown total environment is what every intellect posits at birth; whatever may be attempted in action or discovered in nature will be a fresh feature in that field. Everything relevant to mortal anxiety lies within that immensity, be it an object of earthly fear or pursuit or of religious hope. Animal faith and material destiny move in a relative cosmos.

CHAPTER III

PRESUMABLE PROPERTIES OF SUBSTANCE

THE properties which, willy-nilly, we assign to substance by trusting it and by presuming to act upon it, are relative and functional properties. Has substance no other properties, positive and native to it, which we may discover by observation or experience?

That substance has many native and positive characters is certain: in its diffusion it lends existence to certain eternal essences, and enables them to figure in a flux of events. At each point, then, substance must exemplify some essence, of which, then and there, it creates an instance; but it does so by setting that essence in a frame of external relations; so that substance is always more and other than the essence which it exemplifies at any point. It is also more than the set of external relations, or the natural medium, into which these exchangeable essences fall; for this framework, apart from the exchange of alternative essences which diversify it and individuate its parts, would itself be a mere essence, like geometrical space or time, eternal and unsubstantial. This is not to say that, besides the essences which it exemplifies at each point, and the manner in which it connects and exchanges them, substance need have any *other* essence of its own. Its residual being, or not-being, is antithetical to essence altogether, and irrational. We may

Besides its necessary functions, substance manifests many positive properties.

218

enjoy it, we may enact it, but we cannot conceive it; not because our intellect by accident is inadequate, but because existence, which substance makes continuous, is intrinsically a surd, a flux, and a contradiction.

The question for the natural philosopher is therefore reduced to this: which, if any, of the essences revealed in human experience or observation may we assign to substance and regard as belonging to its essence?

This question might be answered easily and rather gloriously in a single word, All! Every character, every relation, every event which occurs anywhere qualifies substance and is a property of it. We should thus come at once upon a perfectly correct, if perfectly useless, definition of substance: the essence of substance would be that of the universe, or so much of the realm of essence as is ever exemplified in existence, when, where, and in the manner in which it is exemplified. This definition, I say, would be correct, because the essences which substance takes on in detail are certainly forms of substance at those points; while those essences which it takes on in its larger sweeps (or, as I shall call them, its tropes) are forms of substance on that scale and in those cycles. In this way a man is a substance, because his human and his personal essence have become forms of substance in him; and the universe is the sum of all substance, the form of which is called the truth. Even those instances of essence which are not forms of substance in this passive manner, are manifestations of substance by way of active expression or epigenesis; though not embodied in substance they are evoked from it and compose the realm of spirit, which is a natural manifestation of substance in man, but not a true description of it. The freest intuition is free only outwards, in that, like music, it need not look towards substance or towards truth; but, like music, the freest

All exemplified essences are in some respect qualities of substance.

intuition is closely bound to substance by its genesis, and rooted there altogether; so that all the essences appearing in contemplation belong to the essence of substance, as all the subtlest developments of music or dialectic belong to the essence of man.

Nevertheless the proposed definition of substance would be useless: it would merely say that all that exists exists, without indicating what is its tenure of existence or the mode of its attachment to substance; and this is the question which arises in action and which gives the category of substance its meaning. Indeed, if from the truth that all phenomena are manifestations of substance, in some direction and at some remove, we passed to the idea that all phenomena are equally substantial, we should have fallen into a positive error; and the word substance itself would have become superfluous; which is the reason why modern philosophers have dropped it. Not that in dropping the word they have abandoned the category: something somewhere must exist in itself and be substantial; but this self-existence would be made to migrate from the heart of things to their surface, or to the total picture which they make in the mind's eye, or to this mind's eye itself, assumed though perhaps not mentioned. Any of these dislocations of substance would render it irrelevant to action. Action cannot accept phenomena simply as phenomena, but must trace the substantial thread on which they are strung together; for it is quite false that any phenomenon taken in itself is substantial; it is a mere essence, save for its backing in nature, which, although it always exists, is often very recondite, and definable by essences very different from that which it wears on the surface.

The dog in the fable, who dropped the substance for the shadow, might have found substance even in that shadow, namely, water and light reflected from the

But none is a substance in itself.

water; and if he had been a natural philosopher, he might have traced that ray back to the very bone which he had held in his mouth, and had let slip for The dog the sake of its deceptive image. This com- and the plication in the manifestations of substance bone. misled his action, because he was not interested in manifestations at all, but only in a substance which he might assimilate blindly and turn into the hidden substance of himself: and *this* substance was not to be found where he sought it. There is a natural hierarchy in the manifestations of substance; and while no appearance is a mere appearance, but all are in some way appearances of substance, yet some of the essences exhibited to human intuition fit the dynamic movement of nature tightly and consecutively, and can be true guides to action, whereas others are poised delicately there, like a mood or a dream, not long to be traced or trusted; for the flux of substance has other forms beneath to which it proves more faithful. While we halt and disport ourselves at the human level, substance slips on in its merely material career, and that poem is ended. The study of substance is the pursuit of these deepest and most pervasive of its properties, and of the manner in which the rarer properties and the supervening unities are generated in that context. It is the study of physics.

In dreams substance mocks the pursuer; he wastes the emotions of action in a direction in which substance is absent, and action therefore impossible; Pharaoh's but in another direction, namely, in himself, dream. substance is always at hand, and he may ironically trace his dream back to it on waking. Pharaoh's dream was all about substance, yet much interpretation was needed before his fat and lean kine could disclose their relevance to the world of action. They had such relevance initially in his royal preoccupation with animals and with the fat of the land; but this backward reference

of ideas to their seat and their origin is seldom conveyed
by the deliverance of the ideas themselves; when it is,
they become reflection or memory.   In the forward
impulse of perception or policy, ideas have, or are
taken to have, a forward reference to substance as well:
appetition turns them into prophecies.   Fortunately
Pharaoh had at his elbow a prophetic materialist, to
whom ideas were signs, and who readily conceived what
genuine substances might be signified by them; and
the event having justified his prudent guess, the statesman needed to go no further in his interpretation of
ideas: the people's stomach and the king's treasury
were ultimate substances for him.   Had Joseph been a
more curious philosopher, even a treasury or a stomach
might have seemed to him but covering ideas, standing
for undeciphered operations of nature; and he might
have begun to speculate about earth and water, the sun
and the miracle of seeds; but even if his science had
advanced as far as the science of to-day, it would not
have reached anything but some more abstract term,
or more refined covering idea.   He had found substance,
as substance may be found, in the thick of action, in
those harvests and granaries; there he had touched the
hand of the Lord.

There is another fable which renders the matter
more subtly, and dwells more on its ideal side.   Narcissus was not deceived like the dog; he knew
Narcissus. that the fair image was but a reflection of
himself; but in his love of form he was seized with a
sort of desperate enthusiasm, and coveted that celestial
object with an earthly passion; so that his fate was
worse than the dog's, and in plunging after the shadow
he lost not only that fancied substance, but his true
substance and life as well.   Not that self-love need
always be suicidal.   Had Narcissus been content to
enjoy his own substance blindly, in its coursing life
through his members, he might have possessed himself

mightily and long, being all action, all ignorance, all irresponsibility; he might have reverted from the Narcissus of fable to the Narcissus of Freud. But the poets have made him a symbol for a higher fate, for the great deviation of attention from substance to essence. This deviation, as we see in him, has two stages, one confused and mad, at which he stopped, and another sublime and musical, to which he might have proceeded. For Narcissus is the forerunner of Apollo, or Apollo in embryo; he explains the mystery of Apollo having been born so free and so deeply inspired; for high things must have deep and hidden foundations. The foundation of intuition, and of all the free arts, lies in the substance of the self, with its long vegetable and animal evolution; until one day, in the person of Narcissus, attention is arrested on the form which the self lends to all nature, or wears in its own eyes. If at first this intuition is not pure, and Narcissus wildly pursues essence as if it were substance, he becomes Dionysus, inspired but drunk: if on the contrary his intuition liberates the form of substance from its flux, and sees it in its wholeness and in its unsubstantiality, then Narcissus becomes Apollo, inspired but sane.

These parables have a common moral. Ideas, or the forms which things wear in human experience, are unsubstantial in themselves, cheating every action or hope that may be directed upon them in their literal immediate being, or given essence; but they may all be traced, either by interpretation outwards or by reversion inwards to their origin in the self, until they lead us to substance; that is, to something *However unprecedented their form, all things are traceable by their substance.* that can be the butt of action, and in which the effects of action may be fertile and prolonged. Experience and the arts of life thus seem to justify the presumption that all things are natural, even the most ideal, and that nothing, even in a dream, appears by chance, but that all is symptomatic, significant, and grounded in substance.

And as all things unsubstantial may be traced to substance, so all the movements of substance may be Which on its own plane is a continuous process. traced to one another. It is sheer ignorance to stare at anything as if it were inexplicable and self-created, a mere intruder in the world. The universe itself no doubt is groundless and a perpetual miracle; but it is a tame wonder, and terribly self-imitative; and everything in it bears its hallmark and stamp of origin, if we only are clever enough to turn it inside out, and inspect its fabric. The habits of nature are marvellous, but they are habits; and the flux of substance fills quite innocently and automatically the intervals which its own lapse may create. This assumption is not justifiable by induction, because no experience covers any great part of nature, nor that part thoroughly; but it is nevertheless the anchor of rational life. All prudence, all art, all calculation rely upon it, and prosper—in so far as they prosper—by that confidence.

The simplest sort of continuity is persistence, or sustained identity: and this is often found or assumed Some things are traceable because roughly persistent. in the field of action. Leaving my hat and umbrella in the cloak room, I expect, on my departure, to find the same objects. I conceive them to have endured unchanged in the interval. And when I take fresh possession of them, and carry them into quite another place, I conceive that, save for a little wear and tear, they still remain identical. And I assume a similar battered identity in my own person. If things lapsed in nature as they lapse in immediate experience, objects that disappeared at any point would be annihilated, and some new thing, perhaps like them but not the same, would presently be created somewhere else. This magical world may be acceptable to a laughing child, or a desperate sceptic, but it will never do for a sportsman. If the scent is lost for a moment, he must assume that the fox is still in existence, or he could not pursue the chase. To wait and wonder whether another fox might not be created anywhere else at any other time would not be hunting; nor would it be labour, nor art, nor science; it would be treating objects not as substances but as apparitions. That which appears, if it is posited as a thing to be chased, must exist continuously even when it does not appear. The object at each instant must occupy some particular position in the field of action, a place determinable by exploration; and belief and action may be directed upon it when invisible with entire confidence that its path is traceable and calculable.

That substances persist through motion is a veritable postulate of practical reason: not a mock postulate known to be false (as Kant's postulates were apparently meant to be) but one believed to be true, and constantly revived by events. If it were not true, action, and even the thought of action, would be farcical, and would in fact never have arisen. Yet this postulate, as action implies and verifies it, does not extend further than action itself. The huntsman need not assume that his fox will live for ever. Possibly its haunting image, surviving the chase, may of old have suggested to him his totems and animal gods; but in the chase itself only a brief persistence, limited to this particular fox, is posited or proved. Soon this substance is expected to disappear; true, it may feed the hunter or his dogs; yet no theory of a total and absolute indestructibility of substance, through all its transformations, need be broached in practice. The persistence which the human mind tends to attribute to things, especially when they are loved or feared, is less that of their substance than of

Persistence in substance need not be everlasting or universal.

their ghosts. It is a confused intermixture of essences
with facts, of casual circumstances with profound rever-
berations in memory. Experience, even in those of us
who think ourselves enlightened, is full of increments
and losses which seem to us absolute, as if they were
souls, strengths, or illuminations coming from other
spheres. The field of action remains to that extent an
animated chaos in which at best certain magic rhymes
may be detected, which superstition raises into laws.
Were it not for sane instinct, custom, and the steadying
machinery of the arts, we should all be little better than
poets. It is but a thin thread of calculable continuity
that runs through immediate experience: the postulate
of permanence is applicable and reasonable only in the
field of action posited outside, and only in so far as
exact arts and sciences may be able to dominate it.

Might not substance, then, be as intermittent and
spasmodic as experience itself? Might it not be a
fire whose very nature was to lapse: not
merely to lapse inwardly and devour its own
flames, but occasionally to lapse from existence altogether, like the setting sun of
Heraclitus? A different sun, he observed, was created
in the morning; and perhaps not all the intervals or
pauses between existences would be so regular, nor
the existences so much alike. Some sun might be
the last; it would not follow that it had not existed.
So all existence might be occasional, and destined
some day to fail altogether. A playful philosopher,
now that science has again become playful, might
conceive that all things are totally destroyed at each
instant, and fresh things created—I was going to say
" in their place ", but I should rather say in fresh
places, since times and spaces in such a system would
also have no unity and no continuity. Yet these
momentary worlds would still be substantial, in the
transcendental sense; they would not be merely

It might exist dis- cretely at separate moments.

phenomenal, if they were independent, while they lasted, of the notice taken of them by any mind. Per- haps a moralist or a poet might call them unsubstantial, because transitory; but in that sense existence itself would be unsubstantial, and all our categories would become confused. Let us reconcile ourselves once for all to transitive existence: the eternal is ours if we truly honour it, but in another sphere; and mean- time let us inquire what forms of iteration and of persistence appear in the flux of existence, which is substantial because it flows, and at each moment assaults and betrays our charmed conceptions.

It was well known to the ancients, and is confirmed daily, that when things die they leave heirs: the flies that seem to vanish every winter return every summer. And this pertinacity in substance is not always intermittent; a phase of latency, silent but deeply real, often connects the phases of activity. Sleep and night are not nothing: in them substance most certainly endures, and even gathers strength, or unfolds its hidden coils. Then the spirit, in withdrawing into slumber, seems to return into the womb, into a security and naturalness much deeper than its distracted life. It knows that while it sleeps all things wait, last, and ripen; they all breathe inwardly with that same peace which returns to it only in the night. Those heavenly bodies, which when gaped at seemed but twinkling specks, are in reality sleeping giants; they roll with an enormous momentum at prodigious distances, and keep the world in equilibrium. The rocks are rooted in their buried foundations, the bed of the sea stretches beneath it, and holds it; the earth broods over its ominous substance, like a fiery orange with a rind of stone. It is this universal pause and readiness in things, guarding us unwatched, that chiefly supports our sanity and courage. This constancy gives us

But in fact nature is full of in- heritance, potenti- ality, and latent phases.

security; the eyes may close in peace, while the child's dreaming hand, half closing, prepares to grasp a sword.

The ancients also observed how regularly some objects may be transformed into others, as water into ice or vapour; and that there is a certain equivalence through these phases in their quantity or energy. The seasons return, their fruits varying with the weather; the generations repeat themselves, but mixing their breed;

Substance is quantitative and its changes proportionate and measurable.

and there is always a potentiality of reversion to a former constellation of properties, prevented only by cross-currents of change. Even where evolution is not cyclical, but creates new forms, it is proportionate and still conservative; anything does not succeed anywhere to anything else. Nothing new arises except out of seeds differently watered, measurably, locally, conditionally. A limited potentiality, an inherited substance, links all the transformations of things together. They pass their matter on to one another; their matter is the principle of their equivalence and continuity. When objects are mutually convertible, they are substantial: were they disembodied essences it would be neither necessary nor intelligible that one should yield to the other in any order, or with any proportion in quantity or quality. But when substantial things perish, we know very well that their elements are simply dispersed, and go to swell the substance of other parts of nature. A long and victorious husbandry has enabled us to trace these migrations of substance; so much so that it has become a plausible hypothesis, countenanced by many an art and many an experiment, that substance is constant in quantity, and never created or destroyed. Only a certain number of loaves can be baked from a barrel of flour; and it would be a miracle if twelve loaves could satisfy the hunger of five thousand people. Famine and war, commerce and prosperity are evident phases in this natural economy: friction and crowding of substance here, scarcity there, and everywhere a limited, special, temporary opportunity for existence.

It is to be observed, however, that this quantitative limitation in things is, for human experience and science, rather a matter of averages and of proportion between desultory facts than any traceable persistence in particular substances; genesis is roughly subject to calculation and responsive to custom, but its inner texture eludes observation. Nor is this to be *Substance need not endure after the manner of feelings or images in sense.* wondered at, or set down as an argument against substance altogether: because, if we remember how and why substance is posited in the beginning, we shall not expect it to exhibit the sort of permanence which belongs to specious objects. Specious objects are mere essences; in themselves they are eternal and always recoverable in their absolute identity, except for physical difficulties in reproducing the same attitude in the psyche. Substance, on the contrary, is internally in flux. So that the presumption of identity with which we revert to an essence, or to a term in discourse, is likely to be ill-grounded if we transfer it to a thing, the substance of which is always changing its form. Moreover, the very notion of persistence, like all notions, is a specious essence: it is cumulative and emotional and given in that dumb feeling of duration of which a certain specious philosophy has made so much. It is not to be expected that substance should realise internally this specious quality, which may express in human intuition one aspect of its movement. The feeling of blank duration itself covers a slumbering life in the psyche, roughly sustained and rhythmical, like breathing, but by no means changeless or simple. Obvious persistence is a comment made superficially on a physical flux not clearly discerned; whereas the persistence of substance is something integral to that flux itself, rendering its changes changes, and its phases successive or contiguous.

If the elements of substance resembled persistent images in sense, or were indestructible cubes, spheres, Pictorial or pyramids, these Egyptian solids would character hardly possess the sort of permanence im- of geo- metrical pressing the traveller who stops to admire atoms. the Pyramid of Cheops. This pyramid was once built, yet it defies time paradoxically. The stars have the same sublimity, for they ought to burn out or fall from heaven and yet (in our limited experience) they do not: so that an existence seems to us to have put on the eternity of an essence, and by this marvel our own steps and breath and vapid thoughts are rebuked and arrested. But atoms having immutable geometrical forms and no inner substance save pure Being, would be eternal by definition, and not suitable elements of existence at all. They would have no scale for time within them, no sensitiveness to motion or change of relations. Their inner nature would be irrelevant to that flux of existence which it was designed to render intelligible. It would be only their changing arrangement in the void that would determine the field of action. And since the void has pure Being in it no less than an atom (both having geometrical extension for their essence) it is not easy to see how the limits or the position of an atom could themselves be determined. A crumbling pyramid is more substantial than an eternal one.

Indeed if those Egyptian solids were existing bodies If sub- and not merely geometrical essences, their stance takes indestructibility, supposing them indestruct- geometrical forms, it ible, would be a contingent and merely still sup- historical fact. It is evident that a spherical, ports and survives cubical, or pyramidal body *might* at any time them. fall to pieces; it is an atom provisionally, by courtesy, by virtue of its function in a given mechanism;

in its existence and substance, which are centred equally in every part, it is thoroughly divisible. Yet, in admitting this undeniable possibility, or rather this natural presumption, that Egyptian atoms should some day crumble, we still posit and imply persistence in the world; for the principle of existence in those fragments would be the same as in the atoms when they were whole, and the same medium of space and time, or whatever else it may be, and the same fatality of motion and of order would permeate that dust and govern its destinies. It was evidently these deeper properties of substance that kept those atoms whole, if perhaps during some cycle of natural existence they remained indestructible; and among those deeper properties we must count the void in which those atoms could move and the mysterious cohesion and fertility of some of their aggregates, by which nature is diversified and made alive.

The atomic theory is, nevertheless, in one sense, inherent in physics, and alone possible; because the very nature of existence is to be dispersed in *Yet substance is atomic in as much as existence is discrete; and all enveloping unities are only truths about it.* centres, dislocated, corpuscular, granular; the parts must be particulars externally related. Any demand for a unity not a unity of arrangement, derivation, or conjunction turns its back on existence. Indeed these very unities of arrangement, when substance realises them, are not contained in the substance at any point, or at any moment; they are not seated, for instance, in any intuition which may define them or in any perception which may posit them in the world. They belong, if they are realised, to the realm of truth. It is simply true that the parts of substance have assumed that arrangement; and this truth is not proved by the mere intuition of such a unity, which might be specious only, but must be made the goal of a laborious investigation and a practical faith. The seen unities are not false; they are manifestations of substance like the intuitions which we have when we read poetry; but they express our reaction to a manifold object and our gross relation to it, rather than the diffuse substance of that object itself. The unities and arrangements embodied in substance are not separable from it or from its flux; and like substance and its flux these can be known only functionally.

For this reason an atomism which professes to *define* its atoms trespasses against the modesty of our genuine contacts with things. The atomism of De-*Illusion of* mocritus, with the Cartesian notion of sub-*scientific* stance and the Newtonian notion of space, *gnosticism.* time, and matter, are all too graphic and mathematical; they betray their Eleatic·and Pythagorean origin; they share a poetic or mythological gnosticism which thinks to decipher the heart of nature in terms of human intuition. These terms may be admirably chosen and the best possible; but their value is not exhaustive and must always remain symbolical. The persistence of substance can hardly be intrinsically similar to the stubbornness of some ghostly image that will not down.

Great philosophers, having been men of universal mind, have instinctively set the same standard of *Intuitive* accuracy and truth for all their investigations. *knowledge* As there is a possibility of literal or intuitive *or divina-* knowledge in some fields, they have desired *tion is* *proper* such knowledge everywhere; but in physics, *only to* *moral* and in regard to the intrinsic properties of *subjects.* substance, such knowledge is impossible. Intuition lies at the opposite end of the gamut of nature; its simplest object covers an immense complexity, a voluminous heritage, in the animal soul. Where literal knowledge is possible—apart from contemplation of essence, which is complex feeling rather than knowledge—is in literary psychology. Here we often conceive our object exactly as it was or may be: because it is no more improbable that two brothers should feel and think alike than that two similar leaves should sprout on the same tree.   Therefore poetry is, in one sense, truer than science, and more satisfactory to a seasoned and exacting mind.   Poetry reveals one sort of truth completely, because reality in that quarter is no more defined or tangible than poetry itself; and it clarifies human experience of other things also, earthly and divine, without falsifying these things more than experience falsifies them already.   Science, on the contrary, the deeper it goes, gets thinner and thinner and cheats us altogether, unless we discount its symbols.

We may leave it then for literary psychologists and intuitive metaphysicians to record their experience in ways appealing to men of their own mind; and we may leave it for mathematicians to construct possible worlds.   The practical naturalist is concerned only with such properties of substance as are implied, measured, and elicited in his arts and in his explorations.   The study of nature is the most picturesque of studies, and full of joy for the innocent mind; but in natural science all is familiarity and nothing comprehension, save as there is a humorous or devout comprehension in foresight and trust.

I may now add to the indispensable properties of substance others which substance seems to possess, and which, since they too are assumed in practice, may be assumed in natural philosophy.

6. *Substance*, in diversifying the field of nature, *sometimes takes the form of animals in whom there are feelings, images, and thoughts.   These mental facts are immaterial.* They offer no butt for action and exercise no physical influence on one another.

7. The same *mental facts are manifestations of substance*; in their occurrence they are parts of a total natural event which, on its substantial side, belongs

to the plane of action. They are therefore signifi-

cant and relevant to action as signs, being
created and controlled by the flux of substance
beneath.

8. Beneath the intermittence of phenomena, *the phases or modes through which substance flows are continuous.*

9. As far as action and calculation can
extend, *the quantity of substance remains equivalent throughout.*

10. *Each phase or mode of substance, although not contained in its antecedents, is predetermined by them in its place and quality,
and proportionate to them in extent and intensity.*
An event will be repeated if ever the constellation of events which bred it should
recur. This regularity in the genesis of modes
or phases of substance is constantly verified
in action on a small scale. To expect it in
substance is the soul of science and art; but
to expect it in phenomena is superstition.

When, then, in perception, action, memory, or hope
experience is treated as significant, a substance is posited
which must be external to thought, with its
parts external to one another and each a focus
of existence; a substance which passes through various
phases is unequally distributed in the field of action,
and forms a relative cosmos surrounding each agent.
Action on these assumptions makes it further appear
that this substance is the source of phenomena unsubstantial in themselves but significant of the phases
of substance which produce them; that these phases
are continuous and measurable; and that each transformation, though spontaneous in itself, is repeated
whenever the same conditions recur. Now a substance possessing these functions and these characteristics has a familiar name: it is called matter.

Matter is the medium of calculable art. But I have found from the beginning that the impulse to act and the confidence that the opposite partner in action has specific and measurable resources, are the primary expressions of animal faith; also that animal faith is the only principle by which belief in existence of any kind can be justified or suggested to the spirit. It follows that the only object posited by animal faith is matter; and that all those images which in human experience may be names or signs for objects of belief are, in their ultimate signification, so many names or signs for matter. Their perpetual variety indicates the phases through which the flux of matter is passing in the self, or those which the self is positing in the field of action to which it is responsive. Apart from this material signification, those feelings and perceptions are simply intuitions of essences, essences to which no existence in nature can be assigned. The field of action is accordingly the realm of matter; and I will henceforth call it by that name.

CHAPTER IV

PICTORIAL SPACE AND SENTIMENTAL TIME

THE wise men of Ionia perceived long ago that water, air, or fire, by metamorphosis, might make up the whole life of nature. This is now being rediscovered; but with two interesting differences. Exploration and mathematics have changed the scale of our science: we are acquainted with distance, outwards and inwards. On the other hand, religion and romanticism have established the troubled reign of subjectivity, and have endowed immediate experience with a kind of authority which the maritime Greeks, keen-eyed but practical and argumentative, had never dreamt of. They looked in order to understand and to possess; whereas our philosophy, if not our instinct, reverts with relief from understanding and possession to æsthetic life, as to a surer foundation. Our cosmology has spirited away that living substance which, like Zeus, had many names, but under all of them was felt to be fatally revolving, plastic, and mighty. Air has been attenuated to space, the fluid to motion, fire to light— ambiguous essences which are thought of as existing in nature, and forming its elements, yet are also names for feelings or ghostly concepts floating before the mind; and to these last the modern philosopher, when pressed, is inclined to reduce them.

Why shouldn't some astronomer with one foot in

The genuine physics of the ancients has been extended by mathematics and dislocated by idealism.

236

idealism tell us that the universe is nothing but light? If we forget that we eat, work, and die, if we forget that we are animals, may we not plausibly think that nothing exists save a certain coloured brightness playing *in vacuo*? And what is consciousness, which in the nineteenth century passed for the only reality, but an active and burning light? May not formal science, too, be invoked to prove that light is the only revealer and measurer of the material universe? And yet this light, which should be the source of clearness, is itself the most obscure of things, and its name the most ambiguous of names. For in physics light is understood to be a mysterious agency coursing through space, material in that it has a measurable velocity and does material work, and is a form of vibration or radiation emitted by bodies when ignited, and intercepted and reflected by them even when opaque. It traverses space unceasingly in a thousand directions, leaving it perfectly black and cold. This light is invisible: only gross matter shedding it or catching it can become bright. Plants and blind animals—and even the human eye is blind to some of its rays—may bask in it with profit, being deeply penetrated by its electric warmth, as by the healing shafts of Apollo.

Typical ambiguity of the word " light ".

To call this cosmic agency light is a poetic metaphor, as if we called it Phœbus; which indeed we might do without absurdity, since Apollo besides his golden locks had his invisible arrows; and these were the dread reality of the god. Only the obvious essence of brightness shining in intuition is light proper. This is no insidious power, but an open gift, vouchsafed from moment to moment like daily bread to the spirit; an essence appearing and vanishing as we open or shut the eyes; an intensive quality, æsthetic and emotional, proper to images of colour or visual patterns. It has no velocity or direction or substance or pertinacity;

it is incapable of warming anything or doing any work; it is obvious but cannot be caught, proportionate but not to be measured; remote in its spiritual presence from all the functions of that cosmic fire which, according to Heraclitus, shaped, animated, and devoured everything. Yet this visionary light, which can burn only in the hearth of the soul, lends its name to that mathematical measure of astronomical distances. In one sense, light is the messenger of matter, and carries the eye through time and space almost to infinity, and if we trust its reports dehumanises the universe; but in another sense it tinctures this same universe with a surreptitious humanity, for it seems to reduce everything to immediate experience, to the focus of intuition at any moment in any man; so that both its substance and its measure seem to become æsthetic. Thus the dominance of light, in its two acceptations, marks the two developments, and the fundamental confusion, by which modern cosmology differs from that of the ancients.

That the realm of matter, in its own way, is spatial and temporal follows from the conception of this realm as the field of action. In action one state of things must pass into another, something must be precipitated, and each direction and each degree of change must be distinguished from all others, which are its alternatives. Substance, if it is to flow and to have parts, must be distributed in centres, each a focus of external and transitional relations with the rest. Interaction and genesis involve this sort of space and time, or create them. But what this physical space or time may properly be, we could know perfectly only by knowing perfectly the intimate movement and ultimate ranges of matter—not a human task. We know matter, as it behoves us to know it, in the measure in which our highly selective action and mental chronicle of action

Physical space and time are intrinsic to substance and cannot be defined a priori.

penetrate into its meshes: and presently I shall say something concerning our share in this general flux of existence, and our ways of noting it. Physical space and time are integral elements in this realm of matter: they are *physical*, which is as much as to say that they are contingent, to be explored by experiment rather than by reasoning, to be shared by us rather than contemplated. They may change their form if they choose, like any existence, and may manifest a different essence in their new instances.

It is therefore a problem never to be solved except provisionally and locally, how far a human sensation of sentimental time or of pictorial space, or how far any geometrical model of a pure space or time, may fitly express the temporal and spatial dimensions of nature, or be a true measure for them. Over the field of action, in which we exist, logic, which is but our way of thinking, can have no prior control. Substance did not drop into a world with a previous constitution; it was not obliged to squeeze itself into atoms or to spread itself through infinities, so as to verify the precipitate fancies of future philosophers. To ask whether substance must be discrete or continuous, finite or infinite, many or one, is like asking whether the Almighty must think in French or in English. Having no competence in that sphere, why should we have any preferences? Let physical time and space be infinite or finite, discrete or continuous, unreturning or circular, multiplex or single: these would be curious and impressive truths, if they were discoverable, and too great for ignorant opinion.

Meantime the practical arts retain a great advantage over the speculation which seeks to elucidate them: they deal directly with matter, whereas a graphic or dialectical analysis can be immediately concerned only with images which are symbols, or with symbols which are words. When the act of measuring is an actual transition, like a journey, both the metre and the thing measured are material and equally internal to the flux of substance. The measure is then con-

Physical space and time can be measured only by the material processes that traverse them.

gruous and literal; and the disadvantage of perhaps leaving no precise image in intuition—for what, to intuition, is a pace or a mile?—is counterbalanced by the advantage of bridging truly external relations, and catching nature in her own net. A graphic calculus or a map may afterwards be constructed to give definition and a common denominator to the parts of this past or possible performance, and to display it as a whole to intuition—but now in another realm of being from that in which it might actually occur: for it would occur in the realm of matter, and it is surveyed as an essence. This is not a defect in the survey, but the condition of inspection or retrospect, which is the translation of an event into an idea, and not a repetition of the same event. As literature is but childish exclamation modulated and transcribed, so scientific imagination is but sensation steadied and defined. Instead of the flying miscellany of natural images—vivid but treacherous tokens of what nature is doing—science sets up an idol, simpler and more dignified, but still only an idea.

Mathematical space and time are sublimated essences of this sort. They cannot appear in sense as they are defined to be—infinite, equable, and pure;

Mathematical space and time are scientific figments.

yet they remain specious or ideal in their nature, purified extensions or generalisations of the imagery of sense. It is contact with matter, patient empirical art, that guides this idealisation, so that the Egyptian blocks may be fit and four-square, and the planets may not belie the prophet; and this advance in the validity and precision of the symbols used, in spite of their greater tenuity, causes them to be mistaken, as the crude images of sense were at first, for the very essence of matter. Having erected and polished our mathematical idol, we suppose ourselves to behold intuitively what space and time are physically; we even feel confident that it is impossible for them not to exist, or to exist otherwise. The clearness and necessity native to essence when kept in its own realm are thus attributed to the realm of matter, where all is profound fertility and darkness; and having discarded one or two optical illusions, and straightened out one or two perspectives in religious legend, we feel all the freer to endow the residue of our imaginative baggage with a perfect substantiality.

We might have done better, perhaps, like the animals or the saints, if we had continued to trust instinctively in the secret harmonies of the realm of matter, or of the kingdom of God; we might have lived on, imaginatively, in the world of poetry, which is often pragmatic and hygienic enough. But there are natural stages and shifts in human ideation: every age has its peculiar insights and new illusions. The terms of science, like those of sense, are essences describing in human discourse the objects encountered in action. This relative function removes them, and ought to remove them, from any passive or complete iteration of the realm of matter in its intrinsic essence. When the mathematician applies his calculus to nature, he does so tentatively, after having taken a hint from nature herself, by selecting for his unit some simple image which action and comparison of cases have shown to have prophetic value; and in his most wonderful successes, if he is wise, he keeps his distance and his sense of abstraction. Here lies the legitimate magic of poetic intuitions, such as are these intuitions of time and space; that, being incarnations of spirit on some animal occasion, they have a double affinity, here to spirit and there to matter, and that with the authority proper to their intended object they associate the form and accent of the free symbol which names it. What was only interaction becomes also perception, and what was a process becomes also a drama; and these moral overtones, on their new emotional plane, are the first ideas, the beginnings of knowledge, of their natural occasions.

If we ask how it happens that quite fresh essences, spontaneously evoked in intuition, like sounds or words Simple or mathematical fictions, can nevertheless reason why apply to nature, the answer is not far to seek. fiction applies to Ideas apply to their occasions because they fact. arise out of them, mark them, and are a part of the total natural event which controls their development. Mind is a great symptom of health; it appears at victorious moments, changes with them, and recalls them. Even its confusions and agonies are but conflicts in its domination; it would not be there to die, if harmony had not given it birth. The æsthetic originality of sensations and ideas is therefore an innocent privilege, if their practical connections are knit together harmoniously with the environing flux of events. And, on some plane, they *must* be so knit, because sensations and ideas arise only when living beings are actively adjusting, or secretly readjusting, their powers. If the adjustment to the moving environment were perfect, the essences evoked in thought, whatever notes they might freely strike æsthetically, would apply or work perfectly in practice; for it is not the ideas that work there, but the men in whom the ideas have arisen.

Mind is Moreover, in applying any idea a man bred in the must start from a material centre, his own material body, and must use a material scale, since movements to which it neither centre nor scale can be furnished by refers, and logic. Numbering is an action: the essence is con- trolled by of a number in intuition preserves the cumu- them. lative sense of a repeated touching and discrimination of particular things. Measuring is the act

of superposing one material thing on another What
wonder that the notions arising from such operations
apply to their source, and enable the prophet to cry,
as if inspired, that the Lord has ordered all things
in measure and number and weight? These are the
material categories bred in the mind by mechanical
art, and whatever may be later their ideal elaboration,
their validity in the field of action, which is the only
existing world, remains conventional and pragmatic.
An eye sensitive to physical light would have been
useless to the organism, and incidentally would never
have endowed the spirit with the vision of brightness,
were not light mechanically reflected and diversified
by the earthly bodies on which it falls. Signals coming
to the eye would not otherwise be prophetic of rougher
contacts. Nor would pictorial space otherwise have
become what it is for human intelligence, an accurate
and detailed map, drawn according to a private projection, and covering the field of action, or the home-
world of mankind. In consequence, when the sun
rises, it not merely warms the backs of mankind, as
if they were lizards, but it clears away from the spirit
half the terrors of a precarious life. It suddenly extends
the field of grovelling search and opportunity to the
horizon. The gift of specious light, great as it is
æsthetically, would have seemed trivial to the heart,
but for this quicker adjustment to matter and this new
safety expressed in it. Since physical light is an instrument of reaction at long range, specious light, its moral
echo, has become almost a synonym for intelligence.

A chief characteristic of pictorial space,
which betrays its animal origin, is that it has
a centre. This centre is transcendental; that
is to say, it is not determined by any distinction in the parts of space itself, as conceived,
all of which are equally central. The dignity
of being a centre comes to any point of space from

Pictorial space always has a transcendental centre in some animal spirit.

the spirit, which some fatality has lodged there, to the exclusion, at least in its own view, of all other places. These other places appear in that view as removed, and ranged in concentric spheres at greater and greater distances. The cosmos of Ptolemy is the perfect model or systematisation of pictorial space. The choice of the earth for a centre, although arbitrary geometrically, was not arbitrary historically, because Ptolemy and all other human beings found themselves on the earth, and were natives of it. So the fatality which always lodges spirit at some one point in nature, and makes this its centre, is not arbitrary biologically: for wherever there is a living organism it becomes a centre for dramatic action and reaction, and thereby calls down spirit to assume that station, and make it a moving vehicle for one phase of its earthly fortunes. Pictorial space therefore reappears, wherever an animal rises to intuition of his environment, and in each case it has its moral or transcendental centre in that animal; a centre which, being transcendental or moral, moves wherever the animal moves, and is repeated without physical contradiction or rivalry in as many places as are ever inhabited by a watchful animal soul.

The name of this relative centre is *here*. Nature, if it has limits and is all measurable by a single measure (which may be doubted), may have a centre, but not in the same sense as pictorial space; for *here*, in pictorial space, is a centre of occupied position and actual reference, the determinant of far and near, forward and back, up and down, right and left: animal categories imposed on the field of action by action itself, and impossible except in a perspective created by living intently in the act of looking, moving, or reaching out from an occupied centre in a particular direction. This direction could not be chosen, or even conceived, except in sympathy with some organic impulse; in pictorial space all structures and lines of cleavage crystallise about the axis of attention. The centre of the cosmos, on the contrary, if it exists, would be determined by reciprocal material relations between its parts; and the choice of a starting-point in surveying it never would shift that centre, but only lead to it, as if to Rome, by a particular road.

When an image of one's own body is included in pictorial space, as happens almost always in action, this image will roughly correspond with the centre of that action in physical space: vision will be centred in the moving hero, and will follow him in his adventures. For even if nature as a whole has no centre, every organism is a focus for its external and changing *The subjective or practical* here *travels with the sensitive organism.* relations to the rest of the world, and is the centre of a dynamic cosmos relative to itself. Thus pictorial space, spreading round its transcendental point of origin in the attentive spirit, affords a suitable index to that field of action which is its professed object, since the segment of nature implicated in that action actually surrounds and recedes from that action very much as pictorial objects surround the image of the body, and seem to recede from it. In perception, as in painting, distortion is often the secret of significance. Pictorial space achieves something which might have seemed a miracle to a spirit acquainted with matter from the outside, but ignorant of the animal mind, which is the self-consciousness of matter; for pictorial space infuses into its object, physical space, an intrinsic reference to the station, the impulses, and the organs of the creatures ranging within it. This symbolic virtue hangs together with the transcendental status and graphic unity of pictorial space, by virtue of which it forms no part of physical space, but is a new whole symbol for it as a whole. The two belong to different realms of being, like Lucifer and the morning star, that yet bear the same name; and they are connected, not by interfering with or patching one another, but by a spontaneous concomitance and mutual implication, so that to find the one, under certain conditions, is to announce the other. Matter, or physical space, at certain nodes in its organisation, grounds and justifies the biassed sensitiveness of animals to their environment; and this biassed sensitiveness, raised to intuition, forms an ocular-muscular perception of that very space; for the intuitions of animals, at least in action, are not pure or contemplative, but by force of the intent involved in action, signify to the spirit the conditions of its existence—in this case the movement and filling of physical space in that neighbourhood.

Sometimes, as in deep thought, no image of one's own body figures at all in intuition. *Here* then means whatever point in imagined space is the centre of attention. *Here* may be the word on the page which I have reached in reading; or if my attention has passed from the words to the images awakened by them in my fancy, *here* may be Dante's *Purgatorio*, rising solitary out of a glassy sea and lifting its clear-cut terraces in perfect circles, up to the fragrant wood at the summit, whence souls grown too pure for a mild happiness pass into the flame of heaven. *Here* is then at the antipodes of Jerusalem and Calvary; half-way up from the centre of the Earth, which is the Inferno, to the lowest of those concentric celestial spheres, each broader and more luminous, which, as Plotinus would say, are *There*. For, in my contemplative mood, I should be regarding myself as directed away from the earth, and from the Hell in it, and in my pictorial space the Eternal would seem to be the Beyond. But now, perhaps, someone knocks at my door and disturbs my reverie. *Here* is now, if still a purgatory, a purgatory of a very different sort; it is this room in this town where my body finds itself. I look out of the window, and now *here* is Paris;

The objective or contemplative here travels with the object of attention.

I notice on my table Baedeker's guide-books and the *Indicateur des chemins de fer*, and I consider how easily *here* may be transferred to quite another geographical place. As to the *here* of a moment ago, it is not only not here, but it is nowhere. It belongs to Dante's imaginary world. It is a theme from the symphony of essence.

The bond between pictorial space and physical space lies in the organ of intuition, which is a part of the agent in action. As this organ extends its instrumental uses, adjusting the organism at long range to its environment in physical space, so and in the same measure this same organ exercises its expressive or spiritual function, and creates a pictorial space for the spirit of that animal. This intuition is an important element in the total consciousness which that spirit can have of its destiny; it sets the stage in which the image of its body is found always occupying the centre, and marks the vital distinctions of forward and back, up and down, far and near. Such relations, though obviously relative to an animal life, are not intransitive, as if they were the baseless invention of some impenetrable atom coming to life; they express a movement. Indeed, it is hardly conceivable that a point or an arrested structure should feel or think. The organ of intuition is rather so much of nature as is engaged in that movement, and contributes to the choice of the essence which that intuition evokes. It might even be said that the whole universe is the ultimate organ of every intuition, as it is the ultimate object of every belief: but the measure in which this is true is most unequal. All intuitions, and especially that of space, take the point of view of some particular creature at some particular juncture; and if we wish to discover the special organ of an intuition, we may do so by internal evidence, noting the moral centre

The range and objective centres of pictorial space express the scope of its organ in its reaction on other parts of nature.

of the given scene, and its pictorial circumference, as
we might those of a novel. The novel (unless it is an
intentional travesty) will describe the country and age
in which it was written; so the intuition will normally
describe, and will always betray, that centre of vital
relations which is its seat and its author. Thus the
degree in which the intuition transcends or ignores that
centre, becoming possibly an intuition of pure truth,
will mark the degree in which its organ, though particular, is sensitive to the rest of nature.

Besides a specious centre, *here*, pictorial space has
a specious scale: it contains a direct emotional sense
of the large and small, the far and near. Size
and distance are indeed so emotional that they
are more than spatial, and touch the sphere
of sentimental time: the " far " is redolent of the prolonged and dubious adventure of reaching it, and the
" large " taxes the synthetic power of the eye, or the
clasp of the extended arms. Pictorial space itself,
especially when empty and considered absolutely, is
the very model of vastness; it opens in all directions
(something baffling to a hunting animal) and recedes
to immeasurable distances. In its presence the breast
expands, which is glorious, but the will halts, which is
annihilating, and brings tears to the eyes. Therefore
the oppressed souls of heroes sighed in Homer, looking
into the broad heaven. The notion of the romantic
infinite is a sublimation of this helplessness in applying a homely measure to unhomely things; from the
practically inexhaustible we pass to the ideally immeasurable or infinite, and find it at once alluring
and maddening, inevitable and dubious. Romanticism
could not gloat on a more congenial abyss.

The mystery of this mock infinite comes of importing
into an essence, mathematically quite definite, the emotions of an explorer. The innumerable would present
no difficulty if nobody was condemned to enumerate it;

The emotional infinite.

and nobody is. If nature is in some sense infinite, there will be substance found to occupy all its parts, and establish their real relations: but the geo- metrical model of an infinite empty space is only a phantasm visiting the imagination, pic- torial space washed clean. Having no scale, no separable parts, and none but internal necessary relations, it is an essence without existence. Taken in this capacity it is a per- fectly clear and coherent object: a fact which confirms its specious character and derivation *The mathe- matical infinite is a clear essence, which nature suggests to the mind, appropriate but not substantial.* from a sensuous image; because if it were the essence of matter, as Descartes deputed it to be, it would hardly be clear or distinct to human apprehension. For matter, with all existence supported by matter, is unin- telligible, if for no other reason, because it changes. The light of spirit which shines in the darkness cannot see the primeval darkness which begat it and which it dispels; but in so far as its strength avails it consumes that darkness, as it were, for fuel, and sees that which was dark before by the light which it spreads over it. In this way first pictorial space and then geometrical space are cast like a search-light or a net over the field of action, to map and to measure it; but the principle of action, matter in its native unison and flux, escapes intuition, and may be mapped and measured only ex- ternally, even if quite correctly and safely. This is possible because the darkness of matter is not chaotic or malicious; it does not circumvent the light which plays upon it, but only ignores it, and lets it play on. That light is its own child, its own effluence. The harmony between the depths and the surface, the seed and the flower, is as natural as their diversity.

Pictorial spaces are pictorial in various degrees: they range from the simplest essence of extensity, through all images of motion, collapse, swiftness, or scenic con- fusion; or they may culminate in a reposeful landscape,

and in that essence of empty volume or immensity
which, save for the absence of analysis, would fuse with
the notion of geometrical space. Perfectly
Neglected obvious, but not at all geometrical, is the
original
spaces of space revealed by internal sensations, when in
sense. one's insides something is felt moving, it
would be hard to say what, where, or in how many
dimensions. In dizziness and dreams there are lapsing
pictorial spaces; in semi-consciousness there are unmapped unrelated spaces waxing and vanishing. It is
not only the latitude and longitude of visionary places
that are unassignable, but their spatial quality that is
unearthly: the talk about flat-land and four dimensions
is but a thin scientific parody of the uncertainty of
animal sense. Even in rational human experience, the
living intuition of space is endlessly qualified. There
is the scene-painter's space, divided into a few distinct
planes in the direction of vision, but vague beyond and
non-existent behind the observer's back. At the theatre
the house is not in the same space as the play-scene, nor
in the same time—unless you break the dramatic spell,
and substitute the material stage and the paid actors
for the poetic world in which you ought to have been
living. Even in real life, space for most men stops at
the horizon; not sharply, for that would suggest a
beyond, but by fancy merely dying out, so that a beyond
is not needed, and in fact does not exist in that space.
It was in this way that the ancients conceived a round
heaven divided into concentric layers, without thinking
of the infinity beyond; for the empyrean, when that
was invented, was rather an ocean of light than an
abyss of nothingness. The views of storks about space
—and they must be valid pragmatically—would doubtless baffle us altogether, and the logic of them might
seem to us absurd when translated into our language.
Our own topographical knowledge is the fruit of accu-
mulation and synthesis, and doubtless truer of nature

as a whole, though perhaps less penetrating in some dimensions; and its precision renders us intolerant or forgetful of immediate experience even in ourselves. Only in tales or superstitions do we recover at times the elasticity of ignorance, and plunge innocently into as many pictorial spaces as may open out spontaneously before the mind. Even an intelligent man of action will sometimes stop to notice these unauthorised vistas with a humorous affection, as he might play with a child. Yet they may be, in their sporadic way, short cuts to things remote or future, incoherently but vividly reported, like Africa and Norway to the stork; and in any case they are collateral with the elements of our scientific conceptions. Pictures are to knowledge as sound is to language. *Some* true indication is contained in any sensation, since *something* must have happened materially to produce it; but knowledge, synthesis, choice of a centre, and range in apprehension are all adventitious to the existing object: they transfer it from physical to pictorial space, and transpose the parts of it perceived at all into terms of essence.

Pictorial space is one of the dearest possessions of the human spirit: it would be thankless of us to be impatient because it is subjective, as if it ought not to have been so. It might no doubt have had a different sensuous texture, and might have conveyed much the same practical information in that other guise; but it could hardly have been more beautiful than, to the human eye, are the colours of the spectrum, the forms of motion, and the spheres of shadow and of light. If our senses had dogged more faithfully the steps of mutation in matter, we may doubt whether they would have rendered so well the results and scope of those mutations, on the scale of the human body. In science, as in religion, little would be gained by an exchange of idols. Criticism would not be enlightening if it

Pictorial space is beautiful and perhaps transitory.

disgusted us with vision, or led us to quarrel with ideas because they are not things. Ideas are better than things; and one of the happiest fruits of existing in physical space is that pictorial spaces may be based upon it. The wise man is content with his native language: he would not be a better poet or a sharper judge in any other. Pictorial conventions would not have established themselves in the eye or brain if they could not be innocently and harmoniously associated with the business of life; they are to be smilingly welcomed, like strangers coming in the name of the Lord. But the Lord may presently send other messengers: pictorial conventions may vary from age to age and in different races, even if the universe at large is not much changed. Yet this deeper possibility, too, should be remembered by a spirit that would not put all its eggs in one basket: the measure of descriptive truth now possessed by pictorial space need not always belong to it. Its beauty is its own; but if the world fell back into chaos and reconstituted itself differently, our pictorial space would have become obsolete. Other conventions would flourish and other peacocks would spread their tails: all to the greater glory of intuition, so long as intuition survived.

I speak here impulsively of the future; but if the return to chaos were complete, if substance, which is the principle of continuity, were itself destroyed, then there would be no sense in saying that time in the second cosmos was future from the point of view of the first. This firstness and secondness would be reversible, and imputed only because I, from the outside, happened to think of one world before the other. It would be substance in me that alone would actually have passed from the thought of one to the thought of the other, and only my intuition would have connected their essences in a specious

In nature succession is dependent on derivation and mediated by matter.

time. As the space of neither world would lie in the space of the other, so the histories of the two worlds would run irrelevant courses, and be neither before nor after each other, nor simultaneous. For by physical time I understand an order of derivation integral to the flux of matter; so that if two worlds had no material connection, and neither was in any of its parts derived from the other, they could not possibly have positions in the same physical time. The same essence of succession might be exhibited in both; the same kind of temporal vistas might perplex the sentimental inhabitants of each of them; but no date in one would coincide with a date in the other, nor would their respective temporal scales and rates of precipitation have any common measure.

The notion that there is and can be but one time, and that half of it is always intrinsically past and the other half always intrinsically future, belongs to the normal pathology of an animal mind: Specious time, with its moral contrast between past and future, is a vista in the animal mind. it marks the egotistical outlook of an active being endowed with imagination. Such a being will project the moral contrast produced by his momentary absorption in action upon the conditions and history of that action, and upon the universe at large. A perspective of hope and one of reminiscence continually divide for him a specious eternity; and for him the dramatic centre of existence, though always at a different point in physical time, will always be precisely in himself.

Presentness is the coming, lasting, or passing away of an essence, either in matter or in intuition. This presentness is a character intrinsic to all existence, since an essence would not be exemplified in any particular instance unless it came into, or went out of, a medium alien to it. Such coming and going, with the interval (if
Existence and change are intrinsically present.

any) between, constitute the exemplification of that essence, either in the realm of matter or in that of spirit. Thus presentness, taken absolutely, is another name for the actuality which every event possesses in its own day, and which gives it its place for ever in the realm of truth. But taken relatively, as it is more natural to take it, presentness is rather a name for the middle position which every moment of existence occupies between its sources and its results. This presentness is pervasive; a moment does not fail to be eternally present because it never was and never can be present at any other moment. This is the ubiquity of actuality, or if you will, of selfishness: because that very leap and cry which brings each moment to birth cuts it off from everything else; the rest becomes, and must for ever remain, external to it. And this division is as requisite as this actuality: the moment does not, as if by some sin or delusion, cut itself off from some placid unitary continuum in which it ought to have remained embedded; it is not a fragment torn from eternity. On the contrary, its place in eternity is established by that severance. It is one wave in a sea that is nothing but waves. That from which it cuts itself off cuts itself off from it in turn, by the same necessity of its being; and every part of that remainder, with the very same leap and cry, cuts itself off from every other part.

Now life is a rich and complex instance of this precipitation and self-assertion, and of this pervasive presentness. Intuition, when it arises, arises within a physical moment, and expresses a passing condition of the psyche. Feelings and thoughts are parts of natural events; they belong to the self which generates them in one of its physical phases. Intuition creates a synthesis in present sensibility; it is an act of attention occurring here and now. It has not, intrinsically,

Intuition shares this physical presentness, but may conceive temporal perspectives.

any miraculous transcendence, as if it spontaneously revealed distant things as they are or were or shall be. Yet in expressing the moment intuition evokes essences; and these essences, coming as they come in the heat of action, and attributed as they are to the objects of physical pursuit or physical attention, may bring tidings of facts at any distance. Within the life of the organism this distance is primarily a distance in physical time—a distance which intuition synthesises in the feeling of duration. For the animal psyche is retentive and wound up to go on; she is full of survivals and preparations. This gathered experience and this potentiality work within her automatically: but sometimes she becomes aware of them in part, in so far as she learns to project given essences and to develop spatial and temporal perspectives within the specious field of the moment.

This feat is made easy by the frequent complexity of the specious field, in which one feature may be seen to vanish or to appear whilst others persist. The essence of change includes a direction in the felt substitution of term for term; it therefore includes the notion of the earlier absence of something now given, and of the earlier presence of something now absent. This is the very sense of existence and of time, and the key to all intelligence and dominion over reality. It contains *the principle* of transitive knowledge, since the present is aware of the past, and I in this condition think of myself in another condition; and it supplies *an instance* of transitive cognition which is knowledge in the sense of being true; because the essence of transition given in intuition is elicited directly by actual partial transitions in the state of the psyche, and this psyche is a congruent part of nature; so that when the essence of transition given now is projected over all physical time, it is plausibly projected and has every chance of being true.

Thus sentimental time is a genuine, if poetical, version of the march of existence, even as pictorial space is a genuine, if poetical, version of its distribution. The views taken are short, especially towards the future, but being extensible they suggest well enough the unfathomable depths of physical time in both directions; and if the views, being views, must be taken from some arbitrary point, they may be exchanged for one another, thus annulling the bias of each, in so far as the others contradict it. I am far from wishing to assert that the remainder or resultant will be the essence of physical time; but for human purposes a just view enough is obtained if we remember that each *now* and *here* is called so only by one voice, and that all other voices call it a *then* and a *there*. It is inevitable, and yet outrageous, that every day and year, every opinion and interest, should think itself alone truly alive and alone basking in the noon of reality. The present is indeed a true focus, an actual consummation, in so far as spirit is awake in it; and it could not have a universal scope if it had not a particular foundation. To uproot intuition from its soil in animal life would be to kill it, or if somehow it were alleged to survive, to render it homeless in the realm of matter. The body is not a prison only, but a watchtower; and the spirit would live in darkness or die of inanition if it could not open the trap-door of action, downwards towards its foundations and food in matter; or if it could not open the two windows of time, eastward and westward, towards rising or sinking constellations. It is no cruel fate, but its own nature, that imprisons life in the moment, and prevents it from taking just cognisance of any other time save by a great effort of intelligence.

If the present could see the past and the future truly, it would not feel its own pre-eminence; it would

A dramatic view of time is natural and proper to an animal spirit.

substitute their intrinsic essences for the essences of their effects within its own compass, or for its anticipations of them. It would thereby cease to be this waking moment in this animal life, and would rise into a preternatural impartiality and ubiquity. For the double aerial perspective in which a living moment sees the future and the past is a false perspective; it paints in evanescent colours what is in fact a steady procession of realities, all equally vivid and complete; it renders the past faded and dead, and the future uncertain and non-existent. But this is egregious egotism and animal blindness. The past is not faded, except in the eye of the present, and the future is not ambiguous, except to ignorant conjecture. Yet it is only by conjecture or confused reminiscence that the present is able to conceive them. The present had to choose between misrepresentation and blindness: for if it had not seen the past and future in a selfish perspective, it could not have been aware of them at all. In the romantic guise of what is not yet or what is no longer, the fleeting moment is able to recognise outlying existences, and to indicate to its own spirit the direction in which they lie. Flux, by its very essence, cannot be synthesised; it must be undergone. The animal egotism which gives it a centre now and not then, contrary to fact, yet enables the passage from then to now, and from now onwards to another now, to be given in a dramatic synthesis—a synthesis which actual succession excludes. But without synthesis there is no intuition, no feeling: so that the sentimental perspectives of time are the only available forms in which a physical flux could be reported to the spirit.

The least sentimental term in sentimental time is the term *now*, because it marks the junction of fancy with action. *Now* is often a word of command; it

[margin note: Its error is due to relativity, and relativity is necessary to its existence.]

leans towards the future, and seems to be the voice of the present summoning the next moment to arise, and pouncing upon it when it does so. For *now* has in it emotionally all the cheeriness of material change: it comes out of the past as if impatient at not having come sooner, and it passes into the future with alacrity, as if confident of losing nothing by moving on. For it is evident that actual succession can contain nothing but *nows*, so that *now* in a certain way is immortal. But this immortality is only a continual reiteration, a series of moments each without self-possession and without assurance of any other moment; so that if ever the *now* loses its indicative practical force and becomes introspective, it becomes acutely sentimental, a perpetual hope unrealised and a perpetual dying.

The joyous now.

Various other modes of felt time cluster round this travelling *now*. *Just now*, for instance, is already retrospective, and marks a condition of things no longer quite in hand, already an object of intent and of questionable knowledge, yet still so near, that any mistake about it would be more like an illusion of sense than like a false assertion. *Just now* is like a spoken word lingering in the ear, so distinctly that what it was may still be observed, and described by inspection; and yet the description arising is distinguishable from it, and the two may be compared within the field of intuition. For though the voice is silent, I am still able to hear it inwardly; and its increasing uncertainty, its evanescence, is a notable part of what I perceive. At last the reverberation becomes inaudible, and I have only an image formed at intervals by silently repeating the word. If I am able to repeat it, it is not because I can mentally remember it, but I remember it mentally because I am able to repeat it physically. This muted repetition is thereafter my physical

The foreground of absent time.

memory of what that sound was at its loudest; it
suggests the glorious *then*, contrasted with this silent
and empty *now*.

The psyche is full of potential experience—pictures
which she is ready to paint and would wish to hang—
but the question is where, in those vast vague Its middle
galleries of fancied time, she shall hang them. distance.
When the picture is composed and, so to speak, in her
hand, but she can find no hook for it in the direction
of action, she says *not yet*; and unless she drops and
forgets it, she may go on to say *soon*, or *some day*; or
if, diabolically, the place it was about to occupy appears
otherwise filled, she may cry, *too late*. There are
corresponding removes and vacillations in the direction
of the past, where active impulses are not engaged.
A risen image looks for points of attachment in the
realm of truth; the sentimental mind would hardly
entertain it, unless it could pass for somebody's ghost.
A place can be found for almost anything in the fog
of distance, and the most miraculous tale begins with
once upon a time. There is hardly more definiteness,
with added melancholy, in saying *long ago*. The
event has sunk, for sentiment, below the horizon, into
the night where everything sleeps which, though theoretically credited, is not relevant to present action.

All, however, is not flaccidity and weakness in
sentimental time; it has its noble notes in the sublime
always and the tragic *never*. These terms, Imaginary
when true, describe facts in physical time, tragic
and their force comes from that backing, but survey of
it in its
not their sentimental colour; for there is entirety.
nothing tragic in the mere absence of anything from
the universe, and nothing sublime in the presence
there of such elements as may happen to be pervasive,
like matter and change. The sublimity or tragedy
comes from projecting sentimental time, with its
human centre, upon the canvas of nature. *Never* then

proclaims an ultimate despair or relief.   It professes to
banish from the whole past or future some essence
now vividly present to the mind, tempting or horrible;
and the living roots of that possibility here in the soul
render the denial of it in nature violent and marvellous.
That something arresting to thought should be absent
from the field of action causes a cruel division in the
animal spirit; for this spirit can live only by grace of
material circumstances, yet, being a spirit, it can live
only by distinguishing eternal essences.   Its joy lies
in being perpetually promoted to intuition and confirmed in it; but it is distracted if its intuitions are
thwarted, and expel or contradict one another.   Therefore, whenever the spirit finds some steadfast feature
in the world, it breathes, even in the midst of action
and discovery, its native air.   That which exists always,
even if only a type or a law, seems almost raised above
existence: *always* assimilates time to eternity.   Imagination then flatters itself that it dominates the universe,
as it was in the beginning, is now, and ever shall be.
In fact, imagination can never synthesise anything
but its own vistas, in a specious, not a physical time;
but, if the vista had happened to be true, and if physical
time had repeated endlessly the feature now singly
conceived, thought would have marvellously domesticated that crawling monster, prescribing, or seeming to prescribe, how and how far it should uncoil
itself.   In respect to the whole flux of existence such
a boast is gratuitous; but it may be justified in respect
to that field of action on which the spirit immediately
depends.

    Spirit, however scattered its occasions and instances
may be, is always synthetic in its intellectual energy
The   or actuality: it gives the form of totality to
specious its world.   The frontiers may be vague and
present. the features confused, but they could not be
confused or vague if they were not features and frontiers

of a single scene. Synthesis is a prerequisite to the sensation of change. An image of motion or a feeling of lapse is a single feeling and a single image. That exciting experience in which *now*, *now*, keeps ringing like a bell would not be a strained experience of the mind, nor more than so many fresh experiences, if the iteration were not synthesised, each stroke being received by a sensorium already alive, and as it were elastic, so that the dying strokes and others imminent formed with the fresh stroke a single temporal landscape, a wide indefinite *now* open to intuition, which psychologists call the specious present. This intuition no doubt has its basis in the datable physical moment, in a definite phase of the organism; but the temporal landscape given in it is ideal, and has no date and no clear limits; indeed, it is a miniature of all time, as imagination might survey and picture it. A few more details on the same canvas, a closer attention to the remoter vistas, and this specious present might contain all knowledge. All that the most learned historian or the deepest theologian has ever actually conceived must have come to him in the specious present. Unless action concentrates the attention on the forward edge of this prospect, on the budding *now*, the whole leans rather towards the past, and grows more and more extended. It becomes full of things vain for our present purpose. Even when action or scientific observation rescue the specious present from this sentimentality, they leave it ideal, and its field a purely sensuous unit.

Action and scientific observation, though framed within the specious present in perception, ignore it in practice; but arts like music and eloquence Its possible are directed (without knowing it) to enriching richness, this specious present and rendering it, in emotional and some climax, so overwhelmingly pregnant æsthetic. and brilliant, that scientific observation and action

become impossible; as if the flux of things had cul-
minated, collected all its treasures, and wished, at least
for a moment, to stop and possess them. Under such
tension, when the spirit takes flight towards its proper
objects, essence and truth, the body, which cannot
follow, bursts into irrelevant action, such as tears or
applause or laughter or contortions. Synthesis, which
must be material before it can be spiritual, has then
brought to a head more currents than can flow into
any useful channel, and some random outlet must be
found for that physical fullness and that physical impotence. Meantime intuition shines in all its glory.
On lesser occasions, when attention lights up some
particular path in the field of action, spirit, being all
eagerness and appetition, almost seems to be a form of
energy or source of motion in matter. But the fact
that it is always wholly contemplative becomes evident
in its richer moments; for then the specious present
extends far beyond the urgent occasion for action, and
may even drop its conscious relevance to the person
or the hour; and at the same time its vistas will cease
to be sentimental, because the survey of them will have
become intellectual and impartially receptive.

The specious present is dateless, but it is temporal;[1]
it is the vaguely limited foreground of sentimental
time. In it the precipitation proper to existence, the ticking of the great clock is
clearly audible: the bodily feeling of the
moment is complicated in it by after-images
of instants receding, and strained by anticipation of instants to come. As the psyche
can synthesise in memory the fading impressions
that reverberate within her, so she can prefigure and
rehearse the acts for which she is making ready. A
pleasant rumble and a large assurance thus pervade

Flux, synthesised in the specious present, yields the perception of flux.

---

[1] For the exact force of these terms, see *Scepticism and Animal Faith*, p. 270.

animal consciousness in its calmer moments. There is no knife-edge here of present time, nor any exact frontiers, but a virtual possession of the past and even of the future; because the psyche is magnificently confident not only that a future will be forthcoming, but that its paces will be familiar, and easy to deal with; in fact she is quietly putting irons in the fire, and means to have a hand in shaping it. The general character of the future is felt to be as sure as the ebb and flow of the tide, or as the rest of a sentence half spoken; and this assurance, which might seem groundless, is not so, because the psyche is not a detached spirit, examining the world by the light of some absolute logic. She is herself a material engine, a part of that substantial flux which exists only by bridging its intervals, and is defined as much by what it becomes as by what it may have been. That future which is in part her product is, in that measure, her substance transformed, or by its action transforming the surrounding substance.

At bottom, then, the future is no new event, but the rest of this transformation. In an organism like the psyche, it is the present pregnancy of matter that determines the further develop- *The involution of events in the psyche renders her capable of true memory and prophecy.* ment of its forms. Of course this development may be cut short at any point by contacts with other organisms, or with the inorganic; and then, if the psyche survives, she will be diverted in some new direction, at first violent and unpredictable. But if she could understand fully all the substance of which she is a portion, she would dominate in the specious present the remotest future of her universe, as well as its deepest past; for physical time is nothing but the deployment of substance, and the essence of this substance is the form which, if free, it would realise in its deployment. The psyche, then, is not radically deceived in her somnolent confidence in the future, nor in her conviction that she helps to determine it. The future may be largely foreseen, or brought about as intended, even as the past may be largely remembered; the psyche has materials within the moment for both those temporal vistas. It is her egotism here that is in error rather than her faith; for the vivacity of her wishes or momentary fancies may obscure her sense for things at a distance; and beyond the chance limits of the specious present, she may think the future indeterminate and unreal, and the past dead.

The dead past? Certainly all years prior to A.D. 1920 are past at the time when I write these words, and all later years are future, and to me uncertain; yet the reader knows that one of the years perhaps long subsequent to 1920 is as living and sure as 1920 is to me now. My problematic future will be his living present, and both presently a third man's irrevocable past. There is no moment in the whole course of nature (unless there be a first and a last moment) which is not both future and past for an infinity of other moments. In itself, by virtue of its emergence in a world of change, each moment is unstably present, or in the act of elapsing; and by virtue of its position in the order of generation, both pastness and futurity pervade it eternally. Such double abysmal absence is the price which existence pays for its momentary emphasis. Futurity and pastness, the reproach of being not yet and being no longer, fall upon it from different quarters, like lights of different colours; and these same colours, like the red light and the green light of a ship, it itself carries and spreads in opposite directions. And these shafts cross one another with a sort of correspondence in contradiction: the moments which any moment calls past call it future, and those which it calls future call it past.

Contradictory epithets of this sort are compatible

[margin note: Cross-lights of pastness and futurity.]

when they are seen to be relative; but it must be understood that they are the relative aspects of something
which has an absolute nature of its own, to Events can
be the foundation of those relations. And be truly
the absolute nature of moments is to be past or
future only
present: a moment which was not present in relatively,
itself could not be truly past or future in and in case
they are in-
relation to other moments. What I call the trinsically
past and what I call the future are truly past present.
or future *from here*; but if they were *only* past or *only*
future, it would be an egregious error on my part to
believe that they were past or future at all, for they
would exist only in my present memory or expectation.
In their pastness and futurity they would be merely
specious, and they would be nothing but parts of a
present image. If I pretended that they recalled or
forecast anything, I should be deceived; for nothing
of that kind, either in the past or in the future, would
ever rejoice in presentness and exist on its own account.
Thus only false memory and false expectation end in
events intrinsically past or intrinsically future—that is
to say, intrinsically sentimental. False legends and
false hopes indeed have their being only in perspective;
their only substance is the thought of them now, and
it is only as absent that they are ever present.

Romantic idealism, which saturates modern speculation even when not avowed, if it were not halting
and ambiguous, would reduce all time to the Sentimental
picture of time, and establish the solipsism time is the
of the present moment. And the present only time
recognised
moment indeed includes and absorbs all senti- by modern
mental time: apart from its vistas, neither idealism.
the past nor the future would be at all romantic or
unreal. Common sense admits this in respect to the
past. The equal reality of the past with the present,
and its fixity of essence, so that ideas of it may be false
or true, are not seriously questioned. But in respect

to the future, imagination is less respectful of fact, and flounders in an abyss to which it attributes its own vagueness. The prevision which the psyche often has of its future actions, as in planning or calculation, ought to give steadiness to thoughts of the future, in as much as here the causes of future events are already found at work; and the ancients, who were not sentimental, cultivated policy and prophecy, endeavouring to define the future through its signs and causes, as we define the past through its memorials. But modern anticipations are based rather on supposed " laws ", or on intuition of divine purposes; that is, on forms found in the perspective of events, as synthesised in imagination: whereby physical time is asked to march to the music which sentimental time may pipe for it.

In reality, nature moves in a time of her own, everywhere equally present, of which sentimental time is a momentary echo; for sometimes a single pulse of substance may become conscious of its motion, and may fantastically endeavour to embrace the true past and the true future, necessarily external to it, in a single view. This sentimental agony fancy then transfers from its own flutterings to the brisk precipitation and the large somnolence of the general flux, which is neither regretful nor perturbed, and not intent on prolonging one of its phases rather than another. Animal life itself shares this conformity with the flux of things, whenever animal life is perfect; and even perfect intuition shares it, by entirely transmuting motion into light: so that both in rude health and in pure contemplation it either forgets the past and the future altogether, or ceases to be sentimental about them, and learns to feel their direct and native reality, as they feel it themselves.

But the healthy mind transcends it, both in living and in thinking.

CHAPTER V

THE FLUX OF EXISTENCE

SINCE all moments of physical time are intrinsically present, it might seem that real existence was not changeful at all but only, perhaps, asymmetrical, like a frieze of sculptured arrows all pointing one way, or a file of halted soldiers lifting one foot for ever, as if they had meant to march. The illusion of successive events would be produced by the eye glancing along the frieze or the reviewing officer passing down the line. *Hypothesis of a static world in which the sense of change would be an illusion.* This ancient persuasion is founded on much moral reflexion and is appropriate to the intellect composing and recomposing its views of the truth. The realm of truth is indeed eternal and static, and the exploring spirit may traverse it by one or another narrow path in a thousand directions without adding, removing, or changing a single feature of that indestructible labyrinth. But in regard to the realm of existence this suggestion is inapplicable and radically perverse. Indeed, even on this hypothesis, flux would not be abolished but only transferred from the panorama of facts to the living spirit which, in gradually discovering them, would be really passing through a succession of different states. All the questions concerning change, time, and existence would recur in respect to this experience and its temporal order; and the dignity of that eternal truth, arrogating to itself the name of reality, would not help at all to explain our passing illusions, and in comparison with their insistence might itself seem rather shadowy and unimportant.

Moreover, whence should reviewing officers or travelling eyes fetch their mobility, save from that The illusion very world which this hypothesis declares would still to be static? The gift of progressive obser-really change, and vation is no homeless miracle, no illusion this in without a ground; it is a faculty native and obedience to material appropriate to animals. It is quite true that causes. often a movement of attention produces an experience of change before an object, like an inscription, which is materially static; but then it is not a disembodied spirit that freely surveys that monument and notes its parts *seriatim*; an instinctive or trained movement of the eye imposes a temporal order on the words read. Only haste and lack of circumspection in conceiving what spirit is and how it moves could assign to it the origin of change. On the contrary, while spirit is extraordinarily mobile in its existence, it borrows this mobility from the hair-trigger organisation and unstable equilibrium of its organs, and of the stimulations which excite them incessantly. In its own nature, spirit arrests the flux of things, as best it may, in its intuitions, and turns it into a store of synthetic pictures and symbols, sensuous and intellectual. We may therefore say with more reason that the world imposes movement on a spirit which by its own genius would rather be addressed to the eternal, than say that reality seems successive only to a flighty spirit, turning distractedly the leaves of a book written in eternity. Matter, not spirit, is the seat and principle of the flux. Spirit, being an emanation of this flux, seems indeed a pilgrim wandering and almost lost in the wilderness of essence and in the dark treasure-house of truth; but in respect to the realm of matter, spirit is like a child asking questions and making pause, and often brutally run over and crushed by a rush of changes which it cannot understand.

So true is this that even the vistas of sentimental time, although the spirit creates them in its effort to dominate and synthesise the flux of things, yet trouble it a little and seem disquieting. To intense contemplation, memory and pro- phecy come forward and become present, and the present itself recedes into a wonderful unreality and becomes truth. Everything stands together, like a thing accomplished. Prophets do not predict but see, and cry out, even if the vision be of the last day of creation: Behold, the trump blew, and the heavens fell. Such pictorial pro- phecy, like pictorial memory, is a state of trance: it takes us out of changing time altogether, as it is the function of spirit to take us, either into the realm of truth, if the memories or prophecies are clairvoyant, or else into the realm of essence, if they are false fancies. Meantime historical events, since they are conventional stretches containing variations, continually lose and continually gain existence, never being complete and comprehensive, as is the truth about them. They cannot be gathered up or understood, even by those who enact them, without being sublimated and con- gealed into their historical essences and forfeiting their natural flux. The dramatic direction which they may retain in visionary memory, like the visible lack of symmetry in the file of halted soldiers or in the sculp- tured arrows, suggests a movement to the observer only because it induces him to perform one in his survey; but the direction of this survey is reversible, like a film for the cinema. The asymmetrical forms themselves contain no precipitation; they do not destroy and traverse themselves, or take one another's places. They are only a synthetic model or fossil of change.

Spirit endures change but, as far as possible, synthesises it into the truth about it.

Modern philosophers, being contemptuous of essences and without a clear conception of them, usually Hypothesis of an absolute time in which loose facts take their places. assume the reality of change and succession without much scrutiny; they do not stop to inquire where and by what juxtaposition the quality abandoned yields to the quality acquired. If we venture to imagine what is probably in their minds, I think we shall come upon something like this: that the flux is composed of states of existence, mental, material, or simply qualitative, each of which is a unit and contains no variation; yet they succeed and replace one another because they arise in an underlying pervasive medium, absolute time, which itself lapses inherently and inevitably at a uniform rate, so that all its moments are already dated, and at a precise remove from one another. When states of mind or matter or neutral phenomena arise, they must therefore arise at one or another of these dated instants. Although each fact is an absolute reality in itself, and with no intrinsic relevance to any other fact, yet any of them may be successive or simultaneous, if they occur at identical or successive moments in that ever-flowing irreversible time.

This conception of a pure yet physical time, in which events of any sort may arise and take their Its futility. places, needs only to be described and inspected for it to dissolve into puzzles. Each of its moments would be exactly like every other: far from measuring a scale of duration, they would collapse into identity. I have already indicated the sensuous origin and specious character of this ghost: it is an after-image of the *sensation* of time. But let me now admit the hypothesis of such an intuitive phantom being substantial, and the prior locus of all existence. Events will now be rendered successive simply by their position in pure time, apart from any inner continuity or derivation of one from another; and the absolute date of each will be the sole character in it by virtue of which it may be pronounced the source or the result of any other. But absolute dates are intrinsically indiscernible and different only in that one is earlier and another later; so that concrete events will be arranged in sequence only by virtue of a character in them which is absolutely indistinguishable.

Here a subtler suggestion might be made by idealists. Succession, they might say, is a relation between the *characters* of events. As existences, all states of spirit—and for the idealist no other existences are possible—are self-created and, in status, eternal; they are fragments of the one universal mind; but each may be temporal in its deliverance or in the picture it unfolds. If we could compare these scattered spiritual acts—as the idealist is always doing, although on his principles it would be impossible—we should see correspondences, developments, and contradictions in their objects. A feature central in one view might be recognised as the same as a feature quite marginal and faint in another view: the pictured future there might be the living present here, and the pictured past here, in some measure, the present there. Comparing and, as it were, matching these pictures by their rims, we might compose a tolerably continuous landscape; and by identifying the original states of spirit, actually existing each for itself, with those ideal elements which they supplied to this panorama—another illegitimate habit of idealists—we might attribute to those existing states the dates of their objects, as these reappear in our own synthesis. Thus we think to cast specious time, like a butterfly-net, over spirits freely fluttering and dateless in themselves, which altogether escape it: they are not rendered successive by the fact that some of them may repeat the beginning and some the end of what, in our survey, seems a single story.

Hypothesis that succession is a correspondence of perspectives among dateless moments.

It explains away succession and abolishes nature.

It is imperative, then, if we wish to understand existence and the succession of its moments, to disregard any synthesis created in imagination between the essences of these moments, or between what are supposed to have been their essences. Actual succession is a substitution, not a perspective. Now, when this transcendental synthetic glance is discounted, are there other elements left in the experience of change which might serve to describe fitly the nature of a flux actual and physical?

The real flux cannot be synthetised.

Certainly there are such intuitions, else even the most tentative and modest approach to an understanding of nature would be denied us. The feeling of persistence or sheer duration is such an intuition. This feeling is more complex than the insight into the eternity of a given essence, in which there is no drag. It is rather a sense of iteration or failure to lapse in something properly transitory: a strange and questionable arrest where movement is latent or imminent. Such a sense of persistence may become tedious, sublime, or excruciating; it includes an acute tension or sense of existence. It is therefore an admirable expression of the life of nature, emphasising the continuity not without implying the variation. It marks the fact that the flux of existence, although it really never stops, often sustains certain recognisable forms, such as the psyche herself, in a precarious being.

How expressed in the feeling of duration.

The counterpart of continuity, interruption, has the same implication. Total catastrophes in nature might occur; but a wholly new world would not remember or suspect its previous non-existence. The great advance in understanding comes when intuition reveals change in some single respect within a constant object. Doubtless, in strictness, when the world changes in any particular its total essence is renewed, since its balance becomes another; yet the new total essence is—and must be, if

How expressed in felt modifications.

the world is to be consecutive—largely similar to the old one; and this not by a groundless accident or magic law, but because the matter of the earlier phase is inherited by the later. This matter, which alone renders either phase a fact and not a mere essence, carries with it its quantity, its energy, and a progressive redistribution of its parts; so that the very principle of genesis, in lending to each moment of the flux its physical existence, determines the essence which it shall exemplify, and determines it in virtue of the continuity and heredity which must bind moments together materially if they are to be successive chronologically. The same material heritage also determines in what measure or in what detail each successive moment shall differ from the previous one, or how far it shall merely repeat it; and it renders the world, throughout its moments, somewhat amenable to addition, subtraction, multiplication, and division.

If it is true that we cannot bathe twice in the same river, because the water has flowed on, it is true also that the same water which was formerly here is now farther down; so that we might bathe in it again if only we ran down the bank with greater celerity than the water. But our second plunge, though into the same water, would be at another point in the stream: and it is this combination of continuity with instability that we indicate when we speak of a river or a flux. The dialectic of continuity— whether it may be analysed into an infinite number of discrete points or into an indefinite number of intervals —was probably not considered by nature before she began to exist: there is therefore no need to consider it in describing existence. Continuity, for the naturalist, is merely a name for the fact that existence is a transmitted burden, something that goes on and is kept up. In the midst of death we are in life; destruction and

Physical continuity, which is not dialectical, includes instability, and physical change includes continuity.

change are never so complete at any moment as not to continue the previous reality. If each moment made a wholly fresh beginning it would not be a moment in a flux, but simply one member in an original multitude of beings.

Now, this hereditary nature of existence—each moment being *genitum non factum*—is rudely represented in intuition by any phenomenon which partly changes and partly seems to remain the same. Common sense hypostatises this intuition, when it traces and recognises persons and things, supposed to remain identical in a maze of changing relations; and science only carries this inevitable hypostasis a step further when it conceives permanent atoms, or permanent laws, sustaining the flux of things and keeping it continuous and intelligible. Such science is conscientious fiction: there are presumably no atoms and no laws separable from the concrete strains and movements of the flux, by which its substance is intimately modified; but this substance being hereditary, each of its moments assumes a form derived from the previous posture of things, and offering to observation innumerable repetitions, calculable changes, and familiar habits: otherwise neither life nor observation could ever have arisen in the midst of chaos to take note of its existence.

Moving sensible units bear witness to these hereditary modes of flux.

Substance, with its intrinsic deployment and heredity, would certainly remain mysterious to us even if we could inspect it at close quarters, because it involves an unintelligible alloy added to whatever essences we might assign to it. As things stand, however, the mystery is darkened by the great difference in scale between the texture of matter and that of human ideas; and when in mathematics, we pursue and almost seem to attain that inhuman reality, we find ourselves in possession of a perfect method of notation from which everything

Evolution and law are summary views of material derivation.

to be noted has disappeared; and the only truth of our most accurate science turns out to be practical and utterly blind. We must revert, in order to recover our sanity and the subject-matter of our natural science, to crude experience and to the common arts; and here everything is on the human scale. Sunset and sunrise, the obvious repetitions in the generations of men and animals, and in their stock passions, hide movements which in nature are probably knit unbrokenly together, and never quite alike, or obedient to any disembodied law. Seen on the human scale, repetitions are perfectly inexplicable: they suggest to the gaping mind a magical control of events by a monotonous destiny: they suggest superstition. But beneath these trite measures, which human wit casts over things, like a net of proverbs, the natural flux goes its own pace, uncontrolled by any magic or logic. It is *natural*: it passes everywhere from what it was at that point, as the conjunction of elements there prompts it to do, never asking whether that conjunction is new or habitual. It knows no desire for novelty, no obsession by rule; it is as willing to run into repetitions as into catastrophes, and it is as likely to suggest to gross observation a law in one place as a purpose in another. Its order in one place may produce a mind to which its general order seems a chaos.

Physical time is another name for this native instability of matter, which, since it has distinct stations or phases, may be observed by spirit, and since it falls into recurring rhythms may be measured by its own stride. These stages and rhythms are essences; and it is in terms of essence that any possible physics is condemned to describe nature; but the description becomes true in so far as these or equivalent essences are actually embodied in the field of action. It is only by such embodiment in matter that essences

The flux of matter first lends existence to such essences as may define it.

can be loosened, as it were, from their essential setting and turned into the characters of facts; or rather—since their essential setting is eternal and holds them even while embodiments of them are passing through existence—it is only by being distributed in the field of action that essences can add for a moment external and variable relations to those which their proper nature involves.

This descent or incarnation of essences cannot be their own doing, since all essences are inert and non-existent. Even in a dream the objects that impose themselves successively on the spirit, being purely imaginary, have no power to maintain themselves or to generate one another, any more than one word or note in the air has the power, in the absence of a vocal instrument, to breed the next word or the next note. It is the slumbering material psyche that generates those feelings and images out of her disquiet, as when awake she generates those words or notes out of her material exuberance; were it not for her stored troubles no insane anxieties or absurd vicissitudes would disturb her sleep. Even the thinnest creations of spirit, therefore, are products of the realm of matter, and possible only within it. Incarnation is no voluntary emanation from above; it is a dire event, a budding torment, here below. A world of accidents, arbitrary and treacherous, first lends to the eternal a temporal existence and a place in the flux.

Particularity and transition are inherent in this nether form of being. Everything that arises is liable to lapse; everything that exists exists by con-junction with other things on its own plane; it belongs somewhere and to a certain time by virtue of the external relations which pin it there. From this an important consequence follows: Existence can have no general or stable medium deeper than itself, such as an absolute space or time through

The flux flows through no prior medium.

which it should flow and which in some respects would control its formation. The flux is itself absolute and the seat of existence: the substance which flows through things cannot exist between them. It bestows on them their hereditary qualities and quantities, and their place in nature. Without substance each phenomenon would be an insulated essence, lacking all force or movement, either internal or transcendent, and incapable of existing in itself or of imposing itself at any particular moment on any particular mind. But the counterpart is no less true: without those exchangeable forms, without running through those distinct states and positions, substance in turn would fade into an essence. Far from being the natural parent of all scattered particular facts, it would be the impotent possibility of their forms only. It would not be that pregnant and labouring matter which fills the world, but the essence at the opposite end of the ontological scale, pure Being, in which all essences are indeed contained, as it were, in solution, but in which none is suffered to come forward with an irrational emphasis, and impudently to exist. In order to exist substance itself must be something in particular, exclusive at each point of what it is at all others.

Having no prior conditions, existence at each node or centre is what it happens to be, showing such a form, energy, intensity, or consciousness as it happens to show. *It may take any course and contain any events whatsoever.* We must consider and inspect each part separately, by transporting ourselves into it at least ideally, before we can say what that part is intrinsically, or how many parts there are, or what is their order. Relations the facts must indeed have, if they are many: first, the relations eternally contrasting their several essences; and secondly, those accidental and variable relations which render these facts existing instances of their essences, and parts of one fluid world. All the axioms of philosophers declaring the world to be necessarily infinite or everlasting or rational or conscious must be received as applying only to their respective systems: the world meantime is just what it is, has been what it has been, and will be what it will be.

Yet, while the character of each fact is self-declared, its place among other facts (such as our belief in it) depends on contacts and transitions between it and the rest of its world. Did it not come from something different and did it not empty itself into something else, it would not contain within itself that stress, that incompleteness, that pervasive mortality, which precisely mark it as actual and living, and both more and less than a pure essence.

Yet in being realised every essence must acquire natural relations.

If each moment of existence is a centre, and self-assertive, it is so by being a focus of rays gathered into it from external sources and discharged again into eventual effects. By virtue of these connections and transmissions its place is fixed in the flux, and it vindicates its right to be called existent, since it is discoverable, measurable, and dated. All that it possesses besides—its intrinsic essence, its originality, its feeling, if it has feeling—is hidden from the world, escapes physics altogether, and merely marks its degree of inspiration: I mean, how much of the eternal it has managed, in passing, to draw down into itself, to illustrate, or to discover.

How express in human language (all the terms of which, unless they are proper names, designate essences) this mixture of self-assertion and instability proper to any moment of existence? The classic expedient is to analyse existence into matter and form, the matter being transmissible and serving to connect moment with moment and to render the later the offspring of the earlier, while the form serves to characterise each moment and give it individuality

Though all existing matter has form it is condemned endlessly to pass from one form to another.

and limits. This is a correct and—as might be seen by reviewing the alternatives—an inevitable way of expressing the nature of change in rhetorical terms. To the senses, to the passions, to the defining intellect the flux of existence is indeed a flight of eternal essences across a permanent screen, in which alone they have their momentary existence—a screen which sometimes seems to be the vague universe and sometimes one's own soul. Yet these categories, being logical or poetical, are not important to the naturalist. No doubt the naturalist too may speak of forms and of matter; but his forms are aggregates, themselves arising and breaking up; and his matter is something existent, the matter actually transmitted and transmuted by nutrition, generation, or labour. This matter everywhere has a particular quality, structure, and potency; and it not only possesses form, as a geometrical solid possesses it, but it is informed with the peculiar essence of existence also, which includes inner instability. For it is by its place, size, energy, and growth by material composition —qualities all involving external and variable relations —that a geometrical body existing differs from a geometrical solid defined. Aristotle himself derived the existence of any particular thing or substance not from its metaphysical components but from prior complete natural beings; and he even assigned to this ancestral matter what seems to us too fixed a form, since he did not admit any evolution of species. Even if by chance he had been right in respect to the natural history of earthly animals, the same matter in other cycles or in other worlds might evidently have displayed a different morphology. The matter which by taking a particular form becomes a particular thing need never have worn that form before and may never wear it again. Its career is open towards the infinite. Though at each moment it must be something specific, yet, if we consider its unknown plastic stress and the incalculable accidents to which it may be subject, we shall hardly be able to hold it down to any other enduring characters than those involved in its distinctive function: which is to lend existence to certain essences in a certain order, and enable them to succeed and to confront one another in a competitive world.

How penetrate into the inner flow of this existence? Sensuous, dialectical, or moral views of it, however legiti-

This flux not to be understood in graphic terms. mate, are necessarily summary, superficial, and poetical, being created by a psyche biassed and synthetic in her reactions. Mathematical views are more impartial, but wretchedly abstract. Thus, for instance, number is a just category to apply to the field of action, since its elements move as units, but it is a miserable essence to substitute for them. Accurate science has this defect, that it seems to describe the distribution of units of nothing, and to record averages in movements that elude sense, and yet are conceived and posited only in reference to pictorial objects. Meantime existence is no spectacle, though spectacles and calculations may amuse or describe it. In ourselves, and in the objects on our own plane encountered in action, existence is a strain and an incubus, particular, self-centred, substantial. It is in terms of such existence, unstable but burdened and concrete, that an unsophisticated natural philosophy might conceive the realm of matter.

If there is to be lapse, the flux at each point must possess an essence from which it lapses. These points,

Idea of a natural moment. which are the terms of any possible change, I will call *natural moments*. By natural moments, I do not mean instants or cross-sections of the whole flux, where everything is supposed simultaneous; I mean rather any concrete but ultimate elements in the web of existence, within which there is no change or variation of essence, yet which are not merely their essences, but events exemplifying those essences, facts generated and dated in a general flux that outruns them on every side. Within each natural moment there can be no temporal divisions or scale; if a duration is assigned to it at all distinguishable from its intrinsic being, it must be assigned by virtue of some external measure or scale, drawn from an alien medium or perspective in which the moment is supposed to be embedded. In its own person, a natural moment may be called lasting or instantaneous with equal propriety; for its quality is unchangeable, and any variation would simply divide it into several natural moments; it contains no temporal diversity by which it could be collated with different points in a dated scale of time. On the other hand, this undivided moment has material continuity with other moments which generate it and which it generates, so that its life is but one incident, an indivisible beat between states of existence which are not itself yet are its closest kin.

In what does this kinship consist? Not merely in similarity, though some similarity—perhaps only quantitative—is doubtless involved in derivation. Its transitive essence. A natural moment may be followed by a catastrophe and by chaos. Nor is derivation mere juxtaposition, since we have seen that there is no prior medium in which this juxtaposition could occur. There must, then, be something in the inner nature of one natural moment that renders it the derivative from another natural moment, therefore called its source, and productive of a third natural moment which we therefore call its effect. Every natural moment is both traditional and propulsive. It has a beginning and an end, a head and a tail—the head turned towards the end, and the tail towards the beginning. These need not be distinct members within its body; they may be distinguished, like up and down, only by virtue of contrary contacts and tensions; for a natural moment bears quite opposite relations to its source and food on the one side, and to its effects or relics on the other. Many rays, as it were, are focussed in each explosion; and the spark dies by diffusion or excretion of the substance which lent it spasmodic being. Its essence is like that of a valve: it contains a reference to the direction in which matter may flow through it. The moment exists only in act, when the valve is a valve in function; and at that crisis it yields to pressure coming from one side only, while it opens out and empties itself only towards the other side. Or we might liken it to a hyphen or to the sign + ; essentially transitional, as it is existentially transitory. By essence, it overlooks its neighbours on either hand without trespassing on their ground. That a thing by its internal being should have reference to something external—a fact which in the case of knowledge gives so much trouble to logicians—is so far from being an anomaly or an exception that it is the indispensable condition of existing at all: because, apart from that transcendent tension or inherent instability, a natural moment would be simply its essence, and not the act of reaching and dropping that essence, as it must be if it exists or takes place in nature.

I do not think that analytically transition can be otherwise expressed than as a transformation of one thing into another, involving two natural moments, and leaving the bond between them obscure. But it is not analytically that transition may be understood; it is lost when its terms are divided; and yet it is no synthesis of these terms, but a generation—whatever that may be—of one term out of the other. Within each term, however, we may expect to find a synthetic symbol and counterpart of transition. Let me call it the *forward tension* of the natural moment. This name is not meant to attribute to the elements of the flux any

Transition though unintelligible, may be symbolised dramatically or scientifically: it comports a forward tension within the moment.

conscious effort or expectancy; they are restless without the feeling of unrest; yet the analogy implied in the metaphor must be a real analogy, since effort and expectancy are creatures and expressions of this very tension in the flux of matter, when it takes the form of a psyche. *Forward tension*, then, will designate fairly enough whatsoever corresponds, within a natural moment, to the external fact that it occurs between two others, one of which an observer would call its antecedent and the other its consequent. Such a synthetic burden, native to existence in its every node or concretion, may well be represented in physics by a quantum of potential energy, determined by some formula or equation; and we know that the ignorant psyche creates many a poetic index to this same burden in herself, when she conceives sentimental time, and all the dramatic perspectives that people the imagination; for it is only by virtue of the tensions concentrated within her own organism—her memory, will, and intelligence—that the psyche is able to paint a world, which she thinks real, on the canvas of intuition.

That the natural moment has a forward tension becomes the more plausible, or even certain, when we consider that we are describing elements of *existence* (not mathematical or dialectical patterns, which analysis might discover there) and that the field of existence is simply the field of action: for there is no doubt that in action a forward tension is inherent. Nor is it the agent only that has this movement; we have found that his partner in action, the brother-world on which he acts, must have it too, if they are to play the same game, and contribute to the same sequel. We may therefore confidently attribute the forward tension proper to our life to all the rest of nature, down to its primary elements, without attributing to those elements, or to that total,

The nature of natural moments may be found written large in the conventional or dramatic moments of human experience.

any specifically human quality.   On the contrary, that forward tension in us is precisely what we share with all matter, and what renders matter our great companion; for the realms of essence and of truth, to which the spirit looks when it suspends action, are not so much our companions or enemies in this world as our celestial monitors: their perpetual presence does not beset us here but, if we notice it, transports us there. We may therefore appeal to our experience of action on the human scale to suggest to us the nature of action even in the heart of matter, which a mere diminution of mathematical scale or use of the microscope may never reach.

Now, on the human scale, the most obvious units in action are men, and their forward tension is dramatically called their will.   A man's body, if we study it analytically, is enormously complex, and his will highly conditioned and insecure, so that he thinks it free; but if we take him and his will in the flush of action, as factors in the moral world, they count as units.   Each personage in history, each passion or interest in a man's life, may be called a conventional moment. Considered dramatically, each is a single phase of existence internally constant, through which existence is precipitated into its next phase.   How these conventional moments begin, how they end, how matter flows through them, and what determines their inner character while they last are all matters of common knowledge: we call them birth, death, food, and influence.   It is on this analogy that natural moments should be conceived, if we wish to avoid the extravagances of pure theory usurping the place of fact.

A man, with the forward tension of all his instincts
Birth and   and passions, notoriously springs from a seed;
death are   and he develops from the heart of that seed,
proper to   internally, as it transforms and organises the
all natural
moments.   food which comes to it and which it selects.
Seed and food: these are the conditions *a parte priori*

of a man's existence; a seed, to transmit the centre of organisation and impose its specific hereditary form; and food to supply suitable matter to pass through that form and sustain it in existence. So this conventional moment, this individual life, begins and is established: and how does it end? By dissolution, when that hereditary formative energy is exhausted, or crushed by accident, and the matter which it had organised about its centre is dispersed. This matter will take other forms, some of them living; it may breed worms, as the Christian imagination was fond of repeating; but a corpse is not a seed; it is not from there that the next generation is derived; their seed must be plucked from the secret heart of the man in his maturity, essentially uncontrolled and uncontaminated by his personal fortunes. There is a vast difference in character between the beginning and the end: the source is single, concentrated, specific, loaded with precise potentialities; the effects and consequences are diffused, peripheral, miscellaneous, unending. Except the seed of his children, all that a man sheds during his life and at his death is, from the vital point of view, corruption; all that he draws in, in so far as it feeds his flame, is purity and life. He is a pulsation or diastole of his hereditary nature, a bubble waxing till it bursts.

Existence, then, is a passage from potentiality to act, the order of its moments being determined by the direction of realisation within each of them. Actualisation has a direction even within the moment, due to the matter passing through that form. Before and after are not relations in a pure time, but organic, like up and down or right and left. They presuppose a centre, a focus into which matter flows and from which it is dispersed; and this concretion, like a spark or a blow, is irreversible, and separates its occasion and materials on the one hand, in which it was potential, from its effects and remains on the other, in which its potentiality is that of other things. Thus existence is not simply a series of essences solidified, nor a juxtaposition of phenomena; it is the career of a hereditary substance, it is the Life of Matter. And this in both senses of the word life: for it is the history of the fortunes of that plastic enduring being, and it is also the forward tension intrinsic to each moment of that career: an inner tension which is sometimes raised to consciousness and turns to spiritual light, but which animates matter everywhere and renders it transitional. Matter, as if ashamed at the irrationality of having one form rather than another, hastens to exchange it, whatever it may be, for some other form, and this haste is its whole reality; for it can add nothing to the essences which it successively exemplifies except just this: that they are enabled to be exemplified in succession, to be picked up and abandoned. Matter is the invisible wind which, sweeping for no reason over the field of essences, raises some of them into a cloud of dust: and that whirlwind we call existence.

Potentiality seems a vain word, and deceptive; yet it indicates a fact in the realm of truth, since seeds are capable of development into certain organisms only, and these cannot spring from any other source. Yet what this potentiality may be actually is usually unknown to us; we merely assume that it must be something actual, since the state of the seed at any one time must exemplify some individual essence, however complex it may be. Not that this actual state of the potential would pass into the further state, potential in it, if the potential were merely an essence, or a pure phenomenon; an essence or pure phenomenon has no fertility, no implications; it will remain for ever just what it is. It is matter, impatient of form, that fills form with a forward tension, and realises one essence after another; and this tension in matter is ultimately expressed and

Potentiality a retrospective name for material fertility.

rendered conscious in spirit; so that spirit is normally filled with craving, fear, curiosity, and jealousy, clasping to its bosom something precious and unintelligible, only too apt to slip away.

The relation between a man and his father and that between his son and himself, considered in its essence, is identical in the two instances, and always bilateral: there cannot be a child without a parent nor a parent without a child. Yet the flux runs only one way, and from the point of view of each person the felt tensions in the two instances are unilateral, different, and opposite. Even if by miracle grandfather and grandson were identical in essence—as in Greece they often bore the same name— they would be separated and posited as distinct persons by their opposite unilateral relation to the man between, who was son only to the one, and father only to the other. By these contrasting offices and sentiments each generation synthesises the flux of life in its own feeling and action at every moment; and we may reasonably regard this double tension as representing, on the human scale, the irreversible polarity within every natural moment, which indicates and transmits the irreversible direction of genesis. *Instances of parent and child.*

Nor is this universal flux composed of a single strand, like a thin autobiographical melody, sounding only one note at a time. It is many-voiced, like the sea of Homer. We may indeed divide it ideally into instants, each of which cuts through the whole stream and shows its complex visceral face at that juncture; but such a cross-section is not a natural moment. A natural moment is a realised essence of any sort, so long as its realisation continues; and there may be many collateral natural moments. Moments will be collateral if, when traced backwards or forwards according to their inward tensions, they terminate in identical ulterior moments; *Lateral tensions involved.*

and this without being strictly simultaneous through-out the interval, nor divisible on the same scale. So streams that flow from the same lake and empty into the same estuary need not be identical or equal or parallel but must be collateral. Scientific speculation now seems to authorise this view, even for the purposes of calculation, which I should not have expected; but a sceptic will readily admit that the more the sciences deepen their view and discount their assumptions the more they will familiarise us with differences of pace in nature, and incommensurable meanderings. Yet not meanderings beyond the field of action, into a metaphysical region: for unless all these scales and dimensions impinge upon facts posited and acted upon by animal faith, their interesting variety will belong only to the realm of essence, and will not describe this world. This world is not easily probed or understood. Existence is nothing if not complex, elastic, funda-mentally chaotic. Perception, description, and dogma over-simplify and over-regulate everything.

All lateral tensions might be typified, for a living being, in the horrid simultaneity of eating and being eaten. Microbes devour no less efficaciously than wild beasts; and this perpetual inner waste, met by the need of replenishment, is the clearest of demonstrations that matter is the principle of existence. Matter is essentially *food*, an object of competition and a substance fit for assimilation. It is for ever withdrawing itself from one form and assuming another, or being redigested. Food is substance in circulation, shuffling its unities like figures in a dance; and the same generative transition that originally establishes a particular moment of existence is required to maintain and renew it; otherwise that essence is lost. Every living thing must feed, feed perpetually, or it dissolves.

Living beings must be fed laterally if they are to persist recognis-ably.

If, then, we may transfer these fundamental characters of conventional moments to natural moments, we may say that a natural noment arises and exists only by virtue of external supports; first a parent moment to launch it and determine its initial character, and then collateral moments to control that heritage and determine what, and how long, it shall be in act. If ever existence is sustained at all in what we call the same object, or person, or thought, this happens by an external equilibrium which keeps that thing in a state of suspense or of continual self-recovery: each of its external relations tending to transform it, yet all of them together, for the nonce, keeping it as it was.

Lateral tensions condition the formation and exertion of forward tension in any particular moment.

A seed, if it could be thoroughly inspected by a clairvoyant spirit, would reveal the essence which contains or prepares its pregnancy, according to the method of development prevalent in nature, or in that species. But the actual essence of the seed, or of its ultimate fruit, is nothing to the naturalist; for he knows that no seed will mature except under certain fostering external conditions; and to these conditions, not to the unknown essence of the seed, he will trace and attribute the issue. The seed itself could never have been formed or, as it were, expelled from the parent moment, without the food and warmth of a fostering world; and in the act of birth or existence—for these are one in a natural moment—the sequel will be determined and sustained by the lateral tensions which beset it, allowing that sequel and forbidding any other. Everything, then, seems to be a mechanism of circumstances, of which the essences realised at distinct moments are, for the naturalist, only idle signs.

What seems to follow? That the forward tension which I have been attributing to natural moments may be simply the act of escaping in the direction of least resistance, as matter always will. The mysterious potentiality packed in the seed would then not be internal to it, or due to a specially wonderful essence therein embodied. It would be the concentration there of many external relations at work together, a resultant of all the cosmic tensions to which that point was subject. In itself the seed or the moment would not then need to possess any specific character: it might have only a simple or neutral essence, such perhaps as the pure Being which filled the atoms of Democritus; yet, without manifesting any particular bias, it might be ready, as far as its quantity availed, to run and nourish any vortex then evolving, or any self-asserting form. This it would do or not do, according to circumstances; so that all the tensions and heritages of animal life would be but incidents in a universal mechanism.

They may form a universal mechanism.

A diviner like Democritus, or like a modern mathematician hypostatising his notation into the substance of the world, may be willing to prophesy that such is the actual constitution of the universe. Such it may be indeed, at some inhuman depth; and I am willing to admit any such hypothesis on the authority of the learned, because that seems to me to be the direction in which the truth must lie, even if I distrust the means by which those wise men think they have discovered it. Yet however perfectly such a system might transcribe the flux of existence, it would not *be* that flux in person, or in its lapsing life; and science cannot well be truer of it, though true at a deeper level, than are all the vulgar essences which visibly give it character. Somehow the flux has actually gathered and distilled itself into many-coloured natural moments, as into drops; and these are the first and fundamental measures by which we may measure it, and the centres from which we must survey it.

The doctrine that all matter is similar and all laws constant is a mere speculation.

Perhaps in a chaos the only forward tension might be that of the universe as a whole, distended and convulsed by all its lateral tensions indiscriminately. Chaos, however, though doubtless fundamental, is not now complete. If it were, it would not be observable for lack of observers; and we, so long as we behold a world, however chaotic, have the assurance that the flux, for the time being, has been somewhat canalised in our parts of the universe, and that lateral tensions are partly held in check, and turned to sustenance, for the benefit of some persisting organisms; and the forward tensions of these, with their variations and fulfilments, form the drama of natural history.

Moreover, if we may say that in the world at large lateral tensions determine the existence and the forward tension of every part, we may also say, *vice versa*, that the forward tensions of the parts, taken together and meeting, compose the lateral tensions at work at that time; and this way of speaking has some advantages. It recognises that material existence, though everywhere conditioned externally, is everywhere spontaneous. Neither its being nor its singular forward tension are in the least questionable or unwelcome to any innocent moment. It takes itself for granted and leaps, if it can, to the full expansion of its inner powers. That act, or that attempt, is its very existence. Once existing, the moment unhesitatingly exercises its native force in its innate direction, and acts no less freely and efficaciously than it is acted upon. In a contingent world necessity is a conspiracy of accidents.

This precipitation of accidents is the work of matter, shifting its equilibrium and modifying its strains. A flux could neither change nor continue if it were immaterial. Its successive forms, since it takes them up and drops them, are not essences without substance nor facts without

In any case the flux is spontaneous in the part no less than in the whole.

It is inseparable from matter.

derivation. A natural moment marks the existential emergence of a new form—that particular form which circumstances then impose on the matter at hand, as previously disposed; and this moment ends when the balance of tensions which brought it about yields to a fresh equilibrium. This limit of any moment is and is called an end, as that other limit is and is called a beginning; for here there is concretion and there release. The forms are eternal, the matter is old; yet the interplay of the two is full of novelty, and at each point takes a somewhat unprecedented direction. For it is not the old form that creates the new; the old form, if it could do anything, would simply preserve itself; but it is indomitable matter, from the beginning in unstable equilibrium, that fell once into that old form as it falls now into the new, spontaneously and without vows of fidelity. Its potentiality, though unborn, is always specific, since it is involved in the distribution and tensions of the actual matter already in play; its realisation is the flux of existence, creating succession and telling the beads of time.

The dominance of matter in every existing being, even when that being is spiritual, is the great axiom of materialism, to which this whole book is only a corollary. But this axiom would not be consonant with the life of nature if it did not involve a complementary truth which takes away all its partisan bias and half its inhuman sting: I mean the complementary truth that matter is no model devised by the human imagination, like Egyptian atoms or the laws of physics, but is a primeval plastic substance of unknown potentiality, perpetually taking on new forms; the gist of materialism being that these forms are all passive and precarious, while the plastic stress of matter is alone creative and, as far as we can surmise, indestructible.

CHAPTER VI

TROPES

EVENTS have a form as much as things have: even the Greeks, those lovers of statues, were far from insensible to the essence of tragedy or of a happy life. Notion of Now the form of an event is not that event a trope. itself. An event, as I take the word, means a portion of the flux of existence; it is a conventional moment, like the birth of Christ or the battle of Waterloo, composed of natural moments generating one another in a certain order, and embedded in a particular context of other events: so that each event is a particular and can occur only once. Only the *type* of such a sequence, composed of such moments, is the *form* of the event, and this form is a universal. It need never have occurred; if I had said the resurrection of Christ, instead of his birth, the reader might have his doubts about it. The fact that such an essence was exemplified somewhere in an event would be a historical truth; in order to substantiate it, the flux of matter must assume that form; without this material and incidental illustration that type of sequence would remain in the air, in the realm of fiction or of theory. It is especially important at this point to dispel that confusion between essences and facts which makes a quicksand of all philosophy. I will therefore give a separate name to the essence of any event, as

293

distinguished from that event itself, and call it a *trope*.

In what precisely does an event differ from the trope which it exemplifies? I reply (for I must be brief): in being enacted. Any substance differs from the essence of that substance, and any event from the essence of that event, in that it can arise and perish, and this in two ways: externally, by intruding into a field of irrelevant entities, or quitting that field; and then again internally, by changing the order of its parts, each of which, in a thing or an event, has an individuality internal to it, and is a concrete component, not merely a fragment or aspect of the whole. Things and events are contingent and they are compound, even if monotonous or continuously similar: whereas their essences are eternal, and even when complex are not compound but absolutely indissoluble.

A trope is not an event.

Now, in a flux, the total essence realised in the form of its flow during any particular period obviously cannot be realised in any one of its moments, when only this moment exists: it can be realised only progressively, by the order in which those moments arise and vanish. This order is the trope; it is the essence of that sequence seen under the form of eternity; and since existence, in this event, has realised that essence, that essence has descriptive value in respect to this world. It belongs to the realm of truth.

For this reason, a trope is not on the same plane of being as a perspective, because it is not relative to any point of view or native to any psyche: a perspective is only specious, whilst a trope is formal. The flux, of its own initiative and in its own person, falls into that order composed of those elements, whether anyone observes it or not; the trope is a historical truth, the perspective is a

A trope not a perspective.

historical impression. But these relative impressions
or perspectives could never arise if substance and the
flux of substance had no essence of their own to begin
with: that would be tantamount to saying that substance was nothing, that there were no moments and
no centres, and that there was no difference between
a flux and what was not a flux. The nature of existence
is to possess whatsoever nature it possesses with a
treacherous emphasis, dragging that essence, by a sort
of rape, from its essential context into contingent
relations; those relations, being contingent, are variable; and the flux is merely the realisation of this
intrinsic variability involved in existence. The flux
is accordingly always tracing some path through the
realm of essence, and at every point assumes an assignable posture: that is to say, while each natural moment
enriches the flux with its intrinsic quality, the existence of that moment comes by a transformation of
the substance which flows through it and unites it
in a determinate trope with its antecedents and its
consequents.

Thus, in order to describe an event we need to look
forward and back along the path of change, and to note
what each included moment which we are It describes
able to distinguish had for its origin and for its some
results. Observation then discovers a trope, episode
but unless this trope spans all existence, and in existence.
extends endlessly or to some absolute end of time,
the total event which it defines will be like the natural
moments composing it, a mere episode; and this
episode, observed because we happen to belong to the
same epoch, will be caught on the wing, leaving a
margin before, behind, and around it of unexplored contingency. The embosoming reality, by virtue of which
this whole episode takes its place in nature, will remain
unknown. The mind cannot pursue the roots of things
into the darkness; it cannot discover why they exist;

it must be satisfied with noting their passing aspect, which is but an essence; and it must follow the chase, carried by its own galloping substance, to see what aspect they may wear next. The flux, or the path of existence, will elude us if we are content to express it lyrically, by eliciting the intrinsic essences of its single moments; but it may be partly described dramatically, in epic tropes, in terms which are formulæ or types of sequence.

Tropes are not necessarily exhaustive even of that part of the flux in which they may be discovered: Tropes are many heterogeneous tropes may run on to- of many gether, or may appear once only, like a lost sorts, inter- woven and thought. When a man is speaking, there are superposed. tropes in his language; every word uttered being a trope, as well as all inflections and forms of syntax. But these cannot live detached, in a realm of grammar; they can live only when grafted on the wholly different tropes of the nervous system, heart-beats, and circulation of the blood; and these biological tropes are again embedded in others of longer span, belonging to natural and political history. All these measures are more or less on the human scale, familiar but treacherous; because they in turn can only live if supported and filled out by minute incessant vibrations, molecular and ethereal, or by whatever else may mark the primary pulse of nature. In this complex of changes, perhaps endless tropes might be distinguished by a tireless and ingenious observer. Each animal and each philosopher picks out those which fall in with the rhythms and oppositions of his own habits and thoughts: a mile means a thousand paces, and we measure all things by our own stride. These measures are not false on that account; on the contrary, they are true, since the tropes of human existence are natural tropes, belonging to the same flux as all the others, and capable of being their measure. But they are not exclusive, nor exhaustive, nor pre-eminent: and superstition consists in thinking them so.

A sceptic, fearing to fall into such superstition, might even complain that all tropes were merely impressionistic units; that, in fact, they were nothing but perspectives, and that in supposing them to be more, I and all other men (including himself when not sceptical) were dupes of our human interests and habits. But the oversight and self-contradiction inherent in scepticism recurs here unabashed. In obeying our habits and interests we are masters, not dupes; our habits and interests are themselves tropes that must have been established victoriously in the flux, if living creatures defined by those tropes are able to lift their heads out of it and to survey it, no matter how relatively and how partially. Everything cannot be merely imputed. Imputation itself must exist actively, in centres and on occasions which are not imputed but actual. If for instance space, time, and matter were not characterised by definite properties and modes of being, separating them from non-entity and distinguishing them from one another, they would be simply nothing. If in the region indicated by these names— for we use them indicatively in perception and by animal faith—there is anything at all, it must possess the essence which it possesses, of which these names are partial suggestions; although, of course, the true essence of that substance need not at all resemble the images which, in using those names, may occupy any man's fancy.

Scepticism, then, need not be turned into a dogma, into absolute relativism, solipsism, or idealism, nor into a denial of substance and of truth. On the contrary, a scepticism sceptical of itself may become a method of discovery, and in challenging superficial tropes it may reveal deeper ones. And here, in the words " interest " and " habit " I think we have a hint of a principle applicable to the criticism of tropes. No trope is exclusive, as if it could prevent the parallel, higher, lower, or intertwined development of other tropes; but some tropes are *repeated*; they are habitual modes of action or measures constantly maintained; and this circumstance distinguishes them from local harmonies, often the most important æsthetically, which arise only once, by an unprecedented union of circumstances. The advent of Christianity, of the Renaissance, and of the Reformation are important tropes never, we may presume, to be repeated; but birth and death are perpetual in nature, and the habits and passions of each creature, while it lives, are principles of reiteration; they involve repetitions in action, and they find and use repetitions in nature, answering to their own precision of form. Organisms are instruments of repetition; and they rely, for their existence and prosperity, on the repetition of opportunities for the repetition of their acts. Were this reliance not justified, or this mechanism unstable, there could be no life, experience, or art in the world. The more exactly and the more pervasively a trope repeats itself the more it introduces us, if we discover it, into the heart of the flux, and the better it supplies us with an instrument and a background for tracing such rarer tropes as may be discernible occasionally, or such as may arise only once. Moreover, repetition of itself marks the beginning and the end of a trope and rescues it from the arbitrary scope of human apperception.

Tropes realised only once—like the whole history of the world, if there be such a total—are resultant harmonies, which only emotion could regard as reasons for their own existence. Tropes realised occasionally leave open the question of their incidence: why do they appear at certain junctures and not at others? If no reason can

The most repeated are the most ingrained.

Only a pervasive trope can be fundamental.

be given, the flux to that extent is found to be chaotic. If on the contrary their initiation is regular, they are parts of a universal trope, which requires them at those junctures, and connects their occasions by a mechanism deeper than they. This universal trope will be realised everywhere, and contained, not interrupted, in the realisation of all supervening occasional tropes. The flux can be truly and surely measured only by tropes which repeat themselves uninterruptedly on their own plane.

Such a trope is called mechanical: so that to say that the world is fundamentally mechanical is the evident alternative to saying that it is funda- Mechanism mentally chaotic. Nor is it merely by a play is the on words, or a sort of divination, that we are alternative justified in saying so: the thing follows from to chaos. our original trust in the possibility of action, which is the criterion of existence, and the test of substantiality. The agent and his world must both be compacted of matter moving in constant and recurring tropes, if the one is not to be mad and the other treacherous. Men of the world, and women even with more assurance, are quick to foresee or to divine what *must* be going on. Naturally they express this insight in loose human terms; but the trust in repetition and in mechanism is there, else all penetration and all policy would be precluded. To turn this imaginative insight into science is merely a matter of attentive observation, measurement, and transcription of current metaphors into technical terms. The behaviour of animals would then appear to be scanned by tropes continuous with those which scan the behaviour of matter everywhere, if not identical with them. Madness and wild originality, like volcanoes and tornadoes, will be of the greatest help in hastening this assimilation; because the level of mechanism is so deep and its scale so far from the human that it is better revealed in cataclysms, miracles, and diseases than in the placid course of superficial experience.

All this, however, is said in general and from a transcendental point of view: it prejudges nothing as to the particular mechanism which may actually be fundamental. In any case, in calling tropes mechanical, because by hypothesis constantly repeated, we must not assume that they are mathematically necessary, or not vital, or simple, or exclusive. On the contrary, they are contingent and arbitrary, since they are forms of existence, which might just as easily have possessed any other character. They are spanned by all sorts of other tropes, including those native to the human senses and to human logic. They are radically " vital ", if this word means spontaneous and irreducible to any alien principle. As to their simplicity, that is perhaps only a relation to human alacrity or bewilderment in their presence, and no property of their substance or essence. Forms of flux can never be quite simple, since they must contain several terms; in existence they are hardly separable from the tensions which realise them, which probably extend to infinity; so that to speak of simplicity is rather a sign of it in us, than a serious postulate of science.

The fundamental trope arbitrary, vital, not exclusive, and hardly simple.

There is a reason why comparatively simple tropes, called laws, are discoverable in those parts of nature, like the heavens, which we observe from a great distance, and also in those parts, like the depths of matter, which we cannot observe at all, but may imagine in terms relative to their gross aspects and motions. Distance and theory act like a sieve: they eliminate all the detail and leave only average results or total impressions, conveyed by special and highly selective media, such as light and mathematical calculation. The *picture* thus pro-

Laws: how discerned and in what sense true.

duced, if there be a picture at all, is a pure fiction, a
visual or phonetic symbol perfectly subjective and
human; but the law enunciated may be true; that is,
the flux may actually pass through the series of abstract
positions selected, and in its moving equilibrium may
satisfy the equations expressed in the law.

When tropes are called laws, there is danger of
idolatry: for although scientific philosophers often
warn us that a law is merely a formula or an
average, or an equation probably approxi- Law as a
matively realised in a certain plane of events, physical
yet this probability lets loose our action and idol.
expectation; and the force of expectation projects its
confidence into a myth; it erects Law into a metaphysical power compelling events to obey it. This
is the great idol, I will not say of science, but of the
passions which science subserves. Images are as
indispensable in science as they are in worship; a
thorough iconoclast, who should banish all images,
poetical and mathematical no less than sensuous, would
simply make a desert of the mind, and destroy all
science, like all religion; but these necessary images
are vehicles, not ultimate objects of regard. The
quick mind passes through them, here to the instant
fact, there to the supreme essence.

I think that the reality of law can be briefly expressed in two maxims: one, that whatsoever happens
anywhere, happens there spontaneously, as Natural
if it had never occurred before and would causation
never occur again; the other, that whatso- ous, but
ever spontaneously happens once will have habitual.
spontaneously happened before and will spontaneously happen again, wherever similar elements are in
the same relations. The first of these maxims proclaims the contingency, substantiality, originality of
fact everywhere: it is the axiom of empiricism, when
experience is understood practically and not psycho-

logically. The second maxim proclaims the postulate of action and of reason called the uniformity of nature. It is only a postulate, which contingent, substantial, and original facts may at any point disallow; but in so far as they do so, they revert to chaos and render life and art difficult, if not impossible.

" The reign of law " is accordingly only a modern and bombastic equivalent for the ancient naturalness of nature. In so far as the law is more rigid than a habit, it is a human artifice of notation. In so far as it indicates a co-operative march of events mutually generated and destroyed, it is another name for the ways of nature or of God, for the forms which existence can show to spirit. But nature, though highly favourable to spirit, since she has bred it, is not governed by her child; and even in our familiar world the wide margin of incalculable properties by which the calculable part of nature is surrounded—what we sometimes call her secondary and tertiary qualities—proves this most curiously; for in the world of action, as spirit conceives it, spirit itself seems superfluous. And perhaps even in that calculable skeleton of primary qualities, selected because they can be measured and predicted in mathematical tropes, there may be a margin of error; for a law is an essence, eternally identical, and nature is in flux, and probably never the same. Very likely all the movements of matter are more or less elastic or organic: I mean responsive afresh to a total environment never exactly repeated, so that no single law would perfectly define all consecutive changes even in the plane of matter, and every response would be that of a new-born organism to an unprecedented world. There would be nothing magical in this: it would merely distribute the radical contingency of existence throughout its successive phases, without concentrating it in a single initial fact and initial law. But on the human scale, and for fashioning perishable human works, such fundamental instability in nature would remain negligible. Even in a land of earthquakes we live in houses.

Belief in law when hasty is called superstition or, when more cautious, empiricism: but the principle in both cases is the same. Both take expecta- The hazard in empiricism and in superstition. tion for probability; and what probability can there be that an expectation, arising at one point, should define a law for the whole universe? Expectation is an animal attitude resting not at all on induction or probability, but on the fact that animals are wound up to do certain things and vaguely but confidently posit a world in which their readiness may become action. In superstition, as in empiricism, we yield to the vital temptation to ignore reason, and we trust to courage and to whatever idea is uppermost in the mind. Yet in a roundabout way, on the scale and in the period of that animal life, this blind courage is normally justified by the event. For how should the psyche be ready and eager for a particular employment, if in her long evolution she had not been moulded to just that employment by a world which allowed and rewarded it? How should potentialities and propensities be more deeply rooted in her than in the world of which she is an integral part? Certainly, her ideas are specious and her passions precipitate; yet for all their delusions and disarray, they have brought her forward, and she survives; so that things expected, hoped for, and worked for by any prospering animal, are, on the whole and with a difference, likely to happen.

There is then no necessity in the relation between cause and effect, and no assurance that law is constant. Nevertheless, causation is prevalent: Natural status of tropes and laws. were it not prevalent in fact, the expectation of it could never have arisen. But the validity of a prevalent law lies simply in its function as a measure of events; it is no adequate description of them, much less a power bringing them about. Obviously the complete and actual march of events cannot be reduced to anything else than its full and precise self: and even its complete form, being an essence, would be, if considered apart, in another realm from its manifestation. There is no constraint to exist native to these tropes, but it may be true that the flux, which must exhibit some form or other, does for a time and in a certain dimension exhibit this particular trope, or, as we say, obeys this law. A mathematical or pictorial skeleton is thus traced by the economy of thought within the body of nature, leaving all the other dimensions and all the other tropes to hang like garlands about those calculated supports. The skeleton exists, in the sense that by hypothesis this law prevails now in this region; but it is no skeleton in its operative function, like that of an animal; it is no rigid substance within the soft substance of events; it is only a trope, which the thrifty mind selects from the tangle of relations which hold those facts in the mesh of existence. The selection is not made arbitrarily, but in sympathy with the scale and character of the action which that thrifty mind follows in its fortunes and prophesies in its thoughts.

Many a divergence among philosophers may be understood and dispelled by this consideration: that the fundamental tropes in nature, far from excluding other tropes, inevitably produce them. When things are in motion, new relations arise among them by a necessary magic, and they lend themselves to description in various logics or anatomies without interrupting their habitual flux. It is never a just objection to the reality of any trope that it may not be the exclusive trope in the movement of existence, or that there are events which it cannot properly measure. Mathematical tropes may

Necessary inadequacy of tropes to describe the full reality.

pervade the realm of matter, supporting occasional moral and æsthetic tropes which supervene on the mathematical tropes without interrupting them.

Tropes, mathematical or vital, mechanical or historical, all belong to the region of Platonic Ideas; they are unitary patterns distinguishable in the movement of things; they are no part of the moving substance executing those patterns and overflowing them. Yet, if any mind is to perceive that flux, or to distinguish any of its phases, it cannot do so otherwise than by *Being essences, they diversify, but cannot control, existence.* discerning some essence exemplified there, which limits one phase or one moment and divides it from another. Of itself existence has no wholeness: it would not be existence if it were not scattered into moments, each its own centre, reaching out towards one another in the dark, forgetting what they were in what they become, and learning what they will be only by becoming it. It is the very function of flux and of volume in the flux, it is the singular virtue of physical time and space, to make it possible that incompatible things should be equally actual, and irrelevant things closely conjoined. For when anything is actual, the existence of any ulterior thing becomes, to that living moment, eventual, and unnecessary: whether that ulterior thing arises or fails to arise, whether somewhere else it once existed or did not exist, makes no difference here. No difference, I mean, in the instant fact: for that by subterranean processes or substantial derivation, this moment has followed upon others, and will issue in others again, is, if true, an additional circumstance, curious but, in principle, subsidiary: for each of those other moments, and every physical bond between them, would still have to realise and posit itself on its own account, as this moment posits and realises itself here. The brute fact might be enlarged, but it would necessarily remain insulated and absolute in its contingency. No moment, no event, and no world can insure the existence or the character of anything beyond it.

How, then, impose on all existence some trope exhibited by it here and now, and trust that trope to be universal? Why should the flux submit to reproducing this particular pattern, instead of bringing others to light? The contingency of existence is pervasive, and the stress of it may be everywhere much the same, but the forms of existence are likely to be always, as we recede from any fact, increasingly different. The repetitions are as contingent as the novelties; each field of repetition, if we extend the range of observation beyond its limits, proves itself a novelty, as does every species of animal, every art, and every idea. Even if, in fact, some trope is perpetually recurrent, or if one little unchanging world is suspended for ever in the midst of a vacuum destined never to be peopled by other worlds, still this final truth is an accident and almost a paradox: for why should this universe have come to be so trim, when the infinity of essence was tempting it to be otherwise?

Their prevalence is conditional.

It follows that whenever a trope of any sort has been distinguished and found to prevail in nature, as far as our knowledge extends, it need by no means prevail beyond the limit of this domesticated region, nor above or below the level of our human sensibility. It need not even exclude anomalies and outbreaks of chaos in the interstices of the prevalent tropes. In viewing any part of nature as a unit, as we do in the act of discovering a trope, we have necessarily substituted an essence for it. For this reason essences only can be data: the fact which has aroused this intuition and which we posit in these sensuous or grammatical terms, necessarily transcends these terms, and every ideal synthesis of them. It exists on its own moving plane, by tension towards

ulterior facts and by relation to them. Our intuition is
a snapshot: the image it creates yields a word, a law,
a *logos* in another realm of being from the flux which
confronts it. The tropes which we call the laws of
nature cannot therefore exclude other and contrary
manifestations of what nature secretly contains. Egotism
and credulity may protect most of us from troubling
about those foreign possibilities; if there comes any
startling failure in our presumptions—any miracle or
paradox—we are inclined to believe that the marvel
responds to our private interests even more directly and
surely than does the familiar routine of the world; and
the more remote and eccentric the comet that intrudes
into our skies, the clearer proof we read in it of our home
faith. Everything is indeed a support for the religious
spirit, when that spirit is addressed to the truth; but
when it is addressed to imposing on the universe its
own animal habits and animal prosperity, the farther it
ranges the more it is likely to find itself out in the cold.

For fear of this unhomeliness of the infinite, some
philosophers in all ages have adopted a heroic way of
asserting the absolute domination of their
acquired science: they have supposed that the Notion of recurrent cycles.
history of the world is self-repeating and comes
round for ever in a circle. Infinity and familiarity are
thus reconciled; and the limited evidences of human
knowledge do not prevent it from claiming unlimited
authority. The horrid sense of something alien and
undiscoverable beyond receives its quietus. There is,
the inspired philosopher asserts, always something
beyond the known, but it is always a repetition of what
he has discovered: it is this again and again. And so
without further exploration, and without the superhuman labour of changing his habitual categories, the
philosopher realises his dream of finding the trope,
vast or minute, which nature shall be condemned to
exhibit for ever.

To assume such inertia in things, when existence is essentially inventive and spirit the most sublimated and volatile form of it, might seem to be itself a curious instance of inertia: and of inertia in the wrong place, because thought at least might be lively. But the motive and the true sphere for such a love of finality lie in the moral life; there it is indeed imperative to find a master trope, and to stick to it. The psyche (as we shall see presently) is herself a trope, not a substance: but a trope so imbedded in substance as to execute itself energetically, when it has a chance, and not merely to be exhibited passively, by a concourse of other tropes. The psyche is a definite potentiality rooted in a seed, and exhibited unswervingly in the development of that seed, if suitably nourished and allowed to mature. Such an innate but merely potential trope, which an animal strives to realise by his growth and action, has the aspect of a will; it may become conscious: not at first or normally conscious of its own ultimate form, but rather of incidental contrasts between pleasure and pain, success and failure, involved in the realisation of its destiny. In hunger and the chase, in wounds and constraint, an animal gradually learns to distinguish such objects and actions as are good, in that they further the discharge of his innate powers, from such as thwart this discharge and are evil. All experience and wisdom will do nothing but define for him the trope in which his life moves or ought to move; hence the profound marriage of animal life with reason, with definition, with selection. Hence, too, the abusive projection in human philosophy of rules of art upon the flux of existence. The realm of matter, for the moralised spirit, seems to exist only to be mastered, to be reformed, to be painted. Such is indeed its moral function in man, in so far as he profits by its economy. Profit, or the hope of it, rules the thrifty mind, not only in religion, where the edifying

[Marginal note: Moral justification of the demand for fixity.]

aspect of things is deputed to be their essence, but also in science, where the most august philosophers, in order to judge between true and false theories, often employ the childish criterion of simplicity. The flux, however, is not subject to these subjections; and only a speculative spirit, after much discipline, can learn to rejoice with it in its freedom.

CHAPTER VII

TELEOLOGY

WE have already seen that explanation by habit or law is a reduction of events to their rhythms or repetitions;

Like explanation by law, explanation by purpose is verbal only.

we gain no insight into why or how a thing happens by saying that it has often happened before. Did we really wish to understand, we should inquire into the inner elements of such a mutation in any one of its instances: because a thing must happen each time by a concourse of motions there, and not because the same thing happens also in other places; although naturally it will happen again if the conditions which produced it here are repeated. Now a different form of mock explanation appears in what is called teleology, when the ground of things is sought in their excellence, in their harmony with their surroundings, or in the adaptation of organs to their functions and of actions to their intentions.

Such correspondences exist: teleology, if it be only a name for them, is a patent and prevalent fact in nature.

Nature a web of adaptations.

Indeed the adaptation of things to one another is involved in their co-existence: a thing can arise only by finding and taking its place where other things make room for it. Everything in the moving equilibrium of nature is necessarily co-operative. But the question becomes interesting (and unanswerable) when we ask why, at any point, this so singular thing should have found such a singular set of conditions as to permit or compel it to exist there. A wider view, exploring antecedents and consequents, and discovering analogies, may enlarge the prospect, and, as happens in the books of naturalists, may so pleasantly occupy the mind with pictures and stories, that we may stop asking for reasons. And to invoke adaptation itself, as if this were a cause of adaptation, would be to halt at a word, adding perhaps to it, as an element of power, the bated breath with which we pronounce it.

Yet this human scale and these human emotions, which we impose so fatuously on the universe, bear witness, on the plane of thought, to the existence of organisms and of life on the plane of matter; for we should have no emotions and no scale to impose on other things if our own being were not definite, animate, and self-assertive.

In human society teleology takes a special and conscious form: it becomes art. Not only do tropes— which here we call methods—everywhere dominate the scene, but very often the method is explicitly adopted or modified, and the action planned; foresight and intention occupy the first moment of it, and execution of that prevision occupies the second moment. Here the preformation of events and the pre-adaptation of instruments to their uses is a simple fact of history. Knowing how our passions and purposes watchfully realise their avowed ends, may we not reasonably assimilate obscure events to these deliberate actions, the causes of which seem clear to us and intimately confessed? As we do things when we wish, must not all nature, or God working through nature, wish everything when they do it? Must not some idea, seen under the form of the good, guide and attract every movement in nature?

Yes: that is the normal way of speaking, the

Might art be the key to nature?

rhetorical or poetical way of describing nature in human terms from the human point of view. But moral sentiment, poetry, and theology are forms of literature, not of science; they are not wrong in their own sphere, and their rightness becomes intelligible, and takes its place in natural history, when we see its relativity to human experience, and its psychic seat. There, in literature, a sceptic should be the last to quarrel with the use of moral analogies in describing nature: poetry does not contradict science, because in daring to be poetry, it avows a complete ignorance and disdain of the prose of things. Poetry is poetry, and opens up a legitimate vista within its own world, but only to a poetic spirit; in its material existence it is a flood of verbiage incidental to human passions and their rhetorical automatisms. In its biological capacity poetry can be described only in prose; and all its insights reappear as incidents and as subjective creations bred in the realm of matter.

Yes, but only in the realm of art.

Before indicating, in the tentative way which alone is possible, the material basis of teleology, it may be well to examine the logic of it in the imagination; for the contrast between poetry and prose is by no means absolute, and any scrupulous study of moral philosophy compels us to restore that subject, and ourselves who pursue it, to our place in nature. The clearness of moral life after all is only a verbal clearness; a sort of facility and acceleration by which our acts and feelings come to a climax and fulfil their natural tropes. We are left in the dark concerning the manner of this fulfilment. We are even more in the dark as to the ground of the ideas and wishes which, as we say, guide our conduct; when all goes well, we need not stop to question them, but presently when they clash with one another and fail of fulfilment, the

Moral being has physical roots and works only through them.

easy miracle of their power begins to seem dubious, and subterranean bonds between them and the world of action become visible in a new, a biological, direction.

Consider first the existential presence of human wishes and ideas. Is it conceivably an original fact and unconditioned? Why should any wish *All wishes* or idea arise at all here and now? Is the *and ideas* mid-void peopled with them, as with little *have physical* winged heads of cherubs, without bodies and *occasions,* without support? Surely if anything ever had a cause and was evidently secondary, it is human will and fancy; to take them for absolute beings, or original powers, would be to allow theoretical sophistries to blind us to the plainest facts. If I want water, it is because my throat is parched; if I dream of love, it is because sex is ripening within me. Nature has fixed the character, and circumstances have fixed the occasion, for this ferment of desire and conception. Conscious will is a symptom, not a cause; its roots as well as its consequences are invisible to it, material, and often incongruous and astonishing.

But suppose that the mind, like some morose tyrant, determines to shut all doors and windows against the outer world, and to see only by the lamp of *and* self-consciousness. What will be the stuff *physical* of its meditations? Nothing but animal *objects.* wishes and barn-yard ideas; demands for food, air, liberty of motion; dreams of wild things to be chased, eaten, played with, or hidden; or perhaps of fame to be won, empires conquered, friendship and love and praise. How comes absolute free-will or a groundless moral energy to choose these singular objects? Could it not have employed its inviolable leisure and its infinite invention in conceiving something better than such a very humble, cruel, and nasty animal world? And could not its sentiment have been less sentimental, less unctuous and constrained, less tainted by terror and desperate delusion? Why are human love and religion so tormented, if they are masters of the world? If they command miraculously and matter obeys, is it not because matter had first created them and dictated the commands which they were to issue?

Evidence of this, if it were needed, might also be found in the loose character of ideas and wishes They are compared with their fulfilments, even when inadequate they are materially fulfilled. These ideas and feelings accompany- wishes are personal, confused, and incoming action. plete. When a law-giver designs a constitution or an architect an edifice, a thousand contrary principles and suggestions assault his mind. Unless he is very precipitate, or an absolute slave of habit, the plan will take shape in his mind to his own surprise; it will be a sudden concretion of subtle currents and accidents within him, the harmony and relevance of which, if any, we call his genius or his ability. Even when these are greatest, and most seasoned by experience, their prophetic virtue will be only abstract and partial; the event will be a new surprise, as was the idea. For it is hardly possible that the edifice when complete, or the constitution when in actual operation, should produce the same impression on the mind as the plan conceived there originally. The plan arose by a synthesis of acquired impulses within one body: the work arises by a concourse of actions which, even if still those of the same person only, and obedient to the same vital impulses as the idea (as happens in singing, speaking, or making a gesture) yet occur now in the outer world, in a comparatively foreign material, and with a greater admixture of accidental concomitants. Therefore a man's actions and works seem to him less a part of himself than his intentions, but to others seem more so: because to others he is a personage and to himself he is a mind.

Ideas and wishes, then, are mental echoes of movements proper to bodily life; were they not, they could have no application and no relevance to the world. The more accurately they prefigure events and seem to control them by prescribing their tropes, the better they prove their own fidelity to the ruling impulses of matter. Clear ideas are evidences of clean arts; a firm and victorious will bears witness to a strong and opportune economy in the organism. *Scientific psychology itself is a study of behaviour, i.e. of matter.* Indeed, for a scientific psychology behaviour is the only conceivable seat of mind, and intelligence simply a certain plasticity in organisms which enables them to execute tropes in subtle harmony with their material opportunities. True, mind and intelligence are something more in fact. This we perceive when, in reflection, we gather up sensuous images, memories, lyric effusions, and dramatic myths into a literary psychology, which may be remarkably convincing but remains purely literary; for it cannot follow the flux of its subject-matter by observation and measurement, but must recreate it in imagination, and leave it at that. Similarly, the history which interweaves intentions with events and ideas with motions may give a capital description of moral perspectives, but it is simply literature.

Total events in nature are never wholly mental, and it is on their material side, through their substance and physical tensions, that they are derived from previous events and help to shape the events which follow. But this doctrine is based on far-reaching considerations which may often be ignored; and when only the *Mental events, if causal, would not be teleological.* mental side of an event is discovered, the material and substantial side of it may be denied, and states of mind, in their purity, may be regarded as total natural events. It will then seem plausible to regard them as links in the chain of natural causes, for are they not moments in experience, as memory or dramatic reconstruction may survey it? But this amphibious psycho-physics, even if we admitted it, would not be teleological. Each mental event would transmit existence and energy to its successor in proportion to its own intensity and quality, just as if it were a form of matter. It would not thereby exercise any magical moral control over its consequences. Thus intense thought might make the head ache, fear might cause paralysis, amusement laughter, or love a want of appetite and early death. The teleological virtue of wishes and ideas is accordingly something quite distinct from their alleged physical influence; indeed it is only when we disregard this incongruous mechanical efficacy attributed to them that we begin to understand what their teleological virtue would mean: it would mean a miraculous pre-established harmony between the commands or wishes of the spirit and events in the world. It would mean the exercise of divine power, which a well-advised human being could never attribute to himself, but only to the grace of God, perhaps passing through him.

Teleology then retreats into a theology, or into a cosmological idealism, fraught with curious alternatives: The will for a divine mind, if conscious and omniscient invoked, as high theology would make it, would not be if cosmic, would be an event; it would be a decree, a command- mythical. ment, or an eternal glory relative to all events, but on a different plane from any of them. If, on the contrary, the divine will was immanent in the world and intermingled with all natural events, it would evidently not be separate or self-conscious; indeed, it would be only a poetic synonym for the actual fertility of matter, and for the tropes exhibited in its evolution. In either case, after making our bow to this divine will, out of deference to antiquity and to human rhetoric, we should be reduced to studying as far as possible the crawling processes of nature. These will be the seat of such teleology as surely exists, and as a critical philosophy may record without falling into rhetorical ambiguities. Organic life is a circular trope which at each repetition touches or approaches a point which we regard as its culmination, and call maturity. In man, maturity involves feelings, intentions, and spiritual light: but it is idle to regard the whole trope as governed by these top moments in it, which are more highly conditioned, volatile, and immaterial than are their organs, their occasions, or their fruits.

Nature is full of coiled springs and predestined rhythms; of mechanisms so wound up that, as soon as circumstances permit, they unroll themselves through a definite series of phases. A seed, if suitable sown and watered, will grow into one particular sort of plant, and into no other. At the inception of such a trope the pre- destined movement is said to be "potential"; there is a "predisposition" in matter at that point to execute the whole movement. What is this predisposition? Examination of a seed would probably never disclose in it a perfect model of the future flower, any more than examination of a young man's passions, or of his body, would disclose there the poems which these passions might ultimately inspire. Potentiality seems to be an imputed burden, a nominal virtue attributed to the first term of a trope because of the character of the rest of it. Yet, sometimes, as in a seed, the imputed burden is genuine, and potentiality is pregnancy. A true beginning and sufficient cause of what ensues is really found there; but this initial reality need not at all resemble that which it will become. Its nature is internal, hidden, perhaps inexpressible in the terms of human observation at all; so far is it from being an image cast into that well from the outside, or a reflex name given to it in view of the future. The tropes which mark the obvious metres of nature tell nothing

There is an untraced pregnancy in organic matter.

of the inspiration, the secret labour, or the mechanism which brings them forth.

Heredity is an obvious case of repetition; but its temporal scale is so large in respect to an observer of his own species that individualities may seem to him more striking and self-grounded than uniformities. Yet from a little distance, or in an alien species, heredity recedes into a monotonous succession of waves and a multitudinous repetition of objects. Both impressions are just, and nature, here seen at close quarters, reveals the complexity of her endless pulsations. There is a curious involution of the organism in the seed. The seed is not merely the first state of the organism in the offspring but was also a part of a similar organism in the parent. This notable trope is apt to blind us to the mechanism requisite for its repetition. We are solicited by the magic rhyme of it to rest content with explaining the beginning of life by the end, the part by the whole, the actual by the ideal, the existent by the non-existent. Abandoning physics altogether as incapable of solving the mystery, we may wonderingly record the reappearance, by the will of God, of new generations of every species, each after its kind. But as in the Christian sacraments, so here in natural reproduction, the grace of God does not operate without physical continuity in its channels; and it would be by tracing that continuity, and the accidents which often cause it to deviate from its course, that reproduction might be seen in its natural setting. The multitude of successes would not then blind us to the far greater number of failures. To arise in this world and to become something specific is in each instance a fresh and doubtful undertaking.

Prodigious complexity is something to which nature is not averse, like a human artist, but on the contrary is positively prone; and in animals the attainment of

Heredity is a trope revealing the separate and perilous realisation of its instances.

such prodigious complexity is made possible by the fact that a special environment is at hand, in the body of the parent, enabling the young organism to run through its earlier and fundamental phases safely, surely, and quickly. So unerring is this development that the animal is often born complete; yet there is enough wavering, with false starts in directions once taken by the species and since abandoned, to show that the core of the seed need contain no prefigurement of the whole result, but that this result is reached tentatively in reproduction, as it was originally in evolution; only that the ovum is a far better locus for a perfect development of the psyche than was the bleak outer world.

Nevertheless the manner of this quick and spontaneous growth is little understood, and only the total trope remains to furnish our imagination. Seeing its dramatic unity, we feel that the first term must be pregnant with the ultimate issue, as the first act of a good play—assuming human nature and the ways of the world—is pregnant with the last. We forget that poetic genius itself must have natural sources and reason external guides; and we attribute the perpetual attainment of some natural perfection to the miraculous power of the trope realised in it, or to the divine will contemplating that trope and, as if fascinated by its magic beauty, commanding matter to reproduce it for ever and ever.

Final causes certainly exist in the conduct of human beings, yet they are always inadequate to describe the events in which they are manifested, since such events always presuppose a natural occasion and a mechanical impulse; and these cannot flow from the purpose or choice which they make possible and pertinent. The whole operation of final causes therefore requires, beneath and within it, a deeper flow of natural forces which we may darkly assign to fate or matter or chance or the unfathomable will of God. Yet, since without

Final causes exist, but are moral perspectives superposed on natural causation.

this irrational occasion or afflatus those purposes and choices could never have taken shape, it ought to suffice for our reasonable satisfaction if, in some measure, the natural perfections of things are manifested in them, and if there is some degree of harmony between the world and the spirit. Moral tropes have their proper status and dignity if they are actually found in the human aspect of events; they are not rendered false or nugatory merely because the material existence presupposed in them has a different method of progression. Medicine and psychology are now disclosing a truth which men of experience have perceived in all ages, that virtues and vices are equally phases of a controllable physical life: a fact which takes nothing away from their beauty or horror. They are the moral qualities of a natural being.

Mechanical tropes in their turn are incompetent to describe or measure spiritual realities, such as excellence or happiness or spirit itself; nor is it reasonable to require them to do so. They will be amply authenticated if they can serve to trace the whole material backing and occasions of those moral harmonies or spiritual lights. These, in order to arise do not require a different mechanism of their own, or a different occasion; the material mechanism and the material occasion fully suffice to introduce and to justify them. The physical terror of murder has made murder criminal; the animal warmth and transport of love have made love tender and deep. Of course, a deepening of apprehension is required, founded itself on a changed habit, a finer involution of responses in the organism; so that the same things which were done and regarded brutally may be done and regarded with a far-reaching sense of all that they involve. This new sense sees light and glow in the fire, of which the blinder senses could feel only the heat. Hence if either the naturalist or the moralist is a man of a single sense he must be left to grope in his professional half-light. Nature in his children will probably redress the balance.

The fact that natural organisms are far more closely purposeful than works of art, may itself serve to reveal the true superposition of art upon nature. Art is a human, marginal, not indispensable extension of natural teleology. The essential organic tropes, passions, and powers of man must have been first firmly rooted in the race, before anyone could conceive a project, or be able to execute it as conceived. Even highly civilised humanity forms its plans only dreamfully, and is cheated by its own impotence, or by contrary currents, in the execution of them. Often the most fixed purposes and the most vehement efforts are wasted; indeed, they are always wasted in some measure, because no designer can foresee all the circumstances of his work, or its ulterior uses. Any work, when it exists, is a part of the realm of matter, and has its fortunes there, far from all control or intention. The saintly Henry the Sixth founded Eton and King's College for the salvation of souls; they have served admirably together with the playing-fields to form the pensive but quite earthly ethos of the modern Englishman. In the works of nature there is not this division, nor this irony; the uses are not forecast in any purpose, consciously prophetic; they are simply the uses which the thing finds or develops, as it changes under the control of the changing circumstances. Thus the precision of adjustment between organs and functions, far from being a miracle, is in one sense a logical necessity or tautology; since nothing has any functions but those which it has come to have, when plasticity here with stimulus and opportunity there have conspired to establish them.

An organism is a concretion in matter which can feed, defend, and reproduce itself. Its initial form of expansion finds a natural limit, beyond which circum-

Art is a marginal imperfect form of natural organisation.

stances do not suffer it to go: then, unless it perishes altogether, it reproduces itself: that is, it breaks up into parts, some of which repeat the original form of expansion, while the others dissolve into their elements and die. Expansion thus becomes rhythmical, repeating a constant trope; except that, if the force of concretion and accretion is powerful at that centre, and if the circumstances are favourable, that trope may become internally more complex: in other words, the organism may acquire fresh organs. These will reappear in each generation in their due place and season, if the environment continues to give them play; and in this way a race and a species will be established, individual and recognisable, yet subject to private variations and also to generic shifts, by the atrophy of some organs and the development of others.

Brief natural history of organisms.

If, then, we understood genesis we should understand heredity; for an organ cannot arise, either the first time or the last, except spontaneously, and as if it had never existed before. But how can it arise at all? By what genetic impulse does some nucleus of matter modify its parts, and complicate their sympathetic movements, without losing its unity of action in respect to external things? It is for the naturalists to reply, in so far as observation or experiment enables them to trace the actual genesis of bodies; for as to the verbal explanations which they may offer, they are not likely to be on the scale or in the terms proper to the flux or to the concretions of matter at a depth so far below that of human language. Let matter take shape as it will: all that concerns me here is the nature of the teleology present in the result. Organs must arise before they can exercise what we call their function, and this function must be one which the circumstances usually render possible and self-maintaining. Is the philosopher reduced to impressions

Need final causes be operative to form them?

on the human scale? Must he blankly confess that nature is mysteriously inspired, and that matter gathers itself into organisms as if it were magically guided by the love of that life and those achievements of which such organisms will be capable?

Not quite. Moralistic physics is wiser than natural science in not ignoring eventual spiritual issues; but these issues are no factors in generation. On No: the contrary, they are themselves uncertain, because conditioned, and precarious; so that if we purposes reach any depth or honesty in our reflection organisms. we cannot attribute the movement of nature to the antecedent influence of the future good which she might realise. Instead, we must attribute the pursuit of this good, and its eventual realisation, to her previous blind disposition, fortified by the fact that circumstances were favourable to that development: and this last fact is no accident, since (as we have just seen) the adaptation of the parts of nature to one another is necessary to their existence, and nature could not retain any disposition for which circumstances did not make room, at least for the moment. In a word, the teleology present in the world must be distinguished from final causes. The latter are mythical and created by a sort of literary illusion. The germination, definition, and prevalence of any good must be grounded in nature herself, not in human eloquence.

The conditions of existence, as I conceive it, involve change and involve adaptation: perhaps if we ponder these necessities we shall gain some Concretions insight into the origin of organisms and the arise inevitably in secret of life. Each natural moment has a a flux of forward tension, it is a moment of transition. substance. Its present quality was determined by the force of lateral tensions guiding the previous dynamic stress of its substance; and the issue, as this moment passes into the next, will be determined by the lateral tensions to which its inner or forward tension is now subject. Is it not then native and proper to existence in its primary elements to congregate and to roll itself together into shells fashioned by its seeds, and into seeds fostered by its climate? And will not this initial concretion at any point go on swallowing what it can, destroying what it must, and harmonising its own complexity, until some contrary wind or some inner exhaustion disperses its elements? May not this disruption itself become less frequent with the extension of any cosmos, and the better co-ordination of the motions within it? A natural moment may be prolonged or reiterated; it may be caught up in a trope itself indefinitely recurrent, so that associated moments, duly spaced and controlled by their mutual tensions, may for a long time reappear in a fixed order. Any trope will recur if within its substance, or near by, there is generated a fresh natural moment, like the original one, and under similar conditions. Nothing more is required for a swarming or a hereditary life to cover the face of nature.

Every natural moment, in which matter at any point holds some essence unchanged, is fit to be the seed of all creatures and the centre of all thought. Some sequels might be reached only by a great and prosperous development from that moment outward; others might require the dissolution of this complex, and a fresh beginning, in some other direction, from one of its radical elements. But forwards or backwards, everything might be arranged round any nucleus, without the least violence or suppression of its original life, if only it were planted in the requisite soil. This profound naturalness of the greatest complications becomes clear to us in health, when we move spontaneously and think smoothly; it is only in disease that we tremble at our own incredible complexity, and

All matter is fit to be the matter of anything, if circumstances draw it into that form.

that harmony becomes a problem. In fact harmony in
itself is neither more difficult nor rarer than disorder:
that which demands a rare concourse of circumstances
is harmony *of this sort*, *here*; and yet, in the special
circumstances in which anything arises, harmony with
that thing is presupposed, otherwise that particular
thing would not have arisen. When our own ready-
made being and action are the facts in the foreground,
we instinctively and justifiably take it for granted that
surrounding nature is in harmony with them and will
give them suitable play; they are not unconditioned
or omnipotent, but they are co-operative with their
world. It is only when a different harmony, not native
to us, is suggested, that it seems to us impossibly
difficult of attainment and, if actual, miraculous.
Before we could adapt our presumptions and impulses
to that alien order we should need to retrace our steps
and follow that other path of development. Everything that is, except where it is, would be infinitely
improbable.

Thus the very fluidity of the flux, in its moving
equilibrium, causes every concretion that can arise to
arise, and every organism to maintain itself Repetition
which can maintain itself. Such is the and varia-
feeble yet ineradicable sympathy in the poor tion flow
heart of matter towards the whole realm of from the
essence. With many a false start, with a same
momentum and an organic memory often principle.
disastrous, with an inertia always trustfully blind,
existence passes inevitably and in many streams from
what it is to what it can be; it changes in the very act
of continuing, and undermines its condition in surrounding it with developments and supports. Then,
when any of these concretions collapses, as they must
all collapse in turn, it returns to the charge, perhaps
in the same direction, like Sisyphus, or like Proteus,
in quite another. In the first case we speak of repro-

duction, in the second of evolution: but these words do not stand for different forces or principles but only for different results. In reproduction the flux repeats the same trope, in evolution it changes that trope for one more complex or appropriate, imposed by a new balance of forces.

That collapse is inevitable follows from the fact that existence is essentially chaotic. Its parts, perhaps infinite in multitude, will be always readjust- ing their mutual tensions, so that, ultimately, the ground gives way under any edifice. And the catastrophe may ruin more than that confident system; it may radically transmute the elements which composed it, since every essence which matter may wear is arbitrary and, if occasion offers, may be exchanged for some other. Moreover, any trope has limits. The matter which executes or re- produces it, having done so, falls back into the relative chaos which remains the background of everything; so that death, in every instance, is the end of life; and in nature at large death can be only temporarily and imperfectly circumvented by fertility. I speak of fertility in a particular species and within one moral world: for of new creations there is presumably no end, and one perfection can neither remember nor desire another.

Enough for the day is the good thereof.

I confess that the life of the spider, or my own life, is not one which, if I look at it as a whole, seems to me worth realising; and to say that God's ways are not our ways, and that human tastes and scruples are impertinent, is simply to perceive that moral values cannot preside over nature, and that what arises is not the good, in any prior or absolute sense, but only the possible at that juncture: a natural growth which as it takes form becomes a good in its own eyes, or in the eyes of a sympathetic poet. Then this good realised endows with a relative and retrospective excellence all the conditions favourable to its being, as if with prophetic kindness and parental devotion they had conspired to produce it. The spider is a marvel of pertinacity, and I am not without affection for my own arts and ideas; we both of us heartily welcome the occasions for our natural activities; but when those occasions and activities have passed away, they will not be missed.

CHAPTER VIII

THE PSYCHE

OF all tropes the most interesting to the moralist is that which defines a life, and marks its course from

Life not an effect of spirit agitating matter. birth to death in some human creature. But a life is also the most crucial of tropes for the natural philosopher; for here his congenial mathematical categories leave him in the lurch, and he must either recognise their inadequacy to express the intimate flux of substance, or else cut his world in two, appending a purely literary or moral psychology to his mathematical physics. If emotional life preoccupies him, and he cannot simply ignore it, he may even be tempted to revert to the most primitive of dualisms, and to conceive the flux of existence as the resultant of two opposite agents: one an inert matter only capable of sinking into a dead sea of indistinction: the other a supernatural spirit, intrinsically disembodied, but swooping down occasionally upon that torpid matter, like the angel into the pool of Bethesda, and stirring it for a while into life and shape.

Need I give reasons, after all that has preceded,

Matter is, by definition, the principle of all motions. for discarding this last conception? In the first place it would be a materialistic and superstitious view of spirit to regard it as a wind, an effort, or any kind of physical force. On the other hand, in conceiving matter to be inert, merely heavy, and intrinsically blank, we should

328

be forgetting our original reason for positing matter at all; and instead of that existing substance, filling the field of action, and necessarily fertile in everything to be encountered there, we should be considering some casual symbol for matter, such as ignorant sensation or abstract science may have created. To say that matter, as it truly exists, is inert or incapable of spontaneous motion, organisation, life, or thought, would be flatly to contradict the facts: because the real matter, posited in action, and active in our bodies and in all other instruments of action, evidently possesses and involves all those vital properties.

Nevertheless, the venerable tradition which attributes the fashioning of the body to the soul might be retained, if only we could restore to the word " soul " all its primitive earthliness, potency, and mystery. Soul, as often in antiquity, would then signify an animating current widely diffused throughout the cosmos, a breath uncreated and immortal as a whole, but at each point entering some particular body and quitting it, in order to mingle again with the air, the light, the nether darkness, or the life of the god from which it came. Such a warm, fluid, transmissible agent would evidently be material. Industry requires hands: a traceable cause of specific motions must travel through space in particular channels. And indeed, that the soul was material, was once taken for granted both in India and in Greece. On the other hand, the Platonic and Christian tradition has come to identify the soul with a bodiless spirit, a sort of angel, at first neglecting and afterwards denying the biological functions which were the primitive essence of the soul; until in modern times the soul has been discarded altogether and its place taken by consciousness, something which in reality is the last and most highly conditioned of the works of a natural soul.

A soul moulding the body would be itself material.

Thus a soul or an angel became, for the Christian imagination, a supernatural substance, a personal spirit Christian notion of the soul. without material organs, yet somehow still capable of seeing, loving, and thinking, and even of exercising physical force and making its presence felt in particular places. In man, and perhaps in other creatures, an evil fate had imprisoned some of these angelic souls in a natural body, and contaminated them with the vital principle—the old animal heathen soul—proper to such a body. Sometimes, under the influence of Aristotle and of the Apostolic doctrine of the resurrection of the flesh, theologians have endeavoured to bridge the chasm between these two souls, one generative and the other degenerate. Thus the orthodox Catholic doctrine declares that by a special act of creation a rational immortal soul, previously non-existent, is substituted during gestation for the animal soul of the embryo: the new supernatural soul taking on the functions of the previous natural soul in addition to its own, and by that union becoming subject to their influence; an influence which marks the fallen state of the supernatural soul and its participation in the sin of Adam. A forced conjunction of two incompatible beings is obvious here, yet this conjunction is not without its dramatic propriety in expressing theoretically the moral conflicts of the Christian life; and the same incongruities reappear in any doctrine which would make the soul immaterial and its functions physical. A soul essentially generative and directive must be capable of existing unconsciously and of exerting material energy. If it were ever clearly identified with consciousness it would evaporate into a passing feeling or thought, something unsubstantial, volatile, evanescent, non-measurable and non-traceable. Once recognised in its spiritual actuality, this thought would not only be obviously incapable of exercising the vegetative and propulsive functions of animal life, but would loudly call for such an animal life to support its own intuitions and lend them their place in nature and their moral significance.

Avoiding, then, this poetical word, the soul, laden with so many equivocations, I will beg the reader to distinguish sharply two levels of life in the human body, one of which I call *the spirit*, and the other *the psyche*. By spirit I understand the actual light of consciousness falling upon anything—the ultimate invisible emotional fruition of life in feeling and thought. On the other hand, by the psyche I understand Definition a system of tropes, inherited or acquired, of the displayed by living bodies in their growth psyche. and behaviour. This psyche is the specific form of physical life, present and potential, asserting itself in any plant or animal; it will bend to circumstances, but if bent too much it will suddenly snap. The animal or plant will die, and the matter hitherto controlled by that psyche will be scattered. Such a moving equilibrium is at once vital and material, these qualities not being opposed but coincident. Some parcels of matter, called seeds, are predetermined to grow into organisms of a specific habit, producing similar seeds in their turn. Such a habit in matter is a psyche.[1]

In literary psychology the psychic often means simply the mental; and the reader may be disconcerted by the suggestion that the truly psychic, the dynamic life of both body and mind, is on the contrary material. Let me remind him, in that case, of the following fundamental points:

1. The psyche is not another name for consciousness or mind. Everything truly conscious or mental—feeling, intuition, intent—belongs to the realm of spirit. We may say of spirit, but not of the psyche, that its essence is to think. The psyche is a natural fact, the fact that

[1] A further illustration of this definition of the psyche may be found in my *Soliloquies in England*, pp. 217-224.

many organisms are alive, can nourish and reproduce themselves, and on occasion can feel and think. This is not merely a question of the use of words: it is *a deliberate refusal to admit the possibility of any mental machinery*. The machinery of growth, instinct, and action, like the machinery of speech, is all physical: but this sort of physical operation is called psychical, because it falls within the trope of a life, and belongs to the self-defence and self-expression of a living organism. How should any unsophisticated person doubt that the movements of matter have the nature of matter for their principle, and not the nature of spirit?

2. By the word matter I do not understand any human idea of matter popular or scientific, ancient or recent. Matter is properly a name for the actual substance of the natural world, whatever that substance may be. It would therefore be perfectly idle, and beside the point, to take some arbitrary idea of matter and to prove dialectically that from that idea none of the consequences follow with which the true substance of the world is evidently pregnant. What would be thereby proved would not be that matter cannot have the developments which it has, but that that particular idea of matter was wrong or at least inadequate.

3. In calling the psyche material I do not mean to identify her with any piece or kind of substance, an atom or monad or ether or energy. Perhaps all sorts of substances may enter into her system; she is not herself a substance, except relatively to consciousness, of which her movements and harmonies are the organ and the immediate support. She is a *mode* of substance, a trope or habit established in matter; she is made of matter as a cathedral is made of stone, or the worship in it of sounds and motions; but only their respective forms and moral functions render the one a cathedral or a rite, and the other a psyche.

4. The whole life of the psyche, even if hidden by

chance from human observation, is essentially observable: it is the object of biology. Such is the only scientific psychology, as conceived by the ancients, including Aristotle, and now renewed in behaviourism and psycho-analysis. This conception of the psyche also allows the adepts of psychical research to retain a congenial name for the very real region, far removed from everything that I call spiritual, in which occult processes, unusual powers, and subtle survivals may be actually discovered.

Biology aspires to be a part of physics, and this for the best of reasons, since in describing the spontaneous tropes that prevail in the flux of matter, Continuity physics is simply biology universalised. The of physics problem is not where to place the frontier and biology. between two disparate regions, but only to discover how the tropes most obvious in each of them are superposed or grow out of one another. The inanimate world must needs concern the zoologist, since it pervades and unites all living creatures; and the animate world must needs concern the physicist, since it is the crown of nature, the focus where matter concentrates its fires and best shows what it is capable of doing. Obviously, if we could understand the inmost machinery of motion we should understand life, which on the biological level is simply a system of motions.

In one sense, indeed, all matter is alive. Its deadest principles, like gravity and inertia, are principles of motion. The dry dust and the still waters Not all the which the wind sweeps into a vortex, if energies of mingled, will breed. Even celestial matter, matter are properly which might seem too tenuous and glowing vital or to be alive after our fashion, is fertile in light, psychic. which may be, perhaps, the primary stimulus to life, or a first form of it. Yet this universal ethereal trepidation is too diffuse and elusive to seem life to our human judgment, accustomed as we are to the crude contrast between a barking dog and a dead one. Even in animals and plants the life in which, so to speak, nature is interested, the life which is transmitted and preserved, is not their individual life, describable in a biography. Its vegetative continuity takes a course which, from our point of view, seems subterranean and unfriendly; for it does not pass from one complete animal or plant to the next (as the phases of each life succeed one another for the observant spirit), but the child buds at mid-branch, and the tree obdurately outlives its seeded flowers. In fact, individuality and tenacity never are more pronounced than in that old age which, as far as the life of nature is concerned, is so much dead wood and obstructive rubbish. Life at our level has adopted a vehicle which—like all natural vehicles—has a form and a story of its own, apart from the inherited movement which it serves to propagate. The individual has outgrown his character of a mere moment in a flux; his trope is not simply the general trope repeated and passed on. It has become a redundant trope, surrounding that other with epicycles and arabesques and prolongations useless to the march of transmissible life, yet enriching it at its several stations.

It is only metaphorically, therefore, that the general movement of nature can be called a life, or said to be

There is no cosmic soul. animated by a cosmic psyche. Nor would the attribution of these tropes to the universe as a whole explain why they should arise again within it. On the contrary, it is more natural to find fish in the sea than within other fishes. We may rather say that matter, although perhaps everywhere organic or at least ready to be organised, becomes animate only when it forms hereditary organisms; and that a psyche exists only in bodies that can assimilate and redistribute the substances suitable for preserving and propagating their type. Thus the cosmos—not feeding or breeding—can have no psyche, but only psyches within it; and the spirit is no psyche, but always has some psyche beneath, which sustains it.

Embryology, the most obscure part of biology, is accordingly the fundamental part of it. In the present state of knowledge, the psychologist is con- Profound demned to taking summary and superficial obscurity views of his subject, for he sees gross results, of the gross variations, gross repetitions, and all the psychic mechanism. fine, individual, intricate labour of the psyche escapes him. Physiology and organic chemistry work only with ready - made materials, which already possess inexplicable specific virtues and habits; and psycho-analysis, in really opening a trap-door, as disease does, into the dim carpentry of the stage, is compelled to transcribe that intricacy into metaphors. Its reports come to it in hectic language, the latest, most wayward, most hypocritical ebullition of psychic life; while its own theories, for lack of physiological knowledge, must be couched in mythological terms. Thus the psyche remains a mystery in her intrinsic operations; and if something of that mystery seems to hang about the feminine name we are giving her, so much the better: we are warned that we do not, and probably cannot, understand.

What our knowledge of the psyche lacks in precision it makes up, after a fashion, in variety and extent. All that is called knowledge of the world, of human nature, of character, and of the pas- The psyche, like other sions is a sort of auscultation of the psyche; natural and the familiarity of our verbal and dramatic mechanisms, is known to conventions often blinds us to their loose us by her application, and to our profound ignorance fruits. of the true mechanism of life. Not knowing what we are, we at least can discourse abundantly about our books, our words, and our social actions; and these manifestations of the psyche, though peripheral, are faithful enough witnesses to her nature. She is that inner moving equilibrium from which these things radiate, and which they help to restore—the equilibrium by which we live, in the sense of not dying; and to keep us alive is her first and essential function. It follows naturally from this biological office that in each of us she is one, vigilant, and predetermined; that she is selfish and devoted, intrepid and vicious, intelligent and mad; for her quick potentialities are solicited and distracted by all sorts of accidents. She slept at first in a seed; there, and from there, as the seed softened, she distributed her organs and put forth her energies, always busier and busier in her growing body, almost losing control of her members, yet reacting from the centre, perhaps only slowly and partially, upon events at her frontiers. If too deeply thwarted her industry becomes distraction; and what we sometimes call her plan, which is only her propensity, may be developed and transformed, if she finds new openings, until it becomes quite a different plan. But against brutal obstacles she will struggle until death; that is, until her central control, her total equilibrium and power of recuperation, are exhausted. Her death may as easily occur by insurrection within her organism—each part of which is a potential centre on its own account—as by hostile action from outside.

I hardly venture to say more. To watch a plant grow, or draw in its leaves, to observe the animals in a zoological garden, is to gain some knowledge of the psyche; to study embryology or the nervous system or insanity or politics, is (or ought to be) to gain more: and every system of science or religion is rich in this sort of instruction for a critic who studies it in order to distinguish whatever may be arbitrary in it, based on human accidents, and without any but a psychic ground. All the errors ever made about other things, if we understand their cause, enlighten us about ourselves; for the psyche is at once the spring of curiosity and the ground of refraction, selection, and distortion in our ideas. Summary reaction, symbolisation, infection with relativity and subjective colouring begins in the senses and is continued in the passions; and if we succeed in removing, by criticism, this personal equation from our science of other things, the part withdrawn, which remains on our hands, is our indirect knowledge of the psyche.

Each man also has direct experience of the psyche within himself, not so much in his verbal thoughts and distinct images—which if they are knowledge And also at all are knowledge of other things—as in a directly, certain sense of his personal momentum, a though vaguely, by pervasive warmth and power in the inner self-con- man. As he thinks and acts, intent on external sciousness. circumstances, he is not unaware of the knot of latent determinate impulses within him which respond to those circumstances. Our thoughts—which we may be said to know well, in that we know we have had them often before—are about anything and everything. We shuffle and iterate them, and live in them a verbal, heated, histrionic life. Yet we little know *why* we have them, or how they arise and change. Nothing could be more obscure, more physical, than the dynamics of our passions and dreams; yet, especially in moments of suspense or hesitation, nothing could be more intensely felt. There is the coursing of the blood, the waxing and waning of the affections, a thousand starts of smothered eloquence, the coming on of impatience, of invention, of conviction, of sleep. There are laughter and tears, ready to flow quite unbidden, and almost at random. There is our whole past, as it were, knocking at the door; there are our silent hopes; there are our future discourses and decisions working away, like actors rehearsing their parts, at their several fantastic arguments. All this is the psyche's work; and in that sense deeply our own; and our superficial mind is carried by it like a child, cooing or fretting, in his mother's arms. Much of it we feel going on unmistakably within our bodies, and the whole of it in fact goes on there. But the form which belongs to it in its truly physical and psychic character, in its vital bodily tropes, is even less known to us than the mechanism of the heart, or that by which our nerves receive, transmit, and return their signals. The psyche is an object of experience to herself, since what she does at one moment or in one organ she can observe, perhaps, a moment later, or with another organ; yet of her life as a whole she is aware only as we are aware of the engines and the furnaces in a ship in which we travel, half-asleep, or chattering on deck; or as we are aware of a foreign language heard for the first time, perceived in its globular sound and gesticulation and even perhaps in its general issue—that all is probably a dispute about money—yet without distinguishing the words, or the reasons for those precise passionate outbursts. In this way we all endure, without understanding, the existence and the movement of our own psyche: for it is the body that speaks, and the spirit that listens.

The psyche is the self which a man is proud or ashamed of, or probably both at once: not his body in its accidental form, age, and diseases, from which he instinctively distinguishes those initial impulses and thwarted powers which are much more truly himself. And this is the self which, if he lives in a religious age, he may say that he wishes to save, and to find reviving in another world. Yet this self is far from being a stranger to the body; on the contrary, it is more deeply and persistently the essence of the body than is the body itself. It is human, male or female, proper to a particular social and geographical zone; it is still the fountain of youth in old age; it deprecates in a measure the actions and words which circumstances

She is the internal source of the organism and of its action.

may have drawn from it, and which (it feels) do it enormous injustice; and yet the words and actions which it might have wished to produce instead are all words and actions of the same family, slightly more eloquent in the same human language, slightly more glorious in the same social sphere. The psyche is so much of us, and of our works, as is our own doing.

Conflicts between the flesh and the spirit, between habit and idea, between passion and reason, are real conflicts enough, but they are conflicts be- All moral tween one movement in the psyche and conflicts another movement there. Hers is a compound or dualisms are internal life, moulded by compromise, and compacted to her life. of tentative organs, with their several impulses, all initially blind and mechanical. Rarely will any particular psychic impulse or habit move in sympathy with all the rest, or be unquestionably dominant. It follows that what in religion or in moral reflection we call the spirit is a precarious harmony. It is threatened by subject powers always potentially rebellious, and it necessarily regards them as wicked and material in so far as they do not conspire to keep its own flame vivid and pure. And yet the spirit itself has no other fuel. Reason is not a force contrary to the passions, but a harmony possible among them. Except in their interests it could have no ardour, and, except in their world, it could have no point of application, nothing to beautify, nothing to dominate. It is therefore by a complete illusion, though an excusable one, that the spirit denies its material basis, and calls its body a prison or a tomb. The impediments are real, but mutual; and sometimes a second nucleus of passion or fleshliness rises against that nucleus which the spirit expresses, and takes the name of spirit in its turn. Every virtue, and in particular knowledge and thought, have no other root in the world than the co-ordination of their organs with one another and with the material habitat. Certainly such a co-ordination could never arise except in a psyche: the psyche is another name for it: but neither could the psyche have any life to foster and defend, nor any instruments for doing so, if she were not a trope arising in a material flux, and enjoyed a visible dominance there more or less prolonged and extended.

Thus the first function of the psyche in the seed is to create the outer body. With every organ which she brings forth she acquires a new office and a new type of life. These changes and developments are not devised and suggested to the psyche by some disembodied spirit, whispering in her ear. Were they not the natural continuation of her innate tensions she would be justified in regarding these promptings as deceits and snares of the devil. For from the point of view of the psyche (whose innate impulse is the arbiter of morals) every change of purpose is a change for the worse: either a vain complication or a hideous surrender. It is only lateral tensions, circumstances, external pressure, that can compel her to recast her habits and become, to that extent, a new psyche. Surrenders are indeed inevitable when the action for which the soul is ready happens to be impossible, or organs once agile are atrophied by disuse; and new acquisitions of function are inevitable too, when new occasions induce a different mode of action, and preserve and solidify it. The burden of the psyche is in this way continually lightened in one quarter and accumulated in another. If crippled at first by some loss, she may ultimately heal the wound (healing being one of her primary functions) and may live on with her residual equipment all the more nimbly. On the other hand she often hardens herself to some novel exertion which at first was forced and distracting, until that exercise becomes instinctive and necessary to her

Formation and variation of the psyche equally a resultant of material tensions.

health and peace, so that it is performed with alacrity and sureness whenever an occasion occurs. Habituation tames the spirit, or rather kills it in one form and recreates it in another. This forced attention to instrumentalities, this awkwardness, which marks the acquisition of a new art, yields in time to love and mastery; and the spirit rises again from its troubles and threatened death to happiness and confidence.

At bottom, however, the whole psyche is a burden to herself, a terrible inner compulsion to care, to watch, to pursue, and to possess. Yet to evade this predestined career would be a worse fate; and the psyche is more terribly corroded and tormented for not doing, than she would be harassed in doing, or disappointed at having done. Original sin must be purged, the burden discharged, the message delivered. Happiness—for the surface of the psyche is normally happy—lies for her in jogging on without too much foresight or retrospect, along the middle way, exercising her central functions heartily, and reverting to them, as to hearth and home, from those gambler's losses or commitments into which she may be tempted. In this way she may healthfully deliver herself in a long life of her native burden, transmit the same in a healthful measure, and sleep in peace.

Her mission is to discharge an imposed burden.

Sleep is in a manner the normal condition of the psyche, from which in her vegetative and somatic labours she never awakes, unless it be to suffer; and we may fancy that a sort of sub-soul or potential life sleeps, and will always sleep, in the universe of matter, ready to shape it, when opportunity occurs, into the likeness of all essence. Yet as this labour must be in time, and in some one of many alternative courses, the greater part of that sleeping psyche remains unoccupied, and the occupied part anxious and full of the fear of death: from which indeed she cannot escape except by falling asleep again and forgetting, but never really removing, the peril of a new birth.

To be completely mastered by the psyche makes the health, agility, and beauty of the body. This sort of virtue is common among the brutes. It would seem to suffice that a very potent psyche—one to which its matter completely submits—should have entrenched herself in the seed and should surround it later with outworks so staunch and perfect that no ordinary hazard will pierce or bend them. Unquestioning fidelity to type is always a marvel, a victory of form over matter, which delights the contemplative spirit. In fragile organisms, such as children or flowers, this fidelity seems to us an appealing innocence; but in hard-shell organisms, which attempt to resist change by force of rigidity, it seems rather stupid. Brave and proud the conservative psyche may be: she will not suffer minor accidents to distract her from her first vows and native intentions; but against major accidents she has no resource save a total death; and on earth she must be extraordinarily prolific to survive at all.

The peculiarity of the human psyche, on the contrary, is her great relative plasticity. I will not call it intelligence, because that presupposes a fixed good to to be attained, and invention only of new means of attaining it. A total plasticity, that for greater convenience consents to change its most radical direction, would hardly be life; its only assignable purpose would seem to be survival, and even this would be illusory, since the psyche that was to survive would have abdicated in doing so, and would have committed suicide. This the human soul is capable of doing, morally as well as physically, as we see in madness, in conversion, and in the wilder passions; but ordinarily her plasticity remains only a means to a native end, an incidental adjustment in the interests of the major radical passions,

Completely determinate psyches are beautiful but not safe.

which remain supreme at the centre. Yet this alert human psyche, more intelligent than wise, often forgets the treasure locked in the citadel, and lives by preference in her own suburbs, in the outer organs of action and perception. She then becomes distracted, frivolous, loquacious; and we may doubt whether all this agitation and knowingness relieve her of her inner burden, or only add a dreadful fatigue to a profound dissatisfaction.

Nor is this all: friction at the periphery more or less recoils to the centre and modifies the organisation there. Changes of food, temperature, climate, and rhythm may extend to the very substance of the seed whence the next generation is to grow; so that the psyche transmitted is not always exactly similar to the psyche inherited. *Some adaptations extend to the germ.* In the history of the earth, the evolution and transformation of psyches must have gone on from the beginning; and this reconstruction, which in some directions seems to have come to a temporary end and produced stable types of animals, in the human race still continues at an unusual rate. Not so much in the body—unless we regard clothes and weapons as equivalents to fur and claws—but in the singular equipment with instruments by which modern man has surrounded himself, and in the management of which he lives. The changes are so rapid that we can observe and record them: something perhaps impossible and inconceivable to any psyche except the human.

All this may be studied and described behaviouristically, as a chapter in natural history; yet we know that the psyche so occupied has an inner invisible experience, which under these circumstances becomes very complex. The eloquence of language, the multitude of sights and sounds, the keen edge of silent emotion compose a perpetual waking dream—a view *The feeling always involved in psychic life becomes in animals perception and in man thought.* of the world which is not a part of the world and which even in sleep continues and shifts fantastically in many a muted development. This unsubstantial experience, which is alone immediate, is nothing new or paradoxical in kind. The psyche is probably never unconscious; she always feels, in some vague emotional form, the inherent stress of her innumerable operations. Her maturing instincts have their false dawn in her mind; she warms and awakes for a moment at their satisfaction, and simmers pleasantly when replete. But external perception is a keener, more inquisitive form of attention; it is less interested in what is given æsthetically, or even in what might be given, than in the action of things upon one another and on our bodies. At the same time, perception cannot fail to supply us with images—products of the inner psyche, like the feelings of blind animals—which serve to name and to clothe in our poetic consciousness those external objects of her concern. These images and those feelings, together with the constant flow of unspoken words which we call thinking, compose a mental or inner life. Its moments, though probably intent on external material events, are yet directly but symptoms of psychic movements; so that it requires only a shift in apperception to transform all this immediate experience from active consideration of dubious external objects into a certain and accurate index to an internal psychic life.

Not that these moments of spirit, these mental notes and mental vistas, *are* the psychic life in question. Secondary or express- They form a thin flux of consciousness, chiefly ive nature verbal in most of us, which in reflective moods of con- becomes self-consciousness, recollection, auto- sciousness. biography, and literature: all only the topmost synthesis, or play of shooting relations, on the surface of the unconscious. In this capacity, however, as a mental symptom or expression, self-consciousness gives infallible renderings of the agitation beneath. We may therefore use it, in so far as we can recollect it or reconstruct it, to describe the psyche and her passions, just as we use the essences given in perception to describe pictorially those parts of the material world on which the organs of perception react.

Hence a second approach to a science of the psyche, this time not biological or behaviouristic, but personal, through memory and repeatable mental dis- Possibility course; and this imagination of imagination of literary may fill our whole lives, composing a dramatic, psychology. social, religious world in which we suppose ourselves to be living. Such a moral world, the world of humanism, need not mislead in practice the psyche that creates it. Sometimes she may become more interested in this play-world—in religion, landscape, fiction, and eloquence—than in her natural circumstances. Yet all her imaginative life is interfused with language and akin to language, so that it often becomes a convenient or indispensable transcript for the march of things on . the human scale. It may be so disciplined and adjusted to facts as to compose history and literary psychology.

The two sorts of psychology, the scientific and the literary, are clearly distinguished by Aristotle where he says that anger is a name for two different Its relation things, anger being physically a boiling of the to the humours and dialectically a desire for revenge. natural science of Boiling of the humours would be an exterior the psyche. and gross effect of the total movement of the psyche, and the natural history of a passion is far more complicated and far-reaching than any such symptom; yet the boiling is on the same plane as the whole object of biology, on the plane of behaviour, and gives us a first glimpse of what anger is, substantially considered. On the other hand, " a desire for revenge " is a current verbal and dramatic expression for such a passion: this too is summary and might be elaborated in each case into an almost infinite network of motives, memories, likes and dislikes, and delicate juxtapositions of images and words; yet whatever figments we might substitute for the conventional terms " anger " or " desire " would be further literary figments, verbal or intuitive units formed and re-formed by the discoursing spirit, and non-existent in the realm of matter. For this reason the most adequate and confident knowledge of human nature, rendered in literary terms, as in novels and plays, or in the gossip of busybodies, covers only what might be called the reasoned element in life—although it is for the most part foolish at bottom. The same psychology remains helpless in the presence of all the radical passions and all the natural collocations of persons and events by which the life of mind is determined.

Literature and literary philosophy are nevertheless the most natural and eloquent witnesses to the life of the psyche. Literature is conserved speech, speech is significant song, and song is a pure overflow of the psyche in her moments of free play and vital leisure. And this overflow is itself double: biological and ontological. Biologically it resembles the exuberance of the psyche in all her well-fed and happy moments, in the gambols of young animals, the haughtiness of all accomplished strength, or the endless experimentation in colours, forms, and habits characteristic of the psyche in fashioning her strange menagerie of bodies. Yet the ontological overflow, the concomitant emergence of consciousness, alone seems to arrest the wonder, not to say the wrath, of philosophers; and they are so surprised at it, and so wrathful, that they are inclined to deny it, and to call it impossible. I have not myself such an intrinsic knowledge of matter as to be sure that it cannot do that which it does: nor do I see why the proudest man should be ashamed of the parents who after all have produced him. I am not tempted seriously to regard consciousness as the very essence of life or even of being. On the contrary, both my

personal experience and the little I know of nature
at large absolutely convince me that consciousness is
the most highly conditioned of existences, an overtone
of psychic strains, mutations, and harmonies; nor does
its origin seem more mysterious to me than that of
everything else.

Let us, in this important matter, go back to first
principles. From the beginning it was in the very
nature of existence to be involved in indirect
commitments. Being transitive, anything existing is always in the act of becoming something which it was not, and yet which it was
the sufficient cause for producing, according
to those irresponsible impulses which animate
its matter and predetermine its fate. The sequel is
always spontaneous and, if we are not dulled by habit,
seems miraculous; yet it is always natural, since no
other development would have been more so, and
some development was inevitable. Nature is not that
realm of essence where all variety and all relations are
perspicuous and intrinsically necessary. Necessity, in
nature, is only an irrational propulsion which, as a
matter of fact, is prevalent; existence could not have
begun to be, it could not have taken the first step
from one form of being to another, if it had not been
radically mad. But this madness not only has method
in it—a method in itself arbitrary and doubtless variable
—it has also a certain glorious profusion, a rising,
cumulative intensity and volume, coming to a climax
and then dying down. The flux thus runs inevitably
into dramatic episodes, even in its own plane of matter;
episodes in our eyes far more interesting than its general
movement, which is perhaps only itself an episode in
some more radical genesis of existence.

But the tacit commitments of such existence are not
limited to the material plane. Every fact involves many
a truth about it; it casts its shadow through infinite

> Change,
> concretion,
> dissolution,
> and varia-
> tion are
> intrinsic to
> a flux.

distances and makes relevant to it everything that it resembles and everything that it contradicts. By arising and by disappearing it introduces an unalterable event into history; it verifies or stultifies all prophecies concerning it and concerning the place which it fills in the context of nature, and which might have been filled otherwise; and it either justifies or renders false everything that anyone may say or think of it in future.

The eternal truth about it is also involved in it.

Here, then, is a whole infinite world, visible only to the intellect, but actually created and made precise by the blind flux of matter, whatsoever that flux may be. These are the indelible footprints which existence, thoughtlessly running on, neither knows nor cares that it is making, and which yet are its only memorial, its only redemption from death, the eternal truth about it.

Now, when the flux falls into the trope which we call a psyche, existence commits itself unawares to yet another complication; for now the reverberation of its movement in the realm of truth becomes, so to speak, vocal and audible to itself. Not indeed in its entirety—unless there be some divine sensorium to gather all its echoes together—but in snatches. At certain junctures animal life, properly a habit in matter, bursts as with a peal of bells into a new realm of being, into the realm of spirit. When does this happen, and how is this consciousness diversified and guided? We may presume that some slumbering sensibility exists in every living organism, as an echo or foretaste of its vital rhythms; and even when no assignable feeling comes to a head, if there is life at all, there is a sort of field of consciousness, or canvas spread for attention, ready to be occupied by eventual figures. Not by *any* figures, as if essences of their own initiative could come down and appear; but only by certain predetermined classes and intensities of sensation, possible to the particular

Where the flux is a psyche, some truths about it become occasions for feeling.

organs whose suspended animation, or busy growth, spreads that canvas and rings that ground-tone of potential feeling. When ambient influences or inner ripening modify this vital rhythm, or cause the psyche actively to assimilate or to repel that stimulant, organic slumber may easily awake to some special feeling or image. Thus sensations and ideas always follow upon organic reactions and express their quality; and intuition merely supplies a mental term for the animal reaction already at work unconsciously. With each new strain or fresh adjustment, a new feeling darts through the organism; digestive sleep breaks into moral alertness and sharp perception; and, once initiated, these modes of sensibility may persist even in quiescent hours —for they leave neurograms or seeds of habit in the brain—and may be revived in thought and in dreams.

Consciousness, then, in its genesis and natural status, is one of the indirect but inevitable outpourings proper to an existence which is in flux and gathers itself into living bodies. In consciousness the psyche becomes festive, lyrical, rhetorical; she caps her life by considering it, and talking to herself about the absent parts of it. Consciousness is a spiritual synthesis of organic movements; and were it not this, no spirit and no consciousness would ever have any transcendent significance or any subject-matter other than the essences which it might weave together. Yet in fact, on account of its organic seat and material conditions, consciousness is significant. Its every datum is an index, and may become in its eyes a symbol, for its cause. In other words, consciousness is naturally cognitive. Its spiritual essence renders it an imponderable sublimation of organic life, and invisible there; yet it is attached historically, morally, and indicatively to its source, by being knowledge of it.

Being spiritual in essence, yet materially conditioned, consciousness can be knowledge of its source.

Thus, like truth, consciousness is necessarily faithful

to its basis in the flux of nature; it is a commentary on events, in the language of essence; and while its light is contemplative, its movement and intent strictly obey the life of the psyche in which it is kindled.

This knowledge is natural in its origin, validity, and scope.
Hence the whole assertive or dogmatic force of intelligence, by which the spirit ventures to claim knowledge of outspread facts, and not merely to light up and inspect a given essence. This whole extraordinary pretension rests on a vital compulsion, native to the body, imposing animal faith on a spirit in itself contemplative. For in animals the organs are inevitably addressed to intercourse with relevant external things, as well as to internal growth and reproduction. Suspense outwards, towards an object not within her organism, is habitual to the psyche. Her tentacles and her actions hang and grope in mid-air, like a drawbridge confidently let down to meet its appropriate ulterior point of contact and support. Even her vegetative life is prophetic, conscious of maturation, and rich in preparations for coming crises, vaguely prefigured but unhesitatingly pursued. Under such circumstances and with such organs, consciousness could not be pure intuition: it must needs be intuition carried by intent. The intent is adventurous; its object or ulterior development is hidden and merely posited. Yet by thus torturing itself, and uprooting itself from its immediate datum, spirit becomes perception, and perception knowledge, in all its transitive and realistic force. And this perception and knowledge are, for the same reason, normally and virtually true: not true literally, as the fond spirit imagines when it takes some given picture, summary, synthetic, and poetical, for the essence of the world; but true as language may be true, symbolically, pragmatically, and for the range of human experience in that habitat and at that stage in its history.

So much for the claims of spirit to possess knowledge,

and for the range of it. But whence the original qualities
of feeling itself, the choice of essences that shall
appear in intuition, the spectrum of each sense, The
the logic and grammar of each type of intelli- spectrum
gence? How does the psyche arrive at any of sense
                                             and the
of these creations, rather than at any other? categories
Certainly out of her own substance, and by of thought
                                             are original
the natural diversity and fertility of the tropes creations of
which she imposes on her own matter. The the psyche.
presumption of common sense, that these essences
belong in the first place to objects and pass from them
into the organs of sense, and somehow become evident
to spirit in the dark caverns of the brain, is unfortunately
untenable. We find it plausible—in spite of its in-
coherence and the many contrary facts—because we
begin our reflection at the end, armed with our working
conventions and dogmatic habits. We should readily
understand the enormous illusion involved, and the
false reduplication of our data, if we began at the
beginning, where in the natural world the psyche
begins. Surely pleasure and pain, hunger, lust, and
fear, do not first reside in external objects and pass
from them into the mind: and these are the primary,
typical data of intuition. All the rest—colours, sounds,
shapes, specious spaces and times and sensations of
motion—is hatched in the same nest; it all has a
similar psychic seat and dramatic occasion. If such
essences seem to be found in external things, it is for
the good and sufficient reason that outer things are
perceived by us in these sensible terms, and could not
be perceived were not the psyche sensitive, and fertile
in such signals to the spirit. All things might stand
facing one another for ever, clad in all the colours of
the rainbow; and were there no poetic psyche in any
of them, to turn those colours into feelings of colour
and intuitions of the soul, never would anything
perceive anything else.

The psyche is a poet, a creator of language; and there is no presumption that she will perceive material things, including her own substance and movement, at all in the terms or in the order and scale in which they exist materially. On the contrary, only the reactions of her organism are represented in her feelings; and these reactions, which are tropes subsisting only in the realm of truth, resemble in nothing the imponderable feelings which are involved in executing them. The fountain of sense and of sensible qualities lies indeed in the forward and inner tensions of natural moments, with their conjunctions and flow in a psyche. Pain, novel in essence, signalises a special nervous affection, not another pain elsewhere; and this signal is suitable, in as much as just such a cry would be uttered by any psyche in such a predicament, and for all psyches signifies predicaments of that sort. The whole of life is a predicament, complex and prolonged; and the whole of mind is the cry, prolonged and variously modulated, which that predicament wrings from the psyche.

They express directly her own movements and only indirectly and relatively their external occasion.

After the spirit is born, and in the midst of business has begun to take note silently of the actual aspects and essences of things, the psyche may extend her action with more circumspection, in what we call the arts. That pause, as we may think it, for wonder and contemplation, was only, from her housewife's point of view, a pause for breath: in stopping to gaze, she gives herself time to readjust her impulses and increase her range. Having, among other organs, formed the human hand, she may proceed through that instrument to transform matter outside her body; so that artificial instruments and works become, as it were, organs of the psyche too. With this extension of her instruments her spirit, which is the fruition of them in act, also extends its basis.

Psychic origin and control of the arts.

From her centre, where the spirit lives, she may now control and watch a whole political, industrial, and learned world. Civilisation may accumulate for her benefit a great fund of traditions, which will foster the spirit systematically and direct it rationally. Just as in the growth of the embryo there was a marvellous precision and timeliness in the production of the various organs hereditary in the species, so in animal society there is a great, though much looser, predetermination of what the arts shall produce.

Art, as I use the word here, implies moral benefit: the impulsive modification of matter by man to his own confusion and injury I should not call The psyche art, but vice or folly. The tropes of art and all her must be concentric with those of health in subject to the psyche, otherwise they would not, on the disease. whole, extend her dominion or subserve her need of discharging her powers. Nature is everywhere full of vices, partly apathetic, in that the impulse at work does not avail to transmute new matter into its instrument, and partly aberrant, in that the impulse itself runs wild, and destroys, instead of buttressing, its original organ—for without an organ an impulse can neither exist nor operate. Thus the psyche continually creates diseases in her substance, or invents scourges and trammels to oppress her from without, as does a false civilisation, through the mad work of her own hands. These aberrations, if extreme, soon defeat themselves by the ruin which they cause; but often they interweave themselves permanently into the strong woof of life, rendering life wretched but not impossible.

In the very inertia of habit, however, as in inveterate vices, there may be a certain luxury or compensation. Impulse, having taken to that trope, may find a certain pleasure in repeating it, a sort of dogged allegiance and sense of rightness, more intimately native and satisfying than any overt proof of its folly. The virtuous human soul, so to speak, is then long dead and buried, and the omnivorous vice has become a soul in its stead. We are compacted of devils. Love and conscience, like the rest, are initially irrational; and the conservative inner man may strenuously cling to methods in art and to forms of sentiment which defeat his eventual rational nature. The fatal imperative of his daemon may lie deeper in him than any ulterior claim of beauty or happiness.

Thus the spiritual function of the psyche is added to her generative and practical functions, creating a fresh and unprecedented realm of being, the realm of spirit, with its original æsthetic spectrum and moral range and values incommensurable with anything but themselves. Yet this whole evocation is a concomitant function of the same psyche which presides over bodily growth and action. Were it not so, spirit would have no place in time or in nature, no relevance to existence, and indeed, no existence of its own; and even if by a flight of mythological fancy we imagined it existing disembodied, it would thereby have forfeited all its dramatic breathlessness, all its moral aspiration, all its piety and potential wisdom. It would be an abstract intellect without a spiritual life, a hypostasis of the realm of truth or of essence, and not a human virtue. So that the dependence of spirit on animal life is no brutal accident, no inexplicable degradation of a celestial being into the soul of a beast. All the themes and passions of spirit, however spiritual or immaterial in themselves, celebrate the vicissitudes of a natural psyche, like a pure poet celebrating the adventures of lovers and kings.

Meantime she has given birth to spirit and attached it to earthly interests.

CHAPTER IX

PSYCHOLOGISM

IF the movements of matter are due to the nature of matter, not to that of spirit, should not the movements of spirit likewise be due to the nature of spirit, not to that of matter? It might seem so: and a great part of human philosophy has been devoted to exploring this tempting path. Yet the issue has been complete confusion; because the nature of spirit is not, like that of matter, to be a principle of existence and movement, but on the contrary a principle of enjoyment, contemplation, description, and belief; so that while spirit manifests its own nature no less freely than matter does, it does so by freely regarding and commenting on something else, either matter or essence: its primary nature is to be secondary —to be observant and intelligent. As grammar is arbiter of the syntax of speech, yet contains no power to determine when anyone shall speak or what he shall wish to say, so spirit contains no principle to determine its own occasions, its distribution in time and place, or the facts that shall seem to confront it. It cannot originate the animal powers and passions which it comes to express. Existence and movement, even in spirit, are therefore the work of matter; while the perception, the enjoyment, the understanding of both matter and spirit are the life of spirit itself. If we

Misguided attempts to represent spirit as master of its own existence and occasions.

355

deny this, and insist on assigning to spirit the functions proper to matter, *spirit, before we know it, has
become but another name for matter in our philosophy
and in our lives.* In this chapter and in the next I will
endeavour to justify this assertion.

That a material force, or all material forces, should
be called spirit would be nothing new in the history
of language, but rather a reversion to the
primitive meaning of the word. Wind is
invisible but mighty, and it combines a
potentiality of causing total ruin with a
gentler habit of filling our sails and doing
our work for us. Spirit, a synonym for such
a wind, might well be the principle of all action and
of all motion. So conceived, it would be precisely
that sustaining substance and connecting medium
which is requisite to produce feelings consecutively
and responsively to one another. It would be what I
call the psyche, a reservoir and fountain for the redistribution of energy in the material world, a centre
of bodily organisation and action, and simultaneously
an organ of sensation, passion, and thought. When
people feel a power of origination and decision within
them, so that, unless externally hindered, they are free
to do whatever they will, undoubtedly they are not
deceived. It is not the transforming power of the
human heart and brain that any historian of earthly
revolutions would be tempted to deny. Human
energies have polished the earth's surface and pullulate
in it: and it is only too easy for random impulses and
contagious phrases to carry mankind away, like sheep
after a bellwether. But this guiding or organising
or explosive force in animal life is not spirit in any
spiritual sense. It is an obscure, complex, groping
movement of the psyche, or of many psyches in contact: it is a perpetual readjustment of passionate habits
in matter.

Spirit was a name for material force before it was a name for intuition.

When Descartes said that the essence of the soul was to think he gave an excellent definition of spirit; but he initiated a tendency which has dominated modern psychology to its radical disadvantage, the tendency to describe the mind apart from the body and to make psychology merely literary. In his own system the psyche or principle of bodily life was physical and mechanical, and of this true psyche consciousness or thought could only be a concomitant manifestation, and by no means the essence or substance. Nevertheless it was precisely this collateral or ulterior manifestation of the psyche, this conscious spirit, that (because it was the actuality and light of knowledge) became for him and for his followers the one sure existence, and the fulcrum of philosophy: so that since his day philo- But taken sophers have tended to assert that of existence as the we have but this single known or conceivable seat of knowledge, instance—our own feeling or consciousness. spirit may When the relativity of all things to the know- absorb the ledge of them is emphasised, this principle universe. becomes transcendental idealism; but when only the mental nature of all existence, perhaps scattered in many moments and centres, is insisted on, the result is a system of psychological physics which, for convenience, may be called psychologism. This system professes to describe the stuff and constitution of the universe; but it differs from ordinary physics in admitting into its world no elements other than moments of actual experience, as autobiography or dramatic sympathy might catch and describe them. These moments, each only too real in itself, will compose all reality, with nothing latent beneath them, and nothing save other conscious moments possible beyond.

Such a system, though easily conceivable in the abstract, never occurred to the ancients, and would probably never occur to any pure naturalist. Its origin is rather political and poetical: it is humanism become at once radical and sentimental. It sprang up, together with Protestantism and liberalism, out of a worthy but exclusive interest in the inner man. It marks the self-sufficiency of the adult moral individual, forgetful of his origins, and of the external forces which sustain his being. Such reforms often end by abandoning the principle which they seemed at first to exalt, and psychologism in particular may end by denying the existence of consciousness. To one who has never distrusted the orthodox traditions of the human intellect, this conclusion may seem gratuitous and absurd: but it is justified relatively, in compensation for the error of psychologism in making mind absolute, and in pursuance of its critical method: for after all consciousness is directed upon its objects, and knows them before it knows itself.

Psychologism grows out of humanism, which it attempts to make absolute.

The impulse to reduce science to literature was native to humanism and to the whole Renaissance. How much more interesting than logic or theology was the limitless experience which literature could transcribe or suggest! Yet in life a system of science is always involved; and the system assumed by humanists is probably naturalism, which if pressed is materialism; but this is assumed, as all men assume it in daily life, without stopping to defend or to criticise it. To do either would be to become the victim of one of those precarious pedantic dogmatisms which the buxom humanist despises. He lives by a loose naturalism or by a loose religious convention, without examining the principle on which he is living. Nevertheless he is quite positive about the history of the human race, and the variety of its languages, customs, and opinions, including all those conflicting philosophies and religions which, if taken seriously, would prove so inhuman. He may even discourse freely about the

Yet humanism presupposes belief in nature.

causes of events, indulging in prophecy, and leaning towards the higher superstitions, such as the belief in inevitable progress or in laws of history. These prophecies and superstitions, however, can hardly be more than dim perspectives which he thinks he descries in the natural world. History cannot do without geography and material documents and monuments; psychology cannot do without the words and actions of material persons. The humanist inevitably assumes nature reliably at work within and around mankind: a fact which need not prevent him, as it does not prevent the avowed materialist, from relegating the physical world to the background of his thoughts and letting these play by preference on moral and lyrical episodes.

Suppose, however, that we turn this superficial humanism into a dogmatic philosophy and assert that the literary and moral sphere is absolute, so that human experience has always gone on in a vacuum, without any causes, occasions, or existing objects, other than these same successive experiences of particular minds. Would such an all-embracing psychologism compose an adequate system of the universe? For the purposes of the dramatic historian or religious moralist, I think it would. The lives of individuals, as each appears to his own memories and hopes, make up a sort of universal Plutarch, a sufficient handbook for the cure of souls, in which material circumstances need not figure except as picturesque details or landscapes diversifying the experience of those several minds. In sentimental retrospect a man may easily view the scenes of his childhood as having been unsubstantial, and merely a visionary stage-setting to the drama of his young soul. Extending this method to the present and future, we may regard the whole world of history, science, and religion, as internal to the desultory

It may retreat into a personal idealism or monadology.

thoughts in which it is conceived. What a simplification of philosophy, what a lightening of the burden of conventional beliefs! At one stroke the spirit seems to be liberated from all but spiritual preoccupations, and all things are reduced to so many pleasing or oppressive sensations, so many friends or enemies of our internal liberty and peace.

Such were the systems of Berkeley and Leibniz, which though very unequal in their technical elabora-
Berkeley and Leibniz recognised the psychic ground and visionary nature of all phenomena. tion, had this radical merit in common: that they were perfectly lucid and frank about the ideal or visionary nature of all the possible data of experience. These data were all necessarily " inert ideas " or qualities of feeling; they were essences which did not and could not exist on their own account. While they were given they qualified the spirit that contemplated or endured them, and they might then be said to exist " in the mind "; but it was the perception of them that alone really existed; they were incapable of subsisting or generating one another in their own specious or objective plane; they arose and vanished *in toto*, as did the whole phenomenal world, with every movement of attention. Thus all images and terms of thought were impotent and unsubstantial, yet they were not unmeaning; on the contrary, it was the very secret of their being that they were signs. In their variety and movement they composed the language in which spirit might speak to spirit; and Providence caused them to arise, as in a prophetic dream, in order that by their monition and habitual sequence they might forewarn us and make us ready for their future harmonies.

These systems were essentially theological; they invited mankind to substitute a metaphysical faith in a metaphysical power for the animal faith in matter by which we are accustomed to live. Verbally the exchange was easy, and might even be emotionally accepted at certain moments of spiritual exaltation, by a person like Malebranche, accustomed to think religiously; but the religiosity of Berkeley and Leibniz was only official; their idealism was, and was intended to be, perfectly mundane. Common sense, science, and commerce had no cause to take alarm at it, nor religion to take comfort. In their critical analysis they might sincerely persuade themselves that in looking and touching, in talking and travelling, they were in direct and unmediated communion with God or with other spirits; but God, at least, was comfortably pledged never to act otherwise than as if matter were acting for him. The muscular idealist could remain wedded in heart and imagination to that material world which he denied in his verbal doctrine. Learning, business, and propaganda, tar-water and diplomacy, might occupy him far more absorbingly than any prayerful vision of God, or any suspense of wondering hope on the daily manna of sensation.

An ethereal language to express mundane interests.

Indeed, even in theory, these philosophers were but half-idealists. If they had so easily swept matter away from the landscape of nature—which indeed is a mere image—it was only because, wittingly or unwittingly, they had packed away all the potency of matter and all its organisation into the mysterious mechanism of each soul, and into the mysterious interaction of one soul with another. Spirit had not only become again a wind, an invisible power, but each spirit separately, or the swarm of spirits collectively, had become a world of unfathomable generative processes—a world far less observable, and no less mechanical, than the earth and sky of vulgar philosophy. These souls without bodies continued to be full of hidden potentialities and blind passions; they lasted through a time

The soul remained a natural psyche in all its functions and relations.

which being common to them all was not specious and imaginary, but physical and independent of the temporal perspectives within each of them. They were buffeted by collateral contacts or compulsions which virtually subjected them to existence in a physical space. If they did not exert physical force upon one another, at least they interchanged telephonic messages through a sort of central exchange established in the divine mind. Remove matter, thought Berkeley, and you remove all danger of atheism. It did not occur to him to ask in what respect God would differ from matter if the divine function was simply to excite sensation and to supply a medium for psychic telegraphy. He blandly supposed that the alternative to matter was the God of Christianity: but we know that his psychological scepticism, when carried out, will undermine all Christian legend and all Christian cosmology.

A God who was a supreme spirit, like the God of Aristotle and Plotinus, would be immutable: his action God, too, on the world could only occur through an became eternal attraction or effluence, enabling or again a material soliciting matter to take such forms as matter agent. at each point might be capable of taking. If we wish to avoid this conclusion, and to regard divine action as incidental and occasional, God becomes a natural being, like the gods of legend and mythology, living in time, discovering piecemeal his own preferences, recasting his plans, and parrying the blows of fortune or of free-will in others, like any proud animal, with ever-fresh ingenuity and explosions of temper. Such are the moral powers actually at work in the world; some of them might be superhuman; but in any case they would be internal to the field of action, and would inhabit the material agencies by which they were manifested: so that the belief in interaction and intercommunication between so-called

spirits is really a belief in the realm of matter, and in
the interplay there of various living centres.

This conclusion is indeed implicit in the principle
by which the realm of matter is posited in the beginning.
If spirits are agents, they can be discovered This follows
only by being posited in the field of action, from the
and only by virtue of their functions there. nature and
Like matter they will be names for the respon- of animal
sive and calculable energies which are there faith.
at work. But that which fills the field of action, and
is unequally distributed there, being nearer or farther,
mightier or weaker, in discoverable measures; that
which is in perpetual motion, compelling us to act in
time by its definite pressure or allurements; that which
acts within us mysteriously in response, and which
preserves the effects of our action in the form of readiness and habit—this, by definition, is matter itself:
and this definition, I think, is by no means arbitrary,
but scrupulously faithful to the normal force of the
word, and to its spontaneous application. Therefore
the spirits posited by Berkeley, Malebranche, and
Leibniz, or by anyone who thinks of spirits as powers,
are simply mythological names for certain operations of
matter, poetically apprehended, and turned into dramatic units with reference to the observer's interests or
emotions. Human spirits are such mythological units
corresponding to the actions or surviving effects of
human bodies; and God is such a mythological name
for the universal power and operation of matter.

Indeed, the more critical advocates of psychologism
have abandoned, at least in theory, all notion of spirits,
powers, or agents; and for them the universe If feelings
is composed exclusively of momentary feelings, have no
for whose existence, number, quality, or order ground, how
no reason at all can be given or required. It an order?
is perhaps not very clear to a materialist how sensations
arise in bodies; but is it clearer to the pure psychologist

how they should arise in nothing and out of nothing?
It is true that existence is contingent in any case and
ultimately groundless; but in psychologism this initial
marvel is continually recurrent. Sensations and ideas
are supposed to be many: each pops of itself into
existence; yet nothing—since nothing else exists—can
possibly condition their genesis or subtend their
variety. Each, no less than the order of all, is absolutely
uncaused and might just as well have been entirely
different. Nevertheless the advocate of psychologism
seems never to doubt that they all spring up as seasonably
as the leaves of a tree; they seem to be miraculously
revealed to him, who is at any moment only one of them,
in their variegated character and precise distribution.
Something, which he says is nothing, compels each to
bide its own time and makes it cognisant of the existence
and order of the rest.

This assumption of inexplicable transcendent knowledge is so lightly made because psychologism is not an
original or primary conviction, but a critical
reform introduced into a conventional naturalism. Its categories are secondary naturalistic
categories—those of history and social imagination—and they are employed unchallenged after
the primary categories—those of action and practical
art—have been theoretically abandoned. But this reliance on the secondary is fallacious and must be short-
lived. Spirits and laws, for a natural philosopher, are
simply names bestowed humanly on the habits of
bodies. Remove the bodies, and the spirits and laws
have lost their sole natural status and means of manifestation. Nevertheless the literary psychologist may
still live on for a while, like the ruminating camel in the
desert, on the momentum of his unconsumed moral pro-
visions; and he may imagine spirits and laws to retain
their office in respect of his private experience, after
they have lost their meaning and application in nature.

*Moral
society is
an overture
of material
relations.*

He may deny the natural world, and yet suppose himself living in a natural society.

That psychologism leans throughout on a tacit materialism appears clearly in the only principle which, so far as I know, it has ever invoked to describe the course of immediate experience— I mean the principle of association of ideas. This principle is clearly secondary: at best it is a principle of revival, occasionally exemplified in memory and reverie. Even supposing *How, in the absence of animal bodies, shall experience be initiated or controlled?* (what is manifestly false) that we always reviewed events in the order in which they first occurred, how should this law explain the order in which they arose originally? Yet the original order of events is the very subject of natural philosophy—the one thing which science and practical art are concerned to discover and to understand; and of this order association affords no explanation. If psychologism were not implicitly materialistic, it would be a proclamation of complete isolation and helplessness in the midst of a presumable chaos. Each man at each moment would tremblingly be the sensation he was: and if that sensation placed him in the presence of any imagined story or any fantastic world, nothing whatever would indicate that this groundless experience of to-day would have any sequel to-morrow. This is actually the attitude of moral anarchists, such as some of the heroes of modern fiction and some of the authors, who seem actually to take seriously the romantic conceit that experience is something absolute. But sanity assumes the opposite; and the prosperous arts which are the fruit of sanity prove that experience is a perpetually evanescent and most sensitive index to an order of nature beneath it.

Let us still suppose, however, that the universe might be simply a multitude of islets of feeling, each existing for itself. Each would then be distinguished from the rest only by its felt quality or (what is the same thing) by the quality and complexity of the essence revealed in it. There would be a sort of How can absolute sensations be successive? nebula of states of mind; and we should have to ask ourselves in what sense, and in what medium, if in any, they could be said to be successive or in any way earlier or later than one another. I have observed above [1] that when succession is actually enacted and is not merely specious or intuited, it is an external relation: the first state is lost in attaining the second. Now if these states were feelings distinguished only by their essences, they would stand in purely internal and eternal relations to one another; they could not be successive; there would be no possible transition from the one into the other, since there would be neither a flow of substance nor a leaping thought to effect the passage. I need not dwell on the corollary that in that case they could not even exist, but would have receded into their respective essences, and would radically fail to compose the elements or moments of a changing world. Let me admit for the sake of argument that they might exist by virtue of some stress or oscillation internal to each of them: what meaning could there then be in saying that they were successive or existed at different dates? Within each there would be no conceivable evidence of a time when it was not or of a time when it no longer should be. If they are events, as in psychologism they are taken to be, *they must transform something pre-existent, which they at once replace and continue.* They must be portions of a longer event, incidents in an existential field protracted beyond any one of them. Is it not evident that we are positing a physical time beneath and beyond them in which they may be dated and distributed? But I have previously found that physical time cannot be divorced from physical space, nor either of them from the flux of

[1] See pp. 11 and 80.

matter; and this conclusion will impose itself on the critical psychologist quite apart from any mathematical or astronomical arguments which may also support it. For the psychologist differs from the pure logician or poet in that he assumes memory to be constitutionally veracious and self-transcendent, reporting a series of past or outlying events which have been and are materially separate: he is a naturalist and a realist in method. His world has a single history, and involves lateral contacts and forward transmissions which are external to the natural moments concerned. One natural moment is, even for him, *materially* the heir to another and *physically* the neighbour to a third or a fourth. Psychological facts, if they are to be temporal and connected events, are therefore inconceivable except in the realm of matter.

Perhaps a critic inclined to a transcendental view of mind might here take the bull by the horns and might urge that of course psychological facts are not temporal events at all, and that indeed they have only internal relations to one another. What affinity should spiritual existence have to a pervasive and endless flux, when the very nature of spirit is to be synthetic, and in each of its instances an absolute centre of survey and of judgment? How should actual intuitions impinge upon a physical time or be scattered over it like daisies in a field or pins in a pin-cushion? This is an alien relation imputed to spiritual facts by the materialising imagination, which attaches them to bodies and events in a conventional world. In themselves, acts of cognition may picture time but cannot sprawl over it; yet the pictured time in them amply suffices to link them ideally together into phases of a common ideal drama. Like the episodes in a novel or the series of whole numbers, without having any fixed physical date, they may

Suggestion that the essential relations of spiritual moments might suffice to render them ideally successive.

compose an order of logical succession by virtue of their deliverance, if one contains, so to speak, a front view and another a rear view of the same imaginary objects. What to one living moment is a hope, to another living moment is a memory; and these complementary perspectives place them vicariously in one specious time, like the earlier and the later speeches in the same play, without any actual or physical derivation of one cognitive moment from another.

Who would not gladly dwell on these intrinsic contrasts and harmonies in the moral spectrum, by Moral rela- which all possible states of the spirit are tions cannot diversified? But I am not here concerned constitute a physical with establishing any spiritual hierarchy or order. setting up any Jacob's ladder; I am concerned only with the current assumption that feelings and ideas having no material basis may yet have a temporal order. And is it not obvious that if we truly limited our view to the mental sphere, it would be gratuitous ever to posit anything not given? But that which is given at any moment or in any experience is necessarily internal to it. In pure intuition all perspectives contain and exhaust their entire objects; time and space are there specious only. The only thinkable or discoverable sequence touching such states of mind is the sense of succession perhaps given in some of them: a succession which does not connect these states with one another, but only the specious elements, within each, between which it feels a transition. History will all be contained in mirrors, themselves existing in no temporal medium. Each moment of experience will be a monad without windows, but with variously painted walls. It will have no date and no surroundings; like a room in a historical museum it will bear the name and suggest the atmosphere of some age and country otherwise unknowable to us, and now nonexistent; but for the sincere idealist, who posits no truth beyond his living intuition, this represented existence will seem quite satisfying. Without ever needing to quit his museum, he can survey the panorama of all these historic essences in their fabulous progression; the same history being surveyed at each point from a different angle, and knitting all admissible vistas together into one moral world.

We are at the threshold of transcendental idealism: to pass through we need only add this reflection: as all given times or spaces must be imaginary and internal to the act of intuition which surveys them, so the assumed multiplicity of these acts must be itself imaginary and internal to the idea or sense of their multiplicity. Self-consciousness will then have truly swallowed up all its objects, and we shall have passed out of psychologism by the subjective door. We shall have retained and made absolute the activity of spirit: and by force of this initial assurance we shall have destroyed the presuppositions and the problem of psychologism; for we shall no longer posit a naturalistic flux of feelings and ideas, running down somehow in a common time, and somehow divided into separate series called individual lives. Those imagined feelings and ideas, with the conventional divisions and connections established among them, will be reduced to elements in a picture painted by the spirit in the idealist, and existing only under the unity of his apperception, in which they are obviously interrelated and inseparable. The specious world so conceived, we shall see presently, remains material; but the philosopher has become a genuine idealist, because (except when he forgets himself) he attributes no existence to that world apart from his conception.

First way out from psycho-logism: into transcendental idealism.

But psychologism, though inwardly condemned to die, is free to choose among various forms of suicide. Instead of perishing by concentration in the ego, it may perish by diffusion among images, tropes, and phenomena. The ingredients of the universe will still Second way out: into pheno-menalism or pictorial physics. be sought in feelings and acts of intuition which are spiritual events and subjective. Yet the philosopher will not banish from his mind the common assumption that nature exists in her own right and is a perfectly well-known congeries of material objects and events. The consequence is that when he becomes a psychological critic of experience, and endeavours to reform and reconstruct his picture of reality exclusively out of his immediate data, he continues in possession, *de facto* though not *de jure*, of the conventional lines of nature on which to hang the family linen of his mind. Feelings and acts of intuition make manifest certain essences which, although intrinsically only logical, æsthetic, or moral universals, are often impulsively taken for parts of the objects which evoke them; or in other cases, when feelings have only obscure physiological causes, the moral essences given in these feelings are regarded as parts of the body which feels them. Thus a landscape is taken by the innocent tourist to be the intrinsic essence of the region he traverses; and a pain passes mythically for an existing force within the aching part, causing its contraction and all its ensuing acts. When this propensity is dominant in the philosopher, and at the same time he is jealous of the certitude of immediate experience, he is likely to abandon his psychologism by the objective door. He will overlook as far as possible the spiritual centre of his experience and the organic seat and significance of his perceptions, and he will construct out of his given essences, like a poet, a many-coloured garment for nature. His psychologism will become a sort of sensuous realism or pictorial metaphysics. The materials will be ideal, the events subjective, but they will be deployed in a posited time and space, and supplemented hypothetically by imaginary phenomena, so as to compose a panoramic world—a continuum of ephemeral images and impulses having a certain material breadth and interconnection.

Theories of this sort might seem, in one direction, more materialistic than materialism, since they ignore or deny the existence of spirit; but perhaps the omission is more apparent than real. In the lottery of opinion, when schools are bewildered and categories are in solution, spirit may be eliminated in the ostensible result only because it was secretly presupposed in the inquiry. Phenomenalism, logicism, and pictorial realism all start from personal experience and are abstractions from it; they analyse the objects engaging a living spirit which prefers to forget itself, with its perpetually central station and dogmatic energy. What is a phenomenon? Is it an essence given in intuition? Certainly that is what any phenomenon becomes to a radical critic. Or is it a fact posited by an assertive and aggressive mind that regards given essences as substantive existences in their own specious plane? That is what a phenomenon seems to be to animal illusion and dramatic fancy. But the truth is that immediate feeling, whether excited by the eye or by some inner organ, is most thoroughly a product of the living psyche, and expresses her animal passions: how then should the qualities felt in these feelings be detached from the psyche, in which alone they can arise or live? How should they subsist, dead, dried, and insensible, in the external cosmic order of the objects posited and encountered in action?

Nature reduced to a description of nature in visual and mathematical terms.

Nor is it only the trembling visions visiting the soul that suffer and die in that transposition; the dynamic objects for which they are substituted suffer an equal injury. For these are now emptied of their active unfathomable substance, which renders them co-ordinate

with the active self in our own bodies; they are reduced to films and conceived surfaces, if not to mere
Shadowy words or mathematical equations. These thin
character of sensuous or intelligible essences are then
pheno-
menalistic multiplied and hypothetically interpolated *ad*
science. *libitum*, in order to fill the enormous spaces
and the abysses of time which actual experience must
leave unexplored in any world supposed to be continuous
and self-subsisting. Recent science has been very inventive in this direction, and technically profound in
proportion to the intellectual initiative displayed in it;
but, after all, the truth of all these images and tropes,
or even their applicability to nature, depends on their
just contacts, first, with the conventional field of action,
and secondly, with the experience of the questioning
soul.

A philosopher who would place all this literary
psychology and optical physics where they belong,
All object- needs to stand firm in his native centre. He
ive idealisms is a spirit, and his life is a dream; but this
are funda-
mentally dream when trusted and pressed, as it must
subjective. be in action, involves the mysterious fecundity
of a psyche which may breed this sustained dream in
its vegetative and passionate order; and this psyche
in turn involves a material world in which she may
weave her organism and try her fortunes. Her
fecundity as well as her adventures must be initially
blind, since they create in her the first glimmer of
ideas; and they must be mechanical, if they are supposed to depend on the interaction of various psyches,
or various organic impulses, in some medium in which
they have arisen and continue to reside. Above all,
this cosmic flux is nothing phenomenal, nor composed
of visual images or tropes and mathematical laws: it
is in itself what it is, and for us what it does. Our
sensuous and conceptual experience touches but does
not lift the hem of that garment from which its virtue

flows. Phenomena are all like the rainbow, products of a point of view. Permanent or surely recurrent as they may sometimes be, they are so only from a particular station; they vanish on a nearer approach, and change their essence at a different angle. Uprooted from the organ and occasion that support them, they vanish like ghosts without leaving even a bone or a shroud behind. It is only in memory or fancy that any vestige of phenomena remains; only legend can record their order. And these evanescent views have no seat in nature, except perhaps—indirectly and unobservably—in some labouring brain. Traced home, they are moments in some biography, revelations within some personal experience. They lead us back, therefore, to a monadism or solipsism, in which the philosopher finds himself in the presence of nothing but a dream of which he can discern neither the extent nor the meaning. Phenomenalism and its kindred systems may indeed abolish the spirit from their objective cosmos, because this cosmos is itself initially and ultimately visionary, and exists only for the spirit that conceives it.

There are advocates of psychologism to whom the vanity of this conclusion is obvious and who revert from it to the substantial part of their world, namely, to the self or psyche, since it is only there that any phenomenal system can touch actual existence. Yet for them the psyche *Third way out: into panpsychism.* can be composed only of moments of consciousness; feelings and intuitions form her whole substance; and if reality is to lie anywhere deeper than the level of conventional ideas or to explain their origin and composition, it will be necessary very much to extend the field of literary psychology, and to supply no end of unknown feelings and ideas between and beyond those posited by common opinion. Evidence is not wanting to convince us that many such feelings and ideas exist, either buried and ignored in ourselves, or proper to the different quality of other living spirits. Human fancy, if inclined sometimes to invent spirits that do not exist, is also constitutionally incapable of conceiving and crediting the experience of any existing spirits too remote from itself. Nature is in every way richer than our thoughts of nature, and the hypothesis deserves respect that many a form of experience exists, within us and beyond, which our conventional human thoughts cannot appreciate. Such unremembered, dispersed, or alien sensibility is often called unconscious mind—a relative and egotistical name for it, since if alien feelings are unconscious to us, our feelings are no less unconscious to them. Yet perhaps, under this unjust designation, there may lurk a secret reversion to phenomenalism. "Unconscious mind" may suggest an essence or a series of essences which,

Unconscious mind a name for conscious mind elsewhere or for what is not mind at all.

under other circumstances, would be manifest to a mind generated by those circumstances: and these essences may be conceived as existing somehow without any intuition of them, as if they could be formed and dissolved in the dark, by a sort of nebular evolution. But the given or phenomenal is relative to spirit; it cannot arise if not synthesised in an act of intuition; and it cannot be preserved or revived in the unconscious, or set out in a physical time and space to compose a crepuscular mental cosmos, partly illuminated and partly darkened, like the moon. The bright part only will be the field of mind, the rest will be the field of matter; and the field of mind will not be substantially independent or of fixed extent, but will describe so much of the field of matter as the light of intuition or understanding has chanced to play upon. If those unconsidered sensations or wishes are mental at all, they must shine each for itself, even if invisible to one another. A pain or a sound is either felt and heard, or it recedes into the structure, tension, and rhythms of the material world; and only the latter can be designated by the term " unconscious ", if this term be taken absolutely and not relatively. An appeal to the unconscious would then mark the surrender of psychologism.

If we disdain this surrender, and insist on conceiving a universe made up of mental events, may we not posit a compact flux of feelings, such as our waking and dreaming life seems actually to be, only more voluminous, consequential, and complex, so that the interstices of our remembered experience shall be filled in with continuous forgotten feelings and thoughts? And similarly, might not the interstices between the experiences of various selves be filled in with some sort of inner animation, constituting the substance of the world everywhere, even in all the apparently empty stretches of space and time, when these stretches really exist or lapse? This would imply psychic mortar no less than psychic stones. Not only would all reality be a flux of feelings and imagery, as in a dream, but all dreams, divide them as we may into dramatic episodes and private lives, would be continuous and mutually derivative, so that no dream would ever begin save by continuing or uniting previous dreams, nor end save in the act of generating new ones.

Panpsychism a conceivable hypothesis.

This seems to be a logical possibility. Panpsychism is free from that covert reliance on matter by which all other idealisms subsist, and it seems less superficial. Its universe is composed of states of mind generating and emptying into one another; so that while its substance is feeling, to the satisfaction of our pensive self-consciousness and moral pride, this feeling is distributed and condensed just as matter would be in a material world. Therefore while panpsychism seems to cover the whole realm of matter and so to render other matter superfluous, the question is how far it differs from materialism in its texture. Is it anything but materialism strained through a psychological sieve? The use of psychological or even mythological language—as is done in psycho-analysis—would not be of great consequence, if physical facts and relations were always signified: but the axiom of panpsychism is that all facts are mental, and the question arises: How can mental facts compose a natural world? If the relations between them are mental, they are not natural; and if they are natural they are not mental. There is, for instance, a felt continuity in mental life, of which many a moment is conscious, but this felt continuity within given perspectives is not an actual continuity between successive events. The first moment of life begins without consciousness of beginning, and the last moment ends without possible consciousness of having ended. If in any experience the first moment were also the last—as in some sense is always the case, since each moment has a self-existent life which cannot be stretched—this isolated moment of consciousness would not be aware of its punctiform station in the world of events, but would look before and after, and blankly about, as if it had cognitive dominion and large participation in the material universe to which its organ belongs. It has such participation spiritually, being spiritual itself: but the dramatic vista within it cannot enable it to pass physically out of itself into the next actual feeling. Those features in its internal revelation between which a felt continuity obtains are given essences, here forming a perspective in which moments are not self-existent, but imperfectly realised by virtue of felt contrasts, and therefore inseparable. Even if the terms, half-distinguished in this uncertain continuum, were descriptive of ulterior events, the vision of them (with its degree of the partiality and redundance

Marginal note: But in multiplying mental states *ad infinitum* it leaves them without connections.

proper to mental reactions) would be a fresh event on
its own account. It would be as helpless as any other
immaterial fact to flow into other facts, or to lie among
them in a physical time and space.

On the other hand, the existence of continuity in
events, were there no material psyche to synthesise
and collect their successiveness in her enriched powers,
could not yield a sense of continuity, or any other sort
of knowledge. Merely being a fact can never cause a
fact to be discovered. An organ of sense must first
become sensitive to that fact and must impose some
subjective view of it on intuition. In a world of mental
events all the connections of these events must still
remain physical: they cannot be numbered among
those events. It is therefore not true, even on this
view, that the world is composed of mental events
exclusively; they are assumed to impinge on a deeper
medium in which they arise, and which supplies all
their existential relations.

Perhaps without altogether dismissing these considerations, it might be urged that there is one spiritual
reality, the Will, which supplies precisely
the transitive bond required between living   Will is either
moments. What is this Will? All that a   a mental
literary psychologist can consistently under-   phenomenon
stand by the word is the *sense* of willing—   like any
the feeling of glad action, the preferences,   other, and
expectations, wishes, purposes, and decisions   impotent, or
which may traverse his mind. Did he con-   else a physi-
ceive the Will to be a transitive power, by   cal or divine
which ulterior states of mind were positively   power be-
created or transformed, he would be appealing to some-   yond the
thing physical or divine beyond consciousness, some-   range of
thing of which the wishes or decisions occurring in   psycho-
consciousness would be only omens or symptoms.   logism.
Energetic idealists are victims of an illusion: the more
they insist on Will, Life, Vital Impulse, or the Eternal

Feminine, the more decidedly they turn away from
synthetic mind and lay up their treasures in the flux
of matter. What else is that mounting energy which
they feel within themselves and in all nature, and which
they justly recognise as far deeper and more pervasive
than any images or conceptions of the reasoning mind?
An immense and intricate flow of substance has formed
their organisms, and thereby determined their purposes and passions: for evidently purposes, wishes, and
preferences are just as secondary, just as much synthetic
and expressive, as are the data of sense, and all images
and memories. All these are bred in animal organs and
presuppose a prior direction of unconscious life.

Panpsychism accordingly involves and posits the
realm of matter: for it disposes the elements known to
literary psychology in a cosmic system which
Panpsy- they can neither compose nor support. The
chism is
materialism panpsychist merely maintains—what in some
translated
into psycho- sense may be quite true—that the realm of
logical matter is throughout animate; and he chooses
terms. to regard this animation, in deference to his
humanistic and literary habit of mind, as substantial,
ignoring the far deeper fatality, which he can hardly
deny, by which all this animation is distributed: a
fatality which when recognised, posited, and studied,
alone justifies any mind in imagining and addressing
certain other minds, or its own natural destinies.

When the There is a final or vanishing form of pan-
elements of psychism in which this implication is virtually
the psychic
universe are admitted, and the universe is said to be com-
admitted to posed of mind-stuff, or matter of such a sort
be uncon-
scious, the that mind may arise out of it. This is a
distinction radically different theory from the panpsy-
from
materialism chism considered above, in which minds or
becomes sensations, conscious though perhaps feeble
merely
verbal. and vague, were made the stuff of the universe.
That true matter is of such a sort that mind may arise

out of it every materialist must allow; the question is only what conception of matter this circumstance compels or permits us to form. Shall we think of it as dust quickened, or as life dissipated, extinguished, and reduced to atoms?

To assert that the substance of anything, much less of the whole world, was psychic, and to call it mind-stuff, would be inadmissible if we meant that minute but conscious spirits were the stuff of it: we have just seen the manifold impossibility of that. But the phrase becomes legitimate and significant if it serves only to remind us that physical, like spiritual, existence must be intensive centred in each of its parts, and capable of inner change as well as of collateral reduplication. We should never broach existence at all if we cut up phenomena into *minima sensibilia*, or traversed the intellectual landscape in a thousand ways in order to establish, by intense intuition of its essence, all sorts of contrasts and relations between its specious elements. Intellectual landscapes vary with intelligence, not to say with fashion; and *minima sensibilia* vary with the faculties of sense. The actual reality in a man is himself, not his imagined objects: and it is on the level of his active being, and on the analogy of his progressive and self-annihilating existence, that other existences are to be ·conceived.

[marginal note:] Physical existence is more analogous to mind than to ideas.

The substance of nature, thus diffused and, in spots, concentrated into organisms, becomes in these organisms also the substance of mind. It must evidently have been perfectly fitted to produce everything which it actually produces; it may therefore be decorated retrospectively, by a Chinese piety, with all the titles won by its children; indeed, these its eventual manifestations are the sole index which we possess to its intrinsic nature.

Now the fact that substance can sometimes live and

think shows that any pictorial or mathematical description of it cannot be exhaustive or even intensively very penetrating; such descriptions mark rather the external order proper to substance in its diffusion and interaction, and supply a notation suitable for mapping it or building in it. At the same time that which thinks in an animal is unmistakably the same

Though matter may be called mind-stuff, that designation is marginal and not central.

substance as that which lives and moves in him: his mind shares the fortunes of his body and exists only by realising its contacts and its interests. Therefore while the designation of substance as mind-stuff is correct, it is by no means exclusively, or even preeminently proper. Even in animals, not to speak of nature in general, the inclination of existence towards thought is neither radical nor general; and the substance of this world is far more fundamentally designed for sleeping than for waking. In so far as mind has stuff at all under it and is not purely spiritual, the stuff of it is ordinary matter. We can observe and trace the organic bodies which naturally possess feeling, or cause spirit to awake within them; but who shall observe or imagine an organic concourse of unconscious atoms of mind? Moreover, organisation requires a medium as well as a stuff; and the medium in which mind-stuff moves is avowedly physical space and time. But what can exist in space except matter, and what except matter can be the vehicle of true derivation and continuity in a truly lapsing time? Mind-stuff is therefore simply an indirect name for matter, given in deference to an idealistic bias surviving the wreck of idealism; and nothing but a confusing attachment to a psychological vocabulary could counsel its frequent use.

I find, then, that in the psychological sphere, apart from pure feeling or intuition, everything is physical. There is no such thing as mental substance, mental

force, mental machinery, or mental causation. If actual
feelings or intuitions have any ground at all this
ground is physical; if they have a date, place, Summary
or occasion they have it only in the physical and con-
world. Physical, too, is the determination clusion.
of their quality and diversity, of their meaning or
intent, of their affinities and development; physical
their separation into particular lives as well as their
union, in each person, into a particular sequence or
strand of experiences. Physical, finally, is the sole
evidence open to any mind of the existence or character of minds in others. Psychology, therefore, when
it does more than evoke poetically various dramatic
feelings or intuitions, traces the behaviour of living
bodies—which includes their language—interpreting
it in moral terms; and it cannot compose a system of
the universe out of these moral terms abstracted from
their physical backing, because this backing alone
supplies their existential connections and historical
order. Thus psychology reports certain complications
in the realm of matter: and the interpretations which
may be added in terms of spirit depend entirely for
their truth on the existence and spiritual fertility of
that material background.

CHAPTER X

THE LATENT MATERIALISM OF IDEALISTS

WHAT is idealism? I should like to reply: Thought and love fixed upon essence. If this definition were *Idealism a* accepted idealism would be a leaven rather *moral inter-* than a system, because although essence is *est dictating a physical* everywhere present it never occurs alone, *system.* but either as the form of some existing thing or event, or else as a term given in intuition; so that however sceptical or contemplative the philosopher might be, his own existence at least would be a fact eluding his idealism and prerequisite to it. He could become a complete idealist only by forgetting himself, and not inquiring into the origin or meaning of his quite contingent existence and quite arbitrary visions. To arrest attention on pure essence and to be an idealist in a moral or poetic sense, would therefore be possible to a man holding any system of physics. Even a materialist might be a true idealist, if he preferred the study of essence to that of matter or events; but his natural philosophy would keep his poetic ecstasies in their proper place. Such an equilibrium, however, has seldom recommended itself to professed philosophers, whose virtue has impelled them rather to push their favourite insights into the absolute, and assert the universe to be the perfect mirror of their minds. Those who have been idealists by temperament have been accordingly inclined to substitute essence for matter in their theory of the universe. Their hearts, had they not done so, would have been painfully divided; for the most fervent and contemplative idealist is still a man and an animal, and nature has initially directed his attention and passion not on essence, but on fact, on power, on the factors of his material destiny. The more impetuous his idealism and the more unitary his dogmatic mind, the greater need he will find of fusing his physics with his visions, and assigning to the system of essences which fills his imagination the position and the powers of matter. Hence a gnostic physics in which chosen ideas pass for facts and felt values for powers: and it is this superstition, and not the pure study and love of essence, that is commonly known as idealism.

The earliest and noblest form of this idealism was the doctrine of the Platonic Socrates. In somewhat playfully defining the current terms of speech, he very earnestly disentangled the types of moral excellence and the goals of political wisdom. His Ideas were fundamentally ideals, forms which things would approximate in proportion as they approached perfection, each after its kind. It was in this measure also that things deserved their names and could be justly subsumed under their class in the hierarchy of objects important to the legislator and having fixed functions in the economy of life. Nothing could have a nature unless it had a possible perfection: that which rendered a bed " really " a bed, or a bridle " really " a bridle was their respective functions; for it was as better fitted to sleep in soundly or to rein in horses effectively that beds and bridles were better or worse, or were beds and bridles at all. Reality and excellence thus coincided and came from participation in some Idea; for this Platonic sort of reality was altogether supernal and had nothing to do with existence. Filth and hair also existed; but unless

Socratic idealism at first purely moral and spiritual.

they found a use and had a consequent standard of perfection—for instance, as fur or as manure—they fell under ·no Idea, and the rational moralist might ignore them. The wise and prudent man was quick to see the ideal in the material; and he prized existence only for the sake of the ever-bright essence of the good which in a thousand colours and degrees shone darkly through it.

This initial phase of Platonism is pregnant with several different possibilities, all of which, perhaps, have not been noticed or developed. In one direction, for instance, it points to super-naturalism, to the conviction that the soul would never find her true good until she was disembodied and identified in contemplation with the ideas which were her natural food. Only in that heaven would there be happiness, where, as in Nirvana, there would be no change, no division, and in that sense no existence. For if things draw all their virtue from ulterior perfections which they can only embody imperfectly, evidently it would have been simpler and better to have begun at the end, to have always pos-sessed the good in its perfection, and to have been spared the pain and indignity of alienation from it. This view was actually recommended by the Platonic Socrates in his last hours; probably at any other time it would have proved embarrassing, and we need not wonder that it remained in abeyance. Had it been pressed, what would have become of that sane plebeian wisdom of Socrates, austerely reducing all beauty to health, all virtue to circumspect knowledge, and all good to utility for pleasure? Evidently in heaven there would be no place any longer for beds and bridles, for ogling love, or for the restless yearning to bring all things to birth in beauty. Indeed, it is much to be feared that without those humble natural occasions and animal functions demanding to be perfected, per-

All its vir-tue came from its material foundation.

fection itself and the good would have entirely vanished. Had the divine sufficiency of the Ideas in their own realm been seriously maintained, this supernaturalism, by transcending morality and abolishing preference, would have clearly shown that the foundation of Socratic idealism was material.

Matter is indeed indispensable to any system in which the supreme reality is divine and eternal, because without matter that reality could have no manifestation in space, time, persons, and contingent circumstances. This was acknowledged by the Platonists more frankly *Confusion of physical substance with materia prima.* and intelligently than by modern idealists; yet while admitting this fundamental function of matter, they represented it as wholly negative and passive, the forms which it took being imposed upon it from above, by the divine virtue of Ideas regarded as magnets. This view was protected by two equivocations, on which the whole of Platonising physics depends. One equivocation consisted in substituting the essence of materiality, itself an Idea, for the locally existing and variegated substance of material things. The essence of materiality, being defined by negation of all forms, was pure nonentity; its vacuity could be easily proved to contribute nothing to the positive essence of anything; and the bewildered disciple was expected never to perceive that, even if things owed no part of their form to abstract matter, they owed to their concrete matter the possibility of their existence. For if matter was universal inertia, it was also universal potentiality: and by admitting, as Ideas do not, a contingent selection and flux of forms, it admitted life, motion, and particular existences, and enabled one Idea to manifest itself here and another there in varying degrees of perfection.

The other equivocation, intertwined with this, turned on the double use of the word " make " : for a principle of form " makes " a thing what it is, by justifying its title to a certain name or to a certain estimation; whereas its substance and origin cannot lie there, but must be supplied in the flux of existence by matter predisposed to assume that form, and material agencies at hand, able to impose that possible form upon that special matter. For the material cause of anything is not the essence of materiality, but rather a certain quantity of matter already endowed with form, with local existence, and with internal and surrounding tensions calculated to change its condition. This existing matter in its spontaneous movement is the force at work in the genesis of one thing out of another. Ideas at best can be only the formal or final causes of their exemplification: they are not forces at all, but qualities and harmonies resulting from the concourse of material facts: and to say that the form or function of anything " makes " it what it is, is a mere play on the ambiguity of words and a solemn mystification.

Confusion of formal with efficient cause.

That the Ideas are powerless, and that power is perpetually ascribed to them only by a figure of speech, due to a natural impulse in idealists toward indiscriminate eulogy of whatever is formal and describable, I think may be made evident by a single consideration. Platonic Ideas are eternal. Whatsoever hierarchy they may compose, and whatever radiance may issue from them, magically capable of transmuting matter into their likeness, this effluence is perpetual. All the Ideas are always equally inviting and potent: their generous creative virtue pours forth from them impartially at all seasons, in all directions, and to all distances. In a word, they are not physical facts or physical forces at all, but purely logical essences. They are intrinsically without the least bond or the least relevance to any particular point of time or region of space. What-

Eternal forms cannot be the cause of particular incidents.

ever magic attraction they may be reputed to exercise over matter, they will exercise over it equally everywhere and at all times. On the other hand, the face of nature is diversified, and the facts that here exemplify those essences are unevenly distributed, often repeated; and almost always imperfect reproductions of their ideal originals.

Why, then, is any Idea manifested here and not there, perfectly or imperfectly, once, often, or not at all? I know of but one conceivable answer. Because of the different predispositions of the diffuse matter concerned. In respect to any particular event, or to the form of any particular thing or action, the cause of occurrence or non-occurrence can only lie in the material situation at the previous moment—the structure and movement of the substance at hand under those material circumstances. We may rhetorically assign all virtue to the Idea then realised, since this is the marvel open to intuition in which alone the spirit is ultimately interested. Yet it was matter that determined whether that virtue should be exercised in any particular case; so that matter alone is responsible for what occurs, although the Ideas which it brings to light may get all the credit of it.

The cause can only be the varied predispositions of matter.

This predisposition in matter illustrates the fundamental contingency of existence, and in that respect may be likened to absolute free will; we might fancifully say that an absolutely free will in matter was the ground of everything. But such a radical and initial fatality has nothing in it of intelligent freedom, such as appears in actions expressive of the ingrained bent of living creatures, actions adapted to the circumstances, and prophetic of the result which, if fortunate, they are likely to have. Such moral power of self-expression is possible only because that previous

This is a primal accident like absolute free will, but morally free will presupposes a formed nature.

fatality, or free will in the sense of absolutely groundless action, has already established particular psyches
and initiated in them an effort towards specific kinds
of perfection. At whatever point we call a halt in our
backward survey of history, we find extant some
arbitrary state of things, determining the forms which
intelligent judgment and action shall then assume. A
psyche is presupposed distinguishing and declaring
good those characters which, were she omnipotent,
she would impose on everything: characters which
things will hardly acquire in fact, since many forces
besides those centred in the psyche will conspire to
shape the issue. Thus the initiation, distribution, and
transmission of existing forms, when traced to their
source, are entirely the work of matter.

If instead of matter we posit a deity or a moral
force or a special dialectic to be the first principle of
existence, the case is not essentially altered.
Any other efficient cause would be equally contingent and, in respect to spirit, equally material. Such a deity or dialectic or moral force would
then be the primal accident, the groundless
fact, the one form of being which existence
happened to wear in neglect of all other forms;
and that which distinguishes matter from
essence—its exclusive potentialities—would
distinguish that supposed metaphysical agency
just as truly, and just as arbitrarily; so that in respect
to essence, and to the clearness and eventual emancipation of spirit, it would be as material a fact as matter
ever could be. The question, in cosmology, is not
between matter and Ideas but between one sort of
matter and another; and it is for experiment and
science, not for logic, to discover what sort of matter
matter is.

This decisive office of matter remains the same
when Souls are introduced into the Platonic cosmology,
where they tend to absorb the Ideas and to transpose
them into themes or goals of a purely spiritual life.

The transformation is indeed glorious: from being mere essences morally relative to the humblest earthly needs and economy, the Ideas now become spirits shining by their own light, living for themselves, and perfectly fulfilling and enjoy- ing their spontaneous destiny. But all this goes on "Yonder", above, in heaven: "Here", to souls awakening and painfully struggling on earth, those celestial spirits remain mere ideals, patrons or models which we may invoke and aspire to imitate; they can be as little affected or moved by us as if they had remained pure essences. Our existence and our vicissitudes are due to an opposite principle. Why, indeed, did a ray from one of those celestial luminaries fructify in this particular lump of clay, and animate me, and not another, with a felt need and an awakening will, aspiring to contemplate and ultimately to possess that, and no other, heavenly perfection? What called down and buried here, in my private animal psyche, a seed and replica of that particular celestial spirit? Evidently, again, some predisposition, readiness, or responsiveness peculiar to my earthly substance. Perhaps, if my nature at birth was not due to my material heritage, and to the accumulated organisation of an endless series of ancestors, it might be attributed, according to a venerable fable, to my own vicissitudes in previous lives. In this case, if my transmigrations had no beginning, my fatal character—or my fatal acts, making irruption from moment to moment into my character—must be among the primary free constituents of the universe. They must be factors, combining with the other original factors, if any, in determining the flux of existence.

We may give these factors a psychological name and call them wills or acts of will; we may even represent them to be conscious, or prophetic of an intended result; and we may thus assimilate Platonism to panpsychism or to the world of literary psychology. But,

This is true of Platonic souls.

if the previous argument be cogent, we shall not thereby avoid an ultimate materialism. The foundations of existence cannot in any case be other than existent, temporal, and arbitrary. Even if the conscious universe were plaited together out of the biographies of everlasting souls, dramatically interwoven, the realm of matter would still be their only possible theatre. It would establish their conjunctions, fix their dates, measure their journeys, and impose on them, through their bodies, all their providential adventures. Plato, Plotinus, and the Indians never conceived the thing otherwise: and this material underpinning to the migration of souls seems indeed indispensable, if they are to be supposed to communicate and interact, as is requisite for all the offices of charity. The material world could hardly be denied, so long as philosophy remained frankly and dogmatically religious.

Their migrations and conjunctions occur by incarnation in matter.

The case is changed, however, when we adopt a strict monadology and ascribe the illusion of society to the moral burden of each separate soul, and to its infinite capacity for dreaming. Matter then seems really to vanish from the universe; yet all its blind fertility and mysterious involution has entered into the soul. Whether the spiriting away of materialism in this direction is nominal or real may be discovered by the study of modern idealism.

Modern idealism has been in a great measure rooted in psychologism and identical with it: in that measure I have already indicated the surviving materialism on which it leans. But through the transcendental door the Germans long ago abandoned that uninhabitable mansion; and their national idealism may be said to begin where psychologism ends. What, then, are the relations of this national philosophy to materialism?

In the first place, like Platonism, German idealism seems to elude materialism by systematically sub-

stituting concepts for substances and descriptions of
things for the things themselves.   It moves in the
plane of Ideas and leaves obscure their relation   Modern
to particular passing facts.   Or rather, it re-   idealism
duces this relation to identity: for the choice of   a revision
concepts and descriptions is no longer dictated   of Hebrew
by moral preoccupations, or spiritual wisdom;   it is   prophecy.
made in the act of surveying the facts themselves in
the spirit of prophecy.   Its origin is biblical.   Like
the Hebrew prophets, Protestant philosophers tend
to reject the supernatural and to search nature and
history for the divine plan of events.   They are prophets not so much in foretelling the future—though,
by way of warning, they sometimes venture to do so—
as in speaking in the name of the Lord, who is the power
in matter, delivering his judgments and magnifying
his ways.   In contrast to the Platonists, they show
the greatest respect for the flux of existence.   The
Ideas or laws which they proclaim and regard as powers
are simply tropes supposed to be discernable in that
flux.   This discernment is inevitably personal and
relative;   for obviously a moving world, where divisions
are as fluid as positions, is rebellious to any specific
essence, even to fixed patterns or laws of change.
There may be a dialectic inherent in certain attitudes:
but how often does any mind or any revolution obey
it?   The flux of actual existence is untamably complex,
and the tropes visible to the prophet will almost inevitably repeat the outlines of his religious or national
passions, his private insights, or his fine pleasure in
the inner complications of logic or mathematics.   His
prophecy or history, seen from a distance, will seem
only to have added, by its own novelty, one more to
the multitude of unharnessable facts.

But let me suppose that he escapes this fatality, and
traces, for once, perhaps in the person of Hegel, the
exact essence realised in the flux of existence.   The Idea,

or master-trope, enshrined in his system, will then
be a true summary of all truth.   But truth is eternal:
The pro- neither as a whole nor in any of its parts is it
phecy could an existence, but only a description of exist-
not be true ence.   Granting, then, that the truth had
unless
matter con- been revealed to the prophetic idealist and
spired to that he had described existence, on the whole,
realise it
progress- as it actually is, this existence would still,
ively. for that very reason, remain outside of his
mind and of his description.   A description could
not be true, or superior as knowledge to any rival
description, if things of their own accord and in their
own persons had not independently exemplified that
description and rendered the assertion of it true.   Thus
if any descriptive idealism were true, its very truth
would imply and posit the natural world, which is the
realm of matter, existing in itself, and justifying that
description.

I believe that many who call themselves idealists
take this for granted and have never doubted the
substantial existence of nature and society diffused
about them.   If they protest that materialism is absurd
and exploded, they do 'so only because by matter they
understand some pictorial or mathematical idol substituted for the pregnant and unfathomable substance
of things; and they would disown their own idealism
no less decisively, as a rhetorical idol in its turn, if
they understood it to deny the scattered and measurable
existence of the natural world.

There are, however, a few masters of idealism who
Pure ideal- despise such a crude philosophy and insist that
ism, if it ad- descriptions are the only knowable facts and
mits truth descriptive only of their own essence.   Being
or belief at
all, relapses and knowing, they say, are nothing but think-
into psycho- ing, and knowledge grows by closer inspec-
logism. tion of consciousness, not by information
coming from outside or referring to anything ulterior.

Very well: this at least is a radical position; yet if we take it consistently we renounce that claim to truth in our ideas which had originally recommended idealism to the innocent believer. We are abolishing the very notion of truth; and if we retain any system of nature or history, we retain it only as a fashionable mode of thought, a fading dream for the moment entertaining the spirit. Even this pleasing assurance about ourselves, that we may create, survive, and develop our absolute experiences, would forsake us unless we still asserted, with a desperate inconsistency, the transcendent validity of memory and expectation: an assertion which reverts to the belief in truth, and restores psychologism, if not humanism, with all its materialistic implications. We cannot, in fact, outgrow materialism without outgrowing belief altogether. And unless I am much mistaken, it is restiveness under belief of any sort, because it is precarious and a check, while it lasts, on spontaneous life, that has inspired all modern or Protestant philosophy. The assertion of a new belief, contradicting the old, is only a feint in the battle against all dogma. The new belief would prove no less odious, and probably far more absurd, than the old, were it ever seriously established; but its very weakness is a recommendation to a spirit unwilling to be pledged, detesting to be taught, and wedded to nothing but the romantic sport of imposing and deriding its successive illusions. All parties, all ages, Hegel tells us, are mad; yet the folly of all the parts secretly vindicates the rationality of the whole, since every part destroys itself because of its irrationality.

Heraclitus of old had said something of the same sort; but that freer and wiser man was not deceived, or bound to deceive others, concerning the principle of this universal instability. It was fire, it was matter: and what, indeed, is this barbarous self-ignorance and self-treason save

Vague will is the expression of matter ill organised.

the voice of matter, profoundly rebellious to form, and incapable of existing except in the act of leaping from one form to another? Matter, to blind feeling, is but force without, and will within. It seems everywhere instinct with life; yet life and will are not really possible without a modicum of material organisation, stable enough to give foothold and some specific direction to the tentative actions and conquests destined to enlarge it. The paths of life are many, and most of them without issue. Knowledge of nature and of self, in clarifying the blind materialism of action, enlightens this choice of direction, proves it to have been fruitful, and enables it still to be so. The steady habit of matter within, in the psyche, meets and feeds on its steady variations without; and life attains the dignity of the rational animal. Without this definition in character and this recognition of matter, life can only grope and flounder, vehemently agitated by a vague wretchedness, without either courage to confess its limits or lucidity to see its goal.

It is therefore by no means necessary that some satirical critic should point out the fundamental
Idealism materialism of these idealists; it is plainly
transformed confessed by their own aspirations. There
into panthe- is nothing for which they manifest a greater
istic sym-
pathy with contempt than for the merely ideal; they are
existence intent on reality. Reason, Life, and Ideas, when by definition existent and creative, evidently forfeit their original moral values: for they are no longer essentially fulfilments and perfections desired by that which exists, but its actual nature or cause. They have become, like matter, the primal accident; and this fact is far from lowering them in the estimation of the modern enthusiast. The passion at work in his bosom is the will to live; his idealism expresses his vitality, not any squeamish requirements about the conditions of existence or any sure promises concerning

its issue. Why should a few knocks, or a great many holocausts, chill his ardour in living in God's world? His ancestors hardly required a touch of sardonic piety to be edified by the prospect of almost universal damnation. He may well brace himself in his turn to face the same fatality spread thin, and distributed impartially throughout the writhings of history. And if moral judgment is jeopardised or quite surrendered in this brave optimism, moral sentiment still remains; because the happy adventurer is now convinced that in accepting the universe as it is, and appropriating as much of it as possible, he is partaking in the divine life more and more abundantly.

I have said that the Ideas distinguished by Platonists were for the most part ideals never realised in this world; they were the sort of tropes interesting to moralists and poets, and essentially forms of the good. But in modern idealism Ideas are meant to be descriptions of the actual course of nature and history: they are alleged laws. *In pantheism physics has the whip hand.* Now the laws of nature are important in considering the means to an end, but they are not ends nor relevant to the choice of ends. For a Platonist a world governed by natural laws—that is, obeying the habits which it once has formed—would be formless, since its form would not be relevant to the good. It could not become a form of the good until a life arising under those material auspices began to look to it as to a condition of its happiness. In many modern Idealists a dose of this Platonism is mixed with their pantheistic and optimistic ethics, but only to the confusion of thought; for when a sentimentalist becomes a historian, or in self-defence a natural philosopher, he insensibly falsifies the facts and laws which actually hold, in order to insinuate others which have an edifying rather than a descriptive value. Yet it is as little philosophical to beautify reality as to be afraid of it. The face of existence, as open to an omnivorously curious mind, is sublime and fascinating enough, but it is surely more than human, less than moral, other than dialectical. It is something like the universe of Spinoza, which even if stretched a little by his dogmatic logic and idealised by his traditional piety, is essentially the natural world, the realm of matter. This certainly embodies some essence—Spinoza thought it embodied all essences—but the only ideal toward which it moves is that all things shall become what in eternity they are; that nature shall run its course, that every appointed event shall occupy its allotted place, and that opinions shall supersede one another as they do, by a psychological and economic necessity: and this is precisely the picture of the universe painted by modern idealists, when they are strong-minded. Their idealism adds nothing to Spinoza on the ideal side, rather subtracts: but it adds a transcendental preface showing that this picture is the work of thought, as if that improved it.

This pantheism, being Hebraic in origin, sees reality in time rather than in space, and is historical rather than cosmological; and being modern, it approaches reality through the discovery or experience of it, and is fundamentally subjective. But there is no moral idealism left in it, unless it is by making the upshot of history as flattering as possible to local or human interests; in other words, by misrepresenting the truth. This is not to say that pantheism is irreligious; on the contrary, there is a sense in which moral idealism, since it selects, protests, and aspires, is less religious than the unqualified worship of reality. When the heart is bent on the truth, when prudence and the love of prosperity dominate the will, science must insensibly supplant divination, and reverence must be transferred from traditional sanctities to the naked power at work in nature, sanctioning worldly

Respect for matter is the beginning of wisdom.

wisdom and hygienic virtue rather than the maxims of zealots or the dreams of saints. God then becomes a poetic symbol for the maternal tenderness and the paternal strictness of this wonderful world; the ways of God become the subject-matter of physics. Matter, the principle of genesis and the true arbiter of fortune, has often been one of the realities symbolised under the name of God, as truth has often been another; and nothing is more normal than that the magnetism of surrounding substance, with its thousand assaults and its thousand responses, should exercise a sobering guidance over the human soul. As the mere rigidity and grimace of a stock or stone can bring primitive man to his knees, annihilating his waywardness by the relentless authority of its stark Being, so the dis-covered march of nature in its treacherous fecundity can hypnotise the philosopher, and cause him to disown as impious his hopeless private idealisms. It is now his only idealism to be humble, to be wise, to be con-tent with his finitude. This form of religion is more materialistic than materialism, since it assigns to matter a dignity which no profane materialist would assign to it, that of having *moral* authority over the hearts of men.

Yet in some measure matter deserves respect even in the eyes of the Platonist, whose aspiration seems at first sight to be to escape from it; for goodness is a prerogative which matter may acquire, as it acquires beauty, in so far as it falls into living organisms and feeds their capacity for intuition and feeling with an abundance of kindred things. *It is requisite for a full harmony between intelligence and truth.* The avowed materialist also, who professes to be an intelligent animal, cannot but place a part of his happiness in his understanding of the world. It is easier to change one's pleasures than to change the nature of things. Why not adapt these passionate demands of ours — so vague and helpless beyond the circle of our domestic needs—to that larger economy by which we must live, if we are to live at all?   The study of nature and the equalising blows of experience tend to establish this sort of regenerate and disillusioned piety in the place of the arrogant idealisms of the will.   Human utopias begin to seem childish in the face of the facts, and the facts, in their labyrinthine order and polyglot fertility, end by seeming glorious as well as inevitable.   There are always compensations for the brave, even in death; and a part of the soul rejoices and becomes immortal in its sympathies when it countersigns the death-warrant of all the other parts.

This fundamental materialism in all human wisdom leaves the spirit perfectly free to exercise its originality in the sphere of poetry and feeling; but it shows that in so far as spirit takes the form of intelligence and of the love of truth (which is also an ideal passion of the soul) it must assume the presence of an alien universe and must humbly explore its ways, bowing to the strong wind of mutation, the better to endure and to profit by that prevailing stress.   It was in the act of making this assumption that animal sensibility first became intelligence.   In its further explorations, spirit discovers, as far as it is possible or needful, its urgent and compulsory objects, as well as the organs, ailing or healthful, which give it play.   Finally, with this self-knowledge, spirit completes its round and renders its philosophy secure and its ambitions spiritual: for it has now conceived how it came into existence and how it is the natural light by which existence, in its waking moments, understands itself.

THE REALM OF TRUTH

Ille potens sui
laetusque deget cui licet in diem
dixisse, vixi. Cras vel atra
nube polum Pater occupato
vel sole puro : non tamen irritum
quodcumque retro est efficiet, neque
diffinget infectumque reddet
quod fugiens semel hora vexit.
HORACE.

Whatever withdraws us from the power of the
senses, whatever makes the past the distant, or the
future predominate over the present, advances us in
the dignity of thinking beings.
DR. JOHNSON.

It fortifies my soul to know
That, though I wander, Truth is so.
CLOUGH.

PREFACE

AN unsophisticated reader will find no difficulty in understanding the sense in which the word truth is used in this book. It is the sense which the word bears in ordinary conversation; and such refinements as I may be led to suggest are not calculated to subvert the plain signification of the word, but only to clarify and confirm it. In this matter, as in many others, I follow common sense; not indeed in its conventions, not in respect to popular dogmas which may be local, verbal, mythical, and contradictory; but I follow common sense in its general momentum and presuppositions, which are indeed the only possible foundation of science, of literature, and of human intercourse.

Nevertheless, it is the business of philosophers, in using the categories of common sense—as they must if they are to be consistent and intelligible—incidentally to criticize and to reform them. The category of truth in particular has been lately subjected to rough usage: and those who live in the thick of contemporary controversies, particularly in America, may well ask me, with a certain irritation, what on earth I can mean by *truth*. In deference to these experts in logic, let me begin by explaining how I use that word. In fact, I have explained it already on sundry occasions; and I can hardly do better than collect here a few of those incidental explanations. They will pave the way innocently and conveniently to the discussions that are to follow.

401

The truth properly means the sum of all true propositions, what omniscience would assert, the whole ideal system of qualities and relations which the world has exemplified or will exemplify. The truth is all things seen under the form of eternity. . . . Every thinking man always assumes the reality of an actual truth, comprehensive and largely undiscovered, of which he claims to be reporting a portion. What (the psychological critic) rather confusingly calls truth, and wishes to reduce to a pragmatic function, is not this underlying truth, the sum of all true propositions, but merely the abstract quality which all true propositions must have in common, to be called true. By truth he means only correctness. The possibility of correctness in an idea is a great puzzle to him, on account of his idealism, which identifies ideas with their objects; and he asks himself how an idea can ever come to be correct or incorrect, as if it referred to something beyond itself.

The fact is, of course, that an idea can be correct or incorrect only if by the word idea we mean not a datum but an opinion; and the abstract relation of correctness, by virtue of which any opinion is true, is easily stated. An opinion is true if what it is talking about is constituted as the opinion asserts it to be constituted. . . . It is not a question of similarity or derivation between a passive datum and a hidden object; it is a question of identity between a fact asserted and a fact existing. If an opinion could not freely leap to its object, no matter how distant or hypothetical, and assert something of that chosen object, an opinion could not be so much as wrong; for it would not be an opinion about anything.[1]

The experience which perhaps makes even the empiricist awake to the being of truth, and brings it home to any energetic man, is the experience of other people lying. When I am falsely accused, or when I am represented as thinking what I do not think, I rebel against that contradiction to my evident self-knowledge; and as the other man asserts that the liar is myself, and a third person might very well entertain that

---

[1] *Character and Opinion in the United States* (London, Constable & Company, Ltd., 1920), pp. 153-6.

hypothesis and decide against me, I learn that a report may fly in the face of the facts. There is, I then see clearly, a comprehensive standard description for every fact, which those who report it as it happened repeat in part, whereas on the contrary liars contradict it in some particular. And a little further reflection may convince me that even the liar must recognize the fact to some extent, else it would not be *that* fact that he was misrepresenting; and also that honest memory and belief, even when most unimpeachable, are not exhaustive and not themselves the standard for belief or for memory, since they are now clearer and now vaguer, and subject to error and correction. That standard comprehensive description of any fact which neither I nor any man can ever wholly repeat, is the truth about it.[1]

When "truth" is used in the abstract sense of correctness, or the quality which all correct judgments have in common, another word, perhaps "fact" or "reality", would . . . have to be used for that standard comprehensive description of the object to which correct judgments conform. But a fact is not a description of itself; and as to the word "reality", if it is understood to mean existence, it too cannot designate a description, which is an essence only. Facts are transitory: . . . and when they have lapsed, it is only their essence that subsists and that, being partially recovered and assigned to them in a retrospective judgment, can render this judgment true. Opinions are true or false by repeating or contradicting some part of the truth about the facts which they envisage; and this truth about the facts is the standard comprehensive description of them.[2]

Truth is not an opinion, even an ideally true one; because besides the limitation in scope which human opinions, at least, can never escape, even the most complete and accurate opinion would give precedence to some terms, and have a direction of survey; and this direction might be changed or reversed without lapsing into error; so that the truth is the

---

[1] *Scepticism and Animal Faith* (London, Constable & Company, Ltd., 1923), p. 266.
[2] Ibid., p. 267.

field which various true opinions traverse in various directions, and no opinion itself. An even more impressive difference between truth and any true discourse is that discourse is an event; it has a date not that of its subject-matter, even if the subject-matter be existential, and roughly contemporary; and in human beings discourse is conversant almost entirely with the past only, whereas truth is dateless and absolutely identical whether the opinions which seek to reproduce it arise before or after the event which the truth describes.[1]

If there were no absolute truth, all-inclusive and eternal, the desultory views taken from time to time by individuals would themselves be absolute. They would be irrelevant to one another, and incomparable in point of truth, each being without any object but the essence which appeared in it. If views can be more or less correct, and perhaps complementary to one another, it is because they refer to the same system of nature, the complete description of which, covering the whole past and the whole future, would be the absolute truth. This absolute truth is . . . that segment of the realm of essence which happens to be illustrated in existence. The question whether a given essence belongs to this segment or not—that is, whether a suggested idea is or is not true—has a tragic importance for an animal intent on discovering and describing what exists, or has existed, or is destined to exist in his world. He seldom has leisure to dwell on essences apart from their presumable truth; even their beauty and dialectical pattern seem to him rather trivial unless they are significant of facts in the realm of matter, controlling his destiny. I therefore give a special name to this tragic segment of the realm of essence and call it the *Realm of Truth*.[2]

A comprehensive description (of any fact) includes also all the radiations of that fact—I mean, all that perspective of the world of facts and of the realm of essence which is obtained by taking this fact as a centre and viewing everything else only in relation with it. The truth about any fact is therefore infinitely extended, although it grows thinner, so

[1] *Scepticism and Animal Faith.*, p. 268.
[2] *The Realm of Essence* (London, Constable & Company, Ltd., 1928), Preface to Realms of Being, p. xv.

to speak, as you travel from it to further and further facts, or to less and less relevant ideas. It is the splash any fact makes, or the penumbra it spreads, by dropping through the realm of essence. Evidently no opinion can embrace it all, or identify itself with it; nor can it be identified with the facts to which it relates, since they are in flux, and it is eternal.[1]

The eternity of truth is inherent in it: all truths—not a few grand ones—are equally eternal. . . . Inspired people, who are too hot to think, often identify the truth with their own tenets. . . . Eternal truths . . . are then tenets which the remotest ancestors of man are reputed to have held, and which his remotest descendants are forbidden to abandon. Of course there are no eternal tenets: neither the opinions of men, nor mankind, nor anything existent can be eternal; eternity is a property of essences only. Even if all the spirits in heaven and earth had been so far unanimous on any point of doctrine, there is no reason, except the monotony and inertia of nature, why their logic or religion or morals should not change to-morrow from top to bottom, if they all suddenly grew wiser or differently foolish.[2]

The truth, however nobly it may loom before the scientific intellect, is ontologically something secondary. Its eternity is but the wake of the ship of time, a furrow which matter must plough upon the face of essence. Truth must have a subject-matter, it must be the truth about something: and it is the character of this moving object, lending truth and definition to the truth itself, that is substantial and fundamental in the universe.[3]

The tide of evolution carries everything before it, thoughts no less than bodies, and persons no less than nations. Yet all things are eternal in their status, as truth is. The place which an event fills in history is its inalienable place; the character that an act or a feeling possesses in passing is its inalienable character. Now the human mind is not merely animal, not merely absorbed in the felt transition from one

[1] *Scepticism and Animal Faith*, pp. 267–8.
[2] Ibid., pp. 268–9.　　　[3] Ibid., pp. 227–8.

state of life to another. It is partly synthetic, intellectual, contemplative, able to look before and after and to see fleeting things at once in their mutual relations, or, as Spinoza expressed it, under the form of eternity. To see things under the form of eternity is to see them in their historic and moral truth, not as they seemed as they passed, but as they remain when they are over. When a man's life is over, it remains true that he has lived; it remains true that he has been one sort of man and not another. In the infinite mosaic of history that bit has its unfading colour and its perpetual function and effect. A man who understands himself under the form of eternity knows the quality that eternally belongs to him, and knows that he cannot wholly die, even if he would; for when the movement of his life is over, the truth of his life remains. The fact of him is a part for ever of the infinite context of facts. . . . The animals are mortal without knowing it, and doubtless presume, in their folly, that they will live for ever. Man alone knows that he must die; but that very knowledge raises him, in a sense, above mortality, by making him a sharer in the vision of eternal truth. He becomes the spectator of his own tragedy; he sympathizes so much with the fury of the storm that he has no ears left for the shipwrecked sailor, though the sailor were his own soul. The truth is cruel, but it can be loved, and it makes free those who have loved it.[1]

To those who can conceive and love the truth in that sense, this book is addressed.

[1] Introduction to *Spinoza's Ethics* in Everyman's Library (London, J. M. Dent & Sons, 1910), pp. xviii and xix.

CHAPTER I

THERE ARE NO NECESSARY TRUTHS

TRADITION is rich in maxims called necessary truths, such as that $2 + 2 = 4$, that space and time are infinitely divisible, that everything has a cause, and that God, or the most real of beings, necessarily exists. Many such propositions may be necessary, by virtue of the definitions given to their terms; many may be true, in that the facts of nature confirm them; and some may be both necessary logically and true materially, but even then the necessity will come from one quarter and the truth from another.

Logical necessity connects ideal terms.

This conclusion would be evident to anyone who had clearly conceived the nature of infinite Being or the realm of essence; a conception in itself easy and inevitable, when once attention has lighted upon it. So obvious and easy is this conception that it may be regarded as trivial and not worth dwelling on: yet here it finds a momentous echo, which dispels half the doubts and worries of speculation. For if essences, or possible terms of thought, are infinite in number and variety, it follows that every particular fact is contingent, arbitrary, and logically unnecessary, since infinite alternatives were open to existence, if existence had chosen to take a different form. Now it is precisely this unnecessary, arbitrary, contingent chance or fatality, making existence at each point such as it is, that determines what shall be true: that is, what elements of essence shall

But truth, being a radiation of existence, is contingent.

407

figure in that existence. So that, truth being descriptive of existence and existence being contingent, truth will be contingent also.

Let me analyse, on these principles, the four maxims adduced above.

That $2 + 2 = 4$, like all the rest of mathematics, is an equation making explicit certain essential relations between certain terms. Essential relations are all necessary, being based on the definitions or intuitions which distinguish those related terms; though it is by no means necessary or even possible to explore and make explicit in human discourse all the essential relations of the terms selected.[1] Naturally in human mathematics there is a human element. Each intuitive mind darts in its own congenial direction, and sees what a differently intuitive mind might have overlooked: and the range of thought also is human, like its pace and direction. One mind crawls where another wears seven-league boots; yet by whatever leaps or on whatever scale the survey be made, if the essences first chosen are not dropped and confused with others, all explorations will help to fill in the same map, and the science of essence, in that region, will be enriched and consolidated.

Mathematical equations cogent formally.

So far truth has not been broached and mathematics is like music, freely exploring the possibilities of form. And yet, notoriously, mathematics holds true of things; hugs and permeates them far more closely than does confused and inconstant human perception; so that the dream of many exasperated critics of human error has been to assimilate all science to mathematics,

Their applicability a matter of fact.

---

[1] The question does not arise whether mathematical judgments are analytic or synthetic. Psychologically all judgments and all intuitions of the complex are synthetic, because the terms given are distinguished and compared in thought. But if the judgments are necessary, they must be analytical logically, i.e. founded on the nature of the terms.

so as to make knowledge safe by making it, as Locke wished, direct perception of the relations between ideas. Unfortunately, knowledge would then never touch those matters of fact on which Locke was intent. The only serious value of those logical explorations would lie in their possible relevance to the accidents of existence. It is only in that relation and in that measure that mathematical science would cease to be mere play with ideas and would become *true*: that is, in a serious sense, would become *knowledge*. Now the seriousness of mathematics comes precisely of its remarkable and exact relevance to material facts, both familiar and remote: so that mathematical equations, besides being essentially necessary in themselves, are often also true of the world we live in. And this in a surprising measure. For when once any essence falls within the sphere of truth, all its essential relations do so too: and the necessity of these relations will, on that hypothesis, form a necessary complement to a proposition that happens to be true. This same necessity, however, would have nothing to do with truth if the terms it connects were not exemplified in existence.

In this way mathematical calculations far outrunning experiment often turn out to be true of the physical world, as if, *per impossibile*, they could be true *à priori*. But in fact nature, that had to have some form or other, is organized and deployed on principles which, in human language, are called number, shape, and measurable time; categories *They are actually true of the material sphere, at least in the gross.* which for that reason have taken root in human language and science. Yet these categories would have no truth or applicability whatever, if existence were entirely mental and sentimental. They would then be ideal fictions or games of apperception, with their own sporting rules, like the game of chess, but with no cognitive function in respect to the dynamic world in which life would arise, and in which these games would be carried on.

Now as a matter of fact there is a psychological sphere to which logic and mathematics do not apply. There, the truth is dramatic. That $2+2=4$ is not true of ideas. One idea added to another, in actual intuition, makes still only one idea, or it makes three: for the combination, with the relations perceived, forms one complex essence, and yet the original essences remain distinct, as elements in this new whole. This holds of all moral, æsthetic, and historical units: they are merged and reconstituted with every act of apperception. Each essence evoked reverts, when lost sight of, to its limbo of latent forms. It cannot contribute genetically or dynamically, being unsubstantial, to compose the next apparition. Although life in plants and animals may be capable of mathematical treatment at one pervasive material level, none of the vital unities or tropes are so capable. Moreover, this is not due altogether to the imagination superposing its views on the flux of existence: for the special organic unity which breeds imagination and will, and superposes them on events, cannot be itself imaginary, since it creates a specific fact—namely, this very will or imagination. There are therefore levels of reality, and these the most important to mankind, that elude all mathematical axioms.

But irrelevant to the realm of spirit.

In the second maxim adduced, that space and time are infinitely divisible, we pass to an axiom the truth of which is extremely doubtful, even in the physical world. Specious space and time (that is, extension and duration as given to intuition, and space and time as defined geometrically) are indeed infinitely divisible. Scale in them is elastic and utterly unsubstantial, so that

Physical space and time not subject to dialectic.

there is room for the most elaborate ideal event or object within the smallest fraction of time or space. But this hardly seems to be true in the chemical or animal or astronomical spheres, where scale is not variable fantastically: and this for the best of reasons—namely, that in nature empty space and time do not pre-exist, so that existent beings of extensible and unascertainable dimensions may drop into them later; but on the contrary a physical flux, pulsing through natural moments and carrying a definite volume of events with it, creates a real time by its rhythms and a real space by its organic complexity. These native dimensions of the real may indeed be measured and graphically noted in our science, as living music may be measured and noted in a musical score: but the ideal qualities of the medium for such a transcription can no more be imposed on nature by our definitions than the flatness or infinite divisibility of the paper, or the lines of the clef, can impose their graphic qualities upon music.

For want of making this distinction, hopeless difficulties and fatuous assertions have been imported into philosophy. Sometimes nature has been abolished for not conforming to logic: and sometimes logic has corrected nature so as to secure an agreement. Yet the *true* agreement existed from the first, within its natural limits: a friendly concomitance between material events and the free symbolism proper to animal sense or imagination, excited as these must be by those material contacts and organic tensions. There is both precision and poetry in the intricacies of essence, if selectively explored: but the scientific imagination is idolatrous when it interpolates its creations in the dynamic structure of nature. They describe that structure from without, they are not contained within it: they are transcripts, not insights.

When we pass to the third maxim, that everything

has a cause, the balance between necessity and truth is reversed. This maxim has no logical cogency, but the presumption it expresses is backed by a good deal of evidence. In search of necessity we might correct the statement and say that every *effect* has a cause; but this truism would leave us to consider whether every event is actually an effect.

No actual
sequence can
be necessary
and the sum
of causes
can have no
cause.

Certainly not, unless the series of events runs back to infinity: and even in that case—apart from the heavy strain imposed on human imagination and credulity—the question would arise whether every part of every event was caused by its antecedents, or only its initial phase or its approximate outline. The latter is the plausible view, adopted by Aristotle, and reasonable if we believe in the dominance of a conceptual pattern over the flux of existence. Events will fall into certain classes, animals and their passions will exemplify certain permanent types, but there will be a margin of incalculable variation due to accidental conjunctions or lapses in the execution of the dominant themes. And here again, there are alternative possibilities. These lapses or conjunctions may all have mechanical causes, according to deeper laws of matter, traceable beneath the moral morphology of events; or on the contrary, variations may be free and groundless, though kept within certain bounds by the magic of hereditary types; so that the old equilibrium of the cosmos will right itself after each casual oscillation. Or perhaps these oscillations are casual only in appearance, and from the point of view of their antecedents, while by a secret conspiracy they, or some of them, steadily make for one far-off divine event: and it may have been these successive variations, mechanically uncaused but prophetically inspired, that have created, as it were on the way, the stock genera and species of our transitory world.

These would then be restive in their trammels and destined to be superseded. If all variations and free choices were so directed, they might all be said to have a cause, not in the past, but in the future: and the providential harmony of all the parts and of all the incidents would seem, in one sense, to render them necessary. Not that logically a different issue would not be conceivable, but that morally and emotionally it would be "unthinkable" that any absurd accident should ever come groundlessly to mar so perfect a plan.

Nevertheless, the necessity of each element for the perfection of a particular design confers no necessity upon that design as a whole, nor compels nature to adopt it. Whatever regularity or unity the existing world may exhibit, the existence of such unity or regularity remains a perfectly contingent matter of fact.

But have we not heard of an ontologically necessary Being, the essence of which involves existence? We have heard of it: and this typically metaphysical contention brings to a head, and exhibits boldly, the equivocation involved in the idea that any truth is necessarily true. The most real of beings, said St. Anselm, necessarily exists: for evidently if it did not exist, far from being most real, it would not be real at all. Is then reality, we may ask, the same as existence? And can existence have degrees? St. Anselm explains that by greater reality he means more than greater quantity of material being: he means also greater dignity, perfection, and moral greatness. Now, a non-existent essence would woefully lack moral greatness, perfection or dignity: it would be a contemptible ghost, a miserable nothing. Undoubtedly for a care-laden mind seeking salvation—unless it sought salvation from existence—power, which certainly involves

The ontological proof ambiguous.

existence, must be the first mark of reality and value:
what is without power will be without importance.
Granting this, the ontological proof is cogent: the
most powerful of beings necessarily exists, because
power is only another name for the difference which
the existence of one thing makes in the existence of
another. But a less religious or more practical investigator of power might well come to the conclusion
that this greatest, most formidable, and most real of
beings was matter, meaning by this not only the
substance of interacting things but the principles of
their interaction.

At the other pole of reflection, on the contrary,
as among the Indians or the Eleatics, the most real
of things might seem to be pure Being, or the realm
of essence, excluding change and existence altogether:
because in change and existence there is essential
privation. That from which we lapse or to which
we aspire is no longer or not yet; and in being for
the moment something in particular we renounce and
reject Being in every other form. The truly ontological proof, for a pure ontologist, would therefore
assert, not that the most real of beings necessarily
exists, but that the most real of beings necessarily
does not exist. In other words, real would be
identified with necessary Being, or essence, and this
existing world of limitation, contrariety and care would
be pronounced an illusion.

I do not mention this paradox in order to laugh
at St. Anselm or at his many solemn disciples, but
precisely to show that behind the sophistry
of their words there is, or may be, a secret
allegiance to pure and necessary Being.
Their play on the word reality perhaps
masked an instinctive revolt against worldli-
ness, a desire to throw off somehow the
incubus of alien facts and irrational compulsions and

find a way back into safety and peace. They called pure Being most real because to their hearts it was most satisfying. Consequently their argument was fallacious and even ridiculous, if by "necessary existence" we understand a necessity attaching to events or to facts, that is, to contingencies. Yet the same argument breathes a fervent intuition and a final judgment of the spirit, if it intends rather to deny final validity to an existential order which, by definition, is arbitrary, treacherous, and self-destructive: a realm of being over which inessential relations are compulsory and essential relations are powerless.

When we are asked to shift the meaning of terms so that, at least in God, essence may involve existence, we are left in doubt as to the direction in which the assimilation is to take place. Are we to idealize existence so that it may be nothing but essence, or to hypostatize essence so as to make it exist? When we speak of being or reality, are we intent on the miracle of existence, and do we pass from that mystery to the conviction that the divine essence is just this miracle, this absolute power, this abysmal fact? Or free from all trouble or wonder, and in placid intellectual clearness, do we first demonstrate to ourselves the necessity and infinity of possible being or essence; so that for us the miracle of existence becomes rather a scandal? For why should innocent and merely possible being be raised for a moment at this or that point into an insane prominence, impossible to sustain or to justify, whilst all the rest of essence is veiled by a passionate ignorance and proclaimed to be nothing? In the latter case, existence would involve privation, partiality, ignorance, instability, and grotesque pride, with a consequent perpetual misery. Instead of the word existence the ontological argument should then employ the word reality, meaning the fullness and indestructi-

Essence and existence contrasted afresh.

bility—*essential indestructibility*—of being. If we make this substitution, feeling the pregnancy of our terms, we may come to see how the maximum of reality might logically involve infinity, impassiveness, and eternity: all of which are contrary to the limitation, flux, and craving inherent in existence. No essence, not even this essence of existence, has any power to actualize itself in a fact; nor does such actualization bring to any essence an increment in its logical being; only an alien ambiguous status, no sooner acquired than lost.

The existence of God is therefore not a necessary truth: for if the proposition is necessary, its terms can be only essences; and the word God itself would then designate a definable idea, and would not be a proper name indicating an actual power. If, on the contrary, the word is such a proper name, and God is a psychological moral being energizing in space and time, then his existence can be proved only by the evidence of these natural manifestations, not by dialectical reasoning upon the meanings of terms.

CHAPTER II

FACTS ARBITRARY, LOGIC IDEAL

THAT one philosopher should profess to have proved some metaphysical tenet, and that another philosopher should profess to have refuted it, might leave the reader cold. It is not in those regions that he ordinarily feels sure of the truth. Are there no truths obviously necessary to common sense? If I have mislaid my keys, *mustn't* they be somewhere? If a child is born, *mustn't* he have had a father? *Must* is a curious word, pregnant for the satirist: it seems to redouble the certainty of a fact, while really admitting that the fact is only conjectured. The necessity asserted foolishly parades the helplessness of the mind to imagine anything different. Yet this helplessness, on which dogmatism rests, is shameful, and is secretly felt to be shameful. Spirit was born precisely to escape such limitations, to see the contingency and finitude of every fact, and to imagine as many alternatives and extensions as possible, some of which may be true, and may put that casual fact in its true setting. Truth is groped after, not imposed, by the presumptions of the intellect: and if these presumptions often are true, the reason is that they are based upon and adjusted to the actual order of nature, which is thoroughly unnecessary, and most miraculous when most regular. This blessed regularity, logically unforeseeable, is indeed the basis of human safety, wisdom, and science; it teaches us what *must* happen under particular circumstances; but accommodation

Physical necessity is conditional on an order of nature itself not necessary.

417

to the truth in these regions leaves the mind, when not mechanized, full of wonder at the truth.

The mechanized mind, that cannot wonder at the commonplace, is apt to carry its mechanical presump- Practical tions over into logic, as if necessity there certainty too were simply truth to fact. A large mistaken for logical part of the confidence felt in numerical and necessity. geometrical measurements is an emotional confidence. It comes from a sense of what would surely happen to bodies having those numerical or geometrical properties. We seldom stop to consider narrowly the logical relations between defined essences, as pure mathematics would require us to do; but we rely on common knowledge of the world become in ourselves an irresistible mode of imagination; and this precipitation of ideas in ourselves we call necessity in the object. Anything else would be "impossible": that is to say, impossible for us to *believe*. Interest in fact, or confident judgment about fact, here overcomes or confuses interest in essence. Yet wonder at the commonplace—at the stars or a flower or a word—comes to almost everybody at certain moments: because these things are too improbable in themselves and too inexplicably juxtaposed for a spirit whose natural field is the perspicuous.

A rationalistic reader might still ask: "Is there no truth within your realm of essence? Are not Correctness unity and distinctness present in all essences, or error and is it not true to say so? And all that within logic a question you yourself have written, here and else- of art, not of where, about essence, is it not true?" No, truth. I reply, it is not true, nor meant to be true. It is a grammatical or possibly a poetical construction having, like mathematics or theology, a certain internal vitality and interest; but in the direction of truth-finding, such constructions are merely instrumental like any language or any telescope. A man may fall into an error in grammar or in calculation. This is a fault in the practice of his art, at bottom a moral defect, a defect in attention, diligence, and capacity: and in my dialectic I have doubtless often clouded my terms with useless or disturbing allusions. But when consistently and conscientiously worked out and stripped to their fighting weight, my propositions will be logically necessary, being deducible from the definitions or intuitions of the chosen terms, and especially of this chosen term "essence" itself. But logic is only logic: and the systems of relation discoverable amongst essences do not constitute truths, but only other more comprehensive essences, within which the related essences figure as parts. The systems, like the logical elements, become a means of expressing truth only when truth can be otherwise discovered and brought face to face with our deductive reasonings. Truth will then domesticate our logic in the world: until perhaps the dialectical guest so hospitably received forgets his essential foreignness and undertakes to drive the poor native facts out of house and home. Our idealisms, in their moral autonomy, can hardly abstain from claiming a divine right to govern the world, to correct it, or at least to scold it for being so unaccountably wrong. And far from right the world indeed is, and must be, judged by human interests and even by human logic, because man and his moral aspirations are only incidents in the universe; but there is one ideal measure that the actual world cannot fall short of: it cannot be far from true.

This truth, if the world had been chaotic, might have excluded the existence of mind altogether, or kept mind down to the sensuous level; but there was a partial rationality or promise of rationality in things that encouraged the mind to clarify its ideas, and to develop logic. Logic is a child of fact, as spirit in general

Double contact of logic with fact.

is a child of the psyche: a headstrong child quick to forget or deny the sweet milk that has nurtured it; yet the bond with earth remains notwithstanding. It remains not only in the past, fundamentally determining the choice of essences that logic shall play with, but it remains also contemporaneously, in that even the logician's thoughts are controlled at every turn by physical accidents and social pressure. It is important to distinguish this nether contact of logic with fact in the biological genetic direction, from the ideal contact established or rather claimed, when logic is used to express or to extend natural knowledge. Biological contact exists also between vital facts and music; it exists between vital facts and illusions, errors, or myths; but music luckily is not expected (until it is coined into language) to convey *knowledge* of facts. That is the secret of its magnificent development: the life of music is free from everything except its natural sources, from everything except the biological impulses and multiple harmonies internal to the organism. Sight and touch, on the contrary, though no less sensuous, animal and subjective than sound, are more readily and completely caught up by the cognitive impulse, and idolatrously treated as *true*: exactly how literally or consistently, it would be endless to trace.

By the truth, as the reader knows, I understand the complete ideal description of existence; and any part of this description will be a truth, that is, a part of the truth. The ideal complete description of an essence, on the contrary, or of the relations between essences, unless this description is rehearsed psychologically by some living mind, is simply that very essence and those very relations: it can be neither false nor true, but only articulate. And the realm of essence being infinite and omnimodal, any other description of any other essence, or relations between

In respect to essences, all definitions are equally valid, since each selects the essence which it defines.

essences, would be equally articulate up to its own degree of elaboration; so that there would be nothing to choose, in the way of truth, between any two descriptions.

This insight removes a problem sometimes needlessly proposed about the choice of definitions, for instance in the case of number or numbers. Mathematicians are unanimous and clear on the point that $2 + 2 = 4$; but they are obscure and divided as to the nature of 2 and of 1, of $+$ and of $=$. And we are allowed to infer that there is a *true* nature of $=$ and $+$, of 1 and of 2. But that, in logic, is nonsense. Each of these essences is whatever it is by *any* definition: the rest is merely a question of names, perhaps preempted by custom to some one definition rather than to another. Essentially, all conceivable natures and definitions are on a par: the only question is historical and psychological, regarding the prevalence of particular notions in the human mind, or else physical, as to the applicability of these notions to the cosmos. In both directions, obscurity is inevitable, and differences of opinion, if modest, are legitimate. It may be expedient to limit the interpretation of mathematical signs to particular humanly chosen ideas: but other interpretations, perhaps less fertile or useful, would not be essentially less cogent. Truth, then, never enters the field of mathematics at all; and there is no *true* view about the nature of number or numbers, until the discussion veers from mathematics altogether, to physics, history or psychology.

From this it follows that we may intelligently adopt and apply the category of truth to current perceptions and opinions, inasmuch as they profess to be knowledge and are asserted of positive facts: but when, in reflection, we make some supposition deliberately contrary to fact, the relevance of truth to that supposition is exhausted before we begin to develop it.

Suppositions contrary to fact also transcend the realm of truth.

The supposition is admittedly false; and in considering it further we are exploring the relations it may
have in the realm of essence only, where questions
of truth do not arise.   Romantic people think of what
might have been: some danger narrowly escaped,
some bet almost won: possibilities near enough to
the truth to seem false, and perhaps bitter.   In this
moodiness we may say that the poets lie: but the
poets did not lie, they were inspired.   Their suppositions were contrary to fact only by accident, and quite
apart from their innocent intention.   No doubt common waking perception is truer than poetry, and the
poets in their sane moments will not deny it: but
inspiration liberates them from that interest.   The
crucial point is this: that not only are all particular
truths and facts contingent, but the very categories of
fact and truth, like all other essences, if they are
exemplified at all, are exemplified unnecessarily and
by a groundless chance.

Logic, when once its foothold in fact has been
secured at any point, has a moral part to play, and
Contact   this in two directions.   It humanizes the
with truth   world, since we now can think and reason
adds moral
value to   about it with some relevance; and it vivifies
logic.   speculation, by allying the furthest reaches
of it with real life.   Logic traces the radiation of
truth: I mean that when one term of a logical system
is known to describe a fact, the whole system attach-
able to that term becomes, as it were, incandescent,
and forms a part of the aura of truth.   The terms of
logic are themselves originally glimpses of facts: we
deepen this apprehension humanly and morally when
we develop ideally the qualities which a fact truly
wears either in itself or in relation to human faculties
and interests; as a poet deepens his sense of beauty,
if one beauty in his mind recalls another, and he
finds metaphors and musical words that may re-echo

his passion.   But we may also deepen our apprehension by buttressing it with apprehensions of kindred or neighbouring facts, which though interlopers in that argument, support it by analogy or qualify its value.   Here is where allusions, logically redundant, may help to brighten the faint rays of truth still colouring high speculation.   Between the branchings of our logic, that spread aloft forgetful of the truth in which, after all, they are remotely rooted, we may catch fresh glimpses of earth and sky, and so gain, as we go, circumstantial support or correction for our deductions.

Thus grammar, rhetoric, and logic enrich enormously the phenomenon of being alive.   They embroider every image with a thousand latent analogies   *And lends* and concordant rhymes; and they enshrine   *it a tragic* this image in the ideal world to which, after   *force.* all, every image belongs.   Because the truth or applicability of ideas, as of words, though it may be the chief or only source of their importance, is irrelevant to their sensuous or intrinsic character: so that when an idea, weighted with the dignity of truth, is lifted out again from the alien context and accidental occasion which allied it with fact, that idea seems to be clarified and to sing hallelujah; for it finds itself free at last to be itself, and to trace its internal affinities in its native element.   Nor is this merely a sensual or logical holiday for the mind: it is a holiday or holy day also in a religious sense; because weighted with truth as the idea now is, it drags, as it were, the whole workaday world with it into the light.   The world which was but a too familiar fact suddenly becomes beautiful: and at the same time the idea, only a graphic pattern before, now touches the heart and becomes poetical.

Finally, turning the doctrine here defended against itself, we might ask whether it is not necessarily true that the truth is contingent and not necessary. Here again I must repeat that what is necessary logically My own logic, even if made cogent, not therefore true. is not necessarily *true*. In this case, that truth is contingent is a necessary proposition, because facts, by definition, make the truth true and all facts, again by definition, are contingent. But there is no necessity in the choice or in the applicability of such categories as necessity, truth, or fact. These categories are not necessarily true. I find that, as a matter of fact, they are true, or at least true enough: they articulate human thought in a normal way which reality on the whole seems to sanction. They are the lungs and heart-valves of the mind. And while we use these categories, we shall be obliged on pain of talking nonsense to stick to their connotations, and to acknowledge, among other things, that there are no necessary truths. But the possession of such categories is after all a psychological or even a personal accident; and the fact that they are convenient, or even absolutely true in describing the existing world, is a cosmic accident.

The thesis of the first chapter, then, that there are no necessary truths, is itself made necessary only by It is true only in so far as it is applicable. virtue of certain assumed intuitions or definitions which fix the meaning of the terms necessity, contingency, existence, and truth. But no definition and no intuition can render true the term that it distinguishes. My thesis will therefore be a true thesis only in so far as in the realm of existence facts may justify my definitions and may hang together in the way that those definitions require. The case is the same in principle as in the homely equation, $2 + 2 = 4$; only that in arithmetic the terms are simpler and more familiar, so that the necessary relation between them is obvious to more people. It happens at the same time that the application of arithmetic, where it applies, is most constant and exact, so that its truth in those regions is beyond doubt; whereas any general logic applied to describing the universe, however ancient and well tried this logic may be, remains rather a form of human grammar. We are in a region of free intuition and construction, as in music, with no claims to propounding a revealed or a revealing truth.

CHAPTER III

INTERPLAY BETWEEN TRUTH AND LOGIC

HAVING laid down this distinction between logic and truth, and shown that truth, as I define it, is wholly

There is a kind of truth internal to discourse, depending on fidelity.
contingent, I have no desire to quarrel with mankind for using words as they choose, and talking of truth also in cases where there is only consistency. There is much truth, even in my sense, possible in respect to ideas: not only psychological and historical truth, in describing the ideas that may have actually arisen in the human mind, but also formal truth in the description of an accepted idea in terms different from those in which it was couched at first; a change in expression which may serve to analyse that idea and bring out its essential affinities. Mathematics, logic, and a certain kind of psychology may thus create a phenomenological science; that is, a faithful description of some field of essence already selected and duly named; and we must allow that, at least according to the genius of the English language, whatever is faithful and trusty may be called true.

This idiomatic use of the word true is semi-moral. It turns on not belying one's professions and being constant to a plighted troth. Serious thought requires this sort of fidelity. We begin by noticing and liking some idea, and the very earnestness of our attention becomes a pledge in our own minds not to drop that idea, nor adulterously to slip another idea in its place. Truth—truth to it and to ourselves—now demands

426

that we make it clearer and clearer, more and more unmistakable; and perhaps, by an illusion not unknown to lovers, we attribute to our first intuition a prophetic force, as if it had irresistibly predestined us to these later developments. But ideas, if by ideas we mean essences and not impressions, are as Berkeley termed them, inert. They do not compose a world but a vocabulary: and their logical relations, though immutable, have no aggressive force compelling us to notice them. We evoke ideas for a moment of our own motion; and they vanish like sounds and shadows, without leaving a trace. Thus if our intuition had been careless and not vitally rooted, the essence evoked in passing would never have been retained or recovered adequately in a second intuition. Its fleeting definiteness for sense would never have become an express definition for thought. In dismissing and forgetting that image we should then be committing no infidelity. Obviously we could never falsify our old ideas if we never thought of them again.

This drift of ideation, however, which would be innocent if it were purely sensuous, may invade dialectic and explicit recollection, becoming a perpetual fountain of sophistry. Each time we mention a word we may give it a different meaning, and the more we shift and vary, the deeper we may think we go. We lie, either idly or maliciously, when we allow invention to transform our memories; and we contradict ourselves if we allow invention or the flux of accidental thought to vitiate the sense of our original terms. Dialectic then becomes, as in Hegel, a romantic alternation of ideal or moral impulses. Infidelity to one's thoughts is here felt to be truth to one's deeper self and to one's destiny; and it may really be so when the thin pretence to logic covers a shrewd perception of the instability of life. For there

Infidelity to a first meaning is sometimes called dialectic, and may adjust ideas to facts.

are mental reservations and insincerities hiding in our explicit assertions, treasons latent in our promises, and unforeseen social currents destined to carry our thoughts suddenly in new directions. All this may make excellent dramatic history or phenomenology of morals; and if it seems to skirt dangerously a Mephisto-phelean abyss of mockery and biting scorn, it may be rendered unexpectedly edifying by the assurance that our dead selves are stepping-stones to higher things, that the sum of illusions is the only truth, and that a sufficient experience of folly produces wisdom, not by repentance, but by approximation. Yet even suppos-ing that this romantic idealism truly represented the facts, in calling this description of the facts logic we should be turning the irony of logic upon logic itself; and dialectic, far from developing faithfully the im-plications of ideas, would glorify the infidelities of things to those ideas.

Whether glorious or feeble these infidelities are inevitable, since things are in flux and ideas, in the logical sense, are unchangeable. Moreover, History laughs àt politics. there is necessarily some novel idea or pat-tern illustrated in the flux itself, and a special trope in each turn of affairs; so that the truth of history perpetually gives the lie to the maxims of men, and defeats their politics and ambition. Yet looked at from outside, with the wisdom that comes after the fact, people's actions may seem to the his-torian to have been directed upon the ends actually achieved; whereas in fact the result was unintended and probably unforeseen; though it is easier to foresee the future than to command it, and only those seem to command it who pre-figure it with enthusiasm. Infinitely deeper than the logic of our thoughts is the fertility of our destiny; and circumstances keep us alive by continually defeating us. In strictness no man ever succeeds: the only question is whether he shall be defeated by the action of others or by his own action.

The notion that history might be dialectical would hardly have seemed plausible to anybody, had not dialectic been conceived in a satirical sense; as when each speaker in a dialogue refutes the others, and the argument ends in the refutation of everybody. The author in such a case speaks for nature, and laughs at opinions. If he is candid he even laughs at his own opinion, and what he exhibits in his dialectic is not logic triumphant but logic losing itself in the sea of fact.

Nor is captious disputation requisite to this end. So long as logic is not thoroughly purified and abstracted, but is applied to things, a man's most honest ideas may issue in the same contrariety. Existence is once for all irrational and cannot be wholly elucidated in terms of essence. *Ontological divergence between logic and fact.* And since, at the same time, it is only in terms of essence that facts can be described, partiality and instability beset all description. If a thing is small, it is also large, compared with something smaller. If it is good, it is also bad; if true also false. Nor does this hold only of relatives. If a thing has being, or definite character, it also lacks being, because in being what it is it rejects and banishes all that it is not, so that all positive wealth is shadowed by privation.

This famous union of opposites, philosophers being naturally rapt in the excitement of assertion and not having time to be quite honest, gives rise to no less famous fallacies. A first fallacy is this: that the relativity and self-disruption found in the description of facts is transferred to the terms of the description, that is, to the essences confronting each other there. *The union of contraries in things imports no contradiction into essences.* But these essences have no inherent ambiguity

or tendency to pass into their opposites. Large has
no proclivity to mean small, good to mean bad, or
true false, or wealth privation, or being not-being.
If each of these essences could alienate its character,
they could not remain terms in consistent assertions;
they could not be so much as compared or opposed,
and all discourse and perception would sink into black
night. It is only in describing half-hidden, complex,
substantial facts that ambiguities and contradictions
appear; for here essences essentially different (since
each is invincibly itself) are found alternately or simultaneously present. Were the essences not still different
and absolutely fixed in character, there would be no
problem in their co-presence, and no dialectic: only
a flow of indistinguishables, if so much as a flow
could be distinguished.

It may be noted in passing that essences are not
intrinsically predicates or adjectives, but primordial
and distinct forms of possible being. They
The nature become predicates or adjectives when an
of pure animal psyche apprehending them is vitally
Being preoccupied with the pressure of matter,
recalled.
and with reacting upon that pressure; so that the
given essences are taken for portions or qualities of
the dynamic fact by which the psyche is confronted.
Save for that material preoccupation, the spirit would
regard the essences evoked before it in their intrinsic
characters as the adequate furniture of life for the
moment, like an eagle in repose observing the sun.
Moreover, pure Being is not a substance in which
individual essences inhere, so that the essences might
be predicates of it. Pure Being is itself only an
essence. Expressly, it is that which all essences have
in common—namely, character or distinguishableness
and self-identity; but pregnantly, pure Being covers
the whole realm of essence or the sum of all essences,
since all essences are needed to display fully all that

is self-identical and distinguishable, and that has being or character.

A second fallacy incidental to the dialectic of opposites suggests a superstitious origin. Contradiction (which exists only in human language describing facts that in themselves cannot be contradictory) is transferred to the facts themselves, as if a moral uneasiness existed in them compelling them to shift their ground. Heraclitus seems to have hinted at something of the sort, in his oracular fashion: we learn that war is the parent of all things, and that justice or punishment condemns everything definite to destruction, as if it were a sin to be finite. In Hegel the same pantheistic sentiment was doubtless reinforced by intimate acquaintance with self-contradiction and self-dissolution in Protestant theology. Here sometimes there may really have been an uneasy conscience and a conflict of contrary feelings driving the mind to the next stage of enlightenment, and from that stage on. Yet the progress of dialectic even in this field, where there was a primary contradiction between tradition and enquiry, has suffered many reversals and has taken a long time. Not the logic of the beliefs, but the ripeness of society or of private sentiment for a change of view has determined the direction of reform and the halting-places of opinion. In general, it is fabulous to represent phenomenology, or the drama of ideas, as the motive force in history. Phenomena are inert results, æsthetic figments: while the derivation of event from event is a natural flow, with crises and cataclysms here and there, but for the most part lapsing with a serene monotony and a tireless self-repetition. This steady underlying vortex of nature keeps mankind alive and keeps it human: which does not prevent civilizations and empires from rising and falling, not always by mutual conflict

(marginal note:) Natural instability represented mythically as logical contradiction.

or direct succession, but often by some local accretion
of martial and social energy, vegetating spontaneously,
as the Greeks and the Romans vegetated, and sucking
their neighbours up into their more vigorous organism,
not at all by dialectic. Nor is it dialectic, or any
new idea, that commonly destroys the victor in his
turn; ruin comes by the dissolution of his fighting
organization and the changed habits that his very
victory leads him to form. We may personify these
habits in a miracle play, and show how virtues and
vices rule the destinies of nations. Heraclitus had
said so too: every man's character is his dæmon,
presiding over his fate. And this interplay of the
causes of life and death we may call, if we like, the
dialectic of existence.

In Hegel's miracle play there are indeed many
stretches of genuine logic, where he dissects the meanings of given ideas. Such analysis clarifies
its own terms, and no cataclysms of nature
or opinion can annul the validity of the
deductions made from those terms logically.
Whether the deduction is logical or empirical and
arbitrary can be tested by this circumstance: that true
analysis leaves the original idea whole and uncontaminated, in the centre of all the radiating ideas that
may be brought to surround it: whereas in a psychological flux, as in a dream, additions transform the
original datum, identifications are fallacious, progress
is made through oblivion, and the whole torrent is
lost in sand. Yet as the sand itself is a quicksand, and
moves, the romantic historian sees nothing tragic in
the evaporation of his original stream: there will
always be something on foot to undergo interesting
transformations. Hegel's attention was accordingly
not long arrested on pure analysis. Analysis served
chiefly to loosen ideas, and open some breach for
destructive criticism. The point was to produce a

Logic,
sophistry
and truth
in Hegel's
dialectic.

pregnant confusion in which the logician might drop
the thread of his argument and pick up some contrary
fact. The air of this dialectic is thick with the fumes
of earth; this makes its strength and its charm; and
such a picture of mutation, by its very homeliness
and allegiance to truth, confirms my contention that
truth and logical necessity are independent things.

Pleasant as well as tragic is the perpetual excitement of finding that which there was no reason to
expect. If our prudence is discouraged,   Romantic
our vitality is stimulated; and existence, for   chaos.
the romantic soul, becomes a Gothic marvel, infinitely
extensible in quality and quantity, unmapped and
incalculable. If any eternal fitness seems nevertheless
attributable to the course of things, this fitness will
lie entirely in an occasional æsthetic or religious
emotion arising during the process itself.

The taste for chaos, however, is hardly normal,
because even in the act of demanding chaos the mind
throws out a postulate that, by a secret
necessity, this chaos shall never lapse into   Any view
                                                    of reality
order. And what assurance can the em-   when taken
pirical observer or pure experimenter possess   to be true
                                                    becomes
that the indetermination he observes is not   imposing.
specious, and due to the superficial external cognizance
which he takes of events? Might there not be a
rationality in them hidden from his eyes? And,
indeed, it is almost inevitable that, among events
which interest him and remain in his memory, there
should exist some mutual relevance. Every event,
though unnecessary and spontaneous, will probably
be pertinent to what went before, as each fresh episode
in a serial story, unexpected as it may be to the reader,
must somehow be grafted upon the previous characters
and episodes. Even to break in and interrupt an
experience, events must have a certain dramatic continuity, and fall into a temporal and moral order in

the mind that records them. This psychological compulsion soon generates superstitions and prophecies about the secretly meaningful and fatal order of events; and the supposed paths of destiny are explored with as much intellectual ardour and foretaste of truth as were ever the laws of nature.

Cognitive ambition, on the physical side, is inherent in hunting and fighting; and on the spiritual side and Natural origin of dogmatism. for reflection it involves something like a taste for truth. To be deceived is as hateful to the mind as it is dangerous to the body. Impatience and vanity, however, at once intervene; so that it is not facts so much that, dominate human knowledge, in its sweep and intensity, as imagination that lends importance and felt reality to alleged facts. Impetuous thought is then led to claim a double truth: one sort of truth legitimately, truth to inspiration; and another sort of truth abusively, truth to fact. The vital and moral heat inseparable from thinking thus often renders logic dogmatic, and seduces it from its ideal cogency to posing as material truth. The mathematician has this justification, that his original data are simple and true. They have been tested and clarified in daily life from time immemorial; so that his speculative superstructure has a certain diminishing affinity or relevance to material truth, apart from its logical validity. Yet the glory of his science does not reside, for him, in that link with contingent fact, but rather in a certain almost humorous compulsiveness in its logical development: whence its reputation for certitude (not merited in the higher reaches of his speculation) which can make it, even for an empiricist like Locke, the ideal of knowledge.

Here, however, the pride of mathematics, like that of theology, comes before a fall. There is no end of science, no end of learning, in both pursuits; but mathematics, like theology, is not knowledge of anything but itself. *True* knowledge, *natural* knowledge, should be the cognizance that one existing thing takes of another; and this perforce is a form of faith, though justified in continual physical contacts between the knower and the known: whereas mathematics and theology trace ideal relations for their own sake and end in the air.

The bad repute into which logic fell at the Renaissance, for being tautological, might at any moment overtake mathematics, were it not for the utility of mathematics in the applied arts. For in themselves the higher mathematics, in spite of their exactitude, or because of it, have not the direct savour of truth. They are scholastic, they are almost occult; and the hearty shrewd lover of truth distrusts such acrobatic marvels. What he trusts is experiment, exploration, and the warm immediacy of action and passion in his own person; he would like to laugh at all abstract speculation as the most ridiculous of shams. And he would be right in laughing, if logic or mathematics pretended to truth: but that is a claim foisted on them by the dogmatism of common perception, contrary to their proper genius. It is like the claim to truth or utility foisted by pedagogues on the fine arts. Philosophy has too long been pedagogical, and the best schooldays are half-holidays. If liberty has opened a window for us towards the infinite realm of essence, it has not authorized us to regard the prospect visible to us there as the truth about nature. Much less are we authorized to set up our visions as moral standards to which things ought to conform. The order of subordination is the opposite one. Nature being what she is, and we being in consequence what we are, certain special reaches of essence are obvious to our senses and intellect. Sights and sounds, pains and pleasures assail us; and our leisure is free to develop

Logic, when turned into metaphysics, spoils both physics and logic.

in music and language, in mathematics and religion, the moral burden of our animal existence. Nor will this play of ideas be sheer truancy. Our toys may become instruments, our sensations signs; and a part of the truth about nature and about ourselves will be necessarily revealed to us, directly or indirectly, by the mere existence and sequence of those apparitions. Directly, in emotion, perception, and dramatic sympathy, we may learn to know the human world, the world of images, morals, and literature: and indirectly, in close connection with the flow of sensation, we may learn to posit permanent objects and to pick our way among them to good purpose, as a child finds his way home.

CHAPTER IV

PSYCHOLOGICAL APPROACHES TO TRUTH

EVEN if mathematical ideas were less exactly true of the world, the mere possession of them would be indirect evidence that they had some cogni- tive value and were in some way true. If we would show them to be false, we must propose other ideas on the same subject which shall seem truer. But what ideas, truer than those of mathematical physics, can we propose on the subject of the field of action or the dynamic world? Undoubtedly, if reality were confined to spiritual being, mathematics would be useless, and the study of it an idle pastime, if not a vice; and if any spiritual man, like Pascal, got too deeply entangled in mathe- matics, the sad effects might be seen in his self-torture and desperation. A faith founded on logic is an acrobatic and insane faith. It was not logical neces- sity, but hard practical evidence, that first suggested mathematical ideas to the mind and afterwards con- firmed and imposed them. Animal faith honours mathematical science—a fantastic construction in itself —for measuring reliably the footsteps of that stealthy material power that pervades the world. If mathe- matics measures these footsteps perfectly, mathematics is perfectly true. The reality of psychologists—sub- jective presence, whether sensuous or conceptual— belongs to a different moral or æsthetic sphere, not mediated by animal faith and not itself conveying knowledge of truth, true as the account of such experi-

All ideas have some expressive rightness.

437

ence may be which is conveyed later by memory or sympathetic fancy: for often the art of fiction may tell us the truth about the fictions natural to the mind.

Nevertheless, intuition, which is simply sensibility focussed and actually noticing anything, comes upon essences, not things: because in proportion as attention takes notice, and honestly observes what it finds, it suspends that animal faith which was involved in fear or care or the physical impulse to react upon some physical stimulus. When clarified and thoroughly actualized, all data are essences: if the spirit could actualize and clarify everything it would live altogether in its congenial ideal world, as it does, with some lingering qualifications, in mathematics and poetry and music. But in animal life this remains an interlude, something marginal and ulterior. Living attention comes upon essences with a bias, from some particular vital angle: they are stepping-stones in a distracted career. Even if clearly focussed in their own plane, essences do not dictate to us in what direction their relations shall be traced: in themselves they have no movement, no selectiveness, no propulsion. The choice of this or that path, in further intuition, is made by the animal mind, under suasion of casual interests or its own vegetative growth. Poetry does not make itself, poets must make it: and so mathematicians must make mathematics. Narrow paths are thus opened by accident through the compact thicket of essential Being; and later comers, threading the beaten way, may suppose that they are surveying the whole structure of the labyrinth, and discovering the eternal Logos, or self-chosen necessary truth. But the labyrinth, being infinite, offers all choices to the wanderer; and the pattern actually traced was selected by accident.

They are biological products and spontaneously poetical.

Logic is a refined form of grammar. If in my prattle I obey a tendency, and later establish a rule to the effect that nouns shall be either masculine or feminine; and if I obey a tendency and make it a rule that adjectives shall match and prolong the gender of their substantives; *then* it is requisite for propriety of speech that adjectives and nouns should possess gender, and should march in couples, like clerical school children, the girls with girls, and the boys with boys. And this contrast, with this divided way of trooping together, artificial as it is in things without sex, opens the way to the most charming assonances and beckonings of word to word in discourse, enabling us without confusion to pick our way through a minuet of cross-references, as in an ode of Horace. Yet grammar need never have adopted so fantastic a sexual analogy. It did so only because speech is radically expletive, redundant, and exclamatory, as thought is also; and in a creature to whom sexual images are arresting and highly provocative, sexual analogies, however far-fetched, will appear in all sorts of places, particularly when emotion is aroused, and will count for more in the play of description than does the strict truth of the object.

Grammar is biassed (1) by emotional associations.

There are other graver intrusions of the grammatical medium into the deliverance of thought. For instance, the relation of subject to predicate is founded on the circumstance that some words are proper names, and merely demonstrative, like a pointing finger; other words are names of essences, without traceable physical being, but appearing dispersed, repeated, and mysteriously intermittent in all sorts of places or in no place at all, that is to say, in the mind. The proper name, indicating and holding down, as it were, the physical object that concerns us

(2) By the external approach of thought to things, producing a dualism of subject and predicate.

in action, becomes the grammatical subject; and the names of such essences as this subject shares with other things bècome grammatical predicates and adjectives. This grammar registers admirably the education of the mind: for the mind is commonly awakened by some shock, and then proceeds more or less scrupulously to describe the circumstances and the qualities connected with that stimulus.

Moreover, being a spirit beset by animal obsessions, the human mind can retain, compare, and synthesize (3) By its impressions, leaving the flux of existence synthesis in to run on as full and turbid as it will. Yet sensation, perception, this recollection and this withdrawal are and memory. always imperfect. The basis of spirit is itself material, fluid, and self-forgetful: while on the other hand, the knowledge gathered and the pictures painted by the mind are simplified unduly, convention-alized, moralized, reduced to types: and this does violence to the truth, since nature is not human educa-tion hypostatized. Hence the quarrel between the humanities and science; in which science evidently represents the interests of truth. If the problem were scientific, we should have to consider that science also is human, that neither in texture nor in scope can science be identified with the truth: and that the humanities too convey poetical information about historical matters. But the real problem is moral; and even if science presented the truth more honestly than the humanities, we should still have to ask whether these scientific truths were the most important, and even whether the knowledge of truth is the ultimate goal or good of mind. Frankly, it is not, when the mind is free. Spirit is the entelechy or ultimate fruit of life and not a material instrument or means to action; and if once life were safely adjusted and directed amid material circumstances, consciousness of those circum-stances would be superfluous except as it might be interesting; so that truth would take its place side by side with fiction of every sort, to be valued not because true—for merely being true does not make things worth knowing—but only for invigorating and entertaining the mind.   Such is the liberal life; and the humanities have this liberal character, although science also has it, in so far as the truth of it enlarges the imagination.   But such poetic freedom in thinking is premature, and even criminal, when the psyche is living at cross-purposes with the possibilities of life. Health must be established first and organized securely; and then the range and balance of spiritual interests may be left for free genius to determine.

In any case, it would be a vain scruple in the lover of truth to quarrel with his intellect and with the grammar of his thoughts in order to put his ear closer to the ground.   His ear is itself an animal organ, and its deliverance—sound —is the substance of nothing except music. The tread of oncoming reality may be conveyed more impressively or more accurately by one sense than by another: but in the end only intellect and science will be able to reveal the method of that approaching attack, or the method of meeting it by any deliberate or artificial contrivance.   There is no ground for deprecating this intervention of art and reason.   Mind is better than matter in the estimation of mind: and this judgment is final, because only mind is capable of esteeming or judging at all.   Attention to matter is therefore optional for a moral being, and important only when, health having been lost, art is requisite for recovering it; or when, as I was saying just now, attention to matter is spontaneous and self-rewarding, as it is for children and for the true naturalist.   The office of matter is precisely to breed mind and to feed it; and while the fantastic egotistical errors into which mind

This bias legitimate: because mind, though dependent physically, is autonomous morally.

may fall, since it must conceive matter in terms of ideas, might seem laughable to omniscience, those errors do no harm to matter and very little to mind. An unbiassed and literal understanding of matter would be incongruous in an animal; and for pure spirit such understanding remains an ulterior speculative ambition, legitimate certainly, since spirit is potentially omniscient, but rather beside the mark when, being incarnate, that spirit is beset by impurities which it must purge first, before it can ever understand anything or know itself. If it knew itself, spirit would be little pressed to understand the depths of matter, which cannot be changed; but spirit, by existing, does lend to matter a new mental dimension, expressing material organization morally and perhaps gloriously. Better than idly mirroring nature in mind (if it were possible to do so) is to impose an ideal measure upon fluid things, and this not arbitrarily or insignificantly: for the very dependence of spirit, which might seem to condemn it to futility, renders it an index to deeper realities and an organ of truth. Thought would never arise or maintain itself, it would never succeed in imposing formal measures and unities on events, if these events, which include the biological organs of thought, were not already organized and self-distinguished in the bosom of chaos. The very existence of fiction endows fiction with a native relevance to truth.

We are told by certain psychologists that although the dynamic order of events is not *really* mathematical, mathematical fictions must be cultivated because they are *useful in the practical arts.* But why should they be useful if false? And how should they be false if they describe the efficacious order of nature, by which our existence and health and power of speech and thought are notoriously controlled? What better criterion have we of truth than pertinence to action and implica-

Alleged utility of scientific falsifications.

tion in the dynamic order of nature? Primitive imagination no doubt attributes power to wishes and prayers or to formal rhymes and coincidences in the aspects of things; but that is superstition; and we gradually discover the true order of nature by attentive observation of matter, and experiments with it, and calculation of its quantity and movement. If arithmetical and geometrical notions gain such ascendancy over the expert mind, it is precisely because, in their abstraction, they are the surest measure of the concrete. By them we retrace the actual vectors of reality and energy in the living world. What the vitalists call life is, in comparison, but the after-taste and rhetoric of motion.

Irrelevant, then, as the inner cogency of logic may be to the truth, logic nevertheless possesses a natural truth in its first notions, in its chief lines of Mind, deduction, and in many of its developments. without Such applicability rewards later speculation copying or for the early diligence of mankind in study- limiting truth, ing material things, turning and moulding naturally them, and making their image precise in and poetic-ally conforms thought. Ideas are not true because they to it. are clear, but often they have become clear because they were true. This truth gives continual encourage-ment to the dialectitian in tracing his deductions and trusting his insights. Yet he goes too far when with these ideas, framed on the human scale and true and empirically tested on that scale, he presumes to fathom the depths of matter and of time, and to dictate to nature the mechanism of her motions. He ought rather to expect that in some dimensions of being, for instance, in the mind, or at a high degree of complica-tion, as in living bodies, the applicability of his ideal science should cease to be perfect or should fail altogether. Not that in those regions there is less order than in the gross mechanical world: there is evidently more, and a more organic order: but our images and thoughts are not easily adapted to those latitudes and longitudes, and the most signal instances of responsiveness in events seem to us miracles or accidents.

Such limitations are not a fault in human logic or mathematics, as if mankind had been bewitched and ought to begin thinking with other images and other axioms. Even if such a reform of the intellect were possible, and fresh ideal systems were developed, expressly to fit the regions newly explored, the new logic and mathematics would not be likely to fit all reality, or to possess more than a limited and borrowed truth. Nature, we must never forget, is in flux. This flux may move in any number of streams, according to any variety of methods; and even if, at one time, we had obtained an exact formula for everything, presently the flux might take a new turn, and insensibly change its fluid constitution. Then the very accuracy of our earlier measures would render them worthless in a later world.

CHAPTER V

WE have seen that the truth, as I take the word, is subservient to existence: it is ontologically secondary and true of something else. Yet that which is generated by existence may be itself ideal, and often must be so; because the flux of existence is blind and precipitates a thousand accidents of form by merely flowing, accidents supervening on all the material factors concerned in generating them. Truth itself is such a supervening form; not accidental in the sense of being avoidable, since by existing the world fatally determines the truth about itself; but accidental in the sense of adding, at no expense of matter or energy, an impalpable eternal dimension to transitory being. Events did not intend, so to speak, to be recorded; yet in the truth they have left their unintentional mark, their indelible portrait. Even if things escape observation, they cannot escape having been what they were.

Physical being generates ideal relations.

Existence, as it inevitably generates truth, may on special occasions also generate beauty or goodness, but not with the same pervasiveness. Beauty and goodness are far more accidental than truth: they arise only at certain junctures, when various streams of events, already flowing in definite tropes, meet and mingle in a temporary harmony; a harmony which such of these streams as are organized into psyches may feel and rejoice in. Truth, on the other hand, arises by automatic radiation from every region of fact; since no

445

event can occur without rendering it eternally true that such an event and no other fills that point of space and time.

Now as truth, although in itself only a field of essence, radiates from contingent fact, and is determined and limited by it, so truth itself establishes certain harmonies and distinctions dominating the realm of thought.

Truth in turn subtends intelligence.

For thought is originally aroused by events, and directed upon them: it is indicative, and *takes notice*, as we say of young children when their intelligence is dawning. Even when most slumberous and vegetative, consciousness, at least in man, is always partly cognitive, and therefore interested in the truth. Truth thus becomes the arbiter of success in one of the most important functions of life: that of intelligent adjustment on the part of living beings to the conditions under which they live. This adjustment is physical; but the token of it for the spirit comes in foresight, sane imagination, and sentiments pertinent to the facts. In so far as consciousness can become more than vain sensation or blind anguish, it must therefore aspire to possess the truth. The truth will be declared, however partially, by any opinion that prophesies an event before this event arises, or describes it when occurring, or reports it after it has occurred. Such opinions are all incidental to the truth: they may be framed or not, according to the accidents of human life and intelligence. They reproduce the truth in part, as it may be discoverable from their various stations with their various organs; but the truth in its wholeness outruns and completes their several deliverances, and is the standard which these deliverances conform to, in so far as they are true.

This possible discovery of truth, or of some part of the truth, is often confused with truth itself; as if truth were like error, the moral quality of some idea or judgment, when the latter succeeds or (in the case of error) fails to report the fact to which attention for the moment is directed.   But an idea or judgment is only true if it reports the truth, and false if it contradicts the truth.   That which is true is the proposition, relation, or other essence actually illustrated in the facts. If this proposition, relation, or other essence is asserted in a judgment the judgment is true by participation, because it speaks the truth. This participation of true judgment in the truth is neither an ontological reproduction by the judgment (which is an invisible act of the mind) of the object (which may be anything whatever); nor is it a vital compatibility of this judgment with all other judgments on all other subjects.   Not the assertion as a psychological fact is true, but only that which it asserts: and the difference in quality and value between true ideas and false ideas, taken as states of mind, is a moral difference: the true ideas being safer and probably clearer and more humorous than the false, and marking a success on the mind's part in understanding the world, whereas false ideas would mark a failure.   But even this moral quality of enlightening or deceiving us is not an intrinsic passive quality in true or false ideas; as if any clear and distinct idea were true, and any vague sensation or sentiment false.   The opposite is often the case; because a scent, olfactory or intellectual, may be a true scent and may truly discriminate objects in their most important practical relations; whereas the clearest and most distinct images and definitions may be definitions and images of mere essences, and not at all true.

The term "idea", in this connection, is trebly ambiguous. It may mean an essence, the theme or internal object of a feeling or thought. It may also mean the feeling or thought, the moment of living

That which is true in ideas or judgments in what they say, not what they are.

intuition in which such an essence may be distinguished. Finally, it may mean a feeling or thought raised to the self-transcendent value of a belief or judgment, affirming the given essence to be true of some further object. In this last sense, an idea means an opinion, and may be called true or false by assimilation or contrariety to the truth of its object. But an idea that is an innocent feeling or thought, asserting nothing, cannot be true or false: it is a pure intuition of an essence. Much less can the essences given in such intuition be true or false in themselves. They may have been raised elsewhere to the plane of truth, by being exemplified in events: they are not rendered true by being evoked in intuition, as all falsehoods and all fancies are evoked also. An idea, therefore, in the third sense of opinion, can be true or false only if it reports or contradicts some part of the truth: and in order to do this it must be other than an inert essence, and more than a pure feeling or thought. It must be a judgment affirming a given essence of an ulterior object, in which that essence may, in truth, be exemplified or not exemplified.

"Ideas", whether essences, intuitions, or judgments, are never true intrinsically.

Truth, then, though descriptive of existence, has no existence of its own, and remains an ideal standard for any opinions professing to be somewhat true, or true as far as they go. The empirical relations which an opinion, by the action it comports, may have in the world have nothing to do with its truth. If an "idea" is useful, it is useful, not true: and if an idea is beautiful or comforting, it is not therefore true, but comforting only or beautiful; and if an idea, perhaps an illusion, is harmonious with another idea, the two are harmonious, and both together may be a worse illusion than each of them was separately. Nor would perfect coherence in ideas, in the longest of

Nor do "ideas" become true by virtue of their relation as events to other events.

dreams, make the dream true; although if it contained intelligent mutual descriptions of one part of it by another part, those parts would indeed report a part of the truth about one another. Yet the total truth about that dream, as some parts of it might perhaps perceive, would be that it was a dream and all sheer illusion. To reduce truth to coherence is to deny truth, and to usurp that name for a certain comfort and self-complacency in mere thinking. Why trouble about truth, if I can be sure of never discovering my error?

Here we see that curious self-degradation which is latent in egotism. You seem to be making your self and your experience absolute; yet by that very arrogance you cut yourself off from all intellectual dominion over anything else, and renounce the very thought of natural knowledge or genuine truth. And this fate overtakes the empiricist or pragmatist no less than the absolute idealist who frankly admits it, and thinks it the proof of his essential divinity. A desultory experience might indeed contain true thoughts about its own progress, physics being strictly reduced, for the philosopher, to literary psychology. This would allow truth an absolute standing in the fields of psychology and history, and all opinions of historians and psychologists would acknowledge that absolute truth as their standard. But such is not the position of radical or romantic empiricists, who are bent on denying that there is truth about futures, or any fixed truth about the past, each historian making a new "truth", in framing a fresh perspective. Transcendental egotism, with the self-contradictory effort involved in denying truth altogether, thus reappears in empiricism on a smaller scale: with the added inconsistency of positing dogmatically the multiple, consecutive, and well-known moments in which experience and "truths" are to be lodged.

The attempt to ignore the being of truth will be discussed later: here I am concerned only with the increment of physical reference requisite to raise intuition into truth. If spirit were not incarnate, if it had no bodily organ, if in consequence it were not domiciled in the material and temporal world so that certain things did not press upon it and trouble it more than others, if in a word it had no object but the realm of essence, then truth would not need to enter into its thoughts. For, in that infinite field, no truth would be found distinguishable from the structure of pure Being, in which every alternative is equally present. Only if the spirit became by chance self-conscious, and distinguished its survey of essence from the field of essence itself, and wondered why this survey should occur in this particular order and have these arbitrary limits in scope and direction—only then would truth, in its contingent fatality, loom before the mind, truth and fatality coming into being together with existence: because evidently the spirit, with its intensity and insecurity of attention, and its rambling progress, pre-eminently exists.

In reviewing pure essences truth is involved not regarding essence but regarding the history of spirit.

Truth, in dialectic, is decidedly ironical and backhanded. What the reasoning mind demonstrates and discovers is only a certain figure in the tapestry of ideas. This figure is, in that realm of essence, interwoven with every other possible figure, and is in no sense *the true* figure proper to essential Being, because essential Being, by definition, is infinite and contains all figures. Yet the reasoning mind, in threading that particular path in the labyrinth, is really exploring the truth regarding the initial occasions and fundamental categories of its own thinking. In chopping wood or in using words men originally lighted upon the square

Biological freedom of dialectic.

and the triangle, and defined those essences. These essences are true of those blocks or of those conventional concepts and categories of speech; so that any further elaboration, by dialectic, of the essences chosen, is by implication true also of those blocks and those notions. At least it must be so if the original affirmation of the square and triangle was true absolutely: but it may well be that these ideas arrested by thought were only loosely applicable to the existing objects: in which case the more those ideas were elaborated dialectically, the further probably would they stray from the truth.

Existence, as if charged with electricity, turns a whole region of essence into a magnetic field. Not merely do the characters materially embodied in some fact or event become, as it were, incandescent, but all the still opaque essential relations of those characters become pertinent to that existence. A fertile mind will contrast the fact as it is with the fact as it might have been: especially as the movement of external events and the movement of intuition go on at different rates and in incongruous directions. Intuition, for instance, often runs backwards, as evolution cannot do; or jumps over space and time by confusion of similars; while nature endlessly repeats similars, but never identifies them, and never leaves out the alien context that separates them and renders them existentially many. The play of intuition over the realm of essence, though limited and guided by the genius of each psyche, is far freer than the plodding blind course of cosmic events. Imagination makes comparisons, conceives alternatives, regrets that they were not realized, ventures to prophesy their realization, becomes inspired, and ends perhaps by condemning the whole world, and calling it deceptive and false, in contrast to the shining "truth" of what it ought to be. All the errors, illusions, pathetic fallacies, and poetic myths with which the human mind disguises the truth are so many borrowings from outlying regions of essence; characters interpolated in lieu of characters undiscovered, or extensions of the characters actually found.

It is not always fancy, however, or religious passion, that flies from accidental truth to necessary possibilities: cold logic may do so also. Let a fact have any total character you choose: it will at once be true not only that this fact has this character, but that it has not any other character. But all the other characters, which this fact has not, compose the realm of essence in its residual infinity. If this fact be John Smith, it is true not only that he is John and Smith and man and mortal, but that he is *not* Jonah, *not* the whale, *not* Jehovah, *not* any other of the disparate things that infinite patience might enumerate. Thus, by privation and negatively, any fact drags the whole realm of essence into the realm of truth, or rather into that of error; since outlying essences are here introduced, not by genial intuition of their ideal being and sympathy with that variety of forms, but in a faultfinding and depreciatory tone, as things missing and false. It is in this way, perhaps, that a starved Puritan, clutching the bare bones of reality with a material terror, might conceive the realm of essence, and think it the abyss of night.

The impertinence of qualifying the outlying realm of essence as false may confirm the impropriety of qualifying it as true. False and true are nether accidents: and their very contingency renders it impossible for us to say to what extent they may, in the end, colour the realm of essence with truth or falsehood: for there is no knowing how much of essence, in the end, may be exemplified in existence, or may fail to be so exemplified. The congruous interest, in respect to essence, is logical and æsthetic,

All that is not truth becomes, for belief, the field of possible errors.

not documentary or moral. Or, rather, no interest, and no reference to events, is congruous at all, but only the infinite plasticity of intuition playing over the infinite variety of Being.

Before going deeper into this subject, it may be well to make explicit the sort and degree of validity proper to such an argument. Much less is being asked of the goodwill of the reader than he may at first suspect, and nothing at all is being asked of his credulity. I am not defending any belief. The only belief that I myself entertain, because I find it irresistible, is the belief in a realm of matter, the expectation of persistence and order in a natural world; and this is a belief which I am confident the reader shares, although he may prefer to express it in other words. It is only as details in an assumed natural world that the reader and the very book I am writing exist for me at all. But the realms of truth and of essence are in quite another case. To them I assign no existence; in them I demand no belief. They are not to be conceived as hypothetical regions of fact, annexed to the realm of matter, as heaven and hell might be annexed. The smile of the critic who will not be fooled into *believing* in them is entirely justified. They are not proposed as objects of belief. They are proposed as conceptual distinctions and categories of logic; as one of many languages in which the nature of things may be described. Anyone who wishes is free to discard these categories and employ others. The only question will be how he will get on; what sort of intellectual dominion and intellectual life he will achieve; also whether he will really be using other categories in his spontaneous and successful contacts with the world, or only a different jargon in his professional philosophy. Professional philosophies, sincere and even impassioned enough in controversy, are often but poor

Optional character of human logics.

hypocrisies in daily life. But the fortunes of other systems do not concern me. I am addressing those only who are willing, for the time being, to accept my language.

CHAPTER VI

CONVENTIONAL TRUTHS

SUPPOSE I open the newspaper and read: Sun rises
7.35 a.m., sets 3.58 p.m. Apart from some misprint
or other casual error easily corrected, this Current
information is undoubtedly true and accur- information
ate: it is supplied by the Greenwich Obser- probably
true, if taken
vatory. Good sense will prevent me from as it is meant.
taking the statement absolutely or physically, and
making it false. The sun of itself never rises or sets;
and even in relation to human observers it seldom
rises so late or sets so early: this, on the sun's part,
is an extreme wintry laziness. The proposition is
meant to be historical, not general or scientific; and
like all historical propositions, describing incidental
facts, it depends for its truth on its incidence: that
is, on fixing the time and place to which it refers,
as in this case to London on November 25th, 1935.
Nor have we here a precise historical truth in psychological terms, telling us what was the experience of
particular individuals at particular moments. Probably no Londoner saw the sun rise or set on that 25th
of November: if truth were reduced to truths of
experience there would be no truth at all in this
matter. All that is meant is that, at that date, the
astronomical conditions were such that, if there had
been no clouds, no fog and no smoke, the first and
last rays of the sun would have struck the London
chimney-tops at those hours, or would have struck

455

the eyes of any Cockney then looking in the requisite direction from his attic window.

A certain and accurate truth may thus be conveyed in conventional terms which in themselves are loose and inaccurate. Implications as to what has happened physically, and hypotheses as to what might have happened psychologically, may be placed before the human mind by a figure of speech that will not bear pressing, yet is unequivocal enough for human purposes. Almost all the knowledge we have of nature and of history visits our minds in this conventional form, clothed in metaphors and idioms proper to our grammar, and not seriously misleading our action or expectation, though leaving us in ignorance or in childish illusion about the proper texture of the facts.

An animal vision of the universe is, in one sense, never false: it is rooted in the nature of that animal, aroused to consciousness by the circumstances of the moment. These circumstances, as well as that animal endowment, will therefore be expressed in the vision; and when I say "expressed", I do not mean passively betrayed by some quality or detail in this vision, but, since consciousness is implied, I mean noted, described, and known in some measure, and in terms no matter how subjective. In a word, the vision claims to be true; and it possesses truth at least in this fundamental respect, that it has a real object and is not an idle mental phenomenon. It is true enough to be false, and to require correction. For the whole view of mind characteristic of modern philosophy, that mind is a train of self-existing feelings or ideas, is itself false. Mind is spirit; a wakefulness or attention or moral tension aroused in animals by the stress of life: and the prerequisite to the appearance of any feeling or idea is that the animal should be

[margin note:] Truth claimed and actually present in all experience.

alive and awake, attentive, that is, to what is happening, has happened, or is about to happen: so that it belongs to the essence of discoverable existence, as a contemporary philosophy has it, "to-be-in-the-world". The observable details, the sounds, lights, darting pains, curious somatic feelings, etc., are not separately given to pure intuition, as they might be to a disembodied spirit: they come in and from an imposed and assumed world, an object of concern, alarm, desire, or avid possession; and this material incubus is felt and posited as an incubus, as air is felt and posited in the struggle to breathe, not pictorially or ideally, but as a besetting reality. Agony posits it, and sensation or fancy afterwards study and describe it, if they have the leisure. But the greater part of life, and the deeper levels of it always, vaguely but indomitably posit existence in a world; they speak for a living organism floating or struggling in a foreign medium. In positing such existence, and thereby claiming some degree of truth, spirit exists and is incarnate: and this primordial claim to truth is valid; because in fact spirit lives only in animal organisms, and these live only in a habitable world.

Having thus stretched, as it were, the canvas of truth, or a real world to explore, the mind begins to lay on such colours as its palette supplies. These are mixed in the organs of sense; they are lighted up by the passions; yet with this moral light and that sensuous texture they are normally predicated of the object, and used to define its nature: never its substantial nature, for that remains always the dynamic counterpart of the action which arouses attention and evokes faith; but the circumstantial nature of the object, and the form it is to wear in human discourse.

Here are two stages of conceptual illusion, dressing up conventionally the fundamental truth of human knowledge. There is really a world, and there are real objects in each case to be described: but the images of sense used to describe those objects are not found there, but are created by the organs of sense in the observer: and the syntax of thought by which these appearances, which in themselves are pure essences, are turned into predicates of substance, is a mere expedient of human logic: so that while we gain true acquaintance with the real world, in that we distinguish its parts and their relations up to a certain point, we conceive these realities fantastically, making units of them on the human scale, and in human terms. Our ideas are accordingly only subjective signs, while we think them objective qualities; and the whole warp and woof of our knowledge is rhetorical while we think it physically existent and constitutive of the world.

Action, carrying belief with it, meets the reality, while sense and thought supply the poetic appearance.

The exuberance of nature stultifies and overwhelms any specific being that makes itself, or is made, the measure of all things; and the human mind in particular is doubly perplexed when it begins to discover on the one hand that things are not quite as they seem, and on the other hand that its own images and rhetoric are poetical. But an angry or despairing temper of criticism in either direction would be ill-considered. What is there wrong or paradoxical in the fact that the sensations and reactions of an animal must express directly his own nature, and only indirectly the nature of the forces affecting him? And what is there vain or scandalous in emotion, in original sensations, or in the poetic freedom of mind? Undoubtedly the essential potentialities of spirit are not exhausted by a specifically human experience; and intellect cannot help aspiring to omniscience, and to the knowledge of things as they are;

Animal knowledge must be limited in scope and biassed in quality.

and in practice, the conduct as well as the imagination of man stumbles and suffers rude shocks when vital presumptions are contradicted by events. There is accordingly something urgent about truth in our ideas, and something dangerous and ignominious in their falseness. But such urgency and danger touch not the inner rhetoric of thought, but only its practical symbolism, and the concomitant action. We must not be *misled* by imagination; there is no likelihood and no need that, in a miraculous sense, imagination should be clairvoyant.

All troubled and vehement scepticism, therefore, rests or ought to rest on economic considerations. The war against religion, the war against pictorial and logical thinking, is a commercial war. The poor, the hard-pressed, rebel against being taxed for such luxuries. They think mankind cannot afford to be human.

Recent science, both in physics and psychology, has responded, perhaps unwittingly, to this commercial interest. It is proud of not being deceived, and of wasting no energy on superfluous ideas. Physics can be reduced to pointer-readings, psychology to the statistics of behaviour. No doubt they can, for commercial purposes: and it may be convenient, in expert calculations, to abstract from all other considerations. But suppose we were willing to use only mathematical equations in conceiving matter and the dynamic connection of all events: the rest of our experienced or imagined world would then be explicitly transferred to another sphere, let us call it mind; and this variegated experience (not open to psychological science, which treats of behaviour only) would become enormously important and, except for the mechanical or medical expert, alone familiar. Even the expert would continue to

Commercial radicalism in philosophy retains only autobiographical truth.

live in the human world, using his science only in occasional professional excursions beneath the surface of phenomena: and his scientific conception of the underlying forces or processes would be too tenuous (unlike mythology) to draw away his instinctive belief from the pictorial universe of the vulgar. His philosophy, if he stopped to frame one, would probably be empirical and idealistic: he would regard his science not as truer than appearances, but as an intellectual fiction based upon them and somehow serving to predict them. Only autobiography could be quite true.

It is not, however, on the lines of autobiography that mankind conceives the world. Not literary psych-

But physics and even bio- graphy, for mankind, remain pictorial.

ology but pictorial physics dominates the conventional mind. When we walk abroad absorbed in the landscape or in picturesque episodes and street-scenes, a philosophical critic might say that we were occupied with our own sensations, and not with the truth of nature or of society: but though this may be his analysis, it is not our conviction. And even when we are reading history, poetry, or novels, what probably fills our minds is pictorial physics. Suppose I am thinking over the life of Napoleon. I make no attempt to recover his unrecoverable stream of ideas. Instead, I imagine his mother, his military college, his uniforms, his habits, his books, Toulon, and the Tuileries; and I sprinkle over those material scenes a few reported words of the hero. I imagine his life as I might have watched it, not as, in his inner man, he may have experienced it. Yet the scenes I evoke are, to some extent, the very scenes he witnessed and acted in: and I actually re-live a part of his experience in recalling some of the objects that surrounded him. Pictorial physics, or the human aspect of material things, thus forms the principal element possibly common to various minds; and we have no way of imagining other people's emotions save to imagine their predicaments.

A curious compensation results in regard to truth in fiction. Nothing that exists can escape from the purview of truth; and all fictions touch the Established truth at least in this point: that they have fictions are in their day a psychological existence, so standards for that a true history of fictions is conceivable. course. But conventional fictions touch the truth also in a technical way, which is more intimate. In the act of being repeated or communicated, they are named and defined. Their conventional essence becomes a standard essence in human discourse, which may be spoken of congruously or incongruously, truly or falsely, according to the accepted usage. And this is not merely a matter of language and social propriety: because when an essence is once clearly focussed and distinguished in the mind, exactness in reproducing it, or fidelity in expanding it, excites a pleasant feeling of recognition, and euphoria; whereas incompatible variants, passing under the same name, become offensive and, as we say, *false*. Obviously no essence is false to itself; but a violation of convention is false to the context and expectations woven about standard essences in the public mind, that is, in the private mind when socially controlled. There is a vital discord, and the incongruous note that produces it is called a false note.

The vital character of such discords and harmonies justifies a human trait which, at first sight, might seem scandalous to a moralist. Convention, Convention correctness, orthodoxy are far more intim- is naturally ately precious to mankind than truth. The more human world of things seems arid and alien com- and beautiful pared with the inexhaustible world of talk; and a man will laugh at his mistakes about matters of fact, when shame will consume him all his life long if he has slipped into a fault of speech or of manners. Not merely, too, for social reasons, because other people may be laughing at him. The inner beauties of convention are glorious to develop, and its tissue painful to rend. Need I mention music, rhetoric, and social ritual? Perhaps the speculative part of religion, pure myth or metaphysics or theology, will show the power of convention best, because here the inspiration is so potent that it overflows all barriers, overcomes the judgment and claims positive truth for its fictions. Not only in the maniac and the prophet: often at second hand, when social countenance supplies the lack of physical sanctions, and when types of religion, as of language and manners, become things to fight for and to be true to at the sacrifice of all other interests, especially that of truth.

A philosopher who has discovered his principles for himself may wear them with a good grace; but Zeal for one who has adopted them from other tyrant ideas. people is likely to be a fanatic. Nothing infuriates a man more than to be contradicted in the convictions which he has learned with care, accepted on high authority, and made the centre of all his thoughts. Not only are his proud views thereby cheated and mocked, but the fact that this precious orthodoxy was after all acquired, and perhaps not altogether persuasive at first to the inner man, doubles the alarm. The scoffer outside is not without a silent ally within; and the outrage is intolerable that the same world that once taught us all these difficult things and induced us to conform to them at a great secret sacrifice of our inclinations, should now coolly proceed to teach us something different, require us to back our engines and to revise our affections, already so artificially constrained and elaborately stimulated. Our strait-jacket has grown into the flesh, and we are ready to flay any man who would tear it from us. Not only do we regain our freedom with a sigh; we know too well that it will not be freedom but only slavery to a new convention, probably more external and repulsive to our inner nature than were the older traditions. For if those traditions were wrong, it was chiefly because they were too spontaneous, too boldly human and conceited; and anything contrary to them is likely to be doubly contrary to the heart.

All this usurpation of truth by convention is inevitable in a being as richly endowed psychically as man is, so that his inner life is ready to breed world upon world, while at the same time he is so hard pressed by matter and by society, that his imaginative fecundity is *The great deceiver of mankind is man.* continually cut short, and he is compelled instead to attend to the hard facts. Hence all the disappointments of spirit. We are condemned to live dramatically in a world that is not dramatic. Even our direct perceptions make units of objects that are not units; we see creation and destruction where there is only continuity. Memory and reflection repeat this pathetic fallacy, taking experience for their object, where in fact everything is sketchy, evanescent, and ambiguous. Memory and reflection select, recompose, complete and transform the past in the act of repainting it, interpolating miracles and insinuating motives that were never in the original experience but that seem now to clarify and explain it. This second fiction, mythical or intellectual, may serve in one way to penetrate beneath the veil of sense, and render us responsive in poetry and religious symbolism to the deeper currents of nature. Convention in such cases, while filling the imagination with fables and dramas, may really adjust human feelings and actions to the truth; and if mathematical science, in violent abstraction, traces the material movement of things with the greatest accuracy attainable by mind, perhaps religion and traditional precept may more poetically but more voluminously respond to the same movement, in so far as it affects human happiness. Yet such harmony between convention and reality is always imperfect; and the hold that convention has on mankind is not at all proportional to its rational justification. The tight opinionated present feels itself inevitably to be the centre and judge of the universe; and the poor human soul walks in a dream through the paradise of truth, as a child might run blindly through a smiling garden, hugging a paper flower.

CHAPTER VII

DRAMATIC TRUTH

THE dramatic moral climate in which our lives are passed is not other than the climate of matter but only a passionate experience of the same. Society does not present two separable worlds, one the world of men's bodies and another less earthly one, that of men's minds. A world of mere minds, a heaven with its legions of invisible and bodiless angels, if conceived at all, exacts no belief from the sceptic. I am as far as possible a sceptic, and a world of that sort does not figure in my philosophy. On the other hand, a world of mindless automata, like the *bêtes-machines* of Descartes, is a violently artificial object, conceived in purely mathematical and mechanical terms, although the terms in which that object is actually perceived are primarily sensuous and dramatic. The object is a body with the motions perceived or expected in that body; but these bodies do more than amuse the eye. Some are noxious or wild beasts; some are members of your own family. They suckle or hit you; and you know them apart by their works before you distinguish them clearly by their aspect. Even the most crudely physical forces wear a dramatic aspect when their action is violent, or for any reason arouses violent emotion. Spirit in us then rises or falls; and the cause is felt to be the action of spirits and gods: mythical beings not added fancifully to physical beings clearly conceived to be physical, but moral energies recognized

Moral dimensions found in the world are readings of matter in dramatic terms.

465

as the very core and secret of the material facts. That souls exist and that they move bodies is indeed the primary form in which any sensitive soul will conceive the forces of nature.

A soul, a dramatic centre of action and passion, is utterly unlike what in modern philosophy we call consciousness. The soul causes the body to grow, to assume its ancestral shape, to develop all its ancestral instincts, to wake and to sleep by turns. The soul determines what images shall arise in the mind and what emotions, and at the same time determines the responses that the living body shall make to the world. Consciousness is only an inner light kindled in the soul during these vicissitudes, a music, strident or sweet, made by the friction of existence. With this light and music, purified and enlarged, fancy has peopled heaven; but on earth the course of consciousness is helplessly distracted: a miscellany of conventional half-thoughts and evanescent images. A sympathetic intuition of such actual consciousness in another person often comes by imitation or by unison in action. When caught in a common predicament, we involuntarily understand one another. Each feels what everybody else is feeling; and the same thing happens, less voluminously, in ordinary conversation. Such mutual understanding is not in itself dramatic, though the occasion of it may be so; it is neighbourly, attentive, playful, as when we understand a child, a comrade, or an author. Spirit is essentially disinterested, even in tracing the fortunes of spirit. But when physical contagion ceases and this brotherly spell is broken, we remain as profoundly ignorant of the fountains of life in others as in ourselves. The volatile spirit which was ours for a moment is fled we know not where. Hence in consecutive politics or economics the experts are quite

The actual flux of events, either in nature or consciousness, is not dramatic.

DRAMATIC TRUTH

blind, lost in a labyrinth of facts not understood, and appalled at the insidious transformation of these avowed motives and ideas by which action was supposed to be guided.

Dramatic intuition, on the contrary, springs from the passions, that is to say, from the principles of action. A man may be conscious of his passion, in that he feels strangely agitated and is affected by everything in a strange way. But the passion itself is a force, a physical automatism let loose within him, and altogether other and deeper than his consciousness of it. If he attempts to put it into words, or to conceive its proper nature, he is driven to dramatic fictions in one sense more remote from actual passion than were his inarticulate feelings or hot words: he is driven to myth or to dialectic. In a fable, or in a logical trope, he imaginatively draws the outline and traces the movement of that mysterious influence which troubles him; and the truth facing his passion, as he is best able to conceive it, is a dramatic truth.

Here all is expectation, partiality, superstition, hyperbole, rage, and enthusiasm. The accuracy possible in prosaic literary psychology is sacrificed to a summary eloquence. Yet not without compensation in the direction of truth. Dramatic genius can afford to be unfair to the surface facts, to foreshorten, crowd, and caricature everything. It is not interested in accompaniments, however real in themselves, which it finds irrelevant; it is not interested in justice; it is interested only in great issues, and in the secret tendencies that may be making for the ultimate triumph or defeat of one's own soul. If the facts are to be dramatized, they must not be reproduced. They must be recast selectively on a grand scale, and precipitated towards some climax in which the heart is concerned.

Yet if they are to be truly dramatic, these relations must not be invented. They must subsist in the realm of truth. Intuition simply comes to disengage them from what is morally irrelevant, and to trace the red vein of destiny running through the world.

Dramatic intuition, or apt myth, has many forms or stages, from animism to dialectic and wit, from superstition to natural law. These intellectual unities may be true of the world without being parts of it. Every trope discerned in nature, every self-repeating movement, assumes a vital unity in the mind. Whatever happens, when it elicits a living idea, seems to have happened with a purpose. This illusion is normal and even a sign of intellectual force, because the first phase of any trope, when that trope has once been noticed and has taken root in the psyche, comes essentially as merely the beginning of what ought to follow, and a sure omen of the total movement to come. So the first part of a sentence, especially in an inflected language, can hardly appear without prophetic reference to the remainder. In nature, however, any trope may be cut short. It is not a power, as intellectual superstition may fancy, but only a customary rhythm established contingently and subject to interference from every quarter, until it finally becomes unrecognizable or vanishes altogether. Yet so long as it subsists, it describes as well as is humanly possible a whole obscure region of nature from the point of view of some soul. Dramatic fiction may thus reveal to us the gist of existence, as flat experience and prosaic observation could never do.

That which lifts dramatic perception above mere poetry or fiction is its moral origin and its practical sanction. Taken for cool descriptions of the facts,

Mythical units may express important movements otherwise untraceable.

what would the myths of Freud be, or the dialectics of Hegel and Marx, except grotesque fancies? But there is method in this madness. Freud is an alienist, a healer of souls, Hegel fundamentally a theologian, Marx a revolutionary. Each studies a practical momentous problem, how to restore health and sanity, or justify a progressive worldly religion, or provoke and guide a social upheaval. They review the history of their moral problem in its own fantastic terms. They seek to understand and to govern passion by passion. In such treatment—for it is a treatment—the total cosmic truth must be denied or left in the shadow. Instead we have a sort of war-map in which nothing is set down but what touches the campaign of the season. Yet even so, the perspectives opened up may be infinite, since everything in the world touches everything else at a certain remove and at a certain angle; and we may be dramatically enlightened, in the service of our passions, whilst perhaps by these passions themselves we are being intellectually deceived.

The enormous infusion of error that sense, passion, and language bring with them into human knowledge is therefore less misleading than might be supposed. Knowledge is not truth, but a view or expression of the truth; a glimpse of it secured by some animal with special organs under special circumstances. A lover of paradox might say that to be partly wrong is a condition of being partly right; or more soberly, that to be partial is, for knowledge, a condition of existing at all. To be partial and also to be relative: so that all the sensuous colour and local perspective proper to human views, and all the moral bias pervading them, far from rendering knowledge impossible, supply instruments for exploration, divers sensitive centres and divers inks, whereby in divers ways the facts may be recorded.

Error itself a true index to its causes.

A radical instance of dramatic truth appears in sentimental time. Time is not *in truth* sentimental: the past is not fading, the future is not empty or unreal; and when a man is moral and rational he recognizes the intrinsic reality and importance of both those regions, vitally so obscure and intangible. Yet if he could be absolutely rational and moral, if his mind could possess impartially all the past and all the future, he would be dead, he would be deified, he would have become motionless and eternal like the truth itself. The forward direction of his thought and the backward vista of his memory would be neutralized. He would be omnipresent; and this intimate identity of his mind with all possible knowledge would make experience, in any tentative progressive sense, impossible for him. And unless he somehow removed himself from the whole reality of himself and held it at arm's length, even the eternal and complete truth of it would elude him: because he would be that totality, and could not survey it. So the irrational finitude and bias of animal life, far from denying us the truth, summons us to pursue the truth, and gives us, in some measure, the means of attaining it.

Dramatic element inherent in knowledge.

I know how irritating constantly superstitious, rhetorical, moralistic views can be to the truth-lover; yet we must give the devil his due, and consider the consequences of refusing to think humanly when we are human. Thought itself would have to be abandoned in favour of mechanical notation of details. Such notation, in chronicles, statistics and pointer-readings, would not enter the realm of truth at all, if a certain selection and synthesis did not preside over the record: it would otherwise not be descriptive, as truth is, but merely a concomitant echo or mechanical index to certain features in the world; a part of the world, then, and

Foolish effort to eliminate it.

not a part of the truth about the world. To this, indeed, a certain positivistic and ultra-empirical philosophy professes to reduce science, replacing science in act, which is a category of spirit, with the instrumentalities or procedure of science, which lie in the realm of matter. Here, out of respect for the truth, we have an attempt on the part of mind to suppress mind; but although the truth is ontologically no more mental than physical, it is a form, an essence, that intelligence may find in an object, or in a system of objects, and by no means of part or member of that existential reality. Truth is therefore something that only mind can detach, something, as it were, addressed essentially to mind; although in the order of genesis it is the being of truth, the fact that facts exemplify essences and have relations, that makes it possible and appropriate that animals should develop minds: that is, should become aware not only of their organic processes expressed in blind feeling, but should become aware also of the causes or the objects of those feelings, and discover some part of the truth about them.

Truth is therefore not discoverable at all without some vital moral impulse prompting to survey it, and some rhetorical or grammatical faculty, synthesizing that survey and holding it up to attention in the form of a recognizable essence. Dramatic myth, however poetical it may be or merely analogous to the facts, in that at least it responds to the facts reflectively, has entered the arena of truth; it is more cognitive, more intelligent, and more useful than a mechanical record of those facts without any moral synthesis. I think it very doubtful whether, if religion and poetry should dry up altogether, mankind would be nearer the truth; or whether science would gain anything by correcting its philosophical pretensions, for instance the pretension to truth, in order to become merely the technology of the mechanical arts.

Affinity of mind to truth.

Certainly nothing would be gained intellectually: and if we condemned intelligence, as well as imagination, to ticking like a clock, if not to total silence, we might outrage human nature too deeply, and provoke a violent reaction. It is more prudent for the critic of illusion to consider the truth that myth may possess rather than to attempt to escape from myth altogether.

Sanity requires spirit to practise a certain duplicity, and continually to correct its necessary language by a no less necessary mental reservation. We live in this human scene as in a theatre, where an adult mind never loses itself so completely in the play as to forget that the play is a fiction; and he judges it, not for what it pretends to present, but for the stimulus and scope of the presentation. So in the whole verbal, sensuous, and moral medium through which we see the world we may learn not to see the world falsely but to see ourselves truly, and the world in its true relation to ourselves. With this proviso, all the humorous and picturesque aspects of experience may be restored to the world with dramatic truth. The near is truly near, when the station of the speaker is tacitly accepted as the point of reference. The good is truly good, the foreign truly foreign, if the absoluteness of the judgment is made relative to the judge. And this judge is no vagrant pure spirit. He is a man, an animal, a fragment of the material world; and he can no more annul or reverse his hereditary nature, in reference to which things are truly foreign or good, than he can annul the external forces playing upon his organism. Thus in reporting his passionate judgments, as if they were self-justified and obligatory, the dogmatist is unwittingly reporting a truth of natural history—namely, that at that juncture such judgments on his part are normal indexes to the state of the world, and not the least interesting element in it.

This dramatic medium is itself knowable and good.

CHAPTER VIII

MORAL TRUTH

MORAL ideas are usually hybrid. On the one hand, they may contain truth about matters of fact, such as that arsenic is poison, or that a man with more than the desired courage will be called rash, and with less, a coward. On the other hand, in recording these facts the moralist probably adopts and asserts in his own person the preference implied in those eulogistic or disparaging terms. He takes for granted that life is a good, that the approved degree of courage is a virtue, and that cowardice or rashness is a vice. He thus insinuates, as if self-evident, a moral judgment into his historical or psychological observations; and the possible truth of the latter may seem to him to support the truth of the former. But the nerve of moral judgment is preference: and preference is a feeling or an impulse to action which cannot be either false or true.

It might conduce to clearness in this subject if we limited the term *morality* to actual allegiance in sentiment and action to this or that ideal of life; while the history of such allegiances, and of the circumstances and effects involved, would form a descriptive science to be called ethics or the science of manners. Truth in ethics would then be like truth in any other part of natural philosophy, and particularly rich and discoverable: because it would not require us to investigate the mysteries of physics or biology, but would accept

473

large material and historical facts on the human scale, would treat them as units, and would be satisfied with presenting them to the human conscience, to be judged *morally*.   In this *moral* judgment, however, it is hard to see how there could be any truth.   The only truth concerned would be that such a judgment was passed, that it was more or less general and lasting, and more or less passionate.   But there would seem to be no conceivable object or reality in reference to which any type of morality could be called *true*.

Yet how many moralists or political philosophers are content with the support that physical facts and physical forces may lend to their maxims, and do not also claim a moral rightness for these maxims themselves?   Such moral rightness in moral sentiment is either a tautology, meaning that what you prize you prize, and what you want you want, or it is a tangle of confusion.   Any first moral reaction, perhaps of anger, can harden into a fierce absolute command.   Any feeling, nursed and kept close in the dark, may fester into a categorical imperative.   The imperative of life, the imperative of every unchecked impulse, is no doubt categorical; and a certain group of these impulses may easily become a code of duty or honour, traditional in some society, or in mankind at large.   Utility or calculation or what Kant called heteronomy may have nothing to do with such maxims: they may be as spontaneous and free as laughter or love.   But how should these automatisms be *true*?   The word *true* in such a case is unmeaning, except perhaps as a vague term of praise, a mere reiteration of some automatic impulse, as if we cried Amen.   Such repetition might seem harmless; yet verbal self-confirmation, coming to one's notions as it seems from nowhere or from above, tends to fanaticism.   Language then becomes an accomplice and a sanction of the will: and from honest opposition

Fanatical abuse of the word true.

to our enemies in battle, we pass to envenomed refutation of their feelings as false. Each party hugs its maxims not as its own and worth being true to, but as the *only true* maxims. We might dismiss this as excusable heat and vapour, or as a technical solecism; yet when passion usurps the name of truth, the very idea of truth is tarnished and defiled.

Nevertheless, as usage leads us to speak of truth within the spheres of logic and of convention, so it leads us to speak of truth in morals. And there are good reasons for acquiescing in this extension of the range within which judgment may be called true or false. In willing as in knowing there is a good deal of substitution and representation. Moral passions, carried by words and ideas in themselves automatic, may be deceptive, may be hollow; they may pass like storm-clouds over the conscience, tragically misinterpreting the inmost and ultimate allegiance of the soul. Such passions, and the judgments they dictate, may be called false, since besides blinding us to many a matter of fact, they deceive us about our own fundamental needs and demands. Integrity, on the contrary, the clear allegiance of a transparent soul to its radical will, without being true to anything external, makes a man's choices true to himself. It banishes moral illusions. And the same true representation of latent interests may extend to political action; a government or a party may pursue true or false aims, in the sense of being or not being in line with the radical and permanent interests of the people. Thus truth and error may be possible in morals, in so far as they are truths or errors in self-knowledge.

Take, for example, the commandment: *Love thy neighbour as thyself*. Purely hortatory as this seems, it may be almost entirely translated into propositions that would be either true or false. In the sphere

A moral precept may be true or false in respect to moral interests in general.

of action—which if we distinguish moral from spiritual life would also be the sphere of morals— an imperative is an order to a dependent, intended to be, by suggestion, a form of indirect or suspended compulsion. A commandment to love would then be in reality an order to act as if we loved, implying that if we did not do so, our neighbours and God would act as if they did not love us. This would be a true or a false prophecy, and it might guide the will as might any other credible report about the field of action. But love, spiritually considered, is a feeling: and an imperative in the sphere of feeling becomes a little nebulous. How should love be commanded? It might perhaps be awakened by contagion, in return for love—*amor che a nullo amato amar perdona.* Or it might be extended from an object already loved to some kindred object. Then, in terms of pure feeling, the precept might run thus: Love thy neighbour, because God loves him; and thou lovest God, because God loves thee. Or less emotionally: Value others for their own sake, because they too are centres of life and of values. Consider them, as Kant counselled, always as ends and never merely as means. In fact and by nature they are ends to themselves as much as you are an end to yourself. Here, in respect to all living beings, and not merely to other men, we reach a necessary truth, since life means precisely the power in organisms to grow and to propagate, as if they loved their own being.

Yet this ethical truth is not, and cannot become, a moral commandment. The categorical nerve of every imperative is vital, it expresses an actual movement of the will. And evident as the truth may be that life in every form has its intrinsic values, and attributes radiating values to all felt events, it by no means follows that these values are unanimous or

[margin note:] Ethical matters of fact are also involved.

that life in one form can adopt, or morally ought to adopt, the interests of life in every other form. This would indeed be the death of all morality, not the perfection of it. The will of the storm, the will of Neptune or of Jupiter Tonans, cannot with self-knowledge be adopted by the struggling and trembling creature about to be destroyed. The will of the enemy cannot be incorporated into that of the soldier. The will of the tempter, the interests of a rival in love, the tastes of the vulgar, cannot be weighed in the balance against the constitutive will and radical virtue of one's own being. Reason may harmonize the impulses of a soul: it would not be reason but self-betrayal if it abdicated these impulses in a brotherly compromise with cobras, monkeys, idiots, sophists and villains. Against a threatening deity, there is always some protecting deity to be invoked, or some other side of the same deity; and licence may be freely allowed to beasts and barbarians to live in their own way in their own preserves, so long as they do not trespass upon ours. Moreover, there is a mystical insight proper to spirit within ourselves—spirit not being specifically human—that perceives the universal innocence of life in the midst of universal war: but this insight cannot impose on the psyche in which it arises ways contrary to her native ways: nor has impartial spirit any reason for wishing to do so. Life is a form of order, a great rhythmic self-responsive organization in parcels of matter: but it arises in a thousand places and takes a thousand forms. If reason or spirit or any mystic influence whatsoever attempted to impose on each living creature the contrary impulses of all the others, it would induce not universal harmony but universal death. It would solve the moral problem only by dissolving all goods, all arts, all species and all individuals.

But ethical truths cannot inspire or annul natural moral preferences.

Just because moral life is inwardly grounded, physical truths are the only guide that it will willingly

Moral sentiment invents ethical fables.

accept. A contrary purpose merely arouses hostility, but a contrary fact may inspire caution. I remember in childhood the warning of my nurse against swallowing cherry-stones. If I swallowed them, she said, a cherry-tree would grow out of my mouth. This is the principle on which moralists usually recommend their system of morality. The preacher is honestly actuated by an unexplained intense sentiment which he wishes to propagate; and in order to do so he invents circumstances of a startling nature calculated to justify that sentiment. But the method is dangerous. The images evoked under such stress of feeling are likely to be grotesque, like the traditional picture of hell-torments, or the atrocities imputed to an enemy in war; and even if by chance the invention were true, or the fraud never discovered, the sentiments thereby aroused in a half-moralized public would wholly lack the intensity and purity of those that originally animated the preacher. Where he was all moral enthusiasm or sinister superstition, his flock will be lazy, prudential, or prim. For that which creates morality is not facts, nor the consequences of facts, but human terror or desire feeling its way amid those facts and those consequences.

Suppose that instead of laughing at my nurse I had been horrified at my thoughtless sin and terrible

Such sentiment is inevitable.

danger in having swallowed a cherry-stone: then moral experience in me would certainly have become vivid. Sundry *ethical truths* would incidentally become unpleasantly clear, such as that a tree growing out of my mouth would be embarrassing, not to say fatal; or that other little boys lacking that ornament would probably jeer at me. From these ethical truths my mind would be expected to jump automatically to the *moral judgment* that annoyance, derision and especially death are absolute evils, which ought to be avoided. Life indeed involves the moral judgment that life is a good, since, while life lasts, the organism tends to maintain or to restore the continuity and harmony of its functions, defending itself with a blind concentrated fury against mutilation, disease and death. Even when in some tragic moment reflection turns against instinct and prefers physical death to life, not everything in life is judged to be evil; for at least this high condemnation or renunciation of life is regarded as a glorious victory and liberation for the spirit; and what is spirit but the quintessence of life here purified into tragic knowledge, into clear loyalty to what is felt to be best? It is therefore an ethical truth that moral judgments of some sort are inevitable in man. He cannot help having some radical preference. However sublimated this preference may be, it will express his vital feeling, the last cry of his animal nature, morally groundless. This cry may be absolutely sincere and true to the heart; but there is no meaning in saying that the preference so uttered is a truth in itself.

In strictness we might even say that every moral judgment is repugnant to the truth, and that if consciousness fundamentally gave voice to truth rather than to life, and to the animal partiality involved in life, moral sentiment would be impossible. The cry, *How beautiful!* or *How good!* may be sincere, and it may be applauded, but it is never true. If sincere such a cry is also never false, even if not re-echoed by the public conscience; because the public feeling that contradicts it can also never be true, but at best also sincere. Where sentiment is diffused and unanimous, if one person utters those exclamations, all the rest may no doubt murmur, *How true!* And indeed, to that

But if turned into a predicate of things dictates a falsehood.

extent, the judgment will then be *true morally*: that is, it will express the bias of human nature. That mercy is good or the sunset beautiful may be true dramatically and conventionally, for the soul and in the speech of a particular moral society: a society that need not retract its judgments if by chance some harder head or colder heart contradicts them; rather it will judge those contrary judgments to be wicked and blind. And so they will be in respect to the standards of that society. There would be no further meaning, only a greater shrillness, in insisting that they are blind and wicked in themselves. If for the emotional words *beautiful* and *good* we now substitute the analytic words *admired* and *welcome*, all moral contradiction disappears, the fog lifts, and we restore our moral intuitions to their legitimate field, the field of self-knowledge.

This Socratic self-knowledge is not scientific but expressive, not ethical but moral; and here if anywhere, in the discovery of what one ultimately wants and ultimately loves, *moral truth* might be found. This is no easy discovery; and we must be prepared for surprises in morals, no less than in physics, as investigation and analysis proceed. As the blue vault vanishes under the telescope, so moral conventions might dissolve in an enlightened conscience, and we might be abashed to perceive how disconcerting, how revolutionary, how ascetic the inmost oracle of the heart would prove, if only we had ears to hear it. Perhaps a premonition of this ultimate moral disillusion rendered Socrates so endlessly patient, diffident and ironical, so impossible to corrupt and so impossible to deceive.

I think, however, that there was one ethical illusion unextirpated even from the mind of Socrates (as also from that of Emerson); an illusion that warped the moral impartiality of his precepts and rendered him partisan and dogmatic in spite of his intention to be absolutely courteous and fair. He assumed that human nature was single and immutable, and the soul qualitatively identical in all men. The good that glimmered like buried gold in his own heart must lie also in the hearts of others, and only ignorance or sophistry could keep them from seeing it. But the roots of the good are alive; they are far more tentative and curiously entangled than verbal debate might indicate at Athens amid a bevy of rationalizing demagogues and sophists. Even in the individual, in whom actual preference has its only possible seat, ultimate sincerity presupposes a definite psyche, with assignable aspirations; and indeed some degree of definiteness any psyche must possess, else that psyche could not be the hereditary principle of organization in the body or of direction in the will. Yet this vital definiteness is not absolute. At each moment there is a limit, inwards, below which the psyche is not sensitive to variations in her own substance; and there is a margin outwards toward the infinite, beyond which what happens does not affect her specific life. Moreover, the most radical demands of the psyche are not immutable. Unfelt variations in her substance transform and undermine her desires. She is mortal; presently she will make no demands at all; and in the interval, from germination to birth and from childhood to old age, she successively develops and outgrows functions which are essentially temporary. In her origin she was a new equilibrium that changing circumstances had rendered possible; and her organism remains always potentially plastic and internal to the flux of nature at large.

Hence the absence of a need or a passion in one phase of life cannot be taken for an argument that such a need or passion is false or wicked elsewhere. The contrary assumption is the root of much idle

False assumption in dogmatic morals.

censoriousness and injustice in moralists, who are
probably old men, and sapless even in youth, all
their zeal being about phrases and maxims

The problem for the moral imagination.

that run in their heads and desiccate the
rest of their spirit. To reach moral truth,
which like all truth is eternal, we should
have to remember or foresee with absolute clearness the
aspirations of all souls at all moments; and confronting
these aspirations with their occasions, we should have
to measure their relative vanity and physical compatibility. The question is not whether they happen
to be identical or harmonious with our own sentiments.
We are particular creatures at one point in space and
time: and the most contrary goods are beyond mutual
censure, if pursued at different times or by different
spirits.

Moral dogmatism is an attempt to stretch moral
unity beyond the range of natural organization.

Yet conscience, being enlightened will, is indomitably positive.

Spiritually it is a sinister thing, a sin against
spirit elsewhere. Yet politically, and within
the living organism, animal or social, moral
dogmatism is morality itself; it is the effort
of that organism to maintain its health and
attain its perfection. Hatred or contempt
for alien manners and ideas would be absurd in a
philosopher sure of his own ground; he would be
pleased by their zoological variety which like that of
animals in cages would not seriously endanger his
safety, freedom, or peace. But social morality—and
all morality is deeply social—is necessarily divided
at home and threatened from abroad. Invective and
propaganda are instruments in this animal warfare;
they are useful in maintaining discipline, in breaking
the enemy's spirit, and in capturing as many loose
ambient forces as possible to the support of your
particular regimen. Liberals and Pacifists, who
imagine they represent morality in general, are the

first to announce the sure victory of their cause and
the annihilation for ever of all their enemies, that is, of
all moralities in particular.   Yet morality in general,
as we see in truly emancipated circles, is no morality
at all.   The root of morality is animal bias: and to
renounce that bias would be to renounce life.   Even
the most general and tolerant of moral standards—
harmony—is not a good in itself.   There must be an
actual will directed upon harmony in order to render
harmony a good.   Harmony demands many a sacrifice:
in what direction, and at whose cost, shall those
sacrifices be made?   A strong and well-knit nature,
brave with the perfect harmony within, will despise
and detest harmony on a larger scale; it will refuse to
sacrifice any part of its chosen good, and will declare
eternal war on the devil, and on all his obsequious and
insidious agents.

Such, in whatever interest and on whatever scale,
is the nerve of morality.   Reflected in the living soul,
all the rays of nature instantly acquire a moral colour.
Nothing can happen that will not be good or bad in a
thousand directions.   When all living souls are considered, the cross-lights and conflicts of these values
spread an impenetrable tangle, through which it is
impossible for mortal eye to see the ultimate balance
of benefit and injury.   But nature laughs at this
perplexity.   A man is a man, for all the apes and
donkeys in the world.   Instinct reasserts its primacy;
the overwhelming immediacy of some great passion
or hope breaks through the cobwebs of sentimental
idleness, and sets a fresh clear work before us that will
not brook delay.

This self-assertion is not always young and impulsive; it may survive all experience and disillusion,
growing firmer in isolation, and cleaving to the chosen
good even when this is known to be unrealizable.
Such desperate heroism is nevertheless contrary to

all the lower unconsecrated yielding parts of the psyche; and half the martyr's mind, together with the mind of posterity, will judge wholly un-realizable desires to have been unhealthy and undesirable. Moral truth, therefore, even at its purest, by no means bestows moral authority over alien lives. It signifies only complete, enlightened, ultimate sincerity.

Its ultimate deliverance is moral truth.

CHAPTER IX

TRUTH SUPERTEMPORAL

THE relation of truth to time might seem simple
enough if stated in general terms. Make a complete
report of all events occurring in time and   Truth not
there you have the truth. But a complete   an event.
report, though suggested and even in one sense pursued
in all truth-telling, remains always a pure ideal. Be
it in the witness-box or be it in the laboratory, that
"whole truth" which we are pledged to tell can never
be told. It would take too long, much longer than
the events had taken to happen; and our means of
observation are limited, as well as our means of
expression. Moreover, when we enlarge the canvas
and consider the total truth of the universe, we perceive that the impossibility of actually knowing it is
intrinsic. In order that even a superhuman survey of
history should be complete, the last of future events
would have had to occur and to show its colours.
Therefore an actual survey (which would be a fresh
event) could not supervene; or if it supervened it
could not be all-inclusive, since by arising, this
survey itself would have added an important event to
history.

The truth, then, forms an ideal realm of being
impersonal and super-existential. Though everything in the panorama of history be temporal, the
panorama itself is dateless: for evidently the sum and
system of events cannot be one of them. It cannot

occur after anything else or before anything else. Thus the truth about existence differs altogether in ontological quality from existence itself. Life and motion are gone, all scales are equally real, all ages equally present. Intensity, actuality, suffering have become historical. The truth is like the moon, beautiful but dead. On the other hand, the truth is much richer than existence can be at any moment. Not only does it retain the essence of all moments equally, but it contains much that each moment, and even all moments in their inner being, can never contain, since it contains also the systems which these moments form unawares, merely by co-existing and alternating as they do. Truth might be figuratively called the memory of the universe; but it is far more than that, since the destiny of the universe is included in the truth. If we fancifully give the name of memory to the past of the world, we must imagine that memory to be complete and unmixed with error, else it would not contain but contradict the truth of the past; whilst in regard to the future, the truth would still loom before advancing events with a tragic ambiguity, like an oracle heard and known to the infallible, but as yet impossible to decipher. Thus though the truth is created by contingent events, and secondary to them, and though destiny is but the confluence of successive spontaneities, truth nevertheless confronts existence with a divine authority and an insoluble problem of self-knowledge. Nor is it congruous with the nature of life that the truth should be completely revealed to it. Glimpses come only in tragic moments or to strangely disinterested minds; and the revelation is dangerous, even when it seems entrancing. The world at one moment, like Narcissus, may fall in love with its own image, seen in the truth; but at another moment that image may become a Gorgon and may petrify the eye that beholds it.

The truth would not be complete if it left unrecorded that asymmetrical lapse and precipitation of motion in which it cannot participate. In the Change, translated into terms of truth, be- realm of comes the genealogy and measure of change. truth events compose Events become the subject-matter of science perspectives. and history. Constitutional incapacity to change is not a defect on the part of the truth, but on the contrary a proof of its staunchness and its privilege of permeating existence without forfeiting its own ideality. One event cannot be the truth of another. While each fact undergoes change by yielding up its place and substance to a new fact, the truth of that occurrence can be only the *form* of the successive facts with the *form* of the transition between them.

We should doubtless have no notion of change if we did not undergo it; yet it is not by merely passing that facts breed memory or an intuition of Change is time stretching forward and back. It is the revealed not by change enrichment, the complexity, the multiform itself but by tensions of organic life as it flows that enable complex us to feel life flowing. Intellectual syn- tensions within each thesis does not require any existential ele- moment. ment to be in two moments at once; but material energies, rich in vital potentialities, can become conscious of changes on foot. This actually happens when a psyche, organized for growth and sensitive to opportunity, being adjusted both to the past and to the future, feels at each moment the suspense, duration and lapse of time. The canvas is then spread for imagination to paint upon, and history and science do nothing but fill it in. At each moment we are then accompanied by a sense of prolonged events in their wholeness, that is to say, as they lie in the realm of truth. For it is only in the realm of truth that events can be unified or divided. The very concentration of existence in the moving present prevents any contrasts, repetitions, or derivations from actually disrupting that momentary reality; yet this reality, by continually pulsing and changing, renders such contrasts, repetitions and derivations true.

It is precisely this continuity of events and these truths about them that intelligence comes to perceive: not imagining and positing those truths falsely (as the enemies of intelligence would like to suggest) but imagining and positing them truly: because if there were no substantial derivation of event from event, and if generation were not bridged by the truth of generation, no proposition could have an existing object, and all signs and beliefs would be equally vain. For example: there could then be no identity between the child of A and the father of C, since B would be contiguous with each only under a different aspect; nor could the B who had A for his father be identical with the B whom A had for his son. In other words, each flash of change would be a separate universe; and events would therefore have no dates and compose no history.

Such a disruption of nature, or chaos of particulars, is not logically impossible. *It might be the truth*; but in that case all sensation and thought would terminate upon mere essence, and the idea of a flux of experience would be a false idea, since between actual moments there would be no transition, and time would be unrolled into a firmament of simultaneous facts. If chronology can be a true science, memory and dramatic imagination must be organs of truth; they must be truly inspired. The prophets of mutation, who say that all is change, are, against their will, shining instances of intelligence. Far from sinking with every wave, they keep their heads always above water, proclaiming how perpetually and pervasively the ocean flows.

The reality of truth makes intelligence possible logically and supports it biologically.

It might seem, for instance, that the truth changes as fast as the facts which it describes.   On a day before the Ides of March it was true that Julius Cæsar was alive: on the day after that Ides of March it had *become true* that he was dead.   A mind that would keep up with the truth must therefore be as nimble as the flux of existence.   It must be a newspaper mind.

This, on the surface, is an innocent sophism, if not a bit of satire, mocking the inconstancy of things. Idiomatically we might as properly say, "It was then true that Cæsar was living," as we might say, "The truth is that Cæsar was then living."   In using the former phrase we have no thought of denying the latter.   If Julius Cæsar was alive at a certain date, it was then true, it had been true before, and it will be true always that at that date he was or would be or had been alive.   These three assertions, in their deliverance, are identical; and in order to be identical in their deliverance, they have to be different in form, because the report is made in each case from a different point in time, so that the temporal perspectives of the same fact, Cæsar's death on the Ides of March, require different tenses of the verb.   This is a proof of instability in knowledge in contrast to the fixity of truth. For the whispered oracle, *Beware the Ides of March*, the tragic event was future; for the Senators crowding round Pompey's statue it was present; for the historian it is past: and the truth of these several perspectives, each from its own point of origin, is a part of the eternal truth about that event.

Beneath the surface, however, there is no doubt a remnant of metaphysical illusion, by which we transfer to physical time the sentimental colour of our temporal perspectives.   Instead of the physical truth that all men live in their own day and in their own day only, we say "Cæsar lived long ago"; or we may

(marginal note:) Verbal equivocation in transferring the tenses of affirmations to the truths affirmed.

even cry pathetically, "Cæsar is dead, long dead."
We thus slide from a truism to a private perspective,

Sentimental
illusion in
attributing
temporal
perspectives
to physical
time.

and from a private perspective to a dramatic equivocation. For that Cæsar lived *long ago* is true only in relation to our own times; and that he is *dead, long dead*, is not true of him at all, if we mean his life or his consciousness, but at most might be true of his corpse, if that still existed. But words lead us to imagine that things can survive themselves. When Cæsar has ceased to live, we half believe that he continues to exist dead. But nothing exists dead except dead bodies. Facts exist only as they occur, and the essence and truth of them, which are indeed eternal, are non-existent. Names, however, being hereditary, and essences being often exemplified repeatedly or continuously in existence, we tend to attribute the identity proper to the essence or the name to the similar but diffused moments that inherit that name or that essence. But between moments or facts, however similar to one another, there is no identity. The existence of each is internal and self-centred; and each constitutes a primary contingent factor in a world which, as a whole and in its detail, is perfectly contingent and unnecessary. There is therefore metaphysical illusion or idolatry in peopling the world with hypostatic identities and materialized truths: a curious consequence being that truth and essence themselves come to be obscured by confusion with the flux of facts.

Two words in particular are apt to suffer this hypostatis when truth is spoken of as changing: the word *now* and the word *I*. I could once say truly: I am now young. At present I can say truly: I am now old. Therefore it would seem that the truth about me is changed. But it was never true that I am *now* young, if *now* means the year 1936; the *now* of fifty years earlier, though it had the same essence of actuality and was being lived through as breathlessly as the *now* of to-day, was an entirely different moment. And of that concrete moment it could never become true for me to say, Now I am old. The essence of nowness runs like fire along the fuse of time, but the particular spark is different at each point. The various contents of these various *nows* therefore combine perfectly to form the unchangeable truth of history.

The intuitive *now*, which is an essence, confused with the particular *nows*, which are facts.

Even deeper is the metaphysical illusion in hypostatizing the word *I*. Much used to be written concerning personal identity and responsibility: the soul in future had somehow to deserve damnation for its past sins, or for those of Adam. This moral enigma seems to have ceased from troubling, as if people were content to blame each moment for its own folly; but the cognitive problem of memory still perplexes philosophers. Each man uses the word *I* to designate his physical person at all ages, awake or asleep: and the continuity of his body, bearing always the same name, leads him to think of himself as a self-identical being entering into relation with changing things. Yet his body (not to speak of his thoughts) notoriously changes faster than many a tree or river; whilst that in him which bridges time—pictured time only—is not a substantial fact at all but an intellectual faculty called intuition; and the occasions on which this faculty is exercised are themselves movements of the psyche, as transitory and irrevocable as any other events in nature. We may indeed give to all instances of intuition or feeling the common name of spirit, and may say that this spirit is identical at all moments and even in all persons; but such identity is qualitative only. Spirit in all those instances has the same transcendental

And the transcendental *I* confused with the changing person.

status and infinite potential scope; it is everywhere intelligence in act; but this pure spirit or gift of consciousness flashes out only on scattered occasions. It is nothing substantial or permanent or continuous, capable by its prolonged existence of being present at once at every point of time. Such persistence is found only in objects on the human scale, that may be handed down like heirlooms, and still be conventionally identical; yet accurate physics dissolves even that prolonged identity into something formal and imputed; while in extending that analogy to spirit language goes wholly astray. Spirit being the flower of life is intrinsically fresh and self-positing at every moment; there is nothing identical in these moments except their spiritual essence. This essence the word *I* may indicate by its purely grammatical and generic force, when it stands only for the transcendental function of thinking, identical in all thoughts; but these thoughts or instances of thinking, far from being thereby materialized into a continuous fact, become each a transcendental centre for an ideal survey of time. They are lodged in physical time only by virtue of their organs. They are *intrinsically* dateless, as any synthesis of time must be in respect to the events it surveys.

Thus language may lead us to attribute to facts the timelessness of essences, and to create contradictions in knowledge where there is mere instability in existence. It is only when we ignore our own mutation that the truth seems to us to change.

CHAPTER X

COGNITION OF THE FUTURE

IN human life it seems a matter of course to have much knowledge of the past and little of the future. This circumstance is exaggerated by some philosophers into a theory that the past exists now, and that the future is as yet nothing. Common sense hardly goes so far. The past, considered sentimentally as past feelings and adventures, seems rapidly to evaporate and grow ghostly as fresh events crowd upon the scene; while on the other hand all human prudence assumes a future to which the lessons of the past will apply. In mechanics and astronomy, exact predictions are constantly verified; and so, more loosely, is the great volume of daily expectations in human affairs. A cataclysm, perhaps, may intervene; but we feel that this too might have been foreseen had we been wise enough. In any case, there was a future to be known; and if human knowledge in that direction is so largely nebulous, while it is so rich and definite in respect of the past, the cause is to be found in a biological accident. This accident is that man is born helpless and passive, and must shape his instincts under the blows of experience.

The first experience of the human child is to be awake but helpless. He must tentatively acquire the art of walking, talking, and doing every other customary thing; things for which he is imperfectly ready, and which often cross his natural will, so that he is inclined

Knowledge of the past a human peculiarity.

493

to sulk and to attempt the impossible.   Hence a double
scar of defeat and compulsion marks all his progress.
He must skirt again the fatal vices of his ancestors,
and half his virtues have to be imposed upon him
as duties.   Therefore when opportunity smiles upon
him at last, he seldom can leap to meet it without
embarrassment.   His awakened instinct hesitates and
needs to be redirected by a revival of all the jolts
and disappointments and violent jibbings amidst which
it was formed.   He will recall his schooling in doing
what he has learned to do, and in his triumphs he
will still be redigesting his bitter failures.   No such
visionary memories need have accompanied his action,
had the lessons of the past become automatic in the
organism.   Any ghostly survival of the past would
then have signified some impediment or maladjustment in the readiness to live.   But circumstances
alter natures; and in fact the only possible path for
man now runs round the loop of discipline and art,
and these circumlocutions have become integral to
the sort of perfection natural to him.   What he does
seems to him nothing, if he cannot remember what he
has done; and he would hardly care to live if he could
not conceive his background and his limits in living.

Consider, by way of contrast, the triumph of reproduction often approached in nature, when an animal
is born perfect.   In the womb or in the
egg, where all his organs were preformed,
so as to be, in the ripeness of time, unerring in their action, he would have seen
no visions.   Such feelings as he may then have had
would never have been recalled or distinguished in
reflection.   His first daylight perception might well
be that of some lure or some challenge; and his whole
organism would instantly fly and meet it.   Perspectives
would all open towards the future.   The past, for
his consciousness, would remain an empty night and

Instinctive
attention
looks for-
ward rather
than back.

an abyss of nothingness. His astonishment would be equal to his contempt, if he could hear that there were creatures called men, who thought that the future was uncertain, who expected to die, and whose mind was hung round like a mausoleum with skeletons and funeral inscriptions of things non-existent, which they called the past. The life of such a perfect animal, addressed altogether to the future, would be ruled by Passion and Duty, or perhaps it would be more accurate to say, by Honour. He would have an absolute vision of what *must* be done. Circumstances would never contaminate his will, but only call it forth, or defeat it; and the notion of a change of heart, or acceptance of anything short of the one perfect and absolute good, would seem to him the lowest depth of baseness.

I may seem to be writing a fable: yet the deeper parts of the human psyche are formed before birth. All our organs grow and preserve them- Biological selves without memory or experience, yet grounds of with remarkable adaptation to the future, foresight. that is, with biological foresight; and if these organs had a separate consciousness they would be in the same case as a new-fledged insect or a hungry beast. External influences would merely liberate internal powers. Even our outer organs of sense are in this case, since sights and sounds are, in their æsthetic quality, products of the eye and ear; yet their significant side for our lives is not this, but rather the indications they give regarding material facts existing outside at the moment. Suppose that instead of the eye or ear, which are comparatively passive instruments willing to be at rest, the organ were an empty stomach or a ripe sexual apparatus; the feelings involved would be turned, as sounds and colours are turned, upon the forces arousing them, but not as on static objects: rather as on objects of the chase, things to be caught or killed or eaten or possessed. However dumbly and excitedly, it would be a vista towards the future that would absorb the mind; and the intense attention riveted on the present would contain a sensation of imminent action, of something coming, that must and that shall come.

Be it observed that the premonitory knowledge of the future that I speak of is nothing miraculous; no It is not perception of the future. *perception* of something by hypothesis not acting upon the organs of sense. Perception is definable as a sensation turned into knowledge of its ground, that is, of its present occasion. A future occasion can therefore never be known by perception. But it may be known by premonition, by a rehearsal, as in a dream, of the acts to be performed or the visions to be seen later. Evidently an animal governed by instinct alone and incapable of learning anything by experience, would be apt to have such prophetic premonitions. Doubtless they would not contain graphic images, until these were supplied by perception; yet almost any hint will do to launch an innate passion: as children at play in a barnyard will feel the full thrill of standing on mountain-tops or of cutting off heads. The self is as much alive in sport as in battle, and less distracted; and the sheer joy of achievement is never purer than when no reasons or consequences are thought of.

Instinctive life is therefore quite competent to anticipate the moral texture of the future possible to each creature; but that is not all. Premoni- Yet cognitive in function and addressed to the eventual fact. tions are more than anticipations; being carried by a definite impulse to action they are instances of animal faith, and fulfil a requirement essential to knowledge of fact, in that they are beliefs positing a removed object. Such premonitions can be true, because they are assertions regarding the real future.

Moreover, occasions such as might provoke the

expected feelings are almost sure to occur, so that the premonitions are not only capable of being true, but are likely to be so. By hypothesis, the prophetic organism is perfect: but a perfect and incorrigible organization would soon prove fatal unless it were well adapted to the normal environment. We should not be born with lungs if there were no air: and the promise of any instinct, when interpreted realistically, may be trusted, on the average, not to deceive us.

That to which instinct is adapted is likely to come true.

When natural prophecy fails, the failure eliminates the prophet in that particular instance, but it leaves prophecy alive and likely to be verified in the experience of the race. Refutation by the facts can never abolish prophetic vision until the organ of prophecy is destroyed.

Instinctive prophecy survives incidental failures.

Being inwardly inspired, direct knowledge of the future can be only moral and dramatic, and limited to the future experience of the prophet or of the people for whom he speaks. Such fore-knowledge cannot extend to the date or accidental circumstances of its fulfilment, nor to any cosmic facts beyond the range of the self-anticipating life.

It regards only moral issues.

Alleged *perceptions* of the future, as if by telepathy, may be admitted, when they seem to exist, but need not be explained superstitiously. They can hardly be direct intuitions of future events, seeing that no fact, either past or present, is internal to intuition, or given as it occurs in its own medium; and as for the essence which intuition may actually evoke, it may as easily be exemplified in some future fact as in a fact that is past or contemporary. Prophecy may therefore be true conventionally, by anticipating an appearance in human terms, just as memory and perception are true conventionally, by supplying or repeating such an appearance. There is no telepathy in time or even in space,

And is physically conditioned.

taken literally, as if essences flashed themselves about without other agencies; but the psyche in two removed persons may generate the same or partly the same images, through agencies not well known to us.

To be rational, to rely on memory and experience, to study and measure the movement of external things,

Priority of will or instinct over memory even in man.
is that great characteristic of man which has enabled him to construct instruments and to dominate the earth by his science and art. Nevertheless, even in man, this rationality and this accumulated knowledge of the past are something secondary. He is instinctive before he is rational, natural before he is artificial; and we may go further and say that he must look to the future before he can see the past. Memory is a mystery that psychology, as far as I know, has done nothing to penetrate. If it were the literal survival of the past, it would place us in the past, which we should think present, as in a dream; and the sense of pastness would not arise. If it were the revival of a specious past in the present, at a felt remove, with a temporal perspective of antecedent behind antecedent, the imagination would indeed be, so to speak, prophetic backwards; but whence, in that case, the suggestion of a real past with which our memory might be compared, a past which was the intended object of memory, and rendered that memory false or true? No doubt in the field of consciousness at any natural moment there is a sense of duration and lapse, as there is perception of motion; and both motion and lapse, studied analytically, involve a past given as past; or rather a specific part of the present over which a cloud of pastness, more or less transparent, rapidly spreads. If later the cloud seems to break in places, and show us again a bit of what once we saw, the identity of that past datum with our present datum becomes problematical: we may feel that our fresh

intuition (in date, extent and relations manifestly a new intuition) is true as far as it goes, and that we remember the past exactly as it was; but this may be an illusion, inevitable in the absence of any possible fresh control of our recollection by the past occasion itself. The past, then, as far as direct memory and remembered experience can exhibit it, is like the future, a hypothesis in the air, since there is no evidence of the existence of its object except the hypothesis itself, and no possible test of the truth of this hypothesis, except that the compulsion to make it is irresistible.

Even that reflective life, therefore, on which man prides himself would be impossible if the impulse that creates prophecy had died out. The human assurance that there is a past rests on the organic assumption that there is a future. In memory the irresistible impulse to posit a world of action is turned backwards towards a world of origins: a useless and inappropriate turn in itself, because an idea of the past is a mere drag on life, except in the form of poetic legends rich in moral colour; and in that form the idea of the past is not true historically. It is not for its own sake that the past is worth knowing. Consciousness is essentially watchfulness, expectation, anxiety. Sleep would be sweeter; yet the well-fed senses are eager for exercise; or perhaps something foreign horribly invades our peace, and must be shaken off. In a word, Will lies beneath Idea. If the prophetic exercise of mind ever gives place to science, or dramatic to historical truth, it is only because Will has been defeated or intercepted by accidents which we have no means of removing, but may circumvent by some roundabout approach. It then becomes interesting to us to consider what those alien things are in themselves, how they behave on their own initiative, and by what artifice we may so far yield to them as, on the whole, to profit by

Faith and fear inherent in knowledge.

their existence. We rehearse the past, but we rehearse it forward, as it moved when it was present; and even when we plunge backwards in imagination into antiquity, we do so as on a journey of discovery, unearthing one stratum after another, and letting buried truth tempt us on into the depths of its treasure-house.

So much for pointing out that life and mind posit the future initially, and that the same assumption The truth of animates not only each revival of the past in the future is memory, but even the belief in the pastness independent of the events recalled. The past waits to of any animal faculty to be rediscovered as the future waits to be conceive it. fulfilled. This initial assumption is imposed on us by life, and nature makes it dumbly in all her preparations; yet logically the reality of a future is not thereby proved. Existence might collapse at any moment, spirit might vanish; and the truth of history, rounded out to that conclusion, might involve the truth that no time and no events existed beyond. Since existence is essentially contingent, the events composing physical time may be as easily finite as infinite, chaotic as regular; and their course is at liberty, as far as logic goes, to come or not to come to an end. Only visionary, synthetic, geometrical time is necessarily endless and steady.

That the future, if there is a future, will be what it will be, is an identical proposition, and necessary. The future That this pure tautology should have been determinate a cause of anguish to thousands of men, even if not desperately seeking refuge from it in a predeter- mined. thousand confusions, has, I think, a double source: partly in the trick of fancy that identifies vital freedom with chance, and partly in the trick of lan- guage that identifies truth with the knowledge of truth. The truth of the future, like all truth, is eternal, and exactly as definite and complete as what, at any date, is the truth of the past: indeed, it is exactly the same truth, touching what is future from here and past from there. Facts cannot be indistinct or ambiguous in themselves. Suggested facts may exist or may not exist; but if *they* exist, they do so by having the precise character which they have. There is therefore no difficulty placed in the way of knowing the future by any inconsistence or indeterminateness in what the future will contain when it becomes present. The difficulties all come from blankness or want of range in the imagination of the prophet, or from want of affinity between his imagination and the forces by which the future will be really produced. A creature without memory cannot discover the past; one without expectation cannot conceive a future ; one without pre-adaptation cannot conceive the future truly. A creature having only momentary sensations, never fled from or pursued, would know absolutely nothing of the truth of things, since those momentary sensations would reveal essences evoked, not objects encountered, and the very notion of a world or of the truth about it would not arise.

On the other hand, the most intelligent and prophetic mind would be at a loss to predict anything truly, if events in the world had little kinship to one another, jumped into existence underived, and were spanned by no tropes on the scale of the images peopling that mind; for in that case impulses would be perpetually disappointed and calculations foiled. But this impossibility of predicting the future would not arise from any contradiction in that future, nor any ambiguity or incompleteness in the truth about it. It would arise from the accidental absence of tightness and regularity in the world to be discovered. In such a world inferential or intuitive knowledge of the past would be no less impossible than knowledge of the future. We might yield to the social persuasiveness of hearsay or legend; but we should be condemned to renounce all science in retrospect as well as in prophecy.

CHAPTER XI

TRUTH AND CHANCE

SPONTANEOUS oracles and prophecies which had much currency amongst the ancients have now fallen into disrepute. Life having become mechanical, anticipation has become so too. We construct artificial instruments accurately designed for their future uses, and we collect masses of statistics: yet it is extraordinary how blank our imagination is in regard to those events for the sake of which all our measures are taken. Our hands fashion the future, while our heads are full of the past. No harm ensues when the method of action is well established. A half-blind old woman may go on knitting usefully while she babbles old nonsense and vain regrets. Agriculture and trade may continue to prosper, while rival politicians take turns at the government. But in politics the most experienced men are the worst prophets, and the history of parties is a history of blunders. Here and there a genuine Hebrew prophet, like Marx, may divine and seem to direct the future, precisely in those large dramatic turns which the soul is ready for and foresees: the war of classes, which is always latent, may be stimulated into a paroxysm of mutual hatred, until only one class survives. Yet even when such is the genuine promise of the soul, machinery soon intervenes, and the course of events deviates into the unforeseen and the undesired.

When prophecy is trusted, the vital springs of prophecy necessarily feed history also, and the general theory of nature. For if oracular intuition, Classic summary and morally weighted, can predict theory of the future, it will thereby discover the prin- dominant principles ciples that have governed the past also. with inci-The whole universe in that case must have dents occurring by a moral skeleton, such as intuition can "chance". divine. Yet as this moral skeleton is far from specifying the vast detail of events, two levels of truth come to be distinguished: fundamental, generic, universal truths, such as prophets may discern; and homely, accidental truths such as every man daily comes upon. This was the classic view of the universe. Platonic ideas, the genera and species of Aristotle, the axioms of logic, the geometry of bodies, the Ten Commandments, and the decrees of Providence determined the general nature of things and their ultimate destiny: and these were called "eternal truths". But the weather and the fortune of individuals were left to "chance". The tile dropping from the roof on the passer-by had for its intelligible "nature" or function to be a part of that roof, and not to fall from it; if it fell, it fell only by "chance". And the man, going about his normal business, passed by at that moment only by "chance". These accidental conjunctions did not express the true "nature" of anything: they occurred only because different "natures" or principles sometimes collided in the same matter, so that the event was hybrid and abnormal; or, more fundamentally, "chance" appeared in the passive resistance or sluggishness of matter everywhere, blotching the execution of every ideal design.

Truth, in such a system of moralistic physics, could acquire a meaning quite different from that which I assign to the word. Instead of being descriptive of existence, the truth would be a model for

existence: it would exhibit the world purified, transfigured, reduced to its essential principles. The truth
would then paint an inspired, a flattered,
and therefore in my sense a thoroughly
false picture of reality. Yet reality, for a
prophet, demands and justifies this neglect
of what exists only by "chance"; and the
bolder idealists will ultimately deny that
the accidents and evils and appearances

(marginal note:) "Truth" conceived to explain or annul the facts rather than to describe them.

that seem to obscure that prophetic vision have
any reality at all: for having no *raison d'être*, no inner
justification for their momentary apparition, they are
illusions. They collapse and annul themselves when
questioned, and are simply false. The word truth
thus becomes a eulogistic term, as the word reality
does also. Reality will exclude, not include, appearance; and truth will not be the eternal image of all
facts and illusions whatsoever, in the order of their
existence, but rather an *explanation* of existence, a
solution of the puzzle, an awakening from the night-
mare, so that all illusions may be dispelled and may
cease to distract the spirit.

A modern critic would at once perceive that what,
according to classic philosophy, happens by "chance",
gives us the key to all natural causation. The tile
was loosened by the rain, or some other physical
agency; and the man passed by at that moment,
because minor incidents in that day's life had combined to bring him there. That he could not have
prophesied that conjunction merely by proclaiming
his guiding impulses, or by defining the proper function of tiles, only proves that moral impulses and
functions are not primary causes, but tropes sustained
by the organization of animals or arts, which are a
part of nature; and that this animal or technical
organization remains in constant action and reaction
with the mechanical order of nature at large. Any

prophecy founded on passion is therefore extremely loose and precarious: it can foresee at best that single strain in the future which will prolong the prophet's present impulses and powers. Accurate prophecy is possible only where the laws of matter have been studied, and the conjunction of various agencies in the future can be calculated. Amongst these agencies the organized powers and arts of man will be numbered; but circumstances must be reckoned with. The issue will always be partly determined by what the moralist calls "chance"; and the exact conjunction of particular "natures" and particular "chances" might be foretold by a science that had access to all the circumstances.

In regard to "eternal truths", a modern critic, if imperfectly critical, might be inclined merely to substitute natural laws or mathematical logic for the intuitive principles proclaimed by the prophets; but in so doing he would confuse, as the prophets do, the intrinsic eternity of all truth with the length of time during which a particular fact, or a particular trope, may prevail in nature. An "eternal truth" would then mean an everlasting fact; but as the everlastingness of any fact can only be presumed, and as the future or the unknown past might well belie that presumption, "eternal truths" would become presumptive also, and mere articles of faith. Such, indeed, these logical pillars of the universe appear to be when we consider them critically: notions in origin, postulates in function, abstractions in character, and probably not truths at all.

The demands of sanity, though not of logic, were satisfied by this classical philosophy. The nature of things and "eternal truths" determined the future as well as the past, but only within limits. The outlines were fixed, rational, and predictable; but the detail was due to "chance", and there was no knowing how it would befall. Therefore Aristotle and

But what the future will be is predictable only if we admit mechanism or Providence.

his pagan followers could deny the truth of propositions about the future: human predictions of chance events were superstitious, whilst the divine mind possessed only general ideas and was sublimely ignorant of all accidents, whether future or past. On the other hand, no pervasive mechanical laws were admitted by which many of these accidents, or all of them in theory, might be calculated backwards and forwards, in contempt of moralistic categories. Yet this possibility, well known to the ancient atomists, was destined to prove fertile in modern science, and to seem the key to nature; while the intense personal religion of the monotheists demanded a God who should be the sole creator and ruler of the world, and the searcher of all hearts, to their most secret depths. A God who did not foresee the consequences of his acts would be a blind natural force; and one who exercised only an involuntary influence, and thought of nothing but his own thinking, would be too evidently a cold figment of logic. Monotheism thus introduced into the popular mind, in an inevitably mythical form, the radical notions of matter and of truth. Divine omnipotence stood for matter, or the universal dynamic agency in the world; and divine omniscience stood for the truth, eternal and comprehensive.

In being personified, however, these ontological principles were united incongruously, and the notion of truth in particular came to be entangled in artificial difficulties. The truth is not a power, only a description of the works of power, be they what they will. The truth about the future does not therefore compel the future to be what it will be, but on the contrary, the character of that future, due to no matter what causes, or perhaps quite causeless, compels the truth about it to be what that truth eternally is. This was often perceived by theologians in the controversies concerning freedom and necessity. Divine foreknowledge did not influence what it foresaw; but this consideration, though just, was futile, because the omnipotence of God, combined with his foreknowledge, did after all render him responsible for everything foreseen. If we drop the mythical element and consider truth and power in their respective essences, this complication disappears. Truth is absolutely passive, following all the contingent meanderings of existence; and whether these are spanned by large or by small tropes, or rebellious to all measure, is a question of fact for which existence itself must supply the answer. This answer will be the truth.

CHAPTER XII

LOVE AND HATRED OF TRUTH

THE love of truth is often mentioned, the hatred of truth hardly ever, yet the latter is the commoner.

Truth naturally hated rather than loved. People say they love the truth when they pursue it, and they pursue it when unknown: not therefore because of any felt affinity to it in their souls, but probably because they need information for practical purposes, or to solve some conventional riddle. Where known, on the contrary, truth is almost always dismissed or disguised, because the aspect of it is hateful. And this apart from any devilish perversity in the natural man, or accidental vices that may fear the light. On the contrary, the cause is rather the natural man's innocence and courage in thinking himself the measure of all things. Life imposes selfish interests and subjective views on every inhabitant of earth: and in hugging these interests and these views the man hugs what he initially assumes to be the truth and the right. So that aversion from the real truth, a sort of antecedent hatred of it as contrary to presumption, is interwoven into the very fabric of thought.

Images and feelings do not arise without a certain vital enthusiasm in forming or affirming them. To

Sense and fancy pre-empt belief. enjoy them is in some sense to hypostasize them and set them up as models to which other images and feelings should conform. A child will protest and be inwardly wounded if a story once told him is told differently the second

508

time. His little soul has accepted that world, and needs to build upon it undisturbed. Sensation, which makes the foreground of what is called experience, is thus raised by innocent faith to the level of truth. And false these images and feelings would not be, if they provoked no assertions about further objects. They would compose the ingredients of a true biography, although perhaps, when the circumstances are considered, the biography of a dupe.

Now love is a passion, and we might expect it not to be aroused at all by intellectual objects, such as truth, or theory purporting to be true: and yet the bitterest feuds, in families and nations, often turn on the love or hatred of particular beliefs, attacked or defended for the most fantastic reasons. Both sides may perhaps say that they are fighting for the truth; but evidently it is not any circumstantial evidence that supports the claims of the opposed ideas to be veridical; nor is there often much intrinsic beauty in those ideas. The theological notion of the Trinity was little affected by that iota for which nevertheless blood flowed in the streets of Byzantium; yet the metaphysical dignity of the Virgin Mary was involved, and nobody should be suffered to question the truth of a devout image so fondly lodged in the mind.

In such a case the passion concerned is not the love of truth, but a natural joy in thinking freely, and the self-assertion of each mind against all others. If meantime any attention is paid to the truth at all, it is only indirectly, in that the ideal authority of truth is recognized, whilst, by an absurd contradiction, its verdict is dictated to it by violence. The truth is needed, but not respected, not loved but raped; and that barbarous outrage to the truth in the concrete is still a sort of homage to truth as the coveted sanction of fancy.   .

Modern philosophers seem hardly aware of the

extent to which they still reason on these principles. *Occam's Razor*, for instance, or economy as a criterion of truth, is the weapon of a monstrous self-mutilation with which British philosophy, if consistent, would soon have committed suicide.   Only if all ideas were condemned to be blind and ugly, like a secret telegraphic code, would there be a human advantage in having the fewest and the baldest ideas possible: a gain, even then, only because thinking would be a loss, a waste of energy to be reduced to the practicable minimum. As to the truth of simple rather than elaborate ideas, what evidence does nature or history afford for such a presumption?   Is nature sparing of atoms or seeds, of depths of organization and interrelation beyond the reach of human thought?   Doubtless when applied to scholastic entities, conceived as dominant elements or powers (conceived, that is, as limiting the exuberance and waste in nature), Occam's Razor might serve to clear the ground for a richer crop of ideas.   But for what ideas?   I see no lilies of the field, I see only an expanse of coal-dust.

Parsimony in thinking shows indifference to truth.

In fact, most scholastic distinctions were made in the effort to clarify the mind, and bring language nearer to the precise relations of things.   This philosophy was not experimental physics; it did not trace the movements of matter on their own plane; it studied rather the functions that things might have in the life of reason, as classic rhetoric and morals had defined that life.   Such humanism was itself a monument to self-complacency in the home mind and aversion from arctic and torrid truth; but at least in its own dimension it was diligent.   So are modern mathematics and physics, to a degree that renders them more inventive and unintelligible than any philosophy; but though many of their terms, or all, may be figments of human method, they play respectfully round the profound complexity of things; and there is more modesty and love of truth in the better men of science than in the old scholastics, in that they admit that their conventions are largely arbitrary and symbolic.

A false truth is often attributed to human ideas, even when they are not taken for physical objects or powers. Æsthetic, moral or political sentiments, for instance, because they arouse a certain enthusiasm, are proclaimed as truths; individuals and parties entrench themselves within those maxims with all the ferocity of hatred and fear: hatred and fear of the besieging reality, that would prove that no such feelings can express any objective truth, but only the life of some biological or political organism. That every organism must have its own form of life and must love and defend it, goes without saying: but why poison the inevitable conflict of possible forms by insulting your rivals, and saying they have no right to attempt to live? Courage, that in a rational being would be courteous, then borrows the blindness and useless cruelty of instinct; and the legitimate will to live usurps the authority of destiny, which determines what forms of life, at any time and place, may actually prosper. Truly great men, nobly dominant wills, appeal, indeed, to that authority of destiny which they feel working within them: and common moralizing does the same thing when, without anger or false threats, it points to the vanity of some ambitions and the miserable consequences of some vices.

Pre-rational morality asserts its intuitions in defiance of moral truth.

Plato reports the humorous saying of Socrates that dogs are philosophical because they bark at strangers, thereby showing how much they prize knowledge. Intentionally or unintentionally there is a play here upon the word knowledge. This name is given at once, and sophistically, both to familiarity and to

understanding; so that fondness for what we happen
to know and hostility towards what we happen not
to know are identified with the love of truth.

Attachment to familiar ideas shows love not of truth but of comfort.

Yet in fact they are the exact opposite. What
we and the dogs love is our safety, our
home-thoughts, our illusions and our undis-
puted confidence in habit. Undoubtedly,
in controversial moments, we defend our ideas under
the name of great and evident truths, as we defend
our worldly possessions under the name of natural
rights. In this we manifest our animal nature, like
faithful dogs, and are biologically admirable and
morally blameless. There is indeed something candid
and honest in trusting appearance and in being loyal
to convention; but to be dogged about these things
with a clear conscience is hardly possible to an intelligent man. A dull child may tell the truth without
understanding it, not in the least for the love of truth,
but simply for lack of alternatives. Had he a less
sluggish imagination he might have invented some
aimless lie. Stupidity is positivistic, and sometimes,
as in science, literal and uninterpreted reports are useful; they are trustworthy as far as they go, and allow
us to do our own thinking. For the thinking spirit,
however, literalness is simple slavery to appearance or
to convention on the level of sense; a slavery that an
intellectual coward may sometimes love. It saves him
from discovering a truth secretly felt to be inhuman.

Sensuous appearance and spontaneous language are
nevertheless far from hostile to the truth: they are
first steps in the pursuit of it. Nature takes

Fear of being deceived is again not a love of truth but of safety.

good care to discredit our young idolatries,
and drives us from one image to another,
from each thought to some alternative
thought. Not, or not often, by the force
of logic, which indeed would rather tighten
its coils about us, and enclose us in an impenetrable

cocoon of its own weaving. Conviction always abounds in its own sense, as in theology: but what breaks at last through such a charmed circle is wild nature, within and without. A thousand contrary facts, a thousand rebel emotions, drive us from our nest. We find that *there can be no peace in delusion*: and perhaps in this negative and moral guise the idea of truth first insinuates itself into the mind. No spiritual understanding, no generous interest in the truth on its own level and for its own sake: only discomfort in uncertainty, uneasiness about things hidden, and a prudent concern for the future. In positing the future and the hidden and also the past, we have already posited truth, but blindly, without distinguishing intellectually truth, which we might discover and possess, from facts extinct or unborn or incommunicable. We do not in the least care to discover or possess the truth; but we wish to be armed to face the obdurate facts; and our pride recoils from the confusion of finding ourselves mistaken. Better, then, examine everything suspiciously and form no idea, as we should buy no clothes, not likely to wear well. Hence a certain shrewdness and prudence in conceiving matters closely affecting us, each man in his own trade, each woman in her own circle; but this specialized sagacity is remote from the love of truth not only in motive but in scope. The foundation is laid in egotism, in partiality, in injustice; enormous tracts of relevant reality are wilfully ignored; and the result is some slander or some party tenet or some superstition, defended pugnaciously rather because it is preciously false than because it is presumably true. The more these self-indulgent minds fear and hate the truth, the more insistently they give the name of truth to the mask that hides it.

That fiction and convention should usurp in this manner the authority of truth—an authority which, however ideal it may be, is logically absolute—naturally arouses the ire of the critical; and it is not without

Criticism is dogma on a different level.

reason that individual investigators, reformers, and heretics feel that they are champions of the truth. They are, in fact, rebels against imposture. Yet they ordinarily have many stronger and nearer motives for their zeal than love of truth for its own sake: love of ideas, novelties, adventure, controversy, and power. Take the case where bias and ulterior motives seem most radically absent: the case of the scientific empiricist, a compass in one hand and a balance in the other. He may say he is pursuing pure truth. Yet an exact record of his experiments would hardly disclose anything more enlightening than would the sights and gossip of the street. They would be glimpses and gossip about matter, not about human affairs: and this is far from implying that the glimpses or gossip would be truer. On the contrary, it is precisely about the social world that a man's surface impressions are apt to be adequate: the object is like the medium. And indeed the scientific man is not likely to be satisfied with the bare record of his experiments, which would report the strict truth of his investigation. Instead, every experiment will suggest to him some new theory, or will seem to illustrate and confirm some old theory familiar to his mind. So fortified, he may be doubly ready to denounce the errors of his more conventional neighbours, whom he probably dislikes on other grounds, and wishes to supersede in public estimation. Nor is this always the merely inevitable admixture of different passions in a human being. The pure theory advanced is not likely in the end to be truer than the views it replaces. It is often truer in some particular; but when its tendency and oversights are considered, it very seldom increases the harmony between man and nature. Perhaps if

critical and empirical motives governed science absolutely, science would disappear. Autobiography would
replace it, with a perfect democracy of theories, as
so many idle ideas, going with different moods; and
when memory and solipsism had been criticized in
their turn, the so-called zeal for truth would end by
denying the notion of truth altogether.

That would be the second childhood of the mind.
Instead of innocent joy in appearance and in language,
as if nothing could be false, there would be But all
a collapse into idiocy, as if nothing could be dogmas
true. Vigorous critics and innovators are posit, and
far from such apathy. They strip off one honour, the
mask of truth only to substitute another, truth.
as the truer image: and they very likely join the elder
dogmatists in maintaining that in the mask they propose the likeness to the original is perfect. Not all
an honest man's zeal, be he a traditionalist or a reformer,
is arrested at the specific doctrines which he identifies
with the truth: the better part pierces that symbol and
rests in the truth itself, pure and absolute, which
wears that mask for him for the moment. So that
all is not hypocrisy in this partisan or fantastic zeal.
Within the fanatical defence of vested illusions there
may be a sacrificial respect for things beyond us,
whatever those secret realities may be; and the martyr
that on earth is ready to die for some false opinion
may be judged in heaven to have died for the truth.
The very absurdity of a tenet, or its groundlessness,
at least proves that imagination is at work, and groping
for an issue from animal darkness. At least the category of truth has been set up. Appearances, innocent
and perfectly real in themselves, have begun to be
questioned and discounted as deceptive; and this not
merely against the blank background of a posited
substance, known only as a force, but in contrast to
a possible and more adequate description of that

substance and of the manner in which it produces appearances. Intelligence has begun the pursuit of truth.

Does this pursuit ever really deserve the name of love? No doubt there must be a total and exact collocation of facts, and the universe must have a form which we call the truth of it; but why should anyone *love* that collocation, in its perhaps infinite and certainly inhuman minuteness and extent? Why should anyone desire to know what that tiresome truth may be, except for human purposes in the region and on the scale of our gross experience? We may love our pleasures, our perceptions, our dogmas; we may love safety and dominion in action, and victory in argument; but if the truth is none of these things, why should we love it?

Why should respect for truth turn into love?

There is no *reason* why we should love the truth. There is no *reason* why we should love anything. There are only causes that, according to the routine of nature, bring about the love of various things on various occasions. As a matter of fact, nature breeds life, and life is everywhere aflame with love, and with its opposite; and there is also no reason why this spiritual passion—spiritual because it engages and colours the spirit—should stop short at bodily concerns or social affairs, and should not extend to all the relations radiating from bodily life into the realms of truth and of essence. This radiation, as I call it, is in itself passive and merely formal, yet physical organization must take account of it if life is to prosper; and this tension of life towards the eventual, the distant, the past and the future is what becomes conscious and bursts into actuality in spirit. Spirit is a child of truth. Matter in any one of its moments and in any one of its atoms offers no foothold for

The forward strain or cosmic Eros in all existence becomes conscious in spirit.

consciousness: but let certain tropes and cycles be established in the movement of matter, let certain kinds of matter cohere and pulse together in an organism, and behold, consciousness has arisen. Now tropes, cycles, organisms, and pulsations, with all the laws of nature, are units proper to the realm of truth; units that bridge the flux of existence and are suspended over it, as truth and spirit also are suspended. So that in conceiving and loving the truth spirit is not indulging in any caprice; it is surveying with pleasure the soil and the broad reaches of its native country.

Nor is love too warm a term for the sense of this radical affinity. There is cosmic justification for such a passion. Love is, biologically, an emotion proper to generation: and generation, in the cosmos at large, is the same thing as genesis or flux. Love, ever since Hesiod and Empedocles, has therefore been the poetic name for the instability and fecundity of transitive existence everywhere; life passing, and passing joyfully, from each phase to the next, and from one individual to another. Yet this joyful procreation of things is also tragic, because as Lucretius says, nothing is born save by the death of something else. In loving, in breeding, and in bringing up the young we make an unconscious sacrifice of ourselves to posterity. Such is the dominance of love in the realm of matter, where progression is, as it were, horizontal, and the thing generated continues and repeats the nature of its parents. But where the transmitted form is organic, and spirit inhabits it, life and love have also a vertical direction and a synthetic power, such that in precipitating the future, the present evokes some image of the past, and some notion of the outlying realities by which the present and the future are being controlled. In other words, life, in propagating itself, has also generated knowledge, and has become aware of the truth.

This by-product or hypostasis of organic life is also tragic, like physical reproduction, and accepts death; but instead of surrendering one life for another of the same kind and on the same level, we now surmount or disregard physical life altogether, in order to define its form and consider its achievements. This consideration or definition of nature is itself a work of nature, occurring in time and requiring material organs. It therefore partakes of the joy proper to all vital functions in their perfection. The beauty of truth is loved as naturally as the beauty of women, and our ideas are cherished like our children. Enthusiasm and inspiration (which are other names of love addressed to the truth) have no less warmth and breed no less heroism than the love of home or of country.

And transcends the flux ideally by conceiving it.

Thus spirit is born and chooses its aims in sympathy with the movement of organic life, and is simply that movement become emotion and idea. For this radical reason spirit cannot be an independent power coming from nowhere to direct or accelerate animal action. We do not look about us because we love the truth, but we love the truth because we look about us. Were it merely a question of keeping alive or of controlling matter, business would actually be expedited if besides Occam's razor we used, so to speak, Occam's glasses, and reduced our visions of things to pointer-readings, releasing appropriate reactions on our part without further rhetoric. Ignorance, when not materially dangerous, simplifies the fighting mind and is an economic advantage. It renders courage absolute and disturbs no comfortable or harmless illusions. Nature, however, being spontaneous and free, with no end of time before her, despises such thrift and is initially lavish and all-consenting. Her indefinite passive fertility is com-

This movement automatically assigns intrinsic value to truth.

mitted to no antecedent prejudices or desires. She adopts her laws and types unwittingly, as they avail to establish themselves; and they leave untouched her original potentialities. They may become, indeed, positive occasions for playful complications far out-running those special terms and eluding their measure. Such a complication life seems to us to be in respect to mechanism, and consciousness in respect to life. In these cases the new fruit, while having an underivable character proper to itself, will draw all its existential sap from the tree on which it is grafted. Life requires food, warmth and air, yet is none of those things but an organization accruing to them; and spirit feeds on the life of the psyche, while establishing tangential and transcendent interests of its own. When feeling (a form of spirit evoked by organic processes in the body) becomes perception and begins to describe the objects that arouse feeling, spirit is already launched upon the pursuit of truth, an ideal reality altogether transcending the level of the psyche and of her world. When, moreover, the eye and the intellect have adequately surveyed the scene, or gathered the event observed into a dramatic unity, the organ of spirit is satisfied. It is satisfied in the very act by which a truth is discerned; so that by nature this discernment is a joy to the spirit, and the truth automatically conceived becomes an object of love for its own sake.

The vital and fundamentally physical quality of this love of truth appears clearly when it is thwarted. We see daily in young children and in impatient reformers how nothing is more hateful to a passionate being than obstruction, nothing more precious than liberty. The psyche will have her way in the first place, let the result be what it will. Indeed, the primitive horror of being stifled, of being held down and prevented

To stop short of the truth is a vital frustration.

from moving, is doubtless what lends its magic to
the word liberty: any idea of what we might do with
our liberty when we got it would have no such power.
To be checked in our natural actions before we initiate
them produces melancholy: to be checked in the middle
of them produces rage. This intolerableness of suppression extends to the movement of our thoughts.
It was in the act of spinning fine long threads of
relationship that nature first evoked spirit: that web
must not be torn, and nature demands that spirit
should think the truth. We cannot endure to be
cheated, to be deluded, even to suspect that we are
deceiving ourselves. We may be incurious about
remote truths, if our intellect is lazy; but at least we
would not stultify what intellect we have by believing
things positively false. Therefore when authority or
public opinion would hold us down to some manifest
error, however harmless and metaphysical, our impetuous souls resent the outrage. It is not the calm
truth that calls for witnesses: martyrs usually die for
some new error. It is the martyrs that cannot endure
in themselves the arrest of the heart upon thoughts
that the heart despises. No matter how tragic or
arid the truth may be, the spirit follows and loves it,
as the eye follows the light.

Automatic as the love of truth is, and internal as
is the joy of discovering and holding the truth, this
love has nothing narcissistic about it. It is
as far as possible from being joy in the lustre
or harmony of one's ideas. It is a clean,
healthy, sacrificial love. In the form of
childish curiosity it is turned from the
beginning towards alien things, engaging
the impulse to explore, to dissect, and to
dare. The element of courage, united with submission
and humility, belongs to the love of truth even in its
ultimate reaches. Truth, in spite of what Platonists

Yet the standard of truth remains external and the love of truth is a form of worship.

and poets may say, is not at all the same as beauty.
Truth does not arrange or idealize its subject-facts.
It can eliminate nothing. It can transfigure nothing,
except by merely lifting it bodily from the plane of
existence and exhibiting it, not as a present lure or
as a disaster for some native ambition, but as a comedy
or tragedy seen as a whole and liberating the spirit
that understands it. In other words, truth is a moral,
not an æsthetic good. The possession of it is not
free intuition, but knowledge necessary to a man's
moral integrity and intellectual peace.

That conventional truths, as exhibited to the senses,
or in historical narrative or scientific exposition, may
often be impressive æsthetically goes without saying:
but it is not this æsthetic quality that makes their
truth or satisfies the intellect. If truth at first enter-
tains, as falsehood does also, it very soon sobers and
rebukes. It is tragic even in comedy, since it looks
to the end of every career and every achievement.
The very movement of instinctive exploration that
discloses truth, thereby discloses also the relativity,
limits, and fugitiveness of this exploration. It shows
life under the form of eternity, which is the form of
death. Life thereby becomes an offering, a prayer,
a sacrifice offered up to the eternal; and though there
may be incense in that sacrifice, there is also blood.

Such affinity as there is between truth and beauty
has various sources. When the word truth is coloured
idealistically, to mean the types or potential The true is
perfections of things, as when we speak of akin to the
a true friend, evidently if this latent "truth" beautiful
could only be brought out and raised to means "true
actual fact, it would also realize the beautiful. to type".
Love and charity are quick to perceive the latent
perfections of the imperfect; and if we call this (perhaps
imaginary) potentiality the truth, we indeed divine the
principle of beauty also; of that beauty which the

organic impulses of nature would bring to light if they had their way and did not interfere with one another.

Even this partial chaos and mutual destruction, when we see it to be the truth, for the very reason that we are interested in the beauties destroyed, has a cathartic effect. It is sublime; and if we call the sublime a part of the beautiful, the truth, even when distressing and ugly, will be horribly beautiful to us. Both naturalism and romanticism work this vein of merciless poetry. Religion often does the same thing indirectly, and aided by myths: the heart is taught to transmute its affections, so as to make them consonant with the will of God, that is, with the truth. But here we may see the danger of forced assimilations of the true to the good or to the beautiful. False views are often called true, in order to make the truth more consoling; and on the other hand moral and æsthetic values are often distorted by being torn from their roots in an animal soil and stretched on a rack of cosmic dimensions. The starry spaces bring us face to face with depths of reality hidden by the light of day: we find that spectacle beautiful, and sublime in its inhumanity; and the better part of our humanity then seems to be our capacity to rise above ourselves. But it is in fact one part of us that here eludes or rebukes another part. Nature is necessarily full of beauties, since our faculties of perception and sympathy would not subsist if they were not adapted to the facts of nature; and the truth is necessarily satisfying, for the same reason. Yet nature is also full of ugly, cruel and horrible things, and the truth in many ways is desolating: because our nature, though sufficiently harmonious with the universe to exist within it, is nevertheless finite and specific, with essential interests which nature

Also when the beautiful turns to the sublime or over-whelming.

and truth at large cannot but disregard.   The truth, then, is often, in many ways, interesting, beautiful and sublime: but it is not identical with beauty either in quality or extension or status.

Undoubtedly, in their different ways, truth and beauty are both liberating; and when mystics identify them it may be because they are exalted by both above the travail of existence.   In the case of beauty this deliverance is spontaneous and innocent: the spirit takes wing at birth, and flutters from flower to flower, without suspecting that any other fate awaits it.   But the deliverance that comes through the truth comes through sorrow: it is redemption by the cross.   The more inhuman the truth turns out to be, the more dismal or cruel, so much greater is the self-conquest involved in facing it, in casting away false hopes, and entrenching ourselves impregnably in our insignificance.   The very act of recognizing our insignificance, if sincere and not a mask for new claims, removes the sting of that insignificance.   There is even something sadistic in the pleasure with which certain religious minds gloat on their own misery, as if they could never trample enough on their bleeding hearts or dance enough on their graves.   But there is no occasion to exaggerate.   To be finite is not a sin, to be ignorant is not a disgrace: the pleasures of illusion and those of disillusion are equally human.   Pure insight into truth surmounts human bias in both directions impartially, without in the least hating or condemning the life that involves such bias; for to hate or condemn finitude is as finite as to cling to any particular form of finitude with an absolute fury.   Intuition is liberating on every level, in each case defining the proper and adequate object of the faculty concerned.   In sensation, intuition liberates some essence from the obscurity and tangle of fact; from passion it liberates

Also in freeing the spirit from private entanglements.

eloquence, poetry and beauty; from the known world it liberates truth. The operation of each faculty, so perfected, turns into clear joy. To take the full measure of anything, especially of anything living, establishes (quite apart from practical advantages) a spiritual dominion over that thing. You have seen it, you have seen through it, you have seen round it. It no longer can hold you to any weak or unmerited regard. It no longer can torture you with a useless hatred. Moreover, in partly lifting your ignorance, the truth has liberated you from avidity for knowledge. Fortune can never unveil to you more than a part of the truth: such part as is important for you and as you can digest. This part, seen under the form of eternity, can then cease to be external to you; it can become a term and familiar rhythm in your own life. And this part of your life, being absorbed in pure intuition, will no longer seem consciously yours, nor concerned with your personal fortunes. It will be a light revealing the truth to you, and will be lost in the eternity of that which it knows.

Nevertheless, in the dead season of the mind, when every generous faculty is paralysed, it may become incredible that an immaterial reality, or material unreality, like the truth should ever be prized or even conceived. This doubt or denial is incidental to intellectual decay; but that fact does not count from the point of view of the decadence. We must therefore examine the position from within, in its subjective origin and logic.

CHAPTER XIII

DENIALS OF TRUTH

PILATE'S question, *What is truth?* might be asked with varying intentions. It might be a sincere enquiry, assuming that the word truth stood for something assignable, and asking what that thing exactly was. A sincere answer might then be forthcoming, such for instance as is contained in this book. Very likely, however, the original demand would not have concerned so abstract a subject as the ontological nature of truth, considered as a logical category. The question would rather have touched what might be true in the concrete, in some such matter as religion or scientific theory; and then an adequate answer would be wellnigh endless, involving all conventional human knowledge.

The nature of truth in the abstract and in the concrete is largely ascertainable.

Pilate, however, and those who have repeated his question were probably not desirous of learning anything. Their question was merely an exclamation of impatience, uttered in mockery or bravado, or perhaps in despair. If the sentiment were despair, it might be as honest as the innocent desire to know: in both cases we should be assuming the definite reality of the truth, in the one case by looking for it hopefully, and in the other case by thinking of it so grandly and placing it at so great a remove that the hope of ever possessing it would seem to us chimerical. Yet this honest kind of despair could only be momentary, and occasioned

Despair about it a passing mood.

by some inordinate ambition to know all truth or to know the most comprehensive truths infallibly: something not consonant with the nature and station of man. Disappointment there, though sharp, would soon yield to contentment with such knowledge as is natural to us, and humanly interesting. Truth near home, in many a detail, is continually revealed to us; we cannot open a door or receive the answer to a letter without finding verified sundry assumptions made currently by instinct, and being assured that, in some sense, they were true. Amongst these familiar truths any educated man will place the elements of geography, biology, and history: and these, if his mind is open and unprejudiced, will suffice to show him the place of man in nature, the character of his organs of sense, and the images formed by these organs, together with the general history of human opinion. In view of these facts he would become aware that all human *knowledge* of truth, by virtue of its seat and function, must be relative and subjectively coloured. It expresses the sensations and expectations of a specific animal. It is therefore vastly different both in extent and in texture from the literal and complete truth about the universe.

This relativism no doubt shocks and humbles the spontaneously poetic mind. Spirit is initially addressed to omniscience, as it is to perfect freedom and happiness, and even to absolute power. These sweeping ambitions are involved in the synthetic character of spirit, in its moral warmth and in its cognitive transcendence, in idea, over remote times and places; also in its inevitable isolation or egotism: and the same ambitions are encouraged by the real æsthetic and dialectical fertility of mind, when once an organism has flowered into consciousness, and begun to dream. To find itself harnessed to facts that it cannot control, to find

Primitive dogmatism must be renounced.

itself helpless and mistaken, is therefore a hard lesson for the spirit. But this chastening is not fatal; on the contrary, it is positively enlightening and steadying. Not only does appropriate knowledge, in picturesque and infinite vistas, remain open, but spirit can now bring order into its own house, and consecrate itself to its essential vocation without being distracted by vain hopes.

Far, however, from denying or doubting the being of truth, such relativism as to knowledge doubly asserts it. On the one hand, it presupposes much true information about nature and human life; because criticism, even if we call it scepticism, is founded on knowledge. On the other hand, the reality of an unknown truth beyond the human sphere is thereby asserted emphatically and even pathetically: we should not need to beweep our ignorance if there were nothing to know. The post-religious agnosticism widespread in the nineteenth century was suffering from the vacuum left by a lost faith in revelation: in pottering about amongst appearances, and talking about science and progress, it felt secretly empty and bereaved. The truth, which had seemed to shine so warm and near upon a former age, had receded to an infinite distance and been eclipsed for ever. The agnostics often felt some tenderness for their lost illusions: and what they smiled at bitterly, and regarded as inexcusable, was rather the impudence of lay philosophers who ventured to proclaim the absolute truth of their toy systems. That was a double insult to the wise and the sorrowful: it ignored the depths of nature about us; it ignored also the depths of imagination and religion within us, by which the old faith had been inspired. As belief in the reality of material objects is never more acute than in the dark, when we are groping cautiously and intently amongst them, so the reality of overarching

Criticism of knowledge doubly reaffirms the reality of truth.

truth was never more painfully acknowledged than by these agnostics, conscious of not being able to define its form.

Luckily, honest agonies are brief. We become callous to ignorance, as we do to poverty, danger, or solitude: and presently a new healthy equilibrium is established in the mind. Custom and necessity carry us bodily along in conventional speech and action; we live with our images and metaphors without prying too closely into their credentials, as we live with our friends. And if in speculative moments misgivings overtake us, either we deliberately cover our heads with the hood of resignation, or perhaps we are visited by some sudden revelation and conspire with ourselves to trust it. In either case, whether by abstinence or divination, we join mankind in positing a comprehensive and inviolate truth hanging above us, and making our falsehoods false and our truths true.

In Pilate's question, however, we may detect a subtler and more insidious suggestion. He feels he has hold of nothing, and he mocks reality. Mockery is a means of restoring our self-respect by universalizing our own hollowness. As if he said: *Did I ever trouble about truth? No. Then why are these fools talking about it? The truth is that there is no truth.*

Self-contradiction could not be franker. Evidently to deny the truth is to make an assertion, and thereby to allege that there is a truth. Yet a formal refutation of this sort remains rather puerile. It would ignore the depth of irritation and animal courage in that self-contradiction, the scorn of words, the reversion to primitive slumber. Even on the rational level, the verbal contradiction may be easily removed by a *distinguo* which is itself necessary and important. In saying, "The truth is that there is no truth", we use

The real challenge to truth lies in blind impulse.

That which is denied and may be absent is not truth but knowledge of truth.

the word truth in two different senses. In the first clause "truth" means the truth; in the second clause it means *knowledge* of the truth. Now the truth might well be that there were no true human opinions or criteria of certainty: and although a Cretan may not properly say that all Cretans are always liars, a laughing god might say so with perfect consistency. In fact the truth has a superhuman status: so that an absence of true opinions or criteria would not in the least abolish it. Moreover, spirit, which also is human only by accident and may forget its physical seat, can readily conceive an experience that should be inwardly irrelevant to truth altogether, so that within that experience there should be no problems, no alleged true opinions, and no category of truth or of error. It would suffice that such an experience should remain æsthetic and should never posit any removed object, even any removed part of itself. Music, for instance, is in this case: and if certain philosophies, like fine arts, aspire to the condition of music, they actually aspire not indeed to deny but to forget the truth. Of course the most irresponsible dance of feelings and images would be shadowed in all its convolutions by the truth about it, as any existence is inevitably shadowed; but it need not see its own shadow; it need never stop to consider the truth about itself. If the word truth fell somehow from outside into those buzzing ears, the retort might come from within with perfect sincerity: *There is no truth.*

Such, I think, would be the only radical and wholly honest denial of truth: an avowal that, in one's own mind, the notion of truth was absent and needless. Great multitudes of animals would doubtless say so, if they could speak. But in human philosophy the denial of truth is something late and artificial, a contorted, confused, and villainous effort to squirm away from

Background of opportunism in belief.

one's intellectual conscience. In a compact society, where all the world is of one opinion, the worldling will be cocksure of the truth; but when society is loose and decadent, why should he commit himself to any one of a thousand conflicting, exacting, and narrowing systems? To choose rationally he would need to dig down to first principles: but to what first principles? He is probably decayed himself at the core, and can find no first principles there. His obvious course is then to choose at each turn whatever views may be convenient, and to proclaim that there is no truth.

Civilizations are often partly rotten before they are ripe; so that chronologically there may be no great interval between the sophists who deny the being of truth and the philosophers who endeavour to piece the truth together or to defend it, as it may have inspired an earlier age. Thus in Greece the chief Sophists were hardly later than the chief naturalists and law-givers, and earlier than Socrates, Plato, and Aristotle.

In respect to truth the two famous sayings reported of Protagoras suffice to set the essential problem. The maxims "Man," he said, "is the measure of all things, of Prota- of that which is, that it is, and that which goras. is not, that it is not." And he also said, "True is what appears to each man at each moment." I am not concerned with the historical question, vain and insoluble in itself, as to what may have been the exact connotation of these phrases in their author's mind. I take them as public property, to be turned to the best uses of which they are still capable. The first maxim will serve admirably for the first principle of humanism. Humanism begins in the moral sphere, with the perception that every man's nature is, for him, the arbiter of values. So far, this view merely universalizes the Gospel text that the Sabbath was made for man and not man for the Sabbath. From such moral enlightenment, however, we may easily slip into equivocations that will land us in moral chaos. In saying that a man's *nature* is, for him, the arbiter of values, we may understand that nothing is good or bad but *thinking* makes it so. We shall then have confused what a man is with what he thinks he is, and identified his interests with his wishes. Under cover of freedom to be ourselves we shall be denying that we have any true nature; and under cover of asserting our native rights we shall be denying that we have any ultimate interests. Humanism, so understood, will have disintegrated humanity, declared all passions equally good and proclaimed moral anarchy.

These equivocations may extend beyond the sphere of morals and may end in identifying all reality with consciousness. The first maxim of Prota- *Moral* goras, that *man* is the criterion, will have *anarchy* become equivalent to his second maxim, *extended to the* that the criterion is the present *moment*. *intellect.* Yet even in regard to the present moment there is a serious ambiguity. The word which I have translated by "appears," δοκεῖ, might rather mean "seems true", or "is thought to be true". If we took this second meaning seriously, far from denying the being of truth we should be regarding truth as omnipresent, and revealed by every thought or perception. In other words, we should be asserting that consciousness is never a passive feeling but always cognitive, capable of entertaining no appearance without regarding it as a description, and thinking it true. This may well be the case in action, when consciousness is on the wing and carried by animal faith to intend what is not given: but to make this self-transcendence universal would be the extreme of intellectualism, something impossible to attribute to Protagoras or to his modern emulators. Moreover, if all consciousness were cognitive, it could hardly be regarded as always veridical; and this claim to infallibility is only a playful or sarcastic way of saying that no opinion is true in a significant sense, because no moment of consciousness can have a removed object but must necessarily regard only the image or idea then present to the mind.   For this reason I have rendered the term used by Protagoras by "appears" rather than by "seems true" or "is thought to be true"; because the ultimate position can hardly be other than this: that when that which appears is thought true the appearance becomes an illusion; and that this appearance is true only in the sense that it verily appears: in which sense all appearances are true equally.

The Greek Sophists were great men of the world addressing little men of the world: they could not be

This denial of truth assumes the truth of psycho-logism.

expected to push scepticism into the sphere of common sense; its use was merely to discredit speculation and authority.   The Greeks in general were given to speech-making before the crowd.   They might cast ridicule on all reported knowledge, and raise a laugh: they could hardly expect to carry their audience with them, if they denied the existence of that audience, or the intimate shrewd ratiocinations of each man in the crowd, hugging his own thoughts and his own interests.   Therefore the unchallenged and unexpressed presuppositions of all criticism in this school must be the existence of conventional human society and the intelligent egoism of each of its members.   All else in heaven and earth might be challenged with applause, if reduced to these comfortable and convincing terms.

Was the being of truth, then, denied by the Sophists, or could they deny it?   Yes, if we think only

Personal pride hid this from the ancients.

of the truth as proclaimed by particular opinions.   All things *said* to be true might be false.   Whatsoever depended on argument might be challenged by an opposed cleverer argument; whatsoever depended on usage, faith, or preference might be reversed by a contrary pose; so that every man remained free to think and do what he liked, and to deny all authority. This, though with a different moral tone and intention, was also the position of the Sceptics. They despised opinion, and collected contradictory arguments in order to liberate the mind from every pledge and the heart from every earthly bond. These indomitable doubters stood firm as rocks in their philosophy; and even the Sophists were sure of their wisdom and knowingness in playing their chosen parts in the world. For both schools, then, there was an *unspoken truth*: namely, that life was a treacherous predicament in which they found themselves without a reason, and that they were determined, whether nobly or nimbly, to make the best of it. Their moral philosophy left the cosmos problematical, while taking for granted abundant knowledge of human affairs and human character. If that age had had a turn for introspection and autobiography, it might have erected a doctrine of the march of experience. Trust in memory, in expectation, in the mutual communication of many minds might have issued in a system like modern psychologism: the view that all we see, say, and think is false, but that the only truth is that we see, say and think it. If nothing be real except experience, nothing can be true except biography. Society must then be conceived as carried on in a literary medium, with no regard to the natural basis of society. If the ancients never hit upon such a system of biographical metaphysics, the reason doubtless was that they were too intelligent. In filling out their fragmentary natural knowledge with myths, they had originally invented other and more beautiful natural beings to help carry on the world: but when the conflict of theories had made the natural world seem problematical, they preferred to abstain from voluntary follies, and not to credit anything so fantastic as that one sight or sound or pleasure or pain might generate another in a vacuum. It mattered little how events might be generated; the point was bravely to enjoy and endure and mock them as they came. Such spiritual courage, however, is physically barren. Heroic scepticism soon withered, and officious sophistry soon found nobody to listen to it. A new image of truth was rising in the east, evoked by inspiration, frankly miraculous, and destined to be sustained and rekindled for ages only by faith.

The dominance of this imposing speculative doctrine, long identified with the truth, has caused the denial of truth in modern times to assume a special character. It has seemed to go with enlightenment, with science, with the pursuit of truth. How, indeed, should anyone pursue the truth, if he were sure he possessed it? Trust in inspiration is something retrograde: it reinstates the primitive dogmatism of the senses, but reinstates it on the imaginative plane, where the object is some speculative idea or vision of the invisible, in regard to which a clear faith is harder to maintain. Protestants had freely criticized the doctrines of the Church, but only by appealing to the infallible text of the Bible, or to some new inspired image of the truth formed in their private meditations; and each had claimed for his shade of doctrine the authority of absolute truth. In view of so many wrangling "truths", the wiser and more humorous heads could not but distrust all conclusions. Free thought became romantic. Ever to decide what you thought would be to stop thinking, and the eternal search for the truth demanded that you should never find it. But for a humanist or an empiricist a truth never to be found differs little from a nonentity. How then avoid the conviction that fruitful science and adventurous philosophy imply a denial that there is any such thing as truth?

This conviction, suggested by that chaos of inspired opinions which was the weak side of Protestantism, was fortified by what gave Protestantism its *Refuge in* strength—namely, subjective depth and sin- *romantic* cerity. When sensuous dogmatism breaks *subjectivity.* down and we discover an optical illusion, *ipso facto* we discover a scientific truth; and we clarify the contrast, inherent in all investigation, between superficial appearance and material reality. When on the contrary some illusion of the intellect is detected, or we lose faith in a revealed "truth", no other comparable conception is at hand to take the place of the discredited view. Revelation and "truth" go by the board together, and we are driven back upon immediate experience and the inner fountain of ideas. These we must continue to accept, unless we should stop living; but we accept them now only as phenomena of life in ourselves, only as a kind of intellectual music which we cannot help making, because such is the fertility of our genius or the marvellous influence upon us of we know not what cosmic climate.

Some lurid romantic cloud land, in that case, truly envelops and contains us; and though the truth might then seem chaotic to us, because not amenable to our moral or grammatical categories, it would be nevertheless precisely the truth it was, and would display all our random visions and emotions precisely in their true places and true relativity. We should then be talking nonsense when we said we denied the being of truth, this truth being avowedly, in respect to us, that we were in a plastic and ill-determined phase of intelligence, and honourably unwilling to pin our faith on any hasty dogma.

Thus as among the ancients, so among the moderns, the denial of truth is due to palpable confusions between truth and knowledge of truth, between essence and existence, between the ideal and the actual. It might

seem that matters might easily be set right by recalling a few definitions. Yet these verbal equivocations
are not merely perverse: they are incidental
to slow voluminous shifts in morals and
culture. The truth posited by animal faith,
in action or in curiosity, is posited as unknown, as something to be investigated
and discovered; and truth in this transcendent sense
can never be denied by an active mind. But when
animal faith has already expressed itself in coventional
ideas, its own further action finds those ideas obstructive. Truth has now been rashly posited as known.
An idea, an idol, has taken the place of the god originally and intrinsically invoked by the mind, and posited
as unknown. But this is a scandal: how should the
thoughts of the wisest human head coincide with the
intrinsic essence of any object or event, not to speak
of the universe in its totality? The "truth" that the
critic or heretic then denies was itself a blasphemy,
and in denying it he is secretly animated by the love
of truth. What he denies is only the existence of any
view in which truth is contained once for all and
without qualification. Even if we admit prophecy and
supernatural inspiration, the most rapt of prophets can
only signalize, adumbrate, and clothe metaphorically
the truth revealed through his lips, and not fathomed
by his own rational mind: the most explicit of creeds
is called a symbol of the faith. The relation which
any such symbol may bear to the truth is evidently a
historical accident; and the more clearly we perceive
the inevitable, all-comprehensive, eternal being of
truth, the more improbable or even impossible must
seem the notion that any human conception should
ever do it justice.

To deny the truth reported is to posit the truth unreported.

CHAPTER XIV

BEYOND TRUTH

THE temptation to deny the reality of truth does not often attack the mind. It is a suicidal temptation that comes only in moments of surfeit or despair. Commoner and less easily mastered is the temptation to adorn the truth. Indeed, this is not so much a temptation as an original sin; because the truth never appears to us naked, but clothed and masked in sensations and in language, which it takes rare courage even to wish to strip off. No doubt cowardice here, as elsewhere, is folly: for however tragic or desolating the truth may be, it will not be abolished by concealing it, and the facts will operate against us all the more fatally if we childishly insist on not admitting them. Meantime we shall have condemned ourselves to insecurity, confusion, and living with a bad conscience; and we shall have missed the knowledge to which our intellect is by nature addressed: a knowledge that, far from adding to the evils it may discover, masters these evils intellectually and partly balances them by the human and proud pleasure of understanding them.

Nevertheless, the keen air of truth is not for all lungs. The psyche vegetates before she thinks, and when she thinks, far from suspending her vegetative functions, she is merely extending and refining them into a far-reaching sensibility to external influences and probable events. This difficult adjustment has

Loyalty to the truth is wise but difficult.

537

its excitements and rewards; it fills the spirit with images and passions; yet it is a nuisance to the slumbering organism. There would be more comfort in continuing to pulsate in perfect darkness and freedom. It might be more dangerous, but it would feel safer. If shooting pains or dull obstructions disturbed sometimes that pre-natal bliss, they would serve to heighten the love of it and turn it into a positive ideal. And in fact this ideal remains the background and substance of all our later dreams of Elysium and a Golden Age, of Paradise and Nirvana. In contrast with this, intelligence and the facts discovered by intelligence belong to a world of care, of slavery to external things. The truth, for the psyche, remains always an imposition. Sometimes she bows to it sullenly, sometimes she rebels against it, and angrily maintains that her radical feelings are much more to be trusted. In her happiest moments she forgets the quarrel, and builds, with all the materials that experience has given her, a world of her own not too false to live with for a while, and not so true as to check her animal joy in living. She is an artist, and her world must have the truth and the falsity of art.

This art is not all music or verbal fiction: it is also laborious construction in the realm of matter, or in morality and legislation, imposing on the plastic parts of the world a method agreeable to human interests. Heroic men are intent on reality, but less in reverence for what reality may be, or for the truth of it, than in prophecy of what it ought to be, or may speedily be turned into by their agency. The extreme of energy curiously reverts, in respect to truth, to the extreme of primitive somnolence and vegetative egoism. Edens and millenniums reappear, not now as lost but as future. They are defined and demanded by the native force of the psyche; and such premonitions may be

Inspiration that will not conform to the truth must supersede it.

true if the psyche has the means to realize her purposes in action. She will then seem to have not only divined the truth of the future, but miraculously recreated the world in her own image. Such an apparent miracle is physically possible and normal, because the psyche is herself a current in the realm of matter, capable like any other current of cutting a channel for itself between banks that will afterwards seem to have come into being expressly to guide it on its intended course. Yet just those windings were never prefigured by the waters at the spring. Either the prophet, then, will surreptitiously take hints from his worldly wisdom, or he will be compelled to transpose his prophecy into a mere ideal, to be realized, if at all, only in another world, or only within us, that is, only by being steadfastly maintained as an ideal in contrast to the unfortunate truth.

When a man frames a Utopia, and calls it by that name, he frankly avows the rebellion of his inner man against the concrete truth; yet if the roots Truth sought of that vision are very deep in his soul, or in the wrong if the vision is contagious and people confirm place. one another in entertaining it, it will not long be called a Utopia but soon a higher truth, revealed miraculously and accredited by supernatural faith. To extend the word truth to such a region puts a great strain on language and on honesty. A sad waste of spiritual passion comes of looking for truth where, by the nature of things, truth is not to be found: in images, in metaphors, in religion, in moral emotion. These things, excellent or inevitable in their own sphere, are rendered inordinate by that pretension: instead of being poetically beautiful and just, they become scientifically false and morally fanatical. A better language would have invented a word other than truth to express the magic of these visitations. The Greeks hardly asked whether their religion was true, or how far their legends about antiquity might be historical. That would have been a blind and pedantic question. They asked only that their religion should be traditional and legal, propitious to the spirit of the city and to the purgation of private crimes: which myth and worship might well be, without the mechanism of such beneficence being in the least understood. Myths were not true and were not false: they were tales appropriate to tell and to marvel at on specific occasions. They dramatized the true relations of man to nature, reconciling him to the truth without picturing the truth; and by their medicinal influence they rendered his ignorance happy, in the assurance that the truth, if not always friendly to the grosser man, might be liberating in the end to the spirit.

The truth is the chosen object, and therefore the good, of the intellect: of so much of our nature as demands enlightenment and is concerned with circumstances or with the past and future course of existence. But these are not our only interests, and the truth is neither our primary good, nor our ultimate good, nor the synthesis of all goods. By its inclemency, the truth often drives us indoors, to our home comforts and familiar affections; and by its precision and contingency—for many things are not true—it also carries us willingly or unwillingly beyond the truth, into the region of the imagined or the desired or the beautiful. Genius is requisite to divine the truth, but not all kinds of genius take that direction; and a steady affinity to truth, the whole truth, and nothing but the truth, while eminently virtuous and honourable, marks rather a prosaic mind, a cold mind, a mind limited to the safe middle ground of competence and sagacity. Happiness in the truth is like happiness in marriage, fruitful, lasting, and ironical. You could not have chosen better, yet this is not what you dreamt of.

Of spiritual goods it is the most external.

Enthusiasts are consequently seldom satisfied with the truth; they posit something else, much better, warmer, and vaguer. Yet it would chill their enthusiasm to posit this nobler thing as not true, as merely possible or frankly impossible. They have far too dazzling an idea of the truth to recognize the plain truth *That which mystics call truth is something beyond truth.* when they see it: they keep that sacred name for the good, for the all-satisfying, for the ineffable. The consequence is that we have in religion and in idealistic philosophy a baffling reversal of terms: the existent is called appearance, illusion, or privation, whilst something imaginary or notional, or perhaps absolutely blank, is called both reality and truth. That this mystical ultimate good is something in which life issues, or may issue; that it is immediately experienced in moments of ecstasy; that it seems, when found, the sudden solution and quietus for every trouble; all this may be freely admitted by a sober critic; and he will have no serious difficulty in making room for these experiences in his picture of the truth, which should be a description of all existence. Love has a rhetorical habit of heaping all eulogistic terms on one object, no matter how incompatible these terms may be; and in impassioned speculation it is impossible for the most irresponsible intuitions, coming in a trance, not to claim to be called true, although they may annul rather than describe the detail of the world. In reality, the mystic is passing beyond truth. Truth oppresses him, and something beneath or above truth satisfies him completely. He is free to choose; yet however much he may congratulate himself on his flight from existence and from the truth that describes existence, the most that he could legitimately say about his new condition would be that it revealed to him a further region of truth and existence, far superior in his estimation to the region he had abandoned.

The very fact of his salvation would continue to posit the reality of those sins or illusions from which he had been saved: and the truth recognized by him would not be, as he may assert thoughtlessly, *only* his final beatific vision, but this following upon and substituted for his previous experience. If having attained what he calls the truth he shut his eyes to the existence of his previous errors, he would now be hugging the most egregious and egotistical error of all. Not only would he be insisting that a form of being was "true" which perhaps was merely intense and described nothing, but he would be positively denying that this form of being and its relation to all other describable things might be described truly.

Perhaps the fault here touches diction and manners rather than insight. There is insight in saying that existence is privation, since any fact, in being such as it is, prevents itself, and the truth about it, from being all that is different. But only a perverse temper would express this by saying that privation was nothing, and that consequently neither suffering, error, nor finitude could at all exist. We might rather say (though this too is hyperbole) that only privation and finitude, involving suffering and error, made existence possible. But finitude does not involve error, if we assert no more than we know; and privation is not suffering if we are willing to be ourselves.

A less mystical religious way of going beyond truth is to personify it. The truth is not a person: it is not a mind; yet for other reasons we may *The notion* have conceived a vigilant lawgiver and judge, *of an* who will ultimately punish our hidden sins *omniscient* or vindicate our innocence: and evidently *mind per-* such a deity must see in secret, and must *sonifies truth* such a deity must see in secret, and must *poetically.* be omniscient. The truth, in all its detail, scope, and eternity, will then lie open to this divine mind: and if we forget for the moment the other attributes of God, such as power and love, we may say that God not only knows the truth but *is* the truth existing in act. The trick of identifying, or not yet distinguishing, intuition and essence, runs through the history of speculation and breeds a thousand misunderstandings. In this case it would be easy to show that intelligence, though it might eventually traverse all truth in every direction, would in each act of thought be something temporal, progressive, and selective, since it is the utterance of a proposition; so that intelligence moves in another realm of being from truth, intelligence being alive and truth being dead. To represent the truth as living, as the light of universal intuition flooding a divine mind, dramatizes the truth and puts it before us as something to be achieved and possessed. This may pass for a compliment to the truth, and may facilitate an excited love of it. The business of a good myth is precisely to humanize the realities which it plays upon and to render them more amiable. Truth turned into the thought of an omniscient mind is enormously glorified, at least in human eyes; yet this living splendour is not its own. Truth proper is indifferent to being praised or possessed by anybody: its sublimity is of another kind; and a love stimulated by the hope of glory is addressed to dreams of human achievement rather than to a truly divine truth.

The impulse to dramatize the truth is carried further in romantic philosophy. Even when personified, the truth remains too external, too chilling and ominous, for a solipsistic poet, proud of his every mood, and sure only of his present sensation. An endless comedy of vital errors seems to him worthier of a living spirit than a sardonic omniscience. The very notion of truth, though he cannot banish it altogether, becomes elusive and ghostly. Why should a free and unconditioned mind posit a truth at all? Or if the

Romantic impatience of truth cannot abolish truth.

exigencies of acting and thinking compel a man to posit something, why not posit it, why not posit his whole world, as expressly false, like an actor positing the circumstances set down for him in a play? The truth he posits will be a part of his fiction: it will not pledge or contaminate his creative freedom: and he may say in his heart that he has passed beyond truth.

We have already seen that a perfectly happy creature, one free from hindrance and care, might develop a great sensibility without broaching the idea of truth. A Lucifer might convince himself on internal evidence that he was an uncreated spirit, free to invent romantic societies and gay sciences for his endless entertainment. These he would posit beyond truth, that is, as revealing no compulsion and imposing no responsibility. Lucifer might believe in nothing so long as he did nothing. Ideas, when they are mere ideas, leave us as free and as ignorant as if we had never had them. If a spirit could actually exist *in vacuo*, it might harmlessly posit world after world, positing them as false, or as existing merely in idea. Truth would then not be conceived or invoked at all, yet it would not be annulled. It would hover above the dreaming idealist as ironically as ever; since it would be composed of his whole history, past and future, with his successive fictions *ad infinitum*: something surely unknown to him, being entirely different from any of the worlds which, at various moments, he might have (quite truly) posited as false. Had he ever paused to collect his thoughts and review his illusions, he would at that moment have posited his biography not as false but as true: for he would not now conceive himself to be composing an imaginary biography, a novel about himself, but would be convinced that he had really dreamt all those dreams; and if his whole past and whole future could thus be summoned before his conscience, and he saw the whole truth about himself, I am afraid he would *ipso facto* have stopped living, ceased to posit obviously false sciences and imaginary lives, and felt the truth absorb and paralyse his playful spirit.

For mankind, compelled as we are by our animal status to do and to undergo many specific things, the face of truth is more familiar and less be- Active life numbing. We are obliged to believe in reveals the postulates we make, and we are obliged relevant to make them because they are true. Faith confirms it. and truth are thus allied for us from the beginning. A postulate relevant to action is relevant to reality; and where it is action that prompts and controls thought, thought cannot be merely romantic or poetical. It will be initially addressed to immediate and urgent facts; and it will follow the true course and relations of these facts with a rough fidelity. Truth is thus a household presence: not the naked truth nor the divine truth, but truth disguised as a domestic and dressed in homespun. Not to recognize such conventional truths in the home orbit would be idiocy, and to contradict them would be madness.

Yet the same natural life that relies on truth, and is sure of it within this range, inevitably transgresses and overloads the truth which it recognizes. Moral life From childhood up we are carried beyond transcends it. the truth by our passions, by the qualities and perspectives of our senses, by verbal conventions and beliefs, above all by our vehement judgments about good and evil. There is a sense in which all moral life lies beyond truth. Not, of course, that for an external observer, the whole course of our passionate feelings would not fall within the purview of history and be truly describable; but the living spirit, in which this moral life is actualized and enacted, has other interests besides the interest in truth. The modesty of nature calls for a halt in the direction of knowledge, as in all other directions, not only respecting the depth to which we may penetrate the facts, but also respecting the purity and clearness we may claim for our conceptions.

It would be inhuman and fanatical to set up the truth as the only good. The good is the perfection of life for each creature according to its kind; a perfection which man can never reach without knowledge of his immediate circumstances and his own nature. Potentially, spirit has an innate affinity to all truth, and even to all essence; and this, like all other spiritual interests, is disinterestedly addressed to its ideal object, and terminates there. Yet here spirit is lodged in a specific creature, so that the development of these potential interests can be only partial and mutually qualified. Even charity, a disinterested sympathy with spirit in its every predicament, cannot be impartial in all directions and at all removes. Absolutely universal and unbiassed charity would abet contrary impulses and would utterly dissolve the too sympathetic soul. Truth cannot dictate to love. Will and aspiration move entirely beyond the actual, and forbid the human spirit to attune itself to truth only. Nearer things and lovelier things also solicit us. We must turn to them; yet not without a constant speculative reverence for the truth in its divine immensity.

Yet spirit may outrun truth without contradicting it.

THE REALM OF SPIRIT

Ὁ Ἔρως ὑλικός τίς ἐστι, καὶ δαίμων οὗτός ἐστιν ἐκ ψυχῆς. καθ' ὅσον ἐλλείπει τῷ ἀγαθῷ, ἐφίεται δέ, γεγενημένος·

(Love has something material about it, and this spirit is generated out of the psyche in the measure in which she lacks the good, yet yearns after it.)

PLOTINUS, III, 5, 9.

He who knows Brahma advances towards Brahma everywhere. He comes to the lake of enemies; he crosses it by his mind. When they that know only the present come to that lake, they are drowned. . . . As one driving swiftly in a chariot looks down on the two wheels revolving, so he too looks down on day and night, on good deeds and evil deeds and on all the pairs of contraries. Free from good deeds, free from evil deeds, knowing Brahma, he advances towards Brahma.

Kaushitaki-Brahmana-Upanishad, I, 4.

Si mens, dum res non existentes ut sibi praesentes imaginatur, simul sciret, res illas revera non existere, hanc sane imaginandi potentiam virtuti suae naturae, non vitio, tribueret; praesertim si haec imaginandi facultas a sola sua natura penderet, hoc est, si haec mentis imaginandi facultas libera esset.

(If the mind, while calling up non-existent things in imagination, were simultaneously aware that those things did not really exist, it would surely attribute this its power of imagining to a virtue, not to a vice, in its nature; especially if this power of imagining were due solely to the nature of mind, that is, if this imaginative power in the mind were free.)

SPINOZA, *Ethics*, Part II, Prop. XVII, Scholium.

Am farbigen Abglanz haben wir das Leben.
(Light, coloured in refraction, makes our life.)

GOETHE, *Faust*, Part II, Act I, Scene 1.

PREFACE

THE title of this book may tempt some unwary reader with the hope of tidings from a Spirit-World. Such is not my subject. Although not perhaps without a certain affinity to poets and mystics, I am intellectually a convinced materialist; and the singularity of my book is perhaps this, that it traces in spiritual things only their spiritual quality, whilst planting them, as far as their existence is concerned, unequivocally on natural ground, and showing how they spring out of it.

The realm here to be described is therefore not another world, nor even a hidden metaphysical agency alleged to animate the whole universe, or to create it. What I call spirit is only that inner light of actuality or attention which floods all life as men actually live it on earth. It is roughly the same thing as feeling or thought; it might be called consciousness; it might be identified with the *pensée* or *cogitatio* of Descartes and Spinoza. Yet there is an important circumstance that leads me to prefer the term spirit. In modern philosophy the notion of mind has become confused and treacherous, so that in whatever direction we press it into consistency, mind ceases to be mind. Pushed inwards, it may be reduced to a vanishing ego, the grammatical counterpart, impersonal and empty, of all feelings and objects alike. Driven outwards, mind may be lost in its objects, and identified with the existence and movement of a phenomenal world or the history of events. Again, mind may be conceived dynamically, called will or life, and turned into a magic law or impulsion supposed to compel things to

549

become what they are. And it may be conceived analytically and dissolved into a multitude—nowhere assembled—of separate data, or a series of feelings each feeling itself, and none feeling any other. Or instead of data, which after all are thinkable and given, mind may be dissolved into a diffused unconscious substance still paradoxically called feeling, out of which organic bodies and centres of apprehension might be composed. Yet all these results are abdications, and living mind is none of those things. It is a moral stress of varying scope and intensity, full of will and selectiveness, arising in animal bodies, and raising their private vicissitudes into a moral experience. This inner light is indeed requisite for focussing impressions and rendering them mentally present, but it is biologically prior to them, vital and central, a product of combustion, a leaping flame, a fountain and seat of judgment. I therefore call it spirit; not that I think it either a substance or a physical power, or capable of existing by itself, but that it is a personal and moral focus of life, where the perspectives of nature are reversed as in a mirror and attached to the fortunes of the single soul.

My subject is not experience surveyed impartially, as in a book of descriptive psychology, but experience viewed at a certain angle, in the measure in which it torments or educates the spirit. Nor is my subject the whole of moral philosophy or the life of reason; for there all forms of health and government would need to be appreciated, many of which might be, and might be content to remain, purely spontaneous and worldly. Without in the least quarrelling with nature, spirit is in its interests somewhat withdrawn from nature, as are painting and music and history; the very study of nature questioning nature and even in loving and praising nature loving and praising it only for being friendly to the spirit.

A study of the realm of spirit is therefore an exercise in self-knowledge, an effort on the part of spirit to clarify and to discipline itself. Not so much that a new province is added to moral life (although this happens sometimes in religion, poetry, and music, or even in mathematics) as that the common world takes on a new colour, is focussed in a new centre of interest, as when a man falls in love. This transformation or conversion would not be necessary if the psyche and the world moved in perfect harmony, as they do at certain happy moments in childhood and youth; but revision grows possible and urgent for the spirit as it gets more and more entangled in all the contrarieties of existence. Being always alive, and suffering more or less, spirit then becomes aware of its natural claims and interests, in contrast to the endless miscellany of events. The world turns into a school, life into a pilgrimage, and spirit itself, though it be as native to the world as laughter and tears, feels itself a surprised stranger, a monarch mockingly served, a prisoner tortured, or a lover entranced.

The spirit I speak of is thus nothing hypothetical, nothing mythical or cosmic, "whose dwelling is the light of setting suns", or that "circulates" in "the unenduring clouds", and "knows no insulated spot, no chasm, and no solitude".[1] On the contrary, actual spirit is well acquainted with solitude, with insulation, and with chasms, and this not by any accident; and it dwells, not in setting suns, but in human bodies, bodies breeding a thousand passions and diseases by which the spirit also is tormented, so that it congenitally longs at first for happiness and at last for salvation.

That no fabulous diffusion of spirit over infinite spaces could remove this predicament, in which actual spirit finds itself, is vouched for by Indian speculation. There, heavens and hells are posited *ad libitum*, and

[1] Wordsworth.

many gods with many alternative names and virtues. Yet throughout those dazzling confusing spaces, throughout those transmigrations and cataclysms, the spirit takes counsel with itself, observes everything, endures everything, by outlasting everything renounces everything, and by questioning everything liberates itself. The great thundering governing gods of popular religion are far from being the most advanced of spirits in insight or holiness. Insight and holiness may appear anywhere, in anchorite or beggar, in prince or poet, even in a child, when once the illusion of the will is pierced, and the bias of time, place, and person is overcome. All things, in their particular urgency and lure, are then reduced to vain, cruel, and lovely accidents; while the spirit itself withdraws into that infinite potentiality which is the source of its own heat and light. Seen from there our natural loves are not stultified, they remain a part of what the heart desires, but they no longer stand alone; they have counter-weights in eternity; the truth envelops them; and the joy and sorrow of existence are balanced and lost in the peace of being.

The Indians and the mystics are inspired people, and their language does not always bear critical examination. There is a paradox, for instance, in spirit seeming to turn against life and to renounce it, when in spirit life has for the first time become quite alive. But here we fall into a misunderstanding. Spirit can never condemn or undermine natural life; this can be done only by some rival centre of life at the same biological level, tending to steal away matter or energy from its ancestors or neighbours. Spirit may give warnings, it may be austere or ascetic, but it is never competitive: that would be a sure sign of non-spiritual forces at work. Spirit requires no new matter or energy besides that of its organ, but only order and harmony in the matter or energy at hand.

It is therefore charitable and sympathetic to whatever forms life may have taken elsewhere. It loves, but its love is not physical and procreative, multiplying commitments ; rather reflective and spiritual, understanding those commitments, absolving them from their mutual guiltiness, and consoling them for their vanity and ultimate dissolution. In so doing it simply fulfils its own commitment to see things as they are. Such healing intelligence destroys nothing; such charity complicates and embitters nothing; it is neither an accomplice nor an accuser of fate. Spiritual insight is possible only at the top of life; but in fulfilling life it reviews life, and in recollection raises existence into a tragic image. Though this be an image of transiency, vanity, and suffering, there is such joy in forming it, that it often seems unutterably beautiful; or the sheer scope and victory of that revelation may drown all vision in light.

Spirit then seems to have passed beyond existence: which is an ambiguous way of speaking. The detail of existence may have lapsed from view in the sheer intensity of concentrated thought; or thought and spirit with it may actually have ceased to exist, death having been ushered in not by ghastly weakness or violent pain but by a last summing up and a grand finale. That is a question of circumstances, more or less noble and pompous. The liberation of spirit that is internal and essential to spirit has nothing to do with death or with another life, but comes at any moment and pervades all times when intuition supplants convention and passion rises into self-knowledge.

The life of spirit thus has a natural movement and natural goals, which I will now endeavour to describe. But let me not be misunderstood, as if I had taken it upon me to censure everything that is not spiritual. However much a naturalist may celebrate or even share the free life of spirit, he cannot consistently

assign to it more than a relative importance. Salvation
and enlightenment may be all-important from the
spiritual point of view, but this point of view has no
absolute pre-eminence in the universe. It is comparable to our natural interest in human survival, in
science, or in some particular art like music: absolutely
legitimate interests, physically inevitable at certain
junctures, but special and morally optional in the
context of things at large. This relativity is betrayed
by a spontaneous variety and a secret contradiction
even in the ultimate oracles of spirit. Pure intellect ·
may say: *I dominate, I am not dominated.* A pure
heart may answer, *I love, I do not ask to be loved.*
Buddha may be overheard saying: *Overcome the will,
renounce preference, and you have entered Nirvana.*
Who shall gainsay these maxims, or improve upon
them? Yet this desire to cease from willing is
evidently a form of will. So are this selfless love, and
this pride in understanding. Thus the inner life of
spirit is a part of natural life, inevitable and perhaps
tragic. The contrasts we may draw between it and
life in the world can be only partial contrasts. Spirit
pursues a perfection more inward and chastened than
worldly arts and ambitions; but it would not exist or
have a possible perfection to pursue, if it were not a
natural faculty in a natural soul.

CHAPTER I

THE NATURE OF SPIRIT

EVERYTHING that exists is confined to a specific character at a particular place and time; if it escaped from those bonds it would cease to be itself. Such an escape occurs continually in the realm of matter, where everything gradually lapses into something different; and this continuous flux, with its various tempos, composes the great symphony of nature. In living substance, plasticity and fertility are a virtue: matter might say, with Shelley's cloud, *I change but I never die.* That which dies at every turn is only the negligible cloud-rack of the moment, easily replaced or even improved upon. To lament that individuals or even species should vanish would be natural only to some elegiac poet who clung to lost occasions and to remembered forms, not being ready for the next, and lagging sentimentally behind the glorious march of time, always buoyant with victory and strewn with wreckage.

Spirit shares the contingency of existence but surveys it morally.

The case is otherwise when we come to the realm of spirit, as we do in that melancholy poet. Not that spirit is less mobile or elastic than matter. In its ideal vocation, as we shall find, it is infinitely more so. Even in its existence it is as evanescent as any cloud. But the inevitable concentration of existence at each point into something specific rises in the moral world to a higher power. Individuation from being passive and imputed here becomes positive and self-assured. Spirit, in its briefest and feeblest flash, sets up a moral centre for the universe.

Contingence and partiality, in one direction, embitter spiritual life. Why should "I" (that is, spirit in me) be condemned to lodge in this particular body, with these parents and nationality and education and ridiculous fate? Why choose this grotesque centre from which to view the universe? You may say that other people exist in plenty, viewing the universe from their several positions, so that in giving this involuntary pre-eminence to myself I am perhaps not more grotesque than the average man, or even than the most intelligent. But that only makes matters worse, if isolation, partiality, error, and conceit are multiplied indefinitely, and inevitably attached to conscious existence.

In another direction, however, the imprisoned spirit escapes from its cage as no physical fact can escape. Without quitting its accidental station it can look about; it can *imagine* all sorts of things unlike itself; it can take long views over the times and spaces surrounding its temporary home, it can even view itself quizzically from the outside, as in a mirror, and laugh at the odd figure that it cuts. Intelligence is in a humorous position: confinement galls it, it rebels against contingency; yet it sees that without some accidental centre and some specific interests and specific organs, it could neither exist nor have the means of surveying anything. It had better be reconciled to incarnation, if it is at all attached to existence or even to knowledge.

This is the force of intelligence, marvellous if we try to conceive it on the analogy of material being, but perfectly natural and obvious if we look at it congruously and from within.

It is intellectual.

Spirit in each of its instances assumes a transcendental station, and looks out from there on

all the world. Wherever it is, is here; whenever it
is, is now. Yet *here* and *now*, for intelligence, are
not what they are for physical being, or for external
indication, a particular, accidental, dead position.
For intelligence *here* and *now* are movable essences,
to be found wherever spirit may wander; and they
name no particular material point, but the centre
found, at each point, for all distances and directions.
So that the bitterness of confinement is mitigated by
a continual change of prisons, and the accident of
place by the inevitable vastness of the prospect.

A consequence of this intellectual nature of spirit
marks it particularly, or even defines it in popular
philosophy. Spirit is invisible, intangible, And
unapproachable from the outside. The immaterial.
materialist might like to deny its existence; but that is
not the inclination of mankind at large. Only, being
necessarily familiar with material things, and having
shaped language and expectation in conformity with
physical happenings, people find it impossible not to
materialize the spirit of which they are vividly conscious; so that critical philosophy sometimes, in clearing
up the notion of spirit, and removing superstitious and
physical analogies, seems to have nothing left. But
that comes of being, like the primitive mind, preoccupied with matter, and disinclined to conceive spirit
in spiritual terms. This disinclination is not confined
to scoffers: religious philosophers also love to materialize
spirit, in order to make it seem more solid and important, the pure air of a truly spiritual sphere being far too
thin and cold for their lusty constitution.

Let me consider the various ways in which the
notion of spirit is apt to be materialized. The sequel
will then be less exposed to gross misunderstanding.

Spirits, in folklore, legend, and dreams, are often
ghosts; that is, they are visible but intangible spectres
of dead, absent, or supernatural persons. Such appari-

tions, for a critical psychologist, might not be physical facts, since the images have their basis in the ob-

Spirit not a ghost.

server's brain, and are falsely incorporated into outer space: an error that the waking dreamer himself discovers when he attempts to embrace a ghost and finds nothing but air. Genuine believers in the survival and return of the dead, like doubting Thomas and modern Spiritualists, require their spirits to be tangible as well as visible, to come and go and preserve a continuous physical existence, to eat and especially to talk. Their bodies may be called "spiritual", but are conceived as extracts or magical restitutions of the human body, ethereal, astral, but not immaterial. They move about in another world or in the margins of this world, and are not pure intelligences but complete natural individuals, having a body and a soul.

The native land of ghosts is memory, memory transforming sensations, or drowsily confusing, recasting, or exaggerating old impressions into dreams.

But the landscape open to spirit is ghost-like in being purely ideal.

Imagination is fertile; and the old maxim that there is nothing in the mind which was not first in the senses seems to me far from accurate. There is never anything in the mind that *at that time* is not given in a kind of sensation, that is, given directly: but these images are not old images or fragments of old images surviving and recombined, as the fragments of an ancient temple might be built into a modern wall. Images, considered in themselves and objectively, are essences and perfectly immaterial. That which is immaterial has no substance, no persistence, and no effects: it offers no possibility of being stored, divided, redistributed, or recombined. Ideas are not animals that may breed other animals. They may recur, wholly or in part, but only when a living psyche inwardly reverts to much the same movement as on some former occasion. The given essence will then be the same or nearly the same as formerly. But it must be evoked afresh, and unless evoked it has no existence whatever. It is truly a ghost, belief in it is illusion, and its apparition or specious presence depends entirely on the dreaming psyche that weaves it together.

Dreams, and all the sensuous garments that fancy bestows on nature, are made of stuff much more spiritual than any "spirits" supposed to be persisting and active persons, stealthily re-visiting the earth, or sending messages to it from some neighbouring region. The primitive idea that when the body sleeps the spirit may travel to distant places, and receive monitions concerning secret or future things, though poetical, is true in this sense: that in dreams the contribution that the psyche makes to experience predominates over the contribution ordinarily made by external things. This predominance of the psychic we call *inspiration*; the existence and the rush of it are spirit itself. When this predominance is excessive and persists in waking hours, we go mad; any strong passion, in its recklessness and self-assurance, has madness in it. Yet the same inspiration permeates sensibility and desire, perception and thought, all experience being but a dream controlled, and all reason but fancy domesticated and harnessed to human labours. In dreams, when the spirit seems to travel, it merely smoulders like a fire no longer fanned by the wind: and in that withdrawal and concentra-tion, together with much fragmentary nonsense, it may develop and fancifully express its absolute impulses, building the world nearer to the heart's desire. Hence dreams may be morally prophetic: or a more voluminous inspiration, from the same source, may combine with waking intelligence and art to produce some work of genius. The notion that

Marginal note: Inspiration the voice of the psyche rebuking or idealizing external facts.

spirit can escape from the psyche, or comes into us originally, as Aristotle says, from beyond the gates, merely inverts mythologically a natural truth: namely that the spirit is immaterial and transcendental. It issues from the psyche like the genie from Sinbad's bottle, and becomes, in understanding and in judgment, an authority over its source, and a transcendental centre for making a survey of everything.

That the wildest imaginations are, in their origin, native to matter appears clearly in this, that they are produced by drugs. Nor is this incompatible with their æsthetic or prophetic or intellectual value. The priestess at Delphi inhaled the vapours of her cave before uttering her oracles; other ritual practices have an intentionally hypnotic or narcotic influence; wine and music, martial or religious, notoriously rouse the spirit to boldness and to conviction. Nor is this a scandal, as if pure reason could move either the heart or the world. Pure reason is an ideal brought to light in the spirit by the organization of forces all originally irrational and wild: and this organization in turn is a product of long friction and forced adjustments. So much so, that in human life inspiration and reason come to seem holiday marvels, appearing when some suppressed strain or forbidden harmony is allowed to assert itself, in fancy only, during some lull in action. Prophecy is the swan-song of lost causes. The action that accompanies it has no tendency to fulfil it. If it survives like Hebrew prophecy in later Judaism and in Christianity, it becomes a purely spiritual discipline, mystic where it was martial, and ascetic where it was political. The communism of Plato's Republic could be realized only in the cloister.

Spirit is thus, in a certain sense, the native land of ghosts, of ideas, of phenomena; but it is not at all a visible ghost or phenomenon in its own being. Its own essence is an invisible stress; the vital, intellectual, and moral actuality of each moment.

Another way in which spirit may be materialized is by confusion with the psyche and with those cosmic currents by which the psyche is fed. Wind and breath have given their name to spirit, and most aptly. The air is invisible, yet the winds are a terrible reality, and though they may soon be stilled, the calm supervening is no longer deceptive. I have learned that what seemed vacancy was a reservoir of power, that air, ether, and energy filled that apparent void. I discover that innumerable atoms are floating there, ready to make fresh havoc in the world, or to be breathed in and renew life in my breast. What is this life in me but vital oxygen drawn into my lungs; what is this warm breath exhaled but my very spirit and will? Invisible as it is, does it not quicken my body and inspire all my action? Is it not one with the spirit of the winds howling in the storm or ruffling the sea or carrying seeds far and wide over the fertile earth? Is not the world, then, full of spirits? And is not spirit perhaps the one universal power astir in all things, as it stirs in me?

Spirit not a fluid.

Such poetic confusions are spontaneous in a candid mind. They may be corrected by science and by logical analysis; but it would be a foolish philosophy that should ignore the continuities and analogies that run through the universe and that at once impress the attentive poet. The principle of life is not exactly wind or air. Life began in the sea and a great seclusion and darkness are requisite for seeds to germinate and for organic patterns to take shape undisturbed. Storms and struggles come afterwards on occasion; a normal order and distribution of elements, or distinct self-defending organisms, must have arisen first. Yet the currents within and without such organisms or such elements remain continuous. A psyche, the organic order and potentiality in a living body, depends upon ambient forces and reacts upon them; and the sense of this dependence and of this reaction is the spirit.

This spirit is something ontologically altogether incongruous with air, ether, energy, motion, or substance. Spirit is the *witness* of the cosmic dance; in respect to that agitation it is transcendental and epiphenomenal; yet it crowns some impulse, raises it to actual unity and totality, and being the fruition of it, could not arise until that organ had matured. An immense concretion of elements to make a habitat and of tropisms to make an animal must have preceded. Being fetched from such depths, spirit feels a profound kinship with its mothering elements. It suffers with the body and it speaks for the heart. Even if it dreams that it travels to distant spheres, it merely reports in a fable the scope of physical sensibility and the depths from which messages are received. In its station, in its interests, in its language, it always remains at home. To say that it travels, or witnesses the distant, is as if we said that the radio conveyed us to the concert which it conveys to us. The travelling, the waves, the transmissions are all physical. How should they be anything else? Instruments are material; even the composer, when he first conceived those accords, was listening to a spontaneous music bred in his psyche out of theoretically traceable impressions, tensions and outbursts of potential energy within him. The chain of these motions is materially uninterrupted, else the composer's imagined music would never have reached our ears; and spiritual union, both in perception and in passion, depends upon physical concordance. The number of spirits that may have lived through the measures of that

It is the moral fruition of physical life.

melody helps me not at all to hear it now; the physical source must be tapped afresh in each case, and the physical receiver must be capable of vibrating afresh to the message.

Spiritualists and mystics are often more perceptive than rationalists; but they are not for that reason perceptive of spiritual things. They are, more probably, supersensitive materially. They feel influences vibrating through the universe to which the din of vulgar affairs has deafened most of us: and they dream of physical survivals and renewals, of physical Elysiums, with endless vistas of warm physical love or physical peace. They hover, they glide, they wallow; and they think themselves spirits. But there is nothing less spiritual than the shallows of indis-·tinction and of torpid oneness. The universe is perforce one, and its parts easily break down and are lost in one another; but such collapse destroys the very possibility of spirit, which is not an ether or a fluid coursing through space, but a moral focus of recollection, discrimination and judgment.

Language in these subjects is particularly ambiguous and charged with emotion; it serves less to discriminate one thing from another than to attribute to one thing, miraculously, the powers and dignities of something else. So the power of nature is often attributed to spirit or identified with it: with a curious result. For if spirit be only the laws or tendencies discoverable in nature, it is only a form to be found in matter, and not an immaterial invisible inward intensity of being. And there is malice in this abuse of language: for we are expected to conceive that laws or tendencies are thoughts (essences being confused with the intuition of essences) and that nature being describable in those intelligible terms is secretly governed by intelligence: so that we may attribute power also to our own

Confusions about the seat of power.

wishes and imaginations, and depute ourselves to be
co-rulers of the universe.

Now our *selves*, our organisms or persons, undoubtedly play a more or less efficacious part in
physical events. It would be a miracle if our bodies,
with so much stored and redistributable energy as
they contain, did not redirect by their action all sorts
of other motions in the environment. A man habitually identifies himself as much with his body as
with his spirit: and since both are called "I", it is no
wonder if what happens in each is felt to be also the
work of the other. And the connection is radical
and intimate in reality; the problem not being how
the two happen to be united but in what respects we
may justly distinguish them. The difference between
myself as a transcendental centre or spirit and myself
as a fact in the world is, in one sense, unbridgeable;
but not because they are two facts incongruously or
miraculously juxtaposed in the same field, but because
they are realizations of the same fact in two incomparable realms of being. There is only one fact,
more or less complex and extended, an incident in
the flux of existence; and this fact lying in the realm
of matter by virtue of its origin, place, time, and
consequences, contains a transcendental apprehension
of all things, in moral terms and in violent perspective,
taken from itself as centre. Such sensibility is proper
to the natural fact, when this fact is a living animal;
but you can no more pass, at the same level, from
sensation to matter, than you can pass from extension
to duration, from colour to sound, from sound to
meaning, or from logic to love. The organization of
matter is something logically incomparable with its
mere persistence or energy, yet can only exist with
the latter; so spirit is logically incomparable with
body, yet is a moral integration and dignity accruing
to body when body develops a certain degree of

organization and of responsiveness to distant things. Nor does spirit, in its new language, discourse about anything save that very world, with all its radiations, in which it has arisen.

Perhaps it is not logically impossible that spirit should exist without a body: but in that case how should spirit come upon any particular images, interests, or categories? If occu- Treacherous notion of pied with nothing, it would not be a con- disembodied scious being; and if occupied with everything spirit. possible, that is, with the whole realm of essence at once, it would not be the consciousness of a living soul, having a particular moral destiny, but only a hypostasis of intelligence, abstracted from all particular occasions. But can intelligence be abstracted from particular occasions and from problems set by contingent facts? Logic and mathematics would surely never have taken shape if nature had not compelled attention to dwell on certain forms of objects or of language, and rewarded in practice the elaboration of those forms in thought. Indeed spirit, once abstracted from animal. life and independent of all facts, would have forfeited that intensity, trepidation, and movement, that capacity for inquiry and description, which make spirit a focus of knowledge. It would have evaporated into identity with the realm of essence. Even divine spirits, as conceived in human poetry and religion, are thinking, loving, and planning minds, functions which all belong to animal life, and presuppose it.

In some speculative myths spirit is represented as a self-existent potentiality pregnant with the seeds of a particular development; so that spirit, as And of in a dream, gradually creates world upon "Spirit" world, and the experience of them, out of in history. its magic bosom. There is sometimes poetic truth in such myths, but they describe, from some local point of view, a perspective in the realm of matter, not at all the history of spirit. Spirit is not a seed, it is not a potentiality, it is not a power. It is not even— though this touches more nearly its actual character— a grammar of thought or divine Logos, predetermining the structure of creation and its destiny. That, if found anywhere, would be found in the realm of truth; but we may doubt that any alleged Logos, or any psychological system of categories or forms of intuition, prescribes limits to the truth. It prescribes at best one type of logic, one set of senses, in which a particular existent world might be apprehended by its inhabitants.

Yet these myths, as often happens, have a real foothold in the nature of the facts. They catch some transcendental privilege or predica- ment proper to spirit and transfer it, together with the name of spirit, to the spheres of matter or truth. Spirit has an initial vagueness; it awakes, it looks, it waits, it oscil- lates between universal curiosity and primeval sleep. Certainly the feelings and images arising are specific; and spirit has no *a priori* notion of any different feelings or images to contrast with the given ones. Yet it is in no way predisposed or limited to these; it is not essentially, like the psyche, even a slave of habit, so as to think the given necessary and the not given impossible. Spirit is infinitely open. And this is no ontological marvel or mystic affinity of spirit to the absolute. It is merely the natural indistinction of primitive wakefulness, of innocent attention. Spirit is like a child with eyes wide open, heart simple, faith ready, intellect pure. It does not suspect the trouble the world is going to give it. It little knows the contortions, the struggles, the disasters which the world imposes on itself. There is a horrid confusion in attributing to spirit the dogged conservatism and catastrophic evolution of the natural world.

[marginal note:] Spirit essentially open and blank.

To the primitive blankness of spirit corresponds its eventual hospitality to all sorts of things. But this hospitality is not connivance, not complicity. It suffers when thwarted in its proper life of free sympathy and understanding. It is an intellectual hospitality open to all truth, even to all fiction and to all essence, as these things may present themselves. It is not an equal pleasure in them all. Spirit is a product of the psyche; the psyche makes for a specific order and direction of life; spirit congenitally shares in this vitality and this specific impulse. The psyche needs to prepare for all things that may chance in its life: it needs to be universally vigilant, universally retentive. In satisfying this need it forms the spirit, which therefore initially tends to look, to remember, to understand. But the psyche takes this step, so impartial and unprejudiced officially, for a perfectly selfish domestic reason, namely, to prepare the home defences and enlarge the home dominion. The spirit, therefore, is like Goethe's Watchman, who was born to gaze, and possessed all the world in idea, yet was set on that watch-tower for an urgent purpose, with a specific duty to be vigilant. Hence the storms and forest-fires, the invasions or rebellions that he might observe, would not leave him cold, but would distress him in his fidelity, disturb his power of vision, and perhaps bring him and his tower to the ground. Not that spirit trembles for its own being. It is the most volatile of things, and the most evanescent, a flame blown or extinguished by any wind: but no extinction here can prevent it from blazing up there, and its resurrection is as perpetual as its death. What torments it is no selfish fear but a vicarious sympathy with its native psyche and her native world, which it cannot bear to feel dragged hither and thither in tragic confusion, but craves to see everywhere well-ordered and beautiful, *so that it may be better seen and understood.* This is the specific function of spirit, which it lives by fulfilling, and dies if it cannot somehow fulfil. But as it is unresisting yet indomitable in its existence, so it is resourceful in its art, and ultimately victorious; because the worst horrors and absurdities in the world, when they are past or distant, so that life here is not physically disturbed by them, can be raised in the spirit to the level of reflection, becoming mere pictures of hell and marvellous in that capacity. Thus a constant suggestion and echo of sorrow, which cannot but suffuse existence, adds strange dignity to the tragedy and renders the spirit freer from the world and surer in its own intrinsic possessions.

It is not in respect to large cosmic fatalities, such as war and death, that spirit is most perplexed. Love, self-sacrifice, and martyrdom are capable of turning those fatalities into occasions for lyrical joy and tragic liberation. The worst entanglements, from the spirit's point of view, arise within the psyche, in what in religious parlance is called sin. This strangles spirit at its source, because the psyche is primarily directed upon all sorts of ambitions irrelevant to spirit, producing stagnation, inflation, self-contradiction, and hatred of the truth. It is with difficulty that spirit can make itself heard in such a tumult. Spirit is no random blast, no irresponsible free demand, but speaks for a soul reduced to harmony and for the sane mind. This sanity implies not only integrity within, but also adjustment to the outer universe. So that whilst spirit is physically the voice of the soul crying in the wilderness, it becomes vicariously and morally the voice of the wilderness admonishing the soul.

Let me tabulate, as briefly as possible, the principal words and ideas that mark the differences, the bonds, and the confusions that exist between matter and spirit. Such a glossary may help the

Glossary of terms.

reader to criticize his favourite modes of expression and to be patient with those of other people.

BODY. Ancient usage identifies a man with his body, as Homer in the first lines of the Iliad : [1] and in English we still speak of *nobody* and *everybody*. This places man quite correctly in the realm of matter amongst other bodies, but it treats him and them summarily and externally as gross units and dead weights, ignoring their immaterial properties and their subtle physical substance and relations.

ORGANISM. This word still designates the body, since the organization of an organism must exist somewhere and on a particular scale, if it is to exist at all. But a body is an organism only by virtue of its vital power of nutrition and reproduction. By these functions bodily life becomes continuous with the ambient forces on which it feeds and theoretically with the whole dynamic universe. Thus an organism is both a closed system of vital tropes and a nucleus in the general cosmic process.

PSYCHE. The forms of inorganic matter, though distinct from matter logically, are clearly passive: matter may fall into them innumerable times, yet if anywhere disturbed, they show no tendency to reinstate themselves. This tendency defines an organism: its actual form hides a power to maintain or restore that form. This power or potentiality, often concentrated in a seed, dwells in the matter of the organism, but is mysterious; so that for observation the form itself seems to be a power (when locked in that sort of substance or seed) and to work towards its own manifestation. The self-maintaining and reproducing pattern or structure of an organism, conceived as a power, is called a psyche. The psyche, in its moral unity, is a poetic or mythological notion, but needed to mark the hereditary

[1] The wrath of Achilles cast many souls of heroes to Hades and *themselves* to dogs and vultures.

vehement movement in organisms towards specific forms and functions.

ANIMAL. All natural organisms have psyches, and are at the same time in dynamic relations to the whole physical world. When the organism waits for favourable opportunities to unfold itself, the psyche is vegetative; when it goes to seek favourable opportunities, it is animal.

This is an important step in laying the ground for spirit. The unity of the organism subtends the moral unity of the spirit, which raises that unity to an actual and intense existence; the impulse of the psyche, making for a specific perfection of form and action, underlies the spiritual distinction between good and evil; and the power of locomotion gives the spirit occasion for perception and knowledge. Will is no doubt deeper than intelligence in the spirit, as it is in the animal; yet will without intelligence would not be spirit, since it would not distinguish what it willed or what it suffered. So that the passage from vegetation to action seems to produce the passage from a dark physical excitability to the *qui vive* of consciousness.

SOUL. The same thing that looked at from the outside or biologically is called the psyche, looked at morally from within is called the soul. This change of aspect so transforms the object that it might be mistaken for two separate things, one a kind of physical organization and the other a pure spirit. And spirit is in fact involved in feeling and knowing life from the inside: not that spirit is then *self*-conscious, or sees nothing save its own states, but that it is then the medium and focus for apprehension, and imposes on its objects categories and qualities of its own. A psyche, when spirit awakes in it, is turned into a soul. Not only can the career of that psyche now be reviewed in memory, or conceived in prophecy, but many a private impulse or thought never exhibited to the world can now be added to one's history; so that oneself is now not merely the body, its power, and its experience, but also an invisible guest, the soul, dwelling in that body and having motions and hopes of its own. This soul can be conceived to issue out of the body, to pass into a different body, or to remain thinking and talking to itself without a body at all. This, for the psyche, would have been inconceivable; for, as Aristotle shows, the psyche, or specific form of organization and movement, in an elephant, can no more pass into the body of a fly, than the faculty of cutting can pass from an axe into a lyre, or the faculty of making music from the lyre into the axe. The soul, however, having an apparently independent discoursing and desiring faculty, and a power to imagine all sorts of non-existent things, may easily be conceived to pass from one body to another, as by a change of domicile, and to have had forgotten incarnations, with an endless future.

SELF OR PERSON. If memory, dreams, and silent musings seem to detach the soul from bodily life, social relations and moral qualities may re-attach the soul to the world, not now biologically but politically. Politically a man cannot be separated from his body; but it is not by his bodily faculties that he chiefly holds his own in society, or conceives his individuality. He is a person, a self, a character; he has a judicial and economic status; he lives in his ambitions, affections, and repute. All this again, as in the notion of the soul, cannot come about without the secret intervention of spirit: yet these ideas, although spirit must be there to entertain them, are not spiritual ideas; the interests chiefly concerned are those of animal or social bodies. Even moral worth or immortal life are ideals borrowed from animal impulses and animal conditions. In a different biological setting, or in a realm of pure spirits, those social duties and services would be impossible: and the will to live forever is nothing but the animal will to go on living expressed reflectively and transferred, somewhat incongruously, to the social self or historical person.

SPIRIT. Psyches, we have said, take on the character of souls when spirit awakes in them. Spirit is an awareness natural to animals, revealing the world and themselves in it. Other names for spirit are consciousness, attention, feeling, thought, or any word that marks the total *inner* difference between being awake or asleep, alive or dead. This difference is morally absolute; but physically the birth of spirit caps a long growth during which excitability and potentiality of various kinds are concentrated in organisms and become transmissible. The *outer* difference between sleeping and waking, life and death, is not absolute; and we may trace certain divergences between the path of transmission for the psyche and the basis of distribution for the spirit. Life follows the seed, through long periods of unconsciousness and moral nonexistence; whereas spirit lives in the quick interplay of each sensitive individual and the world, and often is at its height when, after keen experience, the brain digests the event at leisure, and the body is sexually quiescent or reduced by old age to a mere husk. In the spirit, by definition, there is nothing persistent or potential. It is pure light and perpetual actuality. Yet the intensity and scope of this moral illumination, as well as the choice of characters lighted up, the order of the scenes and how long each shall last, all hang on the preparations nature may have made for this free entertainment.

CHAPTER II

ON COSMIC ANIMISM

LET us admit that something called spirit exists, and exists invisibly, in a manner of its own, by virtue of an intrinsic moral intensity. Its essence lies in willing, suffering, looking, being pleased, absorbed, or offended. It talks to itself inaudibly, evoking and releasing an infinity of fugitive images, yet sometimes proceeding to a conclusion, to the comparatively fixed possession of an idea. Without being a substance separable from the act of feeling or thinking, this spirit lives through time, as in a dream. It remains spirit throughout, not only in its specific character of witness and living light, but in its capacity for recollecting and prefiguring its experience. It forms designs and develops them dramatically in idea, yet in effect it is helpless and evanescent. It awakes and dies down at no command of its own. Its centre seems to travel, passing from one occasion to another and, for all we can see, arising out of nothing, not once only but often, and often lapsing into nothing again.

Spirit not master of its own existence.

Whence this fevered existence? When does it arise? In what places does it exist? For how long? With what diversity of dramatic experience and intellectual scope?

These are cosmological questions. Whether there are spirits in the mountain-tops, or in the clouds or in the higher parts of the heavens, or wandering ghosts at night, or souls waiting in limbo for re-incarnation or for the resurrection of their bodies, spirit can never

573

discover by withdrawing within itself. The more it is spirit, the less interested it will be in those romantic possibilities. Even the terrible alternative between heaven and hell for their own souls, and for those of all mankind, an alternative which many spiritual persons have faced intellectually, has left them strangely

The question of its origin and distribution is cosmological.

unperturbed; unless indeed they interpreted that doctrine spiritually, as representing the torments or liberation of spirit everywhere and at any time. I think that, on the other hand, theosophists and spiritualists follow a shrewd instinct when, in support of their beliefs, they turn to natural science and to physical phenomena. Matter is the principle of distribution for spirit as for every other feature of the existing world. The "other" world, if it exists, is a neighbour or extension of this world, so that inter-communication may well be possible between the two, travellers may pass from one to the other, and the change of scene need not destroy the identity of the characters or the unity of the play. Supersensitive persons might feel strange influences descending on them from those remote regions. Our habitual ignorance cannot abolish what happens to be unknown to us, or forbid it to exist. Conjecture is therefore free to imagine as much spirit in the world as it pleases, or as the analogies of nature may impose on our dramatic or brotherly sense.

On the other hand, positive belief in imagined spirits, by pressing poetic apprehension into alleged truth, transfers the question to empirical and scientific ground. Such belief has little to do with the subject of this book, which touches rather the internal economy of spirit in whatever world and with whatever companions it may chance to dwell. The landscape of future lives, the private experiences of gods or angels, would place spiritual dilemmas before the spirit no less insistently than human experience places them;

and perhaps the same solutions would suggest themselves there also, negative, ascetic, and mystical in
heaven as well as on earth.   At least, it would probably
be so if those spirits were more spiritual than ourselves
and less ignorant, rather than merely wilder, happier,
and freer.   Thus how wide or how thick may be the
population of spirits in nature is frankly irrelevant to
actual spiritual life, seeking or losing in each instance
a path to inward salvation.   Yet those cosmological
problems cannot help interesting the philosopher who
may be investigating from the outside the origin and
place of spirit in the universe.   I will therefore say a
word about them before proceeding to other matters.

   In the first place, is spirit *distributed* at all?   Might
it not be the fundamental locus of all other things?
This is what spirit itself is inclined to assert
when it becomes thoroughly self-conscious
and perceives its transcendental relation to
every discovery it may make.   The pure
insight here is invincible, but hard to maintain pure.   The flux of existence prevents.
At any moment we may inhale and suck in
the whole universe ideally; but exhaling will
never restore that universe to its natural reality.
Every vista, temporal or spatial, will have been
gathered up into the intense present vision in which
alone it exists.   For discursive thought, however, this
concentrated actuality is a blind alley.   Emotionally
we are enraptured: we have momentarily become God,
a truly solitary and unclouded deity; no scheming,
commanding, responsible creator or governor of a
universe, but a pure fact, a pure possession of all
truth, incapable of creating anything; for to create
effectually would be to generate something external
to oneself, of which this transcendental spirit, by
hypothesis, could know nothing.   The only possible
way for spirit to create is to imagine.   Thus conscious-

The trans-
cendental
priority of
spirit re-
gards only
its experi-
ence, not
its existence
or distribu-
tion.

ness in making itself the seat and criterion of reality, denies itself the privilege of knowledge.

The truth is that knowledge and consciousness are transcendental in regard to ideas, but not in regard to the objects which furnish the occasion and the external control for those ideas. It is merely fatuous to identify our ideas with their objects in theory, but it would be tragic if anyone did so in action. The temptation to do so is real, as we see in dreams; because spirit truly has a vital priority and universality in respect to its eventual knowledge: but this holds only of the single private perspectives, scattered as actual spirit is scattered, along the ups and downs of natural life. Scarcely has imagination in some exalted mystical moments wallowed up all time and change, when that insight lapses, we suffer a jolt, our heaven is clouded over, there is not only thunder and lightning above us, but our very soul begins to cry for help. It turns out that the spirit that had seemed to compose and deploy the universe is itself an incident in the universe, subject to fortune, and broken into moments and into fragmentary views. Even if somewhere, in some superhuman instance, it should be able to embrace all things in idea, it surely exists also elsewhere in other instances in which that omniscience is lost and that peace turned to anguish, when the mind's eye, in which all things were supposed to be painted, peers tearful and half-blind into a dreadful past and an unknown future.

A philosophy, then, reposing entirely on the transcendental dignity of spirit would not represent the cosmos as animated, since there would be no cosmos, only dreams generated by ignorance and delusion; and it would not even represent spirit legitimately as animating the conventional history of the world as attested by documents; for the past too would be a creation of the present. But transcendentalism is

Indian and German idealism represents the cosmos not as animate but as visionary.

seldom taken so strictly. When the Germans talk of
spirit animating history or even nature, they are not
thinking of the actual spirit in themselves, at that
moment framing that vista. They are rather giving
the name of spirit, in a metaphorical sense, to some
tendency or principle or law which they vaguely conceive the facts to obey. Such "spirit" is not a spiritual
reality but what I call an essence or at best a trope:
in itself a conceived rhythm or, if actually executed
by events, a truth about them. So when the Indians
talk of Brahma as the support and only reality of the
universe, they are evoking something to which, in my
vocabulary, the name of spirit cannot belong. This
Brahma is a state of deep sleep in which spirit, matter,
and essence seem to lie concentrated and undeveloped.
The dreamer is felt to be deeper than the dream,
physiologically quite truly: but is this non-dreaming
dreamer a spirit?

I know what the Indians might say about Brahma
at once hearing and not hearing, seeing and not seeing, etc. He *does* hear, in as much as
whenever creatures hear it is only he that   Is Brahma
hears in them. Yet he does *not* hear, since   the absolute
in his own person he is free from all rela-   self truly
                                                a spirit?
tivity or privation, seated in no particular station or
organ, and not subject to the false intrusion of sensation or thought: things which are false because founded
on ignorance of all the rest of infinite Being. Brahma
can lend no ear to these illusions, but annuls them
morally and sleeps on, as the deep sea sleeps on,
unmindful of the vain transitory lights and vain transitory tempests that play upon the surface. Very well:
I have no quarrel with that intuition, or with any
intuition. Yet in terms of the logic implicit in common sense, the Brahma so described would become
actual spirit only when somewhat ruffled by circumstances, and actually hearing, etc. In so far as he

remained asleep in a dead calm, he would be only the non-existent possibility of spirit, the unused category of thought, the unexemplified essence of any consciousness that might arise eventually. The profound reality of Brahma in his deep sleep is surely felt to be much more than that. He pre-eminently exists. He is precisely what is substantial and solid, warm and vital, in all things: the positive potentiality of all universes and of all thoughts. Undoubtedly: but then my name for Brahma would not be spirit but matter; because in my system as the name for the *intrinsic ideal possibility of all things* is essence, so the name for the *existing potentiality of specific things* is matter.

This identification may seem extravagant. The highly subtle notion of Brahma, or transcendental spirit breathing at peace, lies at the opposite pole from stocks and stones, fire and blood. Yet the Indians themselves often identify Brahma with ether, with breath, or even like Thales, with water. It is they, not I, that confuse spirit with the primary substance of things. It has always been under the spell of natural forces that poets have shaped their mythology; and it is still by an intense concentration on mere life, mere duration, or mere dumb existence, that the mystic experiences his identity with the absolute. This identity is hidden, latent, destructive of detail: it is an identity of substance, in a diversity of persons. But the *substance* of spirit is matter as of all other transitory things. Were the notion of spirit not thus fused with that of substance (as it notoriously was by Parmenides) it could never carry that suggestion of indestructible primacy, power, and intimate secret presence in all things which it evidently carries to the devout mind.

The devout mind is pious and anxious, as well as spiritual; it never therefore quite divorces the idea of salvation from that of safety and profit. Now

safety—a treacherous safety—and profit—a temporary
profit—are in the gift of matter, of fortune; and few
would worship spirit if they did not understand it to be the very breath and law of   Religion
material things. But this breath bloweth   not satisfied
where it listeth, and this law is ironical, in immaterial.
that it destroys everything that it fosters. Thus experience of the world turns a clear spirit away from
the world; and substance when recognized in its
indefinite and vain fertility invites the spirit to withdraw within itself. There is thus a kind of co-opera-
tion and understanding between pure matter and pure
spirit. As matter is plastic and blindly prolific, so
spirit, in its inviolate transcendental station, is infinitely open and detached from particulars. It offers,
as it were, an intangible mirror to matter, like a glass
sky traversed by no heavenly bodies but only by
reflected images of earth.

Thus the moral safety of spirit, the joy of its inner
intellectual liberty, seems to the natural man a sublimated echo of material safety and good fortune. The
prophets express salvation in the language of prosperity, as the mystics in that of love. They are not
content that heaven and hell should be merely within
us, or that insight should be its own reward. Though
the chastened spirit may secretly smile, it will be
reputed by the pious to work miracles. Philosophical
demagogues will promise to turn the most vulgar of
generations into gods; and even in the Upanishads the
enthusiastic King, quite convinced at the end of each
lesson that all things are indifferent, cries to the
Brahmin, "I will give thee, O Venerable One, a
thousand cows."

I think, then, that in fundamental sympathy with
Indian wisdom, we may draw the following distinctions
in our own language:

In so far as Brahma is conceived as a universal

readiness for thinking, undetermined to any particular thought, he is the *essence* of pure transcendental spirit, and non-existent until exemplified in some actual intuition.

In so far as he is conceived to be infinitely pregnant and to contain virtually the characters of all possible beings, but without any distinction of subject from object or any actual intuition, Brahma is pure being or the realm of essence.

In so far as this potentiality is conceived to be something real and extant (since avowedly phenomena are not created by pure spirit but produced naturally by a regular development of works and psychic heredities), Brahma is the inner reality of matter.

In so far as within particular psyches Brahma hears, sees, thinks, and suffers, he is existent spirit. He *exists* only diffused; but it is only by attaining his transcendental dignity and cognitive essence that particular psyches can ever hear, see, think, or suffer actually and in a moral sense; so that it is the one pure quality of spirit, it is Brahma himself, that blows through all living beings, whenever they are stirred to consciousness.

This Indian notion of deity corresponds best to our modern insight into the transcendental nature of spirit; for here subjectivism in logic and sentiment is united with naturalism in the description of the world. But our own religious traditions do better justice to the moral and tragic side of the matter. Spirit does not lose its divine nature by becoming incarnate in man, by being rejected by the world, and by suffering and dying. On the contrary, apart from such incarnation God would remain only a natural power or an infinite essence or a vain ideal. If spirit first renders man divine, humanity first renders God moral. We might even read this meaning into the *filioque* clause of the creed, saying that a Holy Spirit could never have proceeded from the Father, if it had not also proceeded from the Son.

Neither transcendental nor Indian idealism can therefore avail to animate the cosmos. They may profess to reduce it to an illusion or to an unconscious work of the spirit; but spirit itself will thereby forfeit its spiritual nature, until, becoming conscious in the vicissitudes of that too real world, it asserts its spirituality by surmounting them. In its reality, then, spirit will be dispersed, and very thinly, in the world which it is alleged to create. *Spiritual falsity of pantheism.*

Might not this dispersion of spirit be admitted and yet the exclusive reality of it be maintained? Might it not exist in an infinite number of instances, with only spiritual relations between them?

I can conceive such a universe, although I know of no philosopher that has described it. Leibniz perhaps came near it, in his ingenious monadology: but his monads were souls, developing through physical time. If he had taken the transcendental unity of spirit seriously, he would have been compelled to break up his personal monads into as many spiritual monads as there were instants of life in each of them; and the relations between these instants, like those between different souls, would have become moral only, subsisting in the realm of truth, without any physical medium of distribution, not even a physical time. Perhaps such was his secret insight, if he ever applied the principle of internal relations to the moments of time; for then the temporal vistas within each moment would correspond with the temporal vistas of all other moments, yet the moments would not occupy distinct dates in any physical time flowing beneath them or through them. *Theory of spiritual monads making up a physical world.*

Distribution into separate souls, each with a consecutive life, is by no means essential to spirit. In our world spirit is so distributed, because a certain persistence on the part of an organism must, according to the established order of nature, precede any sensation; and it is from our animal souls and lives that spirit borrows that moral and dramatic character which marks its most vivid moments in ourselves. Indeed, without expectation, memory, and impulsive preference we should hardly give to intuition the name of spirit. On the other hand, in order to exist at one moment spirit does not require to have existed before, or to exist later; and if Leibniz identified spirit with long-lived souls, and souls again with indestructible atoms, this was due to theological and conceptual commitments that need not detain us.

Such a hypothesis is not one to accept or to disprove. It is a fable; yet the remarkable many-sided **Respects in** competence of Leibniz, in composing it, **which the** distinguished at several crucial points what **monadology** is congruous with the essence of spirit from **does justice** **to spirit.** what is incongruous. Here is a lesson to learn and, in spite of our modern progressive frivolity, never to unlearn again. It is congruous with spirit to be existentially insulated and soliptistic, yet in its solitude to keep an intellectual outlook over its own career, past and future, and over a world felt to surround and control it; for while spirit is enormously active morally and imaginatively, a great dreamer, and full of obsessing cares, yet it is subject at every turn to external fatalities, to surprises and torments; and even when left relatively free, it often feels within itself a sudden tendency to fall asleep, or a sudden tendency to stretch its normal wakefulness to abnormal lengths, as if it could grow omniscient, divinely balanced, and superior to every accident. All this Leibniz admirably indicates in his myth of the everlasting monads, infinite in number, cut off essentially from one another, but each developing (or perhaps reverting) through all the stages of slumber, dream and intelligence.

At the same time it is incongruous with spirit to appear or to operate in the physical world; it can never descend from its transcendental station of witness and judge into the region of objects. It lives, indeed, in a natural society; but that fact can never abolish its spiritual solitude, nor the intrinsic centrality of thought in each of its instances. And the counterpart of this spiritual concentration is the infinity of possible instances of thought. Thus the monadology exhibits in a myth the inwardness and transcendental purity of spirit, its spark-like unity and starlike multiplicity; and all later transcendental idealism only elaborates the notion of this solitary thinking monad of Leibniz, thinking its fated world.

Nevertheless this allegiance to the pure notion of spirit involved Leibniz in hopeless difficulties when, turning his radical transcendentalism into a cosmology, he identified his monad first with the psyche and then, even more extravagantly, with the physical atom; so that the light of consciousness, something essentially warm, moral, and volatile, something *spiritual*, became the substance of the cosmos, comminuted, geometrized, galvanized, and persisting *ad infinitum*. In this sphere the notion of a monad without windows repeats the conceptual atomism of Democritus who wished matter to be composed of indestructible geometrical solids. But ideal fixity of any kind is false to the intimately fluid and relational nature of existence. The natural atom is all windows—all windows at least dynamically; and even in the scheme of Democritus it was the motions, shocks, and congeries of the atoms that supplied the needed orchestration for the life of nature. Indeed, the metaphor of being windowless was not altogether happy even for spirit; for although spirit

[marginal note: But it confuses spirit with the psyche and with matter.]

can admit nothing passively from outside, nothing of
foreign manufacture, yet its inward inventiveness is
fed by external stimuli and made cognitive by anxiety
about ulterior things.   The unity here is that of outlook; and the counterpart of it is a universal curiosity,
an impartial aptness to know and to experience everything whatsoever.   If spirit be without windows, or
rather without doors, it lives by peering perpetually
outwards through that dome of many-coloured but
transparent glass which the psyche has built round it.
The light, however—and this is the main point—is
not that of a sun outside, but of a fire within.   It is
animal life kindled into flame and dramatizing the
world from that focus with the spasmodic chiaroscuro
of good and evil.

The monadology of Leibniz appeared at an unfortunate moment, and hardly received the developments
The psyche, it demanded; for scarcely had the universe
a biological been analysed in Germany into nothing but
unit, dis- souls, when the soul was analysed in Eng-
appears in
psycholo- land into nothing but perceptions.   And it
gism. was a just nemesis: because the soul, if anything, is a poetic name for a biological reality, for the
psyche, a system of tropes in animal life as observable
as the organism and its behaviour.   These physical
facts are the *natura naturata* of natural history; and
the psyche is the same facts synthesized logically into
an ideal *natura naturans*.   It had therefore been a false
step, a step into empty air, to ignore the hereditary
formative psyche and to give the name of soul to
consciousness, however attenuated or dull this consciousness might be said to be.   Degrees of vivacity
in feeling are perhaps only relative and imputed; where
feeling arises at all, it brings its own standard of
intensity.   Leibniz had passed in his monadology,
founded on the logic of parts and wholes, into a
fictitious region; his psychology had become literary,

where perception, introspection, memory, and reasoning exhaust the realities conceived or conceivable. In this literary psychology there is no psyche: there are only images, emotions, dramatic fictions, verbal associations. It was therefore a sort of ironical duty for any shrewd reader of Leibniz to abandon his system, since his critical principle, reducing nature to spiritual monads, reduced his monads at once to passing intuitions; and then we should have only these atomic and homeless intuitions on our hands with which to compose a universe. Our universe would have no souls in it, and no substances or causes; only a cloud of psychological states, existing in no medium and produced by no agency.

Cosmos is not the word to describe such a world; yet the chaos it dissolves into if consistently thought out has one great merit for my present purpose: it is composed exclusively of spirit; an undiluted actuality permeates every part. By examining this system we may see how far spirit alone might go to constitute a world, and by what illusions we might disguise the essential incapacity of spirit to generate itself or to collect its instances into an historical process.

In the first place, there are unavoidable but illegitimate implications in the chief terms that a psychological idealism is compelled to use. The words idealism and idea are themselves illegitimate and constantly ambiguous. An idea is properly an essence, and idealism a system that attributes power to the essences exemplified in things, as if their beauty or clearness had caused matter to assume those forms. But this contradicts the nominalism and the scepticism inherent in any genuine retreat into the passing state of mind. Nor are the names commonly given to these states of mind less misleading. They are not properly "perceptions", for a perception implies an object or an

Yet even literary psychology is saturated with naturalism.

occasion provoking and justifying that perception: whereas in pure psychologism there is never any object save the contents of the mind at the moment, and there is no present occasion, deeper than that state of mind, to determine what that state of mind shall be. "Sensation" and "feeling", in the same way, suggest more than what psychologism can allow: they suggest a plight of the organism, a movement in things, of which the spirit becomes morally aware, without yet discerning any graphic image.   Finally, "idea" remains to render confusion worse confounded: for while still often meaning essence it also means intuition, some episode in the life of spirit, or even the whole passing state of the psyche, in which much more may lie fermenting than the discrimination of any recognizable idea.

All this confusion is involuntary and excusable in a philosophy struggling against common sense and the genius of human language.   Sometimes an effort is made to clear the air, and adopt fresh and more appropriate categories; and we hear less of states of mind and more of phenomena, data, or even objects. But this path leads away from psychologism and back to essences and things; as by another less honourable path, through "unconscious mind" and psychic powers supposed to be spiritual, we return likewise to mother nature.

Much deeper runs the delusion of having super-seded the physical world by a purely spiritual society. Social idealism incoherent. A purely spiritual society is conceivable, but not as modern philosophy may conceive. Such a society would be a community of angels, each singing his note in eternity, notes which might compose a harmony of which each might be somehow aware.   But between these intuitive sorrows or joys there would be no temporal sequence, no communication or causation.   Every phrase of that

music, though there might be musical perspectives
and infinite undertones within it, would in its existence
be without date or place; and these phrases could
neither physically collect, nor physically separate themselves into parallel series, such as common sense conceives human lives to be. A purely spiritual world
would be a monadology of conscious moments, an
ideal symphony of emotions, conspiring or contrasting,
but never meeting, or merging, or generating one
another. If the romantic society of active colliding
and well-known "spirits" conceived, for instance, by
Berkeley, differs so radically from that celestial swarm
of spiritual atoms, the reason is that naturalism survives illegitimately in the habitual assumptions of all
idealists, as of all men. The stuff of modern idealism
is not ideas, it is not spirits, but novelesque literary
psychology; and this psychology, being biographical,
moves in the frame of physical time and physical
evolution. It describes the supposed inner experience
of human souls, born at one date and buried at another
in particular geographical places; souls travelling with
their bodies like the soul of Locke in his coach between
Oxford and London. The psychological philosopher
may reduce his idea of the physical world to a fiction
of the imagination, symbolizing his spiritual relations
with his own past and future, and with other spirits;
but this reduction he makes dialectically in argument
and on paper. He is absolutely debarred from making it in his real belief or daily conceptions not only
because contrary assumptions are involved and ratified
in action, but because, if he did not make these contrary assumptions, his own social idealism would be
blown to the winds.

Men are animals, and human society is an animal
society. Spirit is undoubtedly incarnate in those men,
and may on occasion withdraw into itself mystically
and disengage itself ascetically from the animal interests

of life; but you cannot have it both ways.   If
you are wedded to the flesh and to the world, very

The fiction well, your spirit may enjoy following their
that all fortunes; but then you cannot liberate your-
is spirit
leaves spirit self, save in empty words, from acknowledg-
enslaved to ing their existence and their dominion.   It
matter. is not by calling them fictions, and still
serving them, that you will pass into a spiritual sphere.
Your affections, your self-love, your conceit of freedom
and immortality would need first to be disinfected and
renounced: they are all animal passions, forms of animal
lust, pride, and propulsiveness.   Then, if what remained or supervened seemed to you bliss, you might
say truly that you were a spirit alone with the spirit;
and it would not concern you any longer to deny
matter, as if you were afraid of it or of the notion of
it; for now you would no longer be living competitively
within nature against the rest of nature, but speculatively and disinterestedly in sight of the whole; and
you would be essentially too much above nature to
chafe at being existentially a very small part of it.

Cosmic animism has therefore no real affinity with
spiritual insight or spiritual liberation.   Spiritual
minds may legitimately give names to all things
according to the part these things play in the spiritual
drama; but this is poetry to be understood poetically.
Any dogmatic assertion of the spiritual texture of
things, in turning spirit into power, turns it unwittingly into matter; and the consequences are not confined to a change of vocabulary.   The very notion of
spirit is thereby lost or infected; and the man in
whom spirit seemed to awake becomes again a busy-
body and a worldling, a partisan and a fanatic, a slave
of time, a dupe of place, and a puppet in an evolution
which he calls spiritual, but which is really that of the
material world.

CHAPTER III

THE NATURAL DISTRIBUTION OF SPIRIT

OLDER and saner than any cosmic idealism is the sense that spirit is universally diffused, not by itself but in union with matter. As consciousness is the inner invisible reality of life in our bodies, might it not be the inner invisible reality of things everywhere? The analogy is tempting, and becomes irresistible when, as among kindred living creatures, there is also a close analogy in structure and habit. But the analogy becomes deceptive as we recede from our own species, and ignore the specific conditions of consciousness even in ourselves. We are often unconscious, or almost unconscious : what then quickens consciousness in us, and how far is a similar excitation traceable in nature?

What is the extent of animation in nature?

There are sweeping speculative turns of thought by which, without any accurate inspection, we might assure ourselves that something called spirit pervades the universe. If for instance we define life as spontaneous motion, it becomes evident that matter is everywhere alive; and if we define spirit in the primitive materialistic manner, as the principle and cause of motion, it becomes a truism that matter is everywhere instinct with spirit. But such ways of speaking are intolerable in a critical philosophy, and I have already discarded any definition of spirit that identifies it with physical motions or physical forces. The potential and the dynamic, according to my use of terms, are by definition material;

Vitality of physical forces.

while spirit possesses activity or energy only in the Aristotelian sense of being a perfect realization or ultimate fruition of function. The same use of terms, however, will justify me in saying that a *potentiality* of spirit lies in all life, perhaps in all matter. This does not mean that actual spirit, only very faint, pervades the material world. It means that in the primeval motions and tensions of matter there are rhythms and tropes capable of compounding themselves eventually into living organisms; and we know in our own case that the fortunes of a living organism have a moral import; in other words, carry consciousness or spirit with them.

Throughout nature there are events about which it is possible to care. The forces producing these events seem to form a system, as if each part moved in concert with the other parts, and was affected by their presence and motion: a permeating physical responsiveness that may seem to foreshadow perception and will, and certainly prepares the ground for them. Yet this anticipation is remote. Moral being arises by virtue of the self-recovery and self-defence practised by specific creatures; a world, no matter how organic, if it evolved undisturbed, would have no occasion for sensation or reaction. Moreover (and this cuts deeper) we should remember that the dynamic unity of our world is ignorantly posited by us, as a condition of rational action within it; [1] so that the side of physical reality discoverable to us may be only an excerpt made by our specific sensibility, leaving out all that is beyond our range; and who knows how chaotic that residue may be? No wonder, then, if an image so selected reflects the unity of the selective eye.

It would be a worse impertinence, however, to deny positively that the tremor of change running

[1] Cf. *The Realm of Matter*. Chapter II, toward the end.

through the universe may carry with it some conscious thrill and forward assurance, some music of the spheres; and the distinct parts in turn may be variously haunted by some wraith of intelligence or will, on the same ontological plane as spirit in ourselves. If for that reason, we proclaim the universal presence of spirit in matter, at least we should not forget the dictum of Spinoza that the mind of the universe resembles the human mind as the dogstar resembles the barking animal, in name only. Man lives on food, reproducing himself precariously, dying, and struggling not to die. His experience is all born of pressure and care. But a universe lives on itself, without habitat or neighbours; its mind would therefore be entirely free and automatic, subject to no external stimulus and addressed to no external object. As Sirius and a dog are parts of the same realm of matter, so a universal mind and the human mind would fall within the same category of spirit, and deserve that title. But they would be as different, within that sphere, as it is possible to be.

That which the analogy of nature suggests or even imposes is rather that in matter everywhere there must be a *potentiality* of mind. But what is potentiality? A mere possibility (such as the "possibility of sensation" which Mill made the essence of matter) has no existence or power whatever, except in the language of the philosopher or in his expectations. So with that insidious expression "unconscious mind". This phrase marks something that people are not able or not willing to describe honestly, namely, the *truth* that, under certain additional conditions, a feeling or a thought will arise. The existing facts are either material, and then not to be called states of mind at all; or else (on the hypothesis of psychologism) they are a constellation of previous or contemporary states of mind in the history of spirit: in which case they are not in the least un-

Real potentiality of spirit in matter.

conscious. But philosophical writing has become so slovenly that perhaps a *forgotten* feeling or thought may be called unconscious, because not given at the present moment: in which case all other people's thoughts are always unconscious, and the greater part of one's own. They are indeed for the most part hidden from one another. But properly "unconscious mind" should be intrinsically latent, a process only potentially conscious. This process is now non-mental, that is to say material; because a real potentiality is the actuality of something else. Potential mind, for a psychological idealist, is therefore an absurdity, since in his view all the real antecedents of any sensation or thought must be actual sensations or thoughts elsewhere. But for a materialist the phrase "potential mind", though clumsy, need not be meaningless. A seed is the seat of a real potentiality; it is not a blank; it is not an ideal possibility or essence, but a moment in a material involution and evolution, materially conditioning, under favourable circumstances, the growth of a particular organism. In this sense we might say truly that the potentiality of mind pervades the universe, since doubtless, if the prerequisite material complexities arose at any point, spirit would arise there. Of this we are instinctively sure whenever an animal is born. If the little creature is alive, the little creature is conscious, or will become conscious when duly shaken. All we need do, therefore, in order to discover the distribution of spirit is to study life, to rehearse its movements as sympathetically as possible, putting ourselves in every creature's place, and seeing if spirit in us is thereby really enlarged, or whether we are merely attributing our trite humanity to nature in moral fables.

This subject is not open to science, but only to discernment and imagination. Moral affinity must be felt morally; and if an animation not moral, and in that sense not human, pervades other parts of the world, we must be content to ignore it. In nature, as in a book, we can discover only such thoughts as we are capable of framing. These will be seldom or never the exact thoughts of the author, or of the other animals; yet an author will have existed, and his thoughts will be recoverable if there is a sufficient likeness between the capacities of the writer and the reader, the speaker and the listener. *True mind reading rests on animal sympathy.*

On both sides, at any rate, understanding follows upon inspiration. The most deliberate talker must once have formed his phrases without knowing what they would be; and an intuitive writer, like a sympathetic reader, hears the upwelling thoughts spoken within him, and devoutly listens as he writes. Second thoughts and corrections, contradictions and arguments, merely compare different automatisms that seek to talk one another down. It would be sheer pandemonium, but for two kindly deities that come sooner or later to appease the quarrel. One is Convention, imposing current and communicable ways of talking, apart from actual thought; and the other is Intuition itself, silent and private, surviving the fray and independent of the issue. But neither convention nor actual intuition can penetrate to alien spirit, or disclose its existence. They are tightly subjective and exclusive; and it is only because of their instability that the psyche sometimes passes, in the rough and tumble of life, into the magnetic field of other organisms, and can catch something of their spirit.

The spiritual side of animal life, savage life, ancient or foreign life cannot be approached in the temper of sporting travellers or invading missionaries, or even in that of evolutionary philosophers. We gain nothing by congratulating other creatures on the degree of our special humanity that they may have attained. Insight might *Indefinite elasticity of moral existence.*

begin if we could discover or conceive unsuspected ways of feeling: superhuman courage, fidelity or patience; superhuman scope of the instincts; infra-human absoluteness or intermittance of the passions; even, in so far as such a thing is feasible, some non-human direction or scale of perception. I can call these endowments *super-* or *infra-*human, because I am taking the point of view of spirit as it moves in us; but nothing gives this criterion authority over those different impulses and experiments. The life of spirit is but one ultimate phase of one sort of life. Could we understand the other directions in which nature may move, we should possess other criteria by which our own criterion could be judged, not indeed with greater authority, but with equal justification. Even in ourselves order has some plasticity, and anarchy some allurements. Devils and semi-bestial gods, nymphs and muses were no empty fancies. They were inspired dreams of what existence might be and almost is, either beyond us or in ourselves.

The ancients thought the stars animate and even divine, because the stars know so perfectly what to do.

Order, where there is life, generates spirit.
This hardly seems, to us, a sign of intelligence. We think of mind in romantic modern times as a sort of truant, a disembodied force, interfered with by real things and interfering with them from outside. Both our self-consciousness and our mechanical arts encourage this sentiment. Our intellectuals are rebels, proud to run out of their orbit. At the same time, we live amid machines that have uses entirely foreign to their substance; and our own purposes are artificial, imposed by a variable society or by some variable idea. If one artist or leader shows more genius than another, we think it due to his abstract mind and groundless originality; as if hands were not concerned in doing the work, or the labyrinth of fact in imposing the

action. We are nothing if not critics, but without a criterion for criticism; and we think ideas clever and persuasive for finding fault with reality rather than for expressing it. We thus abstract our minds from ourselves, and imagine that we do as minds what we can do, or can wish to do, only as animals.

Doubtless the stars are not animals, and here the rusticity of fancy in the ancients, who had been pastoral peoples, misled their judgment; but if the stars had been animals, the fact that they knew perfectly what to do would have been a mark in them of great intelligence and sovereignty of spirit. Unfortunately, that relative security and liberty which the stars find in space cannot be enjoyed by animate bodies on earth; the spirit native to us is therefore distracted. But it was a just perception of the ancients that such distraction was a hindrance to spirit, and not, as we moderns are tempted to think, the cause of spirit or an effect of it. Mathematical or static order, like any essence, is in itself lifeless, yet the material process by which such order is achieved or maintained obeys a trope, and adumbrates an organism ; so that the apparently static order of the stars, the mountains, or sublime architecture properly seems to us a high expression of spirit, and a great support to it. To conceive such a harmony, even as static, involves a transitive harmony of motions and tensions in ourselves. The psyche is exalted in rehearsing that order; and quite intelligibly, since organisms exist only by enacting some form of order and defending it, and the psyche is but a name for the success of the organism in so doing. When spirit perceives order in the world, it is therefore quickened by a sort of concourse and applause electrifying all those impulses by which the soul itself and the spirit first came to exist.

If we were justified, then, in attributing spirit to movements in nature not on the human scale, it would be sane and humble in us to think such spirit purer and keener than our own, where those movements were more exact and constant than ours.

Spirit expresses harmony, but the elements of that harmony must be tensions. In the heavens the same idea that described action would fill and satisfy thought; and we might truly say that the stars were guided by a perfect intelligence of their motions and an immortal determination to do their duty. They would have assurance of their destiny forever, and would joyously execute what they foretold. How hazy, how confused, and distressed in comparison, seems a mortal mind! Like all good myths, this notion of the life of the heavens and of Aristotle's God has a moral justification, being the glorification of what tends to occur in us as our minds grow clearer and clearer. Our spirits become freer or, in the cant of to-day, more creative, and we grow happier as our thought and our endeavours express our true potentialities. The psyche has then come to know her resources and her vocation. She is reconciled to herself and to the world in so far as it affects her; she has attained her normal intelligence and virtue. Where these are wanting, we remain tossed by barbaric caprice, benumbed by superstition, rent by internal conflicts. We then cannot help placing our liberty in our ignorance and our pleasures in our vices.

It would be foolish to imagine the spirit dwelling in an absolute void or in the spaces between the worlds or between animals, so that it might slip

It can arise only in an animal psyche. miraculously into any part of nature at random, breeding grapes out of thistles, or inspiring trees to walk and fishes to speak. How should such absolute spirit, even if it had magic powers, ever decide in its own blank, unattached mind what fiats to issue or in what crises to intervene? If it is to act a part in the drama, it must subserve the passion of the play. It must have, as the poet's mind has, its special memories and affinities, to load the dice, to follow a scent, to crave a particular issue. The place of spirit is in a psyche. There must first be a psyche specifically organized, directed upon a particular type of transmissible and defensible life, rich in definite but unknown potentialities. Spirit is incarnate by nature, not by accident. Otherwise it would not possess the lyrical, moral, impassioned character that makes it spiritual. It is intellectual, it thinks ideas; but it is not a realm of ideas hypostasized. It is alive, nothing if not transitive, always on the wing, watching, comparing, suffering, and laughing. It is the consciousness proper to an animal psyche.

This locus of spirit determines in each case its special vocation, turns it perhaps into a moral or social inspiration, when it might have been, in another body at another time, an irresponsible wild sensibility. Perception, impulse, conscience, and hope anchor spirit inwardly in the earth. It cannot imagine, it cannot *It bears inward witness to this fact by its vital and moral bias.* love, what is not somehow native to its home climate. Even its rebellions and contrary dreams are dictated by its animal predicaments. It is a spiritual symptom of vital strains. Ideas do not ask to be conceived; they threaten nothing to the sleeping mind that may neglect to distinguish them. But on the physical side attention and watchfulness are evidently crucial. They enlarge the capacity of an organism to react upon things, to change with them when necessary, and to change them when possible. And how should a pure spirit gratuitously and even blasphemously have pronounced some parts of the creation good and others evil? And why should it embrace as momentous and agonizing the poor fortunes of a particular earthly creature? Logically, rationally, morally this is a scandal, an insoluble mystery, or even, as some think, a hideous sin, meriting the endless torments that ensue upon it.

Turn to the natural history of the matter, and though the mystery remains, since any fact at bottom must be mysterious, the scandal vanishes; and what a self-torturing conscience thought a sin becomes the innocent, inevitable, beautiful impulse in any rhythmic or living thing to persevere in its existence and to grow into all those complexities and extensions that come naturally in its way. Will is but this impulse raised to consciousness, these inwardly rooted potentialities taking shape, and struggling to be born. The impulse and will, though groundless morally, are not groundless physically, but just what at that point they would naturally be; and the potentialities, though limited and specific, are not gratuitous, but fruitful and genial, if only harsh circumstances or their own conflicts do not crush or distort them. Spirit thus depends for sanity, for sweetness and hope, on that same physical order on which it depends for existence.

Our question concerning the distribution of spirit is now virtually answered. While the criterion for Provisional the existence of spirit is internal, namely, conclusion. that it finds itself thinking, the criterion for its distribution is public and historical, namely, the observable distribution of those forms of behaviour with which, in our several persons, we find spirit allied. Evidently this criterion, if scientific in its mode of application, is still subjective in its principle, and open to continual revision. Observers have different degrees of dramatic sensibility, and may see spirits everywhere or nowhere. A true interpretation would need to revise all such intuitive mind-reading. Yet mind-reading, in principle, must always remain intuitive; and where such intuition cannot but mislead, because the nature of the observed physical life differs from the physical life of the observer, all that a critic can do is to discount his personal equation and say: I recognize that there must be spirit, or something like spirit, in other regions, and I salute it and transcribe it, as well as I can, into my human terms; but I see that my myths are myths, and bow to the liberty of alien spirit to blow as it listeth.

A close and credible insight into spiritual life can therefore extend only to the limits of a man's race, temperament, and habit. Spontaneity here may then repeat and understand spontaneity there; and what is intrinsically a poetic exercise, not a metaphysical revelation, may become also, by accident, a true sense of ideal union between many minds.

The outer boundaries of our exploration being thus defined, we may consider the distribution of spirit in man at closer quarters.

There is a false traditional problem about what was called the seat of the soul, or in more modern parlance, the exact point in the brain and instant of time at which consciousness should spring out of the body or should impinge upon it from some fourth moral dimension. The ancients were not troubled by this question; and if it had been put to them, perhaps they might have replied that they failed to localize actual intuition or moral intensity in the natural world because these things being invisible and pneumatic were not to be found at all in that field. The psyche, indeed, was to be found there; and of the psyche they gave various more or less crude accounts, until Aristotle once for all distinguished form from matter, and identified the psyche (which makes the difference between living and dead bodies) not with any physical substance, but with the form which, in an organism, all suitable substances tended to assume and preserve. Even the psyche, then, was not to be found in nature as a particular thing, as for instance a hot vapour issuing from the lips in crises or at the moment of death; yet it could be discerned there intellectually, as

Mind though relevant to physical space and time has no position there.

the form or platonic idea of life in each organism. In other words, the psyche was the system of self-renewing and self-developing tropes reproduced by each species in each of its individuals. In these individuals the psyche was individual, being in each a particular instance or rehearsal of the hereditary type; in the species, the psyche was generic, like the group of faculties which we call human nature. But as to the spirit (which Aristotle called intellect or reason) that was altogether at another level. Intellect and reason were the forms of spirit that interested Aristotle, who had nothing of the poet or sceptic; and he saw that in that direction at least spirit was altogether trans- cendental and not to be found in nature even as a form that matter might acquire. It was pure act, living in and for itself, everywhere its own centre, a court of appeal for perception in which all things sensible are revised, a dialectical field for imagination in which all essences thought of appear.

To inquire *where* this court of appeal or field of ideas may itself lie, is misleading. Intrinsically, as it It not only spontaneously asserts itself and fills itself perceives out, spirit lies nowhere, and has no date. time but keeps pace It is transcendental, that is to say, with- in its own drawn from the sphere of the categories way with physical which it employs, an actual intuition not changes. having by any possibility a position within its own field of view. On the other hand, intuitions or instances of spirit are events ; something therefore precedes and introduces them, and they debouch upon further events. They are also cognitive and moral; they proclaim to themselves the existence of a world which involves them, and which they welcome or reject. Therefore, unless they declare themselves to be illusions and deny their own deliverance (a very complicated case of spiritual distraction) they really have, when viewed from the outside, a date and even a position in space, at least by courtesy or adoption. For they arise at some particular natural crisis, and are relevant to that crisis in duration, in character, and in scope. They are local and temporal instances of an intellectual light which in its cognitive essence sweeps over all space and time.

Now, since intuitions, viewed from outside and taken as events, have a natural locus, might we not define this locus precisely, specifying the exact movement of the organism that elicits each intuition, and the exact instant at which this intuition begins or ceases? Mustn't anything that begins and ends at all, as every actual thought surely does, begin and end at some indivisible instant?

Yes; and we may wait for science to discover, if it can, the precise cerebral commotions subtending different feelings. The times, and even the places, of those commotions will then be the physical times and places of such feelings. But there are elementary considerations that render this assertion ambiguous. In the first place, mathematical instants are not natural moments. In an infinite empty time all instants would be alike and indiscernible; they could not be individuated, because internally they would be nothing and externally the relations defining them would be identical in every case. To talk of a particular instant is therefore meaningless unless it be the limit between distinguishable events. Secondly, natural moments, to whatever simplicity they be reduced, contain at least this internal complexity, that they occur and have a direction. The act by which they arise is different in quality from that by which they lapse. They come and go: which implies that they have an origin and a sequel, and are moments in a variegated flux. Thirdly, in this flux there may be simultaneous differences in the scale of events, not

But structure in physical and mental series is not such that they can be superposed.

merely notional within one image, but physically enacted, as the earth in going round the sun also turns on its axis. These different units could not be contemporary, successive, or coincident, and their scales could not be compared, if they did not measure the same substantial flux, and impinge on the same universe of matter.

Even physical time, then, in which we wish to deploy the life of spirit, cannot be adequately expressed in mathematical or graphic terms. The world is not compacted of essences. The whole Eleatic problem that stretches it on the rack of dialectic is sophistical. Sensuous extension and duration when analysed in respect to the essence given in them yield geometrical space and time, themselves pure essences with no existence of their own. Such imaginary objects can have no authority over the material forces that they may serve to indicate or to measure. Matter flows through these forms and lends them a scale and tempo that are alien to them, being factual and energetic; whereas mathematical quantities are elastic, and there is room for the greatest in the least, as there is not in existing things. The pulses of nature have a pace of their own that is not to be stayed or hurried, and events tramp heavily forward, dividing inequivocably by their beat the distance they travel. Each natural moment lasts as long as it remains itself, and the next begins with the disappearance of that essence, as a pain stops when it ceases to be a pain, and marks its limits without help of latitude or longitude. Yet this weight and momentum of existence within each natural moment traverse that moment without the least hindrance from those ideal limits; on the contrary, the natural moment exists, and is more than an idea, precisely because it has been generated and is the momentary form of a substance

Mathematical form does not exhaust the being even of the realm of matter.

and a force that immediately pass on, and create the next moment. Such is the proper sense of the word *event*, something that comes out of something else, a phase in which some eternal essence is momentarily manifested in a flux of substance.

Now spirit is a form of life, not a hypostasis of logic, and its roots plunge precisely into that dynamic substrate that unites, creates, and destroys in turn all the gross units of the natural world. If, in its outlook, spirit rests in essences, in its origin it springs from matter; only that those tensions, movements, and natural moments which in the material world exist unawares, in spirit rise into actuality, and the essences hitherto stupidly exemplified now begin to be perceived. This is a glorious transformation, though perhaps tragic; and *actuality* has extraordinary ontological privileges.

An actual moment, or moment of spirit, possesses an internal intensive unity, even when aware only of change and distraction. It is not a fragment more or less superficially distinguishable from its medium and surroundings. On the contrary, it arises and develops from its centre outwards, like fire; it bursts forth like a ray of light and proclaims its existence with a great shout. Its objects may overlap and confuse one another, yet each intuition (even the most confused, when the confusion is conscious) is autonomous and self-formed. Their actuality separates them absolutely, and as each exists because it shines, existentially the chasm between them can never be bridged. It may indeed be bridged ideally in various ways and degrees, in representation: by faith and dramatic imagination; by similarity and common reference to the same facts; by common subsistence and historical relations in the realm of truth. How moments of spirit may spiritually support, contradict,

The intrinsic order of the realm of spirit is described in the Divine Comedy.

or fulfil one another is in fact the proper subject of this book. It is fundamentally the same subject as that of Dante's *Divine Comedy*, treated in critical prose instead of in a magnificent biographical and cosmic myth, into which all the fervour and venom of an unhappy life could be infused together with the tenderness of a pure poet. But if we ask what the vision of Dante conveys in the end, by way of a lesson, I think we may say it is this: The morphology of spirit, illustrated by great examples, showing what spirit suffers and what it gains by existing. These myriad lives and these myriad judgments did not produce one another; they grew severally out of human nature in various persons and circumstances; yet here all are marshalled, under the form of eternity, into a hier-archy, into a ladder of salvation, through which spirit may mount to divine insight and freedom, but on any step of which it may halt, down to the depths of rage and madness. Dante had the privilege of living in an age when, over the sea of rage and madness, spirit moved gloriously and universally acknowledged; also the privilege of singing in a young language formed by a Christian people. These privileges led him, how-ever, to take his great myth as almost a truth of physics; so that his respect for the sovereignty of spirit becomes ambiguous and we are not sure how far he is refining his stubborn will into insight and how far he is bowing unwillingly to power. A colder analysis can surmount that doubt. The impossibility of other than moral relations between the moments of spirit follows from their immaterial nature. Immateriality lifts them above the region of interaction, relativity, potentiality, fusion, or flux.

Therefore moments of spirit cannot be situated by their external relations. We must beware of assimil-ating them to physical events bathed in a medium that lends them its substance and determines their position. An intuition does not borrow its unity or its limits from its neighbours. In its own realm, it has no neighbours. It can have only fellow- Every point, witnesses, complementary thoughts, fulfil- as actual, ments real but separate, and enjoyed by central and others. Each thought feeds on its own fuel, primary. and in the act of seeing or positing other things, which it is powerless to create, it must at each moment create itself. Its field of view is finite without being circumscribed, but grows or shrinks with the scope of attention, and changes its structure and contents *ad libitum*, as in a dream. Not the previous thought, but the contemporary flux in the psyche and in all nature, determines what the next thought shall be. Otherwise no one could ever sleep, no one could ever die.

All the phases of spiritual existence have time in them, and local colour, though intrinsically no date, because the time and the pictured place are Time, for internal perspectives within each vista. For them, is not spirit all times are equally present, and its a source but proper and necessary lodging is, as the a vision. *Arabian Nights* have it, "a city among the cities" and above all a heart among the hearts. Experience becomes many-coloured as spirit passes from moment to moment and from place to place, yet to have had this career and to have been divided into these lives remains an accident of fortune. Nothing in spirit could choose those circumstances or fix those limits. The potentialities of spiritual life are infinite and no revolutions in nature can exhaust them; while on the other hand the deeper we go down towards the roots of spirit and the more freely it is suffered to speak, so much the surer and more consistent its oracles become; because the original potentialities of spirit being infinite, they are everywhere the same.

Thus the goodly company of spirits is aptly represented as a gathering of rapturous persons in one assembly, sitting in ranks according to the degree of their achieved enlightenment and charity, while in dark caverns beneath writhe all the writhings ever endured. The occasions are not forgotten, as we see in the speeches of the various souls in Dante. They are remembered and judged, but they are neither re-enacted nor continued. The continuation that is relevant is found realized in the brother-spirits, sitting in the rank above. Or in a more heathen image, we may conceive the inherent relations of spiritual moments to one another as a monadology or legion of daemons, Ariels and Calibans, all free and homeless, each solitary, save for the absorbing presence to it of its imagined world; each spinning in its own thoughts, like a madman, half-prophetic, half-impossible things. This inner isolation of spirit in the wildest rush of life, this essential absence of continuity or derivation between thought and thought, throws them all the more absolutely into the arms of physical nature. There they have arisen, and from there they have drawn their variety. Yet in arising they have escaped that net, each of them has seen the light, no matter how lurid; and their prerogative of being immaterial and intellectual forbids us to distribute them in physical time or space otherwise than by their signification. Each will be, in a moral sense, lost in its theme, riveted to its object, united with what it loves: yet these more or less rhetorical expressions would never suggest themselves, and would lack all point, if they were literally true. It is only because spirit is really not in those places or in those objects, that its occasional absorption in them becomes remarkable; and in the very act of remarking it, spirit recovers its independence, retreats to its transcendental station and wonders at the bewitchment that could seem to disperse it so helplessly amid all those beasts and all those catastrophes.

CHAPTER IV

THE WILL

THE word soul or psyche is a literary symbol standing for the unconscious organic destiny present in living seeds and in living bodies. In this sense the ancients could reasonably speak of a Soul of the World, since the world has a recognizable though imperfect order of movements, *Descriptive use of the word Will.* full of power and beauty. To this animating form or dominant system of tropes, we may give the more modern name of universal Will, provided we are aware of using this term poetically, after the descriptive manner of Schopenhauer and other German philosophers. I will scrupulously write the word, when used in this sense, with a capital, and understand by it *the observable endeavour in things of any sort to develop a specific form and to preserve it.*

Such descriptive use of terms like Will and endeavour is less metaphorical than it might seem. Undoubtedly in literary psychology and in sophisticated modern speech these words are meant to designate movements of the spirit, emotions, expectations, wishes, decisions, commands, or prayers. We are here discussing the realm of spirit, and need not stop to repeat that such a moral and imaginative sphere exists, that there is an immaterial intensity in feeling, and an immaterial light in intuition. But spirit once clearly discerned and admitted, how shall we distinguish its various phases? Suppose I am thirsty: my distress, in so far as it is conscious, is a spiritual trial; but what is it about? About the state of my body; or if perhaps there is only a dream-image that haunts me, it will be an image of water and of myself about to drink, but prevented. Similarly with every other object of passion, even the most impersonally moral or political. There will be some dream-image of what might happen in the world, how people might be living, how they might be shouting for joy, and unanimously asserting everything that I believe. I may imagine that what I long for is a union of pure spirits, but that is a verbal delusion. Spirits cannot be united unless persons are distinguished, and persons can be distinguished only in a physical world. What I long for is life in a world to come, peopled by natural bodies. In my purest will, I am experiencing one physical process and desiring another. My behaviour and the events expected to follow are the sole discoverable parts of the entire history. In these only could my conscious will find evidence of any ideal unanimities.

In using the word Will for these two connected movements in nature, one in human behaviour, the other in its effects and conditions, we are not feigning, then, anything psychological behind or within inanimate processes; we are rather recognizing the original seat of those conflicts and endeavours which agitate the spirit only because, in the first place, they agitate the animal psyche and the material world.[1]

According to this use of terms, the psyche becomes a particular instance of universal Will, found whenever the form to be maintained is organic and preserved by nutrition and reproduction. Then spirit, too, may be called an expression of Will, since it arises at a specially energetic phase in the life of the psyche, namely,

Occasions on which Will in a psyche becomes conscious will or spirit.

----

[1] Hobbes used the word *endeavour* in this way. Had his usage been adopted, English philosophy might have begun with behaviourism instead of ending with it.

when the range of adjustment and control begins to extend beyond the body; for so long as life remains purely vegetative it seems to be unconscious. No doubt there are internal sensations in animals, which may precede external perception; but no organ would be morally sensitive or conscious if cut off from the other organs and from the brain; so that spirit seems to be allied to *messages*, even if these be internal to one organism. We may then say that spirit arises whenever Will in one place finds it profitable to mark, trace, and even imitatively to share the movement of Will elsewhere. By so doing a psyche anticipates attack and defence, putting forth telepathic feelers, as it were, indefinitely far into space and time. To mark, to trace, or to share any and every movement going on in the world is precisely the function of spirit; only that for spirit this marking, tracing, or sharing is purely ideal, and being ideal may tend to become adequate to the life of the object; whereas marking tracing and sharing for the psyche involve only a material response and an instinctive readjustment.

The concomitance of these two phases, one automatic and the other emotional, blinds us to their complete ontological diversity. Each actually involves and instantly suggests the other, so that under the name of either the entire natural event may be safely indicated. But to indicate an event is not to describe it, much less to analyse it. Any feature, any nickname or gesture, suffices to represent to the cursory mind the most complex of facts; and we thread our way automatically through the world, by the help of a few superficial signals to which we hardly attend, while our thoughts go woolgathering or are lost in the haze of bodily sensation. When rarely, in reflective moments, we realize our spiritual solitude, we begin to wonder how nature (all brute accidents) ever came to confront spirit

Harmony conditioned by difference.

(all ideal demands); and the contrast between these conjoined enemies becomes mysterious to us, or even scandalous. Perhaps then we grow speculative, and attempt to reduce nature to a figment of mind, as if the world were an idea to be easily downed or exorcised by another idea; or perhaps we dream of introducing spirit, like a mighty blast, amid the tempests of nature, so as to direct or to pacify them. But these are the illusions of egotism; abounding in its own sense, and ignorant of its foundations. The foundations of spirit are in the life of nature; nothing could be more natural or spontaneous than this running hypostasis of vital changes into prophetic and symbolic intuitions. The world is not only a patient artist in its structure but a rapt poet in its sentiment. Why should it not be? And how should this ever be the case with us if, in essence and potentially, it were not the case in our ancestral substance? Such, whether sophisticated people call it natural or miraculous, is at any rate the fact. Tensions, movements, unities that in the realm of matter are mere forms or tropes, give birth to intensive, moral, and conscious echoes in the realm of spirit. Thereby the fertility of the physical order ceases to be vain, and proves itself to be greater than our partisan minds like at first to admit. In reality, substance and form, mechanism and lyric actuality are interwoven and contrasted in nature's own way: with radical freedom, since opportunity was infinite; yet with blind perseverance, since when one experiment is afoot why should another experiment interrupt it? There is time and there is room for everything in infinity, even for ourselves.

We have therefore no occasion to deny or to minimize the difference between mind and matter. Peace between disparate things is not to be secured by assimilating them. Assimilation would destroy at least one of them, and probably both, and the result would not be a harmony but a material confluence of uniform parts. If reality were all of one kind, elements could agree only by repeating one another or by moving in the same current, like the drops of water in a river. The Will in each molecule—the force by which it coheres— would be unaffected by the direction in which the molecule as a whole might be carried, so long as it was not disrupted; and the politics of the world would remain entirely indifferent to the citizens. Such indifference brings with it a negative peace; the part is not troubled by the whole, and the whole need not trouble about itself, since in the dynamic sphere accommodation imposes itself automatically at every moment and is necessarily perfect. Universal Will, by definition, cannot but be realized, being a name for the continually renewed balance and resultant of all forces.

Ways in which specific Wills may conform to universal Will.

Wholly different are the conditions of harmony when molecules have become plastic organisms, and organisms, always imperfect, have reached great elaboration in incomparable directions. In their fortunes they must continue to conform involuntarily to universal Will, but their different Wills are partly defeated in the process. Compromise may soften this partial defeat by accepting it. We then surrender a native potentiality for the sake of something more opportune, which may graft itself on the original stem and create a new Will no less genuine than the old one. Or if the original Will was strongly organized, the compromise may be only provisional, as when a conquered nationality sullenly vegetates, until an occasion comes for recovering its independence, or as a married pair chafes under the yoke, meditating freedom. But all alien forces are not hostile to a healthy Will that nature has adopted and rendered perennial. Adaptation far from being a compromise or a mutilation, may be a happy development, bringing out latent faculties of the psyche, and enriching life with an increased relevance and responsiveness to different orders of things. A system of moral relations, lying in the realm of truth, will then be found radiating from each organic being, multiplying its connections and increasing its distinction; because these relations will be based on the native affinities of each psyche, and selected freely, so that the more life expands in those congenial lines the more it becomes what it willed to be.

Such is the harmony possible among disparate things, a correlation of different orders of beings, rendering each more distinct, and the whole more diversified. Out of such a harmony, established at the biological level, spirit was born; and the farther and the more perfectly that harmony can spread round the psyche, the better the Will in spirit is fulfilled. Nothing could be ontologically more unlike nature than spirit is; yet nothing could be better able to mould itself, in its own ideal manner, to every detail and convolution in nature, so as to survey it and know it; nothing could diversify and enrich nature more radically, adding a moral dimension to what would otherwise be merely material; and nothing could more freely or triumphantly express its own Will than spirit does by at once feeling and transcending the Will of everything else.

If spirit in us could be entirely dominant we should esteem everything in nature as if it were the inmost part of ourselves, and everything in ourselves as if it were the remotest and the least part of nature. But the actual life of spirit is all compromise, being continually stopped in its flights, and enslaved by some particular passion or illusion. To that extent spirit is not spiritual and exists only in a thwarted effort to be born. Once clear, however, even if only for a moment and in some particular direction, it is out of sight of compromise. It is fed

Pure spirit would find no enemies.

by everything while it wakes and disturbed by nothing while it sleeps. Its existence becomes a pure gain both to itself and to the world that contains it and that thereby completes, in self-knowledge, the cycle of its normal life.

But here we come upon a paradox: that spirit, the most inward of things and the most vital, should find its purest affinities in remote and abstract regions, in mathematics, in music, in truth, in the wider aspects of nature and history, and should find its greatest enemies, its worst torments, at home. The stars are more friendly to it than the mountains, the mountains than the town, the town than the workshop or the garret; and its irreconcilable foes are its own body and its own passions. Yet this was inevitable, in view of the animal roots of spirit in the psyche. An animal organism, in developing smell, sight, and hearing, adjusts itself to external things merely in confirming and steadying its own life. This sensibility to the not-self arises entirely in the self's service. Those far-reaching senses are not speculative in their Will, but defensive or aggressive; and the mechanism that generates and supports them necessarily subserves the welfare of the body. If it did not, it would tend to destroy that body and to annul itself. Yet meantime, by that useful trick of exact adaptation and imitative sympathy, the psyche has automatically generated spiritual sympathy and true intelligence, without in the least requiring these gifts or profiting by them. A purely ideal consciousness of things not hers has sprung up within herself. She has given birth to a spirit that potentially, in its intellectual vocation, infinitely transcends her.

Radical divergence of Will in spirit from Will in the psyche as a whole.

How does this come about? Under what auspices does a moral dimension, mechanically non-existent and biologically idle, attach itself to physical life? I think an answer, of a certain kind, is not far to seek. Every-

thing finite, in the bosom of the infinite, reckons without its host.   The great residuum that it ignores
Non-psychic nevertheless continues to beat against those
processes bounds, like the sea upon a coral island.   And
surrounding
and permeat- not only from the outside.   There is probably
ing the an infinity surging within as well as one
psyche help
to evoke laughing round the corner.   Now a very tight
spirit. and simple organism might resist this double
solicitation almost for ever, or might reappear perpetually almost without change; but the more complex an
organism becomes, the more it will lean upon external
support, and the more everything in it will come to
be an index to the things that it is not.   There are
commitments and dangers enough in vegetative life;
but these are immensely extended by the organ of
spirit, by the whole perceptive, aggressive, and teachably reflex machinery of the animal psyche.   The
human race in particular has entered upon an ambitious
and glorious career, acquiring a dominion over the
universe perceptively and over the earth industrially
that would seem incredible if it were not actual.

Such enterprise on the psyche's part was no blunder,
unless we judge life itself to be a blunder.   Nature has
The price of simply explored the possibilities of organiza-
this sensitive- tion and run the inevitable risk of confusion
ness is moral and disaster.   This is normal, as is also the
distraction.
inner conflict and strain that so complex
an equipment, with its parts working intermittently,
imposes upon the psyche.   A visit to the Zoo may
convince anybody that this is no prerogative of man,
much less a miraculous inroad of spirit into nature.   All
those odd animals are seen straining under the burden
of their oddity.   Many of them are already almost
extinct; many others were extinct long ago.   Perhaps
the oddity of man—that interest of his in things not
edible which issues in art and intelligence—may also
prove fatal; and if so far, on the whole, the experiment

has proved physically useful, it has been at the price of terrible inner conflicts, reaching war and organized tyranny in the race and madness in the individual. In no other creature, probably, is the natural soul so much distracted. In no other has the margin of life encroached so much upon the text; no clean clear margin, such as we may suppose sleep and the placid stretches of contented idleness to be for other animals, but a margin crowded with comments and contradictions and caricatures and cross-references, demanding that we attend to everything at once and live not bravely forward, as other animals do, but continually looking backward, or far ahead, or suspiciously, greedily, impertinently, and frivolously in every direction.

We talk of "life" as if it were unquestionably something precious or even divine. Perhaps a part of the vocation of spirit may be to overcome this prejudice. Life, where it has arisen, is by definition a nucleus of Will, and a point of reference for imputing good and evil; but who should impute good and evil, or in reference to what Will, in those vast cosmic *The Will in matter is deeper than the specific Will of the psyche even in the psyche itself.* regions that surround and that breed life, so that life itself, before it existed, should be declared a good? Physical life and an animal psyche are not ultimate categories; they are not the primary movements or tensions in the universe. The potentialities of matter far outrun any such temporary tropes. The scale on which the psyche operates is a local scale, and the perceptive organs that she develops are biased selective organs. Many deeper or subtler currents, as well as much vaster harmonies, presumably run through the world, and flow unimpeded through the psyche, as through a sieve. In her special interest she can afford to ignore them. But she lives immersed and saturated in them nevertheless; and it was precisely when she availed herself of some of these currents, at first dis-

regarded, that her organs of sense acquired their extra-
bodily range.   Then in becoming physically perceptive
she became, against her primary Will, vitally extra-
verted.   She began to live and to suffer where, materially, she was not; her heart, so to speak, began to travel.
All this was in her simply an organic crisis or fever;
but it set her dreaming, as a fever will in a deep sleep.
For the first time she felt a real pang, the birth-pang
of the spirit, and she saw a clear image, her first notion
of a world.   It was a strange self-displacement, like
falling in love.   In her ambition to grow she had
become so great that she discovered her littleness.
And henceforth it was impossible for her to go back or
to draw in her horns.   If in nostalgia for vegetative
peace she now shut her eyes and risked being mistaken,
her new and formidable friends would escape her, and
she might no longer escape her old enemies, because
her shell would have been broken, and now her greater
sensitiveness and more precarious life would have
multiplied their number and exposed her much more
to their attacks.

Thus a pragmatic mechanism that operates with no
reference to the truth nevertheless must meet and bow
to the truth, in its adjustments; and the truth,
having divine prerogatives, grounded more
deeply and widely in the universe than any
particular life, rewards the respect shown to
it by a miraculous but appropriate gift, namely, by a
vision of the truth.   Clouded as this vision may be, it
is essentially a vision of all reality.   It flashes like sheet-
lightning broadly but unseizably, and only for a moment
in every intuition of the spirit.   With this a disproportionate dignity and ambition breaks in upon animal
life, strangely incongruous, pregnant with repentance
and with exaltation above mortality.   But the psyche
cannot repent, and cannot stop feeding, breeding, and
acting.   She must persist or die; and it is only the

Universal affinities of Will in the spirit.

spirit that can repent for her and suffer for her, until it achieves its own liberty.

In this way, like an ignorant girl, the psyche has become a mother without counting the cost either to herself or to her miraculous child; and the spirit has come undesired into the working world that wanted only another slave and is utterly incapable of understanding or re- specting the divine changeling that has been brought to it. Evidently for the preservation and welfare of an organism fit reactions suffice; a *sense* of those reactions or their occasions is superfluous. And in fact the core of the human psyche, which is like that of other animals, might decline all responsibility for such a dispersion of affection, or even deny that it existed. Adaptation creates intelligence, but does not know that it does so. When the Will in an animal began to react upon and to mimic external objects, it was bent only on absorbing or on dominating those objects materially; the habit of retracing the environ- ment and as it were, sinking into it and catching its rhythm, was something secondary, instrumental and oblique; and the response was strictly practical, touch- ing only what touched the organism. But such a selection cannot be made beforehand. In exploring you cannot first decide what you shall discover; you must explore everything that offers, and then perhaps select the part that it concerns you to study.

Now it is precisely this preliminary but indomitable interest in fact, in form, and in truth for truth's sake that is the Will proper to spirit: a Will that wills heroically what the psyche as a whole willed only condi- tionally and, as it were, unwillingly. For by sensitively adjusting herself to her opportunities she inevitably bred in herself a frank affinity to other things and even to contrary Wills. She found herself hypnotically re- hearsing alien movements, without any possibility of

(marginal note) Automatic acquisition of this affinity in self-defence.

absorbing the substances that so moved. And willy-nilly such an ideal possession of things materially absent is mind; it is spirit. This spirit is spontaneous, disinterested, intellectual in its essence; but it does not live, as sometimes it imagines, on its own resources or by its own power. It is the psyche that creates spirit in becoming materially sensitive to remote things; and it is this living natural individual that in generating spirit renders his vital unity moral, and acquires a mental cognizance of the world and of himself in the midst of it.

We should be antedating the birth of spirit and turning our symbols into myths if we asked whether the psyche *made a mistake* in developing such speculation. She was led into an experiment rich in possibilities and in dangers. It could not be called a mistake even if some day, or in many cases, it proved fatal; because all experiments in the end prove fatal if we regard them as aimed at some specific good; but they all prove fertile as well, since they enable new forms to arise. We shall trace presently some of the conflicts which the Will underlying spirit has caused in the individual and in society; they are biological conflicts, confusions in the play of organic impulses; but it would always be a private judgment, inspired by one or another of these impulses, to say that the psyche *ought* to have remained vegetative, so as to avoid these conflicts, or that in becoming partly disinterested (that is, in generating spirit) she was *false to her own interests*. In her own life, she simply developed new organs—the senses, organic memory, language, the arts—because she had the potency and the occasion to do so; and as to the life of spirit that thereby supervened, she gained and she lost absolutely nothing by it, since spirit is immaterial, neither a drain nor an influence, and merely concomitant to her life, like a shadow, a truth, or a harmony.

If the life of the psyche could ever become *wholly*

Biological automatism not thereby interrupted.

disinterested and sacrificial (which would involve becoming materially passive and barren) the Will achieved would be exclusively the Will in spirit, and in that supreme moment the spirit would live absolutely and sublimely free. But that would mean physical death, or a transport equivalent to a suspension of physical life: a condition that may be approached or traversed, but that cannot be sustained. The Will in spirit therefore does not enjoy the privilege which the Will in the vegetative psyche always retains, the privilege of suspending the experiment by which spirit was evoked, and retreating into unconsciousness. To retreat, or rather to soar, into pure spirit is a continual tendency or goal in intellectual and moral life; it appears in the idea of God, when God is conceived spiritually; it is frequently touched or skirted by the innocent mind; but it cannot be maintained or made the staple of any existence. Spirit is not a substance with a life of its own; if it were, it could never have got entangled in these animal meshes. It is a consciousness of animal aspirations already afoot. Even the aspiration to see, to understand, and to experience everything is at bottom an animal aspiration, that needs to be radically transmuted before it can become a spiritual one. The whole experience of spirit expresses natural predicaments. Spirit suffers hunger and thirst; it hates, it fears, it loves, it inquires, it feels perplexed and forsaken. It is merely the psyche become conscious. Therefore any dream of being pure spirit, omniscient, safe, and joyful, represents only an ideal limit, an ambition intimately involved in being spirit at all, but not attainable in its purity. Sometimes the flame grows brighter, sometimes it sinks, in proportion as the vital synthesis of the moment contracts to the scope of some single interest or trouble, or extends to remoter influences and greater destinies. At best, under the

(margin note: The Will in spirit not separable from the animal Will.)

spell of nature and truth, intuition may almost draw the whole psyche out of her native moulds, and concentrate her energies in intelligence, in fancy, or in worship.

At such moments the Will at work in the spirit becomes unanimous with the Will of nature working beyond the animal soul. In religious par-lance, it becomes identical with the Will of God. Although the spirit always suffers more or less and sometimes suffers cruelly, yet in one sense it is less pathetic, less help-lessly wasted, than the vegetative psyche that never suffers consciously, but simply crops out, struggles, and dies. Spirit dies too, but with the knowledge of its essential capacity to rise again, so that it rather sleeps than dies; and all its sufferings in so many incarnations are properly not its own, but those of the animal organism which for the moment it inhabits, and which but for this descent of spirit, would have been con-demned to grow, to work, and to die without ever loving anything ideally, or knowing its own *raison d'être*. The objects we see the psyche pursuing are results in which she would rest, conditions in which she would prosper, not perfections that, before she evoked spirit, she could ever worship or desire. She lives as long as she can, on any terms, until her mechanism snaps; and her struggles are so vainly persistent and desperate pre-cisely because they are blind. Courage, we call this mechanical impulse, and enlist it morally in our hero-isms; but in the psyche it is a mere potentiality of heroism and also of madness. When instinct prompts, she will boldly lay any wager, and double it against any odds. The advent of spirit cannot abolish these vital impulses and mortal dangers; but in raising them into conscious suffering and love, spirit turns the ignominy of blind existence into nobleness, setting before us some object to suffer for and to pursue. In the very act of becom-ing painful, life has become worth living in its own eyes.

It is the same Will enlightened about its objects and conditions.

CHAPTER V

FREEDOM

THE world continually suffers change, but not complete change; for if it did not preserve some substantial and dynamic continuity it could not be said to subsist through change or even to be a world. But it *exists* by exemplifying various essences successively in a flux; that is to say by an irrational selection, first of the particular character to be presented at any moment, and secondly of the manner in which this contingent character shall be exchanged for the one exemplified next. There is no logical necessity or external compulsion in this process. There is only in certain respects a continuity in movement, quantity and habit, with frequent partial repetitions of form; so that tropes or laws and familiar physical objects may be distinguished in the flux, and may serve in some measure to prophesy how it will presumably flow in the future and how it presumably flowed in the past.

All existence contingent and in that sense free.

From this it follows that every fact and every movement is *free*, since nothing else compelled it to be as it is; and further, each fact or movement is free in positing itself with a certain vehemence or Will, by which it not only exists but seems to enjoy existing and to defy extinction.

Compulsion begins when free action in one direction collides with free action in another. Generative causes never remove freedom; over what should they exercise compulsion? On the contrary, they enable freedom to exist in a new instance and perhaps in a new form. Parents do not trespass on a child's liberty by bringing him into the world. Did they produce him organically perfect they would have endowed him with perfect freedom, as far as his Will was concerned; and if circumstances soon compelled him to do as he would not, or not to do as he would, such an external diminution of liberty would leave his Will no less free and perhaps more precise and defiant. The Will can be enslaved only by one part of it checking or suppressing another part; and this is the sad slavery we inherit from Adam, namely, vital self-contradiction. Each part and act of the Will remains nevertheless an original phase of the Will of nature. The relations between causes and effects, as between parents and children, are fundamentally fraternal. One instance of a law is neither more nor less spontaneous than the next instance; parents and children belong to the same species, and grow on the same bough; the parents have been children, the children are formed to become parents, similar passions animate them and a common fate overhangs them. If, then, nature in producing them has rendered their Will specific and limited, it has not coerced that Will but asserted it, endowing it with special capacities and with affinity to particular goods. Such determination is a prerequisite to bare existence, much more to freedom or to moral life.

To be free you must first be born and have some Will in particular.

At the same time existence, in making each thing and each impulse such as it is, has made it impossible or difficult for it to become anything else, or to pursue any good except that to which it is naturally directed: and this, *to spirit*, is a real and even an intolerable limitation. For spirit too exists by virtue of a specific Will, manifested in special functions and aimed at a special object; and this object, in the case of spirit, is universal knowledge

Special case of spirit.

and universal love. Freedom for spirit would therefore require a supernatural station, from which all
perspectives should be equally visible and equally
neutralized; and it would require infrahuman and
superhuman sympathies, by which an infinite variety
of goods might be appreciated and impartially judged.
In man, in any finite creature, spirit is therefore deeply
enslaved. It tastes freedom, and gets some notion of
it, only in those movements of intuition in which the
animal seat and the animal bias of the Will are forgotten
and intelligence and love, as if disembodied, fly to their
objects without hindrance from the flesh, lifting them
out of the past or the future into immediate presence,
and doing them, ideally, absolute justice, without sinking into the limitations or the confused hatreds inseparable from natural existence.

The ideality of spirit, that drops things in order
to retain only their essences, sometimes gives a new
turn to the notion of freedom. As spirit is *Phenomena,*
free in liberating an idea, we may conceive *though con*
that ideas themselves, or some of them, are *tingent, have*
no Will and
metaphysical powers; and that the Will in *are not free*
all nature is due to the action or attraction *or causal.*
of logical being. Even a power to call oneself into
existence out of nothing is sometimes attributed to
essences or forms, as if that which is always equally
necessary could act, or act freely, or be the cause
of selected and contingent transitory facts. But
phenomena contain no Will or endeavour to persist.
They dawn and fade unconcerned. The force, the
fuel, the food, the machinery all operate beneath those
visible appearances. Thunder itself is but an impotent
sound, fit to frighten children; but there is an invisible
power in heaven that really hurls the bolt. Therefore
philosophical tradition has instinctively placed all initiative and liberty in the Will, not in the Idea. To
attribute power to ideas is superstitious. There is

indeed as much contingency in the *occurrence* of ideas as in any other event: but the material movements that exhibit or call forth those ideas have a previous history and will have subsequent effects, ultimately irrelevant to those ideas. The seed and the soil produce the flower, and a given essence has no more power to create itself, or to call up another essence, than have all the other forms that have never seen the light.

There is a further ground for this superstition about the power of ideas, namely, that *in the psyche* an idea

Psychology of the *idée-force*.

is often a premonition. Some definite impulse, perhaps moulded and qualified by much experience, is at work in the organism; an image of what might be or ought to be the issue, arises beforehand in the spirit; and as the act matures the image perhaps grows brighter and brighter, acquires fresh specifications, and finally is swallowed up in the actual perception of the word, the work, or the action in which the impulse has terminated materially. This perception, though it overwhelms the previous idea by its force and steadiness, often disappoints; there were currents in the psyche, vaguely present to the spirit and beckoning it on, that the result achieved has not satisfied. Often, however, when the prophetic mind was well instructed and rational, what is done is exactly what was foreseen and intended: something that normally happens in routine and daily actions. Yet even here there is sometimes an illusion of success or even of triumph, where the Will has been really defeated. The previous state of the soul may have been confused and painful; there may be a vast relief in the actual birth of something unforeseen, something that at least is definite, in which good points may be found, and which powerfully bends the mind in new directions, towards what now seems possible, and buries those unhappy vague aspirations that now would be grotesque. The chief need of the psyche was to be delivered of her burden: what does it matter in comparison whether the spirit has the satisfaction of seeing realized in matter the very form that it had already seen in thought? Disappointments of this sort may pave the road to a kind of happiness.

If fortune here seems to treat the spirit a little roughly, the spirit may parry the blow, and take a high revenge. When the Will has somehow had *Disillusion* its way, the spirit is apt to sink a little; it is *in victory.* dashed by this earthly fulfilment of its hopes. What was celestial has become terrestrial. What we loved unreservedly has been tarnished and scattered: a thousand vulgar idols have usurped its name. We see how much better it would have been to lay up our treasures where moth and rust do not corrupt and thieves break not in or steal. But is this safe treasury to be found in the clouds or in that most uncertain of regions, the future? We may hope for many good things in the future, most of which can hardly be enjoyed by ourselves; but sure possessions are possible only in the present, which for intuition always gives also a glimpse of the eternal. The spiritual value of our disappointments does not lie merely in producing resignation, or reconciling our chastened wills to the issue. The issue probably has its modest worth, which we do well to prize. But the chief good in having been disappointed is that, if we are firm, we remain inconsolable, having aspired and still aspiring to something better than the event. Then against its Will, fortune will have wedded us to beauties it had no power to create, but only to promise. That promise, externally so foolish, has made us inwardly wise, enabling us to break in spirit through the veil of time, and to recognize a sublime nocturnal firmament above the sky. The spirit cannot be bribed by compensations. It does not wish, it does not need, to be consoled. It is consecrated to a perfection which it loves and from which, in its love, it cannot be separated.

The Will visible in matter and in the laws of nature having been originally free, a doubt arises whether this radically free Will, in once asserting itself, bound itself never to change, or whether, being groundless fundamentally, it may at any moment take a new direction. Looked at under the form of eternity, or as it is in truth, this dilemma becomes indifferent. Existence being intrinsically a flux or process, its essence involves a passage from prior to subsequent terms which are not identical; there is therefore essential novelty at every step; and it makes no difference whether we say that each term arises independently or that the trope that involves and unites the two terms arises as a whole. It will in any case take time to develop, and will in any case be the exact development that it turns out to be. On the human scale we contrast mechanism with tropes, because we ignore the process and progression involved in a mechanical change, treating it as a single stroke, one more instance of an old way that things have of happening, like the apple falling, or the smoke coming from a fire. But the simplest event, being a change, has a trope in it, a beginning and an end, a sort of inner teleology, the beginning being a movement towards that end, and the end the culmination of that transition. Mechanism is therefore just as vital as life; and life, seen at a sufficient distance, when generations become moments and only types and totals are visible, becomes perfectly mechanical. The only question touches the scale of the tropes to be found in nature; and whether the more minute ones continue to run within the larger or whether (as an intuition) the larger transform and obliterate the smaller.

The same optional alternatives appear in theology. Creation may be called a single fiat, since God is con-

Freedom implies initiative but not variability.

ceived to have intended from the beginning all that was to ensue; or we may speak of a gradual creation, since the Will to sustain existence and to continue the same design, must be renewed at each moment, and in each phase of each event. Creative evolution is nothing but a modern name for progressive creation.

An impression nevertheless prevails that if the energy or direction of existence suddenly changed, freedom would be vindicated; whereas if they never change, nature would appear to be self-hypnotized and mechanized. It would seem to be as in marriage. If divorce is possible, the union remains free; but where divorce is out of the question, the vows once made become a fatality. This is really the case to some extent, because Will in men and women contains many other impulses besides the impulse to live together; and married life involves many commitments that the Will in lovers had ignored. Therefore, if no divorce is allowed, the marriage contract loads the dice in every subsequent decision and exercises a real constraint over the other impulses of the Will. But if love wholly unified the soul, as it sometimes thinks it does, so that no comparable passion any longer subsisted, a pledge to love always would be but a claim to immortality, the pure aspiration to be and to remain oneself. It would postulate spiritual freedom: whereas any eventual inconstancy would signify infection by some alien force. Integrity alone can be morally free, being alone compatible with a radical self-knowledge and the perception of an ultimate good. Fluctuations in the Will would prove, on the contrary, that the psyche was pregnant with unharmonized passions or had been transformed by some external influence. It is self-ignorance that leads to actions contrary to one's latent Will, though perhaps willed psychologically; and it is ignorance of the world that leads to actions that, though obedient to

Dispersed freedom hoist with its own petard.

the Will as an impulse, defeat it as a purpose. In both forms ignorance is a cause of helplessness and self-defeat, not (as romantic feeling suggests) a condition of freedom. Without constancy freedom has no momentum or dignity.

On this analogy we may say that, if the same laws of nature always prevailed or if the world had sprung into existence, dynamically complete, the Will in nature would be physically just as free as if force were added in driblets or came in spurts. Moral freedom, however, the universe could not possess unless it were animated by a spirit that saw the whole prophetically and willed it psychologically; in a word, unless God governed it. We are free morally when the spirit in us foresees and intends what we do physically or assents to it while being done: but spiritually we are no less implicated in actions or thoughts which we heartily approve ideally than in those which we perform or utter materially.

A man given to dreaming, planning, imagining, and always talking to himself becomes deeply entangled in such unperformed actions. He may live Psychic in- through many events in fancy that annoy cubation of or even torment him, as in nightmares; but action. even these will have sprung from himself, or from things that have long taken root in him; and when, in the public world, he finds himself actually doing one of those meditated things, or something like it, he will recognize his own work, and feel proud or ashamed of it. Particularly when the thing done was clearly anticipated and planned, with means elaborately conceived to bring it about; for then the man has consciously lived through the first begetting and long gestation of his action, and knows it for his own child. But this felt responsibility implies not that the action was free but that (according to conventional notions of cause and effect) it was thoroughly explicable, and caused by the man's Will, by the deepest and most ancient currents of his being; so that his action is a perfect mirror and revelation of himself—a revelation of himself perhaps appalling to his own conscience. Had the action been separately free, the whole good-and-evil of it being concentrated in its groundless occurrence, the man would find it unaccountable and say he was bewitched, that his body had been magically led to perform it against his proper and habitual Will. This primal Will in himself, responsible for all he does, thinks, and loves freely, is a part of the universal Will in nature, of the groundless character of fact everywhere; and it would be sophistical to pretend that this part of universal Will was due to the other parts, so that the man was not ultimately responsible for being what he was. Who, then, should be responsible for him? The other facts? Or the other instances of Will, willing things quite different from the Will in him? Or perhaps the trope that records the way in which these various Wills hang together? But a trope is not a power, only a description; it simply puts all the included facts in the places which they have always taken spontaneously.

If we said that origins are responsible for aftergrowths (which is not true either analytically or morally) nothing would be responsible for itself, unless we came at last to a first fact. But that notion is questionable. If ever there was a first fact in time, it was probably the simplest of facts; and in what sense could this whole complicated world, physical and moral, be due to that simplest or vaguest nebula from which it sprang? Logically, morally, and under the form of eternity, all facts are first facts. Some elements and processes in nature are certainly more pervasive than others, and simpler; but the complications ensue of their own accord, because those simpler facts are so related that

Responsibility pervades existence.

a new essence or a new trope comes to be exemplified in their movement.   A different Will begins to appear in the world, one that the previous crawling converging Wills in it had never manifested.   But the cataract with its force and music utters the Will of nature no less genuinely, and more loudly, than the brooks and the raindrops that went to make it up; so that the truly primal and responsible Will appears in the total reality and pregnancy of the world, with its groundless elements and free evolution.   The fiat of God and the sin of Adam are equally original, and both are omni-present; for besides the universal Will expressed in all that happens there is independent conation in the parts, making for what might have happened if the total balance of forces had not prevented.

When the unit of action, which is the free fact, seems to pass from the part to the whole, is the freedom of the part thereby lost?   Suppose a young

A free whole qualifies freedom in the parts.

man with a tenor voice, standing on a mountain-top felt a sudden impulse to sing high *C*: the vital freedom in that act would not be questionable.   But suppose he had learned the aria *Ah, quella pira*, and felt a sudden impulse to sing that: would the high *C*, when it came to crown the melody, be less freely uttered than in the other case? Certainly that note would now have been predetermined, not absolutely, but in case this particular aria remained throughout the chosen norm of that action.   High *C* would thus have lost something of its freedom as to the moment when it should come and even as to its coming at all; for if you once set out to sing that particular song this particular challenge cannot be avoided.   You must strike high *C* at the appointed moment or fail in having your Will.   On the other hand your Will now, in spite of being controlled by that of a dead composer, is much more voluminous and potent, and far more deeply your Will than would be the emotional impulse to shout high *C* by itself, without any musical setting. What was an animal cry has become part of a poetical trope and a dramatic climax, so that now there is a reason for your high *C* as well as a cause. Exhilaration may have taken the form of confidence, and confidence that of defiance hurled at all the kingdoms of the world and their wickedness, spread like a map beneath your feet. The Will expressed now dominates a much larger segment of your life and of the moral landscape; the spirit out-poured is more entangled but more richly fed; and this organization of vital freedom may be a step towards spiritual liberation.

Freedom is thus present on various scales in all the forces and tropes in nature: but the psyche being a knot of forces with a particular vehement organic rhythm, repels spontaneity elsewhere as com- Psychic in-justice to pulsion, because it obstructs or disregards nature at her own spontaneity. When she becomes large. conscious these harsh contacts and their sources begin to appear more or less clearly to her spirit, together with the emotions of surprise, hatred, desire, or pleasure proper to her movements on such occasions. In enlightening our vital egoism, spirit must transcend this egoism, else it could not enlighten it. Things that to the psyche are obstructive and dark then recover a new spontaneity in intuition, not their own physical spontaneity but the proper spontaneity of spirit in conceiving them; so that the psychic injustice of treating them as mere lumber or substance to be devoured is partly redressed by the spirit in its first sensuous flight, which turns matter into brilliant images or into comforts and sweets. The world seems alive to children and poets, but with a weak spectacular vitality, full of foolish wonders like a dream. In use and in difficulty this primary fancifulness of spirit is submerged, and everything appears dead, or obdurately

animated by a stupid mechanical Will. Other people
and animals, that were the toys of childhood, now seem
brutal and wicked; and the latent capacity of spirit to
be both poetical and scientific, both sympathetic and
firm, comes late to the surface.

In this long enslavement of free fancy to animal Will
arise certain dramatic or moralistic categories—guilt,
Bewilder-
ment of
spirit that
inherits this
prejudice
contrary to
its own
nature. merit, effort, purpose, responsibility—that
cause great trouble in philosophy, when they
are reflected backward upon the physical
world. If things serve a purpose they are
said to *have* it; but could they have had it
before they acquired the properties that make
them useful to that end? When something costs us
an effort, our *effort* is said to bring it about; but the
effort is imposed on us by our *failure* to perform easily
something that we were already bent upon, and that
would have been better done if it had cost us no effort.
So when action in others or even in ourselves furthers
or defeats our prevalent Will, we call that action right
or wrong, virtuous or guilty. Free and responsible
for itself, in the first instance, is the gross natural event
from which the injury or the benefit visibly comes: the
man, the action, the accident. But if motives, antecedents, or laws of nature are surmised to subtend the
visible event, the responsibility spreads, recedes, grows
thinner and more and more radically involved in the
whole texture of nature; until either the total Will in
things, or in the Creator, becomes alone responsible,
or else, to escape that overwhelming momentum,
separate incidental acts of conscious will are invoked,
without inquiring into their causes.

Freedom may then be attributed to spirit as a
physical agent: something that when scrutinized turns
out to be literally inconceivable. There can be no
physical derivation of a material fact from an immaterial
fact, or vice versa. The two are not to be found in the

same realm of being. In the order of genesis, substance or energy passes, and may be traced, measured, and guided in passing, from one event to another; what follows is a growth from what precedes, partly by inner development, as from a seed, and partly by external accretion or dispersion. A son is not connected with his father merely by similarity and contiguity, though Hume, who was an old bachelor, might let us think so. There is always physical continuity and qualitative inheritance in a natural process, however vast or sudden the transformations. Yet it is logically impossible for matter to move or even to exist without overflowing into other realms of being. Essences must be exemplified, tropes must be adopted, truths must be established; and when the trope is a psyche, spirit too must be evoked, not now by logical necessity but by a free spontaneity in nature, that hypostasizes the moral fortunes of animals into consciousness of those fortunes. Spirit is thus entirely dependent on matter for its existence and distribution, but not by physical derivation; there is only an ontological propriety in this concomitance, to which the self-assertion of spirit contributes an element no less radically distinct and original than the successive phases in the evolution of matter. Matter would never have evolved into animals, had not organization been potential in it from the beginning; and organization would never have awakened consciousness had not essence and truth overarched existence from all eternity, and summed it up, with all its perspectives ready, for spirit to perceive.

Spirit depends on matter for its existence but not for its essence.

There is therefore a spiritual sense in which spirit not only is free and responsible for itself, but extends its connivance and moral dominion over the most distant facts. Not by magic or effort or bluff; only by unanimity. A wish—a consciousness of Will in the spirit—may

True freedom and responsibility of spirit.

easily be fulfilled by a physical event when the wish
has been formed in a psyche accustomed to such events
and ready to prefigure them or, by action, to bring them
about. In a psyche action and readiness for action
have a moral dimension which, by the nature of things,
appears in consciousness. Reflection may then appro-
priately see in a prophetic wish the moral reason or
motive for such events, as warnings may be omens, or
miracles answer to prayer. It was *better* that things
should so happen responsively to a living desire and
as spirit somewhere had invoked them; it was *saner*
and more *reassuring* for that spirit to find itself so
harmonious with fate that its wishes could be granted
and its prophecies fulfilled. But a moral reason or a
prayer answered indicates a harmony, it does not disclose a cause. The Will in the spirit was attuned in
such a case to the dominant or resultant Will in nature:
so that the spirit saw and loved in advance, or in
unison, the very things that nature was primed to
produce.

Where matter and spirit move in harmony spirit
may adopt the Will in nature as the will of God or more
proudly and histrionically as its own will; and the rapt
mystic or the providential leader may feel joyfully
passive or joyfully omnipotent. But when Will here
and Will there are in conflict, each retains such freedom
and responsibility as is proper to its own sphere. Each
felt preference or *idée-force* appearing in consciousness
then figures as a separate instance of local creation,
responsible for its choices, but spiritually only, that is,
responsible for loving that which it loves. The greater
the conflict between Will in the spirit and Will in the
rest of the psyche and of the world, the less responsible
can the spirit feel for subsequent events. Consequences never flow from the mere intent or expectation felt to inspire an action. They flow exclusively
from that action itself in the context of other physical

events; and the contagion or unison often established between spirits is a physical sympathy between persons, who catch each other's attitude and impulse, and feel, no doubt correctly, that they are invisibly sharing the same emotion.

This spiritual union when it exists, is therefore no groundless accident.   Lovers are normally of the same race, exercising a sexual influence of attrac- *It has no* tion, or later perhaps of possession, on one *magic powers* another; and intellectual union, which is no *and its sup-* less spiritual than love, likewise has notorious *posed effects* natural causes.   Through language, gesture, *effects of* and gentle suasion of all sorts, the Will *its causes.* beneath spirit spreads and equalizes itself in groups of persons; and unison in habit brings about unison in feeling and thought.   Spiritual bonds therefore presuppose and require physical assimilation or correspondence; and since the organs of spirit have a common descent and continual contact in society, we loosely speak as if contact and descent existed within the realm of spirit itself: but that is mere verbal equivocation and confusion of thought.   One moment of spirit—one intuition—can no more generate or control another moment than the light actually shed from one candle can generate or extinguish the light actually shed from another.   Actuality exhausts itself, as laughter does, or any emotion.   The causes that brought it about must renew it, if it is ever to reappear in all its freshness and youth.   Those who use the word spirit for physical influences feel a magnetic radiation from the aspect, voice, action, and words of a spirited person; they see him carrying out his threats or his promises, which in their own minds are mere images and words, though in him they were also physical impulses; and they rashly identify those diffusions of energy with spirit itself; for they have so vague a realization of what living spirit would really be, that they make no bones of turning it from an actual intuition or a moment of consciousness into a mythical person, a trope or a power manifested in matter. But the powers and tropes manifested in matter declare the properties of matter itself: spirit meantime is the invisible but immediate fact that matter with its tropes and powers is being observed, conceived, enjoyed, asserted, or desired: a vitality essentially moral, invisible, and private, absolutely actual and thoroughly unsubstantial, always self-existent and totally vanishing as it lives.

Everybody knows this without saying it, because language and the thought guided by language inevitably
fix on objects distinguishable to the senses
Globular
literary units and moving as wholes on the sensuous scale:
not separate and spirit is not one of these objects.
powers.
Language nevertheless does justice to spirit and serves it by the way, in its grammar and syntax, in its emotion, harmony, and intent: because all these relations, that make words "winged", lift language to the level of truth, and render it a good vehicle for spirit. But the indicative character of words, especially of nouns, tends to create globular units, sensuous or mythical, and leads us superstitiously to regard them as primary facts and separate powers. Now a man, his several actions, and the motives that may be conceived to animate him as he acts, are vague globular units of this conventional kind; and freedom and responsibility are attributed to them as wholes, when each is pointed to or named, without any attempt at analysis. Consciousness, when that is distinguished, takes its place in this catalogue of perfectly mythical familiar themes and individual powers; and it becomes paradoxical, and apparently artificial, to distinguish the spiritual element in a phase of daily life from the material and biological elements in it. Had the man not been conscious, people will say, the man would

not have acted as he did: and this is evidently true;
but not because his consciousness impelled his body
materially, but because the impelling vital processes
which involved his action also involved ideas and
emotions like those that his action, dramatically rehearsed, suggests to our own spirit. Had his vital
processes not sufficed to introduce the action, how
should they have sufficed to introduce into his mind
beforehand an idea of what the action might be, or a
desire to perform it? Or how should the sight or the
mere name of that action, reaching our eyes or ears
by purely material means, suffice to make us conceive
that action perfectly and perhaps boil with rage, and
before we know it perform another action to match it?

Spirit, like all forms of life, is glad to be born, and
does not account it violence to have been brought into
existence, although surely that was the most Spirit caught
external and absolute of decrees. But spirit in the war
of Wills
could not have existed before it existed, so becomes
as freely and intelligently to have chosen to conscience.
exist. Its freedom is subsequent, internal, and responsible not physically but morally. Universal Will, in
evolving spirit, satisfied one of its potential impulses;
this impulse is the Will proper to spirit anywhere, the
very breath of our moral freedom, when we become
free; but much contrariety and compulsion precedes
and follows, because the impulse to transcend oneself
cannot animate the universe as a whole, but only the
most sensitive and delicate of its fibres. The special
organ of spirit has an ethereal texture, and its webs
are easily rent. Though without primal malice, but
fatally, universal Will is everywhere a most stormy and
cruel power and constantly contradicts and defeats one
of its impulses by another. It therefore proves in a
thousand ways a good and an evil to itself. Plants
and animals accept this natural chaos, and never swerve
from allegiance to their particular Wills; but when

spirit comes upon the scene, while it too expresses a
particular movement of Will which it cannot abandon
without ceasing to be spirit, it feels at the same time
more or less clearly the conflicting Wills in other
creatures and most intimately the conflicting Wills in
its own psyche or mother-life. In this region the
question of freedom and responsibility first becomes a
riddle and a torment. Shame, remorse, good resolu-
tions, relapses, excuses, and scruples harass the conscience; and if piety aspires to conform all desires to
the universal Will, the responsibility for these troubles
must be placed, if possible, wholly on the private
movements of each psyche.

This, for a philosophic or theological mind, becomes
difficult. The will of the psyche is evidently animal
and hereditary; and although this fact takes
nothing away from the vital freedom of the
passions, it generalizes the seat of responsibility for them. Each of our sins is not the
first of its kind; human nature is to blame;
and who, if not the Creator, is to blame for
human nature? To say that Adam's fall, or each of our
stumblings, contained an element of absolute freedom
is true analytically, and also expresses the felt spontaneity and self-precipitation of action or thought.
Primal Will asserts itself as decisions or ideas take shape
within us; and it is impossible to imagine anything
freer or more due to itself than this growth and budding
of existence, this self-arrangement of matter, by its
own impulse, into some distinct form, which it is
possible to rest in or to repeat. Such is the Will to
exist and to be something in particular.

Such too is the possible sympathy of a living being
with the forms of surrounding or imaginable things.
Attention, with approval or detestation, attaches in this
way to objects and observed actions by a congenital
right; we half become these things in observing them,

Conflict between conscience and conformity to universal Will.

and it would be intolerable to us to erase from them the moral colours that they wear in our living world. Yet when we begin to study nature discursively we see those moral colours spread and fade away as it were, from the centres in which they were focussed, and even to mingle and infect one another with the moral character most contrary to their own. The evil and the good, for intuition, lay at first in each act, in each thought, in each creature; but natural history now assures us that those creatures, with their moral temperaments, were products of evolution, and that the merits and demerits we ascribed to them were relative to our own interests or prejudices. Black and white, that were so absolute, now seem to fuse into a cosmic grey. We scarcely know whom to blame or to praise for anything; the basest passions claim their equal rights; and we are no longer sure that we have any reason for caring what becomes of ourselves.

Perplexity is not relieved by putting this moral contradiction into religious terms. Universal Will may be distributed into divine and human actions, each a primary and absolutely free fiat; yet if the divine will is conceived as enlightened by universal knowledge, all human actions also must have been divinely willed, and spiritually accepted as ingredients in the plan of creation. All our sins and troubles would be providential, everything we detest in ourselves would be ultimately desirable, and all guilt and punishment would be a dreadful blessing that spirit in us was bound at once to hate and to love.

Less sophisticated and contorted is the sense of responsibility that prevails in human society. Alien wills cannot easily be conceived as they are Healthy con-in actual operation; that would require a science of singular triumph of dramatic imagination and the public. sympathy. But they are felt as good or evil, kindly or wicked, in relation to the Will dominant in ourselves at that moment; and a repertory of odious or lovely qualities is formed in the public conscience, quite sufficient for political and educational purposes. Average men, hearty men, men in harmony with their age and nation, assign praise and blame accordingly to gods and to mortals without hesitation. The freedom and responsibility of these natural agents is assumed, since they move of their own accord; and the same responsibility and freedom are attributed to the passions of one's own psyche, the spontaneity of them being actually experienced.

But for a subtler mind, for one divided against itself or acquainted with alien manners and judgments, the force of this local unilateral conscience soon becomes dubious. Not the whole of each criminal is criminal, nor of each saint saintly; there is humanity in the foreigner: and both goods and evils have causes and consequences of a moral colour opposite to their own. A feeble soul may then relax its moral code, blur its sense of what would be best and most beautiful, and having nothing left to fight for, may say that it rises above the fray; but that is impossible for a firm and integrated psyche. Ventilation and enlightenment clarify self-knowledge, as well as understanding of alien things: and self-knowledge is the principle of rational preference. It binds us with indissoluble bonds to the things we love.

Intelligence may slide into willlessness.

The good being thus sharply defined by its very relativity, the living spirit enjoys the same privilege as all other forms of universal Will, and by its inner freedom fixes the goals of its aspiration. It is constantly, even at its birth, distracted from its own good by the intrusion of other impulses seated in the same psyche; but in so far as it awakes to its proper function, and is loyal to itself, it transmutes all things to its own ends, digesting them and,

Specific ambition of spirit.

like a healthy creature, plucking its appropriate food
and rejecting poisons. For even spirit is a form of
Will, involved in the functioning of a special organ;
so that it too has a native unexpressed vocation, in
violation of which it cannot live at ease. Seen from
within, this vocation seems so simple and self-justified
that it ought to meet with no obstacle, since it
antagonizes nothing and interferes with nothing, but
innocently wishes to understand and to love everything. Yet in the psyche where it arises this vocation
is marginal and impossible to realize steadily. Even
the ambition to do so occasionally and ideally within the
spirit's house offends the particular passions shouting
outside, each with its absolute urgency. Each would
monopolize the spirit, which cannot be monopolized,
and yet must listen to every call; so that its distress is
deeper and more constant than that of psyches without
reflection, which as we observe in the brutes, between
the spells of their sudden impulses, live serene and
apathetic, as if all were well with them.

Nor is the free Will of spirit hampered only by
circumstances: it is inwardly divided and confused. It
can triumph only by a perpetual sacrifice. Will here
must sympathize with all Will and must love with all
lovers; yet it must condemn each Will, not for loving
that which it loves but for not loving that which it
does not love; in other words, for not loving the good
in all its possible forms. But all goods cannot be
realized or sanely pursued in any particular life. Only
the specific goals of that place and hour are proper to
that particular concretion of universal Will. To pursue
other goods then or there would be treason; and once
having been born under that star, and vowed to that
allegiance, it would be the height of pusillanimity and
obloquy not to destroy, as far as possible, all obstacles
to that chosen good. No chosen good could ever be
attained otherwise; and what sort of love of all good

would that be, by which the attainment of every particular good was prevented?

Thus spirit comes upon the most tragic of conflicts, the conflict between existence and justice. Beneath the realm of spirit conflicts are whole-hearted on every side, and universal Will has no qualms about contradicting and thwarting itself. That is its business. War is the father of all things that actually arise, since they arise by the confluence of forces; and universal Will has no prior purpose but lives only in the perpetual result. Spirit, on the contrary, is the prophet of all those things that should have arisen and that would have arisen if each vital impulse could have had its way, and reached its glory; so that while universal Will is always satisfied, because it had no special aspiration, spirit which is the breath of all distinct aspirations can never be satisfied, because only one or another by chance is ever fulfilled, and that imperfectly.

It is a martyr to every lost cause.

Yet spirit speaks for something deeper in nature than the upshot visible to cursory science or history; it speaks for *potentialities* in the heart of matter, that have taken at least a first step towards expression. Besides, in its own person, it speaks for the *truth* of that total movement in which these aspirations arise and meet their destiny. What it cannot speak for, except when hypnotized by animal impulse and alienated from itself, is any one aspiration to the exclusion of the others. The aspiration to justice, which is its own essence, would be stultified by such partiality: yet it would be equally stultified if we reproached Will at each point for being specific and exclusive. To be specific and exclusive is the condition for existing at all, for having a vocation, and for establishing an interest, even formal and unconscious, by which to distinguish life from death, benefit from injury. Spirit itself arises by virtue of

And share every joy achieved.

such an interest, suffering and triumphing according
to that criterion.   It has chosen what in its own eyes
is the better part, intelligence, sympathy, universality.
It has thereby chosen for all others that which their
nature, in each case, demands; but for itself spirit has
chosen renunciation, not to be preached to others who
cannot love it, but to be practised inwardly in its own
solitude.   The first thing that spirit must renounce,
if it would begin to be free, is any claim to domination.
Its kingdom is not of this world; and the other world,
where its Will is done, is not a second cosmos, another
physical environment, but this very emancipation and
dominion of spirit over itself, which raises it above
care even for its own existence.   Suffering is not
thereby abolished, either in the world or in the spirit,
so long as the spirit lives in any world; but suffering
is accepted and spiritually overcome by being understood, and by being preferred to the easy injustice of
sharing only one craving, to be satisfied with one sweet.

The freedom and glory of spirit come from its
impotence; by its impotence it is guiltless, by its impotence it is universal, by its impotence it is invulner-
ably supreme.   Its essence is to be light, not to be
power; and it can never be pure light until it is satisfied
with an ideal dominion, not striving to possess or to
change the world, but identifying itself only with the
truth and beauty that rise unbidden from the world
into the realm of spirit.

CHAPTER VI

INTUITION

THE contrast between matter and mind, like a contrast
in sex, is far from defeating a natural union between
them. Nothing could be more intelligible
to a sympathetic observer than such a
differential harmony, when once he aban-
dons the effort to express either fact in the categories
of the other, or to make them pass into one another
materially, as if they could form a single univocal
sequence. Their conjunction is by a spontaneous
conspiracy of complementary qualities. In the material
order, which is dynamic and continuous, this harmony
cannot be contained, since one of the terms lies in
another realm of being; yet that harmony can be prepared. A manifold of motions and tensions is often
organized in an animal, such that all the elements and
occasions are supplied requisite for a moral experience.
Matter could go no further; but when it has gone so
far, spirit has been generated, and does the rest.
Impressions and reflex actions evoke images, voices
acquire meanings, instincts inspire longings. This
completion is no addition to the material process, but
a moral counterpart of what the process was as a whole,
or as we say, of what it *meant*. Such is the natural
link between matter and mind, that bodily life should
excite feeling, and that perception, emotion, and
thought should report material events.

Significance and sanity are great virtues for spirit
in this world, yet they are not inseparable from it in

644

its essence. Left to itself spirit would be omniscient, or would think itself so; and (as is perhaps involved in omniscience) it would feel no regret and no desire. A spirit focussed on particular impressions and troubled about particular events is evidently a foster-child of matter. Why should anything be dangerous to spirit? Why should one essence fascinate or another fatigue? Why should spirit be torn away in tears from what it loves, and beset everywhere by what it hates? Yet such are the first experiences of innocent spirit in this world, and the beginning of its inexplicable trials.

Ignored by intuition when free.

At this late day we know well enough what the material causes of these troubles are, so puzzling to the young spirit. The body must be healthy, well fed, well treated, allowed to grow and develop its faculties. Certainly hygiene will prevent many a woe, and a spirit not smothered or maddened by disease ought to manifest more clearly its innate Will or demands. Souls in this respect are like nations: in health they take everything foreign for a challenge, in disease, everything native for an oppression. What then would be the free and native life of spirit, which it enjoys more and more when conditions are favourable and suffers more and more for missing when they are adverse? What is spirit naturally fit to do?

For the sake of clearness let me state at once the conclusion I shall come to: the reader will then see the details more readily in the particular perspective that concerns us here. This perspective is not psychological or historical, but religious, or rather what the ancients would have called philosophical. The end in view is liberation, or the attainment, if only in glimpses, of the highest good. The steps are to be regarded as steps towards that end. What profit has the spirit in existing, and who are its true friends and true enemies?

Which demands an inward or moral happiness.

To which I reply: The perfect function of spirit is pure intuition. By the very impulse that generates it, intuition tends to become pure. It is the movement of apprehension by which anything is given to consciousness; and there is a natural joy in it, whenever it can live unimpeded by fatigue or pain, and not harassed by care, fear, doubt, desire or any other obsession about the not-given. Distress at its source and distraction about its objects are the enemies of spirit; and its salvation comes when it is freed from all distress or distraction, and becomes pure intuition, be the theme of that intuition simple or complex, a breath of morning air or the sum total of possible knowledge. The datum is never too simple, if it calls forth a whole-hearted response from the soul, and the datum is never too complicated, if it does not overtax and confuse the scope of attention. In both cases equally, intuition will be alert and happy. We see this in the play of young children. Combative, adventurous, or sexual instincts, as yet not ripe and without fit occasions, overflow in play, and play in its first impulse is always joyful. Attention is spontaneous, and action is selective, being confined, or expecting to be confined, to so much as intuition can victoriously discover, trace, dominate and delight in.

By intuition, the reader will perceive, I do not mean divination, or a miraculous way of discovering that which sense and intellect cannot disclose. On the contrary, by intuition I mean direct and obvious possession of the apparent, without commitments of any sort about its truth, significance, or material existence. The deliverance of intuition is some pure essence. The degree of truth or significance that this given essence may have, as revealing a world of action, or as promising other intuitions, is an ulterior question, morally and cognitively important, but itself, when

Relevance to fortune only an incidental advantage.

consciously considered, distracting the spirit from its native and present happiness. We have undeniably a more compact mind and a stronger will when the themes of our intuitions are relevant to our action, and we see with the clearness of genius the movement of things near us, and of society. If we groped about the world always startled and aggrieved, and if we nursed pure intuition only about imaginary things, we should be sick children, and our thin intuitions would grow thinner and wilder, as our troubles grew thick. Nevertheless in the most masterly mind, in the most victorious soldier or legislator, no profit or peace will come to the spirit except in pure intuition, when that dominated world and that brilliant career appear as if in another man's life: a tale, a vision, in which all passion has become light, and all compulsion deliverance. Worldly victories are full of falseness and anguish; there must be a second victory of intuition over all victories before the spirit can triumph.

Such a triumph over nature and human nature can never be complete, and the moments in which it almost exists are rare. Were intuition possible only at the top, in the wisest moments of life, it might be left to the saints and mystics to tell us about it. But intuition is primitive; it is pervasive; we cannot look or think without evoking it in a thousand directions, for without it we should have no emotions, no images, no beliefs. It would be impossible for us to observe similarities, or conjunctions or movements, or to feel implications. Indeed, it would be impossible for us to feel anything or be conscious at all, since intuition is a name for that spiritual wakefulness by which attention discerns characters and distinguishes one character from another.

Yet it is fortune that controls intuition.

Intuition, then, is always with us, but dispersed over occasions that continually confuse and interrupt it. It is comparatively clear in the poet, in the wit, sometimes in the child ; it is the constant friend of the artist lost in his work. All I need do here is to disentangle it, and consider what it would be if it were pure.

In the first place, for a foundation, we may take the Aristotelian definition of intuition, or of any instance First char- of spirit, as the second entelechy, the perfect acteristic of actuality, of organic life. Intuition not only intuition: exists, but is the most intense form of Actuality, or existence existence. Existence, by another definition concentrated which at least in my view is fundamental, into the sense of means flux, process, transition. Had we existence. purely static being we should lapse or rise into essences, and should not exist. Now this point might well provoke some controversy, because in the most opposite quarters, in Buddhism and in British philosophy, the existence of spirit is verbally denied, as being a verbal fiction: according to one party there are only illusions and according to the other party only data. Data and illusions, however, involve intuition; otherwise data could not be given and illusions could not deceive. Moral presence, moral actuality is essential to givenness, as moral deceitfulness is essential to illusion. Intuition crowns the bodily movements that underlie it by taking notice, by being a most acute ideal concentration and moral effect of those movements, so that they now cause clear data, quite unlike their own physical texture, to arise and vanish before pure spirit.

Intuition differs from the graphic or conceptual data so evoked in being itself a process and not an Spiritual image, an event and not an idea, an existence tension and not an essence. It lends to those ideal between and moral data the only existence of which objects and they are capable: it enables them to appear. terms. It justifies, when once we sharpen our concentration on the actually given, the Berkeleyan reduction of data of intuition to inert ideas or essences; also the moral

discovery that essences, if supposed to exist on their
own account, are illusions. There is an intense reality
involved; but this reality is the life of the psyche,
unconscious save precisely where it culminates in
intuition, and raises ideal essences into obsessions.
These obsessions may be calm, steady, and normal,
as when we look at a material object and study it.
Every eye will not paint an identical picture, but each
picture may be clear and sustained at will, or changing
only as the material object itself changes. At other
times the psyche ferments inwardly under insufficient
control from external facts; and the ghosts then called
up, though plainly visible, prove to have no existence
in nature and no definite reference to anything there.
They signify only some inner agitation of the soul,
and they signify even this only for the psychologist, or
on second thoughts. The datum of intuition, when
fully realized and clarified, reveals nothing but itself
to that intuition. It is an essence, and though it may
be a picture of time it knows no temporal neighbours.
It is an idea, a concept, and not a moment in any
existing or evolving world. Intuition though it always
has a natural ground never can have a natural object,
but only an ideal one. Nature has learned to know
itself at this price, that its knowledge should be indirect
and symbolic. It can describe itself only in words,
and had to invent them in order to think.

If these sensible or intelligible symbols seem unreal
in their ideality, the reality of existence in its turn
seems no less ambiguous, since it continually falls between two stools, is by not-being,
by merely ceasing to be one thing and
becoming something different. In intuition,
however, we have an instance of perfect
actuality, a form of being that preeminently exists and
moves (for it is a discovery, an experience) yet is
precisely the act of arresting and defining some clear

Actuality is a physical movement issuing in a definite datum.

essence. This flash of light issues from sundry processes and tensions coming to a head, and fusing their
energies; but the confluence does not remain simply a
fact about those processes: it generates a feeling. This
feeling continually varies, like its physiological ground;
but at each moment it brings some revelation to
consciousness, having a precise logical and moral
character, absolutely individual and like itself, however
nameless and vague it may seem in relation to conventional human categories.

The fruition of an organ, we have noted earlier,[1]
cannot arise until that organ has matured. A first
sensation is therefore, physiologically, a last event. A
full psychic life must have preceded, now perhaps
interrupted, or perhaps brought to a head in some
sudden movement. The vital background is far more
stable, far wider, than the flash of feeling. There was
much more to be felt, if we went in for feeling, and it
was a mere accident that we felt this in particular.
Thus when the Indians tell us that in deep sleep we
return to Brahma, we may say that from the point of
view of spirit they are describing the birth of spirit
itself, representing the absence of consciousness as
consciousness in a perfectly placid, equable, infinitely
potential equilibrium. Logical vacancy would thus
cover vital repletion. So we too, looking at life
naturalistically from the outside, may well feel that
spirit actually slumbers in all things, in a deep sleep
inclined to waking, a sleep, as it were, under tremulous
eyelids. This is not a wholly fanciful notion, because
something very like such a vacant but positive tension
endures in waking life, supplying the background to
all ulterior data. The glance of attention would
disclose nothing distinct if a constant blank field, the
specific datum of expectancy, did not spread round
each image, precede it, limit it, contrast with it, and

[1] Chapter I, p. 8.

swallow it up in the end, much as the sea might swallow up an island or the sky a star—data which could never have been given to intuition except within those broader fields.

Intuition is in some sense always a synthesis, even when the datum is an inarticulate feeling, like a scent or a pain. The very simplicity of such data *Analysis of* proves this, not indeed, to analysis (because *synthesis: it* no analysis is possible of the inarticulate) *is premental.* but to common sense, as soon as the very complex natural occasion for such simple feelings has been discovered. Yet the word synthesis is highly ambiguous and misleading, like other Kantian terms that have become convenient or indispensable. The danger is that what occurs in the realm of matter should be interpreted by literary psychology as occurring in the realm of spirit. In the realm of spirit there is no machinery, nothing compounded, dynamic, mysterious, or latent; therefore there is no synthesis at that level; although intuition momentarily manifests in an open datum, all surface, say in joy, intricate processes that have been going on and combining in the animal psyche since the dawn of creation. The joy felt is a unitary effect of a multiple cause, itself felt only as a fountain of joy. A synthesis may therefore be said to have occurred, but not in consciousness. Consciousness gives the result of that synthesis. It does not give the elements nor the process nor the motive for the given formation. Idealists may say that all these unknown things occur in "unconscious mind", "unconscious mind" being an unfortunate name which they give to bodily life, when they are compelled to acknowledge that the body is not merely an image in the mind but a dynamic heritage prior to consciousness and determining the images that shall appear. This dynamic heritage is the psyche, or the process of life considered objectively and as continuous with the vital heritage in seeds; it is something obscure but indubitably real and taking place in the material world. Being material these processes are not mental; but being hidden and obscure they are most readily distinguished by their occasional moral culmination in some feeling or image. Feelings and images may then be inter- polated dramatically, even where certainly they do not exist, as in thunder and lightning. Such play of fancy is spontaneous in myth and in literary psychology; but to take it literally would be to explain the profound by the superficial, the dynamic by the pictorial, and often the real by the fictitious.

Synthesis, conceived as a fusion of existential elements into a new existential unit, is therefore incongruous with spirit, and belongs to the realm of matter. But before leaving it there, we may notice something proper and indeed essential to spirit that might be confused with an evolutionary synthesis: I mean the intuition of relations or, as called by another Kantian name, the transcendental unity of appercep- tion. When a datum is complex attention in noticing the parts sees them in their common field, and initially qualified by their place there and their mutual relations. These relations may be static, and then, since spirit is volatile, it may return again and again to the same object, emphasizing each time a different feature, and evoking a different essence. These successive intui- tions can never be synthesized. They are events, they are unsubstantial, they blaze for a moment and vanish into nothing. But the deliverances of those moments may supplement one another as descriptions of the object, or as mere experiences; and a subsequent intuition, springing from the organic soil so tilled and fertilized, may repeat those intuitions or variations of them in a fresh description of the object, or poetic suggestion of it in its wholeness and in its destiny.

In intuition there is momentary unity of view but no synthesis.

Imagination may thus evolve, and knowledge may increase, not by an impossible synthesis or breeding together of dead intuitions, but by the training of organisms and the complication of instruments, orchestrating a richer but no less fugitive life in the spirit.

When the object is in motion the perpetual variations in intuition have a double source, for besides the continual renewal of apprehension, always with a somewhat different volume, vivacity and point of view, there is the flux of events, replacing one another before the eyes. Suppose I am watching a procession, or listening to music, or floundering through an improvised speech of my own. The vital continuity of consciousness is not suspended, and there is a comparatively stable background, in my sense of the world and myself in it, against which I notice each new feature. And what is most marvellous, when we consider it, many features that have vanished from the world are still present, though fading, in the temporal perspectives of the spirit. I know that this which has come is not that which is gone, and I can specify many a precise detail in which they differ. Even what is coming, or what ought to come, is present vaguely to my sense, and is recognized as normal or as surprising when it actually appears. Thus intuition transcends in scope the sequence of events toppling over one another in the world, so that the picture of that world in imagination is much wider, much clearer, and much fairer than its aspect at any one instant. There is a nexus of events in the realm of matter, as they fuse and generate one another; there is a history of events in the realm of truth, where their essences, their sequence and all their formal relations for ever confront the spirit; and in the realm of spirit there are partial and ever varied recompositions of events, as intuition catches glimpses of them in different perspectives.

Parts and movements can appear only within the present whole.

If intuition, then, pelts a static object with a variety of views, it lifts a fluid object, or a sequence of events, out of the irreparable flux in which it occurs and keeps its essence and its occurrence in mind, as long as the intuition lasts. The selection of features appearing in such an intuition is made for it by the psyche, under the physical influences of the moment; and here there is a real *synthesis* of tensions and processes. In the intuition the given features are not synthesized but discriminated, being first given in solution under that unity of apprehension without which no intuition could exist at all.

The notion that intuition synthesizes its elements, comes of hypostasizing these elements, and imagining them to be separate existents that intuition must pick out and combine in an adventitious way. But neither intuition nor the features distinguishable in its field are physical objects of that sort, meeting and acting upon one another; they are not wooden pawns that a selective hand must take from the box, move about the chess-board, and sweep into the box again for use on another occasion. We are in the realm of spirit. Here the elements found are pure visionary essences and the spirit finding them is pure light of attention. Essences have no hidden temporal persistence; their so-called subsistence is merely their logical identity. Intuition on its side is not an operation performed by some pre-existing intellect. Intellect exists by intellection; and intuition is a moment of created spirit, not a power applied, but a brief life received. A different simile might express these facts better. Intuitions may be likened to soap-bubbles. Soap-bubbles are impossible to synthesize; if they touch they vanish; yet the surface of one may repeat the iridescence visible on the surface of several others. These colours are not taken from the smaller bubbles, and transferred and rearranged

Illusion that data are substances.

on the larger one: they are reborn in each instance, in each degree of complexity, according to the circumstances of that more or less similar moment. Of those lights, of those spheres, nothing endures; but the soap-suds and the air remain available for bubbles *ad libitum*, and the colours of the rainbow may be drawn upon for ever for decoration without being exhausted. The reshufflings are all material, the pictures are all precarious, and their parts are created and sustained within them by the same rays and the same tensions that create the whole.

In waking life and even in sleep intuition is normally uninterrupted, though what is constant there, amid a stream of changes, is singularly Continuity vague and nameless. Nothing could be of intuition. more worthless to spirit than spirit dozing, when all its specific functions and pleasures are in abeyance. Yet that dim spark of light, like a *veilleuse* in a sick-room, keeps alive the sense of a shadowy ambience from which anything might emerge. Even in alert consciousness this vague background endures; and normally any precise observation or distinct thought is preceded by a momentary pause, as it were for breath, or to take aim. We thus fall back upon our physical resources for foothold before we leap. Then, the observation having been made or the thought formulated, we relapse into the familiar hum of habitual living, with that clear moment marked as with a red letter, to be reverted to if possible upon occasion. Fundamentally, we must remember, all time and all existence are open to spirit; and this virtual omnipresence renders something possible which would be utterly impossible if spirit were not transcendental, but were lodged successively in each of its data: I mean, the reference of a memory to its original, and the possibility of comparing the two and judging the memory to be inadequate. Do we then have two intuitions, one of the original and another of the reproduction? And can a third intuition compare the two? Not in the least. Intuitions are not objects, they are moments of spirit, qualitatively similar in their cognitive essence, which is absolutely intellectual and unpresentable to sense. They differ only in their themes. It is these two themes (which may be rival descriptions of the same fact in the posited natural world) that intuition may compare, when it retreats a little from its two former occasions and sees their two deliverances at once, perhaps together with a third view, taken now of the same object. All views thus form one field of imagination and memory, open to repeated inspection and enlargement; and the diversity of such available ideas supplies all the alternatives between which judgment may waver. For as there is only one ultimate ambition of spirit everywhere, to embrace everything as does the truth, so there is but one total object for multiple consideration, namely, the whole course of nature, physical and moral, with the whole history of spirit included in it, and the whole realm of essence spreading beyond, the logical complement of any special universe.

A survey of the successive is a deeply different fact from the successive events surveyed. Before any

Experience cumulative, intuition comprehensive. survey is possible for the spirit, physical experience and organic memory must accumulate, giving the psyche a wider resonance and fresh capacities for reaction: then these, until the psyche begins to decay, may supply a broadened basis for intuition. This is what fails to happen in the fool : no matter how much he may knock about the world or read in the newspapers, he will never put two and two together. His soul has little synthetic power, and his bubbling intuitions will be as bird-like, as shallow, and as absolute at the end as at the beginning. A great increase in science and in available information therefore does not ensure any greater wisdom in the public. On the contrary, it may occasion universal confusion and frivolity. Materials do not synthesize themselves by being heaped together; a spark of life, a synthesizing force, must arise in some organism; and then a spirit awakened there may rise above the flux, feel events toppling over one another, perceive their variety, their tendency, their promise, and live as much in what they have been and may be as in what, in the passing moment, they actually are. All minds belong to their time and place; such is the condition of their existence that determines their point of view; yet they are minds only in the measure in which they transcend their physical station, and can view their place from other places and their moments from other moments.

Organic rhythms are animated by what we have agreed to call a Will, which if conscious would appear to spirit as pleasure or pain, success or failure. Intuition expresses such a rhythm, such a mode of vital appetition. If the trope initiated were never completed, no intuition or consciousness would arise at all; so that wherever there is consciousness there is an element of organic success, a ground for joy. The organ of apprehension is working successfully. Intuition thus finds itself sympathetically participating in the process of creation, and moving with it. This process cannot stop itself, and its various organs cannot spontaneously rescind their impetus. Nor can spirit put the brake on them, as if it were an independent power, or had a prior bent against the forces that bring it into existence, or would prefer to sleep on. Sleepiness is an intoxication of the organism. But spirit is light, and light, while there is fuel, can never be tired of shining. On the contrary, it clarifies and makes vocal the will that is at work, and does so faithfully and impartially,

Second characteristic of intuition: Vitality.

delivering the message it receives, whether of good or ill omen in the world's affairs.

In primitive will-lessness there could be no Will-not-to-will, and the eternal indifference of Brahma could not prevent the world from arising. Rather that deep sleep was secretly prolific; the whole realm of essence enveloped it like something forgotten yet somehow known which silently invited dreams of all sorts to unfold themselves. Yet when will-lessness is not merely the mutual arrest of innumerable Wills, as perhaps it is in the depths of matter, but is rather, as in spirit, the fruit of Will realized, it retains the image and the love of what was willed, without the propensity to create it. Such clarified will-lessness is the result of experience and discipline, and is will-less only in respect to existence, being still the Will to understand that which exists. Passions and dreams are then recovered without illusion, and experience is gathered together in intuition without being any longer ignorantly traversed through birth and death.

It survives in pure spirit.

There is an oversight possible here that sometimes vitiates asceticism. The vulgar, we feel, move with the blind Will to live; spirit withdraws from that vain and horrible struggle and makes for peace, or even for non-existence. It *may* do so, but only by a revulsion that is physical and temporary. A satirist or an elegiac poet is free to dwell only on what the universal Penelope does at night, when she destroys her day's work; yet in Penelope all is not self-contradiction. Her impulse is not now earnestly to weave and now earnestly to unweave what she has woven; she is busy without conviction and destructive without rage. A shrewd light twinkles in her eye, and her apparent folly serves to defend her liberty; something heroic and humorous within triumphs in the very futility of her action. So

It glories alike in adventure and in reflection.

intuition profits by the vanity of life and quietly takes note, while the cycles of growth and decay succeed one another. To these vicissitudes it adds something different and positive, that covers both movements alike. It does so by virtue of its own Will, at whatever point it arises, and does not tend either to prolong the ascent or hasten the descent of natural seasons. For intuition springs out of a power, present in animal life, to respond from one centre to influences and inheritances coming from a distance, and to trace relations backwards and forwards, in quality and quantity, over all being. The sensitiveness is physical, the intuition spiritual; the one establishes, the other expresses, a vital harmony in the movement of things. There is therefore no hostility to nature in.spirit; where hostility appears we may justly suspect some earthly demon of desire prompting us to hate all that is not food for our own lusts. In nature lusts and conflicts are inevitable, since everything has a Will of its own; yet to note the variety and contradiction of these Wills is a great feat, a great exaltation for the spirit and a great joy. This joy will indeed be mixed with sorrow so long as the psyche is reluctant to change or to die; and consequently, while the old Adam kicks at the pricks, the organ of spirit, in ascetic discipline, cannot but strive to liberate and vivify itself at the expense of all unreconciled passions. But no passion is warmer than the zeal to see, to discover, to master the truth, to rescue the spirit from confusion and slavery, even at the price of perceiving the vanity of life.

In this book I am deliberately taking the point of view of spirit fully awake, contrasting itself with other things, and aspiring to its own freedom and perfection. That is the supreme question for the inner man; but we must not suppose, or seem to expect, that spirit, or anything else, should have been produced with an

Third characteristic: Moral autonomy in physical dependence.

eye towards its ultimate good. That good cannot be chosen or pursued until the creature exists whose good it is to be; you must have a native direction before you can have a goal. Like other natural growths, spirit finds its life taking shape gradually, developing in this direction and in that, retreating, recommencing, piling up great enterprises that collapse in a deluge, or in a confusion of tongues, and only after many readjustments reaching a clear perfection of some particular sort. Nature will move on, and spirit may be launched into other adventures; but a possible culmination will have been attained under the form of eternity in one art, which will unite for ever in mutual understanding all creatures that at any time or place may have that vocation. There are many creatures in many circumstances that possess consciousness; but if we find in one instance what such consciousness would become if it were free and favoured by fortune, we have a criterion for judging, or rather for feeling, its virtue wherever it exists. Intuition, happy in itself and pledged to nothing further, is such a criterion.

This does not mean that pure intuition was established first, for its own sweet sake, and then was rudely disturbed by other processes irrelevant to it. Such is the illusion created in the spirit (an illusion that itself proves a great obstacle to peace) when we presume that, because we are minds, all things ought to minister to us, or even cannot exist save by virtue of our attention to them. This *ought* is the cry of selfishness, this *cannot* the cry of pride. Psyches do not become conscious for the sake of consciousness. They become conscious automatically, in acquiring a special organic responsiveness and heed of relations; and this plunges them into a far more agitated and perilous life than they led before, in their vegetative phase. They are launched into action and passion. Thus spirit is born the twin of trouble. The pure joy and knowledge that should come to it can come only in snatches, or in ultimate concentration and solitude.

Such solitude is not empty; it is solitude in the presence of anything and everything, the solitude of the traveller and witness, the essential stranger, whose proper interest is impartial, but who is caught and jostled in a press of troubles not really his own. Yet it was impossible, *Plastic unity and kindly solitude.* logically as well as physically, that a living spirit should exist where there was no Will, no agent, no environment, no contingency and no fatality. These circumstances and prerequisites supply the interest and theme of the drama. The given predicament might indeed have been different, and the vital impulse different. Such a diversity does not disturb the intrinsic ambition of spirit. Wherever it may arise, at every stage in its manifestation, it will show its true colours modestly and momentarily here, proudly and systematically there. This moral liberty cannot be forfeited while intuition subsists, since this liberty is internal. When on the contrary spirit beats its wings unreconciled against natural bars, it proves how completely it has been deceived about the direction of its possible freedom. It might have been singing in that cage.

False starts and failures are not the spirit's fault. They are its fate, its hereditary slavery, from which it may be freed if it lives long enough. As a first vital harmony brought it forth, a second may redeem it. For we must not suppose that any malice animates nature in regard to *Spiritual freedom may be docile.* spirit, or any reluctance to evoke spirit and give it free rein. On the contrary, the often inopportune existence of spirit, in some sorry and hopeless plight, proves that nature is only too well disposed towards such a development; it emanates from incipient harmonies; and every species of plant and animal, even the most wretched, shows how persistently nature flows into every possible shape. Yet the types established are as specific as they are stubborn, since the first stages have to be hereditary and well protected, if the organism is to be widely diffused or highly elaborate; otherwise the endless potentiality of matter would remain chaotic. We must therefore not be surprised at the fixity of Will in us, physical and moral, or at the consequent peril and suffering besetting us on every side. After a season of incubation while our nature takes shape in the dark, we are born into a world that cannot be altogether friendly. There must be not only buffets and denials, but a more subtle assault of circumstances, contaminating the very psyche in which the spirit lives, and creating strange vices and ambitions. Like a child in a den of thieves, spirit is then taught crime as a duty. Intuition is not suffered to be pure. Scarcely has it begun to distinguish an essence, when it is rudely summoned to confuse it with something different, and in this confusion to become impatient instead of joyful, to hate, to fear, and (what is most insidious) to claim *possession* of its objects, as if they were things or pledges, and not innocent essences. So the interrupted life of intuition is entangled with the incongruous rhythms and conflicts of other organs and of alien things. Yet at this level again a second humbler but wiser life of spirit may begin; piety, religion, and science may insinuate themselves beneath free intuition, darkening its face while deepening its meaning, and turning it from vision into faith and knowledge.

There is indeed a sense in which intuition itself is cognitive from the beginning. It is apprehension of Fourth char- something distinct, capable of being recog- acteristic: nized and spoken of again. Yet this some- Cognition. thing might be a pure feeling or idea, enriching the mind, but conveying no knowledge of anything further. In a pregnant and transcendent sense, therefore, intuition is not knowledge. It is the mere possession of a thought, which need have no object other than the essence revealed in it. So all exercise, play, and fiction, all poetry and music, expand the spirit congenially, give it a tone and cogency perhaps very precious to it, without conveying knowledge of anything else. Yet this purity of intuitive life, though it appears in snatches at any stage, can attain to solidity and permanence only in arts, like language, that have a broad basis and use in the world. The clear profit brought thereby to the spirit may be ultimately only intellectual or æsthetic, a play of ordered imagination; yet imagination has been evoked in the first place by the senses, in physical contact with external things, and it has been corrected and made inveterate by continual experience. Even the purest psychic fictions, such as logic or grammar, would not long hold their own if directly or indirectly they did not reflect the structure of the world. So also a symbolic poet, interested only in the music and emotion of words, must involuntarily feed his art upon nature, if it is to touch his soul.

In some animals perhaps nothing comes to consciousness before the outer senses are stimulated by some sudden change in the environment. Sensation an Intuition then will be an index, in some index even respects, to the assault of an influence and when not to the character of its source. And prob- a sign. ably not merely a passive index but an active perception; because intuition being essentially cognitive and spiritual, it has an intrinsic light to turn upon anything that may confront it; and the psyche being in this case tensely directed upon the source of stimulation, intuition absorbs that vital intent, and becomes animal faith: a specific assurance and expectancy turned towards the not-given.

That attention should be turned towards the not-

given may seem a contradiction in terms, and would
be such if attention were always pure intuition, since
then the datum would be the whole ob-

The leap of intent imposed on spirit by its animal origin. ject, and this object a pure essence.   But in
fact attention is always attracted, in the first
instance, to the not-yet-given, because the
psyche is struggling with a disturbance
or uneasiness of which she has as yet no idea; and this
idea, when it now begins to take shape, indicates that
disturbance or uneasiness without in the least encom-
passing or exhausting the truth about it.   Intuition is
born smothered in intent; and intent is precisely
assurance and expectancy turned towards the not-
given.   The act of recoiling precedes any idea of what
that may be from which we recoil; shaken by the blow,
we look to see what has hit us.   And the act of grasping,
clinging, or pursuing precedes and guides attention to
the object grasped, clung to, or pursued.   *Some*
intuition accompanied the primary movement, else
there would be no consciousness of it; but we hardly
have words for essences so generic and inarticulate as
are given in sheer alarm, lust, impatience, or effort;
these terms, which we say denote "feelings" really
denote, for our adult minds, the occasions and actions
that are visible when we use them.   We never name
our own passions, until we catch them in the mirror
of the world.   Yet the passions are not unconscious:
across the background of the habitual scene—which
may be a blank—a light, a shadow, a suction, a tension
pass and transform themselves as we live on; and we
act under high pressure of an inward fatality or Will
that is conscious of its fury but not until afterwards of
its acts.   Thus attention to the not-given, anxiety,
suspense, precipitation dominate the spirit in the
beginning; and the element of clear intuition, the sense
of what is happening in reality even within the mind,
though always present, remains inarticulate.   In this

way it happens that, though the spirit be essentially joyful, it is born, bred, and propagated in distress.

Tension towards the hidden or distant yields intellectual dominion when it becomes clear intuition; but before being dominion it halts usually at interest, inquiry, or pursuit. And this element of suspense constitutes the trans- *Purgatorial trials of knowledge.* cendent force of true knowledge, which takes the datum of intuition for a sign of something beyond. Such belief involves a claim, as pure intuition does not; it is subject to danger and error, and therefore never puts the cognitive powers of spirit at ease. Spirit instinctively transposes impressions into images, and beliefs into imaginative heirlooms, as in myth and legend, metaphysics and theology. To meditate on an article of faith is to replace it as far as possible by an intuition. Imagination advances as material reference recedes, until in mystical ecstasy possession renders all faith unnecessary.

On the other hand *intelligence* essentially requires postulates, and moves in the sphere of belief; and intelligence rather than idle intuition was what the psyche required when she gave birth to spirit. It was in learning to behave intelligently that she stretched those threads of telepathic communication which when duly· connected struck the first spark of intuition. And we may say that as intuition is cognitive of essence even when not conveying any knowledge of fact, so it is intelligent and conclusive even when not positing any external object. For intuition is an act and has an organ, so that it executes a movement and traverses duration in merely arising. We cannot see or hear without *tracing* the datum; and tracing it would be profitless to the spirit if retracing it were impossible; since an intuition that lost its themes in the act of evoking them would be at best a spiritual atom adrift in infinity and no part of any spiritual life.

Thus memory, consecutive discourse, allegiance to old loves and to old knowledge belong to the grain of spiritual reality; yet they contain faith in the not-given, and thereby transcend intuition. For on a small scale or on a large scale intuition is something ultimate, a culmination of many processes that from the spiritual point of view are subsidiary. All that self-transcendence which is involved in action, in belief, in expectation, must itself be transcended and embraced in intuition, before spirit can be happy. When scattered experience is synthesized in memory and scattered aspirations in worship, they become a single panorama and a single love. The whole course of a life is raised to a present datum possessed virtually in all its details by the dramatic imagination, as all the convolutions of a piece of music are retained virtually in the finale. Then a body of positive knowledge of fact acquires the values of fiction: the man has actually lived through the adventures that on his death-bed or in heaven he sees spread before him as a story: but its spiritual reality now swallows up for him the accident of its material enactment, once upon a time, in his accidental person. He accepts and forgives himself, and ceases to repine at his destiny, because a spirit is now awake in him that is not limited or defiled by those obsessions, now no more its own than those of any other creature. Hope and fear have become vision of the truth: and if that vision is itself lurid and burdened with too much thunder, even the vision of the truth can be dismissed, or sublimated into one pattern among a thousand in the realm of fancy.

Since these phases of spirit do not generate one another but each goes with some special phase of organic life, there is no telling by moral analysis in what order spiritual experience may develop. Moral classifications are possible only if the moments of a

[margin note: Intuition tends to sublimate knowledge into vision.]

given history are distinguished by the relative purity of intuition in them. We might arrange them in a circular or spiral order, from intuition empty to intuition filled with all truth; for according to the Indians, who know more about this than we do, deep sleep, being perfect bliss, must be a kind of intuition, *The spiral of spiritual experience from innocence to ecstasy.* yet empty; and I think an intuition filled with the truth (about which we know more than they did) would be perfect bliss too, if our whole psyche were absorbed in conceiving that truth, with no other wish subsisting. And in that case it would be indifferent that this truth happened to be true rather than mere poetry, since it would be only as poetry that the spirit would entertain it. Pure intuition, even when filled in with infinite detail, would thus revert to the perfect peace of pure Being.

On this hint we might sketch the earthly round of spirit, descending from heaven empty and open to every illusion, and ascending into heaven full, but thoroughly purified. A deep pre-natal sleep might be first broken by a feeling of pressure, which if intensified would become pain. A sense of inescapable duration, a dread of change or a longing for it, would create temporal perspectives, forward and back, into an oncoming future and a receding past, both ambiguously present, and both unseizable. These would form a ghostly world, to which spirit somehow would feel that it belonged, and from which the real world would be hard to disentangle. Yet those vital emotions and those temporal perspectives would have had no consistence, if they had contained no images, and supplied no recognizable ideal terms in which spirit might describe them. Nature and history would thus gradually take shape before the distracted spirit and would reveal to it the secret of its own destiny. Anxiety and craving would dissolve before this redeeming knowledge, and the universe would be clarified into a complex essence, given pure and untroubled to intuition. Spirit, so enlightened, would be again at peace.

When the Indians tell us that such peace is bliss we may be inclined to smile or to call them pessimists, as if only the negation of existence could seem to them good. And when our own religion bids the dead "rest in peace", we may suspect that some early fancy about wandering ghosts survives in our liturgy, contrary to the "hope of glory". But perhaps we are deceived in our cleverness. When peace or deep sleep returns to the spirit the multitudinous vibration of nature that supports spirit has not ceased; it continues and will continue for ever; and new occasions for waking and troubling will break out in a thousand places. Spirit, considered as a natural concomitant of nature, never can rest in peace. Yet at any point, by its own insight summing up nature, it may achieve tranquillity. It is only redeemed spirits, *fidelium animæ*, that can rest in peace: it would be senseless to call down peace on the others. This peace is therefore a quality of life, not of death. And perhaps the bliss of Brahma might be understood in a similar way, when the sense of identity with what is common to all things causes their differences and oppositions, without being historically destroyed, to be balanced and mutually cancelled in our allegiance; so that Brahma is all things, and yet is none of them. As warmth is something diffused and inarticulate, born of infinitesimal pervasive vibrations, so deep sleep may be a nameless happiness, brooding over a sea of troubles. We are justified in distinguishing this state from non-existence not only morally, as escape from all evil, but also physically by virtue of the concourse of Wills in it from all quarters suspended by their mutual incompatibility, yet rich each with its possible good. This latent infinite

Peace implies harmony not emptiness.

aspiration lifts the deep peace of the universal psyche into a limiting instance of spirit, as if love of all good lived there without experience, and therefore without loss.

Love is hardly in itself an object of intuition, since it becomes conscious only when it is love of something; and yet love is independent in origin from the intuition of its object. It colours this object with a quality which is not beauty, or clearness, such as the joy of pure intuition would endow it with. Love seeks posses- *Fifth characteristic: Piety or attachment to its source.* sion. It experiences a physical affinity between the psyche and the object, and attaches the Will to that object like a child to its mother, prior to any clear idea of it; so that here the spirit is caught in the leash, restrained and called back insistently more to an active influence than to the essence that represents it in intuition. Love suffers and hopes; it is attached in its aspirations to something not spiritual; it clothes this something as best it may in spiritual guise, but constantly with the sense or the fear of a misfit, of a disappointment. We sometimes find that the mother we love is not the mother we should have liked; and spirit at every turn has that painful experience. The estrangement flows from the native predicament of spirit in being incarnate, lodged in a particular place, time, and person, while its intrinsic ambition is universal. Love, like knowledge, is of the contingent by the contingent; both knowledge and love are therefore in one sense distracting, since they bind spirit to something particular and pre-existent, other than the spontaneous play of intuition.

Yet these bonds are the first roots of spontaneity itself, giving existence and specific impulse to the spirit, since the whole power in spirit is natural, as the whole glory of nature is spiritual. Detachment presupposes attachment; but attachment, when it becomes conscious in love or knowledge, has already begun to transcend the object of attachment, partly by seeing its limitations and its surroundings in the world, partly by sublimating it into an idea and turning it from the brute fact that it was into a part of the furniture of mind. And how shall any local personal love become just, sure, and enlightened? Not by being disowned (or we should soon be disowning spirit itself) but by being understood and seen to be legitimate and beautiful in its place, as other loves are legitimate and beautiful in their places.

Vital attachment to the life of nature thus has ideal fidelity for its counterpart in the life of spirit. Animal instincts attract attention to specific objects; action and passion, in passing, leave a settled propensity in the psyche to repeat those movements or to recoil from them; and this quickened attention and these well-learned lessons of experience sharpen and fix in the mind the terms of its memory and logic. In this intellectual field experience can be cumulative. Each term retains its meaning; and when further experience or consideration shows that essence in a new light, displaying one or another of its necessary relations to other essences, its identity is not destroyed but vindicated; since its place and function are defined more and more perfectly in the great mosaic of terms composing a coherent language for that spirit. It is in the primary nature of intuition to exhibit something specific, to clarify and define it; and also to keep that definite term *in mind* (as we say), not of course in consciousness except occasionally, but in reserve in the penumbra of essences to which a reference is possible and which silently buttress the meaning and quality of every other essence that may come before us.

Conventionally considered, and from the point of view of language and material knowledge, human ideas are vague and shifting, so that no two men can think

Hence mindfulness and coherence in reflection.

alike and no two readings of the same poem can produce the same impression. But if instead of referring ideas to conventional standards never actually specified, we consider each actual intuition in itself, it is necessarily absolutely clear and definite, revealing the precise essence that it reveals. Some intuitions will be more prolonged or emphatic than others, so that the essence given in them may have a better chance of reappearing in later intuitions, or one almost like it, and of being designated by some word; and it will be only the approach to constancy in the meanings of words or of other signs that will enable the mind to enlarge its scope and to preserve its acquisitions.

In the life of reason this intrinsic growth within intuition may be overlooked, because what interests the moralist is the harmony to be attained between desire and thought on the one side and nature and destiny on the other. The ideal for him is psychic adaptation rather than spiritual freedom, although spiritual freedom would be achieved, perhaps in some at first painful or unpalatable form, if social harmony were once established. Such freedom could be attained, however, only after a great slaughter and sacrifice of spirits; and intuition has its intrinsic reality and value quite as much in the spirits condemned by circumstances as in the spirits approved and declared triumphant. Even such wisdom as the discipline of experience may achieve is bought at a price and is a terrible drag on the *discursive* freedom of spirit, clipping its wings for any far migration. Piety, in domesticating the spirit in one specific region, educates it to be partial, prejudiced and unjust. It seems to attach love to illusion, and life to that which by its very nature is condemned to death. Incompleteness and distraction thus enter into the heart of spirituality, contradicting its native vocation to be clear, comprehensive and free.

The great privilege of the immaterial, however, is to be indomitable. As existence can neither abolish any essence by neglecting it, nor smirch it by dragging it down into the flux of change, so animal life cannot annul the discoveries which it has once made. It may extinguish the light of attention and of memory by destroying the organs and records that might have kept that knowledge alive in the world; but the autonomy of spirit, while spirit lives, is inalienable. The things felt will have been felt, the things loved will have been loved, whatever may ensue; and no contrary judgment supervening will ever have the field to itself. Ignorant as it may be of all contradictions, it will be contradicted; unconscious as it may be of alien goods, the alien goods will exist. So that the clouds that traverse the spirit, in being seen, are in one sense abolished: spirit has outflanked them, set them down to be clouds, and thereby vindicated the supremacy of light and of vision.

Sixth characteristic: Intrinsic authority.

Evidently in the absence of intuition there would be no judgment or valuation at all, no spiritual witness to observe the world or to question it. And if the actual observations or questionings made by anybody be referred to some ulterior authority, that authority can be only that of a further intuition. There is, indeed, the dynamic authority or laughter of things, going their way, doing their work, and crushing all judgments: but this is a triumph for them only in our own estimation. They themselves do not boast; they most humbly and uncomplainingly endure their strains and precipitate their cataclysms. So that intuition shines alone in its moral heaven, among other intuitions; and even these do not shine together in any common medium, but only each in each, when they think of one another.

CHAPTER VII

DISTRACTION

IN languages derived from the Latin the word distraction bears the pleasant sense of an incidental *divertissement*, or change from compulsory to entertaining ideas. In English the word has preserved a deeper meaning of which I will avail myself here. Sense of the term distraction. We are distracted or distraught when torn asunder by contrary and inescapable commitments. From these we may seek refuge in drink, heedlessness, or sport, but still they will poison the sources of our lives, fill our solitude and our dreams, and threaten our sanity. By distraction I understand the alien force that drags the spirit away from the spontaneous exercise of its liberty, and holds it down to the rack of care, doubt, pain, hatred, and vice. And I will distinguish the chief agencies in this distraction, after the picturesque manner of Christian wisdom, as the Flesh, the World, and the Devil.

I have already dropped some hints as to how we may understand this shocking anomaly; for so it would seem to a truly emancipated spirit, to whom everything, including its own movement and destiny, would be an object of sympathetic Distraction something inevitable. interest, but never a source of distraction. Such a spirit would laugh at the hypothesis, perhaps suggested to it by the devil, that it would have lived happy had it been left to its own resources, without a body or a world; for in pure spirit there is evidently nothing to determine what experiences may fall to it, what passions

673

or what impulse to go on living or dreaming at all. Universal Will, even, that part at work in spirit, must be irrational, since if it had been a rational agent it would have sought, but never could have found, a reason for being what it was.   All appetitions, repulsions, selections, and exclusions must first be automatic: they must precede and occasion the rise of intuition, if intuition is to exist temporally and to have any special themes or career.   Emancipated spirit would see clearly that even its emancipation and liberty were gifts of fortune or divine grace; and it would understand at the same time how rare such good fortune is likely to be, and how distracted the life of spirit must be on the whole.

On the whole, but not essentially; for it is only when a certain harmony has been achieved in the psyche that spirit can awake, and this harmony at moments may be almost perfect.   There will then be intuition without distraction.

Instrumentalities that distract as objects may enrich intuition as influences.

You may hear a sound so pure, so musically modulated and sufficient in itself, that no suspicion intervenes of any cause or meaning that this sound might have in the world, much less any thought of yourself hearing, or of your ears or brain. Another day, the sound may be so deafening or piercing that your whole frame winces and trembles, and your hands go up instinctively to the sides of your tortured head.   The body has then awakened spirit only to fill it with horrid concern for that body.   Yet this was not the body's Will, only an effect of maladjustment in its physical economy and adaptation.   When working well, the psyche remains unconscious of instrumentalities.   Your ears may perfectly perform their practical function without sound, as sound, coming to consciousness at all.   Meaning, objects, ideas, remote reported events will alone fill your imagination.   This is normal in interesting conversation: the psyche receives the sounds of the language and conveys their messages to the proper quarters, so that intelligent answers or actions follow; but those sounds never reach the spirit, they remain vibrations without ever becoming data; and intuition evokes only the facts or ideas to be reported. If all the machinery of life could be as familiar and as readily handled as one's native language, it would not need to distract or to detain the spirit at all, but would become transparent and unconscious, or else form a separate sphere of objects, such as words are to the grammarian. No doubt the material intervention of that machinery would qualify the movement by which intuition was finally evoked, as the same thing said in English or in French has not the same exact æsthetic or moral essence for the spirit. Yet this atmosphere enveloping ideas forms no separable object in direct apprehension, but only an indescribable aura, due to the total quality of life concerned. These agencies distract only when they interfere with intuition at the desired level: as when in speaking you catch the tone of your own voice, lose the thread, become embarrassed, and detest yourself and all your peculiarities.

The psyche has limited energies and is seldom in perfect health; each of her achievements (of which spirit is one) therefore suffers from a double Mere in-danger. At the roots, sustenance may fail; complete-ness or lapse only a low or feeble development may be involves no possible, or one in a special eccentric direc- distraction. tion which may seem monstrous judged by what would have ensued if the faculty in question had realized all its potentialities equally. There are animals, there are races, there are circumstances in which spirit may take happy but very limited flights; a little wit, a little fancy, a little innocent pleasure; and no repining, no suspicion that bolder flights are missed. If we regarded such limitation as unfortunate or wrong, we should be condemning every phrase of spiritual life possible to man; because all phases are conditioned and limited by the same power of circumstance that keeps the child a child, and the drudge a drudge. The demand that spirit in all creatures should be passing through the phase which we happen to have reached, needs only to be mentioned to be discredited. It is the very opposite of sympathy with human nature; a wretched exhibition of tyrannical conceit and fatuity. Not the limitations of life should trouble the spirit, for those are inseparable from its existence and definiteness; but only the false promises that nature sometimes gives and then betrays, when some budding affection dries up, or some work begun enthusiastically falls to pieces of itself. This amounts to true cruelty on nature's part, offering a gift and then snatching it back; yet the alternation would be no worse than that between sleeping and waking, if development were merely arrested, as when a child dies; something cruel for the parents, but far from distracting and perhaps a blessing to spirit in the child.

Positive distraction rather indicates a second danger that besets the spirit: not so much failing or lapsing, as being deflected, confused, and deceived by contrary vital motions. In such discord, spirit suffers horribly and is indeed, morally, the only sufferer in all the camps. Yet looked at biologically, spirit in its turn is not always guiltless since its organ too may impede or derange other organs. Sometimes consciousness seems to make cowards of us all; life is spoiled by responsibility for life; care, fear, and indecision poison the innocent pleasure of seeing and feeling and playing the game. The day comes when we can no longer play unless we gamble, adding a dark worldly motive to the free sport. All interests are sicklied over by the shadow of contrary interests, all beliefs by contrary suspicions. The sickly

Any impulse, even the highest working out of season, may corrupt the others.

soldier fights without joy and almost without rage; the
sickly assassin fires the second shot into his own brain.
In all this the paraphernalia of spirit—languages,
maxims, theories, information—overwhelm the primary
Will. So we find the modern man too dubious, too
indifferent, to call a rival out to a duel. He feels
constantly challenged within himself; courage has lost
all charm and all finality. At the moment of his most
confident thrust he perceives that he, too, is wounded,
and the sense of moral disaster all round embitters
every practical effort.

This is an ulterior complication, and spirit seldom
flounders inwardly in that the animal impulses which
buoyed it up have forsaken it. Usually these Unemployed
impulses are only too obstreperous and deter- emotions.
mined; they defy spirit or seduce it. There is a sense
in which spirit is always seduced, seduced by the
radical current of the Will before it awakes to any
clear ideas. It fears, it enjoys, it suffers without
knowing about what. Emotion exists first with a cause
but without any object; and while this condition is
hardly distraction, since there is nothing from which
spirit could be distracted, yet it is an uneasy unsatisfied
state. Alarm summons attention to something, and
attention is baulked if nothing can be found. To feel
alarmed, and not know about what, is ignominious,
and when the trick becomes habitual in the organism,
the spiritual state induced is a form of madness. Yet
madness is often only nature unveiled, a wheel in the
necessary machinery seen working apart; and here we
have but to restore the ideas habitual to the mind
for the emotion to seem sane, even if perhaps mis-
directed.

Love and hatred are often in this case. We are
allured or enraged, yet fundamentally we do not know
what it is that allures or enrages us. We may point
to some rather ordinary person, or to some rather

ordinary event; but why on earth should such devastating feelings overcome us in their presence? The cause lies in the hidden complexity and casual turns of nature in us, in our unconscious Will: and the cause explains the absence of a reason. Emotions arise when Will is precipitated suddenly in some fresh direction; and whatever image meets us at the terminus profits by the colour of the emotion with which we view it. The ordinary creature seems divinely beautiful, rare, and significant; the ordinary event seems an intolerable outrage. The power attributed to those objects is entirely drawn from one's own psyche, ripe for such passions. Therefore mature moralists, when morality was not itself a mere ignorant emotion, talked about the *madness* of passion, the *guilt* of sin, the *folly* of fashion. Yet this is a normal madness, an original sin, a sprightly and charming folly. Life could not have begun or grown interesting without them. The evil involved is constitutional, and the spirit suffers this distraction because it exists, and is a natural being, an emanation of universal Will. Universal Will aims initially at anything and everything, and realizes whatever it can realize, imperfectly of course from the point of view of that special aim. Spirit cannot escape these conditions and this imperfection. It too has infinite possibilities, and contingent occasions. Often we cannot but hate the things we love, and hate ourselves for loving them; and we are right in blaming our fallen nature for these contradictions. It is not in the realm of spirit that they are hatched, but in that of matter, to which our psyches belong. Our souls are diseased, pursuing things that ultimately repel them. And the approach to health cannot come by rescinding our nature but by disentangling and harmonizing it as much as possible, as indeed it naturally endeavours to harmonize itself.

In animals universal Will takes the form of a psyche,

which is no separate supernatural principle, but only a moving harmony or equilibrium maintaining itself more or less perfectly in each organism until death breaks it down altogether. The more vigorous this concretion of vital powers, the more violent will be the protest of the whole organism against any attack, from within or without, that tends to disrupt it. A defensive contraction or concentration ensues; and if we suppose a slumbering consciousness to pre-exist in the psyche, it will awake with a sharp cry, a conscious protest, which we call pain. Pain is a first form of distraction; for it is a summons, a disturbance of that placidity in which spirit slept when merely potential; yet this summons brings nothing to spirit that spirit can light up, diversify, make articulate, or turn into knowledge. As an intuition, if such it may be called, pain is empty, yet as a sensation it is intense, arresting, imperative; so that it exemplifies the very essence of evil for the spirit: to exist in vain, to care intensely in the dark, to be prodded into madness about nothing. The birth of spirit is joyful when it is the dawn of light, disclosing a thousand movements and objects that evoke intuition and excite a discerning love, or even a discerning aversion; but to be born blind and kept alive by force with no foothold, falling as it were spasmodically and helplessly through a horrible vacuum, is to suffer pure torment and be subject to a gratuitous tyranny.

Distraction seen pure in pain.

Now this arrest and contraction which for the spirit is a pain for the psyche is a means of safety: by suspending her diffused vegetative task and rushing to withdraw or protect some injured member, she is fighting for her existence. Nothing therefore, from her point of view (but her views are merely habits!) could be less gratuitous and more opportune than this mobilization, which so distracts the spirit; for the spirit was enjoying

Pain comes with some rude summons to defensive action.

life or enjoying sleep, but the psyche was not sleeping or enjoying life, but only living and obeying faithfully an imperious momentum to live on. She has prudently developed a central exchange in the brain, with a whole plan for coordinate action in cases of danger, with particular nerves, pain-nerves, from every quarter to give the alarm and guide defensive operations. That the pain-nerves *hurt*, that they distract the spirit, she neither knows nor cares; the point is that they should instantly call the blood or the muscles or the hand to the affected part, to protect or to heal it; and if this summons *hurts* because it brings so violent a wrench and stoppage of normal functions, that makes no difference, if only the crisis can be passed, and safely restored. The trouble is that even biologically this machinery remains imperfect. The alarm often arrives late, when the damage has been done and a cure is impossible; or it arrives needlessly, when local unconscious processes would suffice to repair that damage. Often, too, the agitation set up becomes a worse evil than its cause, prolonging itself hysterically with perhaps fatal results. We then have an orgy of pain, as in difficult childbirth, in cramp, neuralgia, or madness. I suspect that this is the case always, in some measure, wherever there is pain: far from being a means to remedial action pain is a sign that the available remedies have failed. If biological organization and adjustments were perfect there would evidently be no internal disorders; and in the case of external accidents nature would apply an anæsthetic automatically, leaving the rest of the psyche undisturbed, while the part concerned did its mending in peace. To diffuse trouble is the worst possible means to correcting it. We may say with better reason of pain what Spinoza said of remorse and pity, that it is bad and useless. The *pain* in remorse and pity is futile, but not the spiritual or tragic *perception* of the evil in question:

for this perception indicates no impediment in the psyche now, but on the contrary an enveloping synthesis by which the old calamity and its neutralization in the vast context of truth are present to the spirit, and radically present for ever. Such tragic insight, such pity and remorse, are parts of the highest good. That which is bad and useless is to protract or repeat pain, physical or moral, at its original level, where it still indicates not synthesis but distraction.

If spirit were all, pain would be utterly dark and inexplicable; but even on the lowest plane we may say that to suffer is to learn. We learn at least *Were the* that we are incarnate; and also that the body *defensive* is subject to some hostile influence and for *reaction per-* *fect it would* the moment helpless before it. Pain ex- *not be* presses disruption, as the sense of relief *painful.* expresses a gradual recovery of vital harmonies, and joy their sudden expansion. If the organism were well adapted and in perfect health attacks from outside would be stimulating rather than painful. The bugle-call to arms would be positively welcomed, as we welcome a challenge to any game in which we are proficient. Bruises and wounds would then be little felt, or would be borne proudly. Even irreparable losses, like blindness, would not spread their blight over the residue of the soul but would rather provoke a new concentration, with perhaps a finer quality of life. Death itself when it supervened would not be painful or feared. Human horror of death is perhaps something exceptional in the universe, arising only when spirit is called back from its natural flights too often, to nurse the agony and bewail the death of others. Simpler better-knit souls might normally die in battle or in sleep, without making a fuss about it.

In pain, in terror, in all such moral suffering as is akin to pain, the enemy is external. There is no disunion in the alarmed soul. Psyche and spirit are on the same side, disturbed by the same irruption. For this reason, when the foreign evil cannot be parried, as in mutilation or approaching death,

Under physical stress souls are simplified and assimilated to one another.

it may be met and almost disarmed by a concentration of life inwards, surrendering the indefensible outworks, and retreating in the end to pure spirit which though existentially the flower of the psyche, morally cannot be caught or finally vanquished, because its interests are not local. Illumination at this point may be reduced, it may be extinguished, but the light is not thereby corrupted or confused: there is no treason, no sin. For the same reason, corporal works of mercy engage the spirit whole-heartedly and more urgently than any ideal object of aspiration. We do not ask whether the wretch lying robbed and wounded by the wayside *deserves* to be helped. He *needs* help, and that suffices to secure unreservedly our spiritual sympathy. His calamity is external to him. In respect to it, there is integrity in his soul, however distracted and criminal may have been the business that led him into this plight. We disregard these circumstances, which we feel to have been accidents in that blind life, snares into which a poor animal soul was drawn insensibly, filth that clotted and distorted it against its primary intent. Now in his extremity the broken ruffian is again a child. He asks only to breathe, to sleep, to be nourished, not to be tormented. And with that elementary Will in him the Will in every spirit is unanimous: all recognize the common enemy, physical misfortune, physical disaster. These may reduce the scope of spirit in each soul, but they remove all antipathy between one soul and another: they inspire humility in each and charity to all.[1]

[1] This sympathy between psyches at certain levels has nothing miraculous about it, as if they lost their individuality and became mere channels for a great reservoir of emotion always actual above them. It is not as if the emotions actual in any man could pass on materially to his neighbour.

Trouble thickens when the enemy disturbing the
soul is not external, but when one vital impulse is
fighting there against another. The spirit
then hardly knows its centre, identifies itself
now with this interest and now with that, or
hangs suspended in an agony of self-contradiction. Moralists are accustomed to give names to
these rival forces, a few stock names for an infinite
variety of passions, and to represent one set or one
principle as alone legitimate. This is convenient in
pedagogy and roughly represents the dominant morality
at a given time in a given society; but even then spirit
will be as often on the side of some rebellious impulse
as on that of the reigning convention. No form of
life can be inherently wrong, since there is no criterion
by which to judge except the inherent direction of life.
But when life is firmly organized in a special way, as
it must be before spirit can appear, some impulses will
be indispensable for it, and others disruptive. Hence
human morality is quite safely and efficiently established by human nature, and maintained by swift
natural sanctions. It is not, and cannot be, perfectly

Psychic organization essential but imperfect.

Each is moved by his own impulses and instincts; and these in a well-
organized animal species will become co-operative without becoming similar,
never actually reproducing in the helpful soul the feelings that the suffering
soul may endure. Charity in Martha will not repeat, as if by physical
contagion, the troubles of her flock, nor will love in Mary repeat the divine
virtues of her Master. The surgeon must remain calm, and the worshipper
prayerful and dependent. Hence a paradox important in the arts: that the
passions most movingly portrayed are passions that nobody has ever felt.
Not only does the poet never actually feel the emotion he is expressing
—he would not be an artist if he did—but the ideal personage he is enacting,
if that personage had existed, would not have felt the pure, the glorified
emotions that the author's words or theme suggest to the public. Not that
real agonies are less terrible, but they are mixed, broken, *distracted*; and
the more intense they are, the nearer they bring the spirit to the edge of
disruption, that is to say, of unconsciousness. Each moment is then
exhausting and blinding in its intensity; and when the storm is over, calm
buries that dreadful past as if at the bottom of the sea. We are neither able
nor willing to recall it. But to the sensitive spectator or to the spirit recovering its native power in epic memory or tragic imagination, the whole is lifted
into the sphere of fable, where ignominious experience becomes a history
of chosen issues in a single distinct and memorable life.

uniform, since various modes of life may be equally possible and successful, and human nature may develop in one direction and wither in another. Yet in each society and in each individual there will be obviously radical needs to satisfy and obvious dangers to avoid.

Even fundamental functions, like nutrition and reproduction, since they engage the same organism, may come into conflict, and each will then be distracting to the spirit in so far as it interferes with the other. Nature in some animals prudently makes the two alternate: each peaceful creature spends his life diligently feeding until the rutting season, when he forgets to eat and will fight any rival to the death for the sake of mating. Evidently to a grazing conscience such love must seem sheer madness, until it discovers that if the mating instinct were suppressed, grazing would soon be extinct also. Hence in the most acquisitive and well-fed human societies universal and early marriage is doubly approved, not only for peopling the state, but for keeping wild love as much as possible from distracting the thrifty mind.

Initially feeding is much more grossly fleshly than making love and much less sprightly, and the images and emotions that fill the spirit are less varied and interesting. Yet in its extensions the need of nutrition carries the spirit farther afield, in hunting, industry, seafaring, and war; so that the oppression that may ultimately come to the soul from these quarters does not seem due to the demands of the body but rather to the world and its hostility. Love is more intimately inspiring; yet it remains visibly rooted in the body, and fixed upon bodily persons; so that its domination seems unnecessary, foreign, tormenting and perhaps degrading to the spirit. Strange that the most fanciful and transporting of passions should be called *par excellence* the concupiscence of the flesh!

Conflicts between primary impulses.

In the perfect exercise of any function the instruments are ignored and attention rests directly on the object, the scene, and the volume of vital music concerned in the action. Such are health and freedom; and then spirit enjoys the life of the flesh without obsession by the flesh. Frank love is not in the least distracting; it is hearty, joyful, and gay; or if any mood follows in which it is viewed at a certain remove, as an odd performance, it still leaves an after-glow of laughter and affection. This harmony between flesh and spirit runs very deep; a premonition of it plays no small part in falling in love and in love-making. We might even say that the final swoon of pleasure celebrated in us this cosmic harmony mystically and for a moment. But human existence is too complicated for spiritual union to be maintained steadily with infra-human and trans-personal forces; a too great flood drowns us in uplifting us, and this coveted victory is a real abdication.

The trouble does not come at all from the flesh being concerned; on the contrary, love turns the flesh into loveliness. It comes entirely from slackness and disorder in the psyche, that cannot time and modulate these impulses so as to keep them pure and friendly to the world in which they flourish. Hence ill-timed cravings, annoyance, shame, hypocrisy and perpetual dissatisfaction. I need not mention the turpitudes of mere sensuality, now ignorant and groping, now vicious and weary; for these in themselves are comparatively trivial and disgusting to their own sense; and the invectives and precautions of ascetic moralists often miss the point, since these things are not what the flesh desires but what it is driven to by ill fortune. Nor need I dwell on the tragic conflicts that distract the spirit when love grows romantic, and passionately resists the irresistible power of time and

Neither matter nor mutation would distract the spirit if the psyche were well ordered.

change.   Pure love is not temporally constant, because time is itself inconstant, and swallows up incessantly every chosen object of love.   Innocent sexual desire, like appetite for food, pursues anything suitable that offers.   It explores, tastes, accepts this, rejects that, and remains always alert.   This playfulness and keenness signify no disdain for what has already been chosen. The spirit cannot forswear any good that it has found, or may find; and no good is truly found until love ceases to be a craving for the unknown and, in face of the known, becomes silent and spiritual.   The object then proves to have been an essence and not an existing person or thing; and among essences there is no jealousy or contradiction, and no decay.

Fidelity to things and persons is a domestic virtue proper to a society centred in the family and its belong-ings.   Affections are then duties, and posses-sions responsibilities.   Such ties, like all moral relations, enrich the soul in confining it and offer a suitable though accidental theme for the spirit; but they are not spiritual ties. In marriage love is socialized and moralized into a lifelong partnership which it would be dishonourable to betray; and community of interests and habits buttresses that love into mutual trust and assistance. A household rather smothers the love that established it.   Nature seems to be repressed there more than obeyed; and the family becomes a political institution and a part of the world, where the fortunes of spirit are entangled in all sorts of interests not those of the heart.

Loop-line through domestic morality.

How might the heart be satisfied?   Certainly not by turning from a first union to others at the same incidental level.   To re-excite a passion physically is not to satisfy it morally; rather to discredit it as morally vain.   Licentiousness becomes horribly tedious; yet spirit can never turn its back on love, any more than on life, since it is their supreme manifestation.   It must accept, honour, transmute and sanctify them. It will therefore retain in compulsory affections that element which is original and spontaneous, because home and country appeal to the heart powerfully, apart from any duty. And it will cull from romantic passion and from loose loves the magic spell in them, without the deception; that is to say, it will distinguish the loveliness in things or the charm in persons from the existing persons and things. These were the vehicle, *that* was the revelation. And the ideal signification, for the spiritual man, is not a new illusion, as if he hoped to pursue the charm and the aroma that have fled from earth into heaven, and there catch them and store them safely in his moral museum. This heavenward evaporation of the good is a metaphor. Charm and aroma cannot be removed from themselves; and in themselves they are incorruptible. Fortune shows them for a moment, then hides them; at any time, in one place or another, they may reappear. The material continuity of life and of objects means nothing to spirit; the point is only that the revelation, wherever it comes, should be as clear and full as possible. That there should be interruptions, that youth should congeal into old age, and that death should end all for each person, follows from the nature of existence. The flux of things is terrible indeed to the distracted spirit, compelled to cling and tremble and whine at the mutations of matter; but those mutations themselves become musical and comic, if once the spirit can free itself and perceive its affinity to the eternal.

A grand passion would open the way best to this transformation: for here the flesh has already conquered the world, and almost conquered itself, since the rapt lover becomes a worshipper, as is *Illusion and revelation in* proper to spirit. Yet there is madness in *the grand* this devotion, and great suffering, because *passion.* the victim is attaching his whole soul to one person and to the caprices of that person, and giving to man, or rather to woman, the things that are God's. Yet this very exaggeration tends to break up the illusion, and to disentangle the secret of love. Here is a fever in the spirit, fed secretly by the flesh, but disproportionate altogether to what the flesh can claim or can give, tormented out of all measure by accidents of little moment, and crucified even in victory. And yet what soul that has ever known a great love would wish not to have known it? The illusion was only a false identification, not a false allegiance. It revealed the potential glory of the beautiful.

Gallantry, marriage, and Platonic love are ways in which the flesh endeavours to make its excuses to free spirit, by showing how amiable, how steady, and how pure it can become. Yet the free spirit is not convinced. Not only do the depths probably remain turbid beneath these surfaces, but love itself, which springs from the heart of nature, has lost its youth and ardour and withered into frivolity or habit or dialectic. Better honest lust in its crudity; for though it be an expense of spirit, yet there is spirit in it, genuine enthusiasm that, when cheated and disgraced, can prompt to repentance. So too the drunkard, in whose vice there are moments of spiritual freedom, repents easily and feels himself a miserable fool. The sordid condition into which he lapses gives the lie too sharply to all the jollity and comfort and irresponsibility that he felt in his cups. If comic insight were to enrich the mind, it would need to be developed into sober intelligence, which has the agility and mastership of wit, without mockery or topsy-turvydom. But when insight ends in laughter, laughter itself fatigues, and dies down suddenly, as if it too had caught us in a false trap. We have lost our bearings and we have cheapened the world; which was not what the spirit longed to do with its freedom. If spirit

Futile escapes and disguises.

suffers and dies in the world, this is only because it loves the world, in the sense of loving the light and joy that are possible in it, or would be possible but for the frustration of one blind impulse by another. Evidently retrenchment is necessary, and surrender of impossible claims; and to surrender them laughing is a short cut to victory and takes place at least in one's own soul for the moment. But this happens only at the level of play and of intellect. The chained dogs below keep on barking in their kennels.

Laughter about fleshly things has various phases, and escapes from distraction in more than one direction. There is first the laughter of victory. As the rude boy jeers at his victims, or the soldier boasts and threatens, so the young lusty rogue laughs at his feats. He has eluded his vigilant elders, has found a propitious nook, has overcome his own awkwardness and the trembling resistance of his partner. How frank and bold he can be now; how clear the world is going to be for him henceforth, how positive, how manageable, how prosaic! But his laughter soon turns into a dead seriousness. This jollity has opened a long chapter of human responsibility, human conflicts and human sorrows.

Comic expressions of love.

There is also, both before and after, the laughter of detachment, of satire, of mockery. We laugh at the ridiculous routine of love-making, its mis- adventures, its delusions. We laugh at the cuckold's horns and at the prude's hypocrisy. We laugh at the one old way out, found at last or missed, from every sentimental labyrinth. There is still a kind of victory, though an intellectual and bitter victory, in this shrewd laughter. Wit in us triumphs, yet human nature, deeper down, remains wounded and ill at ease. The tables have been turned, and now the cynic is laughing at the passion that in the bold lover was laughing at the world. Yet not in this case whole-heartedly,

Satiric descriptions of it.

because the cynic is divided against himself. Sensuality would not amuse him if he were a free observer, such as the Roman satirists pretended to be. He would then instinctively stop laughing and begin to preach. The flesh would appear to him as a mechanical if not disgusting instrument for keeping the world going; a most wasteful and over-wrought instrument, that often defeated and always confused its rational use. But sourness about the flesh is only a forced and hypocritical sentiment. The flesh forms the raw material of human nature and is impossible to discard. He himself has been haunted and troubled from the tenderest age by ill-satisfied fleshly impulses which still engage his fancy no less than his body: and that is why bawdy talk makes him laugh. He knows that somewhere, somehow the flesh will always take its revenge. His satiric scorn is not really merry; it mocks his secret sympathies, and betrays the spiritual confusion at the root of his being. For here is an indispensable impulse that carries on the world well enough from the point of view of universal Will, yet in the individual, probably in himself, works terrible havoc. He laughs ambiguously, half scorning the pleasures he has enjoyed, and still half craving those he has missed.

Things go better when people live simply, like peasants near the earth, and spirit in them is dumb, or entertained only by a few superstitions and a few festive arts or sporting adventures. The flesh is then too little indulged to seem an enemy. Heaven would be to feast, to drink, to dance, and to make love lustily forever. These passions are thus left to grow wild and hungry amid the weeds; labour and an early marriage keeps them within bounds. Fixed and monotonous circumstances seem to render people's characters also fixed and monotonous. They scold and distrust one another, but they have no time to quarrel each with himself.

Hypertrophe of lust in artificial societies.

They lay all their troubles to illness, poverty, bad weather, and ill luck. But in a crowded artificial society, the flesh, with its sentimental overtones, creates an inner focus of life sharply contrasted with worldly circumstances and duties: and the question becomes debatable whether the flesh distracts a spirit properly attached to family, study, work, and public affairs, or whether these worldly interests distract it from the all-important revelation of love. In any case there is distraction. The race is compelled, under pain of extinction, to keep the sexual impulse alive, and powerful enough to overcome all selfish prudence or moral disgust. Love must be flattered and tempted underhand by a thousand social lures and opportunities, while at the same time it must be outwardly restrained, and limited to conventional forms and thrifty habits.

Nor is the straitjacket imposed by society the worst obstruction: deeper trouble comes from the illusions, revulsions, suspicions, and disasters suffered by love itself when given a free rein. At the lower level, it fixes attention on ignoble sub- *Inner contrarieties in love.* human cravings, infects impulse with vice, wastes time and substance and degrades the conscience with ties and memories impossible to acknowledge; while at a higher social level, it attaches duty where the heart is not attached, and attaches the heart where nothing deserves or rewards attachment. Often the ingenuity of love disguises these tragedies by affectionate hypocrisies or accommodations. That is a mild form of repentance, covering the dead sin with flowers; but even avowed repentance is far from solving the problem. A heroic religious asceticism would need to employ the very impulse that it outwardly suppressed, at least if the reform were to be permanent and the new way of life cheerful and sane. Mere repression, without sublimation into a new devotion and enthusiasm, would run great danger of a relapse; or there might ensue a complete philosophical reversal of that repentance, with a return to the vulgar naturalism that decries all discipline as cruel and barren.

These vital contradictions might be solved by a good moral regimen, austere in principle, like the Catholic Church, but charitable in temper and disillusioned about the motives that must rule the world. In regard to the flesh, the enemy to be taken captive is no accidental vice, like gambling or drunkenness, that might be thoroughly extirpated. It is a force intrinsic to human nature; you must make peace with it somehow, or be perpetually distracted. You must tame it, transmute it, employ it to warm your affections and light up your painted world. It will then continue to live in your sense of potentiality, of charity, of wonder, of mystic joy. And this will be no pious deception. The force that seemed an alien demon tormenting you from within was always the very life of nature breaking out in you, and making you akin to the whole world. It may work havoc in your little person; nature is not sparing of havoc; but it may also enlarge your heart into an inner understanding of all things natural and divine.

The sins of the flesh, though the saddest, are therefore the friendliest to the spirit. It may renounce, it will never insult them. They were never themselves hostile to the spirit in intention, only childish gropings of an animal soul caught in the world's trap. It is rather the ill consequences of carnal passion that condemn it, than the quality, dumb longing, of the passion itself; so that for the most part it is the world rather than the flesh that renders the flesh a snare. Evidently in respect to hunger and cold the torments of the body are not due to its own defect, but to a treacherous environment, favourable enough to permit life, but too niggardly to foster it. And from this maladaptation

Transition to distraction by the world.

flows the whole slavery of spirit to the world. In
sympathy with the flesh, it trembles at the multiform
scourges that come from without—from the elements,
from wild animals, from the very family with which
a seemingly happy instinct has surrounded the individual. It is then this family, become a tribe, that
imposes all those duties, initiations, labours, and wars
by which spirit is perpetually pulled hither and thither,
intoxicated, maddened, and fatigued. Even love in
the world cannot be what it was in Eden: it is shadowed
now by responsibility and jealousy. It is beset by a
thousand rival or contrary interests that gain upon it
with time; except perhaps in old age or sickness, when
the old simple affection emerges from the ruins, and
proves its closer kinship with the soul. So all the other
spontaneous powers, in finding their uses, forfeit their
freedom. They drag one another like horses harnessed
to run abreast; and the new half-hostile impulse of
rivalry becomes an artificial spur, turning free play
into bitter passion.

Thus the soul acquires her second, her social, body
with its transpersonal machinery of language, custom,
and industry. I need not stop to describe this political
engine; its phases belong in their principle to the realm
of matter. As they grow organic and harmonious, they
become instruments of reason; and even when most
chaotic, since they form a second political organism
out of animal bodies already well organized, they engage
the spirit of individuals in new adventures, in which
not all is distraction. Labour retains an element of
art, from which it sprang originally in play; government contains an element of paternal foresight and
moral philosophy; and war contains elements of the
chase in action and of chivalry in reflection: things all
charged with spirit and showing how it can overlay
and disinfect the blind complexities of nature. But
here we are concerned with the contrary aspect of

politics, when institutions subject the spirit to forced
and useless labour, and pledge it to hideous passions;
so that, while certainly fed with a more complex
experience and stimulated to higher flights of fancy in
religion and philosophy, it is thereby entangled all the
more helplessly in a vain labyrinth, till perhaps it
loses the very notion of freedom or mastery in any
direction.

A fundamental point in which the political and the
physical worlds are alike hostile to spirit is their
instability. Even this hostility, however, is
not absolute, and for two reasons. In the
first place instability lies at the root of life,
and therefore of spirit also. Were there no
change and no insecurity there could be no expectation
or concern, no interest in what would happen; and
even where the object of interest is static, the interest
in discovering, surveying, describing and redescribing
it, is necessarily a movement. Permanence itself involves a lapse, a duration or continuous passage; yet
the flow may be so equable and silent, it may so
smoothly carry the spirit down a steady current, that
the voyage may seem the very perfection of rest. Were
there less change there would be no spiritual realization
of repose; for eternity lies above or beneath life, and
even to *pass* into eternity (which is the most that spirit,
remaining spirit, can ever do) is still an act and a
transition. If time were ever arrested, the experience
and the thought of eternity would be abolished.

In the second place, the flux of existence, for spirit
in its ultimate insights, is not an evil. Spirit is not
then concerned with its own survival, nor with running
forever its familiar round, like a tame animal. When
free and self-forgetful the spirit ceases to have specific
allegiances, and though each intuition must dart with
fresh zest towards a fresh essence, yet a different
stimulus and a different discovery, when their turn

Timely change not hostile to spirit.

comes, will not be less welcome. Spirit in its own plane feels no inertia, no bonds of habit; those belong only to its basis in animal life. Mutability in things and logical or moral instability in the spirit merely enlarge apprehension, if only the variations do not intellectually confuse or intercept one another. Intuitions must come one by one, but their themes are all eternal.

Therefore elegiac sentiment about the yellow leaf and the nipped flower has little spiritual force, but merely confesses the lag of the psyche in respect to the seasons. Spirit may die, but it can never grow old; nothing obliges it to ruminate upon things past or persistently to renew impulses now belated. And vice versa, nothing requires it to be impatient, or to pine for everything that the present denies. There is a natural desire and foretaste of such things as the psyche is ripe for, and spirit will conceive and prophesy them; but even then insistence on the future, or reliance on it, is unspiritual. The future will come, probably not as we now conceive or demand, and then will be the time for the spirit to enjoy or endure it without delusion. That the briefest life, when pure, is sufficient, appears in the gladness of health and laughter: the child, the happy lover, the conquering intellect rejoice in existing *now*. They are not troubled by any *memento mori*, and need no justification in things to come. The things to come then seem almost as sad and impertinent as things long past, and actual happiness is too inalienably perfect to tremble at mutation, even if mutation were remembered. Spirit, thus freed, surmounts the sophistry of perspectives, by which the noon would be made to shiver at the thought of twilight. Real twilight when it comes has its own beauty, vital and peaceful; but the false twilight of Hades and the Elysian Fields reflects a sense of privation, and adds an imputed sadness or unreality to objects that either exist nowhere or are merely distant and different from our world.

At the same time there is a profound moral gulf between the flux of existence and the life of spirit. In the mind we have foresight and memory, in nature only effects and potentialities. Change when perceived has been synthesized. Contrast, conflict, drama excite thought and fill it with the most interesting themes; but they ruin and torment thought when they work surreptitiously at its foundations, break up its rhythms, swamp it in contradiction and oblivion, and defeat its life without extinguishing it. Representing as it does the victories of the psyche over an inanimate flux and an inorganic environment, spirit lives by transcendence from its centre and responsiveness to outlying things, even to infinity. It would not willingly be cut off from anything or later than the present or earlier than the present, but in the present is conemporaneous with all things and at their very heart. It lives precisely by feeling the co-presence of the successive and the inter-relation of the distant. It would keep all events always present, as it tends to keep them in vivid memory or clear prophecy. The whole and every part are then seen in motion, like episodes in a play; but it would mark a failure in the poet or moralist if he forgot the first act when the second was going on, and had throughout no premonition of the issue. That is the fate of the distracted characters in the play, creatures full of limitations, sentimentality, and impatience, who are trying to preserve the past or command the future, but always in vain, because that which was cannot be again, and that which is coming will have a thousand sources alien to the commanding Will. Spirit envelopes all these sources and all these losses in its virtual omniscience, and while initially living by the life of the parts, corrects

(Marginal note:) Yet to transcend the flux is the essence of spirit.

the blindness of each by an equal participation in all the others; so that although its heart is their heart, its life is not any of their several lives, nor their deaths its death. So long as it remains attached to any one of them blindly, it is defeated in its own Will, and distracted by the inevitable defeats of the vain Wills it has adopted.

The world, then, however familiar superficially, is in its blindness and in its treachery utterly contrary to the spirit. The world is not as it looks, it contradicts what it teaches, it leaves memories which it stultifies, and excites hopes which it betrays.

There has been great insistence in recent philosophy on the terms static and dynamic, but so emotionally that "static" comes to mean not the per- *The dynamic* manent in time but the definite in character, *and the* and "dynamic" not that which exercises *static.* force but simply that which changes. Now instability in existence is at least as characteristic of mind as of matter: and if " dynamic" imply only the continual variation by which one thought yields to another, mind will also be thoroughly dynamic. And it will be dynamic even in an evolutionary or historical sense, if what is meant be that sometimes, on reflection, we find in later phases of thought a logical or moral development of something present in thought earlier. Such moral progression, with dialectic expansion and correction, is inevitable where memory exists, and inherited powers, exercised once, are exercised anew on a changed object, seen in changing lights. The course of experience will be irrelevant to this dialectic, yet the thread of it will be traceable through the labyrinth, until it is broken by accident or lost in its own tangle. And reflection catching rhymes and reasons in the chaos of memory, will fix and impose these tropes on the remembered incidents, or imagine and interweave other incidents to fill out the chosen measure. Thus memory is primarily re-apperceptive, and the first histories are epics and fables. These forms of imagined dynamism, these plots and dramas, are themselves static, and composed precisely because, in such forms, events are memorable. Were these patterns not definite and in that sense static, they could not be conceived or recognized. They are essences. If the love of novelty impels us sometimes to reshuffle them or throw them over altogether, we can be aware of superseding them only if we still see them receding in the distance, while we pick up a new buoy by which to measure our voyage. Mere drift without landmarks would hardly be a change, but only a perpetual sensation of drifting. That the landmarks of spirit are ideal and blown up like bubbles from the unfathomed depths of substance and force, is very true; yet that such bubbles rise to the surface so regularly and mark our course with such varied and responsive lights seems to be proof of relatively static laws in the sea and air. The spirit can count on sufficient stability there, at least in the methods of change; and the fixity of its own terms and achievements, once discerned, laughs at temporal mutation. Spirit has no wish and no power to establish permanent things or persons or types in the world; that is the world's business, if it cares to be conservative, as it must be up to a certain point if it is to rise at all out of chaos, yet as it can never be altogether, since it has chaos in its heart. After running through a cycle or two of evolution, the world might perhaps grow weary, if it had any memory; and the spirit is sometimes tempted to despair in its brief but cruel adventures. What need was there that we should distinguish, that we should care, that we should suffer? No need, surely; yet here is an opportunity, if the spirit is free and unclouded, to see wonderful things, and not rashly for idle amusement but with a participation in divine reality, because our ideas are true. Some are true symbolically of the outer world; others, in a free mind, are true to the organic powers of the psyche, expressed in imagination.

There would be nothing distracting in change if it did not involve deception, or contrary views offered at once to reflection about the same reality. That mere experiences should be various or changeful offends nobody, and simply adds to the gaiety of nations. But for a living being concerned about its destiny, superficial and flighty ideas cannot be satisfying; it cannot help aspiring to knowledge of the obscure and momentous powers that control that destiny and produce those ideas. The variety of these would fortify our spiritual peace if only we could survey their sequence and understand their causes. The problem therefore arises how to fix and deepen our conceptions until they truly describe the ways of the world. This would not involve any arrest or monotony in thought, which is itself a movement. Every moment would still yield a fresh sensation and a new perspective, and all would be well if only changes in ideas co-operated to describe consistently the changes in nature and in themselves. The spirit would then gain continually in scope and wisdom, noting and celebrating the truth in new fictions; because knowledge, unlike truth, is essentially mobile and, both in its terms and in its vistas, poetical. Such suitable harmony between the world and the spirit carries us sanely through daily life; it becomes almost perfect when we are intently watching some exciting event, such as a race. Our perceptions then have the appropriate truth, and so have our emotions; since it is neither possible nor desirable that human ideas should be exhaustive, and the mere sense of losing or winning a bet declares correctly the turn that the race has actually taken in respect to our wager.

Rational variations in ideas.

The natural attachment of spirit to the world follows upon its attachment to the flesh, and is no less necessary in its beginnings. The call for food and shelter establishes the first arts and the call for reproduction establishes the family. How draw the line where the interests of the body begin to yield to the interests of society? But as we pass from one to the other, there is a change in the spiritual climate. Bodily passions, including the impulse to strike and to kill, are violent in their assault like thunderstorms in summer, and often leave behind them amazement and remorse, as if an alien demon had possessed us; yet this demon was himself a spirit, and the profound natural roots of such passions lend them a corresponding depth and even sublimity for the soul. We may have been mad, we may have been criminal, yet something marvellous and divine led us on and dazzled us by its glory. Out of these animal impulses the spirit can weave its refined sentiments of love, honour, and worship.

The world a more external power than the flesh but no less acceptable.

As the dominant influence, however, becomes external, the spirit is drawn further afield, entertained with more knowledge and controlled by stable customs and sanctions; but perhaps the inner fountain of impulse becomes clogged, or dries up altogether. The spirit then resembles a child at school being educated against his will. Perhaps the education succeeds, the lessons grow interesting, compulsory sports absorb every impulse to play, till the mere thought of any pursuit not one of the regular pursuits or any mischief not one of the accepted mischiefs seems strange and repulsive. This might pass for the complete triumph of the world and of a forced morality: but spirit is like Greek fire, it floats on the elements expected to quench it. A tight *Kultur* cannot extinguish it, but merely produces a particularly definite organ for giving it utterance. What is sacrificed at that time and place is only some rival organ that would have had a different spiritual voice. Let the political world do its worst, and while life lasts it will still excite perceptions as clear and feelings as genuine as any that wild nature might have aroused.

The distaste of each temperament or tradition for its rivals is an animal distaste, not to be confused with the interests of spirit in its essence. Spirit is essentially free and potentially infinite; *Suave mari magno.* the nerve of distraction is not the character of the given objects taken in themselves, but the forced attachment of the spirit to their fortunes, which do not really concern it. As a fact, as a pageant, as an object of knowledge no form of the human world would be in the least distracting. The darkest wood does not trouble us, unless we are lost in it, nor the roughest sea, unless we are tossed in it beyond endurance. So the world troubles us by the anxiety and impatience that we feel at its movements, when we are enslaved to interests that are not ours. That the world exists, that it changes, that it struggles with itself for ever and struggles in vain, would only feed and educate the spirit, if the spirit were free. But it is not free: and the causes and degrees of this slavery are the sole ground of division between the Will in nature and the Will in spirit.

Since the Renaissance it has been out of fashion to preach contempt of the world. Writers and academic philosophers are in the world's service, and work for money or reputation; they are no longer impersonal vehicles of an orthodox tradition. *Contentment possible in routine.* There is perhaps an inarticulate feeling in the background that if worldly aims were taxed with vanity, there would be nothing left to live for, and that delusions must be kept up at all costs, or everything would collapse. This feeling, if it exists, is an unavowed pessimism of the deepest dye. Vanity is not escaped but made inescapable; the contempt that religion preached for the pomps and vanities of this world is merely extended to the pomps and vanities of religion. But if absolutely everything is vain, even the desire to escape from vanity, vanity loses its sting and even its meaning, for the notion that things are vain merely because transitory we have seen to be morally confused and superficial. The nerve of true vanity lies elsewhere: in doing something for a further object which cannot be attained in that way. If the worldling aims at nothing beyond his participation in the world, that participation is not vain. It may be called frivolous or stupid, if something different be demanded; but why demand anything different? The existence of the animals is not vain, nor their world contemptible. If we level our morality down to theirs, we deftly escape the reproaches of the preacher.

Such reversion from society to nature has been itself preached by many a false prophet, from the ancient Cynics to Rousseau and his many emulators. I call this gospel false, not because I think animality or rural simplicity or savage independence inferior or wrong: such forms of life exist and the human race may be destined to revert to them or to re-establish something like them in a paradise of anarchy. But I am considering the possible victory of spirit over distraction. To remove certain distracting circumstances may be a relief, but does not essentially fortify the spirit or enlarge its dominion. On the contrary, reversion to animal or mystical solitude, while not excluding union with nature, grounds this union on rudimentary strength or health in the psyche; and this is not only a precarious harmony, but an unspiritual one, like the placidity or the fussiness of animals. Social life lifts the spirit to a more comprehensive intelligence; there

Belated longings to be primitive.

is more constant transcendence of the self in imagination and a richer, more varied, more dramatic world to imagine and to overcome. Intellect is more spiritual than sentiment. A reality traversed by moral and intellectual conflicts excites the spirit to clear, absorbing, varied dramatizations, teaching it to recognize its presence in many another self. If this be a heightened picture of distraction, it is also a deepened exercise in self-transcendence and renunciation. The better we know the world the more inescapable will be our perception of its tragic and comic character, that is to say, of its vanity as an experience and of its richness as a truth. We see that the only profit in experience is its profit for the spirit.

The poor and the very young may imagine that they would be perfectly free and happy if they had plenty of money. Money would procure all Illusion that necessaries and comforts without labour, and wealth is would open the doors of all beautiful places freedom. and all important persons. The world would be at one's feet; and this, be it noted, is what the spirit dreams of in its innocence, never of lying at the world's feet of its own accord. The world is to be that of the *Arabian Nights*, all magic entertainments and easy conquests. But in reality the rich, unless they are more than rich, are slaves to the world, and captives of their successes and their possessions. They must keep earning their money, or defending it, spending it as the world demands, trembling at losing it or finding it insufficient, and countering the endless claims, obligations, and jealousies that it brings. Civilization is a physical growth, like the mechanism of animal bodies; the achievement is wonderful, but the advantage to the spirit thereby elicited is problematic: there will be much new experience and much new suffering. It was poverty that first bred riches in the process of relieving natural wants and hardships; and riches soon covered town and country with variety and softness as verdure covers the earth. They became a great convenience and a great ornament. Civilization is something not impossible to enjoy freely and spiritually, whether we be rich or poor; but in either case freedom and spirituality will be found only by the way, in feeling, in thought, in affection, in love of nature and home and one's art or craft for its own sake. The empty stage of nature has been set for a human drama, with all the paraphernalia of industry, government, and religion; the scene is more elaborate and the story more interesting. But evolution has exacted a terrible price for its benefits by creating a new set of artificial wants and compulsions: the human slavery to labour, war, politics, morality, and imposed religion.

Free labour or art is a transformation of matter to suit the mind, and far from involving distraction **But there may be spiritual freedom in work.** involves the opposite, namely, *application*, or such a happy bending of the eye and hand over some material as may turn it to the service or illustration of some idea. Nor does labour merely copy ideas already clear in the mind, something that for the mind would be a vain repetition. The most precious fruit of application ripens in the mind itself, where in idleness there were only vague or uncertain tendencies to settle into this or that form; an indecision which labour enlightens as it proceeds, making clear what is possible and beautiful in each direction, and revealing its own hidden direction to the mind. For if the marble block contains all possible figures, the intellect said to direct the hand has innate predilections, of which it is initially ignorant, and it is the hand playing with clay, or the eye catching some casual harmony in nature, that reveals to the heart what the heart might love. Free labour or art is simply nature unravelling its potentialities, both in the world and in the mind, and unravelling them together, in so far as they are harmonious in the two spheres. Such labour is therefore a great corrective to distraction, since it concentrates attention on the possible, and trains the Will to discriminate and organize its true intentions.

Why then is mankind universally tormented with having to work or with being out of work? Because the work is imposed or denied socially, not done or omitted freely and individually; because the product is lost to sight, and paid for in money, an abstract and treacherous medium, too easily spent, by which all things necessary or unnecessary must be bought ready-made; and above all because, if the product were traced, it would probably be found to be in the end worthless or worse than worthless. In other words, the working world is distracted in the highest degree, because people are compelled to do what they do not wish to do, and compelled to put up with what does not content them. They are organized, they know not why, into a system of universal slave-labour for the production of rubbish.

It is society that imposes slave labour.

This anonymous engine, grinding rich and poor alike, has a great momentum. In places it runs smoothly and creates what is called progress and prosperity. In other places, its parts collide with one another, and we have crises, panics and wars. That such accidents occur is not itself an accident. Organisms can never be perfect or undeviating in their development. There is always conflict or tension within the system, since the elements are, in substance and method of life, older than the whole, and their private tropes continue to assert themselves within the larger trope that envelops them. If this unifying process is anywhere relaxed, local growths, which we call morbid, or decay and dissolution, appear in the parts. The animal as a whole is in turn a dynamic element in the tribe, and always

Social allegiance secondary and unstable.

in potential conflict with his habitat and his neighbours. Every member of a society wears his loyalties like a garment, which decency and safety do not allow him to discard; yet he remains naked beneath, a wild man and a traitor in his natural person. Therefore any economic or social harmony can be nothing but a compromise or a truce. Society is not an organism at the same level as living individuals that nature reproduces from seeds and endows with potential consciousness. When presently the social tension (which is itself biological) has been relaxed, the bodily functions or private affections or poetic dreams of the individual will absorb the spirit in their turn; and as spirit is, as far as possible, all-embracing, very likely the contrary movements will invade it together, filling it with alternative hatred, now of the world, and now of the passions opposing the world in the private soul.

This state of moral distraction is evidently worse than physical suffering in as much as it overflows more completely into the spiritual sphere. Pain, however intense, remains an alien storm to be roundly cursed, defied, or endured, and leaving a clear sky when it blows over. The spirit may faint or may stifle, but is not divided against itself. Carnal pleasures too, which are but welcome pains, draw the spirit inwards into primal darkness and indistinction. The world, on the contrary, in its thousand aspects, calls forth interest and intelligence. It fills the imagination with knowledge, and paints endless possibilities enticing the Will. Spirit, being the very flame of life, loves to be excited, and whatever excites it appears in the first instance *sub specie boni*, as something interesting and wonderful. The world is alive, beautiful, gay, and tempting. What youth has not burned with indignation at the folly of the past, which has spoiled a world that might easily be made so glorious? When later he finds that the world has again

Consequent moral confusion.

taken a wrong turn, or that his own hopes were misguided, or that at its best the world crushes in him something dearer than any world, the war has passed into the conscience. The court that was to pronounce sentence has become a Babel of quarrelling voices.

This fate overtakes the spirit for having admitted the world into its councils. The world is well enough in its own sphere, being a part of the great cosmos and a natural complication there; yet it is very old, and exasperatingly stubborn in its old ways. The freshness of each spring, when spirit stirs anew over the earth, covers its surface with loveliness without changing its substance or breaking its cyclical habits. Such was not the world that each young soul prefigured, being enraptured less by what it saw than by what it felt the capacity to see. Nor was this feeling spiritually deceptive; only that the object offering itself in each case was inadequate: worth observing but not worth serving. Its incorrigible inertia and endless battles put this world where it belongs; seen in its place and banished from the heart, it ceases to be an enemy. It is an accident, like our brief lives in it, like any game or any aspect of nature. We may safely love it when we know it to be unimportant. Honour makes us amateurs on this stage, and not professionals. With that proviso, the zest of life is as becoming as it is innocent. Even war, since there must be wars, is an inspiriting thing. In animal strife the whole psyche inevitably conspires to defend the body or to pursue the prey; and by the same natural necessity the young patriot or soldier glows with the concentrated ardour of action and hope, shared with his comrades, until every obstacle is cleared away. Nature levies this tax and gives this reward. It was not spirit that established the earth or divided it or caused the tribes to multiply and feuds to arise between them; but the task

The world may be served nobly when it has been overcome spiritually.

once set, heroism and martyrdom are easy for the spirit carried forward by the social Will; and the larger the field the nobler seems the ambition. The work once accomplished, the instrument has done its duty; and death has no terrors for pure spirit, that in enacting each life at once re-kindles and forgets its own light.

Thus in the midst of labour and war—in the worst conflicts of life with matter and of life with life—the spirit is able to rise clear and to attain perfect freedom in art or in heroism. This possibility shows us once more that spirit does not come from or demand another world, or reject any form of life as unworthy. It is ready to participate in any undertaking and to rejoice in every achievement. What it requires is form, distinctness, in that action, so that there may be intuition of its character and of its field: and this intuition in turn cannot attain distinctness and form, cannot become what it aspires to be, unless there is an approach to *wholeness* in the movement that produces it.

This wholeness is approachable in two directions: first, in the occasion, which must be particular and distinguishable from the indefinite flux of events in nature and the infinity of possible growths; and secondly in the depth to which the psyche is engaged on that occasion. For perfect intuition, for utter wholeness and simplicity of spirit, the psyche must be engaged in its entirety, as when the martyr sacrifices his life, or the poet puts his whole soul into his work. And it is in this second direction that the world fails to satisfy the spirit even when tolerable harmony exists in the theme proposed. The lover, the soldier, the artist are not redeemed, they are not turned into spiritual men, by the momentary flash of intuition and rapture that may visit them once or twice in their lives. Nor is it the criminality of the passions concerned that prevents the spirit from accepting them. It does accept them, and raises them

Easy lapse from borrowed inspirations.

to a lyric actuality, which is as truly spiritual as anything can be. But they betray this inspiration; they
become instantly entangled in all sorts of cares, crimes,
trivialities, and dullness. The hero, if his life is saved,
becomes a commonplace man, the lover takes to drink,
the reformer begins to worry about his income, the
poet about publishers and reviewers; and the spirit,
that seemed for a moment to have found a human
home, is turned out again into the wilderness.

Lack of psychic depth also renders unspiritual
those social interests which might seem most superior,
such as politics, philanthropy, religion, and
science. As they dawn in the mind these *The world degrades*
interests are spiritual: enthusiasm for an idea *even science*
or a theory, pious wonder at a story, as in *and religion.*
the religion of a child. But soon, in contact with the
world, such sentiments lose their innocence. Our
charming theory is contradicted by the facts, or by
other theories; we fall out of humour with thought, or
plunge into controversy, where vision daily grows less
and less, and prejudice more and more. And as for
the history of spirit in religion, if it were ever written,
it would make a sad book. In the spellbound child, in
Leopardi's shepherd addressing the moon, in other
shepherds and sailors inventing nymphs and sirens and
gods of the winds, imagination was liberal; it was
poetry touched with wonder and divination. There
was recognition of inscrutable power in things, there
was spontaneous vivid intuition, and there were deep
stirrings of sympathy between the wonders of nature
and the fate of the soul. But this is only one strain in
religion, never entirely lost —because even in the most
artificial constructions of doctrine and precept there is
always some spontaneity, some poetry, some self-surrender; yet the chief source of religion is not spiritual,
liberal, or poetic, but desperately utilitarian. It is
industry appealing to magic, or troubled and made

devious by dreams. The guiding motives are fear and hope, with tyrant custom, both in thought and action, kept alive by the very obscurity of its sources; for when no man knows whence a compulsion has come, how can he know what dreadful thing might not happen, if he rebelled against it? And here his poetic imagination will be aroused again, not freely now, in the face of nature, but under the spell of superstition; and he will invent punishments for his transgressions of custom, over and above those which society imposes, and fantastic rewards for obedience. So that religion, in its radical function, will be an imaginary servant of personal and social interests: it will have been turned from poetry into false science and a false sanction for morals. We know only too well the prolonged inextricable confusion that will ensue in philosophy; but how frequent or how pure the rebirth of spirit may be in that chaos, we cannot tell without such intimate sympathy with alien lives as is seldom possible at a distance. For spirit, though plastic, has a natural simplicity and sameness everywhere; but the prejudices of the world are local, and unintelligible to one another.

Worldly minds are remarkably teachable in matters of science. The truth here does not offend their in-

The world can turn science to its own purposes.

stinctive faith, as it does in moral philosophy. In fact the ways of nature are their own ways. Nature too is a chaos just mitigated enough to keep breaking out, on the surface, into some image of achievement. The mathematical and mechanical order that runs through the material world renders it amenable to industry, but leaves us in a moral wilderness, piling the earth with ruins of civilizations whose souls had perished long before their works. Yet the worldly Will is not daunted. It is not speculative, and the pleasure of rummaging among those ruins and interpreting them controversially against some other archæologist, quite overcomes

any sense of futility in those lost arts or in our own.
Men of affairs are too familiar with the secrets of the
workshop to take any Platonic or religious myth quite
seriously.   It will serve to give a pleasant answer to the
impossible questions of children, or of their own
dreams.   But in reality each Olympian Jove reputed
in turn to rule over us is but a recent god, an invention of the *Zeitgeist*, condemned to fortify his throne
with a terrible anxiety.   Older and more nebulous
deities mock him from their exile, and younger ones,
differently grotesque, are taking shape before his eyes
and preparing to oust him.   There is no resting-place
for the feet of time.   Nor is there any resting-place
for the imagination.   Faith too is a temporary invest-
ment, and thought a comment by the way.   Even the
extreme abstraction that physical science acquires in
the end, when it becomes a mere rule of thumb for
industry or medicine, rather pleases the business man.
What is knowledge after all but a good servant to his
ambition or to his comfort ?   It pledges him to nothing.   He can give his orders and smoke his excellent
cigar with a calm sense that there is nothing in the
world better than what he does or truer than what he
thinks.

Yet this positivism itself is not safe, and human
nature has other impulses that cannot be suppressed.
There are ways in which the world may con- And can
ciliate the spirit.   One, the schoolmaster's tolerate a
way, is to give it a half-holiday and let it run little poetry.
off to the mountains and become romantic.   Romanticism is not a true religion.   It will never liberate the
spirit from the world.   It will rather paint the world
in romantic colours, and let the exciting image make
amends for the dreary fact.   Chaos itself is something
tremendous, tempestuous, a vortex in which it might
seem glorious to revolve and to perish.   What could be
more heroic than to be provisionally free, when you

are ultimately mad?   And this experience of freedom, where there is moral chaos within as well as without, will seem to vitalize the world for the romantic soul, without seriously deranging human society; because romanticism and the people who cultivate it are only a fly-wheel, and may rather help to balance and adorn the engine which they profess to despise.   Far from rebelling against the world, the romantic idealist simply accepts one of the sops that the world offers to its spirited children, when they threaten to become troublesome.   Pleasure is one such sop, praise is another, the challenge of rivalry and victory is a third: and the comforts of idealism, like those of wealth, bind the soul to the world with a chain all the stronger for being self-forged.   What is the world but a system of self-created interests, each sustaining the other, lest it itself collapse in the void?

Sometimes, however, the safety valve of romanticism defeats its purpose, and the spirit's holiday becomes a perpetual truancy.   The lessons of nature may be too well learned, and may undermine those of the world.   This is to become a philosopher.   Human society, in principle, is but another ant-hill: it clings and grows on the earth's surface like moss on the rocks; its passions, its maxims, its interests are variations on the ferocious or diligent habits of other animals.   Language and science take the place among us of the instincts, to us incomprehensible, that govern insects and birds in their vital economy.   Religion itself, when established in society, is for the spirit only a part of the world.   It perplexes, it constrains, it deceives like all those other pompous institutions by which the world carries on its merciless business. Merciless, casual, blind this whole engine of existence certainly is: yet where anything is allowed for a time to run smoothly or bask peacefully or move grandly,

Philosophy undermines the authority of the world without escaping from it.

beauty and joy radiate from. it to the delight of the spirit, which itself radiates, when it can, from the core of life, to observe and to celebrate all that surrounds it.

Philosophy thus strips the human world of all authority and liberates the spirit intellectually; but it cannot strip the world of its power, or even of its ascendancy over the philosopher's soul. He remains an unhappy creature, divided against himself and tempted to play the Pharisee; for in his theoretical pose he professes to dominate the world and benevolently to criticize it, while in his life and person he is hardly less subject than other men to every worldly require- ment, vice, and affectation. And in him, this domina- tion of the flesh and the world over the spirit seems less excusable than in simple honest people, in whom it may be positively amiable and a part of the comedy of existence. So it might be in the philosopher too, if he were frank enough to laugh at himself. For he should never forget that intuition is a surface phenomenon in the psyche, extremely mobile, and usually incomplete: a play of images and feelings lost in passing, and leaving only a general sense of being alive in the world, with fixed habits of language and action to vindicate one's personal identity. Distrac- tion itself is hardly felt as an evil in daily life; inter- ruptions rather enliven us, and we are never happier than when we brush away all reflection and turn to something new. There is a blessed poverty even of the heart; it can be robbed of nothing if it possesses nothing. But the animal soul is eminently tenacious; and it communicates this tenacity to the spirit when mental life has become predominant. A certain degree of definition and method are then established in our ideas and aspirations. Irrelevant matters, contradic- tions, fatigue can then oppress the spirit with a sense of defeat, and distraction becomes a conscious evil.

Perhaps the most insidious way in which the world can distract us is to proclaim loudly how much it needs us. What selfishness for the poet and the philosopher to entrench themselves in their spiritual abstraction, when everywhere else the spirit is suffering and calling for relief! They should be tireless in the service of their fellowmen. Away with your mummified saint! It is a mark of true goodness to live distracted. Such cries are not groundless. Spirit, though it be the function of transcending the self, has a psychic organ, spontaneous like all other organs, and capable of overtaxing the organism as a whole. It is like the Foreign Office in a Government. It may be accused of treason to the country. Many a poor wight thinks too much or feels too much for his own comfort or for doing his work in the world smartly. He may be a dreamer or may go mad. Would that be selfishness in the spirit? Would not an average life in the world have entertained it more and distracted it less? Does it not suffer more keenly and hopelessly than the world does by the hypertrophy of its organ? For the world, this accident means one lunatic more; for the spirit it means *Une Saison en Enfer*. When the world and the spirit part, the world is perhaps no less selfish than the spirit.

Mammon scolds the spirit about its duty.

Unselfishness cannot mean the absence of an organ for the exercise of unselfishness. It may mean the prevalence of social over private interests, shared enthusiasms being called unselfish, and those not shared selfish; and then an intense life in the spirit will be necessarily selfish, because it is rare. Or else, looking at the matter from another angle, we may speak of material, utilitarian, calculated interests on the one hand, and on the other of ideal, impersonal or disinterested interests. The latter might then be called selfless, not because no self possessed them, but because they so possessed the self that all thought of

Analysis of selfishness.

self was banished in pursuing them. Now spirit, by definition, is domination by the not-self, picturing it, fearing or loving it, living absorbed in its life and form. So that to talk of selfishness in the spirit, in this ideal sense, would be a contradiction in terms. To be concerned with the self at all, for spirit, is a horrible distraction, the great disease, the eternal torment. And this slavery to the self would continue unabated, if the world entirely absorbed our love and attention, so that like a distracted mother we rushed to save it, forgetting our own safety. That would be a social impulse overcoming a private one; but it would be merely an exchange of selves and an enlarged selfishness. The same passion that impelled us to help our children or our party, would at the next moment drive us to rend our enemies, to decry all their thoughts, and to detest everything not like ourselves in the universe. The world is a monster of selfishness that in tormenting and devouring its children asks them to be tormented and devoured willingly.

The potential sympathy that spirit has with all life is not purely perceptive but dramatic, because spirit too is a forward movement of attention, developing a theme, and knowing what it is to care and to fail. Yet this sympathy, being spiritual, by no means repeats or imitates the life which it understands, and which probably never understood itself. In the act of surveying and understanding action, spirit raises that action into an image; and the imagination, though likewise a living process, moves at another level. No furtherance or sanction comes from spirit to universal Will. This Will is blind, while spirit virtually perceives the causes and consequences of everything. In feeling the lure, it divines the snare, and in understanding the Will, it understands also the contrary fatality that must ultimately dissolve it. These are

Spirit endures all the passions but tends to understand and to renounce them.

physical monitions; to which is added the inner embarrassment of knowing that all Will is contingent, arbitrary, and doomed to be spiritually unhappy even in
its triumphs.

There is therefore a moral as well as a physical
reason why spirit must transcend the world's Will in
the very act of endowing that Will with a spiritual
value. The physical reason is that spirit, being immaterial, cannot have intrinsically any locus in nature
or do any work there. It must remain undiscoverable
in the object and absent for scientific inspection: while
in the subject its presence is transparent and transcendental, being the hither light that discloses nature
and the hither sentiment that it inspires. Whence
the moral reason for this physical difference of level:
that spirit, being the recorder of time, has its heart
as well as its intrinsic locus in eternity; so that in
rehearsing life, whether in glimpses or in long vistas,
it sees each episode as a whole, yet merely as an
episode.

When events reach the spirit they have already
happened. The contrary might seem to be the case in
prophecy; yet the spirit in the prophet—which we must
not identify with his psyche or his person—actually
sees as a *fait accompli* that which he announces, though
the world, and he in his worldly capacity, have not yet
got round to that event. Similarly in deliberate decisions and actions, the spirit may feel the rising tide
in the psyche surging in this or that direction, till it
bursts into some clear idea or word or deed; but that
whole process went on in the dark, in the bowels of
the world, of which the psyche is a portion; and the
spirit, in great excitement and perturbation felt those
alternatives and decisions of the Will, sometimes with
joy, sometimes with horror: for Will is often like the
wave in Racine, and recoils aghast at the monster that
it has vomited.

It is by no means a duty in animals to be spiritual. Consciousness may easily remain in them a scattered luminosity, actualizing passing sensations and phenomena without creating any well-ordered *realm* of spirit, any transmissible and developing structures of thought, art, or sentiment. Conditional need of being intelligent. If their perceptions did not mislead them, if their expectations were never disappointed, they might be content with an empirical philosophy and a routine of appearances in lieu of truth. If such a round of images cannot satisfy mankind the reason is not that life without a vision of truth would be essentially ignominious. It would be ignominious only to a free spirit, to an active intelligence; but if there were no suffering, the disjointed and frivolous perceptions of a passive dream might be perfectly sufficient. Human empiricists are condemned to find experience often unpleasant, surprising or intolerable; and then their instinct, being wiser than their literary philosophy, looks for a reason, finds it, or imagines what it might be. Thereby intellect in them awakes from its passive slumber, and posits, behind the miscellany of experience, a realm of matter and a realm of truth. *Pathos mathos:* the rebuffs that spirit suffers convince it that it was created and that power and truth confront it from outside.

Even more clearly optional is a sense for the beautiful. If we have it we complicate the simplicity of life, and of satisfaction with whatever may surround us if only it does not physically hurt. Or of noticing the beautiful. Taste would impose sacrifices and labour on mankind for the sake of harmonies that would seem foolish to the positivist. No doubt the essences arrested in intuition probably have some symbolic value in material directions. They signify health and liveliness in the organ of sense, which in turn produce fitness for action. The ground of intuition is always a tension, an openness outward, if not physically in space, at least organically towards some ulterior movement, as in words formulating a thought; yet the quickest and most skilful action, like the happiest phrase, comes automatically, and the spirit accepts it with wonder, as if it were a first-born child. In itself this intuition, when it supervenes, rather arrests action in a touch of trance. We pause and must hold our breath for a moment. Then, having found its distance and taken fresh aim, action begins again. There is therefore plenty of intellectual breath in daily life, in working, fighting, travelling, or migrating. Yet this development is not inevitable. Other animals prefer to reinforce their defences at home, without venturing on a perilous life abroad, and they acquire thick skins and shells, happy in their slow surly movements and dull digestions. To feel joy, to let spirit fly up into the air, they would esteem a gratuitous waste of energy.

In this direction the world constantly pulls. It regards spirit with suspicion, keeps it in leash, and

Incurable conflict between the world and individual Will.

would gladly establish behaviourism in philosophy and in fact abolish spirit altogether. It fails in this, because the organism of the individual is natural and has a psyche, while the organization of the world is mechanical, and is not transmitted by seeds over death and birth, but by an external heritage of dead instruments such as books and tools, with compulsory lessons in using them. Such civilization has no psyche and no spirit of its own; so that its spontaneous equilibriums and variations naturally run counter to the perfection of its living members, and to their living spirit. Is it not a great outrage that this stupid world that has no consciousness should be the parent and master of each individual soul, that alone feels, wills, and morally exists?

It seems so to the baffled child; yet spirit has no materials or instruments of its own with which to build a better world, except in fancy; and even fancy will dry up and lose its charm if not constantly fed by external contacts. Nor is moral penury the only result of secession from the world; a worse consequence is extravagance and anarchy within the spirit. So long as the passions hide or excuse themselves in terms of some conventional morality, spirit seems to have only the flesh and the world for its enemies; but when each passion begins to assert its primary right to life and to liberty, spirit has come upon an enemy in the spiritual sphere. The devil has entered the stage; for by this personage I understand any enemy of spirit that is internal to spirit.

Rebellion of the latter; and enter, The Devil.

How can such a thing be possible? How should spirit oppose or contradict its own nature? It evidently can never do so; and if it were absolute and self-created (as the devil sometimes suggests) it would necessarily be expressed perfectly in all its forms, since these could spring only from its unimpeded energies. But in fact the spirit is earth-born and essentially incarnate, a phase of some psyche; and the psyche in turn is an organic trope in animals that meets with all sorts of over-excitations and hindrances in carrying out its rhythms. Hence spirit may easily be found speaking here for one incipient passion and there for another within the same soul. Different impulses, contrary thoughts may then cross the spirit and bewilder it; for though they may be collated sufficiently for their conflict to be felt, they will be impossible to synthesize or fuse morally into a single vision, or a whole-hearted aspiration. The spirit will be torn by a divided personality and kindled now in one self and now in another, yet conscious in each that the other exists. A mad world of quarrelling demons will have been hatched in the proud intelligence that thought it beneath its dignity to obey the atoms or the stars.

Extreme forms of such distraction we now call insanity; but the same incubus oppresses the ordinary rebellious mind, producing sullenness and hypocrisy, or perhaps issuing in some fanatical heresy or crime. This, as well as frank madness, was once attributed to being possessed by a devil; but I will confine my notion of bedevilment to forms of mental distraction compatible with conventional behaviour and plausible reasoning in words. I conceive the devil after the manner of modern poets as a civilized tempter, intellectually inbred, and perhaps secretly ravaged by some beastly or insane force. He is aggressive and revolutionary, scornful of nature and custom, not merely whimsical and helplessly odd; much less is he to be identified with a genuinely original mind, tending to establish new standards in logic or morals. This might honestly mark the inception of a new type of human nature, perhaps as admissible as the old. The nerve of bedevilment is that it renders *any* harmony impossible either within a man or between man and nature. It is a rebellion of spirit against the sources of spirit; an attempt to be intelligent without docility, spiritual without piety, and victorious without self-surrender. There is nothing devilish in the formation of moral psyches, even if they seem grotesque to our human eyes; nature is full of that sort of monsters, and might be said to be composed of nothing else. The devilishness of a Caliban or an Iago, of a Lucifer or a Mephistopheles, presupposes a normal psyche deranged, the higher faculties having reversed their function and become sycophants to the lower, or else having declared themselves independent in an insane ambition to live by themselves.

The first of these bedevilments merely accepts the natural seductions of the flesh and the world, abdicating

His secondary and perverse character.

any spiritual right to control or reject them; and we see sometimes how an undisciplined spirit, at the end of its rope and corrupted by despair, reverts to this natural servitude with a cynical scorn. This is the servility of Mephistopheles. But normally spiritual experience, as it grows clearer, seems to widen the gulf between the transcendental witness and the spectacle, between the victim and his predicaments; until the innate claims and dignity of the spirit assert themselves as rights, against an even infinite pressure of facts and circumstances. This is the rebellion of Lucifer.

There would be no rebellion but only analysis in noting the transcendental status of spirit, and in seeing that things cannot prove their existence save *Dilemma of* by coming within its range, nor trouble it *solipsism.* save by modifying its moral temperature. Spirit is everywhere the first person, the only speaker of all the parts. Here is a vital necessity, at once a quasi-divine privilege and a fatal animal limitation, a blessing to the humble and a snare to the proud. Shall I wonder and give thanks that in my little mirror such great things can be reflected? Or shall I proclaim myself the universal protagonist, the indispensable Proteus, out of whom all things are formed? And yet is not this a sad omnipotence, or rather a profound impotence, never to have a neighbour, never to find a friend, but always to dream unchallengeably and helplessly of some vapid universe? The spirit, enthroned in the animal heart as in an audience-chamber, may fancy itself a monarch. Can any messenger reach it that it does not admit into its presence? Can any event alarm it, that it does not choose to care about? Can anything but its own will dictate the commands that it shall issue? And as these commands are often obeyed instantly by its own thoughts, the privy counsellors in its presence, ought not all things always to obey likewise? Is it perhaps only irresolution in the spirit, its want of faith and courage, that allows events to fluctuate, to surprise, or to seem disastrous? Might not a spirit that obeyed its own orders give orders to the universe?

Magic is a childlike belief and practice in which the pride of spirit remains instinctive and subordinate to some natural action or desire. A mock art arises, a semblance of accomplishing something mechanically; but the method is capricious, playful, symbolic, out of all natural relation to the intended effect; and the mind jumps to that result, and names it or invokes it mentally, expecting thereby to help the sham operation to bring the result about. But as direct invocation, in prayers or curses, probably fails, a great elaboration is introduced into the magic ceremony, with scrupulous prescription of gestures and words, to see if nature cannot be at last compelled to obey the spirit. Soon these prescribed magical methods form a new code of compulsions, a second mechanical world in which spirit is imprisoned. Instruments here, as in genuine physical arts, still absorb attention and obscure or defeat their supposed purpose, so that nothing will be gained by magic towards liberating the spirit. An experimental study of nature would have served better; because while this too subjects the spirit to a forced discipline, it secures genuine results, genuine wealth, genuine powers over matter, and above all it yields cogent and steady images of things, and methods of thought; whereas magic is as vain as it is pretentious, confused, and idiotic.

The pose of omnipotence.

Magic and madness, battling with the non-existent, find a check at last in the existent, because they waste energy and in the end are self-destructive; yet this control of life by death is loose and eventual, and much wild ceremony and mad thinking flourish always in the world, although in changing forms. Dreams, contagious ambitions, arts, and religions sweep over the

Experience tends to discredit magic but psychic life to renew it.

imagination, and fatigue it. These things have a spiritual air; they are spontaneous, they suspend meaner human entanglements, and show us how easy it is, if we have a little courage, to flout the whole mirage of worldly, legal, scientific conventions. Yet in freeing us from that vast public net these enthusiasms catch us in little private spiders' webs even more strangling. By giving way to mystic or religious passion we do not correct the folly only too natural to all life; we merely exchange many excusable vanities for a single inexcusable one. At least common life in its drudgery has its kindly, comforting and humorous sides, whereas consecrated wretchedness is wretchedness indeed; and we might say of the spirit what Aristotle says of the State, that of bad governments democracy is the least pernicious. In serving many masters that inspire no respect and are always contradicting and replacing one another, at least the spirit may snatch some moments of laughter and freedom.

The sense of omnipotence, though it flatters the ignorant spirit, is only a borrowed pride. The psyche, not the spirit, exerts power and would exert it, if possible, without limits; and even the inner pride of life, the joy of progression and achievement, though only the spirit feels it, is hatched in the growing and conquering psyche. It merely develops the radical animal Will to feed, swallow, clutch, and beget; a Will extended into all sorts of tentative playful actions and contacts, with which the young spirit is greatly entertained. Yet the growth and freedom of spirit are not properly of that kind. They are not prehensile, but self-diffusing; not migratory, but dominating. For spirit the ultimate object is always the same object—the total of events, the truth, the reality. This is an object impossible to appropriate, since it is always more than the given, and also impossible to disown. There is no willing or

All power physical and the lust for it psychical.

final surrender of any part in order to pass to something else; there is a perpetually self-confirming and self-enriching possession of the same treasure, viewed in different lights, traced to new extensions, and kindling varied emotions. The more spirit discovers, the more firmly it anchors itself. Psychic progression on the contrary loses at every step as fast as it gains; strives to gain more, and ends by losing all. The freedom, the initiative, the creative effort inherent in life is psychic, not spiritual. Spirit is stirred and borne along by that movement, but distracted by it, because everything remains inchoate, half ruined before it is completed, half forgotten before it is understood. For this reason the visible works of nature or art are dearer to the spirit than the dark processes of creation, which are necessarily tentative, laborious, often misled, always ultimately abandoned. But a full-blown flower is beautiful, lasts for a while, can be found almost identically blooming again season after season; and when the flowering psyche bursts into words or actions that are memorable, the spirit is not only excited but satisfied. Something has been achieved. The potential has revealed its secret, and time has enriched eternity. There can be no final victory in existence, except in the comment that spirit may make on it.

The dream of spiritual omnipotence is doubly shallow ontologically, because spirit cannot claim any power, not to speak of all power, without misunderstanding its spiritual essence and true dignity, and imagining it might quit its own field for the realm of matter. And the same dream is shallow morally, because omnipotence, if we had it, would merely stimulate our will to try every folly, not recognizing any limits or character to our human nature, or to the vocation of spirit in its very special ideal infinity and peace. We should be more distracted than ever, thinking we might do anything and become everything; as magicians actually are distracted by their nostrums and shams, and as wealth and science are distracted in their worldly triumphs. What could be more vulgar than a Faust with a Mephistopheles to pander to his unsatisfied cravings? What could be flimsier than the philosophies evoked by magic? But Faust has nobler aspirations when he stands alone, when spirit speaks invisibly to him as spirit and not as a tempter exhibiting all the shabby kingdoms of the earth. Science has a side that is not alchemy or spirit-raising; and even despair of science and of philosophy may enlarge the prospect, knock down the barriers, and reveal to us how omnilingual is the truth.

Omnipotence once exploded, the devil may tempt us with omniscience. This is an aspiration far more deeply rooted in the spirit than the childish illusion of power. When the eyes open they open on all reality; what happens to turn up is an accident, and spirit is always ready for more. Indeed the accidental appearance cannot be fully accepted without inquiry about its origin, its background, its promise; so that every perception launches us upon an infinite voyage of discovery.

Less physical is the thirst for experience.

Now the love of knowledge belongs to the essence of spirit. Far from being, as Baconian pragmatism would have it, a love of power, it is a love of imagination; only that imagination needs to be fed by contact with external things and by widening vital rhythms. When the great explorers sailed in search of gold and of spices, imagination within them was dreaming of the wonders they might find, and of the splendours they might display at home after their return. The voyage too would be something glorious, to be described in fabulous books and woven into tapestries. This is a healthy love of knowledge, grounded on

Experience generates spirit when freely synthesized into images and thoughts.

animal quests, but issuing in spiritual entertainment. Had the world turned out to be very small and handy, and the science of it as simple as it seemed to Descartes, spirit would have suffered no disappointment; there would have been more than matter enough for all the wit of man. Perhaps the environing blank would have positively helped to frame in the picture, and make it easier for a religion of the heart to understand and envelop existence.

There is a snare, however, in the very essence of knowledge in that it has to be a form of faith, and faith is something psychic rather than spiritual: an expectation and hope addressed to things not seen, because they would match potentialities in the soul. Actual belief (the expectation or affirmation in it) is a state of the spirit; but spirit could never fall into that state or maintain that assertiveness by a purely spiritual insight, since intuition is of the given and spirit is pure actuality. In knowledge, as distinguished from intuition, there is therefore a postulating element, an element of hunger unsatisfied; the datum hangs in the air, not being accepted for what it is, but taken as an index to a dynamic object that is perhaps non-existent. This adventurous intent, this sense of the ulterior and potential, strains the spirit, spoils intuition, and opens the door to doubt, argument, error, and presumption. Faith belongs to earth and to purgatory: in heaven it would be a lapse into distraction.

But true knowledge is imperfect and demands humility.

Art for this reason is more spiritual than dogma and freer than action. It retains the image of action, and the history of faith without the risk involved in either. Avowed illusion rescues it from illusion unavowed. Now spirit is essentially free, and always an artist and a poet; and intuition, even in the thick of action, where animal faith rules supreme and unchallenged, turns that action into a spectacle and that faith into science or prophetic vision. Time itself, though physically lapsing without arrest or recall in the process of thinking, becomes specious time for the intuition involved, which extends without sharp boundaries over the past, and virtually dominates the future; all ages forming for spirit a single panorama, always reviewable, and traversed by cross-lights, now from this point and now from that.

Omniscience is thus not only an ultimate goal of spirit, but in miniature an inescapable pose. We always profess to know everything, in the *Tragic* sense that nothing can be taken into account *delusion of* by us unless we somehow perceive or imagine *omniscience.* or suspect it. This is the two-edged sword with which transcendentalism, or the cognitive sovereignty of spirit, cuts off its own head. Either we can know nothing, because confined to our passing dream, or we can know nothing because there is nothing but our passing dream to be known. In the first case, spirit is tempted to commit intellectual suicide, in despair at its own essential vanity and madness; in the second case, it is tempted to claim absoluteness and establish anarchy, both in living and knowing, spirit at each moment being declared free to take what direction and nurse what notions it chooses. This does not happen, says the devil, as animal faith assumes, under the influence of circumstances, so that both action and thought might have controlling objects, amid which they might steer a true or a fatal course. It happens, he says, groundlessly, without criterion, and without consequences. Spirit, by virtue of its actuality, is absolutely free and absolutely creative; the counterpart of which is, that spirit must be absolutely solitary and cognitively impotent or vain; since in creating its object at each moment it exhausts its powers, and has no environment that it can refer to or perceive.

In its desperation this solipsism is not without a

profound joy. It is wreaking a metaphysical vengeance on the great tyrant, on fate, nature, and circumstance.

Emancipation by delirium. It is even flouting the alleged authority of one thought over another, the foolish desire of the talking mind to be consecutive, consistent, conclusive. Why should the living obey the dead? Why should the present fear the future? Let me fear nothing, the mad spirit says to itself, let me remember nothing, let me believe nothing. Let me love now what I love now, and call it the love of liberty.

Here we see spirit denying its source and divorcing itself from piety. Piety would attach spirit to nature and to the ancestral order; something con-

Spirituality defying piety. trary to the essential openness of spirit. Even, if need be, in madness, spirit will assert its essential infinity. Is not matter, too, in essence, infinitely plastic? Nature and law are never logically safe. Their antiquity is mere old age, their respectability limitation. Contingency signed their death-warrant at their birth. The sentence may be indefinitely postponed, the time may never seem to come for execution; yet the guillotine is always ready to drop. Free spirit laughs best and laughs last.

Speculatively, this Satanic philosophy has been very little developed, because both the Indian and the Christian tradition are religious; so that, for instance, Fichte or Nietzsche or Dostoievsky takes the spirit to be a soul with a historic or personal career; and the Indians never get rid of their primitive myth about transmigration or inherited Karma. These are psychic speculations involving the realm of matter, since without material documents and conventional naturalistic assumptions about the course of life, neither history nor psychology could begin to be. And if mystical insight or romantic chaotic poetry ever breaks the spell of animal faith, and actually lets the raving spirit hold the stage for a moment, tradition and rationality immediately seize upon the inspired nonsense, as upon an oracle, turn it into some sort of meaning, and infuse into it all those assumptions of common sense which, in its wild sincerity, it had dared to drop. Perhaps the future may explore the immediate more attentively, and give the devil his due. Like dreams, absolute intuition may open into perspectives of any depths and show any degree of complexity; but the complexity is all patent and the depth painted on a surface; because when intelligence and faith are suspended objects collapse into essences, and nothing means more than what it obviously is.

Such is the nemesis that overtakes the pride of knowledge when this retreats into intuition and proclaims itself absolute. How should I (the spirit argues) refer to an object without knowing what it is? Therefore the least suggestion of an object not present to me, and not existing purely in the act of being present to me, is absurd and self-contradictory. Therefore I know everything that exists and I create the world and God and myself by thinking of them. Very well: that is a proof internal to reflection, moving by logical implication from therefore to therefore; but it ends by proving that there is nothing to know, and that every thought is simply about itself. "Knowledge" would be pure intuition tied to the datum, chained in its kennel, condemned to bark for ever at the moon and never bite anything. All the radical irrationality and vanity of the realm of matter would have passed into that of spirit, abolishing in it all detachment, all elevation, all indicative and satiric force; for it would be itself a substance in flux, the helpless and groundless precipitation of existence.

Moreover, this scrupulous scepticism itself covers a hidden animal vice. Pure logic does not argue; it is a labyrinth of paths eternally open, urging nobody to tread them, much less to tread one rather than another. Pure spirit also is selfless. Separation, judgment, scope, while they are essential to a witness that is not an actor, involve no arrogance, so long as this superiority remains spiritual only, impartial, docile to every possibility, respectful to every power, and charitable towards every feeling. Far from posing as creative, incarnate spirit, tossed amid accidents, is humble and a little sad, and such as we find it pictured in Christ; because the divine prerogatives and insights in it render it unearthly, and half kill the natural passions which it understands and yet transcends by understanding. But this transcendence is no denial, no condemnation, either of natural passions or natural beliefs; if it were, it would have abolished the world to be transcended and lost its own function and sublime vocation. Scepticism, insolence, and cognitive paralysis appear only when the natural self, which is an actor in the world and a part of the world, usurps those divine prerogatives proper to pure spirit. The assumption of jurisdiction, of centrality, of comprehensiveness then becomes an insult to the rest of nature. Spirituality has become egotism; and the ego, full of natural pride and jealousy, begins to assert itself defiantly, arguing the absolute freedom of some natural impulse in the self, not because this impulse is natural (as all impulses must be) nor because it is rational (as probably it is not) but because this impulse is *mine*, because it *exists*, because nothing else can abolish its *right to be as it is*. But in reality this self, this psyche, is a natural and precarious growth in the heart of nature, the creature and sport of circumstances; any separation or superiority assumed by it is a lie. And this lie will displace and corrupt those spiritual prerogatives which belong to consciousness, when spirit awakes in the animal soul and begins to *conceive* the world in which it has come to live.

Spirit thereby caught in the trap of egotism.

Such is the odious parody and corruption of divinity which we see in all wilful egotism, be it in a man, in a nation, or in a philosophy. Then spirit, instead of being a deity in swaddling clothes, born helpless and despised, to suffer in all who suffer, and rejoice in all who rejoice, becomes the voice of an animality that has taken to praising itself, unnecessarily and wickedly confirming itself, in the name of heaven, in all its partiality, delusion, injustice, and hate. Universal Will is inevitably self-contradictory and criminal, because it pursues anything and everything for which there is the least opening; and this in a seething and limited realm of matter where hardly any impulse can be followed without running up against another impulse, and in the collision defeating them both. But this blind self-contradiction in Nature is unconscious, and in that sense innocent. By contradiction it advances, until it begins to see; and when it has created spirit, it contradicts itself again. For the Will in spirit is precisely *not to will*, but to understand the lure and the sorrow in all willing. Therefore this specific Will in the spirit becomes in turn distracted whenever spirit identifies itself with any one creature or any one impulse rather than with another, and thus lends a blasphemously divine authority to a bestial preference.

Lucifer, or spirit posing as the champion of spirit, cannot take refuge, like the worldly mind, in being conventional and finding excitement if not happiness in distraction. Honour compels him to digest the truth. At the same time, being spirit in rebellion, he is not willing to accept the moral of his true story. He refuses to admit humbly that spirit may be content with the tortuous but fruitful evolutions of matter. Nothing remains for him but to skulk in his tent, like Achilles, and there eat out his heart in vain protests against vanity.

Moodiness, however, is something grossly psychic

and utterly opposed to the native sprightliness of spirit. How should this pure light dancing on the waves of mutation ever think of posing as a champion of itself against contingency or change or insecurity? That its own gift is to bridge and to transcend the flux of nature ideally, while sharing it existentially, does not authorize it to condemn all other realms of being. On the contrary, pure fidelity to its own vocation would intelligently salute and respect those realms in their several characters, and thereby would achieve its own liberation. We have already seen how mutability feeds intuition, and makes the very life and form of its most interesting objects; there being no greater triumph of unity and eternity, than the synthesis of movement in the truth of movement. And contingency or irrationality in things is no less proper to them and acceptable to a disciplined spirit. In analysing and comparing essences intuition certainly finds necessity; but this very necessity involves that the vast majority of possibles should be excluded from any given universe. This is in no way derogatory either to that particular universe or to the essences it excludes. Will you blame matter for being indefinitely plastic? Will you blame fortune for having shaped this plastic substance into a series of selected forms? Are you displeased at the abstract necessity of being something specific, if you are to exist at all? Are you offended for that reason at any existence? But what could be a more contingent prejudice, or a plainer mark of a particular vital bias, than such insistence on deducing essence from essence, and subjecting the universe to dialectic? I am afraid, when the spirit mopes at the irrationality of things, it is not this inevitable irrationality or contingency in them that troubles it. Intuition is innocently happy in the simplest visions or motions or novelties; it does not first ask that light and beauty should be deducible from something else. These murmurs have an animal source. Things seem questionable when they are by chance unwelcome to a chance disposition in the psyche; and Lucifer is prompted to blame them only by a vital impatience at their inconvenience, and by a private rage.

That things are imperfect, that everywhere, as in the spirit itself, universal Will confuses its own endeavours, and spoils with the right hand what it is making with the left, certainly Inevitable touches the heart with a hopeless sorrow, sadness of generous because it is a sigh at all frus- imperfec- tration, and genuine, because it is a sigh at one's own. tion. Yet even here, the purer the spirit becomes and the more successful in its proper task, the less absolute that universal imperfection will seem. The criterion of perfection must not be imposed from outside. On the path towards some goal which, if missed, was perhaps never really proposed, a thousand minor things may be achieved. The path of failure is strewn with little successes, no less real to a free spirit than the alleged end. And beyond, as well as within, there may be perfections discernible to a plastic intuition. Nor does nature, taken as a whole, *natura naturata*, fail in the least to realize the form or the process selected. The failures, as the Stoics said, are not failures to her: she is victorious in all the defeats of her children. Undoubtedly that is cold comfort to the victims: the victims are free to struggle and curse as much as they like and as long as they can. But spirit is here supposed to have liberated itself from that form of vitality. Even the successes of the psyche now interest us not as prizes gained but as harmonies achieved, as ideas defined, illuminated, made to shine before the spirit in all their perfection. The failures (besides falling into other harmonies in reflection, romantic, comic, pathetic, tragic, scientific) imply and reveal the beauties missed; and for the spirit these suggested perfections are no less estimable than the others that, happening to be realized in some psyche, have attained a greater dynamic definition and emphasis. And all can bide their time. They are eternal; and perhaps a day awaits them when the spirit may not only salute them with respect from a distance, but gaze on them at will, touch, embrace, and espouse them, as perfect companions in some other journey.

To upbraid creation for its imperfections is therefore a piece of insolence in Lucifer. Creation has a perfection of its own; and the imperfection of the creatures, taken each in its broken career, is relative to their special wills, the inevitable risk and eventual punishment involved in finitude. It is an incurable pity, the inherent pathos of existence, that special will should so often have to be disappointed; but that is an argument for charity, not for rage. Spirit too suffers from checks in its scattered instances, yet with this resource, which other forms of Will have not: that it may discern and worship many a harmony not vital to its particular psyche, but contained in some other trope, larger or more abstract or otherwise concrete, such as poetry and music and the plastic arts present to the senses, or as pure thought may trace in the realm of essence. Nor is such intuition at all cold. When the theme is non-human, it has a formal perfection capable sometimes of entrancing; and when the theme is human or moral, charity vivifies it in a chastened mind with feelings perhaps deeper, if calmer, than those endured by the persons concerned, as if by our own past selves. It would be sheer perversity and doggedness to scorn this reconciliation in reflection with things that may have been intolerable in experience. The horror of them is neither denied nor justified, but it is surmounted. The psyche, which is itself a physical episode, cannot

This imperfection itself inevitable.

help being absorbed in passing events, in things to be done or enjoyed here and now at all costs, with absolute rebellion against denial; but the spirit in turn rebels against that distraction, contemplates that necessity, and masters both as far as it can.

CHAPTER VIII

LIBERATION

FROM what does distraction distract the spirit? If the flesh, the world, and the devil impede the proper

No escape possible from nature. movement of life, they must impinge upon something deeper than themselves or degrade something better. But what is this deeper or better thing? Those who regard spirit as a separate substance, and spiritual life as essentially another life in another world, seem to solve the problem clearly; but I fear they would find it still on their hands if they actually passed into that other world. The moral adventure of existence would simply have been extended; and if that life were really life and that world really a world, the spirit would find itself there as much entangled and beset, if not as much tormented, as it ever was in the human body. So too if we suppose spirit to have first inhabited some celestial sphere, according to the Platonic myth. Evidently even in that sphere, if we take the myth literally, the spirit must have been subject to distraction. How else were its incarnations determined, or how else was it tempted to quit heaven at all? From the beginning those two ill-matched horses gave the charioteer no end of trouble. And if we choose a milder fable, and conceive a Garden of Eden where all was health, safety, and abundance, we invoke only an animal placidity, into which spiritual joy might break perhaps at rare intervals and (I should think) wistfully; because animal peace, to spirit, is half cloying, half pathetic, except as some fleeting posture or aspect of it may be caught up and turned into a lyric note or a charming picture.

And why are such pictures or notes momentarily satisfying to the spirit, when the life from which they are drawn, in its monotony and decay, seems so gross and melancholy? Because spirit is essentially a culmination, and perfect happiness a quality to be attained occasionally by natural life, not another nonnatural life existing beyond. To say that we are distracted here because we belong by nature to a different region is simply contrary to fact. Nothing could bloom more naturally or tremble and sing more congruously than spirit does on earth; and the myths about a paradise, past or future, are transparent parables, expressing the rare, transporting, ecstatic quality that distinguishes the culminating moments of natural life from its endless difficulties, hardships, and embroiled hopes. These moments are sometimes the gift of a happy change in circumstances, as when agony ends and lovers are reunited; but sometimes, more spiritually, the supreme moment liberates us from circumstances altogether, and we feel withdrawn into an inner citadel of insight and exaltation. Let us consider how this can be.

Apocalypses and Last Judgments and cosmological wonders interest our moral or political passions: they give us a foretaste—conceivably not false— of catastrophes and triumphs awaiting the human race. They need not be inspired by a narrow partisanship, but may contain spontaneous insights into the genesis and fate of life in a thousand non-human or superhuman forms: dreams of angels and Titans, of Gods and devils. Like inspiration of any kind, such revelations may bring to light and may fortify the rebellion of the psyche against oppression and hopeless routine. So far, the thunders of prophecy, political or cosmic, will give voice to the spirit, and may promise to emancipate it. They may

Liberation does not turn on changes in the facts.

awaken it when perhaps it was sleeping; but they are
not needed and not satisfying. Not needed, because
clear and varied notes enough of the spiritual gamut
are struck spontaneously at every turn in daily life,
even if drowned in the hubbub; and not satisfying,
because those lurid transformations of the scene into
hells and heavens, or into marches and counter-
marches of reforming hosts, only redouble the pressure
of circumstances upon the spirit, and browbeat it into
being joyful or revengeful. All this may involve
fevers and nightmares of singular violence, but short-
lived: nothing can be more dead than dead prophecies.
The shouts of triumph in one camp cannot render the
spirit, which is universal, deaf to the groans of the
other; and by the indefinite prospect of fresh revolutions
and fresh catastrophes, far from being redeemed, the
spirit is tied more excruciatingly than ever to the wheel
of fortune.

The Indians, who gave themselves time to unravel
this question without private prejudices, saw that
salvation could come only by *not* being born
again: not because another life was not
possible and might not be more splendid,
but because, being life, it would be subject
to accident, confusion, and responsibility. It would
be essentially distracted. But not being born again
is a negative solution, and personal. The very
notion of being born again confuses the psyche with
the spirit; for the spirit is inevitably born again so
long as there is consciousness anywhere, whereas the
psyche might perhaps be restored to life by the resurrection or re-creation of a corresponding body, but
would lose its identity in proportion to the transformations suffered by this body and by its habitat. If the
moral heritage or Will of any soul were extinguished
by discipline and penance, so much of the transmissible
energy or burden of existence would be destroyed and

Indian testi-
mony re-
garding
salvation.

the universe would continue to live somewhat diminished in volume. I have not read anywhere that the universe was at last to be totally extinguished by this process, the last man being a saint by whose salvation existence came to an end altogether; nor would such a prospect make any difference in the moral issue. Under the form of eternity that finished history would remain a fact, with all the beauties and horrors that it may have contained; and the spirit said to have quitted it would still be faced by that fact, and be condemned to digest it for ever, if by poetic licence we conceive the spirit to survive disembodied. Salvation, then, must not be the beginning of a new life, which would make salvation again urgent; nor can it be existence without life, which except for dead matter would be a contradiction in terms.

When each sage reaches Nirvana or reverts to perfect identity with Brahma, who then is it that is saved? Certainly not the man, for he has abandoned and disallowed his personal being, even to the extreme of assuring us that *he* never existed at all, but that there was never anything but Brahma existing in him. Not the world; for this, even if with some diminution of potency or debt, continues to wag. And surely not Brahma, or the trance of Nirvana itself, for this has never been and never can be troubled. How then is spirit ever liberated, when in its proper nature it was always free, and in every phase of vital illusion it is still captive?

I think the Indians themselves give us the key to this enigma when they tell us that, in reality, the departed or finite being never existed, but only the One or the Absolute existed in him. This assertion, taken historically or physically, is indeed self-contradictory and contrary to fact: for only the finite and transitory property *exists*. But two genuine insights are conveyed by that mystic

It is an inward transformation.

formula. In the first place, there is one plane, that of matter, or physical energy, on which the universe forms a single dynamic system and is presumably of one substance; so that all other realities, not being possessed of any substance, force, or permanence of their own, are called unrealities by the impulsive realist. On this analogy, mind in its turn may be reduced to an alleged spiritual substance. As the dissolution of bodies or worlds turns them all into water or ether or electricity or dust, so the dissolution of ideas and emotions is conceived to leave pure spirit, deep sleep, Brahma or Nirvana standing. Thus as matter was, in a dynamic sense, the only "reality" in this variegated world, so pure and calm spirit may seem to have been the only lasting "reality" in our distracted consciousness.

Modern philosophy has enabled us to dismiss this notion of an underlying substantial spirit. There is something substantial underlying our feelings and thoughts, but it is the psyche, or the organic life of the body, the substance of which, in its turn, is the common matter of the whole universe. Spirit is as far as possible from being a substance: it is at the other end of the scale, the very flower of appearance, actuality, light and evanescence.

But in the second place the Indians, in telling us that Brahma was always the only reality in our lives, summon us to turn from that physical problem about the one substance in the cosmos to the moral problem of finding the quintessence of peace and joy in ourselves. Their philosophy here takes the same turn that Greek philosophy took in Socrates, and substitutes morals for physics. Now, morally considered, the only "reality" is the good. To say that Brahma is the only reality in our souls will then amount to saying that the only *good* in our thoughts and feelings, and in our

The light which lighteth every man that cometh into the world.

whole existence, comes of pure spirit being alive in us.
In fact spirit in our thoughts and feelings is terribly
distracted; but it can be more or less so; and the nearer
we come, at any moment, to spontaneous, disinterested,
pure intuition, so much more nearly has spirit within
us been freed from ourselves, and so much more
completely have we become, in that act, identical with
Brahma. There was something in us always, since
consciousness awoke, that saw our persons as part of
the world. From the beginning there was a moral
ambiguity in our souls. We might identify ourselves
with the self which we found existing and at work; we
might adopt its passions and limits; we might almost
forget that there might be other selves or other passions
morally as real as our own. Yet such egotism is
naturally unstable and perverse, because in seeing our
persons as part of the world and at work there, spirit
in us cannot help assimilating our action and fate to
that of the other creatures visible in the same world;
and sincerity then compels us either to admit the other
wills as equally important and legitimate with our own
(which would undermine our fighting morality) or else
to detach our genuine allegiance from ourselves also,
regard our passions as follies, our views as illusions,
and identify ourselves not with ourselves, but with the
spirit within us. This spirit will be qualitatively the
same as exists, or may exist, in other creatures also: not
in so far as each accepts and pursues his animal or
political impulses, but only in so far as, like spirit in
us, he detaches himself from those impulses, regards
them as pathetic accidents, and equates them with our
contrasting impulses, and those of all other creatures.

Physically, existentially, historically, nothing will
be changed by this second insight; but morally the
whole natural world, with our own persons in it, will
be removed to a distance. It will have become foreign.
It will touch us, and exist morally for us, only as the

scene of our strange exile, and as being the darkness, the cravings, the confusion in which the spirit finds itself plunged, and from which, with infinite difficulty and uncertainty, it hopes to be delivered.

Thus when the Indians tell us that only ignorance makes us suppose that a world exists or that we have a natural self living in that world, I would understand them to speak of *moral* ignorance only; for they themselves heartily believe, for instance, in the transmigration of souls or (what is morally the same thing) in Karma.

Distraction is called ignorance in that it obscures the true good.

Spirit therefore has a long variegated experience of this ignorance, which is at the same time knowledge of the world, and of the path to salvation; and the created selves that obscure and distract spirit in this process are parts of the vast realm of genesis, with all its earths and heavens. It is not scientific or natural ignorance to discover and understand this too real machinery; but it is ignorance in the heart, ignorance of its spiritual vocation, to attach itself absolutely to anything relative. Those sufferings and triumphs weigh upon spirit only because they arouse spirit; otherwise they would be indifferent and morally null; and they are good rather than evil, true monitors rather than false, only in so far as they liberate spirit and pass into it, as oil shines only when consumed and turned into flame. Once lighted, this flame turns back upon all that it illuminates and upon its own fuel, as upon alien if not hostile facts. Being light, it thinks it shines of itself; but this is only the most inward and subtlest form of its distraction, when it torments itself about its own existence, perpetuity, and prerogatives, instead of simply shining upon all that there may be to shine upon, and consuming all its gross substance in that spiritual office. It is from the fumes of untoward matter obscuring the flame that liberation is needed, not from the fit occasion of this burning.

The burning forms the flame that is to be saved; to be saved from its own impurities, from its obstructions and vacillations, so that it may neither suffer in shining nor fear not to shine.

That it should cease to shine here, upon these circumstances from this odd animal centre, follows from the natural instability of existence, and of the world in which spirit is kindled. To have lighted those things once is enough, if not too much. In any case they cannot The dominance of spirit cannot redeem the whole soul. lapse from the purview of spirit, which is addressed to all truth; they cannot lose their pertinence to that spiritual life which they once diversified; much less can their passing prevent other occasions and other objects from arousing spirit afresh. Frankly, this irrepressible vitality of that fire which by its very essence is continually consuming itself and ceasing to be, devours rather than sustains the animal soul; and those elegiac sentiments which gather round death, loss, old age, and mutation are not in the least modified by the assurance that truth is eternal and that life and beauty may be perpetually renewed in other shapes. On the contrary, both the eternity of truth and the vitality of nature merely perpetuate the reign of death and of sorrow; and far from promising an escape from destruction; they overwhelm the natural soul with a sense of how thorough that destruction is, how pervasive, minute, and hopeless. To be told that spirit may be inwardly emancipated from fortune, and that in innumerable other creatures it may live through endless adventures, sounds like bitter mockery to the poor wight mourning the loss of all his treasures, and shuddering horribly before his open grave. The soul so much concerned about its immortality is not spirit, but is an animal psyche, a principle of natural impulsive life. As thunderbolts, floods, famines and wars, sickness and blindness fill this human soul with horror,

and as social obloquy torments it morally, so when by
a sudden ray of intuition it foresees its own end, it is
appalled and sometimes the thought of resurrection in
the flesh, sometimes that of immortality for the soul
only, arises in reflection to mitigate that despair.

Both these thoughts spring from the same intelligence that brought the knowledge of death. Life is
a perpetual resurrection; and spirit too is
continually being born again. In essence it
is incapable of growing old or weary or
embarrassed by past errors. Wherever there

Ambiguous resurrection and immortality.

is existence there is youth; and death at every stroke by
intercepting memory restores spontaneity. In another
direction all that perishes in time is in truth and for
spirit raised to immortality. Life moves on, but the
achievement of life remains undeniable, even if forgotten. Here are two honest counterparts to death,
not adventitious hopes or hypotheses, but implications
inherent in the fact of death from the first. Resurrection is involved naturally, though not logically, in
death, because life is a self-repeating trope, a rhythm
in which death is the cæsura; and ideal immortality is
implied logically in the truth of any finished life,
which death rounds and frames in its wholeness. The
Phœnix that continually rises again, however, is no
individual psyche, but mere spirit: not impersonal,
since it can exist only in some person, yet not the past
personality of any dead man; only the same rational
light breaking out anew in some fresh creature.
Such a resurrection of the spirit does not liberate it:
on the contrary, in this new incarnation it must begin
its redemption again, or at least continue it, if by a
moral heredity the new psyche takes up the task where
the old psyche left off. This is not only the Indian
and Platonic doctrine but in principle also the Christian.
The number of incarnations is reduced to two (or to
three, if we admit Purgatory), but spirit awakes in the

second life with that degree of moral virtue which it had achieved in the first. This rank it now retains in each soul for ever, either in hell or in heaven; or else, according to Origen and some modern Protestants, it continues its moral adventures in circumstances perhaps more favourable than those it lived in on earth. We are not told whether the test of progress in either case would be an approach to liberation from existence altogether, as the Indians and other mystics aver. Probably not: the picture is rather that of an endless process, monotonous or varied, but essentially quite empirical and naturalistic.

Resurrection is the good old Hebraic hope. Such a prophecy satisfies the moral or political enthusiasm of the prophets and promises relief and compensation to Job. It does not profess to disengage the spirit from accidental bonds. Suppose the prophecy came true and we began to live in the Millennium or in the New Jerusalem. As we walked those golden streets and gazed at those crowned and white-robed phantoms that discoursed music in eternal peace, the still solitary spirit within us might well ask whether all this was not a dream, whether the heart was not deceived and disappointed by it, and whether reality possessed no other dimensions. Spirit would still need to do what it does on earth, what it is the nature of spirit to do everywhere, namely by its own intellectual insight to introduce us into the spheres of truth or of essence, detaching us from each thing with humility and humour, and attaching us to all things with justice, charity and pure joy. Is this what, after all, we should understand by heaven? In that case the heavenly kingdom is already come, and exists potentially within us; and there would be no occasion for spiritual pride to turn its back on heaven, since heaven would open wherever spiritual humility happened to look.

No dramatic eschatology would be involved in such inward salvation. We should simply return to innocence as before nature in us was dis-

Common life has moments of spiritual freedom.

tracted; or we should achieve natural per- fection in some particular faculty, for the moment predominant, say in poetic intuition or in universal sympathy. It is an error to identify spirit with cold intelligence, or to think even intelli- gence primarily cold; however impartial our inspection of truth might become—and it never is wholly impartial —that very impartiality and scope, that very perception of contrary movements crossing or ignoring one another, and all issuing in the least expected or desired of destinies, would excite a tremendous and exhilarat- ing emotion in the heart. Spirit has its lyric triumphs in childhood and in the simple life: wedding-days and moonlight nights and victories in war and soft music and pious trust. It breaks out momentarily in the shabbiest surroundings, in laughter, understanding, and small surrenders of folly to reason. Such moments are far from permanently lifting the soul they visit into a high spiritual sphere; often they come to ne'er-do-wells, poets, actors, or rakes. The spark dies in the burnt paper; yet it had the quality of a flame or a star. All the saint or the sage can add is constancy to that light, so that it colours all their thoughts and actions, turning the material circum- stances into almost indifferent occasions. Yet the least disciplined or integrated of us sometimes feel something within us rising above ourselves, a culmina- tion, a release, a transport beyond distraction. It was but summer lightning, and the sultriness continues unabated; yet that flash has given us a taste of liberty.

This is a spiritual gift, a gift of grace; it is not an earthly or even a moral benefit. Against circumstances and vices there are natural correctives; to apply them is the task of war, medicine, and labour; but easier circumstances or healthier passions will not liberate the spirit from oppression by things not spiritual. Prosperity might even deaden and misguide it more completely than ever misfortune could. For instance, that erotic passion which moralists think of when the flesh is mentioned is a conspicuous source of inspiration and spiritual courage; before it entangles us in sordid complications, it liberates us from the drab world, where everything suddenly seems foreign and worthless. The snares and slavery that love prepares for mankind are like venereal diseases; surprises for the young lover, shocks to his confident emotions, emotions in which nature and spirit seemed at last to have flowed together into an intense harmony.

It is then the flesh as a power that liberates us from the flesh as an obsession. That which is liberated is still love. It may ignore the flesh that breeds it; it may turn its rays away from their source upon the most remote or ethereal objects; it may even consume its substance and exhaust its organ. But that would be the end, not merely of all possible relapses into fleshliness, but of love itself and the blessing of its ultimate visions. Love presupposes a creature addressed to objects naturally harmonious with its deepest needs: otherwise love (if it could be imagined still to subsist) would be a blind unsatisfiable longing, incapable of fixing upon any true object, or even distinguishing the predestined beauty for which it longed.

We find, then, that it was not the flesh in its simple animal functions that imprisoned the spirit, but the world and the mind, complicating those impulses or compelling them to hide, that overwhelmed the young Eros with all manner of extraneous reproaches, jealousies, sorrows, and cares. We should liberate the spirit quite enough from the flesh if we could liberate the flesh from all that, as flesh, distorts, starves, and degrades it.

Spirit is freed by the perfection of the body, not by its absence.

Nor is it liberation for the spirit to be removed from the world. This, too, is physically impossible: but even in the sense in which a hermit or a lover of nature may flee from the world of men, liberation is problematical. It will not ensue if the hermit or poet still takes thought for what he shall eat or drink, what people will think of him, or how he may persuade them to reform their ways. As the flesh is the necessary organ of spirit, so the world is its inevitable environment, and its appointed theme when spirit is intelligent. Perhaps a purely sensuous, musical, or conceptual life might never discern a material or social world beyond the sphere of linked images; but when images are acted upon and understood, when objects, events, possibilities and certainties loom before the mind, then spirit, by becoming intelligent, becomes a conscious and absorbed inhabitant of nature. It lives by finding itself in the world, by seeing how the world wags, by tracing with emotion the tragedies of history. The greater the range or deeper the insight of spirit the more inextricably will it live the life of the world, though not as the world lives it. Ignorance is not liberation; and for that reason the world is such a slave to itself, not in the least understanding its own mechanism or foreseeing its destiny. But spirit, in the measure in which, by attentive study and sympathy, it may have understood the world, will be liberated from it, that is, from distraction by it.

By understanding the world, not by quitting it.

And as for the devil—all that mesh of deceit, which language, imagination, reasoning and self-consciousness weave round the spirit out of its own creations—the devil needs indeed to be exorcised, but cannot be destroyed so long as spirit endures, because in their substance the two are one. We have seen how the distraction of the spirit by the devil reaches its height in insanity and suicide:

By natural faith not by pure reason.

on the way to which there are many stages and devious
paths of sophistication, obsession, delusion, and fanatical pride. We need only follow the thread backward through that diabolical labyrinth to find the gate
to freedom: not always, or perhaps often, a gate by
which we entered or which we recognize as opening
upon fields native to our souls; because we are born in
original sin, hatched within the labyrinth, and accustomed from childhood to be little spitfires and little
devils rather than innocent clear minds. Yet, though
probably never experienced, perfect health and simple
knowledge would have awakened and filled full within
any animal a spirit free from distraction, and so attuned
to its successive intuitions as to find the devil's whisper-
ings inane and utterly repulsive. To this innocence,
armed with the strength of unclouded spiritual wisdom,
we may penitentially return; but only a long discipline
can avail in most cases to smooth out all sophistry and
banish all pride, so that undisturbed by the devil,
spirit may deploy all its notes and all its tints in a new
springtime of inspiration.

Health and knowledge: essentially nothing more is
requisite for liberation from distraction by the flesh,
the world, and the devil. Negatively we Treacherous
may observe this liberation in placid sleep. primitive
A sleeping child is not distracted, yet he is paradise of
indistinction
alive. Nature has given him health; fortune and peace.
has not yet taxed his powers unduly; and while consciousness is in abeyance, the feelings and images ready
to appear, and forming his latent store of knowledge,
will serve perfectly to express his simple contacts with
the world. But spirit in the sleeping child is in what
Aristotle would call its first entelechy: it is ready, it is
perfect, but not employed. It must awake before all
that brimming potentiality can pass into action. And
then, after a first phase of confidence and eager experiment, trouble will begin. Foreseeing this, must we

say with the Indians that liberation can come only by reverting to that deep sleep in which all things are alike and nothing ever happens? It would be foolish to deny both the physical and the moral insight enveloped in this doctrine, but discrimination is needed. There is, let us allow, a universal substance to which we all return and which was always the real force and agent within us; and a worshipper of mere force, permanence, or existence may see in all that is evanescent (that is, in all that is in any honest sense *spiritual*) a vain delusion from which it is blessed to relapse into unconsciousness. This unconsciousness will not be death, because unconscious substance retains all its energy and potentiality, and will still breed, very likely, endless worlds out of itself. But in a spiritual sense is this liberation? Is it even liberation from life, if you are tired of thinking, loving, hating, and hoping, and wish for eternal rest? It would be death indeed to *you*, if that is what you long for: but the unconsciousness of universal substance is immensely alive (else we should not be here, with our troubled phenomenal world) and the end of spiritual troubles in you will not dry up the fountain of spirit or of endless distraction in the universe. The liberation, if you call death a liberation, will therefore be personal only, material and unspiritual. The spirit will not have learned how to live; and to speak of freedom where there is no life, of freedom in non-existence, would surely be an abuse of language.

No: liberation cannot be liberation from spirit itself; and therefore not from those natural circum- stances which make spirit possible. On the other hand, these circumstances plunge the spirit, as we have seen, into all sorts of dis- traction, since the organ of spirit, not by chance but essentially, forms a particular and specific nucleus in the organization of nature. Were not the psyche a special nucleus, subject to

Problem of being emancipated without being starved or uprooted.

external interference and needing external support, it could never have become the organ of spirit, that is, of an intellectual and moral self-transcendence. Living suspended upon circumstances the psyche felt this suspense, reached and covered those circumstances by its concern, and thereby became spirit. Individual life must subsist, with a station from which to survey the world, a set of organs and interests to canalize that survey, to render it graphic, lyrical, tragic, and moral, if ever spirit is to arise or to endure or if in any positive sense it is to be liberated. Yet how shall it be liberated if it must continue, while it exists, to face a world of circumstances not only alien in themselves but often inimical? Between extinction on the one hand, and endless distraction on the other, it might seem that for spirit there were no salvation at all.

Perhaps a surer and more positive idea of liberation may be drawn from observing what spiritual men are than by discussing what they say. They are not all alike. Some are initially spiritual and free, not needing liberation, but birdlike and gay like children, or bovine and steady like peasants. Others who are more sophisticated represent all degrees of regeneration, from comfortable worldly wisdom to the extreme of asceticism. Even frankly mundane sages, like Goethe, while blandly smiling on the world, the flesh and the devil, seem to disinfect those influences by the breadth of their knowledge and sympathy, being too mature to run amok with any one folly. But such equilibrium seems rather the gift of a sound temperament than of a renovating philosophy. Nature at a certain distance and on a large scale looks sublimely calm, as if God lived there; but all is strain, torment, and disaster in the parts, if we take them on the scale of their inner effort and animation. So an Olympian naturalism lives at peace with all the vices, and is more selfish

Appeal to actual types of spirituality.

than sympathetic, thinking that inevitableness and beauty justify nature as they justify woman, no matter how much she may entangle or how much she may suffer.

In such pantheistic allegiance and respect for nature as a whole, spirit may be philosophical, absorbed in curiosity and wonder, impressed by the size, force, complexity, and harmony of the universe; the eyes are open, but the mind is still in leading strings. So it should be in natural science; so it was in that happy childhood of philosophy represented by the Ionian cosmologers. Yet at two points the existence of spirit, with its transcendental rights, is bound to assert itself. The naturalist, being a man, must also be a moralist; and he must find himself dividing this seamless garment of nature, by a sort of optical iridescence, into the shifting colours of good and evil; and he will probably turn his reflection from pure science to giving counsel to his soul and to his country about the wiser way of life. At the same time, within his natural philosophy, he must ultimately notice the existence of sensation and emotion in animals, with his own moral philosophy crowning that immaterial and invisible experience; he must discover the witnessing and judging spirit. This is the adolescence of philosophy, and has its sentimental dangers. Only in the most home-keeping, industrious, unheroic souls will spirit be content, when self-conscious, to accept reality uncritically, and to run every errand of instinct or opportunity with the alacrity of a trained dog. Either overwhelmed by the disproportion between outer and inner forces, they will turn against themselves in the hope of suppressing all moral distinction or rebellion; or they will reserve the moral sphere as a private retreat, a humorous or sarcastic or poetical oasis for the spirit in the environing desert.

Margin note: Worldly wisdom involves a judgment on the world and a choice among the natural virtues.

This last was, at heart, the path chosen by Socrates and his less metaphysical followers, who were not also followers of Plato. Cynics and Cyrenaics, like Confucians and sceptics elsewhere, summoned the spirit to live on its own resources, in studious or domestic peace, dominating the world only intellectually, describing it sometimes scientifically, sometimes satirically, and cultivating abstention from passion and war, and from excessive confidence in fortune or in human virtue. The spirit, as these men saw, was invulnerable in its idyllic modesty, and far more divine than the thundering gods; yet the authority of this spirit over the rest of the human soul remained precarious, and philosophy when honest had to be composed in a minor key. Minor, that is, in its philosophical pretensions, yet often merry and running into *scherzo*; for in fact this homely strain in Socratic wisdom has flowed ever since through all the pleasant fields of literature and worldly wisdom, while religion and science, not always more spiritually, frowned from the heights. For can it be regarded as a triumph of spirit to live, artificially exalted, on its own illusions? The zeal, the trembling anxiety, the fanaticism with which these illusions are sometimes defended betray their non-spiritual source. They represent psychic and political forces struggling to maintain a particular form of life, and dragging the spirit into their vortex, which is by no means identical with the free and natural organ of spirit.

No doubt the metaphysical side of Socratic philosophy, the hypostasis of language and morals into cosmic powers, expressed spiritual enthusiasm, and seemed to support it; yet in the end we find that it contaminated and betrayed the spirit. Earthly warfare against the world is an earthly and worldly business; it impoverishes its own side by condemning too large a part of nature and of human nature, which

(marginal note:) Feeble glow of satire and abstention.

might also have served the spirit; and it constrains such spirit as it fosters into a false alliance with particular opinions and moralities. Spirit soon has to cry aloud to be saved from such salvation. Plato, who had the soul of a poet, knew perfectly how much he was sacrificing to the desperate enterprise of maintaining an impregnable and incorruptible city on earth; and the Church afterwards acknowledged that on earth it was but a Church militant; triumph, liberation, happiness could come only in heaven. Mankind were to remain an enlisted army, heavily armed, narrowly hedged, covered with blood and mire; spirit was to visit them only in the weariness of the twilight, and to rise heavenward in the smoke of their camp-fires.

A dogged allegiance to a particular temperament or country or religion, though it be an animal virtue, is heroic; it keys the whole man up to

More substance yields more fire.

sacrifice and to integrity; so that persons devoted to such a specific allegiance attain a high degree of spirituality more often, perhaps, than sceptics or original philosophers. Yet pantheism, or joyful allegiance to nature as a whole, also has its saints; it too, in one sense, is a special allegiance, since it excludes every irreconcilable passion. Indeed what essential difference can it make to the liberation of spirit from what world or what passions it is liberated? To be liberated, let me repeat, is not to lose or destroy the positive possessions to which the spirit was attached. It is merely to disinfect them, to view them as accidents, to enjoy them without claiming them, to transcend without despising them. So we find the pantheists, when they are spiritual, retreating from this infinitely deployed universe into an inner silence and simplicity that holds infinity, as it were, in suspense; and we also find the disciples of particular religions interpreting their tenets as symbols or occasions for an inward revelation that renders those tenets indifferent.

When St. John of the Cross, for instance, who knew that the accepted facts of religion did not prevent the spirit from passing into the darkest night, tells us that the one guide out of that darkness must be *faith*, what does he understand by this word? The dogmas of the Catholic Church? But those he never seems to have questioned or lost sight of. Any partial heresy seemed to him perverse, and he had no intellectual or historical lights to show him the whole system of Christianity from the outside, as one figment of imagination among many. Faith in that system, as a materially true account of the facts, had not prevented his spiritual desolation. How should it save him from it? The faith to invoke would seem to be rather faith in salvation itself, allegiance to the whole enterprise of the religious life, *Fides caritate formata*, trust that beyond that blank negation and inner death which utter self-surrender involved there would come in the end a positive liberty, a clear vision, a living flame of love. And it could come, it did come; although even the most exquisite poetic inspiration could not avail to express its nature in adequate images. The verses of St. John of the Cross have the lyric brevity, simplicity, and passion that anonymous popular ditties in Spain borrow, perhaps, from the East; there is something so entire, frank and ultimate about such effusions, that they are not unspiritual even when merely amorous or witty. The man who sings them, and perhaps improvises them, sees himself and his feelings from above, as did Catullus when he wrote: *Odi et amo*. Here is a torment that, in seeing how animal it is, has become spiritual. At least it has become awareness of a double life; you are perishing in the sea of fortune and passion, and you are making a philosophy or a poem out of your shipwreck. Or while the whole world is asleep you are slipping out invisibly into the night on the secret errands of your love.

Living flame and traditional fuel in St. John of the Cross.

It was a godsend to Christian mystics that the Song of Solomon was canonical. It countenanced allegories that otherwise might have seemed scandalous. The flesh as we have seen is naturally a breeder of spirit; even vulgar infatuation often touches ultimate insights, defiance of the world, self-surrender. And spontaneous sublimations here may well be used as types of sublimation for all the passions. Yet I find two defects in erotic symbolism, even in the delicate hands of St. John of the Cross, in which it was comparatively safe; because he seems to have had a less erotic temperament, or a more manly control over it, than many other mystics. One defect is that (as in the Song of Solomon itself) the images overpower the thought, if indeed the thought ever existed; and we are charmed by a lascivious picture or a poetic sigh, when we ought to be transported into a perfectly spiritual, entirely sacrificial bliss. The Indians, with their metaphysical intensity, are better guides here. The other defect is that lovers asleep in each other's arms on a bed of roses represent a pleasant death rather than a sublime life. Appeasement of a sensual instinct makes a bad symbol for attainment of intellectual light. The true spiritual sublimation of love is charity, not inebriation, or blind transports, or happy sleep. So that if in its imagery I find erotic mysticism less instructive than Indian concentration on pure spirit, in their issue I find both schools alike too negative, too drowsy, too unintellectual. Blank ecstasy is a form of intoxication, not of disintoxication. Instead of cleansing the lamp, it puts out the light.

St. John of the Cross is now in great favour even among the merely curious in spiritual matters, because he is the most poetical and psychologically expert of mystics; but neither in speculation nor in heroism was his genius of the first order. What the essence of liberation

False erotic symbols.

Appeal to the person of Christ as conceived by the Church.

is might be more readily gathered from St. Francis of Assisi, or from Buddha: one would teach us the cheeriness of utter renunciation, and the other its infinite peace. But I am not writing a history, and will jump at once to the supreme instance obvious to all natives of Christendom. Obvious to believers, because where could spirit be freer or less tainted than in God made man? Obvious also to unbelievers, if they have any discernment; because at the moment when ancient civilization touched the summit of its greatness and of its misery the Hellenized Jews were exiles in the midst of that world; they learned from it without loving it, and were weaned from their own national ambition and bigotry, sublimating these into a purely religious zeal, still filled with prophetic grandeur and fire: and, to be the heart of this new religion, they composed the legend and maxims of Christ. Christ was supreme spirit incarnate in a human creature, suffering and dying guiltlessly in that creature, and immediately rising again and carrying with him into eternity his earthly body strangely transfigured, and thus opening the way of salvation for the spirit in all flesh.

What is this salvation, not as the Christian myth describes it (we have settled our accounts with myth) but as the adored person of Christ exhibits it, and as his followers would experience it if they shared his passion and his resurrection?

Christ in the Gospels continually tells us that he is subject to "the Father", who has "sent" him into this world. Liberation, as a Christian should desire it, cannot be liberation from fortune He is the or domination over it. Spirit is *sent* into Son, accepting his being this world: it does not command this world, and mission much less create it. It may work miracles Father. here, when it feels the silent consent or monition of the Father prompting it to invoke them; but they are secondary, and the fuss the world makes about them is disheartening. "The Father" represents the realm of matter, where the sun shines on the just and the unjust, where to him that hath shall be given, where the lilies of the field flourish and the sparrows fall, where the house built on a rock will stand (for a season), where the poor are always with us, and where there shall be weeping and gnashing of teeth. Miracles belong to that natural sphere, and manifest the hidden sympathies and harmonies between its parts. The spirit notes them, but does not dwell upon them, or value them except as evidences of the unfathomable fatherly power on which spirit itself depends.

Jewish tradition unhesitatingly identified this universal power with Jehovah, conceived at once as a national patron and as the divine vindicator prophetically invoked by an aggressive conscience; but these strains are separable and not spiritual. "The Father" we hear of in the Gospels bears a more intimate and a more universal relation to the spirit. He generates and inspires it, and at the same time subjects it to the chances and cruelties of an impartial natural economy. To this economy the spirit submits painfully yet gladly; because the beauty and terror of that impartiality liberate the spirit itself from its accidental bonds. Family, race, religion, human conceit, human hypocrisy are transfixed by the clear spirit in Christ with a terrible detachment; but where love is refused, this is not because it does not exist; it exists overpoweringly for everything that the Father has created, that is simple, that is young, that suffers and is mangled in the hideous madhouse of this world.

Is universally detached and universally compassionate.

Thus we see by the example of Christ that spirit, even when conceived to have been originally disembodied and voluntarily incarnate, is neither contaminated by its descent nor made proud by its intrinsic elevation. In Christ spirit did not need to

be saved, it was free initially; yet it was inspired to
love and willing to suffer; neither tempted, like the
gods of Greece, to become an accomplice to human
passions, nor like Lucifer to shut itself up in solitary
pride. It was humble towards universal power, wisely
respectful towards the realm of matter. Salvation
could not consist in pretending to be independent, that
is, in becoming mad. It could not consist in correcting
the divine economy, and becoming creative, that is,
in becoming guilty. Humility, piety, is a prerequisite
to spirituality. It is much more than a prudential
virtue, good for those who wish to prosper in the
world. It enables spirit to recognize the truth and
to be inwardly steady, clear, fearless, and without
reproach.

Spirit is not the whole of life, only a child of the
family. The others, the uninspired, cry out even more
urgently and need to be helped first. The
good Samaritan is more spiritual than the Proud towards the proud, and humble towards the humble.
Pharisee. Learning and science and art
scarcely deserve to be mentioned, or only
ironically, in that they refute and stultify
themselves. Spirit, being at once vital and disinterested, cannot but be merciful. Wounds, weakness,
conflicts are the immediate evils; when these are healed,
we may turn to higher things. Nor is this last possible
or necessary to everybody; the parting word rather is:
"Sin no more." Enough, to strike at the source of
each grief, to staunch this wound, stop this pain,
banish this care. Why force anybody to be greater
than he naturally is? There is nothing enlightened
in moral snobbery; and spirit feels more at home amid
simple things, if they are perfect, than in ambitious
minds. Its own perfection consists in charity, in the
perception and love of possible perfections in all other
things.

Thus the innate humility of spirit is turned not only

towards the realm of matter, the universal power on which spirit depends, but also towards the realm of spirit itself, towards all the lives, languages, and loves into which spirit can enter. To corporal works of mercy Christ adds spiritual charities: patience, forgiveness, understanding, defence of the heart against cant, hypocrisy, isolation, and the insanities of conscience. Spirit, that suffers distraction by the disorder of its instruments, rejoices in the salvation and perfectness of all creatures and all aspirations, as in so many preludes or approaches to its own happiness. It is not spirit that sins, but the terrible cross-pressure of a thousand motions in nature that stifle and confuse it, when they allow it to open its lips at all.

St. Paul tells us that Christ liberates us from the law, and therefore from sin, saving us by faith and an infusion of the spirit. This might be (and has been) interpreted so as to countenance moral licence; as the charity of Jesus in the Gospels has been interpreted by sentimental or romantic moderns as an invitation to indulge all their corrupt inclinations. But health and morality are not based on spirit, spirit is based on them; and no spiritual insight can abolish or weaken the difference between what nature allows and rewards and what she punishes and condemns to everlasting torments. The point is that spirit, caught in this vice, suffers guiltlessly for that natural disease and corruption; and to rescue that guiltlessness, to extricate spirit from inner madness as well as from outward oppression, is the double work of mercy proper to Christian charity. The moral economy of the universe is not destroyed or suspended: rewards and punishments, saving miraculous exemptions, take their natural course; but sins are forgiven because they *ought* to be forgiven, because the suffering they bring to the spirit, *the spirit* never deserved.

[margin note:] Sins rightly forgiven because it is always nature that sins and spirit that suffers.

Is it too bold an interpretation of Christian dogma to say that this inevitable innocence of the spirit, in all it suffers, is symbolized by the passion and death of Christ, and by his resurrection? *Its continual passion and death.* The possible liberation of the spirit is not a liberation from suffering or death, but through suffering and death. This suffering and death need not be bloody; often some silent spirit is overwhelmed like a modest brook grown brackish and lost in a tidal river. Suffering and death come from the contrariety of motions in nature and, among these, from the way in which life rises into spirit and sinks away from it. Yet this spirit, however cruelly circumstances may play with it, remains congenitally positive, self-justified, heroic; it has been sent into the world by the very power by which the world was created; and it aspires to live, and to find a good and beautiful world to live in. It loves, and although it suffers only because it loves, it wills to love and to suffer. Our sufferings will chasten and transfigure our attachment to the circumstances and passions that caused those sufferings. Death will soon annul the ignominy that confined spirit in us to our private views and private interests. Even now, by accepting that death in advance, we may identify ourselves dramatically with the spirit in us that endures and surmounts those accidents and laugh at that death, since apart from those accidents spirit in us is identical with spirit everywhere, a divine witness, a divine sufferer, immortal, and only temporarily and involuntarily incarnate in a myriad distracted lives.

So the Cross is a symbol for the true liberation, the ultimate dominion, possible to the spirit in man.[1] Salvation comes by shifting the centre of apprecia-

---

[1] "L'Esprit saura se priver de puissance, de toute espèce de puissance; tel est le plus haut règne. Or, le calvaire annonce cela même, de si éloquente et de si violente façon, que je n'ajouterai aucun commentaire." *Alain, Les Dieux* (the last words of the book).

tion from the human psyche to the divine spirit.
It is a shift within the psyche, otherwise it would
The soul not enter at all into our lives; but in each
redeemed human soul some spark of divine spirit
by grace cohabits with the animal nature of the
remains
human. rest; and shifting the living centre from
some other faculty to this spark, which is the focus
of intellect, by no means abolishes the remaining
faculties; these merely become, for appreciation, peripheral. This means a change of heart, a conversion,
momentarily real, but relapsing and becoming more
or less nominal and merely intended as life goes
on. For genetically and substantially those non-
spiritual faculties were not peripheral but primary,
and the nucleus from which intelligence and spirit
were put forth. So that man is irremediably a
human person assuming and adopting a divine nature,
and not, like the Christ of theology, a divine person
assuming a human nature added to and subordinate
to his native divinity. This religious image is
formed in worship, it expresses an unattainable limit
of aspiration, it is hyperbolic. It represents as a
descent from heaven that inward darkness which is
in fact a presupposition to the idea of heaven. It
would be heaven to shed all these backsliding inclinations and distracting cares, and to live only in the
spirit; but spirit would have nothing to live with and
nothing to live for, if it had begun and ended by being
a spirit. For us to wish to become divine persons
like Christ would be chimerical and, for the pious
Christian, blasphemous; but Christ may come and
dwell within us, transfusing our human nature with
divine light, so that our natural functions, while
continuing to be performed, and performed perhaps
more healthily and beautifully than before, will now
be performed with detachment and humility and an
eye seeing what lies beyond.

The fact that spirit is grafted on the animal psyche and is a continual hypostasis of natural life prevents the sacrifices imposed by spirit from being unrewarded, and the spiritual life from being merely negative. Calvary is not the end: there is the Resurrection. And this post-mortal life has two stages, or two dimensions. One is a rebirth by expansion and re-incarna-tion in all those phases of spirit in which the spirit is free, and therefore self-forgetful. Selflessness can see no difference in value between what is enjoyed here and what is enjoyed there, by one man or by another. Envy is abolished; the very limits of sense and imagina-tion seem virtually to break down; you feel all you have not felt, know all you have not known, live in every one who has ever lived. Yet with a happy partiality; because the endless evils and sufferings which fill actual lives fill them precisely because the will in those creatures has not been liberated. There the spirit cares for what does not concern it, wills things contrary to itself and to one another, and in a word is subject to distraction. This we are now supposed to have overcome: and surely the passions and illusions that are dead in ourselves are not to be replaced in us by adopt-ing the passions and illusions alive in others. Only the clear spirit in each can be identified with the clear spirit in all the rest. The distracted spirit in the world will be succoured with charity, and not hated even in its madness; but only the liberated spirit will be embraced with joy. For this reason hell does not poison heaven. The modern sentiment that heaven could not help being poisoned by the mere existence of such an eternal contradiction to its bliss, though generous, is not intelligent. As all truths fall together into the truth and are perfectly welcome to the intellect, all errors being understood and rejected, so all sane joys add themselves together uncontaminated in the

Spirit may be liberated, first histori-cally, by re-surrection or reincarna-tion.

heart, when the heart is pure; while the sorrows and
hatreds, though perceived, cannot be shared. Pain is
itself a kind of hatred, and however intense it may
be elsewhere, it cannot find its way into a free spirit.
But this very freedom lifts the spirit, in its outlook
and virtual attainment, into the presence of all good,
wherever this good may be realized; so that it now
clings to the earth, and to its native soil, only by the
hidden roots of which it is unconscious, while its head
flowers out and drinks the light from every quarter
of the heavens. Self, so turned into a mere pedestal,
ceases to intercept intuition, yet continues to make
intuition a possible temporal and local fact, and
determines its point of view, language, and perspectives. Spirit continues to live, and to inhabit persons;
but it feels no drag in this attachment, can carry away
and transform its body as it will, and rise into any
heaven to which it has a natural bent.

This I seem to see symbolized in the risen Christ
appearing unannounced, unrecognized, in various disguises; a real body, yet not as it was; the same person,
and yet escaped from his trammels, having finished his
mission, transmitting his work, without regret or
anxiety, into other hands. There remain a few relics
of the man, but the spirit has passed untraceably into
new mansions. If we come sorrowfully at dawn to
the grave where we thought he was laid yesterday, we
behold young men, strangers, sitting by the stone that
has been rolled away, and saying: "He is not here, he
is risen. Why seek ye the living among the dead? He
goeth before you into Galilee. There shall ye see
him."

Such is the escape or migration, or resurrection of
spirit horizontally, in the direction of further instances
and developments. But there is also, and simultaneously, a possible liberation ideally, in the vertical
direction, when at any moment, or habitually, the spirit

in a man recalls its universality, its merely momentary lodgment here, or preoccupation with this trouble, and expands intuitively into the equilibrium of all moments, and the convergence of all insights, under the intense firmament of truth. Here there is no longer any pang of loss, any dubiousness in re-union, any groping in the twilight of birth and death. Birth and death have become integral to life, like the outburst and the close of a phrase in music: there are no winding-sheets or sepulchres or embalmings; we have been initiated into the mystery of the divinity of Christ. In Adam, in the human psyche, the spirit is secondary, dependent, intermittent, only a point of view occasionally taken histrionically, by transcending animal egotism only the better to serve it; but in Christ, in the spirit that then enters into us, the opposite happens. There the centre is divine, and what is put on like a garment or a dramatic mask is human nature. And though this assumption of humanity be voluntary, the very fact that it is voluntary makes it incomplete. The humanity that can coexist with divinity in the same person must be a singularly chastened, subordinated humanity. Such in fact is the humanity depicted in Christ and admitted by Christians into their ideal of life.

In the second place mystically, by identification with pure spirit.

A divine person coming down into the world to redeem it could not adopt its errors or its vices. He could not even adopt its passions, however legitimate or inevitable in the natural man. He could not marry and have a family claiming his special affection in contrast to mankind at large. He could not possess a home or a country that should tether his heart and compel him to defend them. He could not become a national hero, like Joshua or Solomon or Ezra. He might speak figuratively, and with great pity in his heart, of the kingdom to come: but it was not one in which his

Liberated spirit accepts life ascetically.

disciples should sit on thrones, like Cæsar, judging the nations. The first condition was that they should leave their nets by the seashore, take up their cross, and follow him. Nor was this a temporary repentance, because the end of the world was at hand, and it was not worth while making earthly provision. The end of the world is always at hand. The world is transitory, not only because our lives in it are short, but because it is unstable and contradictory and self-devouring essentially. In the true kingdom to come, in the soul transformed into spirit, there would be no anxiety about place or person, no marriage or giving in marriage, no pride of knowledge or power, no rebellion against suffering. These things are in the order of nature. The Father has ordained them. There can be no thought of abolishing them in their sphere. Christ himself came eating and drinking, living with the poor, and even feasting with the rich. Why not, when these things were profoundly indifferent in themselves, and the spirit could strengthen itself and pray in the midst of them whatever they might be?

Christianity was thus a fundamentally new religion, a religion of the spirit. It completely reversed the inspiration of the Jews in their frank original hopes, and rather resembled Neo-Platonism and Buddhism. The Jews did well, from their point of view, to reject it, and the Protestants, from theirs, to reform it so as to revert to the cultus of marriage, thrift, science, and nationality. Nevertheless a religion or philosophy without repentance, without disillusion or asceticism, reckons without its host. The Jews themselves produced Christianity, and the Greeks helped them to do it. After all, it is the spirit that makes human nature human; and in the confused, tormented, corrupt life of Christendom, not only do we find many a bright focus of mercy, sanctity, poetry, speculation, and love, but even the tone and

And also clarifies it emotionally.

habit of the common mind seem shot through with more wit and insight, more merriment and kindness, than in ages and nations that have never asked to be saved. Salvation is demanded, and in one sense is possible, because by virtue of his intelligence man already has one foot in eternity. Each passion, each period of life, each political enterprise, after its heats are over (or even in the midst of them, when spirit shines through) enacts a tragedy which though vain materially need not be vain morally. Error and suffering, by the very change of heart that they provoke, may be offered up as a holocaust; affections lost as joys may be preserved as allegiances; and all experience may be accepted for the insights which it brings. Brings, that is, to the spirit and for the spirit; because if after stumbling we merely plodded on, and if after dying we were merely made flesh again, the wheel of nature would go on grinding brutally for ever, no music would be heard in those spheres, and the soul would have sinned and suffered only to go on sinning and suffering unredeemed.

CHAPTER IX

UNION

LIBERATION is something negative, as freedom itself is; yet the soul feels confident of finding great things to do, if only the enemy would let it alone. This is an illusion, because the soul could not live for a moment without the support and suggestions of the environment; and even if, by an unnatural abstraction, we imagine the soul living on by itself, as in a dream, then, when once the vestiges of its old dependence on the flesh and the world were erased, it would be reduced to feeling itself lingering on in a void, watching the flow of sheer duration, and wishing it might go to sleep. The illusion of a fertile freedom comes of not distinguishing dependence from distraction. The sources of life and Will flow into us, and become ourselves; and so long as we move in harmony with the part of them that remains outside, we think we are our own masters, and even masters over all other things. It is only when there is conflict, and our spontaneity is not only fed and guided by circumstances, but also thwarted by them, that we protest against them, and wish to be free. Liberation, however, would bring no positive benefit, but at best the peace of death, unless it were a mere preliminary to Union.

This, though not always understood by politicians, has always been understood by mystics. Union, even identification, is their constant watchword; and words fail them to describe the fullness and rapture of that

768

consummation. I trust their sincerity, but I doubt their self-knowledge; and in any case we must ask ourselves, since they fail to tell us, *with what* they are united, and *in what sense* union with such a thing may be possible.

To union with what, and to what sort of union?

It would be useless to recite the names given to this supreme object: God, Brahma, the One, the Absolute. The question is what these words stand for; and as a beginning I will take the name given to this ultimate object by Plato and his followers, who are comparatively articulate, and the origin of whose doctrines we are able partly to trace. This name is the Good: it is with the Good that a liberated soul should be united.

Classic reply: To union with the Good.

Socrates, in whose mouth Plato puts his views on this subject, was an austere moralist, what we should call a reactionary and a man of the Right, inveighing against the sophistry and luxury of the age, and idealizing the principles of simpler, harsher, and more religious times. But like all reactionaries that found a new order he was a man of the people, with the tone and manners of that corrupt society which he condemned; and though occasionally he seems to have reached extremes of asceticism and mystic abstraction, which made him the precursor of the Cynics and the monks, he ordinarily passed his days eating and drinking, reasoning and joking, and pushing a plebeian utilitarianism to its most comical consequences. Thus he maintained that his own pop-eyes, upturned nostrils, and voluminous gross mouth were better and more beautiful than regular features, because they served and expressed better the uses of those organs. Such paradoxes, in raising a laugh, were meant to awaken the conscience. Away, they suggested, with all prejudices, all whims, all empty pleasures. There is a true, a perfect, a sublime Good within reach, to which it would

The Socratic Good both utilitarian and spiritual.

be a joy and a deliverance to sacrifice everything else.

This Good, as we learn ultimately, is harmony, to be established by the perfect definition and mutual adjustment of all natural functions, both in the individual and in the State. Nothing could be soberer, more hygienic, more politic. Here is the ancient Greek sage, chosen to legislate for his city in earlier times, but now condemned to legislate only for his own thoughts. Othello's occupation's gone; yet this enforced futility, if it favours exaggeration in the moralist, also favours freedom of mind and tongue, and poetic aspiration. Playfully on a small scale, solemnly in prophetic moments, we find the homely Socrates harping on love. That harmony, that rational Good, which seemed so abstract a conception in argument and so cold and repressive a Utopia in political philosophy, appeals visibly to the heart in everything young and beautiful and positively transports the soul in moments of religious rapture. The Good, then, is not merely a harmony to be established or approached in the economy of nature; it is an influence to be felt, an inner transformation to be experienced, a beatific vision and union with God.

Are we then in the presence of two Goods, and will union with one of them mean something entirely different from union with the other? Not altogether: for dissimilar as the two Goods are in description, they are one in origin and may converge in attainment. Erotic feeling permeates all mysticism; but erotic feeling belongs to the machinery of reproduction, that is to say, to one of the most elaborate and therefore precarious harmonies established by nature in the institution of animal life. No doubt it is precisely when this animal harmony is suspended or deranged that the feeling belonging to it overflows or is sublimated into

The harmony of natural goods becomes a spiritual good called the beautiful.

ideal enthusiasms; but we need not conclude that the ideal enthusiasms cling now to no other, perhaps wider, harmonies and are wholly hectic and diseased. The boys with whom Socrates pretended to be in love were for the most part nonentities and the notion of breeding philosophy out of them was preposterous: yet Plato was among them, and a legitimate Socratic philosophy was begotten in him, and propagated to our own minds. So too those beautiful institutions, which were to be the stepping stones to the highest Good, though never realized as conceived, were missed instances of social harmony that, in other forms, may be often realized; they may actually enlist vivid devotion, and may support materially the happiness found in maintaining them. Even that union with God, more often talked of than experienced, need not be an illusion; because the universe has, at each moment, and in its total career, a particular form, with which everything that exists must needs be in an actual harmony: and nothing forbids some sense of this harmony to resound occasionally in a particular soul, and to overcome it.

I say advisedly, to *overcome* it: because in a union, even if called a union with the Good, some sacrifice is involved. In embracing the greater good, the soul abandons some, or all, of its former affections; it therefore abandons some forms of the Good; and the notion that *all* good can be found in one moment or in one object is merely rhetorical. Often, and not only in an ultimate mystic trance, all other goods may be forgotten; they may cease to be desired; but this exclusiveness of itself suffices to prove that a psyche in a special phase is pronouncing that judgment, and that this judgment, if made dogmatic, is egotistical. The other goods remain good for the other phases of the psyche; and the determination and discipline that fix allegiance and love on a single good, are sacrificial. For that very

Any intense love involves exclusion and sacrifice.

reason they are healthy, noble, and if achieved deliberately, even sublime; since this willingness to surrender
true goods, admitted and felt to be good, for the sake
of one good only, offers to the beloved a supreme proof
of love, and to the world a supreme example of wisdom
and humility.

Commonly the word union is understood eulogisti-
cally, as signifying a new strength and range for the
elements united, so that the gain overbalances

Physical inter- dependence or identity of substance involves no moral union.

any losses involved. Yet in marriage and
other social partnerships the living unit
remains the individual person, and the union
is likely to be partly a disunion and a latent
war. Therefore union, in the eulogistic
sense, must be carefully distinguished from interdependence. Interdependence, whether logical or
physical, may be like the interdependence of the
man hanged and the hangman. Now spirit has no
occasion to aspire to interdependence with the universe
with the truth or with the residual life of the psyche,
because it is allied with these already, genetically,
totally, and compulsorily. This biological bond is
worth mentioning, in view of the confused pantheistic
sentiment that professes to see a marvellous consummation in this necessary cosmic unity or equilibrium.
Conformity with fate or with the will of God (which
cannot be defeated) is a needful though partial factor
in spiritual peace; yet brings peace only when the spirit
conforms spontaneously, in that the order of nature
seems to us magnificent as well as irresistible, and the
intuition of that order becomes our happiest employment. Such epic or stoic sentiments are included, as
occasional events, in the same universal order that
includes every actual crime, folly, and torment; yet
this fact by no means involves logically that spirit
should aspire to nothing in its own life except this
helpless acknowledgment and deadly resignation.

Spirit can aspire to union in a eulogistic sense, only with the object of its congenital love, in union with which its own life would be perfected. Virtual knowledge of the truth, in so far as relevant, and conformity with it, are indeed involved in such a union, because spirit is natively intelligent; but much else is involved also, because spirit is not, as Aristotle supposed, a disembodied act of thinking about thinking, or a hypostasis of general ideas, but is the passionate and delicate flowering of some animal soul, to whom much that exists in the world is inimical, and much would be lovely that does not exist.

Socrates and Plato were therefore true spokesmen and great liberators of the spirit when they made the Good, and not the universe or even the truth, the goal of life, attainment of which was happiness. They thereby placed the object of union in the moral sphere, which is that of spirit; because in material union with the universe, or fusion with the Absolute, no spirit is required or even permitted to survive. There can be no union where there are not at least two things to be united. If one is suppressed, the other may remain, but not the union between them; and if the two are merged in a single thought or feeling this feeling or thought is a new fact, a material resultant, perhaps, of the two previous existents, but not a union between them, since both now have ceased to exist. Union in prayer or in love requires the persistent physical separateness of the two beings united; and their union can be only spiritual, a union in intent, a perfect unanimity. If it were more than that, it would not be a moral union at all, but a material fusion in the dark, with a total extinction of spirit. Everybody achieves that substantial union by dying and being dissolved into cosmic energy and the flux of change. It is a consummation, in some cases, devoutly to be

Fusion with the universe is not union but death.

wished; we may thereby turn into the potentiality of
many a better thing than ever we were actually. Yet
that better thing in its day, and spirit in any of its
instances, can exist only by distinction; not only by
distinguishing one essence from another in intuition
but by distinguishing one object or eventuality from
another in appetition, aspiration, and love. The truth
and the universe will enter into this union only under
the form of the good; that is to say, in so far as they
contribute, by support and by denial, to define both
the adored and the attainable good, both religion and
politics. But it is with the Good only that union is
good; and only with the Good that it is spiritually
possible. Union with anything less, or with anything
more, kills the hope that was to be brought to perfection and damns the soul that was to be saved.

One point, a fundamental point, is thus settled in
our inquiry: The union sought by a liberated spirit is
no fusion of its substance with any other substance, but a
moral unanimity or fellowship with the life of all substances in so far as they support or enlarge its own life.

This first conclusion also arms us with a thread of
spiritual security in our wandering through the labyrinth of religions and philosophies. Are our
steps turned towards discovering the real or
articulating the possible, with no reference
to the good? Then in our philosophic dream
we may accompany great naturalists and
subtle logicians through unending windings; the eye
may range over prospects vastly discursive or intensely
concentrated; we may summon spirits and work magic;
but the Will in us will never swerve from its first animal
direction, from blind craving or idle play. We shall
be studying matter or essence, but not harmony. In
these reaches we shall find the peripatetic Aristotle, the
reasoning Parmenides, the Stoics, Spinoza, and Hegel:
all naturalists and historians in their ultimate allegiance,

The Good also a saving thread through the labyrinth of philosophies.

and never more so than when they raise pure intelligibles or sheer substance or infinite existence into a supreme idol. They may call it God, but it is still fact or truth that they are worshipping, not excellence. Or, weary of that pursuit, we may turn down other paths, less stately and trodden, but more fragrant, where the poets walk. At the end, not far distant (since repentance follows close upon love) we may find some saint in his hermitage or some cynic in his den, or perhaps Epicurus in his little walled garden. Here every alley will be blind, with no thoroughfare. We must turn back into the maze, or stay with these solitaries for ever.

But the thread in our hands may not be broken, and may encourage us to look further; and finally we shall not fail to reach the very centre of the laby- *Moralistic* rinth, where there is a great marvel: Nature *systems of* replanned and twisted into a green temple *nature.* for the mind. Here dignified priests officiate—Pythagoras, Plato, Plotinus—while in a rival sanctuary the Fathers of the Church vehemently preach and gesticulate. Apart, in wider spaces, the Indian teachers sit cross-legged and sleepy, each in his little shrine, and Buddha under his Bo-tree. But the thread we hold fast, the pledge of our safety and sanity, while it suffers us to approach all these arbours, grottoes, and artificial rockeries, will not allow us to enter any of them; if we attempt to step nearer, it pulls us back. Pure Good is not worshipped here. Actual good, which can only be a consummation, a smile suddenly breaking out on the face of nature, or some great gift of fortune to the heart, here is magically materialized into a fantastic monument, not a good realized but a new set of conditions imposed upon the spirit. The Good, falsely petrified, is inverted into a power, limiting the possibilities of the Good; a power here bribing us to accept something not perfect, there forbidding us to love and to praise the inalienably beautiful. But fortunately, we were only dreaming. This inverted universe is in fact undiscoverable and non-existent; those revealed histories were but fables, contrived for the sake of their moral. Inspiration no doubt invented them well, and they in turn may have inspired many a holy life; but, the spell once broken, those deceived passions become mere pantomime and those doctrines dead words. It remains for us to pluck the secret out of that dream, and to trace our guiding thread back to the living Ariadne who spun it.

This Ariadne is the human soul. It is only the psyche that can conceive a good or can love it, or can

They are fables expressing human aspirations.

uphold or misguide the spirit in the pursuit of that good. An original theologian is but a poetizing moralist, and the mystic who thinks he is becoming one with the deity is simply purifying himself and learning to see all things from the point of view of the spirit. For that reason those pious philosophers do not altogether waste their time studying their fabulous universes: for they are but reversed images of the spiritual life, and the deeper the devotee penetrates into their magic economy, the better he learns to know his own heart. He becomes very much wiser, in spite of his fables, than the positivist who rails at them as invented physics, without understanding the moral secret of those inventions.

Yet truth conveyed by a fiction is an ambiguous good, and if it deepens our insight in one direction, it

Hard facts the better counsellors.

is in danger of misleading us in another. The bigoted positivist, who ignores the existence of his own spirit, is unwittingly doing the spirit a clearer service. He does not endeavour to be edifying; yet his views, in their externality and darkness, may serve staunchly for edification, by leading the spirit to a more complete disillusion, a simpler hope, and a greater liberty. The spirit does not need

a universe composed of pure spirits.   It needs a world
that will suffer spirit to live in it.

Now, with gods conceived as powers, or with the
real powers that they personify, a spirit seeking the
Good may make alliances and compromises; Facts, in
it may offer propitiation and undertake closing one
service with a hope of reward.   These are gate to the
the normal expedients of primitive religion: open an-
the calculation is prudential, the aim pre- other.
liminary, and the alliance political.   There is no moral
union involved, and the powers addressed are respected
as much for being dangerous as for being friendly.
Therefore when loyalty is merely political it remains
conditional and essentially unstable.   It is an accidental
method of securing our personal ends.   Yet since the
psyche is plastic, an imposed subjection to some constant calculable power may grow into an easy habit and
a happy allegiance.   The servants of a great king at
once annex pride to their servitude and ambition to
their loyalty.   The power, the kingdom, and the glory
of their master become indistinguishable in their minds
from their own safety, profit, and eminence.   Nature
in this way sometimes overflows calculation and restores
spontaneity where there was at first some ungenerous
artifice.   So polite language turns to wit, labour to art,
superstition to religious devotion; and the ultimate goal
is touched unexpectedly in the midst of a tedious
journey.   The journey continues, but now free from
haste and from despair, since the goal is known to be
always at hand, not before us, but within.

In fine, a spiritual good does not cease to be spiritual
because matter supplies it, or a humble occasion.   We
may eat and drink to the glory of God; but Provided
when, and in what sense?   And when may that the
the arts and sacrifices imposed on us by psyche
external forces become free arts and fresh achieves a
vocations?   I reply: when the psyche has undergone

a radical readaptation to the facts, so that in living in harmony with them, it can live in harmony with itself. This is genuine conversion or *metanoia*, a true education and discipline, that in trimming away all excrescences and parasitic growths allows the plant to shoot up straight to its predestined flower. We see signs of this when asceticism is joyful, limitation avowed, labour interested in its function and excellence, with the heart detached from the issue and set on no particular event. And we see signs of the opposite when the will is merely cowed and suppressed provisionally, the original passions remaining alive under banked fires, and watching for some partial or mock satisfaction. Overt life, social life, then becomes one vast hypocrisy, all duties forced, all virtues conscious, all work sullen and unwilling and bargained for in terms of some irrelevant reward. Something of this ugly lining is visible even in the pursuit of spiritual perfection, when that pursuit is systematic, since conversion is seldom so thorough as wholly to purify the unregenerate will; and some strictly virtuous people are so artificially good that it is only in their lighter and unguarded moments that they are at all tolerable or at all spiritual. The two meanings of the English word *light*, in this respect, seem not wholly divergent, because in order that spirit may be wholly *luminous* it must be also *imponderable*. The creaking of a motor must not be heard in its flight.

Union cannot be attained by sacrificing integrity. With inner integrity a spirit might live in moral harmony with chaos, as the romantic spirit thinks it can live; the only trouble being that chaos could never breed a firm spirit, or any spirit at all; so that your romantic hero draws all his strength from the natural order that he despises, and dreams of a congenial chaos only because his own integrity is shaky and diseased. But admitting, in a myth, that a perfect spirit could exist

Inner integrity the first condition of unity with anything else.

facing a chaotic world, that spirit would make no further claims on that world and would find no fault with it. It would positively love that disorderly order, no matter how many torments and mutual hatreds might be involved. And this tragic exultation, like that of the Stoics, Calvinists and Hegelians, would not become cruel or egotistical, unless, in view of his own Olympian peace, the philosopher denied that the world was a great evil to the world, and tolerable only to a spirit that had overcome and renounced it; a solution easy enough for the fabulous Olympians, but almost unattainable to actual spirit, incarnate in that very world.

Thus we see that it is easier for a free spirit to live in charity and peace with an evil society, than for a distracted spirit to tolerate the most perfect universe. Solitude is morally the most social of states, since it knows no enemies; and the concentration it allows equalizes distances, material and moral, and places the spirit at its own source, from which flow all the radiating varieties of moral life, none of which then seem unnatural or alien. Inwardness makes moral scope possible, the experience obtainable externally being a mere annexation of casual views, without insight or moral understanding. Moving time and endless evolution cannot survey themselves; they straggle and grope along from moment to moment, ignorant of what they were or are going to be, and incapable at each point of conceiving the burden of any other. They can be surveyed only by virtue of a quickened sensibility lodged in particular places within that flux, where long-range organs play upon long-range instincts and unused potentialities in the psyche. Every affection of the organism may then become a perspective for the spirit.

It makes range and insight possible in thought.

There might seem to be a paradox in the love of truth, and in being spiritually exalted by the spectacle of an evil world. If spirit were a power, its first concern would indeed be to reform this world, and (lest it should falter in that endless task) to sharpen and stiffen its own demands, so that the existence of any evil in the world should never pass as a matter of course, and excusable; much less that evil should come to seem an entertaining and pleasant thing, or a necessary shadow and relief to the high-lights of virtue. The least blot should then fill the spirit, to all eternity, with an irreconcilable horror. But spirit is not responsible for the world; it is the world that is responsible for the spirit, and guilty of often tormenting it to no purpose. Yet this happens, so to speak, only by mistake, since consciousness, by its very existence, marks a vital if imperfect harmony already achieved in nature; and the imperfection of this harmony could not be perceived unless the potentiality and need of harmony were at work, impatient to make it perfect. Partial failure is inevitable, because the life of spirit is only a small part of the world's life, and not synchronous with those wider vibrations. Spirit cannot *be* the world; it can only *think* the world; and this function of thinking has conditions that are local and specific: there must be integrity and clear sensibility in some animal psyche. Such perfection of function brings an inner light and happiness. Truth, in the appropriate terms and relevant measure, has been discovered and defined: and this truth is a pure good for the spirit, no matter what disorder, conflict, or dangers in regard to spirit itself the discovery may reveal. Storms are not appalling to the spirit, nor even death; what is appalling is only inner contradiction, delusion, and madness hugging its own torments. Integrity banishes all that; and it renders the truth life-giving and refreshing, like pure air and the solid earth.

This spiritual love of the truth is not love of what the world loves, and therefore not hatred of what the world hates; but is understanding of

(marginal note: Union with the truth not connivance with what the truth reveals.*)*

both those passions. It is therefore a kind of love for the world, a pitying and forgiving insight into its loves, such as the fratricidal world is incapable of feeling towards itself, but such as we might imagine that God would feel for it. He would not *adopt* the passions of his creatures; he would be like a perfectly wise and infinitely sensitive tragic poet, holding all those passions in suspense, as possible sentiments, and seeing their interplay and their moral issue: things to which they themselves, except in some ultimate moment, would remain blind.

Many an old philosopher and theologian has denied that God, if conceived to be pure spirit, could love the world or could have created it. It could only be some Demiurgos, himself a natural wild being full of fatal passions and limitations, that could have contrived so many ingenious ways of using or circumventing the forces of matter, and could have nursed a fatherly fondness for his work and a tendency to pull his too hapless creatures out of the traps that he had covertly laid for them. That seems speculatively correct; yet the notion of God as pure spirit is religiously inadequate. The God of religion must be also a power, the fundamental power in the universe, controlling our destiny: and he must also be the truth or the Logos, that specific contingent pattern which this power imposes on existence. I will return to this point later; here, taking spirit as we find it in ourselves, we may readily see in what sense it cannot help loving the world: cannot help at once enjoying it, and pitying it, and wishing to save the spirits that inhabit it from the troubles they endure.

How spirit may love the world.

In the first place, is not spirit an emanation of animal life? How then should it not enjoy breathing and eating and fighting and loving? How should it not enjoy the sights and sounds that arouse it and stimulate it to fix the terms in which all

By vital sympathy.

its thinking will flow?   Here then, inseparable from the
movement of the world, we find the pleasures of
emotion and of perception, pleasures intrinsically
spiritual.   The vital dependence of spirit on nature
involves a responsive affection towards nature on the
part of spirit.   And this affection (as just now explained) will survive all the buffets of fortune, so long
as the power to think, to observe, or even to protest,
remains in the spirit, the very badness of the world
being a fountain of eloquence in a free mind.

Yet, in the second place, love is an exacting passion,
and we cannot willingly allow the object of it to be
By com-   less than perfect.   When imperfection, folly,
passion and   or shame invade that object, love turns into
concern.   suffering.   Shall we deny the facts?   Shall
we excuse and adopt them, betraying our own honour
and conscience rather than forsake our darlings?   Yet
what would these darlings be without the charms that
we found in them?   Shall we detach our love altogether
from existing beings and platonically worship only
universal Ideas of the Beautiful and the Good?   This
might be wisdom or spiritual insight, but is it love?
And can such sublimation really be professed without
hypocrisy?   Could it be realized without a mortal chill
benumbing the heart?   If ever we have ceased to suffer,
have we not ceased to love?

Whence it follows that a pure spirit that loved all
Good would necessarily suffer with all sufferers, since
they suffer only because they are deprived of something
that has become for them a need and a good.   Union
with the Good might then seem impossible and self-
contradictory, since it involves participation in all evil,
and in all loss of the Good.   And it is very true that
union with the Good, with all Good freed from all evil,
becomes possible only by the prior renunciation of all
impossible or contradicted desires.   We must first let
the sorrow involved in love correct the love that is

vowed to sorrow, not by denying the natural charm of those contradicted sweets, but by not pursuing them or demanding them wherever the natural Will does, or where, at a later moment, it would curse itself for having obtained them. This necessity establishes the double level of moral life, here natural, there spiritual; and it is only at the spiritual level that perfect union with the Good is possible, union with it at the natural level being precarious, blind, and almost always infected with suffering, remorse, and injustice. These two levels are not to be conceived as separated like heaven and earth, or lived in by different persons: they are moral levels within each life, often within one moment, when we partly tremble at our predicament or that of our friends and partly accept our fate and admire their virtues. Our love of the world is natural in so far as it rests on kinship and contagion; it becomes spiritual in so far as it grows disinterested, looks before and after, and discriminates the dead loss from the clear gain.

When sympathy with the world reaches the spiritual level it receives a Christian name and is called charity. This charity is seldom pure or universal, but *By trans-* touches home sentiments with more or less *muting both* spiritual light. We see this in the slowness *sympathy* and hesitation with which the notion of *into charity.* charity was first distinguished. In later Judaism and early Christianity, there was a fervent spirituality of the heart, but the intellect had not discerned the nature of spirit and looked for a miraculous transformation of this world into a celestial society. It was the speedy coming of this mythical revolution that inspired the quite unworldly and ascetic practice of charity that we find praised in the First Epistle to the Corinthians. There was prudence, there was speculative joy, in renouncing this world when this world was dissolving, and in making ready for the next, where only the converted would be admitted. Being forgiven, it was easy to forgive, to be patient, to succour all, and to think evil of none. But such charity was unawares an inner initiation into that new spiritual order which was expected to burst so dramatically into public existence; it involved detachment from all that made the glory of earth, not only from the glories of the heathen or of the natural man, but even from those of the saints, when they were filled with gifts such as prophecy, working miracles, or speaking with tongues, which though called gifts of the spirit were grossly psychical or demonic faculties. These were worthless spiritually without charity, without the insight that renders love universal and the humility that accepts all homely cares, forgives all injuries and, without disclaiming eminence where there is eminence, knows that it is no private possession but a gift of grace. Spirit is not essentially seated more in one man than in another, and in all suffers semi-darkness and tribulation. In all it has an equal need of salvation and an equal capacity for it. Respect for persons and their gifts is worldly; so is enthusiasm for their ambitions. These are seductions for the spirit, blinding it to the simplicity of the Good and of the true love of it.

If thus charity is sympathy with universal Will, it is a sympathy doubly chastened, first by understanding Rationality and then by renunciation. The world is of charity. seen to be in one sense innocent; its great sin is original sin, the sin of being a spontaneous world, self-contradicting and ignorant of its destiny. And this predicament runs deep, to the very centre of the heart. There is no spark of Will anywhere that circumstances might not blow up into the greatest crimes, and the world falls into no error the roots of which might not be found in any soul: so that charity implies repentance, not for this or that slip, but radically for willing otherwise than as God wills. Therefore the true saint unaffectedly thinks himself the greatest of sinners, because he finds in himself, in so far as he is himself and not pure spirit, the potentiality of all sins.   Yet this sinfulness calls for grace and deserves it, because there is still spirit in it, and hunger for the Good.

To blame nature uncharitably is not to understand the circumstantial origin of evil.   Law and morality must needs punish and suppress natural Will whenever it transgresses the prevalent order of society; and they can trace this transgression no further back than to the voluntary *It sees victims in sinners.* acts or thoughts of particular persons who may be fined, imprisoned, executed, or at least banished from good company.   But these are stopping-places conceived on a gross human scale.   Responsibility and freedom no doubt lodge in persons as they do in every contingent unit arising in this contingent world; but for a speculative eye the obliquity of those initiatives is not inherent, nor the evil absolute and all on one side.   The world is as evil for the natural Will as the natural Will is evil for the world.   The true sin is cosmic and constitutional; it is the heritage of Chaos.   This is the sin of which spirit is the innocent victim, which it expiates with undeserved sufferings, and from which it is redeemed if those sufferings and its own insight avail to detach it from the natural Will altogether, not by abolishing that Will (since then spirit would be abolished) but by understanding it and its self-contradictions.

To have passed in this way to the spiritual level is the first prerequisite of charity.   Love here walks hand in hand with renunciation: not followed by renunciation after love has been disappointed but clarified by renunciation at its very dawn.   Not having any stake in the contest, *Its transcendental point of view.* the Will expressed in spirit can rehearse all the other passions, which are not this *intelletto d'amore*, this

understanding and this lesson of passion. Love, when
so universalized and so disentangled, can forgive all
injuries, endure all injustice, malice, or madness, and
this not by an affected meekness, as if one begged to be
trodden upon, but intelligently, justly, in the light of
truth. The initial aspiration of life is everywhere
innocent, the perfection of it would everywhere be
beautiful; and everything is disfigured only by confusion, inopportuneness, and a hostile fate. That
which is here and now impossible, impossible for ever
for me, must be renounced; but it remains a good and
cannot be detested without blindness. It may have
its day in eternity. Charity is a love that outlives
defeat and foresees it, that embraces death and is
immortal; a love not demanding the impossible nor
imagining the false, but knowing the intentions of the
heart in each instance, disregarding the rest, and not
despising the least spark of spirit in the cinders.

Charity comes to assist or modify some work already
afoot, or one that the natural Will might prompt or
Its spiritual might welcome: but the motive is different.
quality.   Animal passions are claims to possession, or
extensions of self-love to wife, children, kindred, or
party. The psyche expands and operates in a wider
field, but remains an animal psyche. Love remains a
pursuit, a need, a demand, and is represented in the
spirit, if at all, by desire or anxiety, that is, by some
form of distraction. Only if at some moment that
natural Will is fulfilled, is the spirit liberated and does
love attain to union. But union for the spirit cannot
lie in physical possession or in material expansion of
its domain, things which impose more problems than
they solve. Union for the spirit can be nothing but
presence; nor need this presence be uninterrupted.
Presence to it anywhere, full presence, is virtual presence to it everywhere else; its treasure is laid up in
heaven, that is to say, in its own depths. Spiritual

love is therefore not anxious and is entirely free from
desire; it lives in the virtual presence of all the fulfilments and all the possibilities that the natural Will
pursues.

The world appreciates charity, and finds it co-
operative, when remedial action is requisite and the
Will is trying to recuperate from its follies. False esteem
Yet morally a spiritual temperament has its and con-
pros and cons, like any other temperament. tamination
Some monarchs who have been spiritual men the world.
—Marcus Aurelius, Saint Louis, Henry VI—have been
unfortunate politically. Their heart was not in the
conduct of affairs, yet they were not strong enough to
recognize their true vocation. A greatly inspired prophet like Buddha would have at once renounced his
throne and his family. Even this might not have
sufficed. The professed and professional prophet is
sometimes entangled in a worse net than a king. He
may be led into self-assertion, into denunciations, into
controversy; he may find himself working reputed
miracles and inspiring fables that he must wink at; he
will probably be utterly misunderstood; a sect betraying
his thought if not his person will follow at his heels.
Martyrdom, in such a case, would not be an escape;
it would turn him into a myth, into an idol. His
spirit would be dead, and more solitary in the other
world than it had been in this; while here his bones
would be encrusted in jewels. Books, laws, and traditional religions, supposed to embody the spirit, are
parts of the world; their effect is compounded of a
thousand influences alien to one another. Undoubtedly, even in their midst, as anywhere in the midst of
nature spirit may be reborn; perhaps a docile intelligent spirit that can avail itself of all symbols without
worshipping any fetich, but more probably a spirit
soured and made wrathful by those very fossils of
spirit. The world then takes sides in spiritual

quarrels, or rather introduces quarrels of its own into that spiritual life which in itself would be free from all human partiality.

If charity be a universal spiritual sympathy with the world how does it seem so contrary to more than half the impulses that flourish there? Only because intelligent sympathy halts wherever one good conflicts with another: and this arrest is a consequence of universal sympathy, not a contradiction to it. As in a complex psyche or a complex world almost all passions are competitive and hostile to one another, charity is reduced to befriending them rather when they are down than when they are up; because when wounded and helpless and already suffering for its rashness, a creature ceases to be aggressive, and its enemies would be vindictive and fiendish if they still continued to assail it. They can afford to leave it alone to its involuntary penance; and charity can then step in with its double work of mercy, corporal in alleviating suffering, spiritual in rendering suffering a means of salvation.

Why charity is chiefly remedial.

This is the rationale of that check which a superstitious moralism would impose on all natural Will. To check any living being for the sake of checking it would be diabolical: the hypertrophy of egotism, when one movement of Will not only asserts itself absolutely against all others, but declares that all others are wicked and ought never to have existed. Moral passion shouts about right and wrong; applying to ends terms proper only to means: that is the feminine eloquence of the psyche, blind to everything but her home interests. To reason and to charity this prejudice is nonsense; it amounts to saying that some goods are good and other goods are bad. All are good, but not all are compatible in the same family.

Good-will on the contrary is the disinterested sympathy of one Will with another; a natural sympathy

in kindred beings, where there is affinity in their Wills,
but requiring spiritual insight before it can turn into
sympathy with aliens and enemies. The
infusion of this insight into natural good-will
has observable stages. A mother will defend
her young with ferocity; their bodies are
extensions of her own; their psyches are colonies of her
psyche; and she will passionately forget herself in
serving them, as the hand forgets itself in defending
the eyes. But as the young grow older, they become
less a part of the mother's life; she will scold, beat,
and enslave them. She will grow jealous and sarcastic
about their separate interests; if she were not human,
and bound to them by economic and legal ties, she
might even lose them in the crowd of young ruffians,
and not know them for her children. Nor is it otherwise in friendship, where there seems to be no material
bond. Friendship is a union in play, in adventure,
in war. It is essentially exclusive, clannish, founded
on sympathies that are common antipathies to all that
is different, a comradeship prized for being segregation,
cut off by special tastes and powers from the rest of
the world. Manly friendship is based on physical
affinity, as brotherhood is, only that instead of being
passive, hereditary, and often annoying, it is freely
chosen and tested in common action and adventure
and in community of thought. It flourishes on sympathy (not confluence) in matters of love and honour.
Personal reserve and idiosyncrasy are accepted tacitly
and always respected; they make no difference in the
common field, and are gladly felt to exist beyond it.
A friend is not the keeper of his friends' souls; mutual
liability is limited, but within the field of their common
life and *virtù*, they feel sure of one another; and this
confidence, when well tried, may be not untouched
with admiration. And here a spiritual element may
supervene. Friends may club together in cultivating

Gradual clarification of good-will into charity.

music or philosophy as they might in mountain climbing: yet if the common ideal object predominates over the social occasions, with their incidental humours, the original personal atmosphere gradually becomes transparent, indifferent, and finally disturbing. Friendship is at an end, and each must tread the winepress alone. Even in the mountain climbing the supreme moments are solitary; the comradeship reigns in the projects, the dangers, and the irrelevant human incidents.

Exclusiveness and pugnacity appear also in all intellectual, political, and religious bodies—called bodies not without unconscious wit. They glow with local affections, with privilege, with scorn and hatred of the damnable outsider. If ever some ray of speculative spirit or universal charity pierces those enclosures, friendship is saddened, party is transcended, religion can be endured only as a human convention and nationality as a physical accident. Whatever measure of truth, beauty, or happiness there may have been in those associations is not denied or diminished; but the heart has travelled beyond; and it is only in an infinite landscape transfiguring their values that they continue to be prized. What was before lived is now understood, and this understanding is a second life in another sphere.

For this reason personal friendships and cliques are discouraged in the cloister. They are distracting and equivocal. Charity should extend equally to all the brethren, without favouritism or attachment. Not that affection is anything but natural and generous; but in the spiritual life it is accidental, as are also the particular doctrines and cults of any religion. They are to be accepted as we have to accept ourselves, not as goals but as points of departure. When we come to a spiritual communion of poets, philosophers, or saints, it is avowedly the divine grace, truth, or beauty flowing through those human channels, and not the human

Union through all channels is interior and only with the Good.

channels, that we profit by and embrace: so much so
that all important spiritual figures necessarily become
mythical, even when they were originally historical.
If they resist this transformation, they become
irrelevant to their spiritual mission, as Shakespeare
the man is irrelevant to the poetic world that we find
in his plays.   The creation of mythical heroes seems
deceptive only to the pedant who insists on proving
them historical or proving them unhistorical.   To the
spirit those *numina* are true, as the gods are; since the
real source of influence in both cases is some diffuse
cosmic power at work in the dark, and exciting these
graphic images in the mind.   We therefore conceive
plastically and love as kindred beings and charitable
powers the powers that actually liberate spirit in ourselves.   They make for the Good; or, as we say, the
Good works through them.   This last, if pressed too
literally, becomes not thinkable, since the Good is a
result, a harmony in the workings of power; yet this
power often serves the Good, which therefore may
dramatically be called its master, commanding its own
realization.

There is a school of theology that would clip the
wings of love, so as to prevent it from ascending and
make it always descend.   Love of the Good,   Charity
they say, is self-centred and erotic; by it we   *versus*
aspire greedily to something that we might   Eros.
enjoy, to the perfection of our own being, in the
possession or presence of something that, for us, is the
Good.   Charity, on the contrary, searches out the
victims of evil, like divine grace poured out regardless
of merit, and dedicates itself to their service.   Forgetting self, it labours to relieve and instruct others.
In a word, these moralists see charity in Martha, a
hard-working Evangelical Christian; but in Mary they
see only a corrupt enthusiast of the Greek decadence,
absorbed in the passions of her own battered soul.

In one sense unselfish love is not only possible but primitive. The Will is directed upon its objects by nature, without any calculation of satisfactions to accrue or torments to be avoided. But it is perfectly impossible that any love should exist not rooted in a psyche and not directed upon an object chosen and pursued by spontaneous Will. There is therefore no love not directed upon the Good, not directed upon something that makes for the fulfilment of the lover's nature. This good may be the good of others, but doing good to others will to that extent be a good for oneself. Or shall we say that a social life, involving friendliness and a sense of duty, is in itself nobler than self-help? If the monkeys agreed always to pick the vermin from one another's skins and never from their own, the operation would indeed have become social but the benefit would remain private. Amiable as the impulse may be to benefit others, this impulse would be cruelly stultified if no benefit could be really conferred; and it is only because Will is already directed upon life, health, food, and liberty that the ministrations of intelligent charity are a benefit and not a nuisance. If to pursue the Good be pronounced selfish the most unselfish charity would be openly serving the selfishness of our neighbours, and secretly serving our own.

Perhaps, however, the good that charity aims to bestow might be no other than charity itself. "The greatest thing in the world" being love, by diffusing love, without any other benefit, we should be saving the world. But should we? Flattered as everyone would be by the idea of being loved and full of ready love in return, yet if it were impossible to benefit anybody, the whole world would be tormented by a perpetual desire to do good and a hopeless inability to do it. But perhaps we may here be the victims of an ambiguity in the word love. Love

Folly of love for love's sake.

may mean loving actions or it may mean the emotion of love. Now the *emotion* of love might be diffused universally, even if no positive natural goods could be secured for society. But then love, love, love would be a vapid sentiment; yet this is the happiness that the sentimental saviours of the world seem to be pursuing. Thinking themselves disciples of St. Paul, or even of Christ, they have removed all disillusion and asceticism from their notion of charity, all austerity from their love, and have become in reality disciples of Rousseau.

The position becomes even more precarious if we extend it to theology. That God is love is an orthodox saying; and even if God were essentially power rather than love, in one sense love would be involved in his being: for power selects what it shall do and this selection *Possible meanings of "God is love."* marks a preference and a kind of love. When the Creator said, *Let there be light,* he exerted power; yet the direction in which he exerted it betrayed an innate affection and proved that he loved light. The Book of Genesis represents God as an artist, loving the world in idea before he had brought it into existence. But a world, like a child, has a life of its own and may soon begin to wander from the parental intention. The parent may even be tempted to disown his offspring; yet the artist, even if disappointed in his work, remembers the Platonic Idea that first inspired him, and still feels its magic. He will be inclined to preserve the erring thing to be revised and corrected. So we learn that God has resumed his labours, this time not to create the world but to redeem it. The absolute artist has been softened into a forgiving father, a miraculous physician, a patient teacher, even a propitiatory victim. God's love of the world has become charity.

Arabian subtlety has known how to refine on these intuitions and to maintain that creation itself was a work of charity. Allah is continually called the Merciful and the Compassionate, even when his decrees are most severe; and there might seem to be a voluntary one-sidedness in these epithets, seeing that Moslem theology makes Allah absolutely omnificent. How should universal Will be moved by charity, when there can be nothing outside to succour or to love? The psyche is not moved by charity to fashion the body, or to react with a healing power on diseases and wounds. Nor is spontaneous unanimity between various psyches an instance of charity: it is not charity that leads a crew to pull together in a race or in a storm. Nevertheless we are told that charity moved the Creator to make the world, because non-existence is the worst of metaphysical evils and the most necessitous. Allah therefore took pity on the unwedded essences of things and entirely without any claims or merits on their part married them to existence. The worst of monsters and of torments has this to be thankful for, that at least it exists. We may smile at such an ambiguous mercy; yet the principle that *giving* is blessing, whether the gift were needed or not, has a great vogue in religion and in society; and even when the gift is needed, the question remains whether the need itself was not an evil. The Prayer Book thanks God for our creation; yet in being created we received nothing but needs with no assurance that they would be satisfied; for what is our organic Will, our psyche, but a vast concourse of needs, some urgent, others latent but brewing and rendering us fundamentally unhappy? Common sense is blunted to such unremitting perceptions, and takes for granted our existence, our needs, and our desire to satisfy them; and on this basis we may unfeignedly thank Providence or Fortune or the charity of mankind for any aid in satisfying them, however inadequate.

Charity has more insight into nature than conscience or self-interest can have; it understands the innocence

(marginal note) Was it a mercy to be created?

of contrary wills and the goodness of contrary goods. For this reason charity seems unnatural or super- natural to the conventional mind. It re- bukes in assisting. But if no will can be un- reservedly abetted by charity, this happens only because natural wills are in conflict; for *Charity is humane, with roots in nature.* although some of them involve worse consequences than others, even the best involve consequences that are unfortunate in some direction. Human wisdom cannot consider everything or really look to the end; and charity must begin at home and never lose its moorings there. Therefore it is always quick to relieve bodily distress. To relieve suffering in anyone's body is an immediate mercy to the spirit there, and can hardly bring an immediate injury to the spirit in anyone else. For the same reason charity gives alms, even when rational economy might hold back; because the benefit is clear, even if undeserved, and the detachment just, even if ill-timed. Thus charity is a second birth of love, aware of many wills and many troubles. It is not creative or constructive of anything positive, unless it be hospitals and almshouses. Institutions produce rival ambitions, rights, and contentions. About all plans and projects charity is disenchanted and sure only of the ever-present propriety of charity itself.

If in saying that God is love we understand that God is charity, we are led to certain consequences perhaps unwelcome to theology. For if the whole essence of deity were bounty, evidently the creator could not exist without the *To deify it involves atheism.* creation; and if the whole essence of deity were mercy, God would depend for his existence on the existence of suffering and sin. These implications are pan- theistic; they are incompatible with Christianity, the religion of charity. But a more insidious consequence follows. If the impulse to give and to help were the very spirit of God (the occasion and demand for such charity being presupposed naturalistically) what would God be but goodness in ourselves, in so far as we are good? This insight may rather satisfy a moralistic and mystical piety, as the pantheistic insight satisfies dialectical wit: but if we say that God is nothing but the brotherly love that we feel for one another, it is clear that we are atheists.

Neither the animal psyche nor the Good to which the psyche aspires can ever be banished from morals. It is natural The psyche introduces the element of pre-Eros en- ference, the distinction between good and lightened. evil, success and failure; and the Good is thus set in its ideal place, as the goal and perfection of a natural life. If we call this vital aspiration Eros, which is its ancient poetic name, we may say that charity is a form of Eros, and thoroughly erotic; for if it were not erotic it would not be a psychic force nor a passion of the spirit. What turns Eros into charity is reason, recollection, comparison, justice. The great tragedy of Eros is its blindness: remove the blindness produced by a too narrow and intense light, remove the bandage that turned vision into dreams, and Eros is charity itself: the pursuit of all Good, guided by all knowledge.

Now sympathy with all good and attention to all knowledge are not possible to an animal psyche in its physical action; they enter the field only as ideals of the spirit, evoked by the psyche in the act of becoming sensitive to *some* sympathy and to *some* knowledge. Correcting a first impulse in consequence, the psyche creates the principle of a rational conscience or of universal justice. The universality of both sympathy and knowledge is posited initially but never attained in act; yet charity (as also science) lives in the light of that ideal. Truth far outruns actual knowledge, or any experience possible to any individual or any species of living beings; and charity far outruns any actual code of politics or morality. Charity extends to all animals and, as the Indians tell us, to all gods, whatever gods there may be; because existence of every type involves difficulty and imperfection, defeat, and essential impermanence, so that everywhere existence deserves compassion and demands transmutation into eternal terms. This the spirit performs instinctively, wherever it can, clearing the gold everywhere from the dross, and laying it up for an eternal treasure.

How is this possible? How shall we be united, even in spirit, with a good that is absent, how recognize a truth inexpressible in our language, or be at peace with a power that is perhaps destroy- *Union with all good is* ing us? There is a way: it is prayer. Prayer *possible only in prayer.* seems sheer foolishness to the world, and rather a puzzle to the materially pious. Why pray, an indoctrinated child may ask, when God loves us, when he knows everything, and when he has already decided what he will do? And the only answer might seem to be the one given in my first Spanish catechism to any hard question: "The Church has doctors that will know how to explain it." We may smile; but in this case the explanation is really at hand if, whether doctors or not, we can distinguish the spirit from the psyche, or in Christian language, the other world from this world. In this world, or for the psyche, prayer is an instrumentality, and it could not be efficacious except magically if incantations, or the unspoken desires of the heart, could compel the powers of nature to obey our commands. This is what superstition expects and asserts, even in the most modern psychology. But for a spiritual religion the idea of compelling God or compelling matter, by magic words or by tears, to do as we wish, is sacrilegious. Magic does not begin to be prayer until it leaves the issue in God's hands, and reconciles itself beforehand to a denial of the need or

the hope expressed. It is not expressed for the preposterous purpose of changing the will of God, or
causing nature to revise the contingency of things,
which seen from within is freedom and seen from
above is fate. It flows out spontaneously from the
fullness of the heart, in confession, in reflection, in
prophetic vistas, in resigned and transmuting union
with the truth and with a different infinite Good at
first hidden from the eyes.

In his life-long prayer the reflective man need not
be especially inclined to address petitions to heaven;
rational prayer is not a means but an end.
Petitions enter into prayer inevitably, because

*Double
interpreta-
tion of the
divine will.*

its language is a social language; and the
spirit has a direction in which it wishes to
move, so that it lives in a perpetual alternative between
I would and *I would not*. It therefore can hardly
conceive anything without gladness or aversion; and
this vital bias comes to clearness, as all things come to
clearness, in prayer. Yet in prayer all these wishes and
sorrows are uttered in the felt presence of omnificent
power and eternal truth; so that all preferences are, as
it were, suspended and neutralized by the sense of
dependence and by the virtual acceptance of the perhaps
contrary fact. The very expression *Thy will be done*
which breathes resignation also defines a hope. The
will of God on the one hand means whatsoever happens;
on the other hand it means that which ought to happen.
In the latter sense it seems as yet not to be done on
earth as it is in heaven; and the Kingdom of God seems
not yet to have come. But this postponement too must
be according to God's will in the first sense; and if it
were not we should not implore him to shorten the
interval and to deliver us from evil. If the will of
God be not conceived as omnificent (that being too
pantheistic for a political religion) and if events are
determined in part by the free-will of other agents, the

ultimate union to be attained in prayer would not be union with God, but with the entire moral society of the universe. With this totality we should have to settle our ultimate accounts, dynamic and ideal, since it would be this conjunction of free agencies, with our own included, that would determine the total destiny and truth of things. A moral theism, in denying that God is omnificent, would still have left omnificence the ultimate court of appeal; and this court would not be composed merely of the sundry free agents visible within it, but also and most importantly of the manner and time of their conjunction, and its effects. Now these conjunctions and effects of various free wills are contingent to any one of them and a primary fatality for them all; yet these unintended conjunctions and results are conceived in orthodox theology to have been foreseen and accepted by God at the creation of the world; so that his will seems to be double. As the designer and ultimate sanction of destiny, God wills whatsoever happens; but as lawgiver, merciful saviour, and moral judge, he wills us, for instance, to do not those things which we do but those which we ought to have done; so that his moral and redeeming will is only one strand in his total handiwork.

But the language of prayer should not be pressed as if, when we are living the life of spirit in its full freedom and transcendence, we were still The langu-
bargaining and plotting in a social and age of prayer diplomatic world. In expressing our needs is poetical. and our sorrows we do not ask ourselves whether we are calling on the Almighty to will what he does not will, or whether we are calling on ourselves to contradict our moral aspirations and to think our evil good. We are probably doing neither. We are recollecting, digesting, purifying our conscience. Essentially, we are addressing nobody; the names and forms of the gods are as mutable as our necessities. Even when we

are expressing a wish, we are doing so in the face of the truth, or of fate impersonally, considering how excellent it would be if fortune came to our assistance. We pray as spontaneously as we curse, and cry *Would to God!* without any theory of divine government. The same exclamation, *ojalá!* is even more familiar in Spain, meaning *May Allah will it!* If the Moslems, the most prayerful and most manly of men, sometimes abstained from petitions as irreverent, they could not abstain from desire; and their most unfeigned prayer was not to God, but concerning God. They could not suppress the feeling how beautiful the beautiful would be, if it came true. And among us now there are good people who pray that there may be a God to pray to.

Moreover, sincere prayer need not affect that hushed tone and demure attitude which we associate with religious devotion in modern times. The spirit may often be sorrowful, but when it thinks, when it dominates, it cannot be afraid. Prayer is essentially *oratio*, the eloquence of destiny; it contains the whole free comment, lament, and jubilation of the spirit, challenging its fate: a continual contrite reconsideration of all things, for which memory and hope supply the materials; so that prayer, as a sincere spirit may utter it, abounds in regrets, praises, aspirations, laughter, and curses, but all transposed from the plane of action to that of reflection and prophecy. Omnificent power and eternal truth mightily sustain this contemplation, rendering it, in so far as it conforms to them, victorious and full of light. Action is not excluded, as it is not in the drama. Prayer may easily glow with an assurance of the direction in which omnificent power, perhaps through our own agency, is carrying the world. We may be fighting with the big battalions, or even leading them; yet in the midst of action that which is proper to spirit is only observation, wonder,

(Marginal note beside paragraph: Need not be timorous or cringing.)

comparison, judgment. What has happened, what is happening, and what is bound to happen fall into a dramatic vista, which the prophet or psalmist develops eloquently in his prayer; and he judges nothing and promises himself nothing except as the agent and messenger of God.

Thus, strange as it may sound to the rationalist who thinks prayer ridiculous, the only perfectly rational form of life for a spirit that has attained self-knowledge is the life of prayer.

To this we must come morally in the end, accepting all inevitable evils for the sake of the good still possible; but there is a partial union that the spirit Transition to may reach vitally at any moment, as in laughter. laughter. Here there is no acceptance of ultimates, only merriment at present absurdities and deceptions. The Olympians did not pray to Fate, they did not *care* enough for that; but being free and happy, they laughed at existence.

There are moments in childhood when spirit breaks through in a clear triumph. Children laugh, they laugh easily, whole-heartedly, at all sorts of things. In laughter there is a release of ten- The pure laughter of sions, as in play; but the tensions released children and in play are vital only, and inarticulate, while the impure. laughter is provoked by release from little obsessions about things already familiar. Things and persons are imposing objects to a child; they seem stolidly committed to be and to remain themselves; but they grow more engaging when they change, and still more when they make faces and pretend not to be what they are. Yet the circle of their tricks and of their stories is soon run, and they become prosaic. In things and persons this commitment to remain as they were may make their individuality and force, but for the spirit it is a restriction. In reality that solemnity and dullness in things and persons is a false pretence. Things are not the essences they put forward; they are configurations of a matter that has indefinite potentialities, just as the spirit has. Any day some unforeseen accident will disclose their inside, or their miscalculation of their powers. The gods have always been laughing at them, and now the spirit in us may laugh too. Even in the silliest fun, when a word meant in one sense is taken in another, there is some release from a false restriction, a little flight from one perch to another; but a pun disappoints if it merely drops us at another chance station. Had it been true wit, it would have kept us on the wing.

Laughter loses this innocence when children lose theirs and become rancorous. In their boasts and jeers we see the difference. These grimaces of egotism are forced, cruel, essentially unhappy. Pure laughter is not malicious, not scornful; it is not a triumph of one self over another, but of the spirit over all selves. It is a joyous form of union with our defeats, in which the spirit is victorious. The bubble once pricked, everybody stands on homelier and firmer ground. In passing, there is exultation at having rung the dirge of something unreal. This pleasure is dear to children, even if a little shrill. They, poor creatures, are being cheated so regularly by their elders, by one another, and by their own fancies, that it is sweet to turn the tables for once and to mock the solemn fools in return. But the enlightenment of children is apt to be a fresh delusion, destined to end not in laughter, but in tears; and tears are not enlightening. They water the roots of passion in the psyche and pile up the fruits of Karma for the world. It is laughter that liberates once for all from error, without taking a new pledge. It therefore unites us freely with whatsoever may truly deserve our troth. Laughter rings the recess-bell in school hours; and then perhaps some ugly little seeds of learning, sown in us against our will, spring up beautiful, free and unrecognized in the playground of the mind.

In after years laughter becomes bitter; we have laughed enough to no purpose and can no longer laugh merrily at the old comedy of things. One *The seamy* half of us has despaired and smiles sadly at *side of* the other half for not having been able to do *cynicism.* so. Meantime, at all ages, laughter can sink into ribaldry and become the by-play of vice, when vice throws off the mask, or wins a trick against its demure enemies. But cynicism is not itself inwardly free; its professed wit (as in the Roman satirists) is not very witty, being tarnished sometimes by savage zeal and sometimes by a base relish for scandal. Nevertheless true merriment may anywhere break in unofficially at the shams of vice as at those of virtue, lifting us out of both to the happy level of understanding.

Sometimes, however, this music changes its stops, and grows solemn. Laughter, for all its innocent spontaneity, is too bodily an affection to be *The victory* wholly satisfying. It lapses sadly into a *of mind.* blank; the next thing is irrelevant and mutes the impulse. When the elevation can be sustained on a wider view, we no longer laugh, but grow speculative, commemorative, even liturgical. The catharsis found in tragedy is only a solemn universalized form of the solution that unravels some comic knot, and leaves us, for a moment, contented with the world. Elegy also leaves us content, not with some gain but with all losses. The *bourgeois* endeavours to explain his love of scandal, of reported crimes, horrors, and ruin, by throwing pleasing considerations into the balance, such as his own safety, or the incidental merits of the report, diction, images, or moral lessons. But this is all beside the point. The nature of spirit and the divine allegiances of spirit have not been discerned. Why is the diction poetical or the imagery sublime or the moral edifying? Because in those intuitions the spirit triumphs over the triumphs of limitation, error, and death. It is not a question of sugaring the pill, but of drinking the fatal cup to the dregs, and being reborn into another life. We should be only lying to ourselves if we pretended that troubles had ceased or that death was not ultimate; but by being ultimate death frames all troubles in, completes the picture, removes it to the plane of historic accidents, and renders it an object fit for intuition to rest in. *Memento mori* may suggest only worms and ghastly corruption; but we might say just as well, *Memento vixisse*, remember that you will have lived. Such is the eternity intrinsically native to spirit and visible from each of its moments, be they few or many. The judgment then passed on the spectacle may be favourable or unfavourable; but it is always a sublime judgment, a true last judgment. David and the Sibyl sing for ever of the Day of Wrath and of the world sunk in ashes, and they are deeply happy.

Spirit could never *see* the truth or conceive it in an actual thought if spirit were not a function of life; and the intuition of eternity must always be a passing or repeated intuition. Now life is a trope in matter, proper to an organism that can restore and reproduce itself. Such life cannot help being precarious. It is inwardly continuous with material processes that outrun it, so that some of its developments will be disruptive and contrary to one another. Life may be killed by life, as it may be stifled by lifeless forces. Therefore the good that a liberated spirit may embrace cannot be the truth, but at best some conception of the truth. This will be more than the truth, in being living and emotional and having an internal movement from potentiality to act; and it will be immensely less than the truth in being always partial, intermittent, and subjectively directed. For it is life, raised to the scintillating light of spirit, that notices this rather than that, sets problems, and finds

Union not with unvarnished truth.

solutions, which are privately exciting scents followed to ends privately gratifying; whereas the truth displays the whole eternal labyrinth of real relations through which question and answer miss their way a thousand times, for once that they find it.

The triumph that inwardly raises spirit to its height is intuition, not knowledge; for when fact and truth have to be regarded, spirit has mortgaged its *The value of* freedom, and is as often depressed as exalted. *knowledge is* Therefore before the truth, or behind it, and *moral.* intercepting knowledge in a thousand ways, arises a ghost of that which is not but might have been: something better than the truth, or worse than the truth, and evoked by fear of what the truth may be. And this play of heated imagination, which the truth if it could speak might call impertinent, flows from the sources of spirit more directly, and prophesies the Good more truly, than knowledge could ever do The function of such free intuition is by no means superseded by eventual knowledge; it persists to enlighten the spirit morally about the truth that may have enlightened it intellectually. Truth is contingent; but spirit, being addressed to essence, can rest only in what is necessary: in the form that a form has, and in the inevitable relation of that form to all others. More deeply, therefore, than with the truth, spirit is concerned with conceiving, loving, or hating what might have been true. Spirit speaks not for the truth or for the intellect alone by which truth is discovered, but speaks for all life, in so far as life has been perfected and harmonized. Even the intellect is an exercise of this spontaneous or poetic faculty that rebels against the intellect; because the categories of the intellect are variable and vital, like those of language, and knowledge, like any other art, trembles between a good and an evil fate.

The fine arts and the traditional religions are vast instruments in the realm of matter, that seem to serve the spirit directly, apart from utility or truth; yet even they carry an immense load of impedimenta. All the

So is the value of imagination. technical, scientific, historical, social, local, and temporal side of art and religion, that absorbs so much blood and ink, has nothing to say to the spirit about the Good. At best, the ground may be thereby cleared for a free spiritual life, which will begin where those distractions end. I do not mean where they end historically, for they can never end while life in this world continues. I mean where they culminate morally and provisionally and yield their spiritual fruits. These fruits are gathered in moments of insight, recollection, and prayer. They are not probably novel fruits historically, but they are always fresh and spontaneous for the spirit that develops them. They are not discoveries of facts in another world, such as religious dogmas seem to a simple mind to report, or such as the arts of fiction add to common reality as it were in a dream. We are not divorced from the facts of this world in order to be subjected to the facts of another world, expected to be better: that is an illusion of the animal Will, unteachable and bent on trying its luck for the second time. We are divorced by a revelation about the old and familiar facts, and remarried to them by a new charity that understands their hidden virtues and forgives their vices; a revelation about our own lives and affections transfiguring them in a superhuman light that robs us of ourselves and of our world, only to return our world and ourselves to us drenched in a truer Lethe, not of forgetfulness but of eternity.

Might not the union to which we aspire be a union with other spirits? Might there not be Union with other spirits only incidental. a supreme spirit, or perfect form of spiritual life, to which all spirits were inwardly directed? At bottom, this suggestion introduces nothing new: if any spirit inwardly aspired to a specific form of life, that form of life would be its good; and if all spirits aspired to the same form of life, that form of life would be the Good, absolute because universally relative. A supreme spirit that should actualize that ideal, as for instance by being omniscient, would possess the Good; and all lovers of the Good would be united with him morally, but not existentially, since the other spirits that aspired to omniscience without possessing it would *ipso facto* not be that supreme spirit itself, and could embrace that good only in prayer. If, on the other hand, we conceive the supreme spirit not as simply actualizing the good pursued by each spirit, but as a power with which all must reckon, union with the supreme spirit could never be wholly spiritual but would remain in some measure political, and such as pious souls without spiritual insight seek to establish in their religion. In seeking union with any other spirit we are therefore seeking either the Good, in that this other spirit realizes the perfection to which we are inwardly addressed; or else we are seeking such conformity with power and with truth as is necessary to the attainment of our proper good.

So the matter seems to end, if we take spirits existentially, and conceive union with them materially, as union in a tug-of-war. But a tug-of-war, and social union generally, does produce spiritual union; not because the spirits pull, as an absurd moral materialism supposes, but because when bodies pull well together, and psyches are akin, spirits for the time being become unanimous. Each has the very purpose, the very hope, that animates each of the others; and this actual spiritual unison is not unconscious. Spirit is divided into spirits by its organs, and into intuitions by its occasions; but we have seen that spiritually it is homogeneous and everywhere transcendental and potentially infinite. When, therefore, in two souls it thinks the same thought or

Spirits can be united only by thinking alike.

sees the same fact, while the intuitions remain two, their object is identical: else we could never think twice of the same thing privately, or ever think of the same thing together. Yet we know that we do so, because we are deeply aware of our animal separateness and cohabitation. The presence of the friend or enemy resets the whole soul, and there is nothing of which we are more quickly conscious than of thinking alike or of thinking differently. This feeling often leads to rash alliances in the world, rash because real cooperation does not depend on spiritual union but on confluence of functions and interests, often more harmonious and cooperative for being diverse: and the *spes animi credula mutui*, in this world, is an *ignis fatuus*. Yet not so in the other world, in the realm of spirit; for there we are not looking for fidelity or active support or common ascendancy over opinion, but for the miraculous rhyming of mind with mind, when a thought, we know not whence or why, re-echoes our thought, confirms and clarifies it, setting it apart from the flux of irrevocable sensation. This spiritual bond is enough: the occasions when it is discovered may or may not recur; the happiness lies in the sense of an intuition once shared, a thought once anchored and become domiciled in history. Then the clearness of the light that had once shone upon us ceases to seem barren: as if a star, burning alone, had news of another star alive with the same fire.

Such unanimity would be a fact in the realm of truth prior to being discovered: and when the discovery brought a sense of spiritual fellowship, the comfort of this added intuition would not make union less spiritual. For we suppose material contact to be absent or impossible, as when our unknown friend is dead or not yet born or perhaps non-human; and what we gain is only fellowship in worship, reduplicating the light that falls, within each of us, upon the realm of ideas. The repetition of insights, though it may fortify an uncertain mind, is not spiritually important, and each angel, according to St. Thomas Aquinas, is the only individual of his species. In fact, the consideration of instances of spirit as events in nature is external to their spiritual import. Their occasions distribute them through physical space and time; but internally, though they are living acts, and in that sense events, they are distributed only by the relations of their subject-matter and individuated only by the ideas that they light up. Intellectually, two exactly similar intuitions make but one idea, being intuitions of the same essence. The multitude of witnesses, therefore, though it has animal weight, adds nothing to the truth or beauty of any revelation. It adds nothing to the happiness of pure life in the spirit.

That no spirit can absorb any other is evident, since spirit (as I use the word) is an act, not a transferable or transformable substance. Therefore any spiritual union actually experienced is necessarily specious and a pure datum of intuition. Not that a real union between spirits may not exist, in that separate minds may be unanimous; but this unanimity would be a fact external to their experience of it, a truth about them, which they might conceive and credit, but which could not in itself be a condition or ecstasy attained by either of them. Yet the union that mystics speak of seems to be emphatically a state into which they pass, internal, certain, and overwhelmingly actual. It has the surprising and all-solving character of a datum: and the character of a datum, by definition, is exactly the same whether it happens to be true or merely imaginary. Therefore the only spiritual union that can be certain, obvious, and intrinsically blissful, must be not a union between two spirits but the unity of a spirit within itself.

Actual union an experience of inner unity.

This conclusion is a corollary from the general critical principle that nothing given exists. That which certainly exists in such a case is only the intuition of that datum, not the datum in its own specious field, which is that of essence. So mystic union resides in intuition; it is not a union of objects or with objects, but a synthesis reached in life and expressed in a given quality of feeling. This is a feeling of union and bliss; but the given union does not exist (it would abolish the universe if it did), only the feeling of union exists; and if the bliss exists for a moment (not without a certain deceptiveness as to its absolute volume and finality) this is only because, in the case of inarticulate feelings, we give the same name to the intuition and to the quality revealed to that intuition. The feeling of bliss exists; the bliss, if taken for a secret reality revealed or for the truth of the universe, certainly does not exist. For the world continues to be just as divided, just as obscure, and just as little blissful as it was before.

Spiritual union with the Good does not, then, alter the general facts or discover any general truth. It is a new dawn within: where the sky was clouded, it is clear, namely, in the mind. The currents that confused and abolished one another before join now in one harmonious deliverance with an all-solving force. And we must not infer that there must be ignorance of the world or a pious monotony involved in this spiritual symphony. On the contrary, the whole torrent and violence of things swells within it and exalts it. There is nothing too painful or too audacious to be included, only it cannot be included as it would exist outside in separation and wilful blindness. The union into which it now enters transmutes it, and is a fact in another realm of being, a creation of the witnessing and recording spirit. Experience cannot

It is an essence given, not a fact discovered.

contain bodily any of its posited objects, or even its own past, in its past existence; it can contain only the thought of them. It obviously cannot make identical the contradictory beliefs and desires afloat in the universe; but it can compose, in thought, a single drama out of their conflict, where the spectacle of their folly turns into wisdom, and their ruin into salvation.

There might seem to be æsthetic cruelty and intellectual selfishness in such an enjoyment of evil at a speculative distance; and this would indeed be the case, if spirit were a power and either produced or did not wish to abolish the horrors of this world, in order to gloat on them from a private heaven. But spirit has no power; and the Will that supports and evokes spirit (and exerts power to that extent) is entirely secondary and sympathetic, being the Will to understand all Will, and to love all the goods that Will anywhere aspires to create. Spirit therefore would not be expressing its own Will if it condoned any evil or was dead to any good; but its nature forbids it to *repeat* within itself the efforts, sufferings, or pleasures that it understands; for it could not then understand or transcend them. Such repetition would be ignominious, and would reduce spirit again to utter captivity, while its vocation is precisely dominion, spiritual dominion, without distraction, responsibility, or power. Not, however, without joy, such as the full exercise of Will necessarily brings when it is conscious.

Thus it is at once a sad, a comic and a glorious spectacle that existence presents to spirit. Spirit would never have *commanded* this performance, like a Nero, if that had been within its power; it understands and feels the inwardness of the matter far too well for that. Yet it watches and records the whole with avidity, though not without tears. How far this liberation of spirit from all it finds afoot differs from selfishness appears in this: that the evils spirit transcends are its own sufferings, since no catastrophe in nature would involve any evil if nature had remained unconscious. Spirit captive has endured whatsoever spirit free may turn into glowing tragedies; and it would contradict its own Will if it did not rejoice in its final freedom. Yet even this tragic wisdom and tearful rapture are imposed on the spirit by a power above it. Had it the choice, perhaps it would renounce this victory also, and humbly prefer silence and peace; but choosing is not its office; it cannot exist before it exists and decide whether or not to bring itself into existence; and if it thinks it can kill itself, that is a psychic illusion, for it cannot prevent its rebirth. Nor is it asked to decide how much is worth enduring in order that something may be enjoyed.

Accepting that which is offered as, be it pious or rebellious, spirit cannot help doing, it may distinguish the direction in which its Good lies. It *Evil, though it may be transmuted in reflection, is not thereby rendered desirable.* lies in the direction of harmony; harmony between the Will and its fortunes, and harmony within the subject-matter open to apprehension. A world without evil in it, that is, without contradiction in the Wills animating the various parts, would be better than a world in conflict. And if this seems to wash the field of experience somewhat too clean, and to diminish too much the risks and excitements of living, this feeling must be pronounced vicious, and a remnant of perfectly mad cruelty and masochism. There are creatures that might, for a moment, find nothing interesting to do, if evils ceased to torment them; yet if they had eyes and hands they might soon find work without torment and images without stain. The thunder of chaos receding would render audible "the music of the spheres": the life of a universe where the Good was not posited but realized.

If we imagine this harmony hypostasized into an actual intuition, we conceive the mind of God in its omniscience and glory. It is therefore per- *If the Good* fectly legitimate to say that the union craved *were hypos-* is union with God, and that when we have *tasized the union with* experience of such union we are merged in *it could be* God indistinguishably and feel that we *only political.* become God. Yet this can be true only of the essence that we have hypostasized into a divine person; and nothing proves that such a God exists or that we have been really united with him, or ceased to be our separate physical selves. On the contrary, if a true union of this kind is to take place between two existing spirits, it must be more than the experience of union, and God must be more than ourselves thinking we have become God. Our experience must be derived from its object and God must be a power infusing that experience into us by an act of grace, as is evidently the case in human love or mutual understanding. There would be no union and no society if our friends were all personages in our own novels; instead of being united with others we should only be deploying ourselves. This inner dialogue is indeed what the life of spirit terminates in at any given point or in any given person: it is all that *experience* can contain. Yet intelligence, which is the cream of experience, transcends experience by revealing to it its own secondary nature, and the existence of its thousand causes and companions; and union with these ambient realities, harmony between these free and independent facts, makes the surprise and the joy of friendship.

Here lies the human advantage that popular positive religion has over mystical insight: it brings *Advantage* us into communion with the gods, and *and dis-* socializes our inner comforts and aspiration *advantage of religious im-* by ascribing them to friendly intercessions *personations.* and divine favours. The myth is deeply true and salutary. We are not self-created spirits, but everything, including our best inspirations, comes to us from beyond ourselves, from the primeval fountains of matter. But the *dramatis personæ* of popular religion are fabulous and grow more and more novelesque as we make them more and more human. Intercourse with these invisible persons is not, even in fancy, an ideal union between spirits, but only social intercourse between psychic agents interacting under common conditions in a natural world. Even miracles, when they are admitted, obey the proprieties and conventions of some divine economy. Rather than the Good hypostasized, God now seems a particular monarch against whom we might rebel or to whom we might swear allegiance. His existence becomes a question of cosmology and political history, to be established by rational evidence.

The point would be important morally, inasmuch as, being a natural psyche with a Will shown in sporadic action, an existing deity might greatly influence the fortunes of other souls. He might be a great friend to some, but others would surely find him an enemy, because

In society the greatest good is only the least of evils.

action in a particular world cannot possibly pursue or secure all particular goods, and the lovers of the goods sacrificed would cry to heaven against God for vengeance. "Heaven" would there signify all Good, unrealizable at any point in an existing world but inviolate in its essential authority and goodness. "God", on the other hand, would signify the power dominant over us for the time being. Job felt the conflict between these two claims to allegiance, that of the Good and that of the Lord; and the Whirlwind enforced the claims of power with a deafening eloquence, utterly unconvincing to the spirit. Many a pagan god might be blameless and perfect, and might point with pride to his mighty works, or even,

like Apollo and the Muses, to his inspiring or healing
influence. He might, in a sense, be holy, in that he
realized his chosen good absolutely, and remained
steadfast, whatever monstrous growths chaos might
vomit around him. But before a god of power could
speak persuasively to the spirit he would need in his
own person to be spiritual and religious. He would
need to be inspired by a perfect understanding and
love of all goods. In his action, however powerful
he might be, he could never bring all these goods at
once into existence. Probably, as no power can assure
itself against the intrusion of some other power, he
would be incapable of bringing even some goods into
existence in perfect order and uncontaminated; so
that his choice of the greatest possible good at each
moment would really be a choice of the least of evils.
To such a patient and merciful power spirit might
well cry, *Though thou slay me, yet will I trust in thee*;
and there would be a spiritual union possible with
the antecedent Will of God, addressed to universal
Good, as well as political submission and piety towards
his consequent Will, determining actual events.

Essentially, however, it is not with the gods of
popular religion that spiritual union is possible: they
are not themselves at peace with mankind, Without
with one another, or with the universe. denying the
Mystics are normally believers in the ortho- gods, spirit
doxy of their day, not being curious about union within
facts nor thinking opinion very important; itself.
yet they cannot help piercing the reigning myths, not
critically but interpretatively, and reaching truths about
the spiritual life at once more abstruse than traditional
dogmas and more intimate. Why does the mystic keep
his vigils and fasts, if not to escape from subjection to
things external, and in the first place from the cravings
and illusions of his individual self, the most accidental
of seats for the spirit and, as he feels, the most unworthy?

It would be a sorry failure to relapse in the end into the worship of earthly prosperity or disputatious learning, or into subjection to new accidental passions and hypnotic powers; and what else are the benefits proposed by popular religions?   Paradises, as the Indians know, are fit rewards for active virtue, temporal rewards for occasional good conduct; but paradises are but stepping-stones for the spirit; and what does it matter whether the stepping-stone be a lump of gold or of granite, if only the foot neither slips nor sticks there, but leaps easily to safety and freedom?   And this safety and freedom cannot be found in union with any existing being.   If we say it is union with Brahma we must understand by Brahma pure spirit present in all its instances, not any one instance, however extraordinary; and if in order to avoid mythology we speak rather of Nirvana, we must understand by this no passive lapse from existence but a moral victory over it, occasionally possible, though never physically final. What is suspended is not existence but ignorance, and what is gained is not indifference but equilibrium.

That spirit should have its centre in itself, wherever and whenever it may exist, so that all its adventures

Spirit always a consummation, never a finality. must be ideal and all its symbols internal and specious, follows from its transcendental nature. This nature was clearly if inadequately expressed by Aristotle when he called it *intellect in act*; an act being a spontaneous, transitional, momentary exercise of life, and intellect being such an act in an animal psyche that has become perfectly cognitive and conscious.   But intellect is only the side of spirit that is addressed to knowledge and system; and life may be perfectly actualized also in feeling and in imagination.   Everywhere, however, this actuality will be conscious light, the dawn of attention making something present: so that spirit can neither escape from itself nor be confined to any given object or sentiment. For these are present only in act, by being felt or conceived; and they have no hold on spirit, to prevent it from living on, and being differently active. That which can hold spirit down to steady objects and fixed categories is only the power of matter, which also elicits spirit itself; and the healthy limitations of the psyche give to each special spirit its special circle of sane thoughts. But an act is necessarily self-limited and self-delivered: what it does or thinks it can never undo or unthink; and spirit may shine again in another act, similar or dissimilar to the last, according to psychic and physical occasions.

The idea of final union with anything specific, even with omniscience or with pure Being, therefore contradicts the very nature of spirit. In one sense there is always union with so much as the spirit has clearly felt or conceived, since it is the same act that makes the actuality of spirit and the actuality of the feeling or thought. But in another sense, there is never union, never completion or finality, since an absorbed datum dies with the actual absorption in it; and no act, dying as it must in the process of living, can abolish or prevent a further act.

A sustained act would be perfectly possible if there were, as Aristotle supposed, perfectly sustained celestial motions. But everlasting sameness is something non-natural and a fabulous materialization of ideal eternity. Eternity belongs properly only to essences and truths, and may be extended by assimilation to intuitions in their deliverance, but never in their existence. In their existence intuitions are events: they arise and vanish; and in the interval they illustrate a *nunc stans*, since they fill a natural moment and actualize some essence or truth, in itself eternal. But the duration of such an actual *nunc stans* is not to be measured astronomically in fractions of a second or in light-years. It is a unit, however long

The nunc *stans how possible.*

sustained or however fugitive, in the realm of spirit, spiritually individuated by its quality and deliverance, not by its station (which it borrows from its organ) in physical time and space. For although each intuition has a date and a home in the physical world, if viewed from the outside or historically, when viewed from within each always stands in the middle of the temporal and spatial universe, introducing a moral centre into a flux where probably no centre exists physically.

These moral centres are as many as they happen to be; so that the realm of spirit is intrinsically a democracy (as the realm of truth is not), spirit being everywhere sovereign in its own right. This sovereignty, however, is only spiritual, as human equality, when not a sham, is only spiritual; and the sovereignty of each at home expressly invites and rejoices in the home sovereignty of all the others. For spirit exists; it is not a tyrannical idea, to be imposed on spirit; and existence is intrinsically dispersed, tireless, inexhaustible in its youth, ready to die and to be reborn, to discover and to re-discover, to sing sometimes an old song and sometimes a new one. The only totality or finality is ideal, it is the truth; but no view of the truth can be final in the life of spirit. Even omniscience, if it were possible, would not be final there; it would be a single instance of spirit, a supremely complex intuition. Simpler and partly ignorant intuitions would remain possible, and perhaps better. The truth that is requisite for the honour and peace of spirit is not omniscience but the absence of delusions; and this, where humility exists, does not demand infinite information. So it happens also when a man surveys his personal history. There is no contribution of experience that need be excluded from recollection, but the new total at each moment forms a new object, caught in a new intuition. The various

The galaxy of spirit.

perspectives have arisen in the same world; they contain errors and contradictions if turned into absolute dogmas and made to debate every point face to face, as if they stood or ought to stand in one another's shoes; but seen in their origin and causes, they are always complementary, explicable naturally, and unified objectively in the realm of truth. Yet actually, in the realm of spirit, every intuition is a flying spark, private, momentary, and saved from total death only by its ideal bonds and its inner vision of eternity. Each spark, by the radiation of its light, has revealed for a moment one region of heaven; and in that heaven it is united, with its friends by mutual confirmation, with its enemies by the common risks of existence and a common appeal to the jurisdiction of fact. Intent on the same reality, material or ideal, and spreading over different parts of it, all intuitions, the greatest with the least, form the galaxy of spirit.

This is an unwitting conspiracy of free natural beings, each springing from its own seed in its own country, and growing into whatsoever may flow from the potentialities of its substance and fortunes. The union is a fact in the realm of truth: the fact that many spirits or instances of spirit exist in the same universe, partly similar, partly dissimilar, sometimes unanimous, sometimes complementary in their insights. I say again, complementary rather than contradictory; because although judgments may be contradictory if expressed in words, they become supplementary phases in the history of judgment, when this history is surveyed as a whole. They may be judgments about different objects; or in regard to the same object, they may express different fractions of the relations between that object and different souls. The Babel is but the totality of languages; and if each seems gibberish to the others, there is always some analogy in their logics, for they are languages, and some

Thoughts remain individual.

identity in their object, since they exist in the same world. So the galaxy of spirits has a natural orderliness in its moral confusion, and each spirit, in its solitude, a great kinship to all the others. Even if some or all, at the Last Judgment, should discover this spiritual society, which they had always composed without knowing it, no mind would become another mind, or like another; for even their common discovery of their relations would present these relations, in each case, in a different perspective; and an omniscient mind, in holding all perspectives at once in suspense, would differ enormously from all the other minds held by one perspective exclusively. Were not these personal histories and feelings eternally distinct, they could never orchestrate their celestial symphony.

On the other hand, it is not persons, in their personal limitations, that can enter into a spiritual union; for
the limitations are transcended in being

Persons become transparent. understood, one's own limitations as well as other people's. Persons become translucent, like the souls in Dante's *Paradise*, and what each sees in the others is only that part of the truth which they saw. It is in them that this part became visible, for the truth is not visible to itself; therefore this remains a union of spirits, of thoughts living and thinking each its special thought. But the rest of the man disappears; as in reading a book, the material book is forgotten, and the reader lives in rehearsing the author's thoughts without thinking of the author. At least this happens when the book is interesting and the author was himself lost in his subject; the realm of spirit is not to be entered by literary peacocks, or by bibliophiles that do not read, but hoard their books, pat them, and talk about them. So in communion between spirits, the man or the god is rendered invisible by the light he diffuses, and we are inwardly united only with so much of him as by his gifts or his grace can exist also beyond his

person and can become a part of ourselves. For
the spirit, therefore, the dead are still living, and
the living are present *numina*, like the remembered
dead.

This is not to say that the real existence of persons,
or that contact or friendship with them, has not a real
function, and one prior to the function of
ideas. Friends are important for the spirit,   The nest
and the
as a man's own identity and fortunes are   wings.
important. Without such special occasions and attachments, spirit would have no foothold in nature
and could not exist. Occasions, we have said, distribute spirit among psyches and divide each spirit
into intuitions. Yet intuition itself is born out of
a synthesis, and the field it opens up embraces, in
conception, all that the flux of existence may have
diversified and separated. The world was not made
for the spirit, nor by the spirit, as the beautiful is; but
for this very reason the world and the truth about the
world have a tutelary function, and a guiding function,
in the life of spirit. They are the gates through which
the garden of the beautiful may be safely entered, the
walls by which that garden is circumscribed and
defended. The first step towards union with the Good
is to have settled one's accounts with the world and
with the truth. After that, truth and fiction may be
entertained together, and the difference between them
may be ignored. Yet this licence, which the world
takes for incompetence or madness in spiritual men,
would really be madness or incompetence if it were not
founded on health, on adjustment to universal power,
and on a deep ironical allegiance to the truth. When
such moral health is presupposed the perspectives of
truth and of fiction may be developed together, with
no spiritual fear of either, since the agile spirit can
digest both.

If union must be unity within the spirit, might we

not say finally that the Good is the existence of spirit itself? Not at all. Spirit is evidently a prerequisite to union within the spirit; but spirit is more often distracted than harmonious; and the attainment of harmony depends on many other causes than those that suffice to evoke spirit. The causes and conditions of the Good are not themselves good: else matter and universal Will would be good, and more radically good than spirit, since they are needed to generate it. The Good lies not behind all this movement but before it; it is the end that life proposes to itself when conscious and rational. Each endeavour furnishes spirit, which is by nature sympathetic, with an initial criterion of values; whatsoever helps each flower to grow seems good to the dramatizing spirit, and whatsoever blights it, seems evil. But how shall the relative value of these endeavours be judged? The most considered judgment could only express some other instance of initial Will, a preference as contingent and groundless as those it criticizes. Shall the spirit succumb to this universal egotism and judge that whatsoever in the universe conduces to the free exercise of spirit shall be pronounced good, and whatsoever hinders that exercise shall be pronounced evil?

Such a shamelessly egotistical judgment is in fact implicit in so much of unconscious Will as rushes blindly to create spirit. But the peculiarity of spirit, when once it exists, is not to be blind, and to be eternally ashamed of egotism. Its Will is not to will, but to understand all Will; and so without willing any of the ends that universal Will pursues (not even the Will to create spirit) it sees the beauty of all those ends, including the beauty of its own impartial but enamoured vision. Spirit too is only an incident in the life of nature; the Will to be spiritual can as little be pronounced to be absolutely good as can any other natural impulse; yet

Spirit not itself the Good.

Understanding and love must make no claims for themselves.

like any other natural impulse, when once launched into life, it inevitably becomes a criterion, by which all other things may be judged relatively.

Therefore the spirit, if free to criticize its enemies, is free also to judge its own aspirations tragically or satirically; and the higher flights of wisdom and self-knowledge have always done so. Never, however, when spirit is vigorous and free, can it judge any fate coldly or any aspiration unsympathetically; because to be sympathetic and warm towards all endeavours (though they may know nothing of themselves) is the very essence of spirit; and how then should it not be so towards its own endeavours? Yet this acceptance and pursuit of its specific aims will never be safe or pure until they are qualified by a prior complete renunciation of all illusions about them. The spirit can never be altogether spiritual, or morally other than a caprice of blind Will, until it has traversed the *Dark Night* described by Saint John of the Cross, and adopted his motto: *Nothing, Nothing, Nothing.* It is only on this understanding that all things may be understood without confusion, loved without disgrace, and touched without infection, or that a life of action, for the spirit, can be a life of prayer. Henceforth we are playing a part: we do not become kings because we may wear a crown upon this stage, nor fools because it is set down for us to talk nonsense. We may give commands, when they are in character, without arrogance, follow our fortunes without greed, and declare our affections without fear of disillusion. The disillusion has come already, and the affection flows out notwithstanding, without any claims. We know that the power that creates us and shapes our passions and prompts our acts is the Poet's, and not our own; that our knowledge is but faith moving in the dark, our joy a gift of grace, our immortality a subtle translation

The great witness is the great victim.

of time into eternity, where all that we have missed is ours, and where what we call ours is the least part of ourselves. We are not impatient of injustice. It is not the fate that overtakes us that makes our dignity but the detachment with which we suffer it. All belongs to the necessary passion and death of the spirit, that to-day rides upon an ass into its kingdom, to be crucified to-morrow between two thieves, and on the third day to rise again from the dead.

In the animal psyche the passions follow one another or battle for supremacy, and the distracted spirit runs helter-skelter among them, im-pressed by the sophistical arguments which each of them offers for itself; but if the psyche grows integrated and rational, its centre, which is the organ of spirit, becomes dominant, and all those eloquent passions begin to be compared and judged, and their probable issue to be foreknown and dis-counted. The waves will not be stilled, but they will now beat against a rock. And with inner security comes a great inner clearness. We may now become aware of the world to any depth, in any degree of com-plexity. We shall have reduced our psychic centre to its precise function as a centre; and from this centre, in duly shaded perspectives, the spirit may spread its silent light over all nature and all essence.

Spirit con-centrated is clarified.

By so fortifying the spirit we shall not have saved the world; all its titular saviours have left the world much as it was. But we can reconcile ourselves with the world by doing it justice. It is a natural process: why should it have been other than it happens to be? We shall also have reconciled ourselves with our own destiny. Materially, we could not be more than poor animal experiments, lame yet wonderful, defeated yet breaking out in places into a jubilant sympathy with all creation. Spirit may live in its universal affinities, forgiving itself its ignorant errors and childish woes.

It could not have suffered if it had not loved, and to love is to have eyes for the beautiful. This privilege is bought at a great price, but spirit speaks for a part of universal Will, for that part which becomes conscious. It is therefore essentially brave, as it is essentially enamoured; and the goal once seen, it cannot count the cost.

Intermittence is intrinsic to life, to feeling, to thought; so are partiality and finitude. Spirit cannot achieve unity or perfection physically; the living flame must dance. It suffices that its light should fall on things steadfast and true, worthy to be discerned and returned to and treasured; so that though spirit be everywhere halting in achievement it may be always perfect *And is united with all things, thinking itself nothing.* in allegiance. Its happiness must always remain volatile, and its union with the Good ideal. This union is achieved not by physical possession or identity, but by intellectual worship, in which spirit, forgetting itself, becomes pure vision and pure love. Then to the spirit that has renounced all things, all things are restored: and having renounced itself also, it cannot resist any inspiration or think evil of any good, but embraces them all in the eternal object of its worship, not as they may have existed in the world in passing and in conflict, but as they lie ideally reconciled in the bosom of the Good, at peace at last with themselves and with one another.

CHAPTER X

HAVING, after sixteen years, brought this work at last to an end, let me look back and consider how far the performance has been true to the intention.

I said in the Preface to *Scepticism and Animal Faith*, "Here is one more system of philosophy"; and I pro-

The plan of this work and the execution.

ceeded to warn the reader that this system would not aspire to be new or personal or metaphysical or a system of the universe. It would be a revision of the categories of common sense, faithful in spirit to orthodox human tradition, and endeavouring only to clarify those categories and disentangle the confusions that inevitably arise when spontaneous fancy comes up against an intricate inhuman world.

Unfortunately, as some of my readers think, my own fancy is too spontaneous, interfering with an accurate and orderly exposition of facts and arguments: so that, contrary to my promise, my system is personal and new-fangled, without being original, and is extravagantly metaphysical in places, as for example in regard to the realm of essence. Nor does it escape being, in effect, a system of the universe, since the realm of matter, conceived mechanically, here forms the groundwork of all existence, the realm of spirit being only a sort of invisible vegetation flourishing in some of the stars, and the realm of truth a history of those happenings; while the realm of essence is but an infinite void presupposed, a part of which is occupied by the other realities.

Is this a fair report? I think it is, in the sense that such a photograph might be taken of my system in a bad light at a great distance. The impression would truly proceed from the object, but would not render its true characteristics. My philosophy neither is nor wishes to be scientific; not even in the sense in which, in temper and method, the *Summa* of St. Thomas might be called scientific. My philosophy is like that of the ancients a discipline of the mind and heart, a lay religion. In saying that I did not intend it to be personal, I meant that I was to rely on the common and notorious state of mankind, and to discount as much as possible the special circumstances and influences to which I might have been subject. I did not mean that my philosophy was not to spring from the inner man and not to embrace all my faculties and interests working together, but was to be a dry compilation of other men's theories and arguments, with judicial comments. I like theories and arguments when they are spontaneous and not used to refute one another; but they come to me as refinements or excursions. The large facts, the great interests by which theories and arguments are to be judged, are known to me, as to everyone else, in the daily process of living. My philosophy endeavours to enlighten this process morally, and to define its ultimate issues.

This philosophy is ordinary reflection systematized, or lay religion.

Philosophy so conceived, though it need not be new, ought certainly to be fresh. There must always be some variation in thinking the most orthodox thoughts, and I hardly know how much novelty of this kind may have crept into my ideas; but my happiness lay in understanding the ancients (or thinking I understood them) rather than

Not meant to found a new sect.

in contradicting them; and I should dislike to frame an unprecedented opinion, unless at least I thought it more congruous with common sense than what people repeat habitually, and better fitted to become conventional. I should prefer that something of me should subsist anonymously buried in the public mind, than that my name should remain attached for a few years to some technical curiosity.

That this system was to be frankly ontological, and not humanistic like my earlier writings, was obvious from the very title, *Realms of Being*, and was admitted from the beginning, since three of the four realms distinguished were non-material and two of them non-existential. The system is therefore quite properly called metaphysical, in the current literary sense of the word. But I was reserving the term metaphysics for a particular, though widespread, abuse of super-material categories; an abuse that occurs whenever logical, moral, or psychological figments are turned into substances or powers and placed beneath or behind the material world, to create, govern, or explain it. When I aver that my ontology is not metaphysics, I do not mean that I admit nothing but "data" or "sensations" into my philosophy. I mean that I regard all immaterial things, in so far as they exist or are true, as qualities, products, or ideal implications of the physical world. Nature certainly could not have existed or produced our minds, if it had adopted no form or method of existing; but this form or method is arbitrary, contingent, and essentially variable, so that in its ideal essence it has no power or prerogative to impose itself on existence. Physics, not metaphysics, therefore reveals to us, as far as it goes, the *foundations of things*; and ontology is a subsequent excursus of the mind, as in non-Euclidean geometry, over all that the facts may suggest to the fancy.

Ontological but naturalistic.

From this it appears how far my system is from being a description of the universe. It is immensely more, since it contains, or might contain, *The place of science in this system.* everything that logic, poetry, or religion might invent; yet it is immensely less, since it remains absolutely passive and modest in respect to the facts reported by natural science and by credible history. My very flights into the supra-material render me docile to the darkness and contingency of this world. In respect to the facts I am ready to accept anything that the experts may tell us for the moment, to accept it as I do the weather, without cavil but without excessive confidence. When I was younger what was pompously called Science wore an imposing aspect. There was a well-dressed Royal Family in the intellectual world, expected to rule indefinitely: sovereign axioms, immutable laws, and regent hypotheses. We had Newtonian space and time, the conservation of energy, and Darwinian evolution: Now there is a democracy of theories elected for short terms of office, speaking shop-dialects, and hardly presented or presentable to the public eye. The investigator's technique takes the lead, not the exigences of popularizing eloquence. The frontiers of this science seem less secure, with vast claims to undiscovered or undiscoverable regions; and first principles at home are wobbly and vague. Yet this looseness in thought goes with ingenuity in methods and multiplicity of contacts; and it serves to dispel an illusion that better-digested science might create: the illusion that scientific ideas reveal the literal and intimate essence of reality, as the images of sense certainly do not. But the fact is that both sense and science are relatively and virtually true, being appropriate to the organ employed and to the depth to which this organ may penetrate into the structure of things or may trace their movement. The senses do this well enough, in their own terms, for the uses of animal and social life; but modern science approaches the dynamism of nature by means of artificial instruments and experiments: hence its astonishing mechnical applications, and its moral and pictorial blindness. It studies methods rather than objects; it works indirectly if not directly in the service of industrialism, which needs to manipulate and not to understand; and if it succeeds in its manipulations it has done its duty. But this is a very special development, perhaps temporary, and certainly not fundamental in human knowledge. The images of sense will be with us while the human race endures. They will always yield our classical and personal view of nature. The stars will remain the visible stars, no matter what science may tell us about them; earth, water, air, and fire will still confront the spirit, and survive the disintegration that chemistry may subject them to. Ultimately the authority of science will always depend on the evidence of sense and on the analogy of familiar objects and events.

So too with the authority of history, which is much more closely bound up than physics with the life of The place spirit. History extends a man's dramatic of history. view of his own life and of contemporary society into the past, by the aid of documents and monuments. History is true or plausible fiction, such as we compose instinctively concerning one another's motives and mind and even concerning our own. This current knowledge that we have of ourselves is most slippery and deceptive: our memories, expectations, and reading of other people's minds would run wild in a moment, if they were not controlled by well-certified physical facts; and it is the course of physical events, observed on the human scale, that guides psychological imagination in reconstructing the past, in so far as imagination can be guided at all. Drop that thread, and you have passed at once into poetry and legend.

In general, it would avoid misunderstanding to remember that essence, matter, truth, and spirit are not,
in my view, separate cosmological regions, The limits of
separately substantial, and then juxtaposed. scepticism.
They are summary categories of logic, meant to
describe a single natural dynamic process, and to dismiss from organized reflection all unnecessary objects
of faith. Essence is not an object of faith, but a least
ultimate term in scepticism, showing how little evidence
there can be for faith of any sort, since all data are in
themselves dream-data, actual in that we evolve them,
like a pain, but false in that they do not otherwise exist.
And in regard to the realm of matter I propose no
theories, but only ask a preliminary question, namely:
What presuppositions do we make in pursuing knowledge of anything? And I reply: We presuppose that
there is some real object or event to be known or
reported, prior or subsequent to the report that reaches
us. In other words, we presuppose existent facts about
which our affirmations may be false or true. About
these facts our knowledge will be true, as far as it goes,
if we have access to them and discount the relativity
and partiality of our perceptions and theories. To
assert this principle of realism is no more than honesty.
Such trust in animal faith is involved in action and in
the impulse to look for, to describe, or to make anything. It is the first presupposition of intelligence and
sanity, and any scepticism that denies it asserts it.

Similarly what I lay down about the realm of spirit
involves no system of idealism, psychological or
Platonic, no eschatology, no providential or magic
philosophy of history. On this subject, too, I am
as sceptical as it is possible for me to be with sincerity;
but just as I would reject all hypostasized myths, so
I would reject all affectation of disbelief where life
and action render belief inevitable and perpetually
renew it. I posit therefore that the realm of matter is

animated by spirit, as in myself, so in my fellow-creatures, as far as my sympathies avail to conceive that animation spontaneously, or my experience, reflectively, to confirm my divinations. Even in regard to one's inner history one's notions are insecure, unless they are controlled by external evidence, like that of old actions or old letters; and self-knowledge grows less out of memory than out of discipline and concentration of thought, because spirit is not a phenomenology of spirit but the act of witnessing, reviewing, and judging natural facts. In regard to the extent and detail of the realm of spirit, then, all must be hypothesis and literary fiction, to be indulged in by poets, historians, and critics as their genius may prompt or their prudence allow. In reconstructing the *moral* history of spirit, however, we are not left without guidance. There is a traditional language, the language of poetry and religion, in which the essential fortunes of spirit are recorded, and these traditions impose themselves, like other external facts, upon each new soul; yet they count spiritually only in so far as they are confirmed or rediscovered in each case. Spirit cannot live except alone.

In regard to my intended allegiance to common sense, I confess that in several important matters I

Divergences from common sense. have not been able to maintain it. There are too many traditional equivocations and inconsistencies in human language, for instance in respect to spirit, which in current parlance retains its original sense of breath or invisible force, while also used, as I use it, for intellectual light. There are also too many vestiges of myth and superstition in moral and religious convictions. And in fact it was not common *opinion* that I respected or wished to follow, especially not the common opinions of my time, which I instinctively abhorred. It was rather the common *intellect* that I wished to adopt and to fortify in myself, after the manner of Aristotle; and even this not from any absolute reverence for the intellect, as if it were infallible or universally competent, but because I felt myself to be inevitably an accomplice in that vital adventure. I must think humanly or I could not think at all. My allegiance to common sense is distinctly not religious but political or grammatical, and therefore from a spiritual point of view accidental: something particularly obvious to a man whose spiritual attachments lie in one quarter and his linguistic attachments in another.

To have drawn this distinction between the natural and the spiritual sphere I do not regard as itself a break from human orthodoxy. All intellectual nations have had prophets, poets, and mystics whom they have honoured as certainly wiser than the vulgar rationalist; and this because in every man there is an alternation and opposition between the outer and the inner life. While in the rush of action and talk he must rely on conventional assumptions, in repose, in sorrow, in art, in love, or in prayer he is aware of passing to another order of considerations, unreal to the world, but most important to himself. Perhaps he thinks there are two worlds, or two criteria of truth: but this is precisely one of the points where I part company with tradition. To double the world would unspiritualize the spiritual sphere: to double the truth would make both truths halting and false. There is only one world, the natural world, and only one truth about it; but this world has a spiritual life possible in it, which looks not to another world but to the beauty and perfection that this world suggests, approaches, and misses. On this point, although I am perfectly willing to stand alone, I rather expect that posterity may agree with me: not that mankind will ever accept or remember my philosophy, but that, by fellowship with what is perennial in their hearts, I shall have had a foretaste of their sentiments.

[side note: Matter and spirit not two worlds.]

The primitive mind is inevitably superstitious; that is to say, it attributes power to appearances and turns accidents into laws. All that is requisite in order to transform such superstition into a critical philosophy is to trace back all power to the continuous transformation of physical forces, in other words, to matter; and at the same time, by the same insight, to recognize all appearances to be mere appearances, and all accidents mere accidents, sensible signs of power manifest to the spirit, but having no substance or power in themselves.

This simple dissolution of superstition yields three of my realms of being: matter, as the region and method of power; essence, as the proper nature of appearances and relations; and spirit as the witness or moral sensibility that is subject to the double assault of material events and of dramatic illusions. There remains the realm of truth, which is the total history and destiny of matter and spirit, or the enormously complex essence which they exemplify by existing.

This rejection of superstition preserves the original categories of the animal mind: power succumbed to, feared or exerted, and images distinguished. But the animal mind, and the psychologism that tends to revert to it, do not keep these two categories distinct, but employ them together; and this for a manifest reason. Man, as Aristotle would say, is a compound; he exists at once in the realm of matter and in that of spirit. It is as an individual animal, one person with two natures, that he is named, and finds himself acting and talking. He constantly exerts power, sometimes visibly by bodily acts; but often the physical sources of his power are hidden from his mind, or not attended to, and he attributes his action to his ideas. But his ideas have no place in the traceable sequence of material events; they brood over that flux like the invisible gods or the laws of nature. This magic of laws, images, and words he interpolates into the hidden continuities of matter; and as his thoughts are fed by passion more than by observation, his beliefs remain inveterately mythical. To be essentially poetical seems to me a virtue and not a vice in the mind; and the illusion involved when thought professes to be transparently cognitive may easily be corrected. It is corrected instinctively in poetry, which ceases to deceive without ceasing to be significant; and it might be corrected in science if data as well as theories were recognized to be only symbols, deceptive to the idolater, who takes them for substances, but true indications to the enlightened man, who takes them for signs. This recognition of the ideal character of the given seems to me to emancipate the spirit from a horrible net of contradictions in its cognitive pretensions and to restore it to its proper poetic and religious function.

The critics will tell the public that I run hopelessly away from common sense in denying the material efficacy of spirit. Yet this is a misunder- *The in-* standing, because neither the critics nor the *efficacy of* public take the word spirit in my sense. *spirit inher-* They understand by it the self, the soul, *nature.* the psyche: and nothing could be farther from me than to deny the interaction of the psyche—that is, of bodily life—with surrounding events. The continuity of these motions, outside a man, in through his senses, out through his impulses, into his actions and influence, is perfectly obvious. His senses and impulses will not be aroused without arousing his spirit; so that it is quite true that if he had been unconscious most of his actions would have been different, or rather would not have occurred at all. He would have been asleep. In sleep, it is not spirit that departs or determines to close the eyes, but the eyes that close of themselves, and shut the world out from the spirit. With eyes closed, a man will certainly not act as if his eyes were open:

and when the physical cause of his lethargy or gropings is so evident, it is sheer myth to suppose the cause to be the absence of light in his mind. That light is eclipsed, as everyone can prove experimentally at any moment, because the eyes are closed. Spirit is therefore a concomitant effect of physical causes and not a separate cause descending from another world.

To read actions in terms of spirit and to divide the thought that doubtless accompanied them is perfectly legitimate in principle although often mistaken in practice. I call it literary psychology and believe that when the mind-reader and the mind read are genetically akin, it may be more literally true than any other kind of knowledge. Yet it is essentially divination, not science. Scientific psychology must be behaviouristic: it can discover, not what spirits feel or think, but what people are likely to say and do under specific conditions. This science cannot prevent people from being erratic; but if they are so, it will not be because spirit in them intervenes, but because there is or may be an indeterminable element in erratic psyches, as in erratic atoms or stars. Spirit in those cases will be erratic too, and may possibly go quite mad and dissolve into a chaos of shocks and images. I do not, then, deny either the efficacy or the indetermination of human action or Will, but only a miraculous interference of spirit or of visionary objects with the flux of matter.

Knowledge of it is intensive but insecure.

The universe, however broken and inconsequential may be its course, is what it is as a whole; but this totality is itself contingent; so that while I have not the least faith or hope in indeterminism, I see that all regularity is relative and factual, and by no means imposed on existence by any essence or law. The freedom that so many people, learned and unlearned, passionately wish to possess is a vital freedom, freedom

Psychic versus spiritual freedom.

to be themselves, and to bring to light the potentialities of their psyches, all knocking at the door of life. This freedom exists; and though variously modified by the acquired habits of the psyche, it belongs fundamentally to all life, if not to all change. Everything is what it is by its own initiative, not because some other thing was like it earlier, and compelled it to repeat that essence. Essences are all passive, and the flux of existence is as self-guided at every point as at the beginning.

As to the freedom proper to spirit, this is no power to move matter by magic, but the fact of being sometimes liberated from distraction and permitted to be pure spirit. Magic may be real enough, the magic of a word or an act, grafted upon the invisible influences that course through the material world; but no spiritual religion, in availing itself of magic and miracles, regards them as the measure of spirit. A spiritual man may say: "Take up thy bed and walk." That is the psyche speaking to the psyche. But when he says "Thy sins are forgiven thee," the spirit is speaking to the spirit.

That God is a spirit, though the text be orthodox, has never been the popular belief, nor have theologians taken it seriously. As a man seldom identifies himself with the spirit in him, but at best speaks of spirit as something higher than has descended upon him and possessed him, so in thinking of God the dominant *Universal power deserves reverence, but is not a spirit.* consideration is that God is a power at work in the world, as man is an agent there; and as man attributes his actions to his feelings, so he introduces feelings into the powers in nature, according to their operation. But this mythology, like his own psychology, is in the air, and criticism should lead him to attribute to his gods *only the powers which they exercise*; as to-day, if we speak of the Muses, we mean only the inspiration actual in artists, with its obscure natural sources, and not nine invisible young ladies whispering our thoughts to us. So God in Spinoza becomes identical with Nature, speculatively magnified; and if I retained the word God, as I do not in this connection, my result would be even more scandalous, since God, conceived merely as a power, would become identical with matter, the omnificent substance and force in everything. It should be remembered, however, that sunshine and rain, the stars and the harvests, justify many of the emotions and virtues cultivated by religion; and it is in the economy of nature that divine beneficence, justice, and wrath are manifested. If mankind had always lived without contact with open rural nature, as does the proletariat in large modern cities, mankind would have had no religion, but would have perished believing that it could be saved by its wishes and votes and the eloquence of politicians. Disrespect for matter, ignorance of the real seat and method of substance and power, therefore kills the belief in God at its roots.

By definition there is an *ens realissimum*, though this be but a blanket-name to cover all the radical, pervasive, and terrible influences to which the spirit is subject. When people ask, Does God exist? the question is really verbal. They are asking whether the reality signified by the notion of God, if we understood that reality better, could still bear the name of God, or had better be designated by some other word. This is at bottom the whole question in dispute between theists and atheists.

Now in this verbal sense, and in respect to popular religion that thinks of God as the creator of the world and the dispenser of fortune, my philosophy is atheistic. It puts all substance and power into the realm of matter; and although this realm presupposes essence, creates spirit, and involves truth, yet in its dynamic procedure it takes no account of those accompaniments, and excludes the spiritual and moral vitality implied in the word God.

Sense in which this system is atheistic.

God, at least for Jews, Christians, and Moslems, must be a power that is a spirit, and a spirit that is a sovereign power. As I place spirit and power at opposite ends of the ontological scale, and of cosmic evolution, making spirit the fruit and enjoyment of power, but no part of its radical energy, I must be pronounced an atheist in this company. I am not even a pantheist, as if I regarded the whole realm of matter as an organ of spirit; for then, even if the dynamic order were purely mechanical, the omnipresence of spirit and the pervasive ministration of matter to moral ends, would allow us to say that the universe was a divine body with a divine mind. But that, in my opinion, is a false extension of spirit, where the animal and moral conditions for perfection and for consciousness are absent; so that while I regard spirit as the culmination of life, at least in our planet, I am far from regarding all nature as directed upon spirit, or intelligible to it, or good in its eyes.

Still the question is not settled, since there are developments even in the Hebraic idea of God, that transcend the spheres of power and of con- *Truth and* sciousness; and there are also other religious *essence* traditions, Indian and Greek, in which I *neither identical* might seem less heretical. I have revived, *with the* in a form clearer than is customary, the *idea of God* perennial notions of truth and of pure Being, *nor separable from it.* or as I call it, the realm of essence. I should not myself identify either of these notions with the idea of God. Truth is but the complete character of the universe seen under the form of eternity; and essence, in its infinity, is but the field of all the complementary characters that any given character excludes. Both this infinity and that eternity transcend mutation, transition, and local emphasis, and therefore transcend life. Neither can be a living God; yet unless the idea of God somehow included them it would remain a wholly mythical poetic idea without philosophic or rational warrant. And if the existence of divine forces were to be shown empirically, by miracles or historical evidences of design, we should have new but limited knowledge of nature, and not any inward, speculative, or religious revelation. Therefore it is not surprising that the most concentrated and speculative minds, if not the most religious, should have regarded sometimes truth and sometimes pure Being as the supreme reality.

That pure Being should be thought of as alone real and divine may seem strange, yet is explicable, because Esoteric the sense of instability and vanity in all deification of existing things, supervening upon animal pure Being. love of life and of self, produces a spiritual longing for peace and security in a heaven where all that is possible shall be understood and nothing that is transitory shall be loved. Then pure Being, something neutral, infinite, and eternal, may become the focus of the prayerful mind. Dialectically too for its unity and omnipresence, and æsthetically for the clearness of all its modes, pure essence can fascinate the intellect, as we see in the Eleatics and Pythagoreans. In Spinoza the flight from contingency leads to the same goal; for although we perceive nothing of substance except agitated extension and agitated thought, yet, when he comes to define that substance ideally, what he defines is neither matter nor mind, but precisely the realm of essence, namely, infinite Being, deployed in an infinite number of attributes, each attribute again deployed in an infinite number of modes. It is true that, without the least shadow of evidence, he attributes existence to this enormously imaginary Being, and identifies it with his Nature-or-God; but that is a vestige of idolatry. As for me, partial as I am to the realm of essence, and happy in the presence of non-existent objects, when they are beautiful or significant, it would never occur to me to eulogize *all* essence. That would be treason to human nature and to the

Good; because even if much that to the human mind is tedious or horrible might be acceptable from some other point of view, animal or divine, that would be because some living psyche found its happiness in that object. For as Spinoza himself says,[1] the great advantage that the imaginary may have over the true is that free intuition evokes it; whereas in the perception or report of matters of fact, vital spontaneity cannot be perfect, but is constrained by the occasion, by the distribution and unhappy changes in its objects, and by irrelevant stimulation or lapses of attention. Perfection is better than truth; but perfection itself is relative to a definite existing nature and its spontaneous functions; so that to worship infinite Being as good or sublime, and to make a God of it, inverts the moral order. There would be a better excuse for worshipping matter, since it is matter that feeds and kills us, and these are the functions that popular religion first attributes to the deity. But to worship essence, which can do nothing, merely because it is infinite and ineffaceable, would be a refined madness, fortunately not likely to prove contagious when its true object is understood. Shreds and echoes of such aberrations nevertheless mingle in religious tradition, adding a touch of false mystery to honest piety, or of common superstition to spiritual life.

The realm of truth has a much closer relation to the object of human religion. Many truths are important, and all truth is a sublime standard _Intellectual_ of reference for science, for speculation, and _deification_ for the conscience suffering from doubt or _of the truth._ injustice. To appeal to God, or to feel God's eye upon us, is a dramatic way of invoking the inexorable truth. But is the truth God, or is God merely a name for the truth? Not properly speaking: and we may verify this judgment by observing how the philosophers

[1] See the motto opposite the title-page.

whose highest category might seem to be the truth, for instance Plato or Hegel, have to subtract all detail from nature in order to obtain Ideas or an Idea that might be identified with God: and how even after that thinning of the full truth, they would be unmistakable atheists, unless they added a living intuition, a personal psyche, to the Idea or Ideas, in order to raise them from the realm of truth into that of spirit.

When this is done, we reach the orthodox philosophical notion of God in Aristotle and Plotinus. Here Mythical deification of the Good. God is by no means the truth, being ignorant of all facts: but he is an influence, radiating from the realized enjoyment of all perfections in one act of thought; the effect being to diffuse those perfections, as far as matter permits, through the whole realm of matter and of created or fallen spirit. This theology is sublime, refining into pure spirit the turbid life of the universe: but that life remains as turbid as it was before, because this theology is mythical. The Good from which all goods are supposed to be derived, is a hypostasis of their common quality of goodness, not realizable psychologically, nor even ideally; because each possible good is specific, and the enjoyment of them all at once would be the enjoyment of none separately, as alone it can *exist*. So that as the God of Aristotle and Plotinus is avowedly ignorant of all facts, knowing only types of perfection, so he is ignorant of all actually realized goods, except the single one of his own rapture. This sun feels itself burning and sheds universal light; but it is blind to all refraction, to all colour, and to all shadow.

Truth, then, and excellence, even when reduced to a moral outline or programme of the cosmos, cannot A God must be a spirit. be sublimated into a deity. Deity must be spirit; and it must be a supreme instance of spirit, freed from all the trammels that depress spirit in ourselves. It must be posited, as spirit in any instance may posit spirit elsewhere, socially and naturalistically, as a separate invisible existence.

Does my philosophy compel or allow me to posit such a divine spirit or spirits? Certainly it does not compel me, nor does it even invite me to do so with any plausibility; because spirit, in my system, must be the spirit of some body, the consciousness of some natural life; and we find no bodies or psyches in nature that suggest to us, as they did to the ancients, a divine animation. I know that pantheistic poets retain that feeling, yet I have but scant respect for it. It seems to me to be vitiated by two childish fallacies: one, to attribute spirit to sunsets and storms known to be mechanical accidents; the other, to imagine that, if spirit animated such phenomena, it would have any kinship with human aspirations. Genuine mythology would see divine fecundity where there is exuberance, and divine fury where there is destruction; and it would grow feebler and feebler, and more and more literary, as it began to humanize those fables, and to find "books in the running brooks, sermons in stones, and good in everything."

The genuine inspiration of modern religion is moral, and drawn from the difficulties, hopes, and joys of the spirit. In this capacity, as expressing the inner life, it may be interesting; but it has absolutely no standing-ground in external fact, and therefore supplies no evidence of the existence of non-human spirits.

That divine spirits may nevertheless exist, without their bodies being visible to us, or their influence such as to awaken in us any sense of their presence, I should be the last to deny. Our science cannot fathom the realm of matter, either inwards or outwards; and there can be no just presumption that, beyond the dynamic cosmos to which we have access, other worlds rich in things unimaginable to us may not exist. But such

Any existing Gods would be cosmic incidents.

blank possibilities are uninstructive, and they benumb religion rather than stimulate it. The God of tradition might himself wonder how many other gods unknown to him might not exist, and he might be shaken by that thought in his presumptive omnipotence and omniscience. The bastions of any existing heaven may some day be stormed. Security lies in a different dimension, where no cosmic thieves can break in or steal. It lies not in being protected by spirits beyond us, but in the nature of the spirit within.

When this exclusively spiritual autonomy of spirit is thoroughly understood, the existential dependence of spirit becomes inoffensive. Inoffensive, I mean, to the philosopher examining the nature and dignity of spirit; not inoffensive to the spirit itself, enduring the accidents of fortune. But these accidents, cruel as they may be, are the indispensable occasions for asserting the autonomy of spirit now in one place now in another, and exercising all its spiritual rights. If spirit were not physically distributed and evoked among the animals, and perhaps among the stars, it would have no home in nature, no point of view fixed for each incarnation, no moral character, no tragic interests, no comic shifts of perspective. In a word, spirit could not exist unless its existence were natural. That it should be subject to all the accidents, lapses, conflicts, intermittences, and self-contradictions proper to life and death was set down once for all in its birth-certificate; yet the newborn creature, for all that, is born a spirit. Existence is not so jejune as an analytic positivism would make it; it is no collection of successive data; it vibrates with potentiality, momentum, interaction and tension. It is existence by being a perpetual passage from non-existence back to non-existence, in respect to all its moments and most of its forms; and this fact, that makes existence painful to spirit, alone allows spirit to exist,

The existence of spirit is as natural as any other existence.

since it exists precisely by feeling potentiality, momentum, interaction and tension. But in feeling them it ideally eludes them, in that it combines and unites their fleeting essences in single pictures and perspectives, whereas the facts themselves can never be fused or unified without being abolished. Spirit, by being immersed in the flux, perceives the flux and by perceiving it lends it the only immortality of which it is capable. Here, in the scope of vision, seeing the relations of things, it asserts an intellectual dominion over its parent world. This is an absolutely unchallengeable dominion in its own sphere, into which matter can never rise; although by suppressing spirit in any given instance, matter may always dip again into the darkness of a total flux, and remain subject only to its own impetus.

Spirit, then, belongs here below, not yonder, ἐκεῖ, in the Platonic heaven. In placing it here, in the animal psyche, my system takes its place in the train of Democritus and Epicurus who, although they did not deny the existence of gods, assigned to them no dominion over nature, and in that sense may be called atheists. *Analogy between this ontology and the doctrine of the Trinity.* Yet, seen in another light, religiously rather than cosmologically, my treatment of these four realms of being may be regarded as a reduction of Christian theology and spiritual discipline to their secret interior source. In particular my analysis transposes the doctrine of the Trinity into terms of pure ontology and moral dialectic.

At the foundation there is one total groundless reality, breaking in upon nothingness with an overwhelming irrational force. This reality lies in the primordial elements and motions of things, with their interlocked potentialities and momentum. Here the presence and pressure of existence confronts us, the unfathomable mystery of the actual. Reason, that loves *Matter, or primordial substance and power, corresponds to the Father.*

the perspicuous and the logically necessary, might like
to dismiss this incubus, but cannot; and impatience
towards unreason is itself irrational, since any different
state of the facts would be equally groundless.   Moreover, as Heraclitus perceived, everything existent does
itself justice by presently disappearing, and soon this
incubus ceases to oppress each particular soul.   This,
however, is no speculative solution; for not only will
the incubus continue to oppress spirit in others, but
even if everything save the present moment of spirit
were abolished or had never existed, the truth would
remain that here spirit had been confronted by fate:
and this indelible fact suffices to prove the existence of
a vehemently actual and absolute power.

This assault of reality, in the force of whatsoever
exists or happens, I call matter or the realm of matter;
but evidently this very power is signified by the First
Person of the Trinity, the Father, almighty creator of
heaven and earth and of all things visible and invisible.

Yet all things, according to the Nicene creed, were
perforce created through the Son; and this dogma which

Power can-
not be
exercised
without
appealing to
form.

might seem unintelligible, becomes clear if
we consider that power could not possibly
produce anything unless it borrowed some
form from the realm of essence and imposed
that form on itself and on its works.   Power
would be annulled before it began to exert itself unless
it did or produced something specific, something
eternally distinct and recognizable in its character.
The Son is thus an indispensable partner and vehicle
for the life of the Father.

The same creed tells us that the Son was *begotten
not made*, that is to say, came through an inner impulse,
without plan or foresight, from the substance of the
Father; as in nature it is absurd to imagine that the
shape taken by things was an aim pursued in their
taking it.   Design and creation are secondary incidents,

possible only when experience has supplied models for invention and when special organs, already formed, have acquired a definite capacity for free play and variation. Blind spontaneity must generate, and not make, the instruments and the goals of deliberate action.

If we interpret in this way the Father to be power and the Son to be form, we see at once how the essence or quality of each is independent and incomparable, while their existence is one and inseparable. To exercise power is to select and adopt form: by which selection or adoption power ceases to be a merely explosive and empty strain, and form ceases to be an infinite undiscriminated field of possibilities.

In its own direction essence is entirely irrelevant to existence, equally necessary in every part, yet only logically necessary. But by the intervention of irrational power (as for instance in the propensity or compulsion to think) the infinity of essence is determined to a particular complex or series of forms: and this happens not only at each moment in each thinking mind, but in the flux of existence at large. This complex or series of forms exemplified in the universe composes the truth about it; and this is the side of reality approachable by the intellect. It is the Logos, comparable with the heaven of Platonic Ideas, with the God of Aristotle, and with νοῦς, the second hypostasis in the trinity of Plotinus.

The selective fiat of power limits actual form to the Logos or the truth.

This Logos is just as much God as is the Father, since power or substance cannot exist without form. But form also cannot exist without substance and power to extricate it from infinity and render it actual; so that the Father and the Son are not two separable existents, but two incommensurable and equally original features of existence itself. And the priority of substance indicated by the name Father, who *generates* the Son, appears only on the naturalistic side; because in nature

In the beginning the Word was with God.

substance and power take up one form after another, and endure throughout the transformation, thus seeming fundamental, while the form, though there must always be *some* form, seems accidental.   But in a deity, or in the universe seen under the form of eternity, the Logos is as primitive as the Will; and to the intellect form might even seem the prior element, as if the Will were magnetized by the Idea, rather than the Idea evoked or generated by the Will.   Perhaps on this account Aristotle and Hegel place no power above the Idea or Logos of the world, making form magically dynamic; but I think this is doubly untenable.   It is untenable naturalistically, because, as Schopenhauer perceived, an inarticulate force, a blind compulsion or attraction, breeds, not indeed the forms themselves which are eternal and do not need to be begotten, but breeds the intuition or illustration of any form.   And the priority of the Logos is untenable dialectically, because the Logos is only a selection from the realm of essence, and nothing in pure essence could authorize the self-assertion or dominance of one feature to the exclusion of the rest.   Plato and Leibniz therefore had to introduce the Good or the notion of the Best Possible to make the inevitable selection.   But this, in both cases, was a subterfuge of apologetics, an appeal to moral considerations which are out of place.   Nothing can be more naturalistic than moral preference, in which the love of life, the fears and the lusts of the psyche speak the absolute language of passion.

Now love and pursuit of the Good, though they cannot be prior to power and to essence, also arise on

The procession of the spirit.

occasion, when matter and form, by a contingent fusion, have themselves become actual; and this third dimension of reality is spirit. Christian theology has been much less curious and penetrating in regard to the Holy Ghost than in regard to the Father and to the Son; so that the Nicene creed, as if to excuse the Church for its negligence, says that we virtually adore the Holy Ghost when we explicitly adore the Father or the Son. Yet, from the human point of view this is an anomaly, since it is the Holy Ghost that speaks through the prophets, vivifies us, and tells us all we know about the Son and the Father. But there is a secret reason for this silence on what is nearest to ourselves. The ancients could never out-grow their mythologizing turn of thought. When they conceived power or form they infused into them, poetically, the moral intensity of spirit. Power—the crash of a thunderbolt or the dark potentiality in a seed —had to be intentional and intelligent; and form had to become an intellectual intuition of form. The Father and the Son were accordingly conceived to be spirits on their own account: all the more when they were identified with Jehovah and with Christ, perfectly familiar as persons to the religious mind. Therefore, when it came to the Holy Ghost there was nothing positive to add, rather the positive character of those more individual divine persons to subtract, and only a vague influence to mention, which could perfectly well flow from them without involving a third personality.

Suppose, however, we abstain from personifications for a moment and consider our terms in their essential meaning and relations. We learn in the Its equal Nicene creed that the Holy Ghost *spoke* by divinity. the prophets, but this past tense is accidental, for we also hear that he proceeds from the Father and from the Son and is the universal lord and life-giver: a procession, dominion, and vivification that must be understood logically rather than temporally, like all crucial points in Platonic speculation. The spirit *gives* life in the sense that life would nowhere be morally worthy of the name if spirit were not actual there; but the *source* of spirit itself lies in the Father and the Son,

or in my language in matter organized into the form
of a psyche. It is not one instance of spirit that creates
another, but nature that rises into spirit at the crest
of every wave. And this spirit speaks by all prophets,
that is, by all voices inspired by power and by truth:
an utterance which is itself the ultimate manifestation
of power, and the first pure and non-material actualization of form. So that it is in the Holy Ghost that the
Father and the Son are first truly vivified and united
and adore and glorify one another. We may therefore
say that spirit, for all its dependence, is no less divine
than are form and power, and integral to reality. For
without stretching over the physical continuum of
space and time after the manner of power, or being
indelible and eternal, like essence and truth, spirit has
its own supremacy. It is original and morally prior
in its sphere, and necessary to the perfection of those
elements from which it flows. It lives in moments
and in spots; yet from any station it may survey everything, rescuing its causes from ignorance of themselves.
By the least joy it can redeem them from futility, and
by the least pain it can wring the conscience of the
Fates and challenge their selfish somnolence.

This moral cry and authority of spirit, unexampled
in the seething world, makes it the judge as well
as spectator of everything, and subjects it
Its incarna-
tion and   inevitably to every sort of contrariety and
passion.   suffering. I know that theology does not
say so directly: but indirectly we learn that Christ was
conceived by the Holy Ghost; and St. Paul often speaks
of "Christ" and of the "Spirit" indifferently as dwelling
within him; while speculative theologians are not wanting who say that the incarnation and passion of Christ
were essential features from the beginning in the design
of creation, and would have occurred even apart from
the sin of Adam. And when we eliminate the mythical
and legendary parts of this theology, and consider only

its spiritual burden, I think it becomes clear that the divine element especially incarnate in human existence is spirit; not that matter or essence can be wanting, but that the novel fact and great characteristic here is the passion of the spirit. This passion would certainly not have overcome the spirit in heaven, where the harmony between power and form is perfect, and life is for ever at its topmost ecstasy, as in the God of Aristotle. But that again is sheer myth; and as matter can *exist* only in some form, and form only in some matter, so spirit can *exist* only incarnate in the flux of matter and form, where nothing is stable or is perfect, if perfect at all, for more than a moment. Passion is therefore inseparable from spirit in its actual existence, and exposes it to perpetual obscuration and suffering.

Obscuration and suffering bring temptation with them, and spirit is tempted sometimes to love evil, and be content with lies, and sometimes to Its degrada-defy its sources and conditions, to deny tion. matter, to despise form, and to pose as itself the only power and the only arbiter of truth, self-tortured and absolute. But this is itself the greatest of lies and the sin of the spirit against its own vocation. Spirit proceeds, it is always proceeding, from the Father and from the Son; and, if it would not grow mad and suicidal, it must go about the Father's business, and repeat the eternal Word that it hears spoken in heaven.

It was not the Holy Ghost that denied his dependence on the Father and on the Son: it was Lucifer. And Lucifer thereby lost his brightness and quickly became Satan, Mephistopheles, Caliban, and Puck.

That spiritual ruin should be possible is a proof that spirit is secondary: spirit could not run into dissolution and death, as it does constantly, if *Parendo* there were not sources and conditions of its *tutior* life that might betray it, or from which its *libertas.* immediate organ might break away. Nor will it do to invoke the absolute contingency of fact, and to say that the worst of dreams might as easily be groundless as the best of philosophies, or that absolute free spirit might indulge in both by turns. For there is the inner difference felt by spirit itself between the absurd and the beautiful, between hell and heaven; and spirit, though equally alive in both, is not equally at peace in both, or in enjoyment of its chosen good. This good is therefore chosen for it, before being chosen by it; a thousand errors must be corrected before that good can be clearly distinguished and possessed. There is an order of reason, a Logos, prescribed for spirit, and within which alone it can find its possible good. If spirit, taken abstractly, might embrace all essence impartially, finding Being in evil as much or more than in good, spirit in the concrete, as it actually exists, is directed upon order, and upon a definite selected order, beyond which it is swamped, lost, tortured and maddened. Chiefly, no doubt, this narrow path is prescribed for spirit by the realm of matter, where its organ and its fortunes must take shape; but even when expatiating in the realm of essence, where freedom might seem infinite, living spirit can make its way only systematically, as in mathematics or in music. Chaos itself then seems only an infinite complex of orders. In tracing any of these possible orders, a certain fidelity of intention, a serious self-limitation and consistency are requisite: whereby the vital presuppositions and conditions of spiritual life are manifested. In other words, the Holy Ghost is not the first person of the Trinity, but the third, proceeding both from the Father and from the Son. Consciousness is a gift of nature, happiness is a fruit of piety and order: and spirit, being the final fruition of existence, absolutely needs the other realms to evoke and to feed it.

Nor is spirit brought to light once for all, in one supreme instance; for its essence is to think, to love, to be awake, watchful, and transitive. The Word must be *uttered*; and such utterance cannot be either momentary or endlessly repeated; it must progress, vary, and complete itself in endless ways. *Spirit exists in multitudinous inspirations.* As the potentiality of matter and life is probably indefinite, and the variety of essence certainly inexhaustible, so spirit has an infinity of its own, the infinity of the renewable. One cry of moral actuality breaking out from the heart, leaves the heart free to repeat or not to repeat it; and the repetition if it comes will vary it. One pleasure cannot prescribe the quality of another pleasure, or cause or prevent its existence; nor can one thought annul the deliverance of another thought. The occasion and the bounty of nature must provide. Authority thus belongs to the Father, revelation comes by the Son, and Spirit descends to those predestined by the Father to receive it. Then, in the galaxy of spirit, the lesser with the greater lights become partakers in his glory.

This analogy between Christian theology and my ontology must not be pressed: the one is a dogma, the other a language: a language based not on *This system not a cosmology but a grammar of the spirit.* inspiration but on analysis, and meant only to render articulate the dumb experience of the soul. I am not concerned in these *Realms of Being* with alleged separate substances or independent regions. I am endeavouring only to distinguish the *types* of reality that I encounter; and the lines of cleavage that I discern are moral and logical, not physical, chasms. Yet I find this language applicable, and in that sense true. Theology could not possibly be true unless revealed miraculously; and I presume that most of my readers would agree that miraculous revelations are creatures of the heart. Religion itself sometimes calls its dogmas mysteries and its creeds symbols, as if admitting the difference in kind between imagination and truth. So discounted

and disinfected, the speculations of intense and consecrated minds have a great authority, especially when
they have proved acceptable to mankind, and have
become the companions and vehicles of a spiritual
discipline. They do not thereby become miraculously
true; nevertheless they reveal inner and outer harmonies
established with long labour and sacrifice in the human
soul. There they remain fountains of wisdom and self-
knowledge, at which we may still drink in solitude.
Perhaps the day may return when mankind will drink
at them again in society.

INDEX

Abstraction not the principle of essence, 16, 32–40; incidental of discourse, 37

Action, posits the field for physics, 201; excludes doubt, 201; distinguishes fact from fancy, 213; moves in a relative cosmos, 213–214

Actuality, 648–657, 816–821

Agnosticism, 527

Alain, 761, *note*

America, 401

Animal faith, the basis of physics, 195, 198, 831; animal defined, 570

Anselm, Saint, 413, 414

Apollo, a symbol for intuition, 224; for light, 237

Aristotle, 62, 212, 279, 330, 333, 345, 362, 503, 506, 530, 560, 571, 590, 599, 600, 723, 749, 816, 817, 832, 834, 842

Art, requires prior organisation, 321; extends the range of the psyche, 352; implies benefit, 353

Art or free labour, 704, 705

Association of ideas, 365

Atheism, 837–840

Athens, 481

Atomic theory, its generic truth, 231

Atoms, pictorial units, 230; contingent, 231; not existing as defined, 232, 274

Beauty arrests attention on essences, 8; is itself typical of essence, 152–154; how related to truth, 521–523

Before and after, organic relations, 285

Behaviour, the object of scientific psychology, 315, 345, 346

Being eminently possessed by essence, 23, 24; contrasted with existence, 47; only an essence, 414–416

Being, Pure, is infinitely pregnant, 50; is positive and inclusive, 57; not identical with the idea of God, 58

Berkeley, 170, 360–363, 427, 587

Body defined, 569

Brahma, 579, 658, 739–741, 769, 816

Buddha, xxii, 552, 757, 775, 787

Byzantium, 509

Cæsar, 489, 490

Categorical imperative, 474, 476

Catholic philosophy, v, 168

Causation, not necessary, 412, 413; underlies "chance," 504

Change, not an illusion, 267, 268; not internal to intuitions, 271; how represented there, 272, 273; synthesised in intuition, 487; not evil, 694–701

Chaos, fundamental, 291; would be re-established by a sincere psychologism, 365

Charity, 783, 788, 791–797

Christ, 730, 757–766

Clough, 400

Coherence, not truth, 448, 449, 520

Common sense criticised, 832–835